PEARSON EDEXCEL INTERNATIONAL GCSE (9–1)

MATHEMATICS A

Exam Practice Book

David Turner
Ian Potts

Published by Pearson Education Limited, 80 Strand, London, WC2R 0RL.

www.pearson.com/international-schools

Copies of official specifications for all Pearson Edexcel qualifications may be found on the website: https://qualifications.pearson.com

Text © Pearson Education Limited 2022
Development edited by Keith Gallick
Copy edited by Krysia Winska
Proofread by Christine Bruce, Jackie Mace, Linnet Bruce
Designed by Pearson Education Limited
Typeset by Straive
Picture research by Straive
Original illustrations © Pearson Education Limited Year 2022
Cover design © Pearson Education Limited Year 2022
Inside front cover: [Shutterstock.com/Dmitry Lobanov]

The rights of David Turner and Ian Potts to be identified as authors of this work have been asserted by them in accordance with the Copyright, Designs and Patents Act 1988.

First published 2022

24 23 22
IMP 10 9 8 7 6 5 4 3 2 1

British Library Cataloguing in Publication Data
A catalogue record for this book is available from the British Library

ISBN 978 1 292 39496 1

Copyright notice
All rights reserved. No part of this publication may be reproduced in any form or by any means (including photocopying or storing it in any medium by electronic means and whether or not transiently or incidentally to some other use of this publication) without the written permission of the copyright owner, except in accordance with the provisions of the Copyright, Designs and Patents Act 1988 or under the terms of a licence issued by the Copyright Licensing Agency, 5th Floor, Shackleton House, 4 Battlebridge Lane, London, SE1 2HX (www.cla.co.uk). Applications for the copyright owner's written permission should be addressed to the publisher.

Printed by Neografia in Slovakia

Cover Acknowledgements:

Shutterstock: nattanan726/Shutterstock

Text Acknowledgements:

Pearson Education: 3H 2004 May Q3 338; 2014 JanR 3H Q10 340; Adapted 3H 2013 Jan Q4 341; Adapted 3H 2007 Nov Q18 341; 3H 2015 JuneR Q20 342; Adapted 4H 2015 JuneR Q17 343; Adapted Edexcel GCSE Mock set 3 Nov 2017 3H Q12 347; Adapted Edexcel iGCSE Jan 13 3H Q20 348; Adapted Edexcel IGCSE May 12 4H Q22 349; Adapted Edexcel IGCSE June 2013 Q18 254; Adapted Edexcel IGCSE May 2012 3H Q13 258; Adapted Edexcel IGCSE 4H Jan 2016 Q20 259; Adapted 4H Jan 2013 Q25 360; Adapted Edexcel Q17 IGCSE 4H 2017 38; Adapted Edexcel 2016 3H Jan Q17 38; Adapted Edexcel Jan 2015 4HR Q16 39; Adapted IGCSE Edexcel 2014 4HR May Q18 39; Adapted from Edexcel June 2018 IGCSE 24 4HR 60; Edexcel GCSE Nov2015-2H Q15b 60; Adapted from Edexcel GCSE(9-1) Mock Set 3 Autumn 2017 1H 20 60; Adapted Edexcel IGCSE Nov 2007 6H Q25 77; Adapted Edexcel IGCSE Jan 2014 4HR Q 21 78; Adapted Edexcel IGCSE 3HR June 2015 Q23 78; Adapted IGCSE Edexcel 2017 Jan 4H Q21 78; Adapted Edexcel IGCSE 2018 Jan 3H Q25 79; Adapted from Edexcel GCSE Nov 2005 6H Q14b 87; Adapted from Edexcel IGCSE 3H June 2018 Q5 102; Adapted from IGCSE Edexcel 3HR June 2016 Q9 102; Adapted Edexcel IGCSE Jan 2016 4H Q20 121; Adapted IGCSE Jan 2015 3H Q14 121; Adapted Edexcel IGCSE 2015 June 4HR Q17 122; Adapted Edexcel IGCSE 2017 4HR Q17 122; Adapted from Edexcel 2014 Jan 4H Q17 198; Adapted from Edexcel IGCSE 2017 June 4H Q21 199; Adapted from Edexcel IGCSE 2017 3HR Q21 199; Adapted from Edexcel IGCSE 2013 4H Q19 199; Adapted Edexcel IGCSE Jan 2016 3HR Q15 215; Adapted Edexcel IGCSE 2016 3HR Q14 221; Adapted Edexcel IGCSE 2016 3H Q16 222

Photos Acknowledgements:

123RF: Boris Sosnovyy/123rf 29; Rafal Glebowski/123RF 53; carlo zolesio/123RF 63; cheskyw/123RF 69; Burmakin Andrey/123RF 72; Achim Prill/123RF 86; Dennis Jacobsen/123RF 104; Brent Hofacker/123RF 105; luckybusiness/123RF 106; Ian Grainger/123RF 106; efetova/123RF 116; dolgachov/123rf.com 145; Michael Eisenhut/123RF 147; Miguel Perfectti/123RF 158; perig76/123RF 178; Samransak Lomlim/123RF 180; tabuday/123RF 214; Maria Dryfhout/123RF 215; Maksym Bondarchuk/123rf.com 53; maxpro/123RF 138; carlotta vitrani/123RF 103; **Shutterstock:** JPC-PROD/Shutterstock 4; Charles Bowman/Shutterstock 8; Syda Productions/Shutterstock 12; panitanphoto/Shutterstock 20; Cornel Constantin/Shutterstock 25; andersphoto/Shutterstock 26; M_Agency/Shutterstock 26; Alexey Boldin/Shutterstock 33; eAlisa/Shutterstock 35; Elena Veselova/Shutterstock 44; sportpoint/Shutterstock 42; YoYosha/Shutterstock 49; BAZA Production/Shutterstock 49; Gilang Prihardono/Shutterstock 53; KSPTT/Shutterstock 56; Steve Byland/Shutterstock 57; Melinda Fawver/Shutterstock 69; StockEU/Shutterstock 75; Volodymyr Burdiak/Shutterstock 85; George Dolgikh/Shutterstock 102; hxdbzxy/Shutterstock 108; Maxim Khytra/Shutterstock 108; branislavpudar/Shutterstock 126; Rido/Shutterstock 128; P Maxwell Photography/Shutterstock 129; Suhani Design/Shutterstock 133; Timof/Shutterstock 143; trek6500/Shutterstock 148; Adam Vilimek/Shutterstock 153; kei907/Shutterstock 154; Weslley Silva/Shutterstock 155; eakasarn/Shutterstock 156; vipman/Shutterstock 157; Young Swee Ming/Shutterstock 157; exopixel/Shutterstock 157; Grandpa/Shutterstock 158; Dan Thornberg/Shutterstock 173; Cristopher Orange/Shutterstock 177; Tasha Art/Shutterstock 179; ZouZou/Shutterstock 210; Bardocz Peter/Shutterstock 219; fotodrobik/Shutterstock 52; Paolo Bona/Shutterstock 149; StudioByTheSea/Shutterstock 53; BAZA Production/Shutterstock 29; zphoto/Shutterstock 45; IgorZh/Shutterstock 112; omers/Shutterstock 89; 187633/Shutterstock 21; Stephen Mcsweeny/Shutterstock 42; Julia Sudnitskaya/Shutterstock 90; judyjump/Shutterstock 181; Mauricio Graiki/Shutterstock 189; Imagebug/Shutterstock 32; richard pross/Shutterstock 217; DasyaDasya/Shutterstock 223; Lukas Gojda/Shutterstock 225; EvrenKalinbacak/Shutterstock 137; Joe Ravi/Shutterstock 10; Atsushi Hirao/Shutterstock 19; Kolpakova Svetlana/Shutterstock 19; sungsu han/Shutterstock 48; Vevchic/Shutterstock 67; NZGMW/Shutterstock 68; 3dmitruk/Shutterstock 89; Rawpixel.com/Shutterstock 94; sunsinger/Shutterstock 100; New Africa/Shutterstock 128; PostMeridiemPhotos/Shutterstock 129; marketlan/Shutterstock 176; Goldilock Project/Shutterstock 66; Red Fox studio/Shutterstock 5; Photographee.eu/Shutterstock 51; S.Pytel/Shutterstock 63; Martin M303/Shutterstock 64; dotshock/Shutterstock 65; fotoliza/Shutterstock 65; FamVeld/Shutterstock 43; Val Thoermer/Shutterstock 56; Africa Studio/Shutterstock 101; Joao Seabra/Shutterstock 155; Hananeko_Studio/Shutterstock 179; fourlights/Shutterstock 111; **Alamy:** Rowan Romeyn/Alamy Stock Photo 12; ART Collection/Alamy Stock Photo 72; Maxim Kazmin/Alamy Stock Photo 115; Shreekant Jadhav/ephotocorp/Alamy Stock Photo 146; Melissa Jooste/Alamy Stock Photo 183; Pat Tuson/Alamy Stock Photo 220; pcpexclusive/Alamy Stock Photo 127; Guerilla/Alamy Stock Photo 5; Elles Rijsdijk/Alamy Stock Photo 41; **Getty Images:** MARK GARLICK/SCIENCE PHOTO LIBRARY/Getty Images 25; Arslan Awan/iStock/Getty Images 25; AmpleSpace/iStock/Getty Images 45; 10'000 Hours/DigitalVision/Getty Images 150; ronstik/iStock/Getty Images 151; lilithlita/iStock/Getty Images 152; fotoARION - Specialist in product and business photography/Getty Images 154; RossHelen/iStock/Getty Images 182; ImageGap/iStock/Getty Images 47; MARK GARLICK/SCIENCE PHOTO LIBRARY/Getty Images viii; Arslan Awan/iStock/Getty Images viii; **Tsz-shan Kwok:** Tsz-shan Kwok/Pearson Education Asia Ltd 73

All other images © Pearson Education

Endorsement Statement
In order to ensure that this resource offers high-quality support for the associated Pearson qualification, it has been through a review process by the awarding body. This process confirmed that this resource fully covers the teaching and learning content of the specification at which it is aimed. It also confirms that it demonstrates an appropriate balance between the development of subject skills, knowledge and understanding, in addition to preparation for assessment.

Endorsement does not cover any guidance on assessment activities or processes (e.g. practice questions or advice on how to answer assessment questions), included in the resource nor does it prescribe any particular approach to the teaching or delivery of a related course.

While the publishers have made every attempt to ensure that advice on the qualification and its assessment is accurate, the official specification and associated assessment guidance materials are the only authoritative source of information and should always be referred to for definitive guidance. Pearson examiners have not contributed to any sections in this resource relevant to examination papers for which they have responsibility.

Examiners will not use endorsed resources as a source of material for any assessment set by Pearson. Endorsement of a resource does not mean that the resource is required to achieve this Pearson qualification, nor does it mean that it is the only suitable material available to support the qualification, and any resource lists produced by the awarding body shall include this and other appropriate resources.

CONTENTS

COURSE STRUCTURE	**iv**
ABOUT THIS BOOK	**viii**
ASSESSMENT OVERVIEW	**ix**
FORMULAE SHEET – HIGHER TIER	**xi**
UNIT 1	**2**
UNIT 2	**22**
UNIT 3	**46**
UNIT 4	**66**
UNIT 5	**84**
UNIT 6	**104**
UNIT 7	**129**
UNIT 8	**151**
UNIT 9	**176**
UNIT 10	**202**
EXAMINATION PRACTICE PAPERS	**223**
GLOSSARY	**249**
ANSWERS	**254**
EXAMINATION PRACTICE PAPER ANSWERS	**366**

UNIT 1

NUMBER 1 — 2
- EQUIVALENT FRACTIONS
- SIMPLIFYING FRACTIONS
- FOUR RULES OF FRACTIONS
- DIRECTED NUMBER
- BIDMAS
- SIGNIFICANT FIGURES AND DECIMAL PLACES

ALGEBRA 1 — 6
- SIMPLIFYING ALGEBRAIC EXPRESSIONS
- SOLVING EQUATIONS

GRAPHS 1 — 8
- GRADIENT OF A STRAIGHT LINE
- PLOTTING STRAIGHT-LINE GRAPHS
- STRAIGHT-LINE CONVERSION GRAPHS

SHAPE AND SPACE 1 — 13
- ANGLE PROPERTIES
- POLYGONS
- SIMILAR TRIANGLES
- CONSTRUCTIONS

SETS 1 — 18
- BASIC IDEAS
- VENN DIAGRAMS WITH TWO SETS

UNIT 2

NUMBER 2 — 22
- STANDARD FORM
- PERCENTAGES
- PERCENTAGE INCREASE AND DECREASE

ALGEBRA 2 — 27
- MULTIPLYING AND DIVIDING FRACTIONS
- SOLVING EQUATIONS WITH ROOTS AND POWERS
- POSITIVE INTEGER INDICES
- LINEAR INEQUALITIES

GRAPHS 2 — 30
- FINDING THE EQUATION OF A STRAIGHT LINE
- SKETCHING STRAIGHT-LINE GRAPHS
- SOLVING SIMULTANEOUS EQUATIONS GRAPHICALLY

SHAPE AND SPACE 2 — 34
- PYTHAGORAS' THEOREM
- ANGLES IN A SEMICIRCLE
- ANGLE AT CENTRE IS TWICE THAT AT CIRCUMFERENCE
- ANGLES IN SAME SEGMENT ARE EQUAL
- OPPOSITE ANGLES OF A CYCLIC QUADRILATERAL SUM TO 180°

HANDLING DATA 1 — 40
- COLLECTING AND DISPLAYING DATA
- MEAN, MEDIAN, MODE AND RANGE

UNIT 3

NUMBER 3 — 46
- MULTIPLES, FACTORS AND PRIME FACTORS
- HCF AND LCM
- RATIO

ALGEBRA 3 — 50
- SIMPLE FACTORISING
- SIMPLIFYING FRACTIONS
- EQUATIONS WITH FRACTIONS
- SIMULTANEOUS EQUATIONS

GRAPHS 3 — 54
- DISTANCE–TIME GRAPHS
- SPEED–TIME GRAPHS

SHAPE AND SPACE 3 — 58
- TANGENT RATIO
- SINE AND COSINE RATIOS

HANDLING DATA 2 — 61
- FREQUENCY TABLES (CONTINUOUS DATA) AND HISTOGRAMS (EQUAL CLASSES); MEAN, MEDIAN AND MODE

COURSE STRUCTURE

UNIT 4

NUMBER 4 — 66
- COMPOUND PERCENTAGES (INCLUDING DEPRECIATION)
- REVERSE PERCENTAGES

ALGEBRA 4 — 70
- CHANGE OF SUBJECT
- USING FORMULAE

GRAPHS 4 — 74
- QUADRATIC GRAPHS: $y = ax^2 + bx + c$
- USING GRAPHS TO SOLVE $ax^2 + bx + c = 0$

SHAPE AND SPACE 4 — 76
- TRIGONOMETRY AND PYTHAGORAS' THEOREM IN 3D; ANGLE BETWEEN TWO LINES, AND ANGLE BETWEEN A LINE AND A PLANE

HANDLING DATA 3 — 80
- DISPERSION (DISCRETE DATA)
- DISPERSION (CONTINUOUS DATA)

UNIT 5

NUMBER 5 — 84
- ESTIMATING USING STANDARD FORM
- UPPER AND LOWER BOUNDS

ALGEBRA 5 — 88
- MULTIPLYING BRACKETS
- FACTORISING
- SOLVING EQUATIONS BY FACTORISING
- PROBLEMS

GRAPHS 5 — 91
- GRAPHICAL LINEAR INEQUALITIES
- PERPENDICULAR LINES
- MIDPOINTS
- PYTHAGORAS' THEOREM

SHAPE AND SPACE 5 — 95
- TRANSLATIONS
- REFLECTIONS
- ROTATIONS
- ENLARGEMENTS
- COMBINED TRANSFORMATIONS

HANDLING DATA 4 — 99
- PROBABILITY FROM A SAMPLE SPACE AND PROBABILITY OF THE COMPLEMENT OF AN EVENT
- EXPERIMENTAL PROBABILITY, THEORETICAL PROBABILITY, RELATIVE FREQUENCY AND EXPECTED FREQUENCY

UNIT 6

NUMBER 6 — 104
- DIRECT PROPORTION
- INVERSE PROPORTION
- NEGATIVE AND FRACTIONAL INDICES

ALGEBRA 6 — 109
- DIRECT PROPORTION – LINEAR
- DIRECT PROPORTION – NON-LINEAR
- INVERSE PROPORTION
- NEGATIVE AND FRACTIONAL INDICES

SEQUENCES 1 — 113
- CONTINUING SEQUENCES
- THE DIFFERENCE METHOD
- FINDING A FORMULA
- MIXED QUESTIONS
- ARITHMETIC SERIES

SHAPE AND SPACE 6 — 117
- INTERSECTING CHORD THEOREMS
- ALTERNATE SEGMENT THEOREM

SETS 2 — 123
- SHADING SETS
- TWO SET PROBLEMS
- THREE SET PROBLEMS
- DESCRIBING SETS ALGEBRAICALLY

UNIT 7

NUMBER 7 — 129
- CALCULATOR WORK
- RECURRING DECIMALS

ALGEBRA 7 — 131
- FACTORISING QUADRATICS
- COMPLETING THE SQUARE
- QUADRATIC FORMULA
- QUADRATIC INEQUALITIES
- MIXED QUESTIONS
- PROBLEMS LEADING TO QUADRATIC EQUATIONS

GRAPHS 6 — 134
- CUBIC GRAPHS: $y = ax^3 + bx^2 + cx + d$
- RECIPROCAL GRAPHS: $y = \frac{a}{x}$

SHAPE AND SPACE 7 — 138
- MENSURATION (2D)
- MENSURATION (3D)
- SIMILAR FIGURES

SETS 3 — 144
- PROBABILITY USING VENN DIAGRAMS
- CONDITIONAL PROBABILITY USING VENN DIAGRAMS

UNIT 8

NUMBER 8 — 151
- CONVERTING MEASUREMENTS
- COMPOUND MEASURE

ALGEBRA 8 — 158
- FUNCTION NOTATION
- DOMAIN AND RANGE
- COMPOSITE FUNCTIONS
- INVERSE FUNCTIONS
- MIXED QUESTIONS

GRAPHS 7 — 163
- USING GRAPHS TO SOLVE QUADRATIC EQUATIONS
- USING GRAPHS TO SOLVE OTHER EQUATIONS
- USING GRAPHS TO SOLVE SIMULTANEOUS LINEAR AND NON-LINEAR EQUATIONS

SHAPE AND SPACE 8 — 168
- VECTOR OPERATIONS
- SIMPLE GEOMETRIC PROOFS
- VECTOR MODELLING

HANDLING DATA 5 — 173
- MULTIPLICATION (INDEPENDENT EVENTS) AND ADDITION RULES (MUTUALLY EXCLUSIVE EVENTS)
- TREE DIAGRAMS (TWO BRANCHES)

UNIT 9

NUMBER 9 — 176
- FINANCIAL ARITHMETIC
- COMPARATIVE COSTS

ALGEBRA 9 — 181
- SIMULTANEOUS EQUATIONS WITH ONE LINEAR AND ONE NON-LINEAR
- PROOF BY COUNTER EXAMPLE
- NUMBER PROOFS
- PROOFS USING COMPLETING THE SQUARE
- OTHER PROOFS

GRAPHS 8 — 186
- TANGENTS TO CURVES
- INTERPRETING TANGENTS
- TRANSFORMING GRAPHS

SHAPE AND SPACE 9 — 194
- TRIGONOMETRIC GRAPHS
- SINE RULE AND COSINE RULE
- AREA OF A TRIANGLE

HANDLING DATA 6 — 198
- CONSTRUCTING AND INTERPRETING HISTOGRAMS (UNEQUAL CLASSES)

COURSE STRUCTURE

UNIT 10

NUMBER 10 — 202
- RATIONAL AND IRRATIONAL NUMBERS
- SIMPLIFYING SURDS
- RATIONALISING THE DENOMINATOR
- MIXED QUESTIONS

ALGEBRA 10 — 206
- SIMPLIFYING ALGEBRAIC FRACTIONS
- ADDING AND SUBTRACTING ALGEBRAIC FRACTIONS
- MULTIPLYING AND DIVIDING ALGEBRAIC FRACTIONS
- EQUATIONS WITH FRACTIONS
- MIXED QUESTIONS

GRAPHS 9 — 209
- DIFFERENTIATING INTEGER POWERS OF x
- GRADIENT OF A CURVE
- FINDING TURNING POINTS
- LINEAR KINEMATICS
- PRACTICAL PROBLEMS

SHAPE AND SPACE 10 — 214
- GEOMETRIC PROBLEMS
- NAVIGATION AND BEARINGS

HANDLING DATA 7 — 217
- CONDITIONAL PROBABILITY
- TREE DIAGRAMS (MORE THAN TWO BRANCHES)
- PROBABILITY TABLES

EXAMINATION PRACTICE PAPERS — 223
- EXAMINATION PRACTICE PAPERS 1A — 223
- EXAMINATION PRACTICE PAPERS 1B — 230
- EXAMINATION PRACTICE PAPERS 2A — 235
- EXAMINATION PRACTICE PAPERS 2B — 242

GLOSSARY — 249

ANSWERS — 254
- NUMBER 1 — 254
- ALGEBRA 1 — 256
- GRAPHS 1 — 257
- SHAPE AND SPACE 1 — 259
- SETS 1 — 262
- NUMBER 2 — 263
- ALGEBRA 2 — 265
- GRAPHS 2 — 267
- SHAPE AND SPACE 2 — 271
- HANDLING DATA 1 — 273
- NUMBER 3 — 275
- ALGEBRA 3 — 277
- GRAPHS 3 — 279
- SHAPE AND SPACE 3 — 281
- HANDLING DATA 2 — 283
- NUMBER 4 — 285
- ALGEBRA 4 — 286
- GRAPHS 4 — 289
- SHAPE AND SPACE 4 — 290
- HANDLING DATA 3 — 293
- NUMBER 5 — 295
- ALGEBRA 5 — 296
- GRAPHS 5 — 298
- SHAPE AND SPACE 5 — 301
- HANDLING DATA 4 — 303
- NUMBER 6 — 305
- ALGEBRA 6 — 308
- SEQUENCES 1 — 310
- SHAPE AND SPACE 6 — 312
- SETS 2 — 314
- NUMBER 7 — 318
- ALGEBRA 7 — 319
- GRAPHS 6 — 321
- SHAPE AND SPACE 7 — 324
- SETS 3 — 326
- NUMBER 8 — 329
- ALGEBRA 8 — 332
- GRAPHS 7 — 335
- SHAPE AND SPACE 8 — 337
- HANDLING DATA 5 — 340
- NUMBER 9 — 343
- ALGEBRA 9 — 344
- GRAPHS 8 — 346
- SHAPE AND SPACE 9 — 350
- HANDLING DATA 6 — 352
- NUMBER 10 — 354
- ALGEBRA 10 — 356
- GRAPHS 9 — 358
- SHAPE AND SPACE 10 — 361
- HANDLING DATA 7 — 363

ANSWERS — 366
- EXAMINATION PRACTICE PAPERS 1A SOLUTIONS — 366
- EXAMINATION PRACTICE PAPERS 1B SOLUTIONS — 370
- EXAMINATION PRACTICE PAPERS 2A SOLUTIONS — 373
- EXAMINATION PRACTICE PAPERS 2B SOLUTIONS — 378

ABOUT THIS BOOK

This Exam Practice Book is written for students following the Pearson Edexcel International GCSE (9–1) Maths A Higher Tier specification. It can be used to accompany the two Student Books available for the course.

The book contains ten units of work each containing five sections in the topic areas: *Number, Algebra, Graphs, Shape and Space, Sets, Handling Data* and *Sequences*. Each section contains a Basic Skills Exercise to reinforce topics and an Exam Practice Exercise containing exam style questions. There is a particular focus on higher order problem solving and reasoning skills.

The book also contains four Examination Practice Papers, modelled on past papers, to help prepare students for the exam.

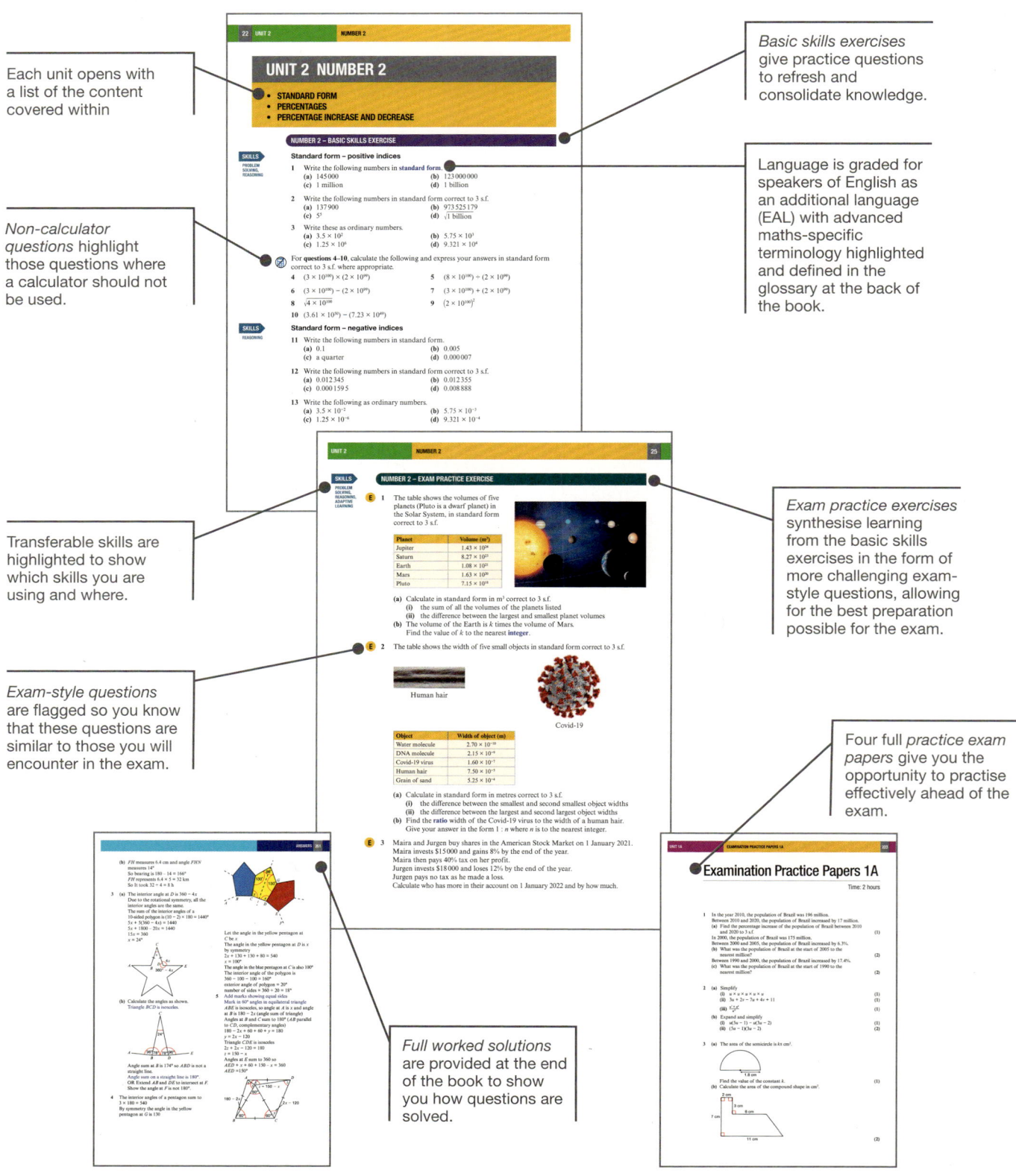

Each unit opens with a list of the content covered within

Basic skills exercises give practice questions to refresh and consolidate knowledge.

Non-calculator questions highlight those questions where a calculator should not be used.

Language is graded for speakers of English as an additional language (EAL) with advanced maths-specific terminology highlighted and defined in the glossary at the back of the book.

Transferable skills are highlighted to show which skills you are using and where.

Exam practice exercises synthesise learning from the basic skills exercises in the form of more challenging exam-style questions, allowing for the best preparation possible for the exam.

Exam-style questions are flagged so you know that these questions are similar to those you will encounter in the exam.

Four full *practice exam papers* give you the opportunity to practise effectively ahead of the exam.

Full worked solutions are provided at the end of the book to show you how questions are solved.

ASSESSMENT OVERVIEW

The following tables give an overview of the assessment for this course.

We recommend that you study this information closely to help ensure that you are fully prepared for this course and know exactly what to expect in the assessment.

PAPER 1	PERCENTAGE	MARK	TIME	AVAILABILITY
HIGHER TIER MATHS A Written examination paper Paper code 4MA1/1H Externally set and assessed by Pearson Edexcel	50%	100	2 hours	January and June examination series First assessment June 2018

PAPER 2	PERCENTAGE	MARK	TIME	AVAILABILITY
HIGHER TIER MATHS A Written examination paper Paper code 4MA1/2H Externally set and assessed by Pearson Edexcel	50%	100	2 hours	January and June examination series First assessment June 2018

ASSESSMENT OBJECTIVES AND WEIGHTINGS

ASSESSMENT OBJECTIVE	DESCRIPTION	% IN INTERNATIONAL GCSE
AO1	Demonstrate knowledge, understanding and skills in number and algebra: • numbers and the numbering system • calculations • solving numerical problems • equations, formulae and identities • sequences, functions and graphs	57–63%
AO2	Demonstrate knowledge, understanding and skills in shape, space and measures: • geometry and trigonometry • vectors and transformation geometry	22–28%
AO3	Demonstrate knowledge, understanding and skills in handling data: • statistics • probability	12–18%

ASSESSMENT OVERVIEW

ASSESSMENT SUMMARY

The Pearson Edexcel International GCSE (9–1) in Mathematics (Specification A) **Higher Tier** requires students to demonstrate application and understanding of the following topics.

NUMBER
- Use numerical skills in a purely mathematical way and in real-life situations.

ALGEBRA
- Use letters as equivalent to numbers and as variables.
- Understand the distinction between expressions, equations and formulae.
- Use algebra to set up and solve problems.
- Demonstrate manipulative skills.
- Construct and use graphs.

GEOMETRY
- Use the properties of angles.
- Understand a range of transformations.
- Work within the metric system.
- Understand ideas of space and shape.
- Use ruler, compasses and protractor appropriately.

STATISTICS
- Understand basic ideas of statistical averages.
- Use a range of statistical techniques.
- Use basic ideas of probability.

Students should also be able to demonstrate **problem-solving skills** by translating problems in mathematical or non-mathematical contexts into a process or a series of mathematical processes.

Students should be able to demonstrate **reasoning skills** by
- making deductions and drawing conclusions from mathematical information
- constructing chains of reasoning
- presenting arguments and proofs
- interpreting and communicating information accurately.

CALCULATORS

Students will be expected to have access to a suitable electronic calculator for both examination papers. The electronic calculator to be used by students attempting **Higher Tier** examination papers (1H and 2H) should have these functions as a minimum:

$+, -, \times, \div, x^2, \sqrt{x}$, memory, brackets, x^y, $x^{\frac{1}{y}}$, $\bar{x}$, Σx, Σfx, standard form, sine, cosine, tangent and their inverses.

PROHIBITIONS

Calculators with any of the following facilities are prohibited in all examinations:
- databanks
- retrieval of text or formulae
- QWERTY keyboards
- built-in symbolic algebra manipulations
- symbolic differentiation or integration.

FORMULAE SHEET – HIGHER TIER

Arithmetic series

Sum to n terms, $S_n = \dfrac{n}{2}[2a + (n-1)d]$

The quadratic equation

The solutions of $ax^2 + bx + c = 0$ where $a \neq 0$ are given by:

$$x = \dfrac{-b \pm \sqrt{b^2 - 4ac}}{2a}$$

Area of trapezium $= \dfrac{1}{2}(a+b)h$

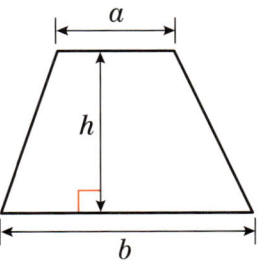

Trigonometry

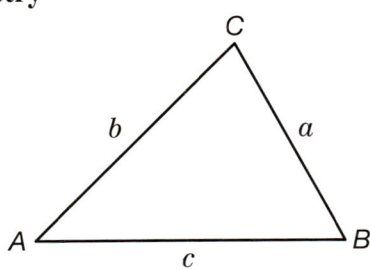

In any triangle ABC

Sine Rule $\dfrac{a}{\sin A} = \dfrac{b}{\sin B} = \dfrac{c}{\sin C}$

Cosine Rule $a^2 = b^2 + c^2 - 2bc \cos A$

Area of triangle $= \dfrac{1}{2} ab \sin C$

Volume of cone $= \dfrac{1}{3}\pi r^2 h$

Curved surface area of cone $= \pi r l$

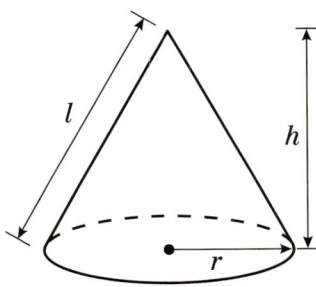

Volume of prism = area of cross section × length

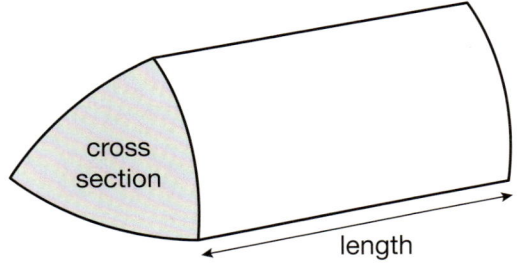

Volume of cylinder $= \pi r^2 h$
Curved surface area of cylinder $= 2\pi r h$

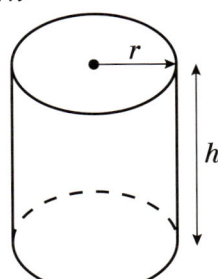

Volume of sphere $= \dfrac{4}{3}\pi r^3$

Surface area of sphere $= 4\pi r^2$

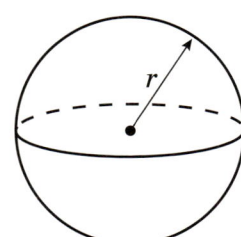

UNIT 1 NUMBER 1

- **EQUIVALENT FRACTIONS**
- **SIMPLIFYING FRACTIONS**
- **FOUR RULES OF FRACTIONS**
- **DIRECTED NUMBER**
- **BIDMAS**
- **SIGNIFICANT FIGURES AND DECIMAL PLACES**

NUMBER 1 – BASIC SKILLS EXERCISE

Do NOT use your calculator for this exercise. You need a good knowledge of numerical fractions to be able to work out algebraic fractions, which cannot be done on a calculator.

Equivalent fractions

1 Find the value of x.

(a) $\frac{3}{4} = \frac{x}{3.6}$ (b) $\frac{3}{7} = \frac{24}{x}$

(c) $3\frac{1}{4} = \frac{x}{8}$ (d) $2\frac{5}{6} = \frac{34}{x}$

2 Show that $4\frac{1}{3}, \frac{52}{12}$ and $\frac{6.5}{1.5}$ all represent the same number.

SKILLS
ANALYSIS

Simplifying fractions

3 Write as fractions or **mixed numbers** in their lowest terms (simplest form)

(a) $\frac{28}{84}$ (b) $\frac{210}{441}$

(c) $\frac{41}{12}$ (d) $\frac{156}{42}$

(e) $\frac{0.4}{14}$ (f) $\frac{2}{3.6}$

SKILLS
PROBLEM SOLVING

Four rules of fractions

For questions 4–8 show that

4 $\frac{8}{9} \times 3\frac{1}{2} \div 2\frac{1}{3} = 1\frac{1}{3}$

5 $4\frac{2}{3} - 2\frac{1}{2} + 1\frac{3}{4} = 3\frac{11}{22}$

6 $\frac{0.12}{32} \div \frac{0.024}{7.2} = 1\frac{1}{8}$

7 $\frac{1}{4} - \left(\frac{1}{4} \times \frac{1}{4}\right) + \left(\frac{1}{4} \div \frac{1}{4}\right) = 1\frac{3}{16}$

8 $\dfrac{4}{2 + \dfrac{2}{3+4}} = 1\frac{3}{4}$

Directed number

  9 Work out
    (a) −4 + 12   (b) −4 − 12
    (c) −4 × 12   (d) −4 ÷ 12
    (e) −4 × −12

BIDMAS

 10 Work out
    (a) 12 − 3 × 3   (b) 8 ÷ 2(2 + 2)
    (c) 8 ÷ 2 × 2   (d) $4(3^2 + 2) - 12 \div 2$
    (e) $\sqrt{(3(4 + 2^2) - 8)}$ (f) $(12 + (4^2 \div 8)) \div (3 \times 2^2 - 5)$

Significant figures and decimal places

11 Write each of these correct to 3 **significant figures** (s.f.).
    (a) 12 340   (b) 12 350
    (c) 12 349   (d) 438 599
    (e) 54 999   (f) 0.012 95
    (g) 1.012 95   (h) 0.009 999

12 Write each of these correct to 3 **decimal places** (d.p.).
    (a) 2944   (b) 1.2949
    (c) 1.2951   (d) 1.200 49
    (e) 0.100 499   (f) 340.0054
    (g) 0.9995   (h) 0.000 499

NUMBER 1 – EXAM PRACTICE EXERCISE

Do NOT use your calculator for this exercise. You need a good knowledge of numerical fractions to be able to work out algebraic fractions, which cannot be done on a calculator.

1 (a) Show that $4\frac{2}{3} \div 3\frac{5}{9} - 1\frac{3}{8} = -\frac{1}{16}$

(b) Hayat, Karim and Ferhana shared a pizza.

Hayat ate $\frac{1}{4}$ of the pizza.

Karim ate $\frac{2}{7}$ of the pizza.

Ferhana ate $\frac{3}{14}$ of the pizza.

(i) Who ate the most? You must show **working** to justify your answer.

(ii) Show that $\frac{1}{4}$ of the pizza remained.

2 (a) Write the number 0.001 854 8 correct to
(i) 3 d.p.
(ii) 3 s.f.
(iii) 2 d.p.
(iv) 2 s.f.

(b) Pedro wrote $\frac{9}{2} - \frac{25}{10} = \frac{9-25}{2-10} = \frac{-16}{-8} = 2$

The answer is correct, but the method is wrong.
(i) Find one mistake Pedro made.
(ii) Show clearly how to work it out correctly.

3 (a) Show that $1 \div 2 \times (5^2 \div 4 - 6 \times 3^2 \div 2^3) = -\frac{1}{4}$

(b) $\frac{1}{u} + \frac{1}{v} = \frac{1}{f}$

Work out f as a fraction when $u = 2\frac{2}{3}$ and $v = 1\frac{1}{5}$

Give your answer as a fraction in its simplest form.

4 (a) There are $187\frac{1}{2}$ ml of hand sanitiser left in a dispenser.

The dispenser gives $3\frac{1}{8}$ ml of sanitiser each time it is pressed.

How many times can the dispenser be pressed before the sanitiser runs out?

(b) Part of a train timetable is shown in the table.

Station	Departure time
Granada	13:18
Antequera	14:30
Sevilla	16:06

Show that the journey time from Granada to Antequera is $\frac{3}{7}$ of the journey time from Granada to Sevilla.

E 5 (a) In a school, $\frac{5}{11}$ of the students are in the lower school while the rest are in the upper school.

$\frac{7}{12}$ of the upper school play football.

$\frac{3}{10}$ of the lower school play football.

Show that $\frac{5}{11}$ of the students at the school play football.

Show each stage of your working.

(b) At a prom, $\frac{23}{45}$ of the students are in year 12 while the rest are in year 13.

$\frac{5}{12}$ of the students wear glasses.

What is the smallest possible number of students at the prom?
Show each stage of your working.

UNIT 1 ALGEBRA 1

- **SIMPLIFYING ALGEBRAIC EXPRESSIONS**
- **SOLVING EQUATIONS**

ALGEBRA 1 – BASIC SKILLS EXERCISE

Simplifying algebraic expressions

For questions **1–8**, **simplify** each expression as much as possible.

1 $2xy + 2xz$
2 $3xy - xy$
3 $5a + 5 + 5a$
4 $a + 6b - a + b$
5 $3a \times 3b$
6 $a^3 \times 7a^2$
7 $a \times 5a^2 \times a^3$
8 $(2a)^3 \times (3a)^2$

For questions **9–12**, **expand** the brackets and simplify as much as possible.

9 $6(2a - b)$
10 $4(3a + 4b)$
11 $-(2a + b - a)$
12 $8b - 2(a + b)$

SKILLS
REASONING

Solving equations

For questions **13–18**, solve for t.

13 $3t - 1 = 14$
14 $2t + 9 = 5$
15 $1 - 2t = 7$
16 $1 - \frac{t}{3} = 4$
17 $\frac{t}{7} = 7$
18 $\frac{7}{t} = 7$

For questions **19–22**, solve for y.

19 $3(y - 2) = -12$
20 $4(y + 3) = 8$
21 $3(y + \frac{1}{2}) = 6$
22 $5(y - 1) = 4$

For questions **23–26**, solve for z.

23 $5z + 6 = 2z + 3$
24 $3z - 1 = 7z - 9$
25 $3 + 2z = 18 - 3z$
26 $2 - 4z = 1 - 5z$

For questions **27–30**, solve for x.

27 $2(x + 5) - (x + 4) = 8$
28 $4(x + 2) - 5(x - 3) = 24$
29 $5(2x + 3) - 3(4x - 1) = 12$
30 $3(3x + 2) - 5(2x - 2) = 7(3x - 4)$

UNIT 1 — ALGEBRA 1

ALGEBRA 1 – EXAM PRACTICE EXERCISE

SKILLS — PROBLEM SOLVING, REASONING

E 1 The **sum** of three **consecutive**, even numbers is 648.
The smallest number is x.
(a) Form an equation in x.
(b) Solve your equation to find the three numbers.

E 2 The diagram shows a triangle ABC.
$AB = AC$
BCD is a straight line.
(a) Form an equation in x.
(b) Solve your equation and find the size of each angle in the triangle.

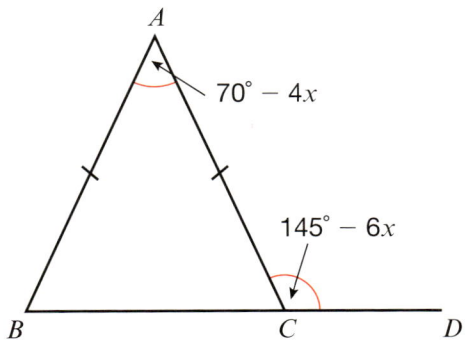

E 3 The length of a mobile phone is twice the width.
There is a border around the screen.
The border is 1.5 cm wide at the top and bottom.
The border is 0.25 cm wide at the sides.
The **perimeter** of the screen is 32 cm.
Let the width of the phone be x cm.
(a) Form an equation in x.
(b) Hence find the area of the screen in cm².

E 4 A piece of wire is 30 cm long.
It is cut into two unequal pieces.
One piece is bent into a circle.
The other is bent into a square enclosing the circle, as shown in the diagram.
Find the length of each piece of wire in cm to 3 s.f.

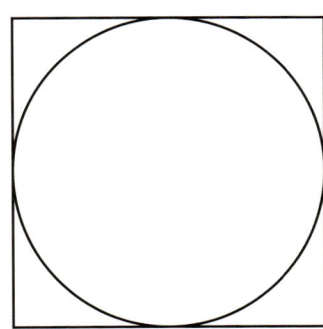

E 5 (a) Find the first time after 12:00 that the hands of a clock are at right angles.
Let x be the number of minutes after 12:00.
Give your answer to the nearest second.
(b) At 12:00 the hands of a clock are directly in line.
Find the first time after 12:00 that the hands of a clock are directly in line again.
Give your answer to the nearest second.

UNIT 1 GRAPHS 1

- **GRADIENT OF A STRAIGHT LINE**
- **PLOTTING STRAIGHT-LINE GRAPHS**
- **STRAIGHT-LINE CONVERSION GRAPHS**

GRAPHS 1 – BASIC SKILLS EXERCISE

Gradient of a straight line

1. Find the **gradient** of the straight line joining A to B when
   (a) A is $(-1, -2)$ and B is $(2, 4)$
   (b) A is $(-5, -1)$ and B is $(-1, -3)$

2. A ski slope has a gradient of $\frac{3}{4}$
   Work out the value of h.

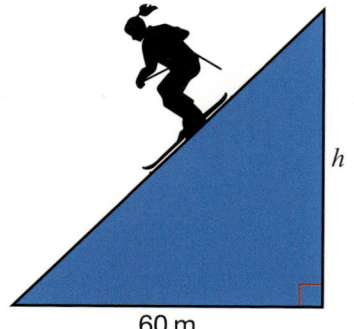

3. This tree is leaning with gradient 18.
   Work out the value of d.

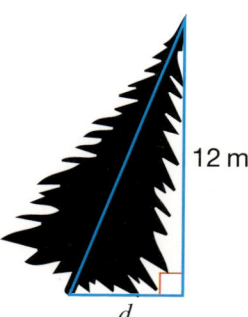

4. The lift in the Spinnaker Tower at Portsmouth, England, is not vertical.
   The top of the lift is 100 m above the ground but 350 cm off the vertical.
   What is the gradient of the lift?
   Give your answer to 3 s.f.

5 The gradient of the line joining $A(p, 2)$ to $B(6, -3)$ is $-\frac{1}{2}$
   Find the value of p.

6 Do the points $A(-1, -3)$, $B(2, 3)$ and $C(92, 185)$ lie on a straight line?
   Justify your answer.

7 The points $A(-2, 5)$, $B(1, 1)$ and $C(49, p)$ lie on a straight line.
   Find the value of p.

8 The line joining the points $A(1, q)$ to $B(2, 8)$ has twice the gradient of the line joining $C(1, -2)$ to $D(3, q)$.
   Find the value of q.

Plotting straight-line graphs

9 Which of these points lie on the line $y - 5x + 3 = 0$?
   $A(3, 12)$ $B(-5, -26)$ $C(0, 3)$ $D(-52, 263)$

10 This table of values for a straight-line graph contains one mistake in the y-values. Find and correct the mistake.

x	−2	0	2	4	6
y	5	2	1	−1	−3

11 Find the values of a, b and c in this table of values for a straight-line graph.

x	−3	a	0	1	3	c
y	11	8	2	−1	b	−10

12 (a) Make a table of values for $y = 3 - 2x$ and $2y - x + 2 = 0$ using $x = \{-2, 0, 2, 4\}$ and then draw both graphs on one set of axes for $-2 \leq x \leq 4$
   (b) Write down the gradient and y-**intercept** of both graphs.
   (c) Write down the intersection point of the two graphs.

Straight-line conversion graphs

13 One kilogram (kg) is approximately equal to 2.2 pounds (lb) weight.
   (a) Use this information to draw a conversion graph from kg to lb for $0 \leq$ kg ≤ 5
   (b) Use your graph to convert
      (i) 3.5 kg to lb
      (ii) 4 lb to kg

14 The graph shows the cost, C, for a taxi ride plotted against the distance, d km, travelled.

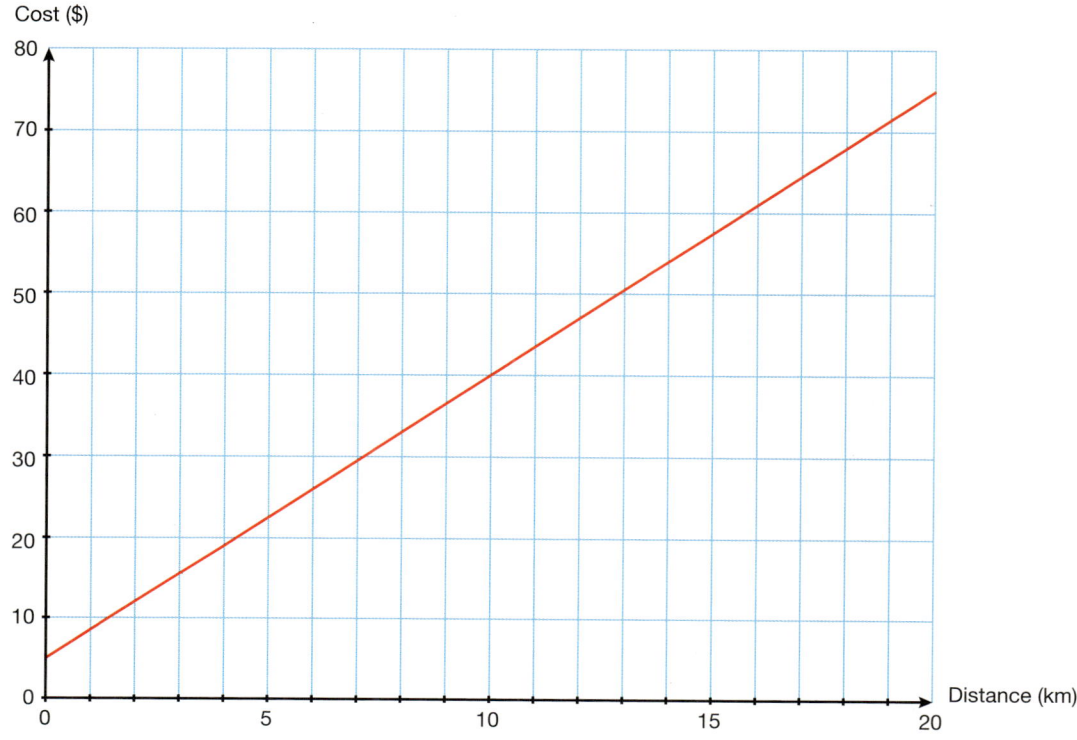

(a) What is the cost for a taxi ride of 16 km?
(b) A taxi ride cost $30.
What was the distance travelled?
(c) Kobe is 6 km from home and has $20. If they take a taxi as far as they can and then walk the rest of the way home, how far will they have to walk?

GRAPHS 1 – EXAM PRACTICE EXERCISE

1 (a) A shed has the dimensions shown in the diagram.
The roof has a gradient of $\frac{1}{3}$.
Find w, the width of the shed.

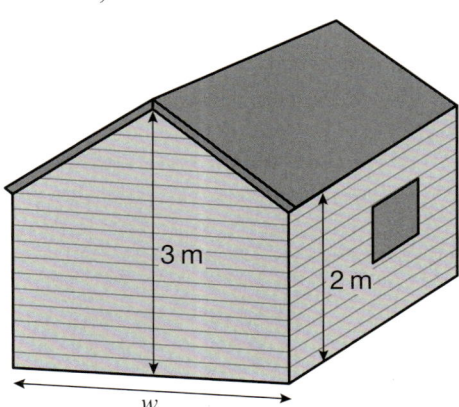

(b) The straight line joining the points $(p - 1, p - 9)$ and $(p + 7, 5p - 9)$ has a gradient of $\frac{1}{2}$.
Find the value of p.

2 The points $A(-16, -10)$, $B(29, 20)$, $C(45, -12)$ and $D(0, -42)$ form the **vertices** of a **quadrilateral**.
(a) Use gradients to prove that $ABCD$ is a **parallelogram**.
(b) Show that the line AB does not pass through the origin.

3 Jodie's new phone contract costs £20 every month.
The first 300 minutes of calls every month are free.
Each month, after the first 300 minutes of calls she is charged per minute.
The formula for the cost, £C, against the time, t minutes, of calls per month is

$C = 20$ for $0 \le t \le 300$, $C = 0.02t + 14$ for $t > 300$

(a) Complete the table and then draw a graph of C against t for $0 \le t \le 1800$

t (mins)	0	300	1000	1800
C (£)				

(b) How much is she charged per minute if she makes more than 300 minutes of calls in a month?
(c) One month Jodie's bill read: 'Call time: 16 hours 40 minutes: cost £38.50.'
Should Jodie complain?
Give a reason for your answer.

E 4 In 1980 the area of the Arctic Sea ice was 7.7 × 10⁶ km².
The area was decreasing by 86 000 km² each year.

The formula for the area of Arctic Sea ice, y km², x years after 1980 is given by $y = mx + c$.

(a) Find the value of the constants m and c.

(b) Complete the table and then draw the graph of y against x for $1980 \leq x \leq 2000$

x (years after 1980)	0	20	40
y (area in km²)			

(c) Use the graph to find
   (i) the area of sea ice in the year 2000 in km²
   (ii) the year when the area of sea ice was 5 × 10⁶ km²

E 5 Lily has bought a 3D printer.
This uses a thin plastic wire (filament) wound onto a reel.

An empty reel with no filament weighs 200 g.
A full reel with 330 m of filament weighs 1.2 kg.

(a) Complete the table and then draw a conversion graph for the length, L m, of filament against the weight, W g, of a reel for $200 \leq W \leq 1200$

Weight, W (g)	200	1200
Length, L (m)		

(b) Use your graph to find
   (i) the length of filament on a reel that weighs 900 g
   (ii) the weight of a reel with 100 m of filament on it

(c) Write down the formula connecting L and W in the form $L = mW + c$, where m and c are constants.

UNIT 1 SHAPE AND SPACE 1

- **ANGLE PROPERTIES**
- **POLYGONS**
- **SIMILAR TRIANGLES**
- **CONSTRUCTIONS**

SHAPE AND SPACE 1 – BASIC SKILLS EXERCISE

Angle properties

For questions 1–4, calculate the size of each lettered angle.

1

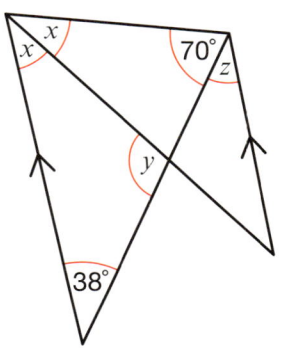

2

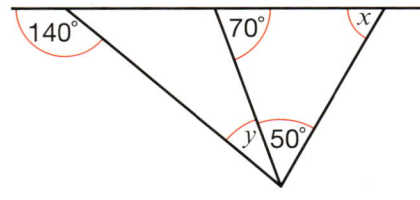

3

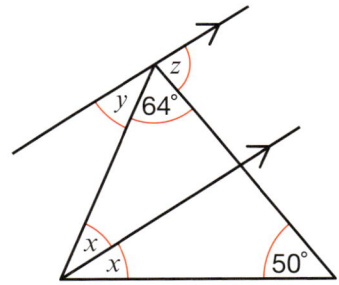

4

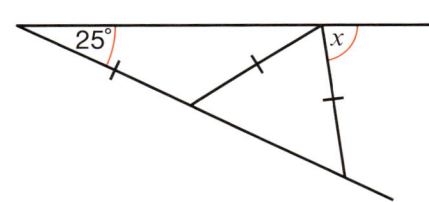

5 A triangle *ABC* has **exterior angles** as shown.
(a) Find the value of *x*.
(b) Show that *ABC* is an isosceles triangle.

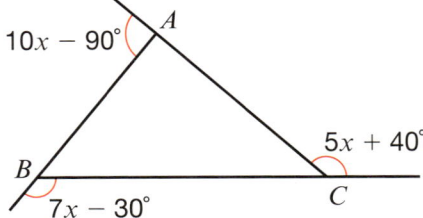

SKILLS
REASONING

6 The **interior angles** of a quadrilateral *ABCD* are shown in the diagram.
   (a) Find the value of *x*.
   (b) Show that the quadrilateral is a **trapezium**.

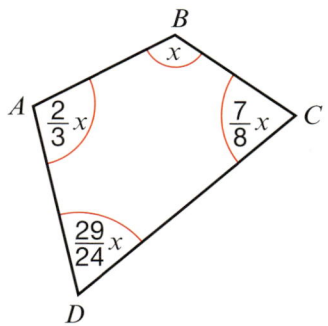

7 Find the smallest angle between the hands of a clock at 20:06.

Polygons

8 Calculate the values of *x*, *y* and *z*.

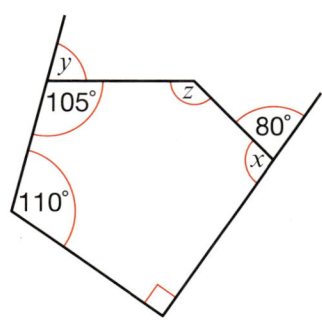

SKILLS
REASONING

9 *ABCDE* is a regular pentagon.
   (a) Find angle *x*.
   (b) Prove that *AB* is parallel to *CE*.
       Give reasons for each step of your working.

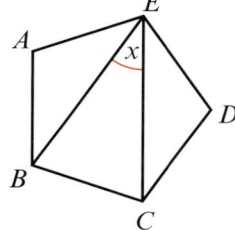

10 A regular **polygon** has 20 sides. Find the size of the interior angle.

11 The sum of the interior angles of a regular polygon is 3060°. How many sides does it have?

12 The diagram shows part of a regular polygon.
    (a) Find the number of sides of the polygon.
    (b) Find the sum of the interior angles.

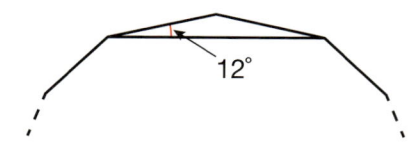

SKILLS
REASONING

Similar triangles

13 Calculate *a*.

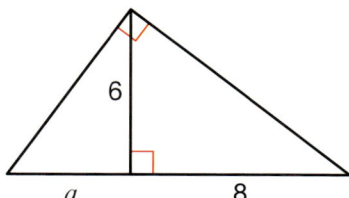

14 Calculate a and b.

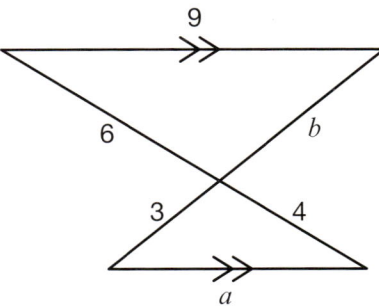

15 Calculate a and b.

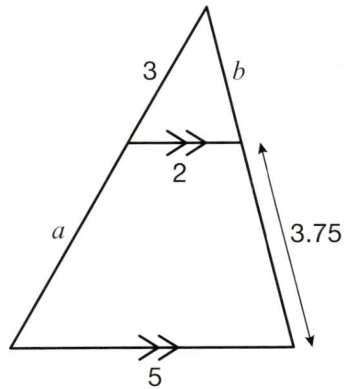

Constructions

In questions 16–18, use a ruler and compasses only and show all construction lines.

16 (a) Construct the triangle ABC where $AB = 10$ cm, $AC = 12$ cm and $BC = 8$ cm.
   (b) Construct the bisector of angle A, and extend it to meet BC at the point D.
   (c) Measure DC.

17 (a) Draw the line segment $AC = 8$ cm and construct the perpendicular bisector of AC.
   (b) Hence draw the rhombus $ABCD$ that has diagonal $AC = 8$ cm and diagonal $BD = 12$ cm.
   (c) Measure the side length of the rhombus.

18 In a game, a clue is buried within a triangle formed by an Oak tree (O), an Apple tree (A) and a Plum tree (P). $OA = 16$ m, $AP = 18$ m and $OP = 20$ m.
   (a) Construct a scale drawing of the triangle OAP using a scale of 1 cm to 2 m.
   (b) The clue, C, is equidistant from the A and P and 12 m from O.
       Find the distance of the clue from P.

SHAPE AND SPACE 1 – EXAM PRACTICE EXERCISE

1 **(a)** *PQS* is an isosceles triangle with *PQ* = *QS*.
PRS is another isosceles triangle with *PR* = *PS*.
Find the value of *x*.

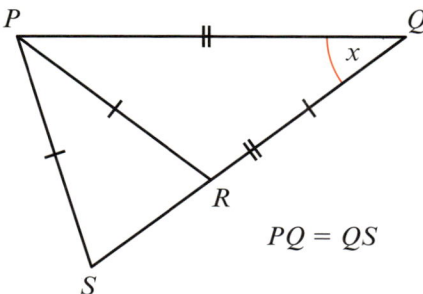

PQ = *QS*

(b) The diagram shows some **right-angled triangles**.
AC = 20 cm, *BC* = 21 cm
D is a point on *AB* such that angle *CDB* = 90°.
Use **similar triangles** to find the length marked *x*.
Give your answer as an **improper fraction** in its simplest terms.

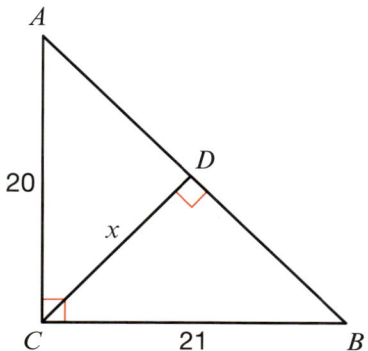

2 Rupinder sets sail from a harbour, *H*.
She sails 35 km on a **bearing** of 030° to a buoy, *B*.
She then sails 28 km on a bearing of 270° to her fishing grounds, *F*.
(a) Construct a scale drawing of her voyage using a scale of 1 cm to 5 km.
Use a ruler and **compasses** only.
You must show all your construction lines.
(b) Rupinder sails straight back to the harbour at an average speed of 4 km/h.
   (i) Use a **protractor** to find the bearing she sailed on.
   (ii) Use a ruler to calculate the time it took in hours.

E 3 The diagram shows a star *ABCDE*.
The star has 5 vertices.
The star has **rotational symmetry** of order 5.
BC = *CD*
Angle *BCD* = *x*
Angle *CDE* = 4*x*
(a) Calculate the value of *x*.
(b) Show that *ABDE* is not a straight line.

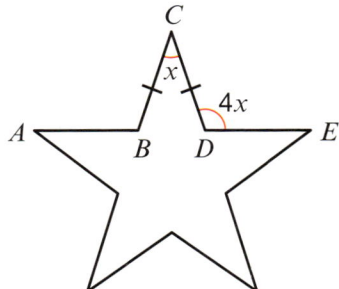

E 4 The diagram shows part of a regular polygon *ABCDEF*.
The polygon is surrounded by pentagons that have one line of symmetry.
Two interior angles of the pentagons are 130° and 80° as shown on the diagram.
Find the number of sides of the regular polygon.

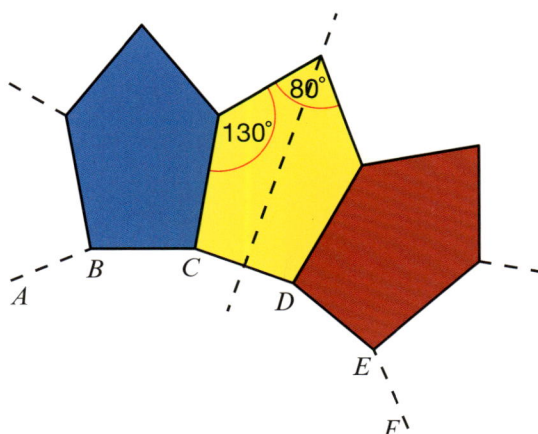

E 5 *ABCD* is a **rhombus**.
BCE is an **equilateral triangle** with *E* lying inside the rhombus.
Angle *AEB* = *x*
Prove that angle *AED* is 150°.
You must explain each step of your working.

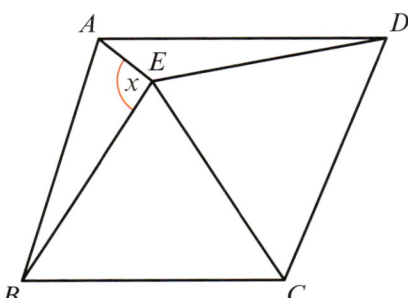

UNIT 1 SETS 1

- **BASIC IDEAS**
- **VENN DIAGRAMS WITH TWO SETS**

SETS 1 – BASIC SKILLS EXERCISE

Basic ideas

1. Write down two more members of the following **sets**.
   (a) {3, 6, 9, 12, …}
   (b) {−1, −2, −3, …}
   (c) {football, cricket, swimming, …}
   (d) {Ford, Toyota, Rolls-Royce, …}

2. Use a rule to describe each set in **question 1**.

3. List these sets.
   (a) {even numbers between 1 and 9}
   (b) {square numbers between 2 and 20}
   (c) {months of the year beginning with J}
   (d) {colours on traffic lights}

4. Which of these statements are true and which are false?
   (a) $3 \in$ {odd numbers}
   (b) $5 \notin$ {factors of 10}
   (c) lion $\notin$ {animals with four legs}
   (d) triangle $\in$ {polygons}

5. Which are examples of the empty set?
   (a) {square numbers between 10 and 15}
   (b) {birds with four legs}
   (c) {fish with teeth}
   (d) {common factors of 32 and 45}

SKILLS
REASONING

Venn diagrams with two sets

6. $\mathscr{E}$ = {positive integers between 1 and 11 inclusive}, A = {multiples of 2}, B = {multiples of 4}
   (a) Illustrate this information on a **Venn diagram**.
   (b) List the set A' and describe it in words.
   (c) What is $n(B')$?
   (d) Is $B \subset A$? Explain your answer.

7 ℰ = {odd numbers between 1 and 21 inclusive}, M = {multiples of 5}, F = {factors of 20}
  (a) Why is 10 ∈ M false?
  (b) List M.
  (c) Find n(F).
  (d) List M ∩ F.

8 Draw Venn diagrams to illustrate the following statements.
  (a) A ∩ B = ∅
  (b) A ∩ B ≠ ∅
  (c) A ∩ B = A
  (d) A ∪ B = A

9 ℰ = {A, E, I, O, U}, W = {capital letters that have straight lines in them}
  S = {capital letters that have curved parts in them}
  (a) List the sets W, W′, S and S′.
  (b) Draw a Venn diagram to represent the information.
  (c) What is
    (i) W ∪ S
    (ii) W ∩ S?

10 The following information was obtained about all the fast-food restaurants in a town: 6 sold tacos and burritos, 4 sold burritos only, 9 sold tacos, while 2 served neither tacos nor burritos.
  (a) Draw a Venn diagram to represent all of this information.
  (b) How many fast-food restaurants are there in the town?

SETS 1 – EXAM PRACTICE EXERCISE

E 1 (a) Which of these statements are true and which are false?
 (i)   circle $\in$ {polygons}
 (ii) $y = x + 2 \notin$ {straight-line graphs with gradient 2}
 (iii) $-1 \notin$ {solutions of $x^2 = 1$}
 (iv) square $\notin$ {parallelograms}

(b) The Venn diagram shows four events A, B, C and D.

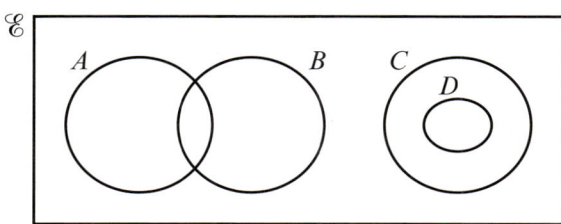

Choose a statement from the box below that correctly describes the relationship between
 (i) A and C
 (ii) D and C
 (iii) A and B

$A \subset B$ $C \cup D = D$ $A \cap B \neq \varnothing$ $A \cup C = \mathcal{E}$ $C \cup D = C$ $A \cap C = \varnothing$

E 2 (a) $\mathcal{E}$ = {even integers between 1 and 15 inclusive},
 A = {multiples of 4}, $n(B) = 4$, $A \cap B = \varnothing$
 List $A \cup B$.

(b) $n(\mathcal{E}) = 17$, $n(D') = 9$, $C \cap D \neq \varnothing$ and $n(C' \cap D) = 6$
 (i)   Find $n(D)$.
 (ii) Find $n(C \cap D)$.
 (iii) Draw a Venn diagram to illustrate this information.

E 3 Thirty students were asked to choose either Art, or Biology, or both subjects.
Three students forgot to make a choice.
Twenty-five students chose Biology.

Use a Venn diagram to find how many students chose both subjects.

E 4 ℰ = {all triangles}, I = {isosceles triangles}, R = {right-angled triangles}
(a) Draw a Venn diagram to illustrate the sets I and R.
(b) Calculate the three angles of a member of $I \cap R$.
E = {equilateral triangles}
(c) Add set E to your Venn diagram.

E 5 (a) $n(ℰ) = 33$
$n(A) = x$
$n(B) = 2x + 7$
$n(A \cap B) = \frac{x}{2}$
$n((A \cup B)') = 17 - x$
Find $n(A' \cap B)$.

(b) A group of students use the social media sites Beetle and Iota.
$\frac{3}{4}$ use Beetle.
$\frac{5}{24}$ use Iota only.
Two students use neither.
(i) How many students are in the group?
(ii) If $\frac{11}{24}$ use Beetle only, how many use both Beetle and Iota?

UNIT 2 NUMBER 2

- STANDARD FORM
- PERCENTAGES
- PERCENTAGE INCREASE AND DECREASE

NUMBER 2 – BASIC SKILLS EXERCISE

SKILLS
PROBLEM SOLVING, REASONING

Standard form – positive indices

1. Write the following numbers in **standard form**.
   (a) 145 000
   (b) 123 000 000
   (c) 1 million
   (d) 1 billion

2. Write the following numbers in standard form correct to 3 s.f.
   (a) 137 900
   (b) 973 525 179
   (c) 5^5
   (d) $\sqrt{1 \text{ billion}}$

3. Write these as ordinary numbers.
   (a) 3.5×10^2
   (b) 5.75×10^3
   (c) 1.25×10^6
   (d) 9.321×10^4

For **questions 4–10**, calculate the following and express your answers in standard form correct to 3 s.f. where appropriate.

4. $(3 \times 10^{100}) \times (2 \times 10^{99})$
5. $(8 \times 10^{100}) \div (2 \times 10^{99})$

6. $(3 \times 10^{100}) - (2 \times 10^{99})$
7. $(3 \times 10^{100}) + (2 \times 10^{99})$

8. $\sqrt{4 \times 10^{100}}$
9. $(2 \times 10^{100})^2$

10. $(3.61 \times 10^{50}) - (7.23 \times 10^{49})$

SKILLS
REASONING

Standard form – negative indices

11. Write the following numbers in standard form.
    (a) 0.1
    (b) 0.005
    (c) a quarter
    (d) 0.000 007

12. Write the following numbers in standard form correct to 3 s.f.
    (a) 0.012 345
    (b) 0.012 355
    (c) 0.000 159 5
    (d) 0.008 888

13. Write the following as ordinary numbers.
    (a) 3.5×10^{-2}
    (b) 5.75×10^{-3}
    (c) 1.25×10^{-6}
    (d) 9.321×10^{-4}

For **questions 14–24**, calculate the following and express your answers in standard form correct to 3 s.f. where appropriate.

14 $(3 \times 10^{-100}) \times (2 \times 10^{-99})$

15 $(8 \times 10^{-100}) \div (2 \times 10^{-99})$

16 $(3 \times 10^{-100}) - (2 \times 10^{-99})$

17 $(3 \times 10^{-100}) + (2 \times 10^{-99})$

18 $\sqrt{4 \times 10^{-100}}$

19 $(2 \times 10^{-100})^2$

20 $(1.36 \times 10^{-3})^2$

21 $(3.75 \times 10^{-5})^2 \times (4.35 \times 10^{-7})^2$

22 $\sqrt{5.785 \times 10^{-12}}$

23 $\sqrt{\dfrac{3.85 \times 10^{-9}}{1.47 \times 10^{-3}}}$

24 $\sqrt[3]{\dfrac{3.85 \times 10^{-9}}{1.47 \times 10^{-3}}}$

25 If $p = 9.47 \times 10^{-5}$ and $q = 4.31 \times 10^{-3}$ calculate the following in standard form correct to 3 s.f.
  (a) pq
  (b) pq^2
  (c) p^2q
  (d) $\left(\dfrac{p}{q}\right)^2$

SKILLS
ADAPTIVE LEARNING

Standard form – applied problems

26 The smallest mammal is the Kitti's hog-nosed bat in Thailand which has a body length of 29 mm. Calculate this length in km. Give your answer in standard form correct to 3 s.f.

27 One of the biggest known stars is the M-class supergiant Betelgeuse which has a **diameter** of 980 million km.
  (a) Assuming it to be a sphere, calculate its surface area in mm², giving your answer in standard form correct to 3 s.f.
  (b) Given that the Earth has a **radius** of 6370 km, express its surface area as a percentage of Betelgeuse's. Give your answer in standard form correct to 3 s.f.

28 Kalyan Ramji Sain of India grew a moustache to a length of 339 mm over a 17-year period between 1976 and 1993. Calculate the speed of his moustache growth in km/s. Give your answer in standard form correct to 3 s.f.

29 The speed of sound is 3×10^8 m/s which is equal to p km per year. Find p in standard form correct to 3 s.f.

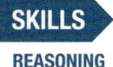
SKILLS
REASONING

Percentages

30 Write these percentages as fractions in their lowest possible terms.
  (a) 25%
  (b) 10%
  (c) 75%
  (d) 60%
  (e) 35%

31 Find 10% of 1500 m.

32 Find 15% of $2400.

33 Find 10% of 5% of 8400 g.

34 Express 12 cm as a percentage of 1.5 m.

35 Express 1 cm² as a percentage of 1 m².

36 Ahmed buys a model boat for £120, then sells it for £75.
    What is his percentage loss?

37 Mari buys a painting for €1250, then sells it for €1400.
    What is her percentage profit?

Percentage increase and decrease

38 Increase 1500 m by 10%.

39 Increase 320 kg by 65%.

40 Decrease $1200 by 24%.

41 Decrease 25 000 cm² by 15%.

42 A mobile phone from Pineapple Net is advertised at a 25% reduction in Winter sales. Its price before the sale is $120. What is the sale price?

43 Jermaine's pocket money is €15 per week. His weekly rate is increased by 15%. How much will he receive at the end of a year at the new rate?

44 Sami buys a computer game for £36 after the cost has been reduced by 36%. What was the original cost?

45 Jamal's fastest time for the 400 m is 70 seconds. In his next race he improves by 10% and in the race after that he improves from this time by 10% again.
    (a) What is his new fastest time?
    (b) What is his overall percentage improvement?

46 Ning was 1.25 m tall. One year later she was 10% taller and in the next year her height increased a further 12% from her new height.
    (a) What is her height after both increases?
    (b) What is her overall percentage height increase over the two years?

47 Umberto has a salary of €120 000. Calculate his new salary if it is
    (a) increased by 10% then decreased by 10%
    (b) increased by x% then decreased by x%

48 Increase x by y%.

49 Decrease x by y%.

50 Find the percentage increase of the area of a square if its side is increased by 20%.

NUMBER 2 – EXAM PRACTICE EXERCISE

SKILLS
PROBLEM SOLVING, REASONING, ADAPTIVE LEARNING

E 1 The table shows the volumes of five planets (Pluto is a dwarf planet) in the Solar System, in standard form correct to 3 s.f.

Planet	Volume (m³)
Jupiter	1.43×10^{24}
Saturn	8.27×10^{23}
Earth	1.08×10^{21}
Mars	1.63×10^{20}
Pluto	7.15×10^{18}

(a) Calculate in standard form in m³ correct to 3 s.f.
 (i) the sum of all the volumes of the planets listed
 (ii) the difference between the largest and smallest planet volumes
(b) The volume of the Earth is k times the volume of Mars.
 Find the value of k to the nearest **integer**.

E 2 The table shows the width of five small objects in standard form correct to 3 s.f.

Human hair

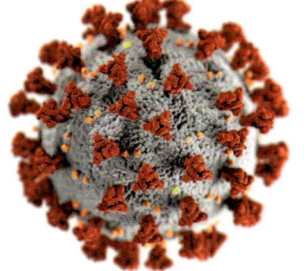

Covid-19

Object	Width of object (m)
Water molecule	2.70×10^{-10}
DNA molecule	2.15×10^{-9}
Covid-19 virus	1.60×10^{-7}
Human hair	7.50×10^{-5}
Grain of sand	5.25×10^{-4}

(a) Calculate in standard form in metres correct to 3 s.f.
 (i) the difference between the smallest and second smallest object widths
 (ii) the difference between the largest and second largest object widths
(b) Find the **ratio** width of the Covid-19 virus to the width of a human hair.
 Give your answer in the form $1 : n$ where n is to the nearest integer.

E 3 Maira and Jurgen buy shares in the American Stock Market on 1 January 2021.
Maira invests $15 000 and gains 8% by the end of the year.
Maira then pays 40% tax on her profit.
Jurgen invests $18 000 and loses 12% by the end of the year.
Jurgen pays no tax as he made a loss.
Calculate who has more in their account on 1 January 2022 and by how much.

4 The table shows the population of London in four different years.

Year	Population (millions)
1900	5.00
1950	8.20
2000	7.27
2020	9.30

(a) Express London's population in 1900 as a percentage of its population in 2000.
(b) Find the percentage change in London's population from
  (i) 1950 to 2000
  (ii) 1900 to 2020
Give all your answers correct to 3 s.f.

5 The table below shows the number of medical doctors working in the four countries of the UK in 2019.

Country	Women	Men
England	98 974	107 221
Scotland	11 012	9766
Wales	4711	5531
Northern Ireland	3337	3207

(a) Which of the four countries has the highest percentage of doctors that are women?

The total number of doctors that are men increases by $k\%$ to 130 754.

(b) Find the value of k.
Give all your answers correct to 3 s.f. where appropriate and show full working to justify your conclusions.

UNIT 2 ALGEBRA 2

- **MULTIPLYING AND DIVIDING FRACTIONS**
- **SOLVING EQUATIONS WITH ROOTS AND POWERS**
- **POSITIVE INTEGER INDICES**
- **LINEAR INEQUALITIES**

ALGEBRA 2 – BASIC SKILLS EXERCISE

Multiplying and dividing fractions

For **questions 1–18**, simplify the expressions, giving your answer as a single fraction.

1. $\frac{12}{3x}$
2. $\frac{4a^2}{2a}$
3. $\frac{4x^2y}{2xy^2}$
4. $\frac{16x^3y}{4xy}$
5. $\frac{15a^3bd}{21(ab)^2}$
6. $\frac{2x}{3} \times \frac{6}{x}$
7. $\frac{x}{y} \times \frac{z}{y} \times \frac{y^2}{x}$
8. $\frac{3x}{4} \div \frac{3x}{4}$
9. $\frac{4ab^2}{c} \div \frac{ab}{c^2}$
10. $\frac{a^2}{b} \div \frac{a}{c} \div \frac{ac}{b^2}$
11. $\frac{2x}{3} + \frac{3x}{4}$
12. $\frac{1}{2x} + \frac{2}{3x}$
13. $\frac{4z}{3} - \frac{2z}{5}$
14. $\frac{1}{x} - \frac{2}{5x}$
15. $\frac{2x}{3} - \frac{x}{3} \times \frac{x}{2}$
16. $\left(\frac{2x}{3} - \frac{x}{3}\right) \times \frac{x}{2}$
17. $\left(\frac{a}{b} + \frac{b}{a}\right) \div \frac{1}{ab}$
18. $\frac{a}{b} + \frac{b}{a} \div \frac{1}{ab}$

Solving equations with roots and powers

For **questions 19–28**, solve the equations.

19. $3x^2 + 1 = 49$
20. $\frac{x^2}{2} + 3 = 11$
21. $\frac{x^2 + 3}{2} = 6$
22. $\frac{2x^3 - 14}{5} = 8$
23. $\frac{5(19 - x^4)}{6} = 2\frac{1}{2}$
24. $\sqrt{x} + 8 = 10$
25. $3\sqrt{x} - 2 = 7$
26. $2\sqrt{x} + 5 = 1$
27. $\frac{3\sqrt{11x + 1}}{5} = 6$
28. $5\sqrt{x} - 4 = 2(4\sqrt{x} - 5)$

Positive integer indices

For **questions 29–36**, simplify the expressions, giving your answer in **index** form.

29. $3 \times 3^5 \times 3^4$
30. $a \times a^3 \times a^2$
31. $5^9 \div 5^2$
32. $x^{12} \div x^{10}$
33. $(4^3)^2$
34. $(y^6)^3$
35. $(7^3)^4 \div 7^8$
36. $(z^2)^4 \div z^5$

Linear inequalities

37 Find the correct symbol, <, > or =, to insert in the box.
    (a) $2 \square -2$ **(b)** $-2 \square -5$
    (c) $20\% \square \frac{1}{4}$ **(d)** $-0.3 \square -\frac{1}{3}$

38 Show the following inequalities on a number line.
    (a) $x \leq -1$
    (b) $x > -3$
    (c) $-2 \leq x < 1$

39 Write down the inequalities represented by the following number lines.
    (a)

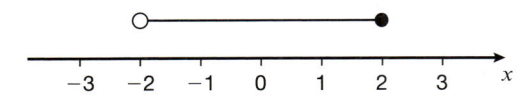

    (b)

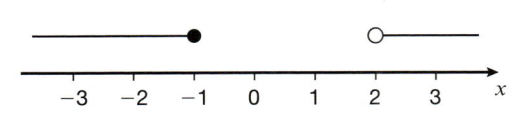

For **questions 40–43**, solve the inequality.
40 $5x - 1 \leq 9$ **41** $x + 7 < 3x - 1$
42 $4(1 - x) > 12$ **43** $2(x + 1) \leq 2 + x < 10 + 3x$

ALGEBRA 2 – EXAM PRACTICE EXERCISE

1 (a) Simplify fully $\dfrac{12x^3y^2z}{5x^2y^4} \div \dfrac{8xz}{15y^3} \times \dfrac{yz}{9x^2}$

(b) Show that $1 - \left[\dfrac{1}{x^2} \div \left(\dfrac{1}{x} - \dfrac{3x}{x^2}\right)\right]$ can be written as $\dfrac{ax+1}{ax}$ where a is an integer to be found.

2 There are three children in a family.
Ava, Ben and Charlie are the three children.
Ava is y years old.
Ben is four years younger than Ava.
Charlie is twice as old as Ben.
The sum of their ages in completed years is greater than 27 but less than 41.
(a) Write down two inequalities in y that show this information.
(b) Find the maximum ages of each child.
(c) Find the minimum ages of each child.

3 (a) $a^{\sqrt{x+1}} \div a^3 = a$

Find the value of x.

(b) (i) Show clearly that $\dfrac{1}{1 + \dfrac{1}{a}} = \dfrac{a}{a+1}$

(ii) Simplify $\dfrac{1}{1 + \dfrac{1}{1 + \dfrac{1}{a}}}$

4 David goes on a journey.
He travels for the first third of his journey at an average speed of 60 km/h.
He then travels for the rest of his journey at an average speed of 40 km/h.
The total time for his journey is 1.5 hours.
Let $3x$ be the total distance travelled.
Find the total distance, in km, of David's journey.

5 When two resistances with values a and b ohms are placed in parallel, the overall resistance, R ohms, is given by $\dfrac{1}{R} = \dfrac{1}{a} + \dfrac{1}{b}$
(a) Show that $R = \dfrac{ab}{a+b}$

The original value of a is increased by 1 ohm.
The original value of b is decreased by 1 ohm ($b > 1$).

(b) Show that the percentage change in R is given by $\dfrac{b-a-1}{ab} \times 100$

UNIT 2 GRAPHS 2

- **FINDING THE EQUATION OF A STRAIGHT LINE**
- **SKETCHING STRAIGHT-LINE GRAPHS**
- **SOLVING SIMULTANEOUS EQUATIONS GRAPHICALLY**

GRAPHS 2 – BASIC SKILLS EXERCISE

Finding the equation of a straight line

For **questions 1–4**, find the equation of the straight line with

1. gradient 3 passing through (0, −1)
2. gradient $-\frac{1}{4}$ passing through (0, 2)
3. gradient 1 passing through (1, 1)
4. gradient 2 passing through (0, 1)

For **questions 5–8**, find the equation of the straight line parallel to

5. $y = \frac{1}{3}x - 1$ passing through (0, 4)
6. $y = 4x + 8$ passing through (0, −2)
7. $y = -0.4x + 7$ passing through (0, 1)
8. $y = 0.2x + 3$ passing through (0, 0)

For **questions 9–12**, find the equation of the straight line joining A to B where

9. $A = (2, 8)$, $B = (4, 4)$
10. $A = (1, 2)$, $B = (7, 4)$
11. $A = (-6, 2)$, $B = (10, -6)$
12. $A = (-2, -11)$, $B = (2, 1)$

Sketching straight-line graphs

For **questions 13–16**, write down the gradient and y-intercept of the line and then **sketch** the graph.

13. $y = 3x + 2$
14. $y = \frac{1}{4}x - 1$
15. $y = -2x$
16. $y = 2 - x$

For **questions 17–20**, find where the graph crosses the axes and then sketch the graph.

17. $4x + y = 12$
18. $x + 3y = 15$
19. $x - 5y = 10$
20. $2x - 7y = 1$

SKILLS

INTERPRETATION

Solving simultaneous equations graphically

21 (a) Copy and complete the tables, then draw both graphs on the same set of axes for $0 \leq x \leq 6$

x	0	3	6
$y = x + 3$			

x	0	3	6
$y = 6 - x$			

(b) Use your graphs to solve the **simultaneous equations** $y = x + 3$ and $y = 6 - x$

22 (a) On the same axes, draw the graphs of $y = 3 - x$ and $y = 2x - 4$ for $0 \leq x \leq 6$

(b) Use your graphs to solve the simultaneous equations $y = 3 - x$ and $y = 2x - 4$

For **questions 23–26**, solve the simultaneous equations graphically, using $0 \leq x \leq 6$ in each question.

23 $y = 3x - 5$ and $y = x - 1$

24 $y = 4 - \frac{1}{2}x$ and $y = 6 - x$

25 $y = 6 - \frac{1}{2}x$ and $y = x - 2$

26 $y = \frac{1}{2}x - 2$ and $y = 6 - 2x$

UNIT 2 — GRAPHS 2

GRAPHS 2 – EXAM PRACTICE EXERCISE

SKILLS — PROBLEM SOLVING, INTERPRETATION

E 1 L is the line $3x + 4y = 12$
Line M is parallel to $y = 2x - 4$
L and M **intersect** the x-axis at the same point.
(a) Find the equation of line M.
(b) Find the area of the triangle formed by L, M and the y-axis.

E 2 Line A is $y = \frac{1}{2}x + 2$, line B is $y + 2x = 2$, line C is $2y + 1 = x$ and line D is $y = 7 - 2x$
The points of intersection of these lines form the vertices of a square.
(a) Show that opposite sides of the square are parallel.
(b) Find the perimeter of the square.

E 3 Mia is x years old and Priya is y years old.
Ten years ago, Mia was six times as old as Priya.
In ten years' time, Mia will be twice as old as Priya.

(a) Complete the table.

Age (years)	Mia	Priya
Now	x	y
10 years ago		
10 years' time		

(b) Use the completed table to find and simplify two equations in x and y.
(c) Use a graphical method to solve the equations to find the ages of Mia and Priya. Use scales of $0 \leq x \leq 50$ and $0 \leq y \leq 20$

4 One month Abdul used his phone for 200 minutes.
He sent 200 texts.
His bill came to $28.
Next month he used his phone for 100 minutes.
He sent 300 texts.
His bill was $22.
Let the cost per minute of a phone call be p cents.
Let the cost of sending a text message be t cents.
(a) Show by **clear** algebraic working that $p + t = 14$ and $p + 3t = 22$
(b) Draw both equations on one set of axes for $0 \leq t \leq 14$ and $0 \leq p \leq 14$
(c) Find Abdul's bill when he uses his phone for 150 minutes and sends 250 texts.

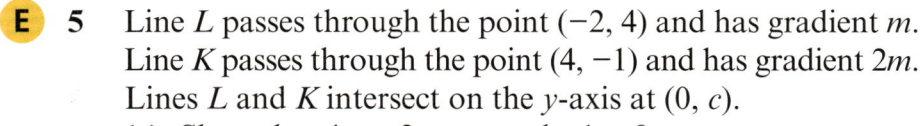

5 Line L passes through the point $(-2, 4)$ and has gradient m.
Line K passes through the point $(4, -1)$ and has gradient $2m$.
Lines L and K intersect on the y-axis at $(0, c)$.
(a) Show that $4 = -2m + c$ and $-1 = 8m + c$
(b) Solve the two simultaneous equations $4 = -2m + c$ and $-1 = 8m + c$ algebraically.
(c) Find the area enclosed by L, K and the x-axis.

UNIT 2 SHAPE AND SPACE 2

- **PYTHAGORAS' THEOREM**
- **ANGLES IN A SEMICIRCLE**
- **ANGLE AT CENTRE IS TWICE THAT AT CIRCUMFERENCE**
- **ANGLES IN SAME SEGMENT ARE EQUAL**
- **OPPOSITE ANGLES OF A CYCLIC QUADRILATERAL SUM TO 180°**

SHAPE AND SPACE 2 – BASIC SKILLS EXERCISE

SKILLS
REASONING

Pythagoras' theorem

1 Calculate a.

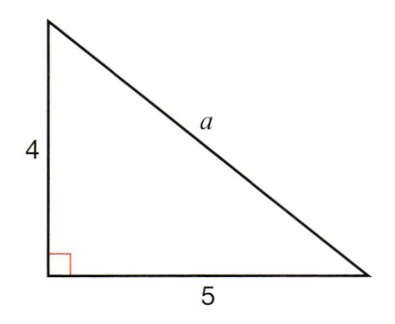

2 Calculate b.

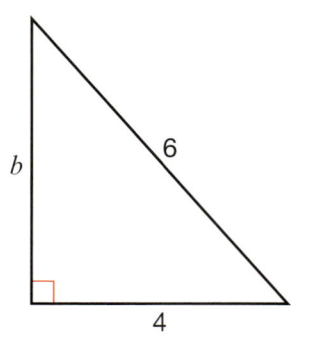

3 Calculate c.

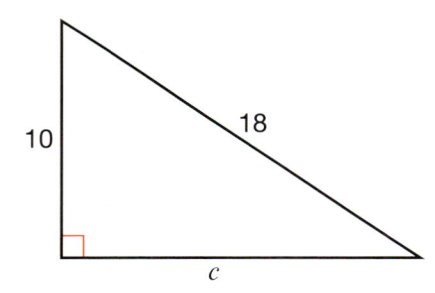

4 $ABCD$ is a rectangular piece of paper. Find the length AC.

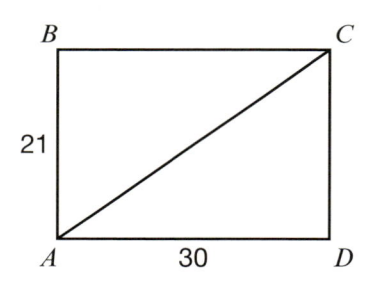

5 Calculate a.

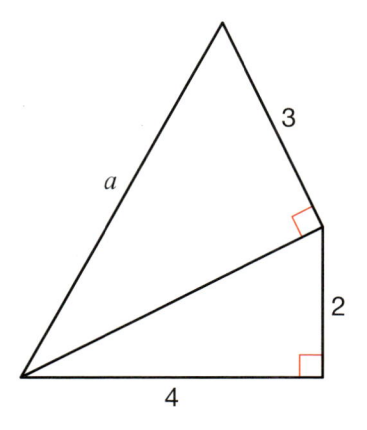

6 Calculate a.

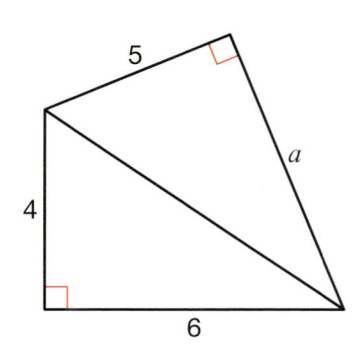

7 **(a)** Calculate the radius of the circle.
(b) Calculate a.

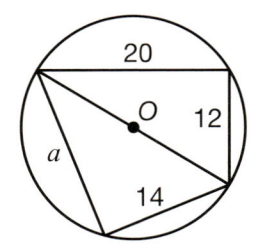

8 The diagram shows a circle with radius 5 cm.
$AB = 8$ cm and X is the midpoint of AB.
Find
(a) XC
(b) AC

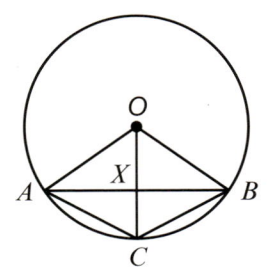

9 Show that the distance between the two points $A(1, 7)$ and $B(4, -8)$ is given by $k\sqrt{26}$ where k is a constant to be found.

10 Show that the area of a square, A, in which **adjacent** vertices are given by (a, b) and (c, d), is given by $A = (a - c)^2 + (b - d)^2$

11 A Border Collie dog is herding some sheep. She starts at point O before travelling 10 m North, 20 m West, 30 m North, 40 m East and finally 50 m North, in that order, before stopping at point P.

Show that the distance $OP = 10\sqrt{ab}$, where a and b are both **prime numbers** to be found.

12 Show that the length of the internal diagonal of a **cube** of side $10x$ is given by $10\sqrt{kx}$ where k is a constant to be found.

SKILLS
ANALYSIS

Angles in a semicircle

For **questions 13–18**, find the size of each lettered angle.

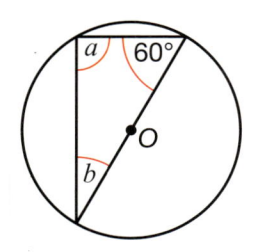

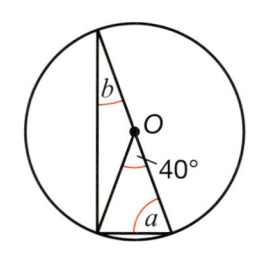

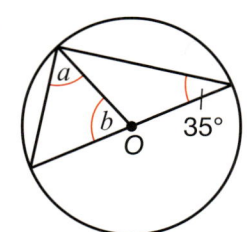

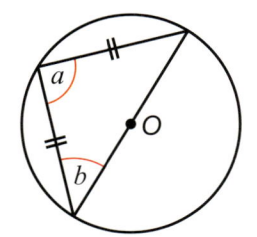

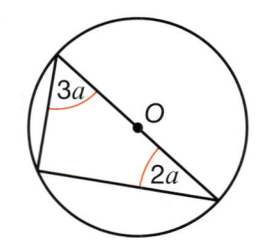

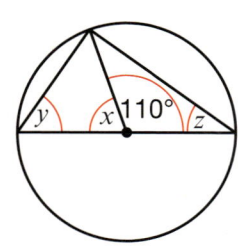

13, 14, 15, 16, 17, 18

SKILLS
ANALYSIS, REASONING

Angle at centre is twice that at circumference

For **questions 19–27**, find the size of each lettered angle.

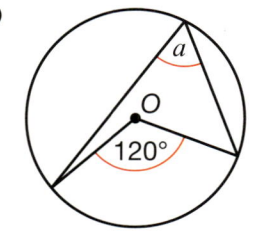

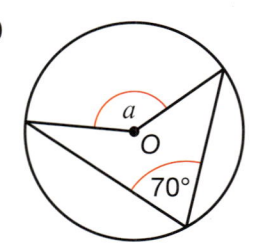

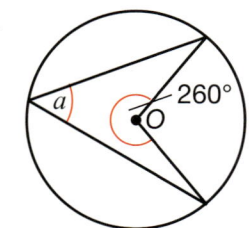

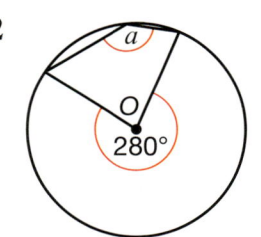

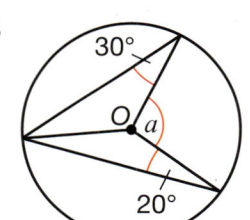

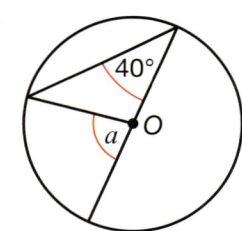

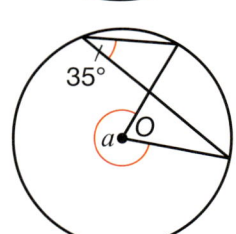

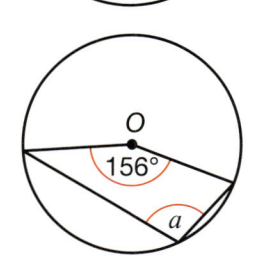

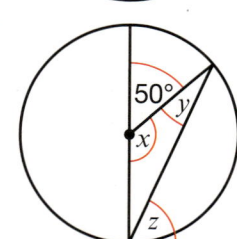

19, 20, 21, 22, 23, 24, 25, 26, 27

UNIT 2   SHAPE AND SPACE 2   37

SKILLS
ANALYSIS, REASONING

Angles in same segment are equal

For **questions 28–31**, find the size of each lettered angle.

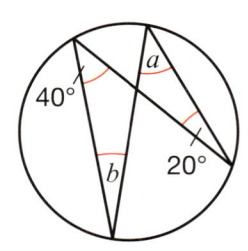

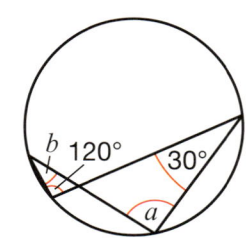

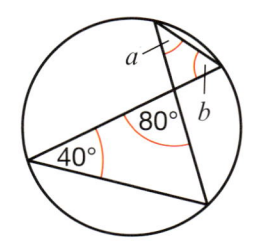

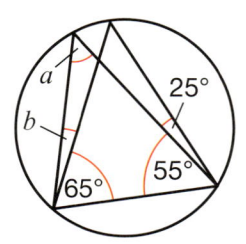

28

29

30

31

SKILLS
REASONING

Opposite angles of a cyclic quadrilateral sum to 180°

For **questions 32–36**, find the size of each lettered angle.

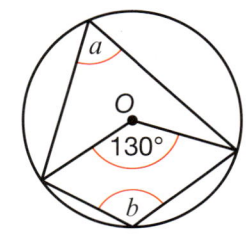

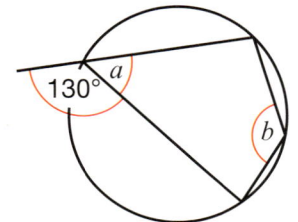

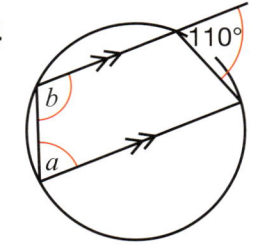

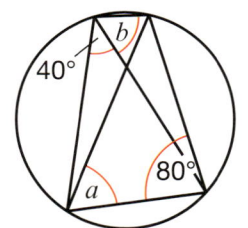

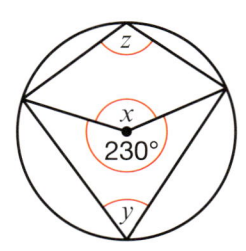

32

33

34

35

36

SHAPE AND SPACE 2 – EXAM PRACTICE EXERCISE

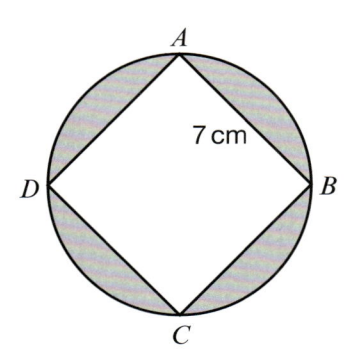

E 1

A, B, C and D are points on a circle.
ABCD is a square of side 7 cm.

(a) The area of the shaded region as a percentage of the whole circle area is $m(\pi - 2)\%$. Find the exact value of the constant m.

(b) The diagram is now enlarged by a **scale factor** of 4 about the centre of the circle. Show that the area of one of the shaded regions on the enlarged circle is given by $n(\pi - 2)$ cm², where n is a constant to be found.

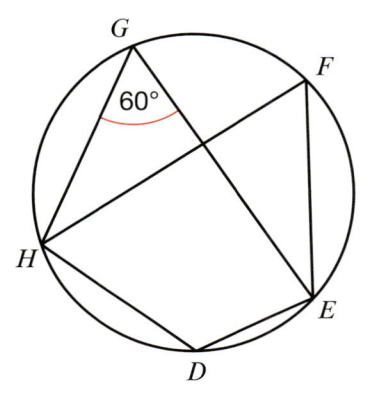

E 2

D, E, F, G and H are points on a circle.
Angle $EGH = 60°$.
The point P is on the minor **arc** GF such that angle HDP : angle EDP = 1 : 2
Calculate angle HFP giving reasons for each step of your working.

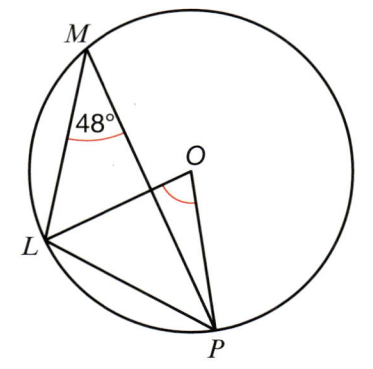

E 3

L, M and P are points on a circle, centre O.
Angle $LMP = 48°$.
Line MP trisects angle OPL such that angle MPL > angle MPO.
Calculate angle MLP giving reasons for each step of your working.

E 4

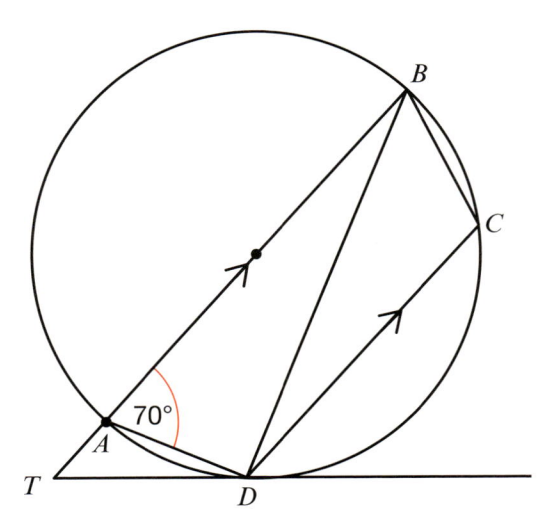

A, B, C and D are points on a circle.
AB is a diameter of the circle. DC is parallel to AB.
Angle BAD = 70°.
The **tangent** to the circle at D meets the line AB extended at T.
(a) Calculate angle ADC.
(b) Calculate angle ATD, stating reasons for all steps in your working.

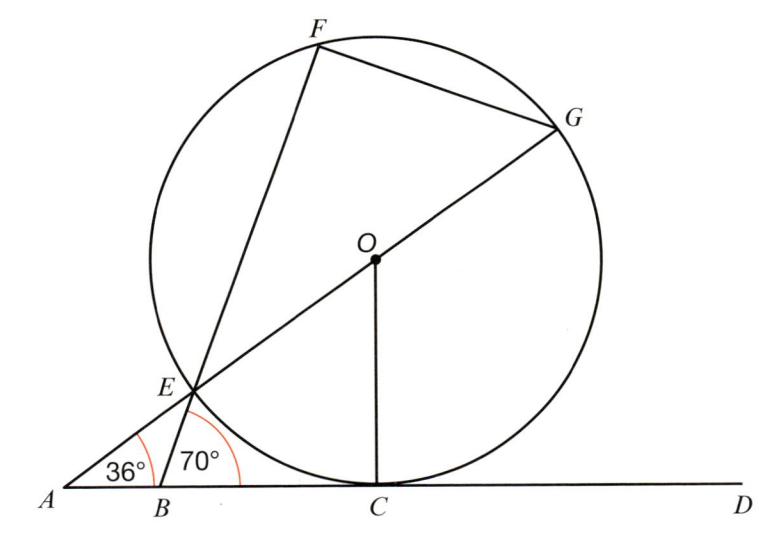

E 5

ABCD is the tangent at C to a circle, centre O.
E, F and G are points on the circle.
AEOG and BEF are straight lines.
Angle BAE = 36° Angle EBC = 70°
(a) By giving reasons for each step of your working, calculate
    (i) angle OCG
    (ii) angle FGO
(b) Given that the radius of the circle is r and $CG = 4s$, show that
    $EC = 2\sqrt{(r-2s)(r+2s)}$

UNIT 2 HANDLING DATA 1

- **COLLECTING AND DISPLAYING DATA**
- **MEAN, MEDIAN, MODE AND RANGE**

HANDLING DATA 1 – BASIC SKILLS EXERCISE

Collecting and displaying data

1 Classify the following data as discrete, continuous or categorical.
   (a) Make of phone
   (b) Number of goals scored
   (c) Height of a horse
   (d) Number of coins
   (e) Time to eat a pizza
   (f) Hair colour

2 Dalilah decides to check the **random** number generator on her calculator. She generates 30 random numbers between 1 and 5 with the following results.

   | 3 | 2 | 4 | 1 | 5 | 4 | 2 | 2 | 1 | 3 | 2 | 1 | 5 | 5 | 4 | 2 | 2 | 1 | 2 | 1 | 5 | 4 | 5 | 5 | 5 | 2 | 1 | 2 | 2 | 2 |

   (a) Copy and complete the tally chart for this data.

Number	Tally	Frequency
1	̸̸̸̸̸̸|̸̸̸| I	6
2		
3		
4		
5		

   (b) Draw a **bar chart** to represent this data.
   (c) What conclusions can you draw?

3 Ella surveys the number of revision guides owned by the members of her class. The table shows the data from the survey.

   | 21 | 6 | 9 | 17 | 7 | 3 | 11 | 5 | 19 | 25 | 30 | 13 | 22 | 24 | 20 |
   | 26 | 4 | 22 | 24 | 4 | 23 | 16 | 5 | 4 | 18 | 22 | 24 | 16 | 26 | 18 |

   (a) Construct a tally chart for the data using groups
       1–5, 6–10, 11–15, 16–20, 21–25, 26–30.
   (b) Draw a bar chart to illustrate the data.
   (c) Comment on the distribution of the number of revision guides owned.

4 The table shows the number of televisions sold at a shop over two years.

	January–April	May–August	September–December	Total
Year 1	64		72	178
Year 2		24		
Total			109	294

(a) Copy and complete the table.
(b) Draw a comparative bar chart to illustrate this data.
(c) Comment on the difference in television sales between the years.

5 A survey of pet owners gives these results.
55% have a cat.
30% have a bird.
5% have fish.
x% have a rabbit.
2.5% have some other pet.

(a) Find what percentage have a rabbit.
(b) Display this information on a **pie chart**, marking the size of the angles clearly.

6 The pie chart shows the results of a survey that asked people what drink they had for breakfast.

Breakfast drink survey
- Other 40°
- Coffee 88°
- Orange juice
- Milk 72°
- Tea 104°

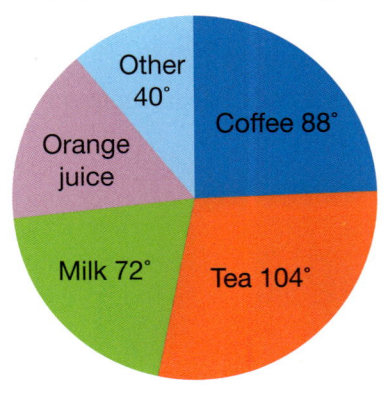

The number of people who had orange juice was 14.
Calculate how many people drank each of the other drinks.

Mean, median, mode and range

SKILLS
ANALYSIS

7 A research group were asked to name their favourite single-digit number.
These are the results:
5, 7, 9, 1, 7, 3, 6, 7, 2, 4, 7, 0
Find the **mean**, **median** and **mode** of these numbers.

8 These are the number of times that each pupil in 7R has been late this term.
0, 4, 5, 1, 3, 4, 6, 0, 1, 2, 3, 0, 0, 2, 6, 5, 4, 0, 1, 3, 2, 0, 4, 3, 2, 1, 1, 4, 6, 0
   (a) Find the mean, median and mode of this data.
   (b) Which average would the head teacher prefer to use in her termly report to the Governors?

9 The mean number of texts per day that Abena sent in one week was 32.
The numbers of texts sent on the first six days were 25, 36, 41, 27, 19 and 28.
How many texts did she send on the seventh day?

10 These are the numbers of goals Ella scored in each match **last** season:
0, 1, 0, 0, 2, 0, 1, 1, 3, 0

   (a) Find the mean, median and mode of this data.
   This season Ella has played in 12 matches.
   The mean number of goals he has scored this season is 1.25.
   (b) What is the mean number of goals scored over both seasons?
       Give your answer correct to 3 s.f.

11 Jess is trying to qualify for the Olympics in the heptathlon.
She needs a mean score of at least 857 points over the seven events.
After six events her mean score is 840.
What must she score in her last event in order to qualify?

12 A country consists of three states: A, B and C. The table below gives data for the mean number of people infected during a recent flu epidemic.

State	A	B	C
Population in millions	21	26	18
Mean number of infections	0.1	0.09	0.15

Find the mean number of infections for the whole country.
Give your answer to 2 d.p.

13 The numbers 52, x, 61, y, 86 and 92 are written in ascending order.
They have a mean of 70 and a median of 67.
Find x and y.

14 The numbers x, 13, 15, 23, 32 and y are written in ascending order.
They have a **range** of 35 and a mean of 22.
Find x and y.

15 The first 19 prime numbers are squared and the mean calculated.
The answer is 1314.
The 20th prime number is 71.
What is the mean of the first 20 prime numbers squared?

UNIT 2 — HANDLING DATA 1

HANDLING DATA 1 – EXAM PRACTICE EXERCISE

SKILLS — PROBLEM SOLVING, ANALYSIS

E 1 The table shows the numbers of ice creams sold in one week by a shop.

Day 1	Day 2	Day 3	Day 4	Day 5	Day 6	Day 7
32	29	83	32	35	95	86

(a) Find the mean, median and mode of the numbers of ice creams sold.
Over the next three weeks, average daily sales were: mean 60, median 38 and mode 38.
The manager wants to work out the average sales over the whole four-week period.

(b) (i) Explain why only one of the three averages can be calculated.
(ii) Calculate this average.

E 2 The table shows the sales of three different tablets called Burn, Apricot and Song.

Make	Sales in millions
Burn	5.2
Apricot	4.9
Song	4.8

Burn produces the following chart in its sales brochure.

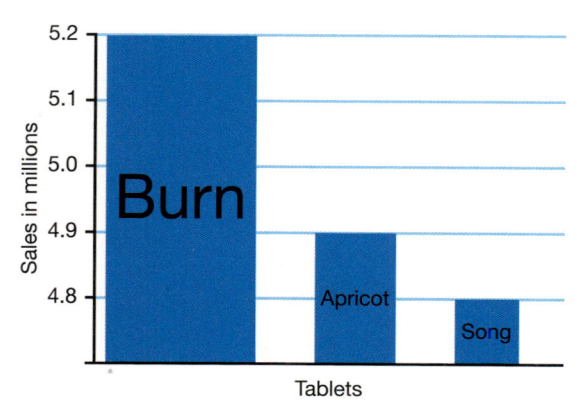

(a) Give two reasons why the chart is misleading.
(b) Draw a bar chart to give a fair representation of the sales figures.

E 3 The table and pie chart show the numbers of grades that were obtained in exams by pupils in a school.

Grade	Number of pupils	Angle
A	p	100°
B	q	60°
C	r	70°
D	s	80°
E	40	t

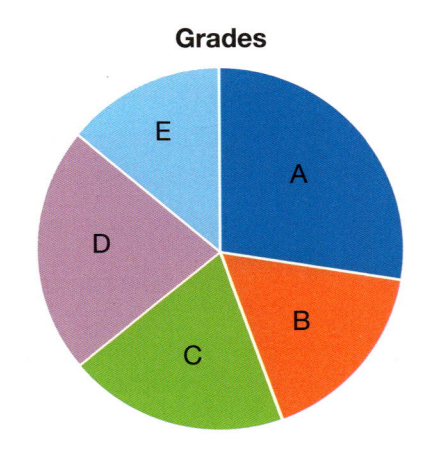

Find the values of p, q, r, s and t.

E 4 (a) The mean of 12, 16, 21 and 27 is 19.
Each of these numbers is multiplied by a.
Show that the mean is also multiplied by a.

(b) There are two sets of numbers, A and B.
Set A has n numbers with a mean of x.
Set B has m numbers with a mean of y.
The two sets are combined to form set C.
Find a formula for the mean of set C.

E 5 (a) The numbers 6, a, 8, b, 14, c, 21 and d are in ascending order.
The mean is 14.
The median is 13.
The range is 19.
The mode is 8.
Find a, b, c and d.

(b) w, x, y and z are four **different** integers written in ascending order.
The mean of these integers is 17.
The range is 8.
The median is 16.
Find the integers.

UNIT 3 NUMBER 3

- **MULTIPLES, FACTORS AND PRIME FACTORS**
- **HCF AND LCM**
- **RATIO**

NUMBER 3 – BASIC SKILLS EXERCISE

SKILLS
ANALYSIS

Multiples, factors and prime factors

1. List the first four **multiples** of
   (a) 7
   (b) 11
   (c) 17

2. Find all the **factors**, in numerical order, of
   (a) 15
   (b) 20
   (c) 98

3. Express as a **product** of **prime factors** in index form
   (a) 945
   (b) 24×945
   (c) 945^3
   (d) 9.45×10^4

4. $n = 2^3 \times 3^2 \times 5 \times 7^2$
   Express in prime factor form
   (a) $2n^2$
   (b) $(2n)^2$

5. $N = 7.2 \times 10^7$
   Find the largest factor of N that is an odd number.

SKILLS
PROBLEM SOLVING

HCF and LCM

6. Find the HCF and LCM of
   (a) 60 and 70
   (b) 140 and 84
   (c) 525, 40 and 441

7. $A = 2^4 \times 3 \times 7 \times 11^2$, $B = 3^2 \times 5^3 \times 11$ and $C = 2^2 \times 3 \times 5 \times 7^2$
   Find the HCF and LCM of A, B and C, giving your answers in prime factor form.

8. The HCF of a and 12 is 3 and $a < 30$
   Find the two possible values of a.

9. Find the HCF and LCM of
   (a) $20pq$ and $35pq$
   (b) $2x^2yz$ and $12xy^2z^2$
   (c) $12a^2b^3c^4$ and $18a^4b^3c^2$

10. The LCM of two numbers is 12. One of the numbers is 12.
    (a) Write down all the possibilities for the other number.
    (b) Describe the set of numbers you have written down.

11 Sofia and Valentina are swimming 50-m lengths of a swimming pool.
    Sofia takes 48 seconds for each length, while Valentina takes 45 seconds.
    If they both start together, after what time will they first be both together at one end of the swimming pool?

12 Two houses are decorated with flashing lights. The first house has lights that flash every 0.88 seconds and the second house has lights that flash every 1.1 seconds. The lights have just flashed together. How long before they next flash together?

Ratio

13 Write these ratios in their simplest form.
    (a) 40 : 88
    (b) 4 : 20 : 68
    (c) 0.15 : 0.2 : 3.5
    (d) $3x^2y : 12xy^2 : 60xy$

14 Write these ratios in the form 1 : n.
    (a) 5 : 120
    (b) 3 min : 1 day
    (c) 4 cm/s : 10 m/s
    (d) 10 cm/s : 9 km/h

15 The ratio of 3 : x is the same as the ratio of x : 27.
    Find x.

16 (a) Divide 360 minutes in the ratio 4 : 5.
    (b) Divide €133 in the ratio 1 : 2 : 4.
    (c) Divide €1000 in the ratio 1 : 2 : 3 : 4.
    (d) Divide 352 km in the ratio 2 : 3 : 6.

17 Work out the difference between the largest and the smallest share if £3450 is divided in the ratio 2 : 6 : 7.

18 The ratio of Karl's age to Petra's age is 4 : 9. If Karl is 12 years old, how old is Petra?

19 x is 75% more than y. What is the ratio $x : y$ in its simplest terms with x and y as integers?

20 The ratio of the charging times for three different electric cars is 7 : 8 : 9. The shortest charging time is 3 hours 30 minutes. What is the longest charging time?

21 The Olympic triathlon is a race over 51.5 km involving swimming, cycling and running. The ratio of distances of swimming to cycling to running is 3 : 80 : 20. What is the distance swum in km?

22 The ratio of the masses of two sloths is 3 : 5. The difference between their masses is 6 kg. What is the mass of each sloth in kg?

23 A piece of wood is cut into three smaller pieces in the ratio 2 : 3 : 5. The difference in length between the two longest pieces is 120 cm. What was the length of the original piece of wood in cm?

24 The ratio of the weights of sugar, milk and flour in a recipe is 4 : 5 : 7. The difference in weight between the sugar and milk is 60 g. What is the weight of the flour in grams?

25 $a : b = 1 : 2$ and $b : c = 9 : 5$
Find the ratio $a : b : c$ in its simplest form, where a, b and c are integers.

26 $3a = 2b$ and $b : c = 4 : 5$
Find the ratio $a : c$ in its simplest form, where a and c are integers.

27 A, B and C are three angles of a triangle in the ratio $3 : 5 : x$ respectively. Angle C is 60°. Find x.

28 A bed of roses consists of r roses. The ratio of pink roses to white roses is 2 : 3 and the ratio of white roses to red roses is 7 : 5. Find the number of red roses in terms of r.

29 The diagram shows a square inscribed within a circle of radius r.
The vertices of the square lie on the **circumference** of the circle.
Show that the ratio of the area of the circle : area of the square is $\pi : 2$

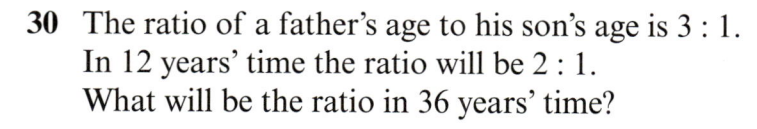

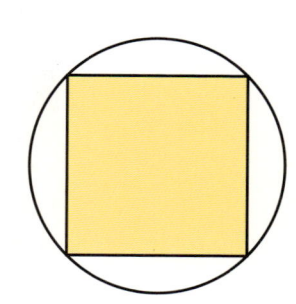

30 The ratio of a father's age to his son's age is 3 : 1.
In 12 years' time the ratio will be 2 : 1.
What will be the ratio in 36 years' time?

NUMBER 3 – EXAM PRACTICE EXERCISE

1 (a) Find the greatest factor of one million that is odd.
   (b) The HCF of x and 525 is 21.
       The LCM of x and 525 is 3150.
       Find x.

2 (a) The HCF of x and y is 3.
       The LCM of x and y is 60.
       $3 < x < y < 60$
       Find x and y.
   (b) $a = 2^x \times 3^y \times 5$ and $b = 2^y \times 3^x \times 7$
       The LCM of a and b is 45 360.
       The HCF of a and b is 36.
       $a < b$
       Find x and y.

3 (a) The points A, B, C and D lie on a straight line in that order.
       $AB : BD = 1 : 3$ and $AC : CD = 11 : 13$
       Work out $AB : BC : CD$.
   (b) The population of a village is in the following ratios.
       men : children = 11 : 3 and women : children = 5 : 2
       (i) Find the ratio men : women : children in its simplest form.
       There are 42 more men than women in the village.
       (ii) Find the number of children in the village.

4 A restaurant sells four types of pizza: Veggie, Cheese, Meat and Mushroom.
One evening it sold 140 pizzas, of which 40% were Mushroom.
The ratio of Veggie : Cheese : Meat was 2 : 5 : 7
How many more Meat pizzas were sold than Veggie pizzas?

5 A group of volunteers are making up food parcels for a food bank.
They have 720 pints of milk, 1260 loaves of bread and 1800 cans of beans.
Each food parcel must contain the same and there must be nothing left over.
What is the greatest number of parcels that can be prepared, and what will be in each parcel?

UNIT 3 ALGEBRA 3

- **SIMPLE FACTORISING**
- **SIMPLIFYING FRACTIONS**
- **EQUATIONS WITH FRACTIONS**
- **SIMULTANEOUS EQUATIONS**

ALGEBRA 3 – BASIC SKILLS EXERCISE

Simple factorising

For **questions 1–6**, **factorise** the expression completely.

1. $7a - a^2$
2. $3x - 12x^2$
3. $a^2b + b^2a$
4. $4xy - 8x^2y^2$
5. $\frac{1}{3}pq^2r^3 + \frac{2}{3}p^3q^2r$
6. $2x(x + 1) - 5(x + 1)$

Simplifying fractions

For **questions 7–12**, simplify the fraction.

7. $\frac{3x^2 + 12x}{3x}$
8. $\frac{ab + a^2b}{ab}$
9. $\frac{2x^2 + 2xy}{x + y}$
10. $\frac{30}{xy^2} \div \frac{6x^2}{x^2y}$
11. $\frac{x+1}{3} - \frac{x-5}{21}$
12. $\frac{x^3 + 2x^2}{x + y} \times \frac{x^2y + xy^2}{x^2 + 2x}$

Equations with fractions

For **questions 13–26**, solve the equation, showing full working.

13. $\frac{x}{8} = \frac{3}{4}$
14. $\frac{5x}{6} = \frac{1}{2}$
15. $\frac{x+1}{4} = \frac{x-2}{3}$
16. $\frac{x-4}{5} = 0$
17. $\frac{3(x-2)}{4} = 9$
18. $\frac{2x}{5} + x = 21$
19. $\frac{3}{x} = 15$
20. $\frac{8}{3x} = 4$
21. $-\frac{1}{7} = \frac{7}{x}$
22. $\frac{9}{2x} = 6$
23. $\frac{2}{x} = \frac{x}{8}$
24. $x - \frac{64}{x} = 0$
25. $\frac{10x-3}{3} + \frac{5x+2}{4} = 5$
26. $\frac{1}{4} + \frac{5}{x} = \frac{13}{12}$

27 Xavier, Yi and Zazoo run a business together. They recently received a refund of £11 000, which they decide to share. Yi receives three times as much as Zazoo. Xavier receives half of the amount Yi receives.
How much do they each receive?

Simultaneous equations

For **questions 28–31**, use elimination to solve the simultaneous equations. Show full working.

28 $2x + y = 9$
$x - y = 3$

29 $3x + 2y = 13$
$2x - y = 4$

30 $x + 3y = 7$
$y - x = 1$

31 $x + y = 2$
$2x + 3y = 5$

For **questions 32–35**, use substitution to solve the simultaneous equations. Show full working.

32 $x = y - 3$
$x + 2y = 9$

33 $y = x + 7$
$3x + y = 11$

34 $y = x - 2$
$4x - y = 11$

35 $x = y + 4$
$2x + 5y = 22$

For **questions 36–39**, solve the simultaneous equations, showing full working.

36 $3x + 2y = 8$
$2x - 3y = 1$

37 $2x + 3y = 7$
$x = 4y - 2$

38 $y = 3x + 8$
$x + 2y = 9$

39 $4x - 3y = 26$
$2x + y + 10 = 0$

40 If $x : y = 8 : 5$ and $x - y = 9$, find x and y.

41 There are 20 seats in a house.
Some are stools with three legs, and some are chairs with four legs.
The total number of legs is 74.
How many stools are there?

ALGEBRA 3 – EXAM PRACTICE EXERCISE

1 (a) Factorise fully

   (i) $\frac{2}{5}p^2r^3 - \frac{4}{5}p^3r^2$ (ii) $x(3-x) - (3-x)$

   (b) Simplify fully

   (i) $\frac{10x^2 + 5x}{5x} - 1$ (ii) $\frac{3x^3y + 9x^2y^2}{x^2 + 3xy}$

   (c) Show that $\frac{x^2 - xy}{xy^2 + y^3} \div \frac{xy - y^2}{x^3 + x^2y}$ can be written as $\left(\frac{x}{y}\right)^n$ and find the value of n.

2 (a) Solve these equations, showing full working.

   (i) $\frac{2(x+1)}{5} - \frac{3(x+1)}{10} = x$ (ii) $\frac{36}{x} - 4x = 0$

   (b) Anna, Bobbie and Carla share $16 000.
   Anna gets $500 plus half of Bobbie's amount, while Bobbie gets 40% more than Carla. How much does each receive?

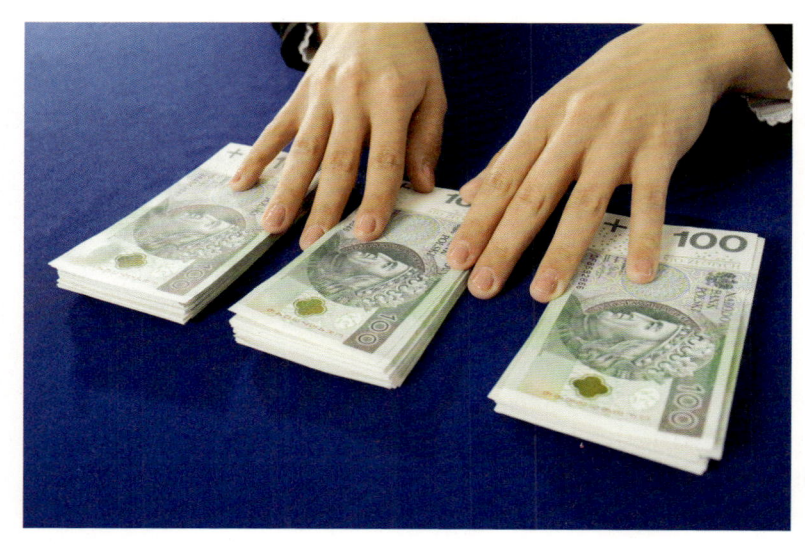

3 The triangle *ABC* is isosceles.
Angle $B = 2x + y$
Angle $C = 4y - 2x - 15$
The ratio $x : y = 3 : 5$.
Find the ratio Angle *A* : Angle *B*.

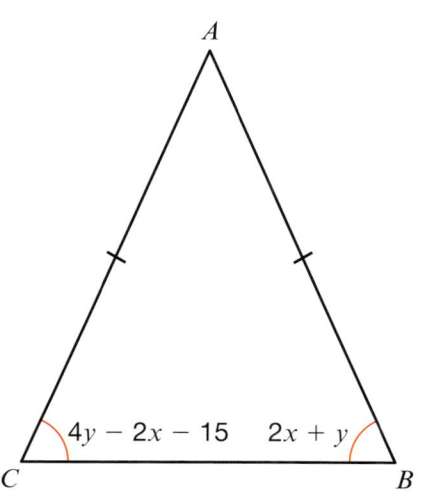

E 4 (a) The curve $y = x^2 + ax + b$ passes through the points (2, 12) and (−1, −6).
Find the equation of the curve.

(b) Rahim is buying some trees for a conservation project.
Twenty ash trees and thirty beech trees will cost him $3100.
Thirty ash trees and twenty beech trees will cost him $2900.
Find the cost of each type of tree.

E 5 The price of a bike is x dollars, and the price of a laptop is y dollars.

When both prices are increased by $100, the ratio of the price of the bike to the price of the laptop is 4 : 3.
When both prices are decreased by $100, the ratio of the price of the bike to the price of the laptop is 11 : 7.
Find the price of the bike and the price of the laptop.

UNIT 3 GRAPHS 3

- **DISTANCE–TIME GRAPHS**
- **SPEED–TIME GRAPHS**

GRAPHS 3 – BASIC SKILLS EXERCISE

SKILLS
INTERPRETATION

Distance–time graphs

1. Find the speed of the bicycle's journey shown in the distance–time graph.

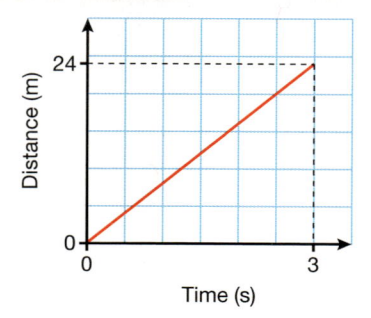

2. Find the speed of the boat's journey shown in the distance–time graph.

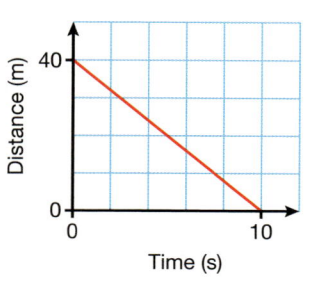

3. An insect's journey is shown in the distance–time graph.
   Find
   (a) the insect's outward journey speed in m/s
   (b) how long the insect remained stationary
   (c) the insect's return journey speed in m/s

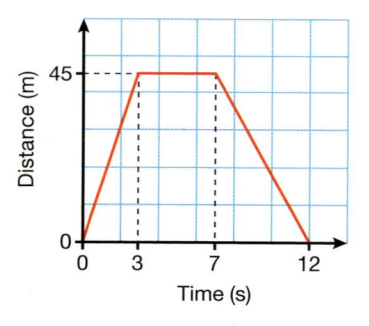

4. **Sketch** distance–time graphs that show the journey of Seb
   (a) going to school at a constant speed
   (b) returning from school at a constant speed

5. **Sketch** distance–time graphs that show the journey of Khalid
   (a) going to the train station at a gradually increasing speed
   (b) returning from the train station at a gradually decreasing speed

6. **Sketch** a distance–time graph for a flying duck such that its entire journey is described as:

   An initial constant speed, followed by a gradual reduction in speed until the duck is stationary, after which it gradually accelerates to reach a constant speed faster than its initial speed.

UNIT 3 — GRAPHS 3

SKILLS
INTERPRETATION

Speed–time graphs

7 Find the **acceleration** of the boat's journey shown in the speed–time graph.

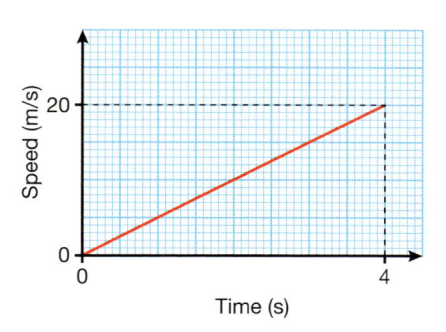

8 Find the acceleration of the train's journey shown in the speed–time graph.

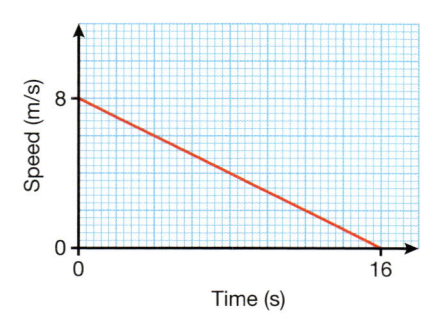

9 Johann's journey is shown in the speed–time graph. Find Johann's
   (a) initial acceleration
   (b) acceleration at 30 seconds
   (c) final acceleration
   (d) mean speed for the whole journey

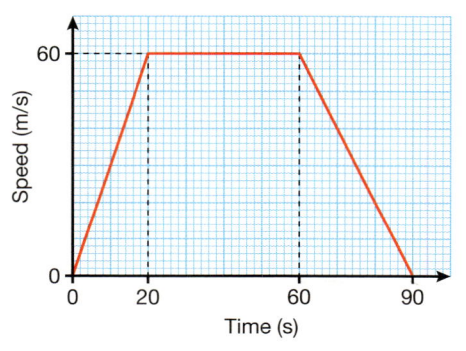

10 A model aeroplane accelerates from rest to 10 m/s in 20 s, remains at that speed for 30 s and then slows steadily to rest in 10 s.
   (a) Draw the speed–time graph for the aeroplane's journey.
   (b) Use this graph to find the aeroplane's
      (i) initial acceleration
      (ii) final acceleration
      (iii) mean speed over the whole 60 second journey

11 Sketch speed–time graphs that show
   (a) constant acceleration
   (b) zero acceleration
   (c) constant deceleration

12 Sketch speed–time graphs that show
   (a) increasing acceleration
   (b) constant speed
   (c) decreasing acceleration

GRAPHS 3 – EXAM PRACTICE EXERCISE

1 Luke leaves home at 08:00, and cycles to Martha's house at a speed of 20 km/h for one hour.
He stays there for two hours before returning home at a speed of 30 km/h.
(a) Draw a distance–time graph to illustrate Luke's journey.
(b) Use this graph to find the time Luke returns home.

2 Mrs Lam leaves home for work at 07:00, driving at a constant speed of 60 km/h.
After 45 minutes she increases her speed to 80 km/h for a further 45 minutes.
She stays at work for 4 hours before she returns home at 70 km/h to meet Mr Lam who gets home at 2 pm.
Draw a distance–time graph and use it to find out if Mrs Lam arrives home late to meet her husband.

3 Marie runs on a straight road.
She starts from rest and then travels with a constant acceleration for a period of 10 seconds until she reaches a speed of 5 m/s.
She continues to run at this speed for t seconds.
She then has a constant deceleration until she stops running.
She has run 1 km in 5 minutes.

(a) Draw the speed–time graph to show Marie's 1-km run.
(b) Calculate
  (i) the value of t
  (ii) Marie's final acceleration in m/s^2 correct to 3 s.f.

E 4 A hawk constantly accelerates from rest to 12 m/s in 6 seconds followed by a further constant acceleration to 18 m/s in 3 seconds. It then remains at 18 m/s for 10 seconds and then retards at a constant rate treble the initial acceleration before coming to rest.

(a) Draw the speed–time graph for the hawk's flight.
(b) Find the hawk's final **retardation** in m/s².
(c) Find the mean speed for the whole length of the hawk's flight in m/s to 3 s.f.

E 5 At the school Sports Day, Ivan wins the 400 m in 62.5 seconds.
(a) Calculate his mean speed in
  (i) m/s
  (ii) km/h

The speed–time graph of Ivan's race is shown.

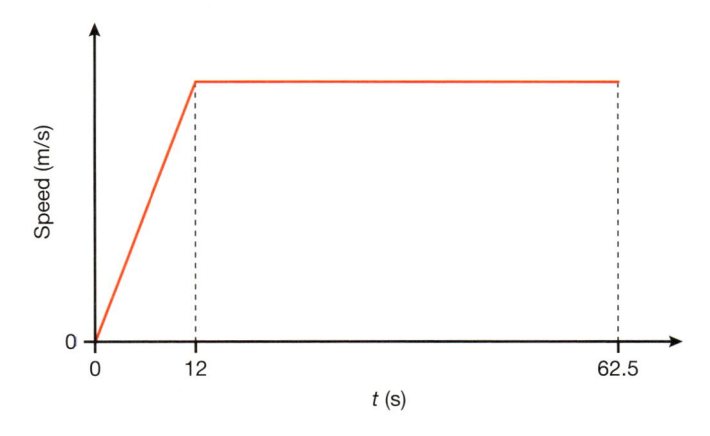

(b) Calculate his maximum speed in m/s.
(c) Find his initial acceleration in m/s².

UNIT 3 SHAPE AND SPACE 3

- **TANGENT RATIO**
- **SINE AND COSINE RATIOS**

SHAPE AND SPACE 3 – BASIC SKILLS EXERCISE

SKILLS
PROBLEM SOLVING, ANALYSIS, REASONING

Tangent ratio

For **questions 1–4**, find the values of x and y correct to 3 s.f. where appropriate.

1 (triangle with 10 m vertical side, angles 40° and 10° at top, base split into x and y)

2 (triangle with 7 cm base on right, angles 15° and 30° at top, base split with y)

3 (triangle with 25° angle, base 14 cm, with x and 60° angle, y)

4 (triangle with 20 cm top, 60° and 50° angles, x and y)

For **questions 5–8**, find the value of θ correct to 3 s.f.

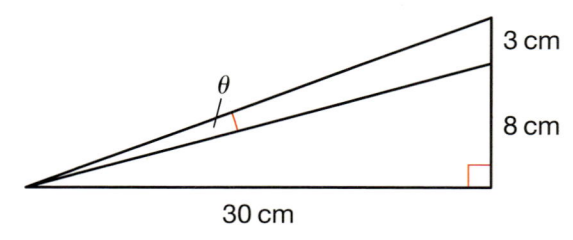

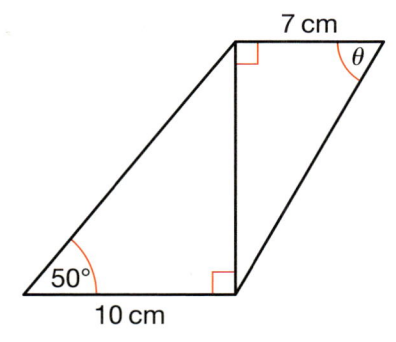

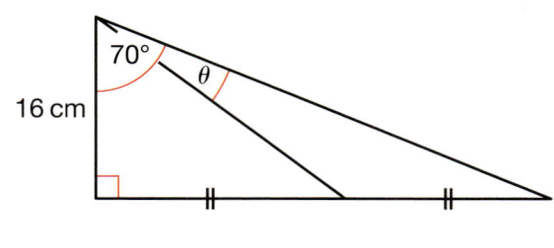

5 (triangle with 27° angle, base split 15 cm and 8 cm, θ at top)

6 (triangle with 30 cm base, 3 cm and 8 cm right side, θ)

7 (shape with 7 cm, 10 cm, 50° angle, θ)

8 (triangle with 16 cm, 70°, θ)

9 Find the **acute angle** that the line $y = 3x - 7$ makes with the x-axis.

10 The area of an equilateral triangle is $1000\ \text{cm}^2$.
Calculate the perimeter of the triangle in cm correct to 3 s.f.

Sine and cosine ratios

For **questions 11–14**, find the values of x and y.

11

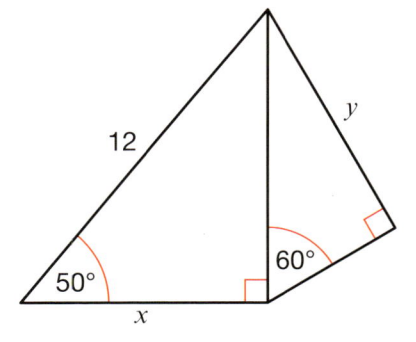

12

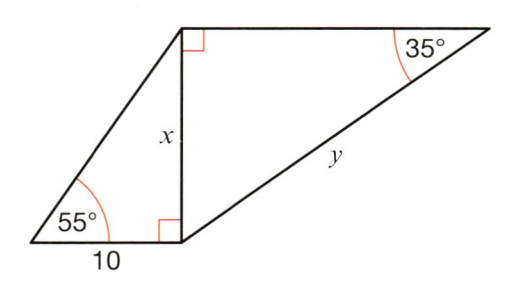

13

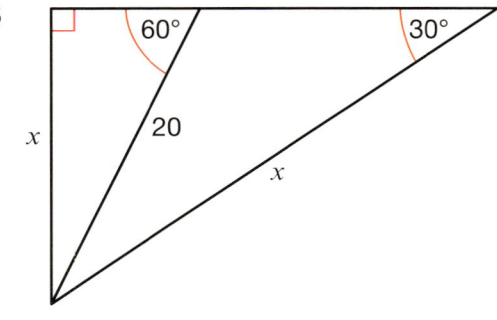

14

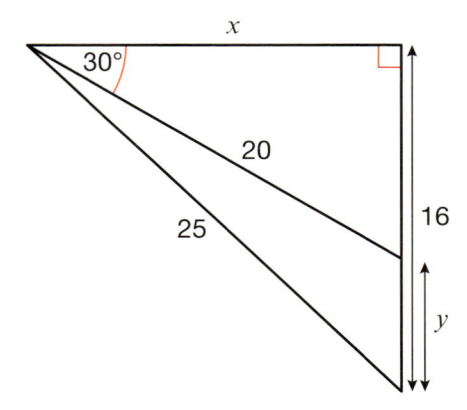

For **questions 15–18**, find the value of θ.

15

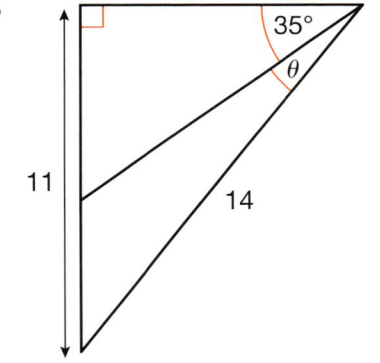

16

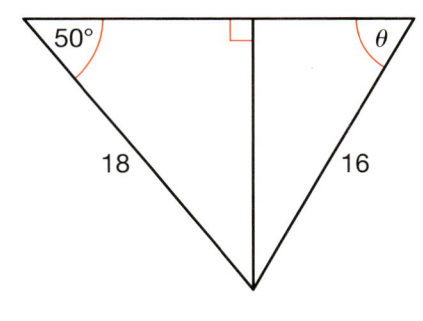

17

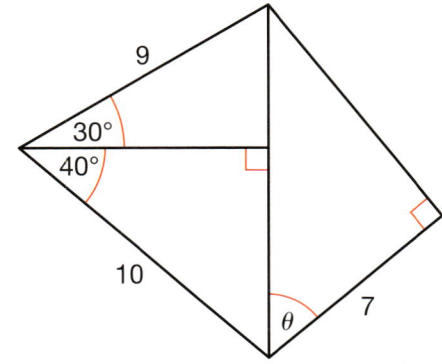

18

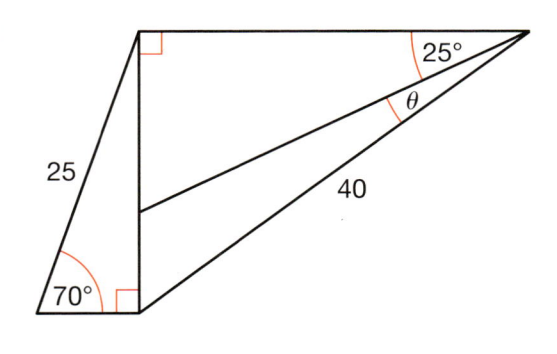

19 A 4.2-m ladder makes an angle of 20° with a vertical wall. Calculate the distance of the foot of the ladder from the base of the wall.

20 Jamila runs from point A on a constant bearing of 300° at 5 m/s for 15 minutes at which point she stops at point B. Calculate, correct to 3 s.f., how far Jamila has run
(a) from A
(b) North from A
(c) West from A

SHAPE AND SPACE 3 – EXAM PRACTICE EXERCISE

E 1 An equilateral triangle of side 10 has an area equal to a circle. The circumference of the circle, c, is given by $c = 10 \times \pi^a \times 3^b$, where a and b are constants.
Find the values of a and b.

E 2 A regular pentagon is drawn inside a circle of radius 6.8 cm.
Each **vertex** of the pentagon lies on the circle.
(a) Calculate the perimeter of the pentagon in cm correct to 3 s.f.
The shaded area as a percentage of the circle is $p\%$ correct to 3 s.f.
(b) Calculate the value of p.

E 3 B, C and D are points on the circumference of a circle, centre O.
BOD is a diameter of the circle.
The percentage area of the circle not occupied by the triangle BCD is $p\%$ to 3 s.f.
Calculate the value of p.

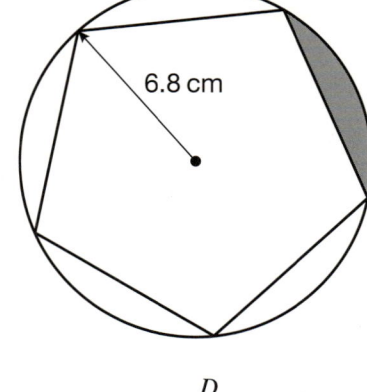

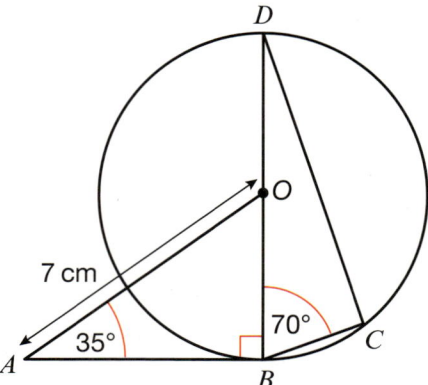

E 4 The diagram shows three right-angled triangles.
(a) Show that $y = \frac{3}{4}n$
(b) The total area of the irregular pentagon is $\frac{37\sqrt{3}}{2}$
Find the value of n.

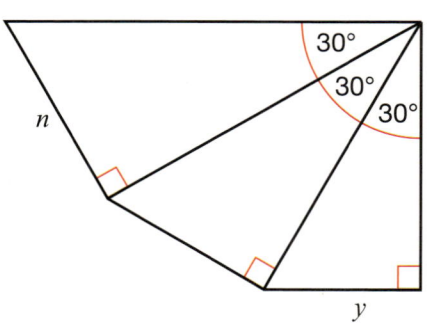

E 5 A regular hexagon has side length a.
(a) Show that the area of this hexagon $A = \frac{3\sqrt{3}}{2}a^2$
(b) An equilateral triangle of side 2 has the same area as a regular hexagon of perimeter P.
Show that $P = \sqrt{3} \times 2^k$, where k is to be found.

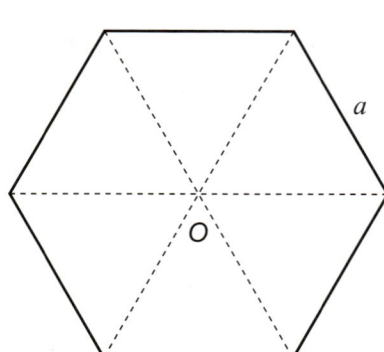

UNIT 3 HANDLING DATA 2

- **FREQUENCY TABLES (CONTINUOUS DATA) AND HISTOGRAMS (EQUAL CLASSES); MEAN, MEDIAN AND MODE**

HANDLING DATA 2 – BASIC SKILLS EXERCISE

SKILLS
PROBLEM SOLVING, ANALYSIS

Frequency tables (continuous data) and histograms (equal classes); mean, median and mode

1. These are the times, t, in seconds that it took a class to solve a mathematical puzzle.

t (s)	$40 \leq t < 45$	$45 \leq t < 50$	$50 \leq t < 55$	$55 \leq t < 60$	$60 \leq t < 65$	$65 \leq t < 70$	$70 \leq t < 75$	$75 \leq t < 80$
Frequency	12	5	8	4	2	10	4	5

(a) Draw a **histogram** to represent this information.
(b) What percentage of the class took less than 1 minute to solve the puzzle?

2. This **frequency** table shows the times taken by competitors on a charity fun run.

Time (min)	$60 \leq t < 70$	$70 \leq t < 80$	$80 \leq t < 90$	$90 \leq t < 100$	$100 \leq t < 110$	$110 \leq t < 120$
Frequency	8	14	26	17	13	7

(a) How many competitors were there?
(b) Draw a histogram to display this information.
(c) What percentage of the competitors took at least 100 minutes?

3. The weight marked on a packet of Super Breakfast Snaps is 500 g.
A **sample** of 50 packets of the cereal has the weights shown in the table.

Weight w (g)	$490 \leq w < 495$	$495 \leq w < 500$	$500 \leq w < 505$	$505 \leq w < 510$	$510 \leq w < 515$	$515 \leq w < 520$	$520 \leq w < 525$
Frequency	1	3	10	18	1	5	2

(a) Draw a histogram to display the distribution of weights of the 50 cereal packets.
(b) Does evidence suggest that the 500g printed on the cereal packet is a mean weight or a minimum weight?

4. This frequency table shows the speeds of some cars on a road.

Speed s (km/h)	$30 \leq s < 35$	$35 \leq s < 40$	$40 \leq s < 45$	$45 \leq s < 50$	$50 \leq s < 55$	$55 \leq s < 60$
Frequency	4	18	43	54	5	2

(a) How many cars had their speeds recorded?
(b) Draw a histogram to display this information.
(c) What do you think the speed limit is on this road? Give a reason for your answer.

5. This frequency table shows how much time per week 120 teenagers spent watching television.

Time t (h)	$0 \leq t < 2$	$2 \leq t < 4$	$4 \leq t < 6$	$6 \leq t < 8$	$8 \leq t < 10$	$10 \leq t < 12$	$12 \leq t < 14$
Frequency	18	12	10		21	25	19

(a) What is the frequency for the group $6 \leq t < 8$?
(b) Draw a histogram to display the information.
(c) What percentage watched between 4 and 10 hours of television per week?

6. Olga is interested in how much encouragement her Maths teacher gives the class. She counts the number of times her teacher says "Good" during a lesson. The table shows her results for a term.
   (a) How many Maths lessons did Olga have during the term?
   (b) Write down the **modal class**.
   (c) Calculate an estimate for the mean number of "Good"s per lesson.

Number of "Good"s	Frequency
1–5	3
6–10	7
11–15	14
16–20	16
21–25	10

7. As part of her routine examination a vet weighs every cat she sees in her surgery. The table shows her results for a week.
   (a) How many cats did she see that week?
   (b) Write down the modal class.
   (c) Calculate an estimate of the mean mass of these cats.

Mass m (kg)	Number of cats
$0 < m \leq 2$	2
$2 < m \leq 4$	6
$4 < m \leq 6$	10
$6 < m \leq 8$	5
$8 < m \leq 10$	1

8. The times of some cross-country runners in a race are given in the table.
   (a) How many runners took part in the race?
   (b) Write down the modal **class**.
   (c) Calculate an estimate of the mean time of these runners.
   (d) State the class which contains the median time.

Time t (min)	Frequency
$11.5 < t \leq 14.5$	3
$14.5 < t \leq 17.5$	7
$17.5 < t \leq 20.5$	11
$20.5 < t \leq 23.5$	4

9. The table shows information about the ages in completed years of students who sing in the choir.
   (a) How many students sing in the choir?
   (b) Write down the modal class.
   (c) Calculate the mean of these ages.
   (d) Another student joins the choir on her 13th birthday. Will the mean increase or decrease? Give a reason for your answer.

Age a (years)	Frequency
$12 \leq a < 13$	8
$13 \leq a < 14$	5
$14 \leq a < 15$	9
$15 \leq a < 16$	6
$16 \leq a < 17$	4

10. In a primary school competition to grow the tallest sunflower, the following heights (in metres) were obtained.
    1.32, 1.87, 2.03, 1.56, 1.95, 1.48, 1.12, 2.15
    (a) Calculate the mean and median heights of these sunflowers.
    (b) The 2.15 m height had been recorded incorrectly and was actually 2.75 m. Calculate the new mean height.

11. A group of ten girls has a mean height of 1.42 m.
    (a) What is the total height of all ten girls?
       One girl with height 1.57 m leaves the group.
    (b) What is the mean height of the remaining girls?

12. The lengths of tracks in minutes on a streaming music album were as follows:
    6.2, 3.6, 10.8, 2.4, 2.3, 8.7, 14.7, 10.9
    (a) Calculate the mean and median length of tracks on the album.
    (b) The time of 10.9 had been misread and was actually 16.9. Calculate the correct mean length.

13 A football team of eleven players has a mean height of 1.83 m. One player is injured and is replaced by a player of height 1.85 m. The new mean height of the team is 1.84 m. What is the height of the injured player?

14 Shuhan is doing a Biology project using two groups of worms. The mean length of the first group of ten worms is 8.3 cm.
(a) What is the total length of all the worms in the first group?
The mean of the second group of 8 worms is 10.7 cm.
(b) Calculate the mean length of all eighteen worms.

15 The mean time of Alec's first five matches in a chess tournament is 10 minutes and 20 seconds. After his sixth match, his mean time is 12 minutes and 16 seconds. How long did Alec's sixth match last?

16 Two squads of swimmers raced over 100 m and their group times were recorded:
Dolphins: mean time = 125 s   size of group = 20
Marlins: mean time = 130 s   size of group = 5
(a) Calculate the combined mean time of the Dolphins and the Marlins.
A timing error has occurred such that all swimmers' recorded times need adjusting.
Dolphins required 5 seconds to be added to each swimmer's time.
Marlins required 5 seconds to be subtracted from each swimmer's time.
(b) Calculate the new combined mean time of the Dolphins and the Marlins.

UNIT 3 — HANDLING DATA 2

HANDLING DATA 2 – EXAM PRACTICE EXERCISE

SKILLS: PROBLEM SOLVING, ANALYSIS

E 1 Each day for a month Ross keeps a record of the number of calls he makes on his mobile phone. The table shows the results.
  (a) In which month did Ross do his survey?
  (b) Write down the modal class interval.
  (c) Work out an estimate of the mean number of calls made per day.

Number of calls	Frequency
1–5	2
6–10	4
11–15	7
16–20	9
21–25	6

E 2 The table shows the number of words in some essays written in an English exam.
  (a) How many students took the exam?
  (b) Write down the modal class interval.
  (c) Calculate an estimate of the mean number of words per essay.

Number of words	Number of essays
401–600	150
601–800	425
801–1000	350
1001–1200	75

E 3 A Munro is the name given to any mountain in Scotland over 3000 feet in height. The table shows the distribution of Munros by height.
  (a) How many Munros are there in Scotland?
  (b) Write down the modal class interval.
  (c) Calculate an estimate of the mean height of a Munro, giving your answer to the nearest ten feet.

Height h (feet)	Frequency
$3000 < h \leq 3300$	300
$3300 < h \leq 3600$	135
$3600 < h \leq 3900$	80
$3900 < h \leq 4200$	20
$4200 < h \leq 4500$	5

E 4 The table shows the maximum speed of serve of 50 players in a professional tennis tournament.
(a) What value, in terms of x, should go in the blank space in the frequency column of the table?

The calculation of the estimate of the mean speed gave the result 107.8 mph.
(b) Calculate the value of x.

Speed s (mph)	Frequency
$90 < s \leq 100$	x
$100 < s \leq 110$	23
$110 < s \leq 120$	
$120 < s \leq 130$	5

E 5 The delayed times of trains at La Gare du Nord, Paris, on 1 January 2020 are shown in the table:

Delay d (min)	Midpoint x	No. of trains f	fx
$0 \leq d < 30$		10	
$30 \leq d < 60$		14	
$60 \leq d < 90$		16	
$90 \leq d < 120$		11	
$120 \leq d < 150$		8	
$150 \leq d < 180$		1	
		$\Sigma f =$	$\Sigma fx =$

(a) Copy and complete the table to find the total number of delayed trains.
(b) Use this value to estimate the mean delay of these trains.
(c) Why is this value only an estimate?
(d) Define the median class interval and state it.

UNIT 4 NUMBER 4

- **COMPOUND PERCENTAGES (INCLUDING DEPRECIATION)**
- **REVERSE PERCENTAGES**

NUMBER 4 – BASIC SKILLS EXERCISE

Compound percentages (including depreciation)

1. $500 is invested at 7% **compound interest** per year. Find the value of the investment after
   - (a) 1 year
   - (b) 2 years
   - (c) 3 years
   - (d) 4 years

2. £100 is invested at 4% compound interest per year. Find the value of the investment after
   - (a) 1 year
   - (b) 2 years
   - (c) 5 years
   - (d) 10 years

3. A valuable oil painting is worth ฿25 000 and **appreciates** by 5% per year. How much is it worth after
   - (a) 1 year
   - (b) 2 years
   - (c) 5 years
   - (d) 20 years?

4. A brand new car is purchased for ¥45 000 and **depreciates** by 8% per year. How much is it worth after
   - (a) 1 year
   - (b) 2 years
   - (c) 5 years
   - (d) 10 years?

5. €2500 is invested at 6% compound interest per year. Calculate
   - (a) its value after 5 years
   - (b) after how many years its value has doubled

6. $1000 is invested at 3% compound interest per year. Calculate
   - (a) its value after 10 years
   - (b) after how many years its value has increased by 50%

7. The population of a tropical island is increasing at the **rate** of 3.5% per year. How long will it take for the population to double?

8. An antique glass bowl was valued at ₹10 000 at the end of 2017. This value increased by 25% in 2018 and then by 22% in 2019. Its value fell by 30% in 2020. What was its value on 1 January 2021?

9. A 60-km glacier is shrinking by 6% every year. Find its length, in km, after
   - (a) 10 years
   - (b) 30 years

10 A 100-g sample of a radioactive element loses 2% of its **mass** every year.
Find the mass remaining, in grams, after
(a) 1 year (b) 5 years (c) 10 years

11 A saucepan contains 2 litres of boiling soup. The soup loses 0.25% of its volume every second.
How many litres of soup remain after 1 minute?

12 A government target is to increase electric car production by 85% over the next 10 years. Show that a monthly increase of 0.5% will *not* be enough to meet this target, but a monthly increase of 0.52% *will* meet the target.

Reverse percentages

13 An antique silk rug is worth KD12 000 after it has appreciated by 5% per year for ten consecutive years. How much was it worth ten years ago?

14 A valuable wooden carving is valued at $7500 after it has appreciated by 12% per year for five consecutive years. How much was it worth
(a) five years ago (b) two years ago?

15 A television is worth €525 after it has depreciated by 7% per year for three consecutive years. How much was it worth three years ago?

16 A farm tractor is worth £11 500 after it has depreciated by 9% per year for four consecutive years. How much was it worth
(a) four years ago (b) two years ago?

17 Ali sells her goat for $150, giving her a profit of 25%. Find the original price she paid for the goat.

18 Liam sells a bag of rice for $24, giving him a profit of 20%. Find the original price he paid for the rice.

19 Pierre sells an oil painting for €2125, giving him a loss of 15%. Find the original price he paid for the painting.

20 Guvinda ran 400 m in 77.6 seconds, which was an improvement of 3% on her original time. Find her original time.

21 In a sale the price of the Banana computer is $495 after a 17.5% price cut. What was the price before the sale?

22 A conservationist released some rare birds onto an island, which increased the population of these birds by 25% to a total of 60 birds.
How many birds did she release?
(This happened recently on the Galapagos Islands involving a rare finch studied by Charles Darwin.)

23 A valuable clock has an original price of $x. It is sold for $5000 after its original price has been increased by 5% and then by 10%. Find x.

24 A stone garden statue has an original price of €y. It is sold for €2500 after its original price has been increased by 15% and then by 20%. Find y.

25 A doll's house has an original price of £x. It is sold for £350 after its original price has been decreased by 5% and then by 10%. Find x.

26 A mountain bike has an original price of €y. It is sold for €1750 after its original price has been decreased by 15% and then by 20%. Find y.

27 An antique chair has an original price of $p. It is sold for $1250 after its original price has been increased by 7% and then decreased by 9%. Find p.

28 An apartment in New York has a value of $q. It is sold for $1 million after its original price decreases by 10% and then increases by 25%. Find q.

29 A pearl necklace has a value of €7500 after it has appreciated by 3% per year for 3 years. Find its original value 3 years ago.

30 A shirt signed by a world famous footballer has a value of £1800 after it has depreciated by 5% per year for 5 years. Find its original value 5 years ago.

31 An electric car is purchased for £60 000.
It depreciates by R% in the first year and by $R - 10$% in the second year.
The value of the car at the end of the second year is £30 000.
Work out the value of R correct to 3 s.f.

32 A restaurant increases the area of its circular pizzas by 15% to 730 cm².
What is the percentage increase in radius correct to 3 s.f.?

33 A 120 000 hectare forest is shrinking at a rate of 1.25% per month.
Find what area, in hectares
(a) has been lost in the last 4 years
(b) will be lost in the next 4 years

34 During the last 20 years the carbon dioxide level in the atmosphere has been increasing at 0.5% per year.
In 2020 the level in the atmosphere was 412 parts per million (ppm).
(a) What was the carbon dioxide level, in ppm, in the year 2000?
(b) Assuming the level continues to increase at the same rate, what will the carbon dioxide level, in ppm, be in 2040?

NUMBER 4 – EXAM PRACTICE EXERCISE

E 1 Alexa invests $50 000 in a savings account for 5 years at 3.5% compound interest per year.
At the end of the 5 years, a tax deduction of 35% of the total interest is made from the savings account.
Work out the percentage increase from Alexa's original investment at the end of the 5 years, after the tax deduction has been made.

E 2 Ruben invests €12 000 in a savings account for 10 years.
The savings account pays compound interest at a **rate** of 3.25% per year for the first 3 years and then 2.25% per year for all subsequent years.
Work out the percentage increase from Ruben's original investment at the end of the 10 years.

E 3 A new electric car is purchased for £50 000.
The value of the car depreciates by $P\%$ per year.
The value of the car at the end of the 3rd year is £25 000.
Work out the value of P to 3 s.f.

E 4 (a) The height of a tree is H m.
After a further three years' growth of 7.5% per year its height is 12 m.
Work out the value of H to 3 s.f.
(b) Three years ago Tim was x metres tall.
Over the next three years his annual growth rates were 7.5%, 5% and 2.5%.
Tim is now 1.8 metres tall.
Work out the value of x to 3 s.f.

E 5 (a) The price of 1 kg of gold on 1 January 2020 was £46 800.
The price of 1 kg of gold on 1 January 2015 showed a 15.2% decrease from its price on 1 January 2020.
Work out the price of 1 kg of gold on 1 January 2015 to the nearest pound (£).
(b) Between 1 January 2015 and 1 January 2020, the price of 1 kg of platinum increased by 18%, which represented an increase of €3848.
Work out the price of 1 kg of platinum on 1 January 2015 to the nearest euro (€).

UNIT 4 ALGEBRA 4

- **CHANGE OF SUBJECT**
- **USING FORMULAE**

ALGEBRA 4 – BASIC SKILLS EXERCISE

Change of subject – equations

For **questions 1–12**, make x the **subject** of the equation.

1. $a(b - x) = c^2$
2. $\frac{ax + b}{c} = d$
3. $\frac{a + c}{bx} = d$
4. $\frac{x^2}{a} - b = c$
5. $c - \frac{a}{x^2} = b$
6. $a(\sqrt{x} - b) = c$
7. $a\sqrt{x - b} = c$
8. $c - dx = ex + f$
9. $\frac{x + a}{x + b} = c$
10. $a(x - b) = c(d - x)$
11. $p = \sqrt{s + \frac{x}{t}}$
12. $r = \frac{sx}{s - x}$

Change of subject – formulae

For **questions 13–24**, make the letter in brackets the subject.

13. $V = \frac{1}{3} \pi r^2 h$ (h)
14. $V = \frac{4}{3} \pi r^3$ (r)
15. $v^2 = u^2 + 2as$ (s)
16. $A = 2\pi r(r + h)$ (h)
17. $S = \frac{n}{2}\{2a + (n - 1)d\}$ (a)
18. $s = ut + \frac{1}{2}at^2$ (a)
19. $S = \frac{a(1 - r^n)}{1 - r}$ (a)
20. $\frac{x^2}{a^2} + \frac{y^2}{b^2} = 1$ (x)
21. $T = 2\pi\sqrt{\frac{l}{g}}$ (l)
22. $F = G\frac{mM}{r^2}$ (r)
23. $F = \frac{k}{\sqrt[3]{d}}$ (d)
24. $m = \sqrt{\frac{6a + r}{5r}}$ (r)

Using formulae

25 $A = \frac{1}{2} ab\sin C$

Find b when $A = 6$, $a = 6$ and $C = 30$

26 $A = \frac{1}{2}(a + b)h$

Find a when $A = 35$, $b = 6$ and $h = 5$

27 $\frac{a}{\sin A} = \frac{b}{\sin B}$

Find A when $a = 6$, $b = 4$ and $B = 30$

28 $a^2 = b^2 + c^2 - 2bc\cos A$
Find $\cos A$ when $a = 5$, $b = 7$ and $c = 5$

29 $\frac{1}{u} + \frac{1}{v} = \frac{1}{f}$

Find v when $u = 4$ and $f = 2.5$

30 $x = \frac{-b + \sqrt{b^2 - 4ac}}{2a}$

Find c when $a = 1$, $b = -2$ and $x = 3$

ALGEBRA 4 – EXAM PRACTICE EXERCISE

E 1 A home improvements shop gives the formula $N = 2 + 0.4A$ to find the number, N, of rolls of wallpaper needed to paper a room with wall area A m². Windows and doors are ignored when calculating the wall area.

(a) Meghan wishes to wallpaper a rectangular room measuring 5 m long by 4 m wide by 2.6 m high.
Find the number of rolls of wallpaper she needs to buy.

(b) Juan buys 15 rolls of wallpaper for his room.
What are the maximum and minimum wall areas of his room in m²?

E 2 The diagram shows a pattern of shapes made by joining cubes of side 1 cm.

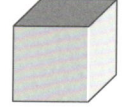

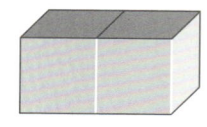

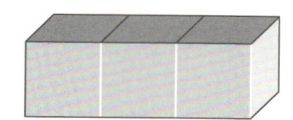

Shape number 1   Shape number 2   Shape number 3

A is the surface area of shape number n.
(a) Find a formula for A in terms of n.
(b) What shape number has a surface area of 214 cm²?
(c) Use your formula to explain why it is impossible to have a surface area that is an odd number.

E 3 Isaac Newton invented a temperature scale with temperature measured in °N.
The formula to convert a temperature N in °N to a temperature C in degrees Celsius is $C = \frac{100N}{33}$

The formula for converting a temperature C in degrees Celsius to a temperature F in degrees Fahrenheit is $F = \frac{9C + 160}{5}$

(a) Show that the formula to convert °N to °F is $F = \frac{60N + 352}{11}$

(b) What temperature is the same on both the °N and °F scales?
Give your answer to 1 d.p.

E 4 The time, t seconds, for a pendulum of length l metres to complete one swing is given by

$$t = 2\pi\sqrt{\frac{l}{9.8}}$$

(a) Rearrange the formula to make l the subject.

(b) A pendulum is designed to make a complete swing every second.
When it is made and measured it is found to be 5% too long.
What will be the percentage increase in the time taken to complete one swing?
Give your answer to 2 s.f.

E 5 The diagram shows part of the graph $y = ax^2 + bx + c$
Peter estimates the area, A, between the curve, the axes and the line $x = 2$
He draws two trapezia as shown in the diagram and calculates their area.

(a) Show that the formula for the area Peter calculates is
$A = 3a + 2b + 2c$
A formula for the exact area is
$A = \frac{8a}{3} + 2b + 2c$

(b) Show that the percentage error in Peter's answer is $\frac{100a}{8a + 6b + 6c}$ %

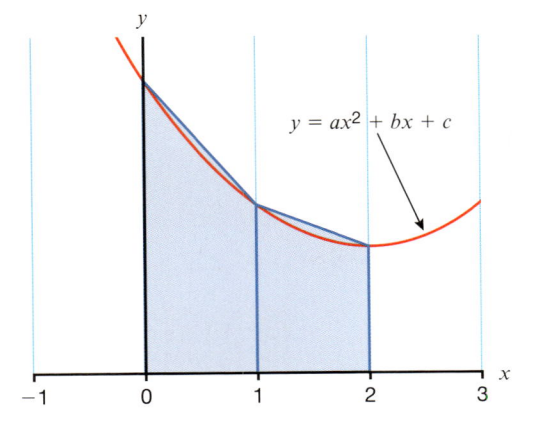

UNIT 4 GRAPHS 4

- **QUADRATIC GRAPHS:** $y = ax^2 + bx + c$
- **USING GRAPHS TO SOLVE** $ax^2 + bx + c = 0$

GRAPHS 4 – BASIC SKILLS EXERCISE

SKILLS
ANALYSIS, REASONING

Quadratic graphs: $y = ax^2 + bx + c$

For **questions 1–4**, complete the table of values.

1 $y = x^2 + x + 3$

x	−2	−1	0	1	2	3
y	5		3			

2 $y = x^2 + x − 5$

x	−2	−1	0	1	2	3
y			−5	−3		

3 $y = x^2 + 2x + 7$

x	−3	−2	−1	0	1	2	3	4
y			6		10			

4 $y = x^2 + 3x − 4$

x	−3	−2	−1	0	1	2	3	4
y			6		0			

SKILLS
PROBLEM SOLVING

Using graphs to solve $ax^2 + bx + c = 0$

5 Draw the graph of $y = x^2 − x − 2$ for $−3 \leq x \leq 3$ and use this graph to solve the equation $x^2 − x − 2 = 0$

6 Draw the graph of $y = x^2 + x − 6$ for $−4 \leq x \leq 4$ and use this graph to solve the equation $x^2 + x = 6$

7 Draw the graph of $y = x^2 − 2x − 8$ for $−3 \leq x \leq 5$ and use this graph to solve the equation $x^2 = 2x + 8$

8 Draw the graph of
  (a) $y = 2x^2 − 3x − 1$ for $−2 \leq x \leq 3$ and use it to solve the equation $2x^2 − 3x − 1 = 0$
  (b) $y = −2x^2 + 3x + 1$ for $−2 \leq x \leq 3$ and use it to solve the equation $−2x^2 + 3x + 1 = 0$

GRAPHS 4 – EXAM PRACTICE EXERCISE

1 The distance y m fallen by a free-falling parachutist t seconds after jumping out of an aeroplane is given by the equation $y = 5t^2$ for $0 \leq t \leq 5$
  (a) Draw the graph of y against t for $0 \leq t \leq 5$
  (b) Use your graph to estimate
    (i) the distance fallen after 3.5 s
    (ii) the number of seconds it takes the parachutist to fall 25 m

2 The partially completed table for $y = 2x^2 - 7x + p$ is shown below.

x	0	1	2	3	4	5
y	5					

  (a) By making a suitable substitution for x, find the value of p.
  (b) Copy and complete the table and then draw the graph for $0 \leq x \leq 5$
  (c) Use the graph to solve the equation $2x^2 - 7x + p = 0$

3 The partially completed table for $y = 2x^2 + px + q$ is shown below.

x	-2	-1	0	1	2	3	4
y			-3				13

  (a) By making suitable substitutions for x, find the values of p and q.
  (b) Copy and complete the table and then draw the graph for $-2 \leq x \leq 4$
  (c) Use the graph to solve the equation $2x^2 + px + q = 0$

4 The profit p (£1000s) made by a new coffee shop, t months after opening, is given by the equation $p = 10t - kt^2$, valid for $0 \leq t \leq 4$, where k is a constant.
  (a) Use this table to find the value of k, and then copy and complete the table.

t	0	1	2	3	4
p		7			

  (b) Draw the graph of p against t for $0 \leq t \leq 4$
  (c) Use it to estimate
    (i) the greatest profit made by the coffee shop and when it occurred
    (ii) when the coffee shop starts to make a loss

5 Consider the graph of $y = px^2 + qx + r$ where p, q and r are integers.
  Sketch the following graphs if
  (a) $p > 0$, $q = 0$ and $r > 0$
  (b) $p > 0$, $q = 0$ and $r < 0$
  (c) $p = 0$, $q > 0$ and $r > 0$
  (d) $p < 0$, $q = 0$ and $r > 0$

UNIT 4 SHAPE AND SPACE 4

- **TRIGONOMETRY AND PYTHAGORAS' THEOREM IN 3D; ANGLE BETWEEN TWO LINES, AND ANGLE BETWEEN A LINE AND A PLANE**

SHAPE AND SPACE 4 – BASIC SKILLS EXERCISE

SKILLS
CRITICAL THINKING, PROBLEM SOLVING, REASONING

Trigonometry and Pythagoras' theorem in 3D; angle between two lines, and angle between a line and a plane

1. *ABCDEFGH* is a cuboid. Find
   (a) the length *FH*
   (b) the length *BH*
   (c) angle *BHF*

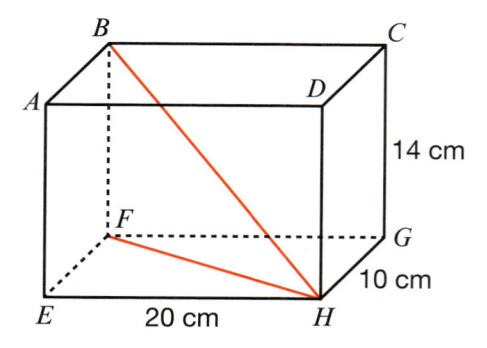

2. *VABCD* is a right pyramid on a square base. Find
   (a) the length *AC*
   (b) the pyramid's height
   (c) angle *AVB*
   (d) the total surface area of the pyramid including its base

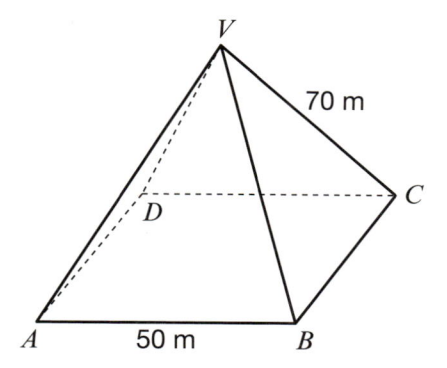

3   A ski-slope is shown.
    Calculate
    (a) the angle that *BF* makes with the base *ADEF*
    (b) the length *DF*
    (c) the angle that *CF* makes with the base *ADEF*
    M is the midpoint of *BC*.
    A skier travels directly from *M* to *F* in 30 seconds.
    (d) Calculate the speed of the skier in m/s to 3 s.f.

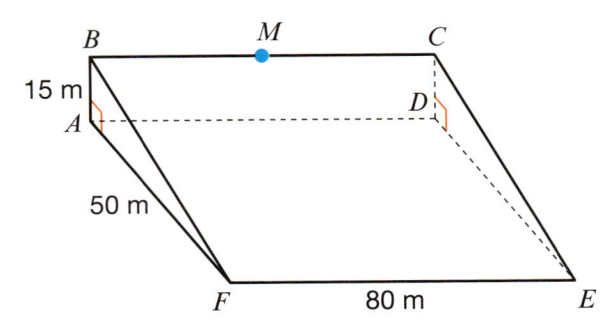

4   A parrot is at the top of a 15 m tree when it sees a mouse due West at an **angle of depression** of 15°. At the same moment, it observes a rabbit due South, also at an angle of depression of 15°.
    If the mouse and rabbit are both on level ground, calculate the distance between them at this instant in metres to 3 s.f.

5   A diagonal of the cube *ABCDEFGH* is shown. If $DF = 10\sqrt{3}$ cm, show that the total surface area of the cube is 600 cm².

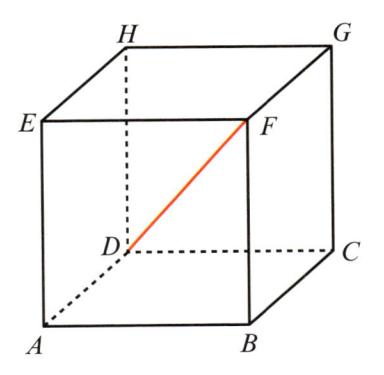

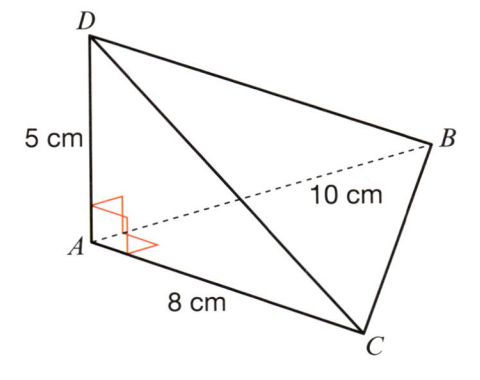

6   The diagram shows a **tetrahedron**.
    AD is **perpendicular** to both *AB* and *AC*.
    $AB = 10$ cm. $AC = 8$ cm. $AD = 5$ cm. Angle $BAC = 90°$
    Calculate the area of triangle *BCD* to 3 s.f.

SHAPE AND SPACE 4 – EXAM PRACTICE EXERCISE

E 1 The diagram shows a solid right cone.
The base of the cone is a horizontal circle, centre O, with a radius of 5 cm.
AB is a diameter of the base and VO is the vertical height of the cone.
The total surface area of the cone is 75π cm².
Calculate
(a) the slant height of the cone
(b) the angle AVB

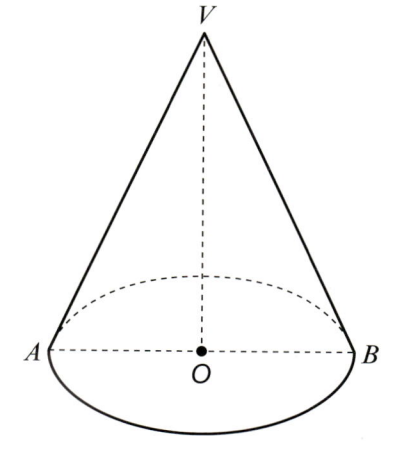

E 2 A, B and C are points on horizontal ground.
B is due North of A and AB is 14 m.
C is due East of A and AC is 25 m.
A vertical flagpole, TX, has its base at the point X on BC such that the angle AXC is a right angle.
The height of the flagpole, TX, is 10 m.
M is a point on XC such that $XM : MC = 3 : 1$
Calculate the angle of depression from T to M to 3 s.f.

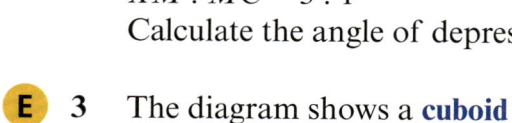

E 3 The diagram shows a **cuboid** $ABCDEFGH$.

$AB = 21$ cm and $CH = 9$ cm
$BC : CH = 4 : 3$
K is a point on EH such that
$EK : KH = 2 : 1$
Calculate to 3 s.f.
(a) the angle AKB
(b) the angle between the line AK and the **plane** $ABCD$

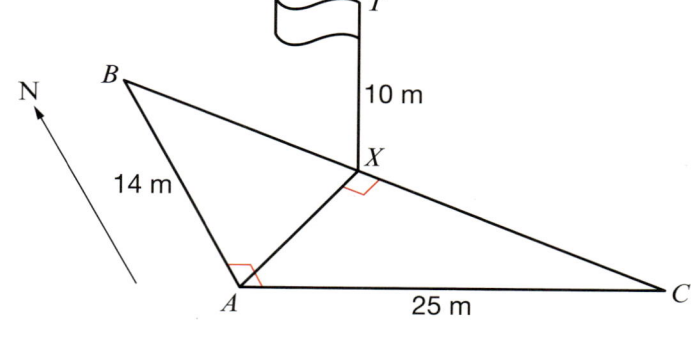

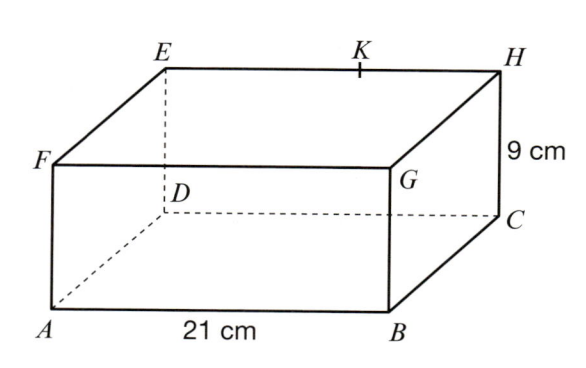

E 4 An aircraft is flying due East at a constant speed and constant height of 2000 m. At *T*, the aircraft's **angle of elevation** from *O* is 25°, and on a bearing from *O* of 310°. One minute later, it is at *R* and due North of *O*.

RSWT is a rectangle and the points *O*, *W* and *S* are on horizontal ground.

Find to 3 s.f.
(a) the lengths *OW* and *OS*
(b) the angle of elevation of the aircraft, *ROS*
(c) the speed of the aircraft in km/h

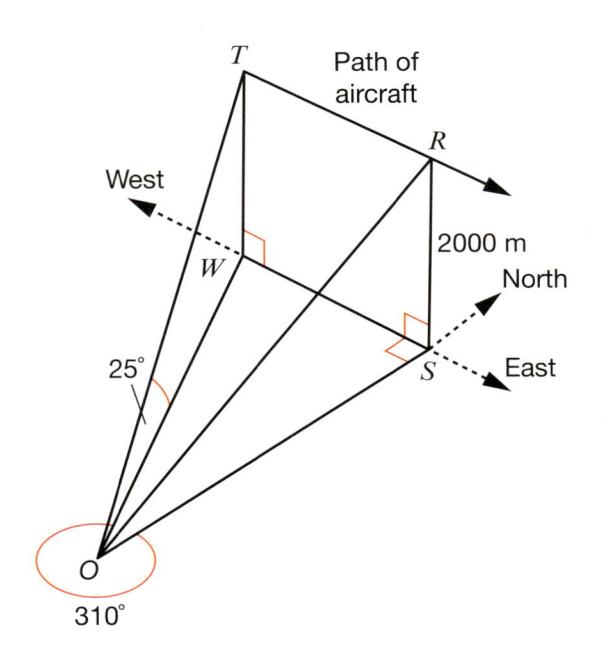

E 5 The diagram shows a pyramid with horizontal base *ABCDE*.
ABCDE is a regular pentagon, centre *O* and side 8 cm.
The vertex *P* is vertical above *O*.
M is the midpoint of *CD*.
OP = 10 cm
(a) Find the angle between *PM* and plane *ABCDE* to 3 s.f.
The weight of the empty pyramid is *w* grams.
The pyramid is now completely filled with water.
The weight of the pyramid full of water is 1 kg.
(b) Calculate *w* to 3 s.f.
(density of water = 1000 kg/m³)

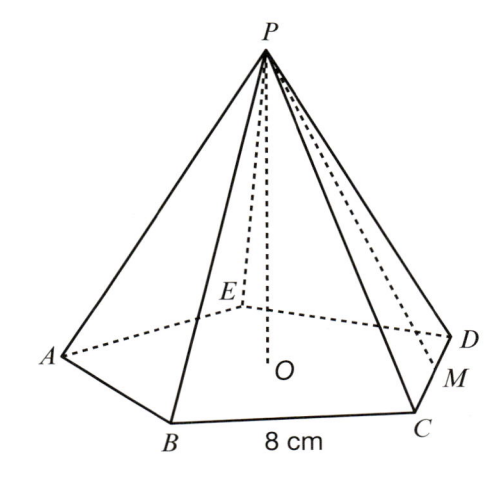

UNIT 4 HANDLING DATA 3

- **DISPERSION (DISCRETE DATA)**
- **DISPERSION (CONTINUOUS DATA)**

HANDLING DATA 3 – BASIC SKILLS EXERCISE

SKILLS
PROBLEM SOLVING, ANALYSIS

Dispersion (discrete data)

For **questions 1–4**, find the median, **quartiles**, range and **interquartile range** of the sets of numbers.

1. 5, 6, 8, 1, 0, 7, 6
2. 2, 5, 9, 0, 6, 1, 8, 1, 8, 6, 5, 0, 5, 5, 2
3. 2, 11, 8, 5, 1, 3, 0, 6, 4
4. 60, 83, 90, 59, 62, 83, 71, 46, 50, 82, 87, 21, 39

For **questions 5–8**, find the median, quartiles, range and interquartile range of the sets of numbers.

5. 4, 5, 5, 7, 8, 9, 0, 6, 8, 5, 9, 5, 4, 8, 7, 9, 3, 5, 8
6. 5.1, 3.9, 9.0, 9.4, 0.9, 2.5, 4.6, 9.9, 1.8, 2.1, 2.9
7. 39, 51, 32, 57, 77, 45, 70, 70, 89, 5, 83, 67, 77
8. 0.21, 0.57, 0.58, 0.46, 0.91, 0.46, 0.78, 0.55
9. The frequency table shows how many detentions students in Mr Tonge's class received last term. Find the median, quartiles, range and interquartile range of the number of detentions.

Number of detentions	Frequency
0	10
1	5
2	3
3	8
4	4
5	1

10. The frequency table shows how many books students in Ms Twitchitt's class read last term. Find the median, quartiles, range and interquartile range of the number of books read.

Number of books	Frequency
0	6
1	8
2	11
3	5
4	2
5	1

UNIT 4   HANDLING DATA 3

SKILLS

PROBLEM SOLVING, ANALYSIS

Dispersion (continuous data)

11 The frequency table gives the amount of time some students spent on the internet last night.
   (a) Construct a **cumulative frequency** table for the data.
   (b) Draw the cumulative frequency curve.
   (c) Use your curve to estimate the median, quartiles and interquartile range for the length of time spent on the internet.
   (d) How many students spent more than 32 minutes on the internet last night?

Time t (min)	Frequency
$0 < t \le 10$	3
$10 < t \le 20$	7
$20 < t \le 30$	15
$30 < t \le 40$	27
$40 < t \le 50$	19
$50 < t \le 60$	9

12 The frequency table shows the results of a spot check of speeds of some vehicles on a motorway.
   (a) Construct a cumulative frequency table for the data.
   (b) Draw the cumulative frequency curve.
   (c) Use your curve to estimate the median, quartiles and interquartile range for the speeds of vehicles.
   (d) What percentage of vehicles were travelling at less than 63 mph?

Speed s (mph)	Frequency
$s \le 55$	0
$55 < s \le 60$	6
$60 < s \le 65$	19
$65 < s \le 70$	46
$70 < s \le 75$	14
$75 < s \le 80$	5

13 The frequency table gives the birth weight of two random samples of babies from different countries.
   (a) Construct cumulative frequency tables for the data.
   (b) Draw the cumulative frequency curves on one set of axes.
   (c) Use your curves to estimate the median and interquartile range of birth weights for both countries.
   (d) Comment on the difference between the two samples.

Weight w (kg)	Frequency Country A	Frequency Country B
$w \le 2.0$	0	0
$2.0 < w \le 2.5$	14	0
$2.5 < w \le 3.0$	29	3
$3.0 < w \le 3.5$	23	20
$3.5 < w \le 4.0$	14	51
$4.0 < w \le 4.5$	0	6

HANDLING DATA 3 – EXAM PRACTICE EXERCISE

E 1 The table shows the number of phone calls that Tina made each day in June. Find the median, quartiles, range and interquartile range for the number of phone calls made each day.

16	25	18	39	31	13
35	15	38	17	27	11
19	23	31	18	23	29
14	22	34	21	33	30
35	25	29	17	24	21

E 2 The frequency table shows the weights of some chocolate bars in a gift box.
(a) Construct a cumulative frequency table for the data.
(b) Draw the cumulative frequency curve.
(c) Use your graph to estimate the median and interquartile range for the weights of the chocolate bars.
(d) What percentage of chocolate bars weigh more than 75 grams?

Weight w (g)	Frequency
$66 < w \le 68$	5
$68 < w \le 70$	13
$70 < w \le 72$	18
$72 < w \le 74$	10
$74 < w \le 76$	8
$76 < w \le 78$	6

E 3 The frequency table gives the amount of time some students spent on their mobile phones last night.
(a) Construct a cumulative frequency table for the data.
(b) Draw the cumulative frequency curve.
(c) Use your curve to estimate the median, quartiles and interquartile range for the amount of time spent on a mobile phone.
(d) What percentage of students spent between 45 minutes and 95 minutes on mobile phones last night?

Time t (min)	Frequency
$0 < t \le 20$	3
$20 < t \le 40$	7
$40 < t \le 60$	11
$60 < t \le 80$	10
$80 < t \le 100$	21
$100 < t \le 120$	25
$120 < t \le 140$	23

UNIT 4   **HANDLING DATA 3**   83

E 4   The frequency table gives the reaction times of a group of volunteers before and after drinking a can of fizzy drink.
     (a) Construct cumulative frequency tables for the data.
     (b) Draw the cumulative frequency curves on one set of axes.
     (c) Use your curves to estimate the median and interquartile range for both sets of reaction times.
     (d) Comment on the difference the drink makes to reaction times.

Time t (milliseconds)	Frequency before drink	Frequency after drink
$t \leq 160$	0	0
$160 < t \leq 180$	10	0
$180 < t \leq 200$	35	0
$200 < t \leq 220$	31	8
$220 < t \leq 240$	4	41
$240 < t \leq 260$	0	25
$260 < t \leq 280$	0	6

E 5   The frequency table gives the diameters of two random samples of tree trunks taken from two different woods, Short Wood and Waley Wood.
     (a) Construct cumulative frequency tables for the data.
     (b) Draw the cumulative frequency curves on one set of axes.
     (c) Use your curves to estimate the median and interquartile range for the diameters of the tree trunks for both woods.
     (d) Comment on the differences between the woods.

Diameter d (cm)	Frequency Short Wood	Frequency Waley Wood
$0 < d \leq 10$	6	2
$10 < d \leq 20$	9	3
$20 < d \leq 30$	12	7
$30 < d \leq 40$	23	38
$40 < d \leq 50$	21	42
$50 < d \leq 60$	14	6
$60 < d \leq 70$	10	2
$70 < d \leq 80$	5	0

UNIT 5 NUMBER 5

- **ESTIMATING USING STANDARD FORM**
- **UPPER AND LOWER BOUNDS**

NUMBER 5 – BASIC SKILLS EXERCISE

Estimating using standard form – positive indices

For **questions 1–12**, **estimate** the following in standard form, correct to 1 s.f.

1. $(1.9 \times 10^3) \times (5.1 \times 10^4)$
2. $(4.9 \times 10^7) \times (8.1 \times 10^5)$
3. $(6.8 \times 10^6) \times (7.9 \times 10^8)$
4. $(1.1 \times 10^6) \times (9.9 \times 10^4)$
5. $(7.9 \times 10^5) \div (4.1 \times 10^3)$
6. $(3.9 \times 10^7) \div (1.8 \times 10^4)$
7. $(8.9 \times 10^9) \div (1.9 \times 10^2)$
8. $(9.7 \times 10^{12}) \div (1.9 \times 10^4)$
9. $18\,000\,000 \times 19\,000\,000$
10. $49\,000 \times 61\,000\,000\,000$
11. $21\,800\,000 \div 19\,700$
12. $79\,950\,000\,000\,000 \div 3900$

Estimating using standard form – negative indices

For **questions 13–18**, **estimate** the following in standard form, correct to 1 s.f.

13. $0.005\,912 \times 290\,000\,000$
14. $0.000\,007\,987 \div 0.001\,967$
15. $(3.89 \times 10^{-7}) \times (5.91 \times 10^{-6})$
16. $4\,890\,000\,000 \times 0.011$
17. $(5.81 \times 10^{-5}) \div (2.98 \times 10^{-6})$
18. $(7.71 \times 10^{-3}) + (3.98 \times 10^{-4})$

Upper and lower bounds

For **questions 19–25**, calculate all answers to 3 s.f.

19. If $w = \frac{ac}{b}$, and $a = 2.5 \pm 0.1$, $b = 3.5 \pm 0.1$ and $c = 4.5 \pm 0.1$, calculate the **upper bound** and **lower bound** of w.

20. If $x = \frac{a+b}{c}$, and $a = 5.5 \pm 0.3$, $b = 3.5 \pm 0.5$ and $c = 2.5 \pm 0.1$, calculate the upper bound and lower bound of x.

21. If $y = \frac{a+b}{c-d}$, and $a = 1.5 \pm 0.1$, $b = 2.5 \pm 0.1$, $c = 5.5 \pm 0.1$ and $d = 3.5 \pm 0.1$, calculate the upper bound and lower bound of y.

22. If $z = \frac{a-b}{c+d}$, and $a = 10.5 \pm 0.1$, $b = 2.5 \pm 0.1$, $c = 1.5 \pm 0.1$ and $d = 3.5 \pm 0.1$, calculate the upper bound and lower bound of z.

23. If $w = \sqrt{\frac{a^2 - b^2}{\pi c}}$, and $a = 7.5 \pm 0.1$, $b = 1.5 \pm 0.1$ and $c = 3.5 \pm 0.1$, calculate the upper bound and lower bound of w.

24 If $w = \left(\frac{a}{b-c}\right)^3$ and $a = 2.5 \pm 0.1$, $b = 8.5 \pm 0.1$ and $c = 3.5 \pm 0.1$, calculate the upper bound and lower bound of w.

25 If $y = \frac{10 \sin a}{b-c}$, and $a = 30° \pm 0.5°$, $b = 2.9 \pm 0.1$ and $c = 1.2 \pm 0.1$, calculate the upper bound and lower bound of y.

26 A circular Persian rug has a diameter of 4 m to the nearest metre. Find, to 3 s.f., the upper and lower bounds of the

(a) area

(b) perimeter

27 $W = \frac{a-b}{\sin(c)}$, where $a = 7.35$, $b = 1.42$ and $c = 150°$ are all measured to 3 s.f. Calculate the upper and lower bounds of W correct to 3 s.f.

28 A cylindrical fish tank of diameter 120 cm and height 80 cm is to be filled with water.
The dimensions are given to the nearest 10 cm.
A bucket has a capacity of exactly 10 litres and is used to completely fill the tank.
If N is the number of buckets of water required to complete this job, find the upper and lower bounds of N to the nearest integer.
(1 litre = 1000 cm³)

29 A white rhinoceros exerts a downward force of 22 000 N measured to the nearest 100 N.
Each foot of the rhinoceros has an area of 350 cm² measured to the nearest 50 cm².
Assuming the animal's weight is evenly distributed and that the pressure exerted on **each** foot is given as P N/cm², calculate the upper and lower bounds of P correct to 2 s.f.

30 An equilateral triangle has a perimeter of 1200 mm measured to the nearest 100 mm. Calculate the upper and lower bounds of the area, A, in mm² of the triangle. Give your answer correct to 2 s.f.

86 UNIT 5 — NUMBER 5

NUMBER 5 – EXAM PRACTICE EXERCISE

SKILLS
PROBLEM SOLVING, REASONING, ADAPTIVE LEARNING

E 1 Hector is measuring the height, h in metres, of a tall building.
The dimensions a, b and α are all **rounded** to the nearest integer.
$a = 2$ m, $b = 100$ m and $\alpha = 40°$

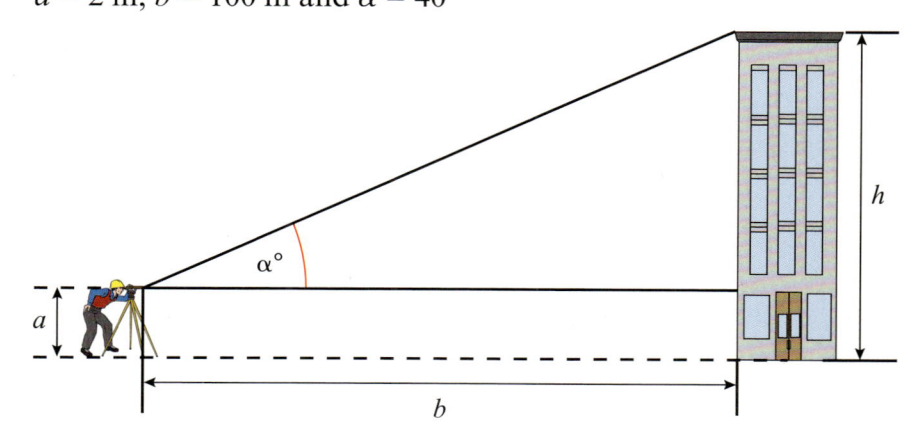

Calculate in metres to 3 s.f.
(a) the upper bound of h
(b) the lower bound of h

E 2 A metal block rests on a horizontal table.
The block has a square base of side 12 cm measured to the nearest cm.
Its weight produces a 50 N downward force on the table measured to the nearest 10 N.
The pressure exerted on the table is P N/cm².
Calculate to 2 s.f.
(a) the upper bound of P
(b) the lower bound of P

E 3 A mouse runs around a circular track of diameter 2.5 m measured to 2 s.f.
The mouse takes 2.5 seconds to complete one circuit.
This time is measured to the nearest 0.5 seconds.
The speed of the mouse around one circuit of the track is V m/s.
Calculate to 2 s.f.
(a) the upper bound of V
(b) the lower bound of V

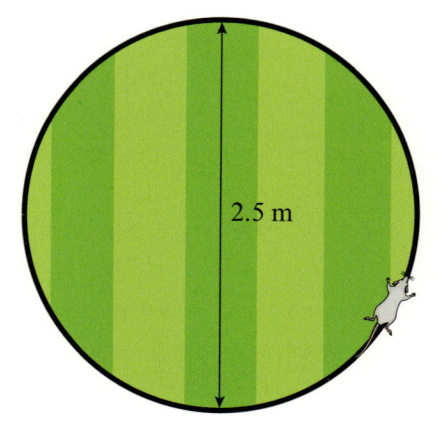

E 4 O is the centre of both circles.
The radius of the outer circle is R cm and the radius of the inner circle is r cm.
$R = 12.8$ and $r = 10.3$ both correct to 3 s.f.
The shaded area is A cm².
Show that $p\pi \leq A < q\pi$, where p and q are constants to be found to 2 s.f.

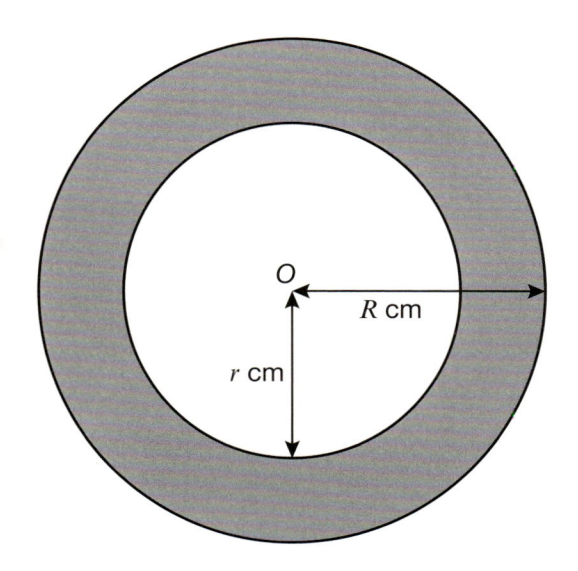

E 5 T is defined by the formula
$T = 10^z$, where $z = \frac{a-b}{c+d}$
The values of a, b, c and d are all measured to 3 s.f.
$a = 12.5$, $b = 3.25$, $c = 1.75$ and $d = 3.85$
Calculate to 2 s.f.
(a) the upper bound value of T
(b) the lower bound value of T

UNIT 5 ALGEBRA 5

- MULTIPLYING BRACKETS
- FACTORISING
- SOLVING EQUATIONS BY FACTORISING
- PROBLEMS

ALGEBRA 5 – BASIC SKILLS EXERCISE

Multiplying brackets

For **questions 1–10**, **multiply out** and fully simplify the expressions.

1. $(x - 5)(x + 2)$
2. $(x + 8)^2$
3. $(x^2 - 5)^2$
4. $(4x - 3)(2x + 2)$
5. $x(2x + 1)(5x - 2)$
6. $(x + 2)(x - 3)^2$
7. $(3x + 5)(3x - 5)(x - 2)$
8. $(2x - 3)^3$
9. $(2x - 2)(x + 2) - (x + 1)^2$
10. $4x(x - 3) - (2x - 3)^2$

Factorising

For **questions 11–14**, write the expressions in factorised form.

11. $(x^2 + 3)(2x + 1) + (x^2 + 3)(1 - 2x)$
12. $(4x + 1)^2 - (4x + 1)(x + 1)$
13. $\pi(4x + 3) - 3(4x + 3)$
14. $2x(1 - \cos x) - 3(1 - \cos x)$

Solving equations by factorising

For **questions 15–30**, solve the equations by factorising, showing full algebraic working.

15. $x^2 - 7x + 12 = 0$
16. $x^2 + 8x - 9 = 0$
17. $x^2 - 11x = 0$
18. $x + x^2 = 20$
19. $3x^2 + x - 10 = 0$
20. $4x^2 = 5x + 6$
21. $6x^2 - 10x + 6 = 3x$
22. $10x^2 + 9x = 40$
23. $(x - 3)(x + 5) = 9$
24. $x(2x + 1) = 6 - 3x$
25. $0.4x^2 - 1.8x = 1$
26. $4x^3 + 14x^2 + 12x = 0$
27. $x^4 + 36 = 13x^2$
28. $(x + 2)(x + 3) = (x + 2)(x - 4)$
29. $1 + \frac{4}{x^2} = \frac{5}{x}$
30. $x^{-2} + x^{-1} - 6 = 0$

Problems

Show full algebraic working. All quadratic equations to be solved by factorising.

31 The right-angled triangle and the rectangle have the same area. Find the value of x.

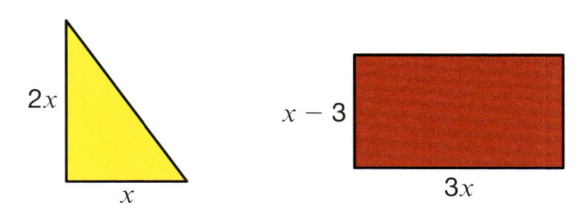

32 A rectangular carpet has a length of $x + 2$ m, a width of x m and an area of 15 m². Find the value of x.

33 A monkey throws a coconut from the top of a 14 m high palm tree. After t seconds the coconut has fallen a distance x m, where $x = 5t^2 + 3t$
Find how long it takes for the coconut to hit the ground.

34 Two integers differ by 4. The sum of the squares of these integers is 208. Find the two integers.

35 The **hypotenuse** of a right-angled triangle measures $4x - 3$ cm; the other two sides measure $x + 1$ cm and $2x + 4$ cm. Find the area of the triangle.

36 (a) Factorise $a^2 - b^2$
   (b) $N = 2^{24} - 1$. Using part (a) or otherwise, write N as the product of two integers both greater than 1000.

ALGEBRA 5 – EXAM PRACTICE EXERCISE

All quadratic equations in this exercise to be solved by factorising.

E 1 The angles of a quadrilateral are as shown in the diagram.
Prove that *ABCD* is a **cyclic quadrilateral**.

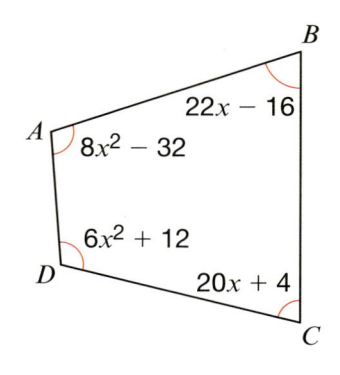

E 2 (a) A trapezium has two parallel sides of lengths $3x + 5$ cm and $x + 1$ cm. The distance between the parallel sides is $x + 3$ cm and the area of the trapezium is 35 cm². Find the value of x.

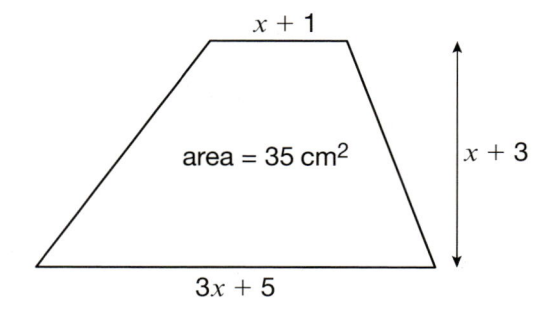

(b) Find the perimeter, in cm, of this right-angled triangle.

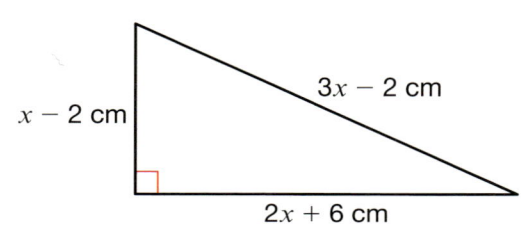

E 3 (a) $x^2 + px + 6$ has one factor $(x + 2)$.
Find the other factor and the value of p.

(b) (i) Factorise $2x^2 - 11x - 21$

(ii) Hence or otherwise solve
$2\left(x + \tfrac{1}{2}\right)^2 - 11\left(x + \tfrac{1}{2}\right) = 21$

E 4 (a) A quadratic equation has the two solutions $x = 5$ and $x = -\tfrac{2}{3}$
Find the quadratic equation in the form $ax^2 + bx + c = 0$

(b) $x^2 - 6x + p = 0$ has only one solution.
Find the value of p and the solution.

E 5 Priti spent $20 on some jars of fruit smoothies.
Each jar cost the same.
In another shop, she sees that the same jars of drink are each 20 cents cheaper.
She calculates that she could have bought five more jars for the same $20.
Let x be the number of jars she bought.

(a) Show that $x^2 + 5x - 500 = 0$

(b) How many jars did she buy?

(c) What was the price of each jars?

UNIT 5 GRAPHS 5

- **GRAPHICAL LINEAR INEQUALITIES**
- **PERPENDICULAR LINES**
- **MIDPOINTS**
- **PYTHAGORAS' THEOREM**

GRAPHS 5 – BASIC SKILLS EXERCISE

Graphical linear inequalities

For **questions 1–6**, state the inequalities that describe the **unshaded** region.

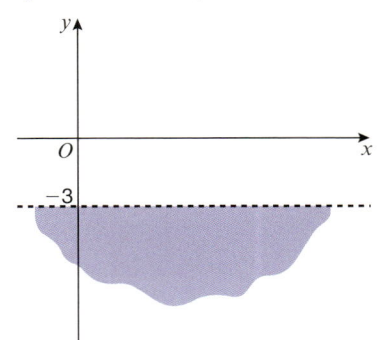

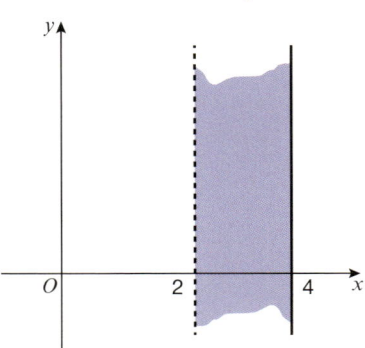

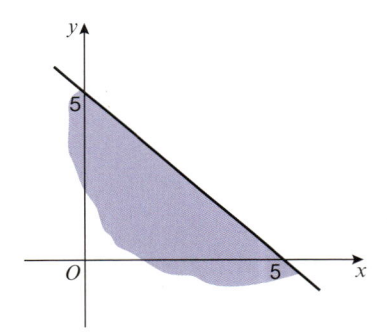

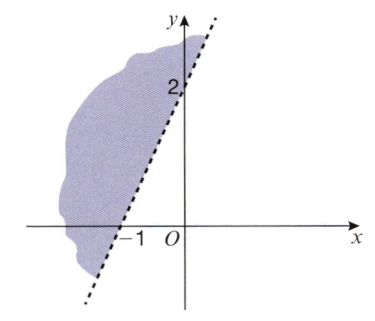

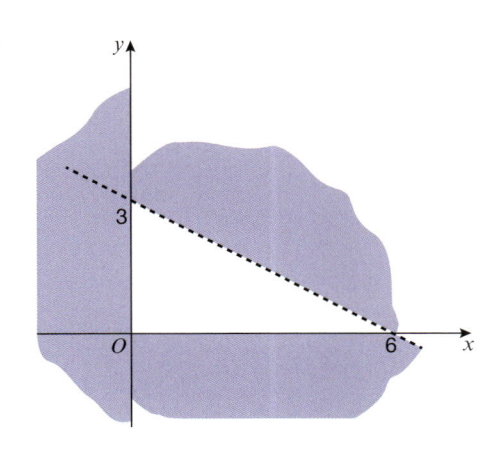

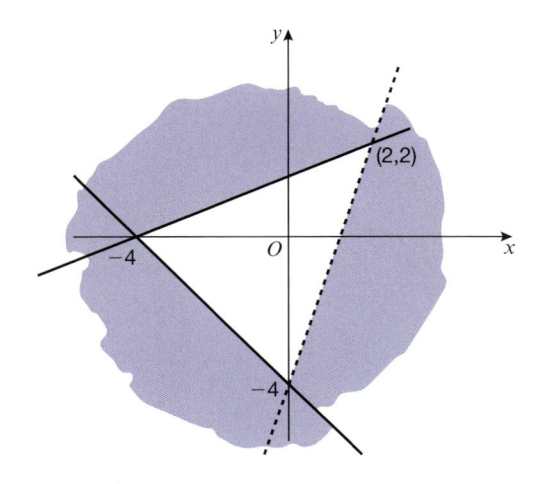

For **questions 7–10**, illustrate the inequalities on a graph, shading the **unwanted** region.

7 $x + y \geq 2$ and $x < 2$
8 $y \leq x + 1$ and $y > -1$
9 $x > -2$, $y \leq 4$ and $2y - 4 > x$
10 $x \leq 6$, $y + 1 < x$ and $2y + x > 4$

Perpendicular lines

11 Find the gradients of the lines parallel and perpendicular to AB when
   (a) A is $(-2, 4)$ and B is $(2, 1)$
   (b) A is $(-3, -2)$ and B is $(4, 4)$

12 Which of the following lines are perpendicular?
   (a) $4x + 3y = 12$
   (b) $3x + 4y = 12$
   (c) $3y = 4x - 1$
   (d) $4y = 3x + 7$

13 Show, by considering gradients, that the points $A(3, 0)$, $B(12, 3)$ and $C(1, 6)$ form a right-angled triangle.

14 Line L is $3x + 7y = 12$. Line M passes through $(-4, -9)$ and $(5, 12)$. Show that L and M are perpendicular.

15 Find the equation of the line that is perpendicular to $9x - 5y = -3$ and passes through $(9, -3)$.

16 Line L is $y + 4x + 2 = 0$. Line M passes through $(3, 3)$ and $(p, 1)$ and is perpendicular to line L. Find p.

Midpoints

17 Find the midpoint of AB when
   (a) A is the point $(-3, 1)$ and B is the point $(-1, -4)$
   (b) A is the point $(-3, 5)$ and B is the point $(26, -31)$

18 B is the point $(6, -1)$. $M(2, 1)$ is the midpoint of AB.
   Find the coordinates of A.

19 $A(-4, 1)$, $B(4, 3)$, $C(7, 1)$ and $D(-1, -1)$ are the four vertices of a parallelogram.
   Show that the diagonals bisect each other.

20 A is the point $(4, 1)$ and B is the point $(-2, -1)$.
   Find the equation of the perpendicular **bisector** of AB.

21 A median of a triangle is a line from one vertex to the midpoint of the opposite side. Show that $2y = x + 2$ is a median of triangle ABC where A is the point $(-4, -1)$, B is the point $(-1, 3)$ and C is the point $(5, 1)$.

Pythagoras' theorem

22 Find the distance between the points A and B when
   (a) A is the point $(-6, -2)$ and B is the point $(6, 3)$
   (b) A is the point $(-5, 7)$ and B is the point $(4, -5)$

23 A is the point $(-1, -3)$ and B is the point $(7, 3)$.
   AB is the diameter of a circle.
   Show that $P(1, \sqrt{21})$ lies on the circle.

24 The vertices of a triangle ABC are $A(-1, -1)$, $B(2\sqrt{3} - 1, 1)$ and $C(2\sqrt{3} - 1, -3)$.
   Show that ABC is an equilateral triangle.

25 Line *L* is tangent to a circle with centre $C(-1, 1)$.
Line *L* touches the circle at the point $T(2, -1)$.
Find the radius of the circle and the equation of line *L*.

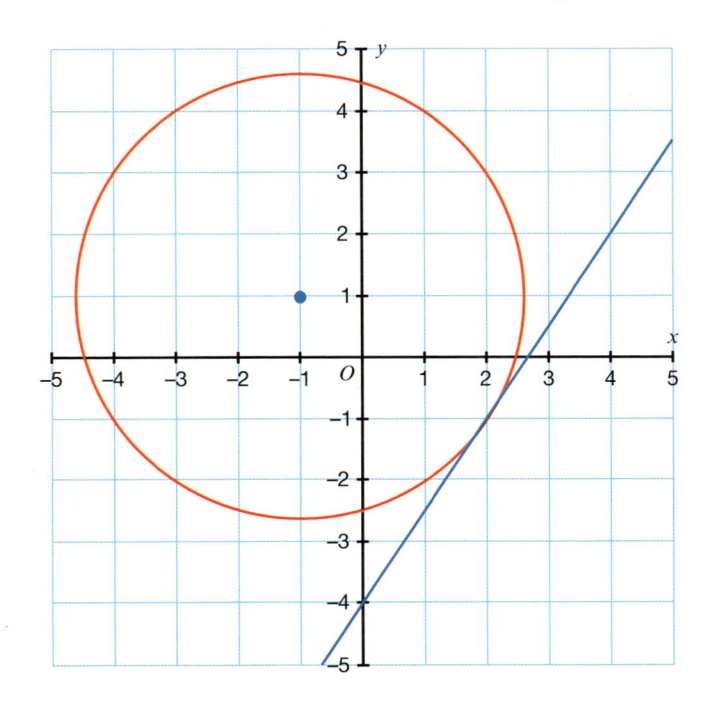

26 The points $A(2, 1)$ and *B* lie on the line $2y = x$
The distance AB is $\sqrt{20}$
Work out the two possible values of the coordinates of *B*.

94 UNIT 5 — GRAPHS 5

SKILLS
PROBLEM SOLVING, REASONING, ADAPTIVE LEARNING

GRAPHS 5 – EXAM PRACTICE EXERCISE

E 1 The grid shows a region R.
Find three inequalities that define region R.

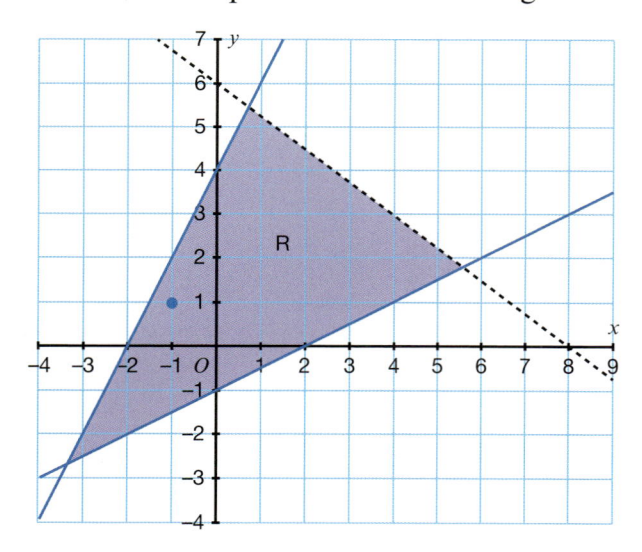

E 2 L is the line $2x + 5y = 20$
The line M passes through the points $(k, 10)$ and $(3, k)$.
L is perpendicular to M.
Work out the value of k.

E 3 The points $A(-4, -3)$, $B(3, 21)$ and $C(11, 17)$ are the three vertices of a triangle.
(a) Show that ABC is an isosceles triangle.
M is the midpoint of BC.
(b) Show that AM is perpendicular to BC.
(c) Show that the distance $AM = 11\sqrt{5}$

E 4 Point P is $(-2, 1)$ and point Q is $(8, -4)$.
Point R lies on the line $y = x$
PR is perpendicular to QR.
Work out the two possible values of the coordinates of R.

E 5 Saoirse is on an orienteering course.

She is at the point $(7, -2)$ where 1 unit = 100 m
A road is given by $4y + 4 = 3x$
Show that the shortest distance of Saoirse to the road is 500 m.

UNIT 5 SHAPE AND SPACE 5

- TRANSLATIONS
- REFLECTIONS
- ROTATIONS
- ENLARGEMENTS
- COMBINED TRANSFORMATIONS

SHAPE AND SPACE 5 – BASIC SKILLS EXERCISE

Translations

1. Find the image of point (1, 2) after it has been **translated** by the **vector** $\binom{5}{8}$.

2. Find the image of point (3, 4) after it has been translated by the vector $\binom{-1}{7}$.

3. Find the translation vector that moves point (5, 6) to point (7, 8).

4. The point $P(-1, 6)$ is translated by the vector $\binom{6}{6}$ to point Q.
   Find the distance of Q from the origin.

Reflections

5. The image of point $P(a, b)$ after it has been reflected in the x-axis is (1, 2).
   Find the coordinates of P.

6. The image of point $Q(a, b)$ after it has been reflected in the y-axis is (3, 4).
   Find the coordinates of Q.

7. The image of point $R(a, b)$ after it has been reflected in the line $y = x$ is (5, 6).
   Find the coordinates of R.

8. The image of point $S(a, b)$ after it has been reflected in the line $x = 4$ is (7, 8).
   Find the coordinates of S.

Rotations

9. Find the image of the point (1, 2) after it has been rotated 90° clockwise about (0, 0).

10. Find the image of the point (3, 4) after it has been rotated 90° anti clockwise about (0, 0).

11. Describe fully the rotation that transforms the point (5, 6) to point (−5, −6).

12. Describe fully the rotation that transforms the point (7, 8) to point (6, 7).

Enlargements

SKILLS
REASONING

13 A triangle is enlarged by scale factor 2 with centre (0, 0).
    It has a vertex at point $A(1, 2)$.
    Find the coordinates of the image of A after this transformation.

14 A circle is enlarged by scale factor 3 with centre (0, 0).
    It has a point $A(3, 4)$ on its circumference.
    Find the coordinates of the image of point A after this transformation.

15 A regular pentagon of side 10 cm is enlarged by a scale factor of 2 with centre (0, 0).
    Find the perimeter of the pentagon's image in cm.

16 A regular octagon of side 10 cm is enlarged by a scale factor of $\frac{1}{2}$ with centre (0, 0).
    Find the perimeter of the octagon's image in cm.

Combined transformations

SKILLS
PROBLEM SOLVING, REASONING

17 Find the image of point $P(3, 4)$ after it has been
    (a) reflected in the x-axis
    (b) reflected in the y-axis
    (c) rotated about 0 by 90° in a clockwise direction
    (d) translated by vector $\begin{pmatrix} 7 \\ -6 \end{pmatrix}$

18 Find the image of point $Q(-3, 5)$ after it has been
    (a) reflected in $y = 0$
    (b) reflected in $x = 0$
    (c) rotated about 0 by +90°
    (d) translated by vector $\begin{pmatrix} -5 \\ 3 \end{pmatrix}$

19 Draw a set of axes for $-8 \leq x \leq 16$ and $-8 \leq y \leq 10$.
    Draw the triangle ABC, where A is (1, 2), B is (1, 6) and C is (8, 2).
    On the same axes, draw the image of triangle ABC after it has been
    (a) reflected in the x-axis
    (b) rotated about 0 by 90° in an anti clockwise direction
    (c) translated by vector $\begin{pmatrix} -5 \\ 4 \end{pmatrix}$
    (d) enlarged by a scale factor of 2 about a centre of enlargement (0, 4)

20 (a) Reflect the flag F in the y-axis and label the image A.
    (b) Reflect A in the line $y = x$ and label its image B.
    (c) Describe fully the single transformation which takes F to B.
    (d) Reflect A in the line $x = 2$ and label this image C.
    (e) Describe the single transformation which takes F to C.

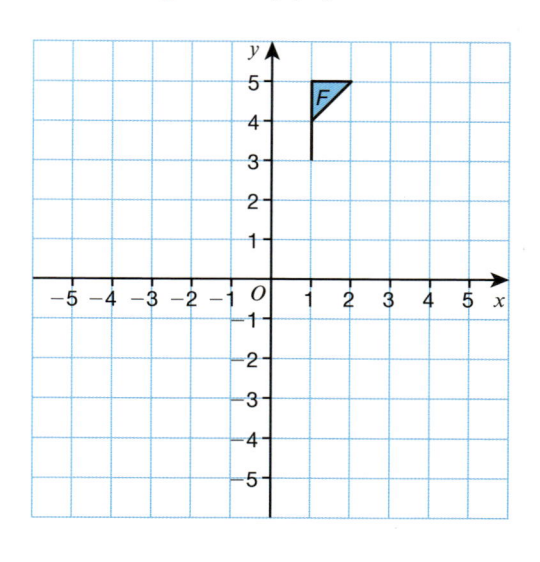

UNIT 5   SHAPE AND SPACE 5   97

SKILLS

PROBLEM SOLVING, REASONING

SHAPE AND SPACE 5 – EXAM PRACTICE EXERCISE

E 1 The image of a point $P(x, y)$ is at point $Q(4, 8)$ **after** P has undergone the following transformations in the order:
  Reflection in the x-axis.
  Rotation by 90° in a clockwise direction about 0.
  Translation by vector $\binom{3}{-3}$.
Find the values of x and y.

E 2 The image of triangle ABC is at $J(2, 3)$, $K(2, 5)$, $L(6, 3)$ **after** it has undergone the following transformations in the order:
  Reflection in the y-axis.
  Rotation by 90° in an anti clockwise direction about 0.
  Translation by vector $\binom{-3}{4}$.
Find the co ordinates of triangle ABC.

E 3

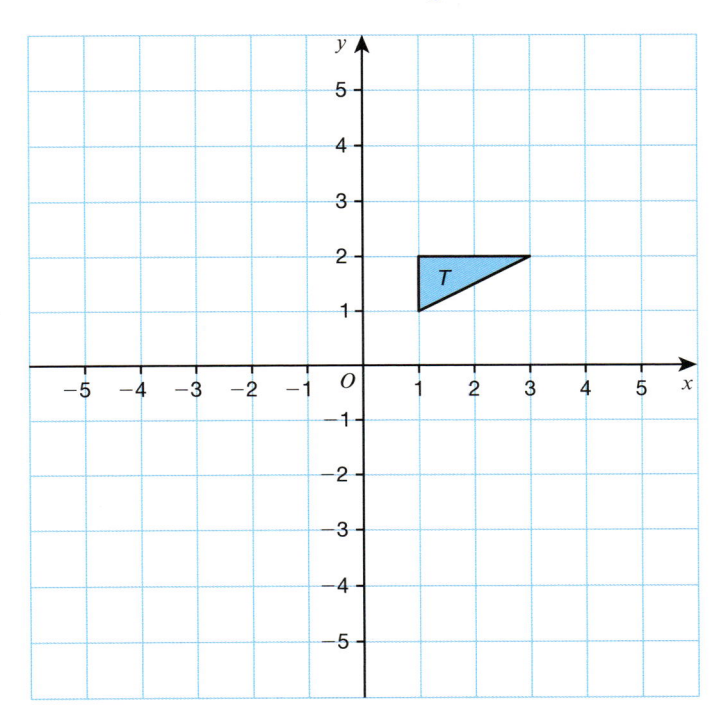

(a) Triangle T undergoes the following transformations.
  (i) A is the image of T after a reflection in $y = x$. Draw A.
  (ii) B is the image of A after a 180° rotation about $(1, 1)$. Draw B.
(b) C is the image of B after a 180° rotation about $(0, 2)$. Draw C.
(c) Describe the single transformation that **maps** triangle A to triangle C.

E 4 Triangle *T* is shown in the diagram.
- (a) *T* is reflected in line *L* to form image *A*. Draw triangle *A*.
- (b) *A* is reflected in $y = -1$ to form image *B*. Draw triangle *B*.
- (c) *T* undergoes a translation by vector $\begin{pmatrix} -2 \\ -3 \end{pmatrix}$ to form image *C*. Draw triangle *C*.
- (d) *T* is enlarged by scale factor 2 with centre (3, 2) to form image *D*. Draw triangle *D*.
- (e) Describe fully the transformation which maps *T* to *B*.
- (f) Describe fully the transformation which maps *C* to *D*.

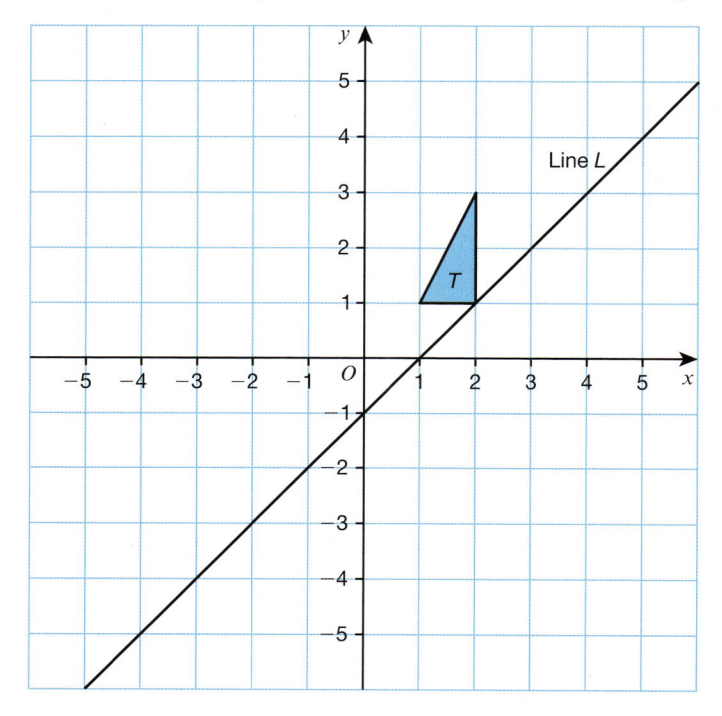

E 5 A regular hexagon with perimeter 12 cm has its centre at (0, 0).

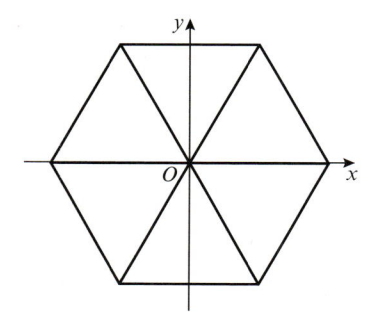

The hexagon is translated by vector $\begin{pmatrix} 6 \\ 6 \end{pmatrix}$.

It is then enlarged by scale factor 6 about (0, 0).
- (a) The original hexagon has a vertex at point $A(1, \sqrt{3})$. Find the image of point *A* after the translation.
- (b) Show that the area of the image of the hexagon after the enlargement is given by $2^a \times 3^b$ cm², where *a* and *b* are constants to be found.

UNIT 5 HANDLING DATA 4

- **PROBABILITY FROM A SAMPLE SPACE AND PROBABILITY OF THE COMPLEMENT OF AN EVENT**
- **EXPERIMENTAL PROBABILITY, THEORETICAL PROBABILITY, RELATIVE FREQUENCY AND EXPECTED FREQUENCY**

HANDLING DATA 4 – BASIC SKILLS EXERCISE

SKILLS

ANALYSIS, REASONING, ADAPTIVE LEARNING

Probability from a sample space and probability of the complement of an event

1. The probability of it snowing in New York on 25 December is 0.2.
   What is the probability of New York not experiencing snow on that day?

2. A box contains twelve roses. Four are white, two are red and six are pink.
   Sacha picks out one rose at random. What is the probability that it is
   - (a) pink
   - (b) not red
   - (c) white, red or pink
   - (d) yellow?

3. One letter is randomly chosen from this sentence.
   'I have hardly ever known a mathematician who was capable of reasoning'.
   What is the probability of the letter being
   - (a) an 'e'
   - (b) an 'a'
   - (c) a consonant (non-vowel)
   - (d) a 'z'?

4. Jamal receives 50 emails. 32 are from England, 12 are from the USA and the rest are from China.
   He chooses one email at random to read first. What is the probability that it is from
   - (a) France
   - (b) the USA or China
   - (c) England
   - (d) not England?

5. A card is randomly selected from a pack of 52 playing cards. Calculate the probability that it is
   - (a) a Queen
   - (b) a King or a Jack
   - (c) not a heart
   - (d) a red picture card (a picture card is a Jack, Queen or King)

6. A fair eight-sided dice has numbered **faces** from 1 to 8. After it is rolled, find the probability of obtaining a
   - (a) 3
   - (b) prime number
   - (c) a number of at least 3
   - (d) a number of at most 5

7. A box contains one red marble and three green marbles. Two are taken at random.
   - (a) Write down all the possible outcomes in a table.
   - (b) Use this table to find the probability of obtaining one marble of each colour.

8 Two fair six-sided dice are rolled and their scores are multiplied.
   (a) Write down all the possible outcomes in a table.
   (b) Use this table to find the probability of the following scores being obtained.
       (i) 36
       (ii) 11
       (iii) a multiple of 5
       (iv) at least 20

9 Three discs are in a black box and are numbered 10, 30 and 50. Four discs are in a white box and these are numbered 9, 16, 25 and 36. Two discs, one from each box, are randomly selected and the *highest* number of the two is noted.
   (a) Construct a suitable 'probability space' table.
   (b) Use this table to find the probability of the following numbers being obtained.
       (i) 10
       (ii) a prime number
       (iii) an even number
       (iv) a square number

10 Three vets record the number of horses which are cured after being given a particular medicine.

Vet	Number of horses given medicine	Number of horses cured
Mr Stamp	18	16
Mrs Khan	14	11
Miss Abu	10	9

Calculate the probability that
   (a) a horse given the medicine by Mr Stamp or Miss Abu will be cured
   (b) a horse given the medicine by Mrs Khan or Miss Abu will not be cured

Mr Stamp, Mrs Khan and Miss Abu treated 90, 84 and 99 horses respectively with the medicine.
   (c) How many horses would you expect not to be cured from this group?

11 Baby Kiera has two toy boxes. The pink box contains a triangle, a circle and a star whilst the blue box contains a square, a rectangle and a star. She randomly picks one shape from each box to play with.
   She is happy as long as at least one of these shapes is a star.
   (a) Construct a suitable 'probability space' table.
   (b) Use this table to find the probability that
       (i) Kiera is happy
       (ii) Kiera is not happy

12 A garden fish pond contains 40 Koi Carp, of which x are golden and the others are white. If 20 more golden Koi Carp are added to the pond, the probability of catching a golden Koi Carp is doubled.
   Find x.

SKILLS
PROBLEM SOLVING, REASONING, ADAPTIVE LEARNING

Experimental probability, theoretical probability, relative frequency and expected frequency

13 Gita wishes to estimate her probability of scoring a goal in hockey from a penalty. She does this by taking 10 penalties in succession, with the following results.
Score: S   Miss: M
S S M M M S S S M S
Use a **relative frequency** diagram to estimate the probability of scoring.

14 A fair six-sided dice is rolled 120 times. How many times would you expect to roll a multiple of three?

15 Zak decides to guess each answer in a Physics multiple choice test. There are 20 questions, each with four options A, B, C and D. How many questions should Zak expect to get right?

16 Yara is the first person to buy raffle tickets in a draw from 250 tickets with a single grand prize.
Calculate the probability that Yara wins the prize on her sixth ticket.

17 Two bags contain ten identical discs with numbers printed on each one.
Bag A contains discs with the first five prime numbers.
Bag B contains discs with the next five prime numbers.
A disc is taken from each bag and the numbers are added together to give a total.
(a) Draw a sample space diagram to show all the possible totals which could be produced.
(b) If one number is randomly selected from these totals 50 times, how many would you expect to pick which contain a zero? Justify your reasoning.

18 A letter is chosen randomly from the word SYMMETRICAL and replaced before the next random pick. If this is done 99 times in total, how many letters would you expect to have obtained which have a line of symmetry?

HANDLING DATA 4 – EXAM PRACTICE EXERCISE

E 1 Here is a biased five-sided spinner.
Jack spins the spinner once.
The table shows information about the probabilities that the spinner lands on red, blue, black, white or green.

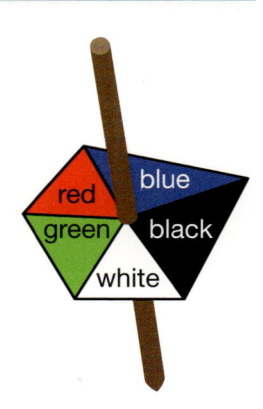

Colour	red	blue	black	white	green
Probability	x	$2x$	$3x$	x	x

(a) Find the probability that the spinner lands on black.
(b) Find the probability that the spinner does *not* land on red or green.

Lydia spins the spinner 100 times. It lands on one colour 25 times.

(c) State which colour is most likely to have been spun, explaining your reasons clearly.

E 2 Li rolls a six-sided biased dice once.
The table shows the probabilities that the dice will land on 1, 2, 3, 5 or 6.

Number	1	2	3	4	5	6
Probability	0.15	0.1	0.05		0.2	0.15

(a) Find the probability that Li rolls a prime number.

Li rolls the dice 100 times and she notes that two numbers turn up a total of 40 times.

(b) Find which two numbers were the most likely to have been rolled, explaining your reasons clearly.

E 3 The table below shows the favourite drinks of a group of students.

	Milkshake	Orange juice	Tea	Coffee	Total
Year 10		10	7	5	
Year 11	3	12	4		26
Total					50

(a) Complete the table.

A student is picked at random.

(b) What is the probability that this student is
  (i) a Year 10 student who prefers milkshake
  (ii) a Year 11 student who does not prefer tea or coffee?

(c) Given that a Year 10 student is picked at random, what is the probability that he does not prefer milkshake?

E 4 The table below shows the highest common factors (HCF) of different pairs of numbers.

	35	42	120
20	5	2	
63	7		3
96		6	

(a) Complete the table.

Jensen picks a HCF at random from the table.

(b) What is the probability that the HCF picked out is
 (i) an even number
 (ii) a prime number or a triangular number?

Jensen randomly chooses a HCF from the table 90 times.

(c) How many of these numbers would you expect to be odd?
 Explain your reasoning.

E 5 An aquarium contains 60 jellyfish.
A total of x jellyfish are purple and the rest are white.
Forty more white jellyfish are added to the aquarium.
The probability of a white jellyfish being taken out randomly has now trebled.
What is the probability that a randomly removed jellyfish is purple?

UNIT 6 NUMBER 6

- **DIRECT PROPORTION**
- **INVERSE PROPORTION**
- **NEGATIVE AND FRACTIONAL INDICES**

NUMBER 6 – BASIC SKILLS EXERCISE

Direct proportion

1. Which of these pairs of quantities are in **direct proportion**?
   (a) 3 melons cost $1.26, 7 melons cost $2.94
   (b) 275 ml of water costs 50 cents, 500 ml costs 80 cents
   (c) A car used 12 litres of fuel to travel 254 km, it used 15 litres to travel 317.5 km

2. If a 1.2 GB download takes 20 minutes 27 seconds, how long will a 1.9 GB download take at the same speed?

3. Which perfume is the better value, Brand A at €60 for 25 ml or Brand B at €70 for 30 ml?

4. At blast off, a space rocket uses 104.5 tonnes of fuel in 9.5 seconds. Assuming it continues to use fuel at the same rate, find
   (a) how much fuel is used in one minute
   (b) how long it takes to use 297 tonnes of fuel

5. During its migration a bird called the bar-tailed godwit flew for 11 days, covering a distance of 12 000 km without stopping.

   Assuming it flew at a constant rate, find
   (a) how far it travelled in one minute
   (b) how long it would take to fly from London to Edinburgh, a distance of 534 km

6   The cost of a wedding cake is directly proportional to the number of people it will serve.

Number of people	50		160	200
Cost (£)		200	400	

   (a) Copy and complete the table.
   (b) A cake costs £875. How many people will it serve?

7   Kit does an experiment timing how long it takes for a hot drink to cool down. The table gives his results.

Time (min)	0	5	15	30
Temperature (°C)	63	58	49	36

   Kit claims the temperature drop is proportional to the time taken.
   Show that Kit is wrong.

8   A bar of chocolate weighs 85 grams and contains 20 squares.

   The label states that the chocolate contains 30% cocoa solids.
   A recipe needs at least 15 grams of cocoa solids.
   What is the minimum number of squares of chocolate needed for the recipe?

Inverse proportion

9   In the table, three pairs of values are in **inverse proportion** and one pair is not.

x	2	3	4	6
y	18	12	10	6

   Which pair is not in inverse proportion?

10 The number of scarves sold by a shop is inversely proportional to the temperature. Copy and complete the table.

Number of scarves	120		40	32	
Temperature (°C)		8		15	20

11 The time taken to download a music track from an online streaming service is inversely proportional to the internet speed.
   (a) When the internet speed is 64 megabits per second, how long does it take to download a 24 megabyte song?
   (b) A 15 megabyte song takes 0.25 seconds to download. What is the internet speed in megabits per second?

12 The number of days it takes to clean an office block's windows is inversely proportional to the number of window cleaners.
It takes three window cleaners 8 days to clean the windows of an office block.
  (a) How long would it take two window cleaners to clean the windows of the same office block?
  (b) How many window cleaners are required to clean the windows of the same office block in 4 days?

13 The time it takes to check in at an airport is inversely proportional to the number of check-in desks open.
When 3 desks are open it takes $\frac{3}{4}$ hour to check in.
  (a) How long will it take to check in if 5 desks are open?
  (b) How many desks are open if it takes 15 minutes to check in?

14 The time taken for an ice cube to melt is inversely proportional to the temperature of the drink.
When the temperature of the drink is 20 °C it takes 9 minutes for an ice cube to melt.
  (a) How long will an ice cube take to melt in a drink with a temperature of 15 °C?
  (b) An ice cube takes 24 minutes to melt. What was the temperature of the drink?

15 The time taken to serve a wedding banquet is inversely proportional to the number of waiters and proportional to the number of guests.
It takes 12 waiters three minutes to serve a wedding banquet to 60 guests.
  (a) How many waiters would be needed to serve a wedding banquet to 60 guests in two minutes?
  (b) A wedding banquet for 100 guests was served in 90 seconds. How many waiters were used?

16 A bumble bee has to travel 150 km to produce 1 g of honey.
  (a) A hive contains 10 000 bees and produces 1 kg of honey.
   What is the mean distance flown by each bee in km?
  (b) A hive produces 12 kg of honey and the mean distance flown by each bee is 45 km.
   How many bees are in the hive?

Negative and fractional indices

For **questions 17–26**, without using a calculator, write each expression as a fraction or integer in its simplest form, showing each step of your working.

17 5^{-2}

18 $(3^{-1})^3$

19 4×4^{-3}

20 $7^4 \div 7^6$

21 $5^{-8} \div 5^{-7}$

22 $2^{-2} \times 3^{-3}$

23 $2^{-3} \div 3^{-2}$

24 $2^{10} \times 4^{-5}$

25 $3^{-9} \times 3^7 \div 3^{-4}$

26 $6^{-8} \times 3^7 \div 2^{-9}$

For **questions 27–36**, without using a calculator, evaluate each expression, showing each stage of your working.

27 $49^{-\frac{1}{2}}$

28 $64^{-\frac{2}{3}}$

29 $\left(\frac{4}{25}\right)^{\frac{3}{2}}$

30 $\left(\frac{81}{16}\right)^{-\frac{3}{4}}$

31 $\left(3\frac{3}{8}\right)^{\frac{2}{3}}$

32 $\left(1\frac{9}{16}\right)^{\frac{1}{2}} \div \left(1\frac{7}{9}\right)^{-\frac{1}{2}}$

33 $32^{-\frac{3}{5}} \times 16^{\frac{3}{4}}$

34 $27^{-\frac{2}{3}} \div 3^{-1}$

35 $64^{\frac{2}{3}} \div 32^{-\frac{2}{5}} \times 8^{-\frac{2}{3}}$

36 $8^{\frac{2}{3}} + 25^{-\frac{3}{2}} \div 5^{-4}$

For **questions 37–44**, find x.

37 $3^x = 81$

38 $12^x = 1$

39 $16^x = 4$

40 $8^x = \frac{1}{4}$

41 $8^{\frac{x}{3}} = 1$

42 $16^x = 8$

43 $3^{2x-1} = 1$

44 $2^{(x^2+x-2)} = 1$

NUMBER 6 – EXAM PRACTICE EXERCISE

E 1 A factory has 5 similar machines that can produce 30 000 shoes in 20 days.

The factory receives an order for 36 000 shoes to be delivered in 16 days' time.
Kiko orders some more machines of the same type to fulfil the order.
The 5 machines will work for 6 days before the extra machines can be installed and start work.
How many machines should Kiko buy to fulfil the order?

E 2 In a particular ocean, the temperature of water is $T\,°C$ at a depth of d metres.
T decreases linearly with d for $0 \leq d \leq 700$
T is inversely proportional to d for $d \geq 700$
The temperature at the surface ($d = 0$ m) is 20 °C.
The temperature at a depth of 500 m is 10 °C.

A certain species of fish can only survive at temperatures greater than 4 °C.
What is the maximum depth at which the fish can be found?

E 3 In this question, do not use a calculator and show each step of your working.

(a) Show that $(5^4)^{\frac{3}{8}} \times (5^{10})^{-\frac{1}{4}} \div 100^{-\frac{1}{2}} = 2$

(b) Show that $27\sqrt{27} = 81\sqrt{3}$

(c) $27\sqrt{27} = 9^k$. Show that $k = \frac{9}{4}$

E 4 For each part of the question, find k as an improper fraction in its lowest terms.

(a) $8 = 4^k$ (b) $2\sqrt{32} = 4^k$ (c) $\frac{1}{32} = 8^k$

E 5 (a) If $x = 2^3$ and $y = 3^2$, express the following in terms of x and y.

(i) 6 (ii) $4\sqrt{3}$ (iii) $\frac{1}{3\sqrt{4}}$

(b) $2^a \times 3^b = \frac{3\sqrt{6}}{8}$

Find the values of a and b.

UNIT 6 ALGEBRA 6

- **DIRECT PROPORTION – LINEAR**
- **DIRECT PROPORTION – NON-LINEAR**
- **INVERSE PROPORTION**
- **NEGATIVE AND FRACTIONAL INDICES**

ALGEBRA 6 – BASIC SKILLS EXERCISE

Direct proportion – linear

1. y is directly proportional to x. If $y = 18$ when $x = 2$, find
   (a) the formula for y in terms of x
   (b) the value of y when $x = 10$
   (c) the value of x when $y = 45$

2. a is directly proportional to b. Copy and complete the following table.

b	10	15	
a	200		600

3. The variable y is directly proportional to x, and $y = 24$ when $x = 3$. Find
   (a) the formula for y in terms of x
   (b) the value of y when $x = 10$
   (c) the value of x when $y = 40$

Direct proportion – non-linear

4. x varies directly as the cube root of y. If $x = 12$ when $y = 27$, find
   (a) the formula for y in terms of x
   (b) the value of y when $x = 32$

5. y varies directly as the square of x. If $y = 10$ when $x = 5$, find
   (a) the formula for y in terms of x
   (b) the value of y when $x = 15$
   (c) the value of x when $y = 15$

6. p is directly proportional to the square root of q. If $p = 100$ when $q = 25$, find
   (a) the formula for p in terms of q
   (b) the value of p when $q = 64$
   (c) the value of q when $p = 50$

7. The vertical distance a stone falls from a cliff, d m, is directly proportional to the square of the time, t seconds. If the stone falls 45 metres in 3 seconds, find
   (a) the formula for d in terms of t
   (b) the value of d when $t = 2$ seconds
   (c) the value of t when $d = 90$ m

8   The price of an art book, €p, varies directly as the square of the number of coloured pictures, n, that it contains. If a €150 art book contains ten coloured pictures, find
    (a) the formula for p in terms of n
    (b) the price of an art book containing 12 coloured pictures
    (c) the number of coloured pictures contained in a €600 art book

9   y is directly proportional to the cube of x. If y = 32 when x = 2, find
    (a) the formula for y in terms of x
    (b) the value of y when x = 4
    (c) the value of x when y = 864

10 The energy of a meteorite, e kilo-joules (kJ), is directly proportional to the square of its speed, v m/s. If a meteorite travelling at 10 m/s has energy of 50 kJ, find
    (a) the formula for e in terms of v
    (b) e when v = 50 m/s
    (c) v when the energy is 10^6 J

11 The surface area, A m², of an inflatable toy is proportional to the square of its height, h m. The surface area = 60 m² when the height = 2 m. Find
    (a) the formula for A in terms of h
    (b) the value of A when h = 3 m
    (c) the value of h when A = 540 m²

SKILLS

ANALYSIS

Inverse proportion

12 y is inversely proportional to x, and y = 16 when x = 3. Find
    (a) the formula for y in terms of x
    (b) the value of y when x = 8
    (c) the value of x when y = 12

13 p is inversely proportional to q. If p = 5 when q = 10, find
    (a) the formula for p in terms of q
    (b) p when q = 20
    (c) q when p = 20

14 y is inversely proportional to the square of x. If y = 20 when x = 2, find
    (a) the formula for y in terms of x
    (b) y when x = 4
    (c) x when y = 0.5

15 p is inversely proportional to the square root of q. If p = 500 when q = 25, find
    (a) the formula for p in terms of q
    (b) p when q = 100
    (c) q when p = 50

16 p squared is inversely proportional to the cube of q. If p = 10 when q = 2, find
    (a) the formula for p in terms of q
    (b) p when q = 4
    (c) q when p = 5

17 a is inversely proportional to the cube root of b. Copy and complete the table.

b	125	8	
a	2		10

18 A machine produces coins, of a fixed thickness, from a given volume of metal. The number of coins, N, produced is inversely proportional to square of the diameter, d. If 4000 coins of diameter 1.5 cm are made, find
  (a) the formula for N in terms of d
  (b) the number of coins that can be produced of diameter 2 cm
  (c) the diameter if 1000 coins are produced

Negative and fractional indices

For **questions 19–42**, find the value of x.

19 $\sqrt{a} = a^x$ **20** $\frac{1}{a} = a^x$ **21** $\frac{1}{a^2} = a^x$ **22** $\frac{1}{a^3} = a^x$

23 $\sqrt[3]{a} = a^x$ **24** $\frac{1}{\sqrt{a}} = a^x$ **25** $\frac{1}{\sqrt[3]{a}} = a^x$ **26** $\frac{1}{\sqrt[4]{a}} = a^x$

27 $\sqrt{9} = 3^x$ **28** $9^{\frac{1}{x}} = 3$ **29** $8^{\frac{1}{x}} = 2$ **30** $125^{\frac{1}{x}} = 5$

31 $2^x = \frac{1}{32}$ **32** $4^x = \frac{1}{256}$ **33** $5^x = \frac{1}{625}$ **34** $7^x = \frac{1}{343}$

35 $125^{\frac{1}{3}} = (5^x)$ **36** $216^{\frac{1}{3}} = (6^2)^x$ **37** $729^{\frac{1}{3}} = (3^x)^2$ **38** $10000^{\frac{1}{4}} = (10^{2x})^2$

39 $\left(\frac{2}{3}\right)^x = \sqrt{\frac{16}{81}}$ **40** $\left(\frac{3}{5}\right)^x = \sqrt{\frac{81}{625}}$ **41** $\left(\frac{2}{3}\right)^{2x} = \sqrt{\frac{81}{16}}$ **42** $(\sqrt{x})^{\frac{1}{2}} = 1000^{\frac{1}{3}}$

For **questions 43–50**, simplify the expressions.

43 $a^{\frac{1}{2}} \times a^{-\frac{5}{2}}$ **44** $b^{\frac{1}{3}} \times b^{-\frac{4}{3}}$ **45** $c^{\frac{2}{3}} \div c^{-\frac{4}{3}}$ **46** $d^{-\frac{4}{3}} \div d^{-\frac{11}{4}}$

47 $\left(e^{\frac{2}{3}}\right)^{-\frac{3}{2}}$ **48** $\left(f^{\frac{3}{5}}\right)^{-\frac{10}{3}}$ **49** $\left(g^{-\frac{1}{2}}\right)^{\frac{2}{3}}$ **50** $\left(h^{-\frac{4}{5}}\right)^{-\frac{5}{2}}$

For **questions 51–54**, solve the equations to find the values of x and y.

51 $(a^x b^y)^{\frac{2}{3}} = a^{\frac{1}{5}} \times b^{-\frac{3}{5}}$ **52** $\sqrt[4]{a^6 b^{-4}} = a^{2x} \times b^{2y-1}$

53 $\sqrt[3]{\frac{a^x}{b^y}} = a^{\frac{2}{3}} \times b^{\frac{1}{5}}$ **54** $\sqrt[4]{\frac{a^{x+1}}{b^{y+1}}} = a^{\frac{2}{5}} \div b^{\frac{5}{6}}$

55 Solve for x:
$a^{2x-1} = 1$

56 Solve for x:
$a^{(x-3)(x-4)} = 10^0$

ALGEBRA 6 – EXAM PRACTICE EXERCISE

1 The cost, $C, of a circular wedding cake is directly proportional to its diameter, d cm.
A 49 cm diameter cake costs $60. Find
(a) the formula for C in terms of d
(b) the cost of a cake with a diameter of 650 mm
(c) the diameter, in cm, of a cake costing $80

2 The population of a termite hill, n thousand, is inversely proportional to the square of its age, t years.
If a termite hill has a population of one million after six months, find
(a) the formula for n in terms of t
(b) the value of n after two years
(c) the value of t when the population is one thousand

3 Tidal waves (tsunamis) are the result of earthquakes in the sea bed. Their speed, v m/s, is directly proportional to the square root of the ocean depth, d m.
If a tsunami travels at 9.8 m/s at an ocean depth of 10 m, find
(a) the formula for v in terms of d
(b) the value of v when
   (i) $d = 50$ m
   (ii) $d = 1$ km
(c) the value of d when $v = 1$ m/s
(d) the ocean depth at the point where the fastest ever tsunami was recorded at 790 km/h

4 x, y and z are three related variables.
x is directly proportional to z^3.
x is also directly proportional to y^2.
$z = 50$ when $y = 25$
Calculate the value of z when $y = 10$
Give your answer to 3 s.f.

5 $a = 5^m$ and $b = 5^n$
$ab = 125$ and $\left(\dfrac{a^2}{b}\right)^2 = \dfrac{1}{5^9}$
Find the values of m and n.

UNIT 6 SEQUENCES 1

- CONTINUING SEQUENCES
- THE DIFFERENCE METHOD
- FINDING A FORMULA
- MIXED QUESTIONS
- ARITHMETIC SERIES

SEQUENCES 1 – BASIC SKILLS EXERCISE

SKILLS
PROBLEM SOLVING

Continuing sequences

For **questions 1–6**, write down the next three terms of the sequence.

1 $2, 5\frac{1}{2}, 9, 12\frac{1}{2}, \ldots$

2 $1, 0.8, 0.6, 0.4, \ldots$

3 $1, \frac{1}{2}, \frac{1}{4}, \frac{1}{8}, \ldots$

4 $200, 40, 8, 1.6, \ldots$

5 $-\frac{1}{9}, \frac{1}{3}, -1, 3, \ldots$

6 $0, 3, 8, 15, 24, \ldots$

For **questions 7–12**, write down the first four terms of the sequence.

7 nth term $= 6n - 8$

8 nth term $= 84 - 4n$

9 nth term $= \frac{1}{3}(n - 2)$

10 nth term $= n + \frac{1}{n}$

11 nth term $= n(2n + 1)$

12 nth term $= \frac{3 - 2n}{2 + n}$

SKILLS
ANALYSIS

The difference method

For **questions 13–18**, find the next three terms of the sequence using the difference method.

13 $1, 6, 14, 25, 39, \ldots$

14 $7, 12, 14, 13, 9, \ldots$

15 $4, 0, -2, -2, 0, \ldots$

16 $2, 4, 10, 20, 34, 52, \ldots$

17 $5, 8, 10, 11, 11, 10, \ldots$

18 $3, -1, -4, -6, -7, -7, \ldots$

SKILLS
ANALYSIS, REASONING

Finding a formula

For **questions 19–24**, find a formula for the nth term of the sequence.

19 $5, 7, 9, 11, \ldots$

20 $26, 23, 20, 17, \ldots$

21 $0, \frac{1}{3}, \frac{2}{4}, \frac{3}{5}, \frac{4}{6}$

22 $1, 4, 7, 10, \ldots$

23 $9, 5, 1, -3, \ldots$

24 $1, 2, 4, 8, 16, \ldots$

Mixed questions

25 Is −218 a member of the sequence 75, 72, 69, 66, …?

26 Find the first member of the sequence −18, −13, −8, −3, … that is greater than 1000.

27 The nth term of the sequence −3, 1, 5, 9, … is equal to the nth term of the sequence 12, 15, 18, 21, …
Find the value of n.

28 The nth term of the sequence given by $n^2 - 4$ is equal to the nth term of the sequence 19, 30, 41, 52, …
Find the equal term.

29 The nth term of a sequence is given by $\frac{1}{3n+1}$
Which is the first term less than 0.02?

30 The first four terms of the sequence whose nth term is given by $n^2 + an + b$ are 3, 3, 5, 9.
Find the values of a and b.

Arithmetic series

31 Find the sum of the first 20 terms of 6 + 11 + 16 + 21 + …

32 Find the sum of − 2 − 6 − 10 − 14 − … − 42 − 46

33 The first and last terms of an **arithmetic series** with 38 terms are 1 and 297.
Find the sum of the series.

34 Find the sum of the first 100 multiples of four.

35 The last four terms of an arithmetic series with 68 terms are …440 + 447 + 454 + 461
Find the first term and the sum.

36 The sum to ten terms of an arithmetic series is 120.
 (a) If the first term is 3, find the **common difference**.
 (b) If the common difference is 3, find the first term.

37 The 7th term of an arithmetic series is 37 and the 18th term is 92.
Find the sum from the 10th to the 20th terms.

38 The first term of an arithmetic series is 6 and the common difference is 3. The sum to n terms is 270. Find n.

39 Find the sum of the first 80 even numbers that are not multiples of three.

40 The last term of an arithmetic series with 17 terms is 103. The sum is 935.
Find the first term and the common difference.

41 The sum of $-11 - 9 - 7 - 5 \ldots$ is 540.
Find the last term.

42 The sum of the first ten terms of an arithmetic series is 145.
The sum of the next ten terms is 645.
Find the first term and the common difference.

43 The 12th term of an arithmetic series is 64 and the sum to 12 terms is 504.
Find the sum to 24 terms.

44 The kth term of an arithmetic series is $4k - 1$
Show that the sum to n terms is $n(2n + 1)$

45 The first term of an arithmetic series is 48 and the common difference is -3.
(a) The kth term is zero. Find the value of k.
(b) Find the largest positive value of the sum of the series.

SEQUENCES 1 – EXAM PRACTICE EXERCISE

E 1 Here are the first five terms of an **arithmetic sequence** S.

  1 5 9 13 17

(a) Find the next three terms and the nth term of the sequence S.

The first and third terms of S are square numbers.
(b) Find the positions of the next two terms of S that are square numbers.

These positions form a new sequence T starting 1, 3, …
(c) Use sequence T to find the sixth square number of S.

E 2 Here are the first five terms of a sequence S.

$$\frac{2}{3} \quad \frac{3}{5} \quad \frac{4}{7} \quad \frac{5}{9} \quad \frac{6}{11}$$

(a) Find an expression, in terms of n, for the nth term of the sequence.

(b) Show that $\frac{99}{195}$ is not a member of the sequence.

(c) Which is the first member of the sequence to have a value less than 0.52?

E 3 The first three terms of an arithmetic series are $4x + 10$, $10x - 9$ and $12x - 10$
Find the sum from the 20th to the 30th terms.

E 4 The fifth term of an arithmetic series S is 56.
S_n denotes the sum of the first n terms.
The sum of the first five terms, S_5, is 300.
$S_5 : S_n = 6 : 11$
Find the two possible values of n.

E 5 (a) $10 100 is to be divided in the ratio 1 : 2 : 3 : 4 …. 99 : 100
Show that the smallest and largest shares are $2 and $200 respectively.
(b) £A is to be divided in the ratio of 1 : 2 : 3 : 4 … $(n - 1) : n$.

Show that the smallest and largest shares are £$\frac{2A}{n(n+1)}$ and £$\frac{2A}{n+1}$ respectively.

UNIT 6 SHAPE AND SPACE 6

- **INTERSECTING CHORD THEOREMS**
- **ALTERNATE SEGMENT THEOREM**

SHAPE AND SPACE 6 – BASIC SKILLS EXERCISE

SKILLS

PROBLEM SOLVING, ANALYSIS

Intersecting chord theorems

For **questions 1–14,** find the value of x.

1.

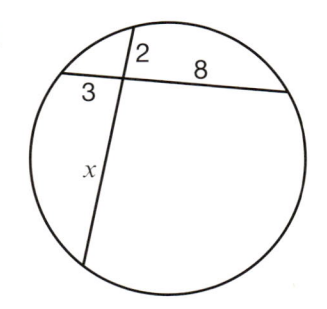

2.

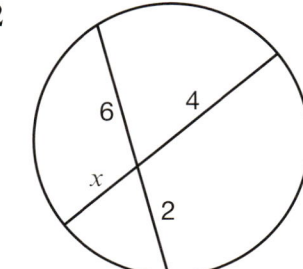

3.

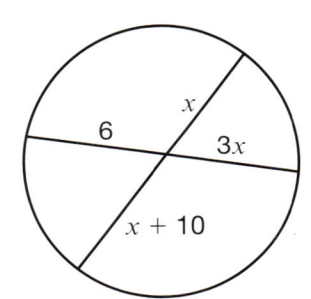

4.

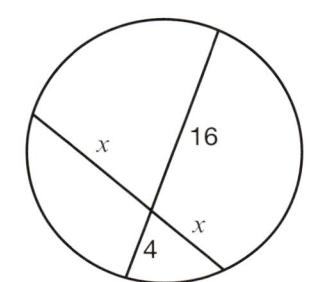

5.

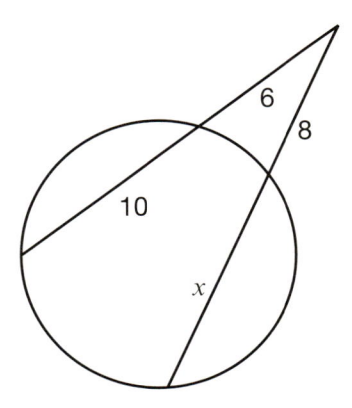

6.

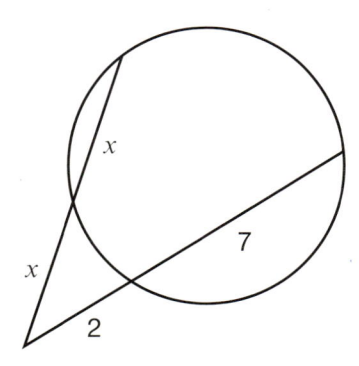

7.

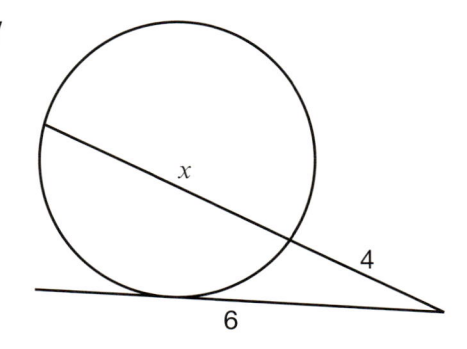

8.

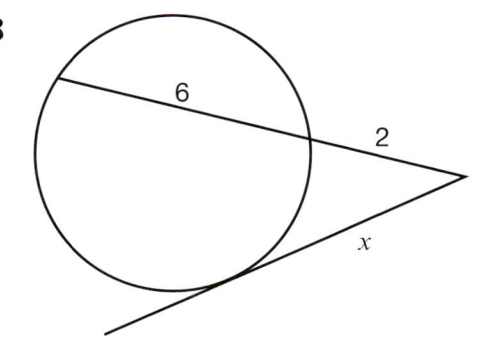

9

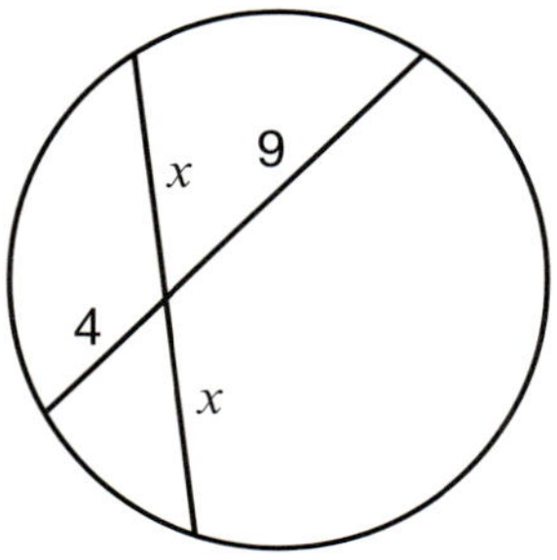

10

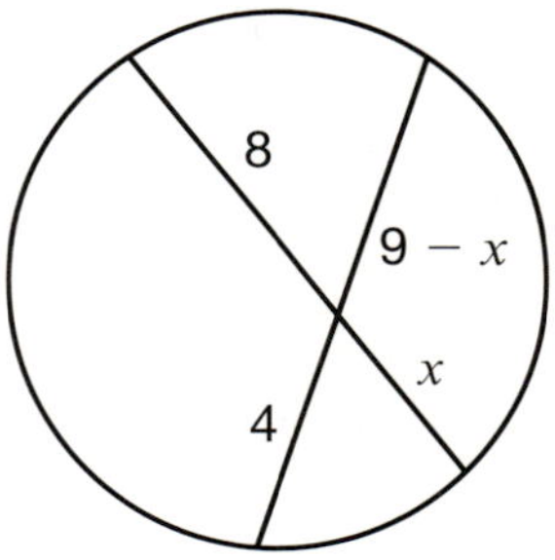

11

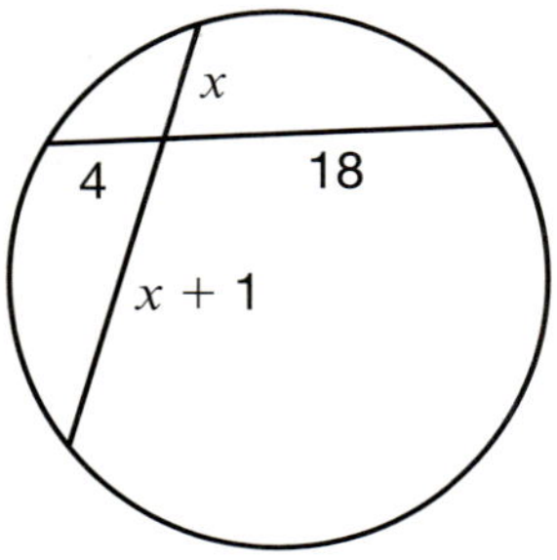

12

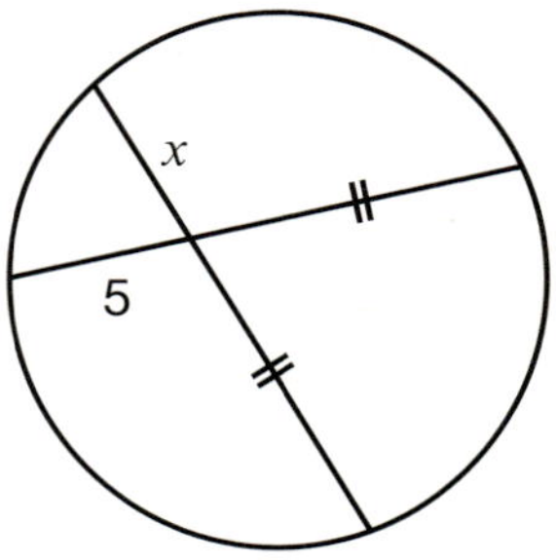

13

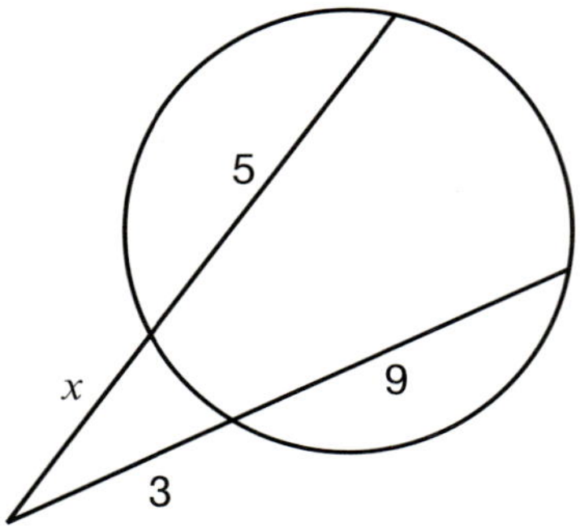

14

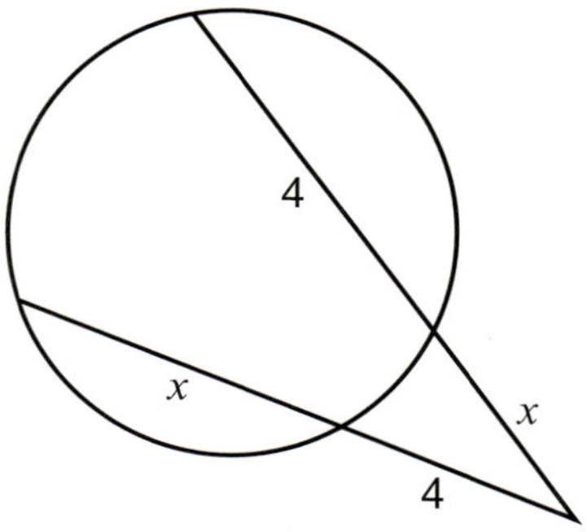

15 Solve the following to find x.

(a)

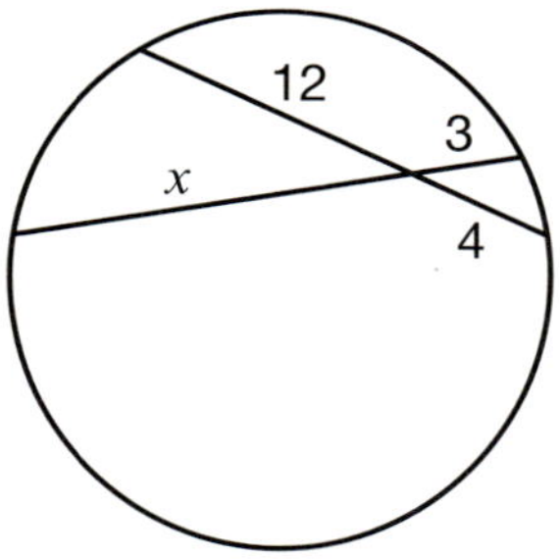

(b)

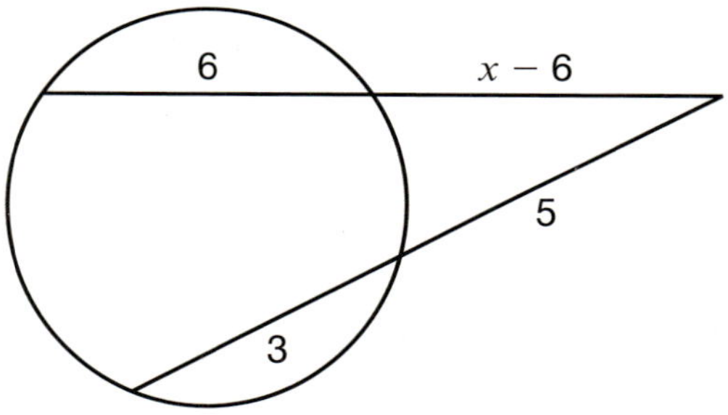

UNIT 6   SHAPE AND SPACE 6   119

SKILLS
ANALYSIS

Alternate segment theorem

For **questions 16–31**, find the value of a.

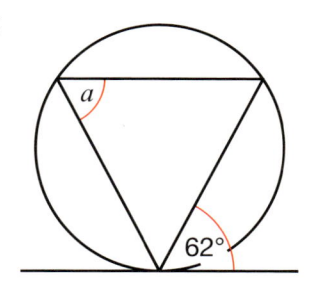

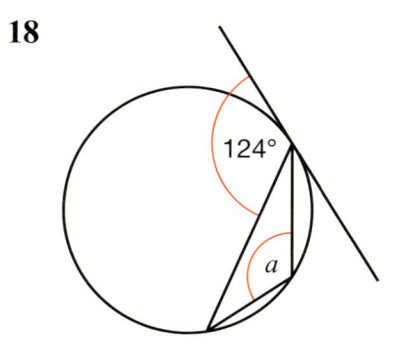

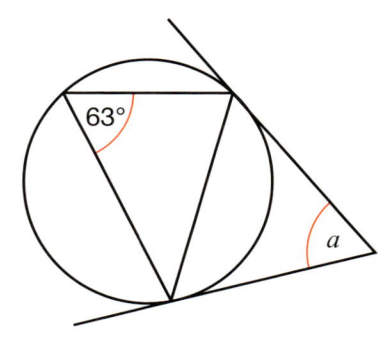

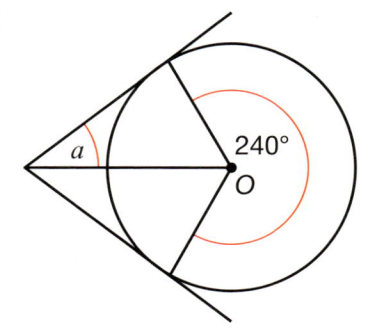

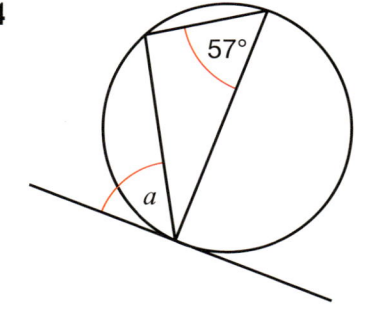

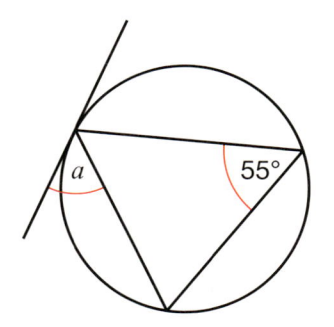

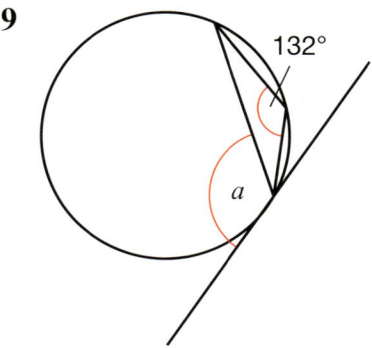

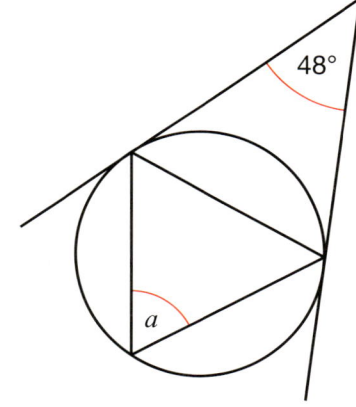

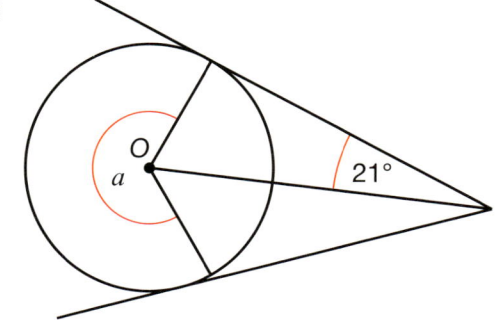

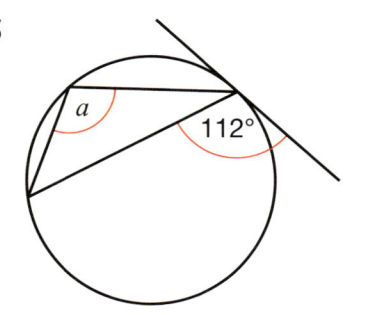

16

17 55°

18 124°

19 132°

20 63°

21 48°

22 240°, O

23 O, 21°

24 57°

25 112°

26

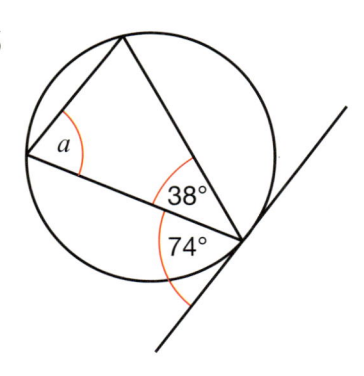

27

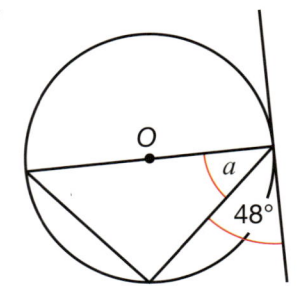

28

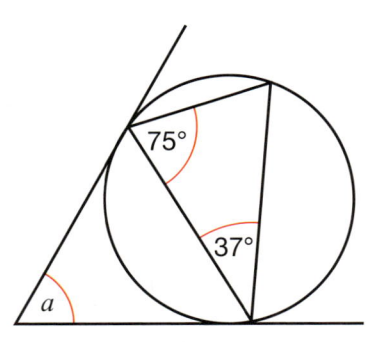

29

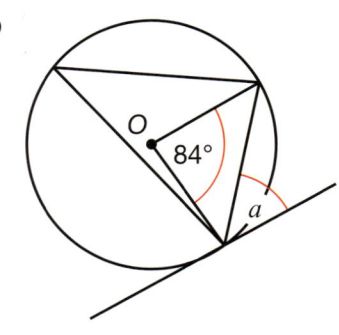

30

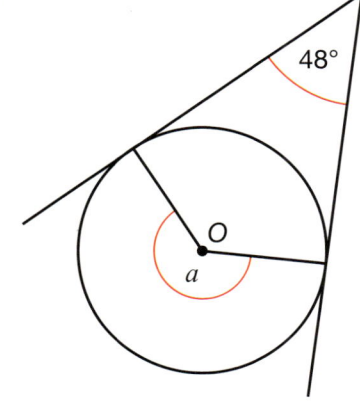

31

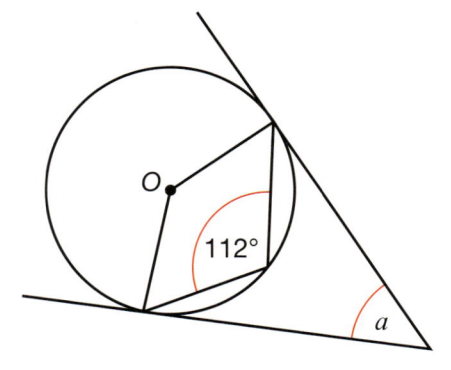

32 Solve the following to find the angles x, y and z.

(a)

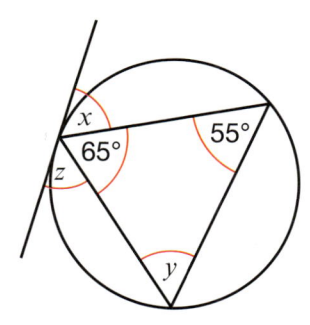

(b)

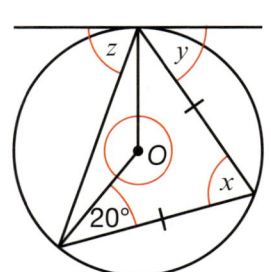

SHAPE AND SPACE 6 – EXAM PRACTICE EXERCISE

1 A, B, C and D are points on a circle.
PAB and PDC are straight lines.
$PA = 10$ cm, $PD = 8$ cm and $DC = 7$ cm.
Give answers to 3 s.f. where appropriate.

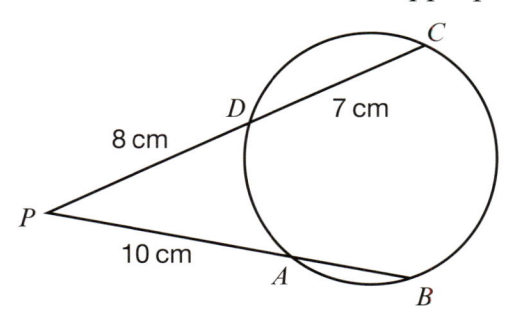

(a) Calculate the length AB.
If angle $DPA = 40°$, calculate
(b) length BC
(c) angle BCD

2 P, Q, R and S are points on a circle, centre O.
QS is a diameter of the circle.
QS and PR intersect at the point T.
$OS = 5$ cm, $QT = 3$ cm and $TR = 6$ cm.
Give answers to 3 s.f. where appropriate.

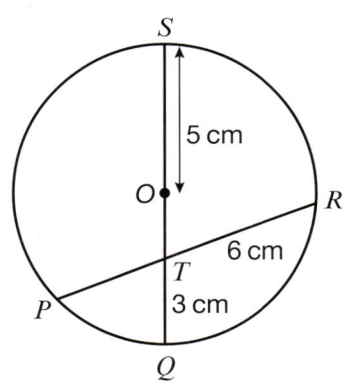

(a) Calculate the length PR.
If angle $OTR = 74°$, calculate
(b) length RS
(c) angle QPT

E 3 Points *A*, *B* and *D* are on the circumference of a circle, centre *O*.
CDE is a tangent to the circle.
angle *BDC* = 68°
(a) Calculate the size of angle *BOD*.
(b) Given that *AO* = *r* and *AB* = 2*s*,
show that $BD = 2\sqrt{(r+s)(r-s)}$
State reasons for each step of your working.

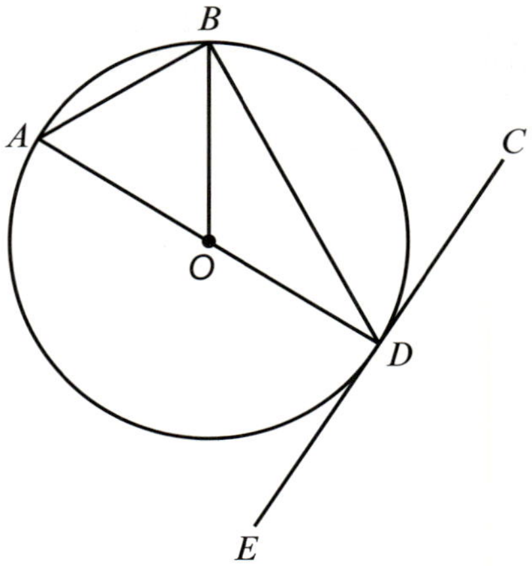

E 4 *J*, *K*, *L* and *M* are points on the circumference of a circle.
GJH is the tangent to the circle at *J*.
MK and *JL* intersect at the point *P*.
GML is a straight line.
angle *HJK* = 62° angle *JKM* = 21° angle *JGL* = 78°
Calculate, stating reasons for each step of your working
(a) angle *KJL*
(b) angle *GMK*

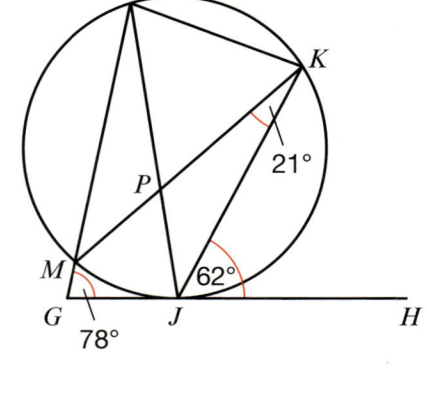

E 5 *A*, *B* and *C* are points on the circumference of a circle, centre *O*.
DAE is a tangent to the circle.
(a) Calculate the angles
(i) *CAO*
(ii) *ABC*
(b) A point *F* is placed on minor arc *AB* such that line *AF* bisects angle *BAE*.
Calculate angle *ABF*.
State reasons for each step of your working.

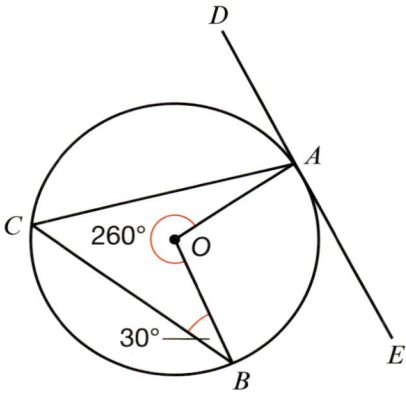

UNIT 6 SETS 2

- **SHADING SETS**
- **TWO SET PROBLEMS**
- **THREE SET PROBLEMS**
- **DESCRIBING SETS ALGEBRAICALLY**

SETS 2 – BASIC SKILLS EXERCISE

SKILLS
ANALYSIS

Shading sets

1 On separate copies of the diagram, shade the following sets.

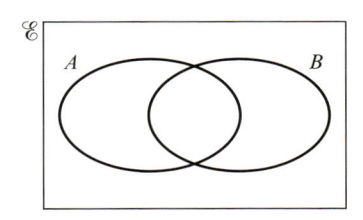

(a) $A' \cap B'$ (b) $(A \cap B)'$
(c) $A' \cup B'$ (d) $(A \cup B)'$

2 On separate copies of the diagram, shade the following sets.

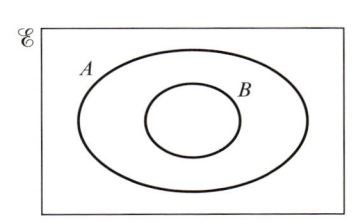

(a) $A \cap B'$ (b) $A' \cap B$
(c) $A \cup B$ (d) $A \cup B'$

3 On separate copies of the diagram, shade the following sets.

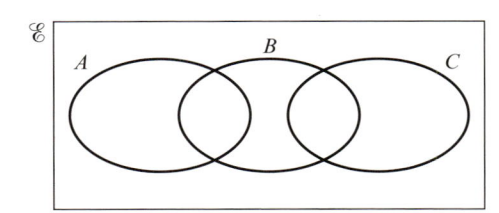

(a) $(A \cup C) \cap B$ (b) $(A \cup B)' \cap C$
(c) $(A \cap B)' \cap C$ (d) $(A \cap C)'$

4 On separate copies of the diagram, shade the following sets.

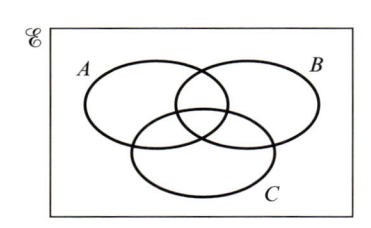

(a) $(A \cup B)' \cap C$
(b) $(A \cap B) \cup (A \cap C)$
(c) $(A \cap C) \cup B$
(d) $(A \cap B)' \cup C$

5 Describe the shaded sets using set notation.

(a)

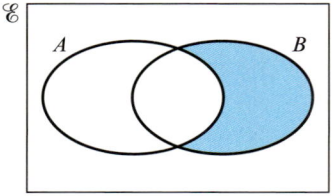

(b)

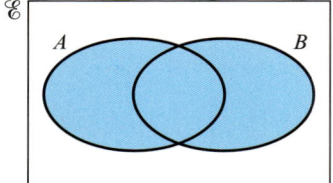

6 Describe the shaded sets using set notation.

(a)

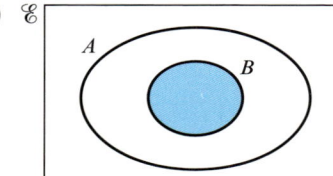

(b)

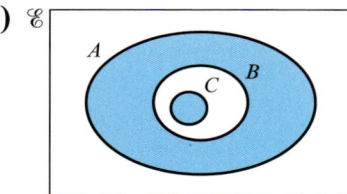

Two set problems

7 $\mathscr{E}$ = all cats, O = cats over 10 years old, T = Tabby cats. Describe in words.
  (a) $O \cap T = \varnothing$
  (b) $(O \cup T)' \neq \varnothing$

8 In a class of 30 students, 6 play the drums, 12 play the guitar, while 4 students play both. How many students play neither instrument?

9 In a hockey team of 11 players, 9 have brown hair, 3 have green eyes and 1 has neither. How many players have both brown hair and green eyes?

10 In a group of 40 teenagers all except one have a mobile phone. 18 of the phones can receive 5G and 12 of the phones are pink. 13 phones are neither pink nor can receive 5G.
How many pink phones cannot receive 5G?

11 Of the animals in a field, 18 are sheep while 8 are black but not sheep.
Five of the animals are neither sheep nor black.
How many animals are in the field?

Three-set problems

12 The incomplete Venn diagram shows a **universal set** $\mathscr{E}$ and three sets A, B and C. The numbers shown represent numbers of elements.

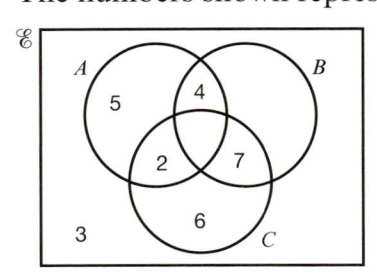

$n(C') = 20$, $n(B) = 20$
Find
  (a) $n(A \cup B')$
  (b) $n(A' \cap C)$

13 Draw a Venn diagram showing the relationship between isosceles triangles, equilateral triangles and right-angled triangles.

14 In a group of pensioners, 40 play bowls, 55 play golf, 30 play tennis and 8 play nothing. 12 play bowls and golf, 18 play golf and tennis and 10 play tennis and bowls. 5 play all three sports.
How many pensioners are there?

15 A group of 40 teenagers all enjoy water sports. 22 enjoy wind surfing, 23 enjoy swimming and 17 enjoy diving. 12 enjoy wind surfing and swimming, 6 enjoy swimming and diving and 7 enjoy wind surfing and diving.
How many enjoy all three?

Describing sets algebraically

16 List the following sets where
$\mathscr{E}$ = {integers}
(a) $A = \{x: -1 \leq x < 2\}$
(b) $B = \{x: 4 < 2x \leq 10\}$
(c) $C = \{x: -5 < 3x \leq 3\}$
(d) $D = \{x: 0 < x^2 \leq 20\}$
(e) $E = \{x: x^2 - 4 = 0\}$
(f) $F = \{x: -1 < \frac{1}{2}x \leq 3\}$

17 Describe the following sets algebraically where $\mathscr{E}$ = {integers}
(a) A = {integers less than 5}
(b) B = {integers greater than or equal to −8}
(c) C = {integers between −2 and 4}
(d) D = {integers between 3 and 8 inclusive}
(e) $E = \{-2, -1, 0, 1, 2\}$
(f) F = {even integers between 2 and 10}

UNIT 6 SETS 2

SETS 2 – EXAM PRACTICE EXERCISE

1 (a) Two sets A and B are such that $A \cap B \neq \emptyset$
Show the following sets by shading Venn diagrams.
(i) $(A \cup B')'$
(ii) $A' \cap B'$

(b) It is claimed that 68% of the population exercise by jogging, while 39% exercise by swimming.

(i) What could be the largest percentages that do both?
(ii) What could be the smallest percentages that do both?

2 $\mathcal{E}$ = {Suzie's clothes}, D = {Dresses}, T = {T shirts} and G = {Green clothes}
(a) $G \cap T \neq \emptyset$. Describe what this means in words.
(b) $D \subset G$. Describe what this means in words.
(c) Illustrate all this information on a Venn diagram.

3 There are 34 horses and 24 donkeys in a rescue home.

31 of them do not have microchips.
Twice as many donkeys as horses have microchips.
How many horses do not have microchips?

E 4 There are 50 cars in a car park.
19 are blue, 7 are green and 6 are soft tops.
5 are green but not soft tops.
23 are neither blue nor green nor soft tops.
x are blue and soft tops.
Use a Venn diagram to find x.

E 5 In a group of 60 teenagers all but 15 like at least one out of peppermints, chocolates and toffees.
10 like peppermints only, 7 like chocolates only and 12 like toffees only.
4 like peppermints and toffees but not chocolates.
6 like peppermints and chocolates.
9 like chocolates and toffees.
x like all three.

(a) Draw a Venn diagram to represent this information.
(b) Find an expression, in terms of x, for the number who like peppermints and chocolates but not toffees.
(c) How many like all three?

UNIT 7 NUMBER 7

- **CALCULATOR WORK**
- **RECURRING DECIMALS**

NUMBER 7 – BASIC SKILLS EXERCISE

SKILLS
ANALYSIS

Calculator work

For **questions 1–12**, use your calculator to find the answer to the calculation, correct to 3 s.f.

1. $1.2 + 1.2^2$
2. $1.2 + 1.2^2 + 1.2^3$
3. $\dfrac{251.7 + 3.6 \times 10^2}{2.5 \times 10^3}$
4. $4\frac{2}{7} + 1.35^3$
5. $\dfrac{11.2 + 3.7}{\sqrt{6.3}}$
6. $\dfrac{\sqrt{21.3}}{17.3 - 2.6}$
7. $\left(\dfrac{3.5 \times 10^3}{6.7 \times 10^2}\right)^2$
8. $\sqrt{5.75 \times 10^{12}}$
9. $(2^3 + 3^4 + 4^3 + 3^2)^2$
10. $\sqrt{3^4 + 3^4 + 3^4}$
11. $\sqrt{3.82 \times 10^7} \div \sqrt{6.7 \times 10^{-5}}$
12. $\sqrt{9.5^3 - 5.9^3}$

For **questions 13–18**, use your calculator to find the answer, correct to 3 s.f.

13. $\left(\dfrac{1}{2.5 \times 10^{-3}} - \dfrac{1}{2.6 \times 10^{-3}}\right)^5$
14. $\sqrt{5 + \sqrt{5 + \sqrt{5 + \sqrt{5 + \sqrt{5}}}}}$
15. $\sqrt[3]{10 + \sqrt[3]{10 + \sqrt[3]{10 + \sqrt[3]{10 + \sqrt[3]{10}}}}}$
16. $\dfrac{1}{\sqrt{\pi^3 \times 10^{-3}}}$
17. $\sqrt[3]{5.5 \times 10^3 \times \tan(30)°}$
18. $\tan\left(\sqrt{\dfrac{10\pi^3}{\pi^2 - 1}}\right)$

SKILLS
ANALYSIS

Recurring decimals

For **questions 19–38**, use algebra to show that the **recurring decimal** equals the given fraction.

19. $0.\dot{1} = \dfrac{1}{9}$
20. $0.\dot{2} = \dfrac{2}{9}$
21. $0.\dot{3} = \dfrac{3}{9}$
22. $0.\dot{3}\dot{6} = \dfrac{36}{99}$
23. $0.\dot{6}\dot{3} = \dfrac{63}{99}$
24. $0.\dot{1}\dot{7} = \dfrac{17}{99}$
25. $0.\dot{7}\dot{1} = \dfrac{71}{99}$
26. $0.\dot{9} = 1$
27. $0.\dot{1}\dot{2} = \dfrac{12}{99}$
28. $0.\dot{3}\dot{4} = \dfrac{34}{99}$
29. $0.0\dot{2} = \dfrac{1}{45}$
30. $0.0\dot{7} = \dfrac{7}{90}$
31. $0.\dot{0}7\dot{5} = \dfrac{25}{333}$
32. $0.\dot{1}2\dot{3} = \dfrac{41}{333}$
33. $0.\dot{1}23\dot{4} = \dfrac{1234}{9999}$
34. $0.\dot{2}46\dot{8} = \dfrac{2468}{9999}$
35. $0.7\dot{3} = \dfrac{11}{15}$
36. $0.3\dot{7} = \dfrac{17}{45}$
37. $0.001\dot{7} = \dfrac{2}{1125}$
38. $0.023\dot{4} = \dfrac{211}{9000}$

SKILLS
PROBLEM SOLVING, ANALYSIS

NUMBER 7 – EXAM PRACTICE EXERCISE

E 1 $m = \dfrac{7.5 \times 10^5}{9.5 \times 10^4}$ and $n = \sqrt{10^m}$

Find the values of the following.
Give your answers in standard form to 3 s.f.

(a) mn
(b) $(n - m)(n + m)$
(c) $10^{\left(\dfrac{m^5}{n}\right)}$

E 2 Calculate the following.
Give your answers in standard form to 3 s.f.

(a) $\sqrt{2\pi + \sqrt{3\pi + \sqrt{5\pi + \sqrt{7\pi}}}}$

(b) $\dfrac{\sqrt[5]{5} + \sqrt[3]{3} + \sqrt{2}}{\sqrt[7]{7} \times 10^{-7}}$

(c) $\dfrac{\pi^{33} - \pi^{22}}{\pi^{12}}$

E 3 $x = 2.3 \times 10^2$, $y = 5.7 \times 10^{-2}$ and $z = \pi^2$
Find the values of the following.
Give your answers to 3 s.f.

(a) $\sin(xyz)$
(b) $\cos\left(\dfrac{z^2}{xy}\right)$
(c) $\tan(xy^2 z)$

E 4 Show, by using algebra, that $0.0\dot{2}\dot{3} + 0.1\dot{7} = \dfrac{p}{q}$, where p and q are integers.

Express the fraction in its simplest form.
Show clear working.

E 5 Show with clear algebraic working that

(a) $0.\dot{x}\dot{y} = \dfrac{10x + y}{99}$

(b) $5.\dot{x}\dot{y}\dot{z} = \dfrac{4995 + 100x + 10y + z}{999}$

UNIT 7 ALGEBRA 7

- **FACTORISING QUADRATICS**
- **COMPLETING THE SQUARE**
- **QUADRATIC FORMULA**
- **QUADRATIC INEQUALITIES**
- **MIXED QUESTIONS**
- **PROBLEMS LEADING TO QUADRATIC EQUATIONS**

ALGEBRA 7 – BASIC SKILLS EXERCISE

Factorising quadratics

For **questions 1–8**, solve the equations by factorising, showing clear algebraic working.

1. $x^2 - 11x + 30 = 0$
2. $x^2 - 4x - 5 = 0$
3. $4 + 3x - x^2 = 0$
4. $5x^2 + 35x + 60 = 0$
5. $28 = 28x - 7x^2$
6. $9x^2 = 18x$
7. $(x - 4)(x + 2) = 7$
8. $x(3x - 20) = 2(x - 4)^2$

Completing the square

For **questions 9–14**, solve the equations by completing the square, showing clear algebraic working.
Give your answers in **surd** form.

9. $x^2 + 6x + 6 = 0$
10. $5x^2 + 15x + 5 = 0$
11. $2x^2 - 12x = 5$
12. $3x^2 = 3 + 12x$
13. $(3x + 3)(x + 1) = 8$
14. $5(x + 2)(x - 2) = 2(5x - 4)$

Quadratic formula

For **questions 15–20**, solve the equations using the quadratic formula, showing clear algebraic working.
Give your answers to 3 s.f.

15. $x^2 - 6x + 7 = 0$
16. $3x^2 = 7x + 2$
17. $10 + 3x = 2x^2$
18. $x^2 + 62.2x + 248.6 = 0$
19. $1.2x^2 + 3.5x - 1.5 = 0$
20. $2.5x^2 + 6.5x + 0.9 = 0$

Quadratic inequalities

For **questions 21–26**, solve the quadratic inequalities, showing clear algebraic working.

21. $x^2 + 2x - 15 > 0$
22. $x^2 \leq 5x + 14$
23. $6x^2 < x + 1$
24. $x^2 + 2x > 5$
25. $x^2 + 2 < 4x$
26. $2x + 24 \leq x^2 \leq 2x + 6$

Mixed questions

27. The solutions of $x^2 + bx + c = 0$ are $x = -7$ and $x = 1$. Find b and c.
28. Solve $x^2 + 2\pi x - 3\pi^2 = 0$ by factorising, giving your answer in terms of π.
29. Solve $x^2 + (p + q)x + pq = 0$ by factorising, giving your answers in terms of p and q.
30. Write $6x - x^2$ in the form $p - (x - q)^2$ where p and q are to be found.
31. $x^2 + bx + c = 0$ has solutions $x = 1 \pm \sqrt{5}$. Find b and c.

SKILLS
CRITICAL THINKING, PROBLEM SOLVING

Problems leading to quadratic equations

32 The sum of the squares of two consecutive odd numbers is 202.
    Find the numbers.

33 The **chords** of a circle intersect as shown.
    Use the intersecting chords theorem to find x.

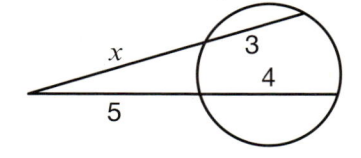

34 $f(x) = x^2 - 4x + 9$
    (a) Show that $f(x)$ can be written as $(x - a)^2 + b$
    (b) Find the equation of the line of symmetry of $y = f(x)$
    (c) Find the minimum value of $y = f(x)$

35 The curve $y = x^2 + bx + c$ intersects the axes at (2, 0) and (3, 0).
    Find b and c.

36 The perimeter of a rectangular lawn is 26 m and the area is 40 m².
    Find the dimensions of the lawn.

37 The hypotenuse of a right-angled triangle is 4 cm long and the perimeter is 9 cm.
    Find the lengths of the other two sides.

38 A circular pond of radius 2 m is surrounded by a path of constant width.
    The area of the path is the same as the area of the pond.
    Find the width of the path.

39 The four interior angles of a quadrilateral $ABCD$ are
    $A = 9x - 3$, $B = 2x^2 + 22$, $C = 15x + 30$ and $D = x^2 - 4$
    Show that $ABCD$ is a trapezium.

40 A rectangular picture has side lengths $(x + 5)$ cm and $3x$ cm.

    The area of the picture must be greater than 600 cm² and less than 700 cm².
    Find the range of possible values of x.

41 A rectangle and a right-angled triangle
    have sides with lengths as shown in
    the diagram.
    Find the range of values of x such
    that the area of the rectangle is greater
    than the area of the triangle.

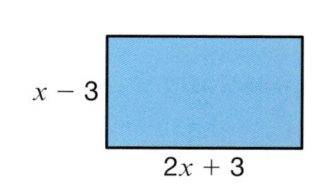

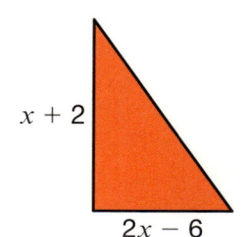

UNIT 7 — ALGEBRA 7

SKILLS
CRITICAL THINKING, PROBLEM SOLVING, ADAPTIVE LEARNING

ALGEBRA 7 – EXAM PRACTICE EXERCISE

Give answers to 3 s.f. where appropriate.

E 1 $f(x) = 3 - 12x - 3x^2$
(a) Write $f(x)$ in the form $a(x - b)^2 + c$, where a, b and c are constants.
(b) Solve $f(x) = 0$, giving your answers in surd form.
(c) Sketch $y = f(x)$, marking clearly the intersections with the axes, the **axis of symmetry** and the **maximum point**.

E 2 A fuel tank for a vehicle is a **cylinder** with hemispherical ends.
The length of the cylinder is 20 cm, the radius is r cm and the total surface area is A cm².
To keep weight to a minimum, $A \leq 800\pi$ cm²
(a) Find the range of possible values of r.
(b) What is the maximum volume of a tank with $A \leq 800\pi$ cm²?

E 3 The four interior angles of a quadrilateral $ABCD$ are
$A = 2x^2 + 50$, $B = 3x^2 - 18$, $C = 3x + 40$ and $D = 12x + 18$

(a) Show that $ABCD$ is a cyclic quadrilateral.
The diameter of the circle passing through A, B, C and D is d cm long.
AB is 3 cm shorter than d and BC is 2 cm shorter than d.
(b) Find d, giving your answer in surd form.

E 4 Kris is designing a garden.
The garden is a rectangle measuring 8 m by 6 m.
The garden is bisected by straight pathways x m wide to form four flower beds.
(a) Show that the total area of the pathways is $14x - x^2$.
The ratio of the area of the pathways to the total area of the garden is 1 : 4.
(b) Find the value of x.

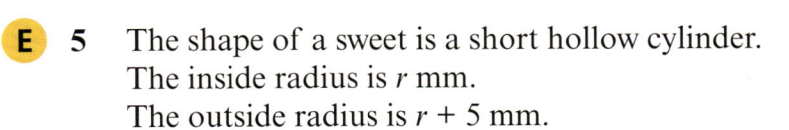

E 5 The shape of a sweet is a short hollow cylinder.
The inside radius is r mm.
The outside radius is $r + 5$ mm.
The length of the sweet is 3 mm.
The ratio of the volume of the sweet to the volume of the hole is 4 : 1.
(a) Show that $4r^2 - 10r - 25 = 0$
60% of the volume of the sweet is sugar.
(b) Find the volume of sugar in the sweet in cm³.

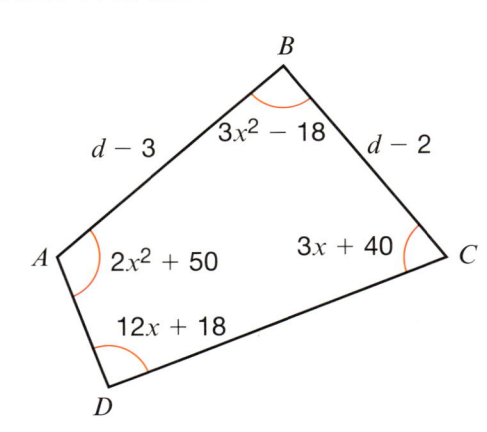

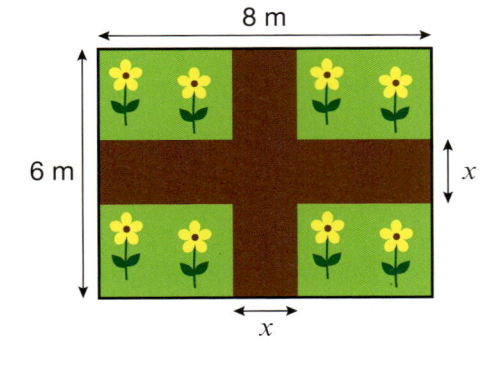

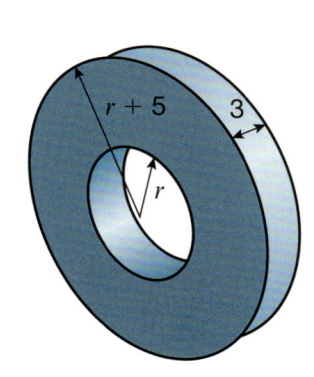

UNIT 7 GRAPHS 6

- **CUBIC GRAPHS:** $y = ax^3 + bx^2 + cx + d$
- **RECIPROCAL GRAPHS:** $y = \frac{a}{x}$

GRAPHS 6 – BASIC SKILLS EXERCISE

SKILLS
ANALYSIS

Cubic graphs: $y = ax^3 + bx^2 + cx + d$

1. (a) Copy and complete the table for the equation $y = x^3 - 3x^2 + 3$

x	−2	−1	0	1	2	3	4
y	−17		3				

   (b) Use the table to draw the graph of $y = x^3 - 3x^2 + 3$ for $-2 \leq x \leq 4$

2. (a) Copy and complete the table for the equation $y = 2x^3 - 3x^2 - 4x + 1$

x	−2	−1	0	1	2	3	4
y	−19		1				

   (b) Use the table to draw the graph of $y = 2x^3 - 3x^2 - 4x + 1$ for $-2 \leq x \leq 4$

3. (a) If $y = x^3 + ax^2 + 2x + 9$, where a is a constant, for $-2 \leq x \leq 5$, use the table to find the value of a and hence copy and complete the table.

x	−2	−1	0	1	2	3	4	5
y			9					19

   (b) Use the table to draw the graph of $y = x^3 + ax^2 + 2x + 9$ for $-2 \leq x \leq 5$
   (c) Find the values of x at which the curve cuts the x-axis.

4. (a) If $y = x^3 + ax^2 + 9x + b$, where a and b are constant, for $-1 \leq x \leq 6$, use the table to find the values of a and b and hence copy and complete the table.

x	−1	0	1	2	3	4	5	6
y		8						26

   (b) Use the table to draw the graph of $y = x^3 + ax^2 + 9x + b$ for $-1 \leq x \leq 6$
   (c) Find the values of x at which the curve cuts the x-axis.

UNIT 7 GRAPHS 6

SKILLS
ANALYSIS

Reciprocal graphs: $y = \dfrac{a}{x}$

5 The profit, p ($1000s), made by Giggle, a new internet search engine, t months after its opening, is given by $p = \dfrac{20}{t}$, valid for $1 \le t \le 12$

(a) Copy and complete the table and use it to draw the graph of p against t for $1 \le t \le 12$

t	1	2	4	6	8	10	12
p	20		5				

(b) Use your graph to find
   (i) after how many months Giggle makes a profit of $15 000
   (ii) Giggle's profit after nine months
(c) Giggle's profit at one month is reduced by x% after five months. Find x.

6 (a) If $y = \dfrac{k}{x}$, where k is a constant, for $1 \le x \le 6$, use the table to find the value of k and hence copy and complete the table.

x	1	2	3	4	5	6
y						2

(b) Use the table to draw the graph of $y = \dfrac{k}{x}$ for $1 \le x \le 6$

7 (a) If $y = ax + \dfrac{4}{x}$, where a is a constant, for $1 \le x \le 6$, use the table to find the value of a and hence copy and complete the table.

x	1	2	3	4	5	6
y	8					

(b) Use the table to draw the graph of $y = ax + \dfrac{4}{x}$ for $1 \le x \le 6$
(c) Find the coordinates of the lowest value of y for this graph.

8 $y = -x^3 - \dfrac{200}{x} - \dfrac{200}{x^2} + 410$ for $1 \le x \le 7$

(a) Copy and complete the table to 3 s.f. for non-integer values.

x	1	2	3	4	5	6	7
y	9						37.8

(b) Use the table to draw the graph of $y = -x^3 - \dfrac{200}{x} - \dfrac{200}{x^2} + 410$ for $1 \le x \le 7$
(c) Use the graph to
   (i) find the maximum value of y in this **domain**
   (ii) solve $x^3 + \dfrac{200}{x} + \dfrac{200}{x^2} = 210$ for $1 \le x \le 7$

GRAPHS 6 – EXAM PRACTICE EXERCISE

E 1 The depth, d m, of water in a tidal harbour, t hours after midnight, is given by $d = t^3 - 8t^2 + 12t + 18$, for $0 \leq t \leq 6$

(a) Complete the table and use it to draw the graph of d against t for $0 \leq t \leq 6$

t	0	1	2	3	4	5	6
d	18		18				

(b) Use your graph to find the maximum depth of the harbour water and at what time this occurs.

(c) An oil tanker requires at least 10 m water depth to dock in the harbour. Between what times should the oil tanker be kept out of the harbour?

E 2 The temperature, T (°C), in Paris on 1 April t hours after 07:00 is given by $T = t^3 + at^2 + 8t + b$, for $0 \leq t \leq 5$, where a and b are constants.

(a) Use the table to find the value of a and b and hence complete the table.

t	0	1	2	3	4	5
T	10					25

(b) Use the table to draw the graph of T against t for $0 \leq t \leq 5$

(c) Find the lowest temperature in this time period and when it occurs.

E 3 The wind speed, w (miles per hour), in Florida during the hurricane season is monitored t hours after midnight on 1 January, such that w in terms of t is given by $w = t^3 - 6t^2 + 4t + 25$, valid for $0 \leq t \leq 6$

(a) Copy and complete the table.

t	0	1	2	3	4	5	6
w	25						

(b) Draw the graph of w against t for $0 \leq t \leq 6$ and use it to find
  (i) the wind speed at 04:30
  (ii) the time at which the wind speed is 20 mph

E 4 The population of a colony of woodlice, w, t months after 1 January is given by $w = \dfrac{2000}{t}$, valid for $0 \leq t \leq 6$

(a) Copy and complete the table.

t	1	2	3	4	5	6
w	2000					

(b) Draw the graph of w against t for $1 \leq t \leq 6$ and use it to find
  (i) the population on 15 April
  (ii) the date when the population is reduced by 60% from what it was on 1 February

E 5 The speed, V (m/s), of a cyclist on a mountainous section of the Tour de France, t minutes after 12:00, is given by $v = at + \dfrac{b}{t}$, for $1 \leq t \leq 10$, where a and b are constants.

(a) Copy and complete the table.

t	1	2	4	6	8	10
v	25					52

(b) Use the table to draw the graph of v against t, for $0 \leq t \leq 10$

(c) Use the graph to find
  (i) the speed at which the cyclist is travelling on the steepest section and the time at which this occurs
  (ii) the time after which the cyclist's speed is at least 25 m/s

UNIT 7 SHAPE AND SPACE 7

- **MENSURATION (2D)**
- **MENSURATION (3D)**
- **SIMILAR FIGURES**

SHAPE AND SPACE 7 – BASIC SKILLS EXERCISE

Give answers to 3 s.f. unless specified otherwise.

Mensuration (2D)

1 Calculate the area and perimeter of each of these shapes.

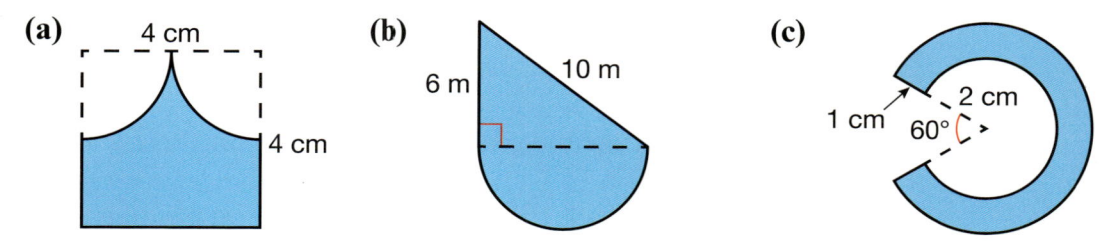

(a) 4 cm, 4 cm

(b) 6 m, 10 m

(c) 1 cm, 2 cm, 60°

2 The perimeter of a **semicircle** is 24 cm. Find the radius in cm and area in cm².

3 The shape is a **sector** of a circle with centre O. The area of the shape is 14 cm².

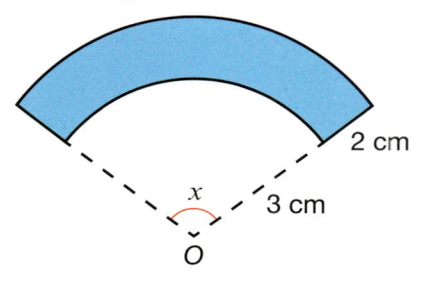

2 cm, 3 cm, x, O

Find the angle x and the perimeter in cm.

4 The diagram shows a square inscribed in a circle.

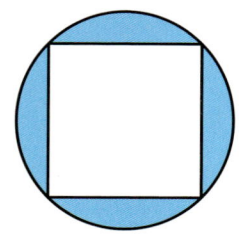

The vertices of the square lie on the circumference of the circle.
The area of the circle is 81π cm².
Find the area of the shaded region in cm² correct to 4 s.f.

5   The diagram shows the sector of a circle *ABCD* with centre *O*.
    angle *AOB* = 30° *OA* : *AD* = 3 : 1

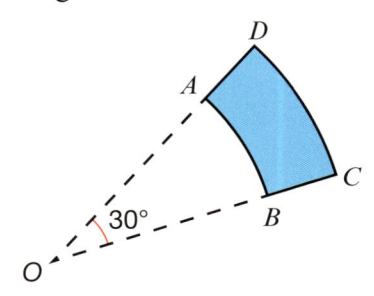

    The perimeter of the shaded area is 18 cm.
    Find the shaded area in cm².

6   The diagram shows a shape made from a sector of a circle with radius 10 mm and centre *O* and an isosceles triangle *OAB*.

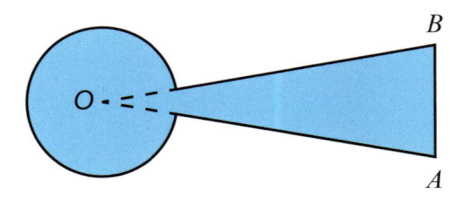

    Angle *AOB* = 15° and *OA* = 50 mm
    Find the perimeter in mm and the area of the shape in mm².

Mensuration (3D)

7   The **total** surface area of a solid **hemisphere** is 108π cm².
    Find the radius in cm and the volume in cm³.

8   The ratio of the area of **one** end of a cylinder to the curved surface area is 2 : 5.
    The ratio of the radius to the height = $r : h$ where r and h are integers.
    Find $r : h$.

9   The object shown is a cylinder with a conical hole.
    The cylinder is 20 mm in diameter and 25 mm tall.
    The cone has a base diameter of 10 mm and is 15 mm deep.
    Find, to 4 s.f.
    (a) the total surface area in mm²
    (b) the volume of the object in mm³

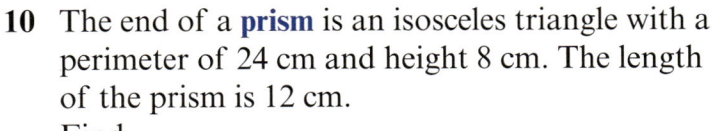

10 The end of a **prism** is an isosceles triangle with a perimeter of 24 cm and height 8 cm. The length of the prism is 12 cm.
    Find
    (a) the volume in cm³
    (b) the total surface area in cm²

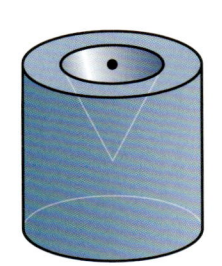

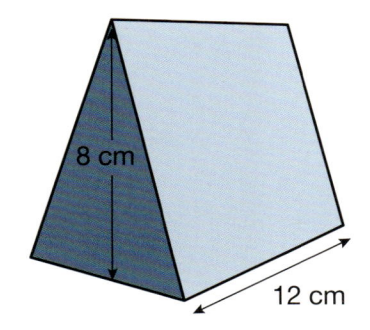

11 The top of a slice of cake is a sector of a circle with radius 9 cm. The perimeter of the top is 22 cm. The slice is 7 cm tall.
    Find
    (a) the angle x in degrees
    (b) the volume in cm³
    (c) the total surface area in cm²

12 The diagram shows a square-based pyramid.

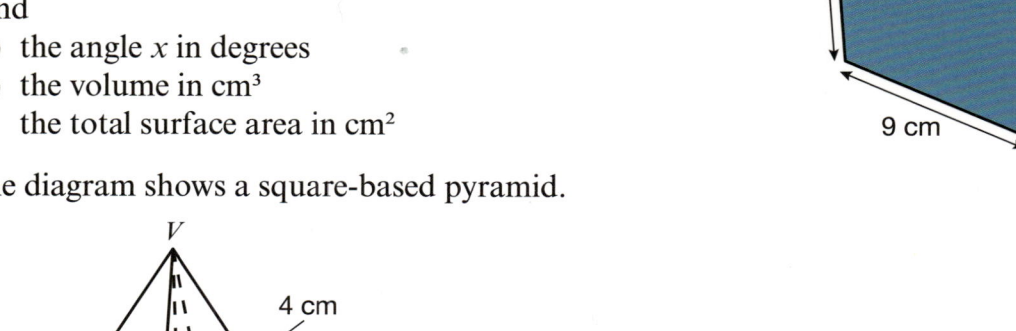

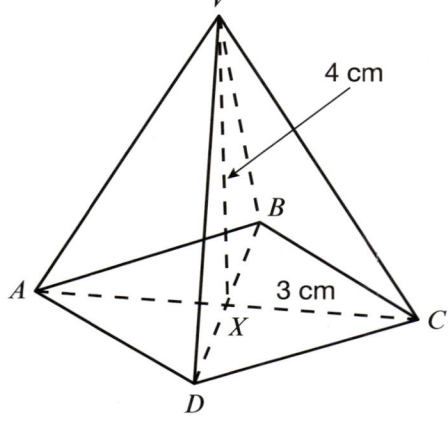

   Point X is the intersection of the diagonals AC and BD.
   The vertex, V, is directly above X.
   $VX = 4$ cm and $XC = 3$ cm
   (a) Find the volume of the pyramid in cm³.
   (b) Show that the total surface area = $18 + 6\sqrt{41}$ cm².
   Volume of a pyramid = $\frac{1}{3}$ × base area × height

Similar figures

13 The two triangles are **similar**.

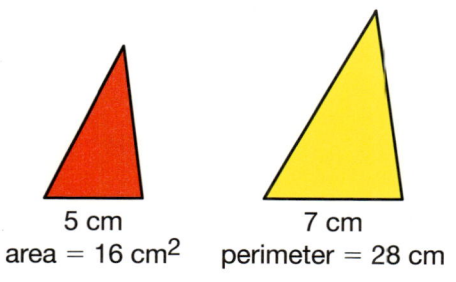

    5 cm   7 cm
    area = 16 cm² perimeter = 28 cm

    Find
    (a) the perimeter of the smaller triangle in cm
    (b) the area of the larger triangle in cm²

14 The two shapes are similar.

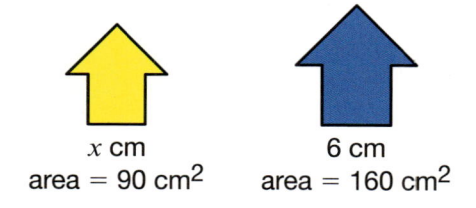

    x cm   6 cm
    area = 90 cm²   area = 160 cm²

    Find the length marked x.

15 In the diagram, DE is parallel to BC and AE : EB = 2 : 3. The area of BCDE is a.

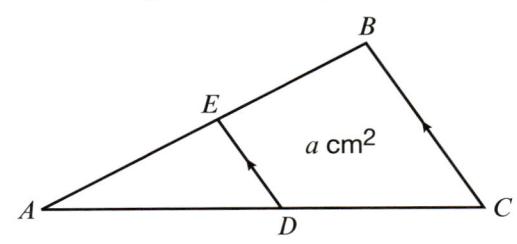

Find the area in cm² of triangle ADE in terms of a.

16 The two packets of cereal are similar.

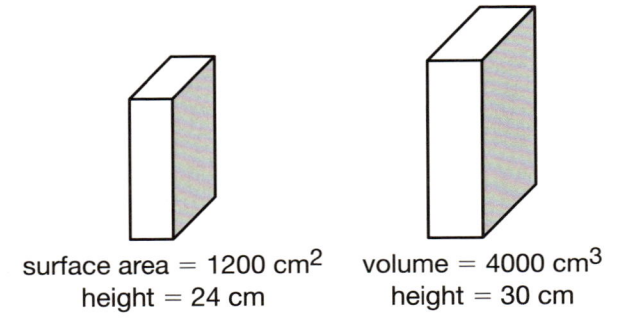

surface area = 1200 cm²
height = 24 cm

volume = 4000 cm³
height = 30 cm

Find, to 4 s.f.
(a) the volume of the smaller packet in cm³
(b) the surface area of the larger packet in cm²

17 Three bottles, A, B and C, are similar.

The ratio of the surface areas of A to B is 4 : 9.
The ratio of the volumes of B to C is 1 : 8.
The ratio of the heights of A to C is 1 : n.
Find n.

18 The volume of Earth is 1.08×10^{12} km³ and its diameter is 12 740 km.
The volume of the Moon is 2.20×10^{10} km³ and its surface area is 3.8×10^{7} km².
Calculate
(a) the diameter of the Moon in km
(b) the surface area of Earth in km²
Assume Earth and the Moon are similar.

UNIT 7 — SHAPE AND SPACE 7

SHAPE AND SPACE 7 – EXAM PRACTICE EXERCISE

SKILLS
PROBLEM SOLVING,
REASONING,
DECISION MAKING,
ADAPTIVE LEARNING

Give your answers to 3 s.f. unless specified otherwise.

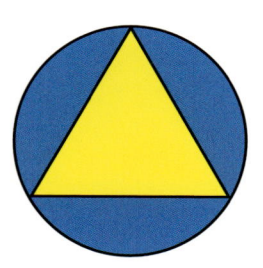

E 1 The diagram shows an equilateral triangle inscribed in a circle.

The vertices of the triangle lie on the circumference of the circle.
The area of the circle is $k\pi$ cm².

Show that the blue area is $k\left(\pi - \dfrac{3\sqrt{3}}{4}\right)$ cm²

E 2 The inside of a mug is in the shape of a cylinder.
The internal height is equal to the internal diameter.
The sum of the internal base area and the internal curved surface area is 250 cm².
(a) Find the capacity of the mug in cm³.
Give your answer to 2 s.f.
A similar mug has an internal base area and internal curved surface area that total 360 cm².
(b) Show that the ratio of the capacities of the mugs is 216 : 125.

E 3 A jeweller has a cube of gold with side length 3.0 cm.
The cube is melted down and made into a hollow cylinder of length l mm.
The external diameter of the cylinder is 5.0 mm and the internal diameter is 3.0 mm.
The cylinder is then cut into pieces 6.0 mm long to thread onto a necklace.
All dimensions are correct to 2 s.f.

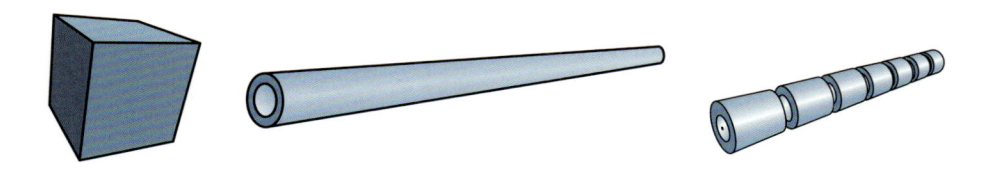

Calculate the maximum number of pieces that can be cut from the cylinder.

E 4 A hollow cylinder has an internal radius of r cm, an external radius of kr cm and a height of r cm.

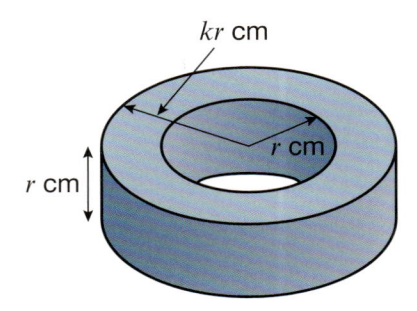

The sum of the areas of both flat ends = A cm²
The total curved surface area (inside and outside) = B cm²
(a) Show that the ratio $A : B = (k - 1) : 1$
The height of a similar cylinder is $2r$ cm
(b) Show that the ratio $A : B$ does not change.

E 5 A solid cone has volume V cm³ and total surface area A cm².
The area of the base of the cone is a cm².
The cone is cut parallel to its base and the top piece removed to leave a truncated cone, as shown in the diagram.
The area of the top of the truncated cone is $\frac{a}{4}$ cm².

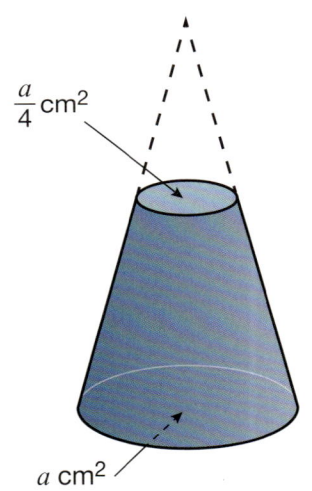

(a) Find the volume of the truncated cone in terms of V.
(b) Show that the **total** surface area of the truncated cone = $\frac{3A}{4} + \frac{a}{2}$ cm².

UNIT 7 SETS 3

- **PROBABILITY USING VENN DIAGRAMS**
- **CONDITIONAL PROBABILITY USING VENN DIAGRAMS**

SETS 3 – BASIC SKILLS EXERCISE

SKILLS
PROBLEM SOLVING, ANALYSIS

Probability using Venn diagrams

1. In a class of 30 students:
   20 have read book A,
   23 have read book B,
   3 students have read neither book.
   (a) Draw a Venn diagram to illustrate this information.
   (b) A student is selected at random. Find the probability that
      (i) the student has read both books
      (ii) the student has read book A or book B but not both books

2. In the Venn diagram, the numbers refer to the number of elements in a set.
   $n(A) = 38$, $P(B') = 0.72$
   (a) Complete the Venn diagram.
   An element is selected at random.
   (b) Find
      (i) $P(B)$
      (ii) $P(A \cup B)$
      (iii) $P(A \cap B)$

3. $P(A) = 0.6$, $P(B) = 0.5$ and $P(A \cup B) = 0.9$
   Find (a) $P(A \cap B)$
        (b) $P(A \cup B')$

4. The Venn diagram shows the results of a survey about three television programmes, A (Adventure), B (Blinders) and C (Celebrity). The numbers in the diagram refer to the number of people who watched these programmes one night.
   (a) How many people were in the survey?
   (b) How many people watched
      (i) A or B
      (ii) A and C?
   A person is selected at random.
   (c) Find the probability that they
      (i) watched B
      (ii) watched A and C but not B
      (iii) watched exactly one programme

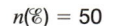

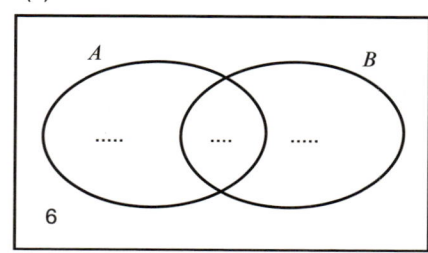

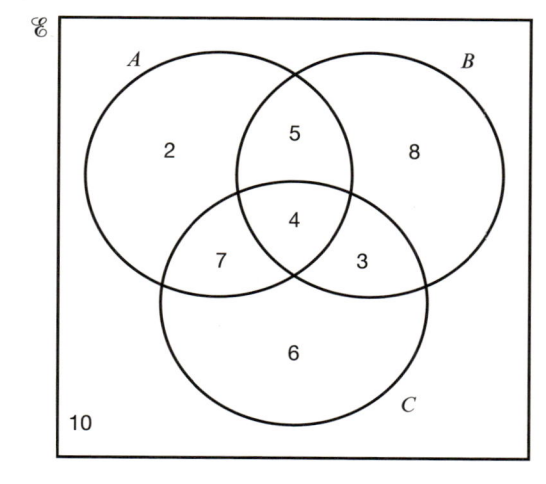

5 Three sets X, Y and Z have the following properties:
$P(X) = 0.5$, $P(Y) = 0.43$, $P(Z) = 0.47$,
$P(X \cap Y) = 0.24$, $P(X \cap Z) = 0.27$, $P(Y \cap Z) = 0.22$ and $P(X \cap Y \cap Z) = 0.13$
An element is selected at random. Find
(a) $P(X \cup Y)$
(b) $P(Y \cap Z')$
(c) $P(X \cap (Y \cup Z'))$

Conditional probability using Venn diagrams

6 $P(A) = 0.4$, $P(A \cap B) = 0.1$ and $P((A \cup B)') = 0.5$
(a) Find $P(B)$
An element is selected at random from Set A.
(b) Find the probability that the element is also in Set B.

7 There are 50 students in an orchestra.

11 play the piano,
15 play the guitar,
30 play neither instrument.
A student who plays the piano is selected at random.
Find the probability that this student also plays the guitar.

8 A universal set has 100 elements. $n(A) = 70$, $n(B) = 50$ and $B \subset A$
(a) An element is selected at random from Set A.
Find the probability that the element is also in set B.
(b) An element is selected at random from Set B.
Find the probability that the element is also in set A.

9 $B = \{$Bramley apples$\}$ and $R = \{$Rotten apples$\}$
In a box of 100 apples:
$P(B) = 0.5$
$P(R) = 0.4$
A rotten apple is selected at random. The probability of it being a Bramley apple is 0.1
(a) Draw a Venn diagram to show this information.
(b) Find $P((B \cup R)')$
(c) A Bramley apple is selected at random. Find the probability that it is rotten.

10 P(A) = 0.75, P($A' \cap B$) = 0.3 P(B') **given** A has occurred = $\frac{2}{3}$
   Find (a) P(B)
         (b) P(A') **given** that B has occurred

11 The Venn diagram shows the relationship between German cars (G) and black cars (B) in a car park.

$n(\mathcal{E}) = 200$

Venn diagram: G contains $2x+1$; intersection contains $3x-6$; B contains $4x-3$; outside both: 100.

(a) Find the value of x
(b) Find P(B)
(c) A German car is selected at random. Find the probability it is also a black car.
(d) A black car is selected at random. Find the probability it is also a German car.

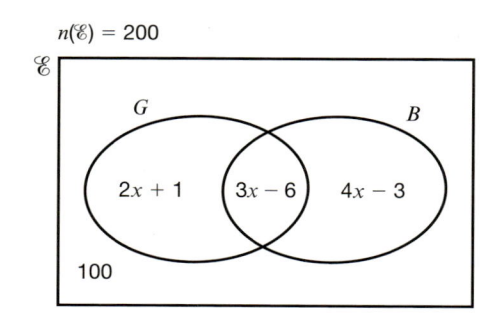

12 A mathematics test consists of two sections, one with a calculator (C) and one without a calculator (NC).
1000 students took both tests.
100 failed both tests.
750 passed the calculator test.
700 passed the non-calculator test.
Find the probability that a student selected at random has
(a) passed both tests
(b) passed both tests **given** they passed the calculator test
(c) passed the calculator test **given** they only passed one test

13 There are 3 overlapping sets A, B and C within the universal set.
$n(\mathcal{E}) = 100$
$n(B) = 32$
P($A \cap C$) **given** B has occurred = $\frac{1}{8}$

Find P($A \cap B \cap C$).

14 A fair 12-sided dice numbered 1–12 is rolled.
R = {number rolled is prime}
E = {number rolled is even}
O = {number rolled is odd}
(a) Draw a Venn diagram to show R, E and O.
(b) Find
   (i) P($R \cap E$)
   (ii) P($R \cap E \cap O$)
   (iii) P(($R \cup E$)$'$)
(c) An odd number is rolled. Find the probability it is prime.

15 The Venn diagram shows the number of people in an adventure club who have climbed the three highest mountains in Scotland, Wales and England.

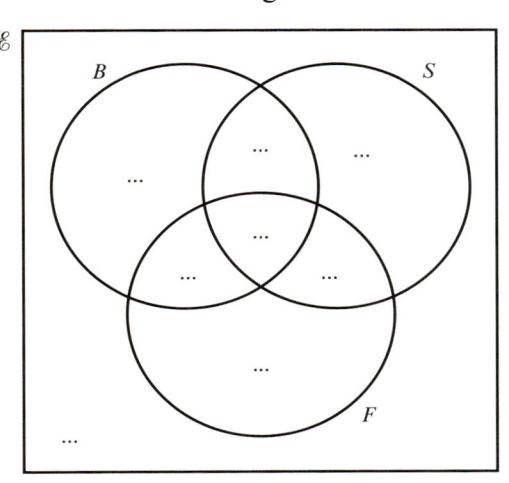

B = {climbed Ben Nevis}
S = {climbed Snowdon}
F = {Scafell Pike}
The club has 48 members.
12 have not climbed any of these mountains.
27 have climbed Ben Nevis.
29 have climbed Snowdon.
21 have climbed Scafell Pike.
21 have climbed Ben Nevis and Snowdon.
14 have climbed Snowdon and Scafell Pike.
15 have climbed Scafell Pike and Ben Nevis.

(a) Complete the Venn diagram to show the number of people in each **subset**.
(b) A member is chosen at random. Find the probability that the member has
  (i) climbed all three mountains
  (ii) climbed exactly two mountains
(c) A member who has climbed Scafell Pike or Snowdon or both is chosen at random. Find the probability that this member has also climbed Ben Nevis.

SETS 3 – EXAM PRACTICE EXERCISE

1 There are 1000 spectators at a rugby match.

H = {spectators wearing a hat} and S = {spectators wearing a scarf}
The Venn diagram shows the relationship between these sets.
(a) Find the value of x.
(b) A spectator is chosen at random.
 Find the probability that
 (i) the spectator is wearing a hat or a scarf or both
 (ii) the spectator is wearing a hat or a scarf but not both
(c) A spectator who is wearing a scarf is chosen at random. Find the probability that this spectator is also wearing a hat.

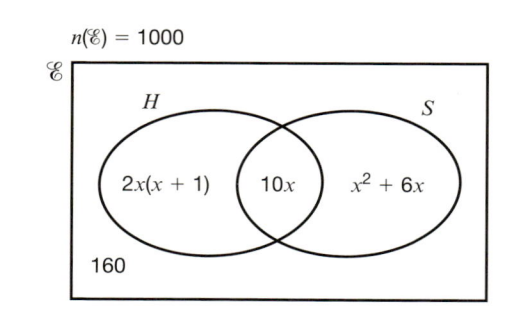

$n(\mathcal{E}) = 1000$

Venn diagram: H contains $2x(x+1)$, intersection $10x$, S contains $x^2 + 6x$, outside 160.

2 100 people were asked what type of exercise they took during the last week. The results were as follows.
40 had taken no exercise.
35 had been for a walk.
26 had been for a swim.
10 had done all three forms of exercise.
17 had been for a walk and been on a run.
13 had been for a walk and been for a swim.
15 had been on a run and been for a swim.
W = {Walkers}
S = {Swimmers}
R = {Runners} 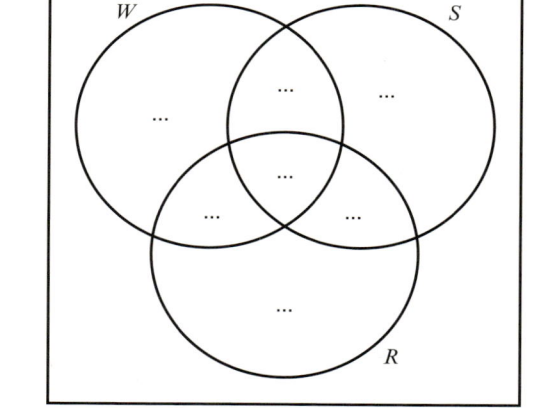
(a) Complete the Venn diagram to show the number of people in each subset.
A person is selected at random.
(b) Find the probability that this person
 (i) had been on a run
 (ii) had been on a run only
 (iii) had been for a walk and on a run but had not been swimming
(c) A person who went on a run is selected at random.
 Find the probability that this person also went swimming.

UNIT 7   **SETS 3**   149

E 3 The diagram shows three sets, *A*, *B* and *C*.
$n(A) = 50$, $n(B) = 70$, $n(C) = 60$
The letters in the subsets refer to the number of elements in that subset.
There are no elements outside the three sets.
P(*A*) **given** that *B* has occurred = 0.2
P(*C*) **given** than *A* has occurred = 0.32
(a) Complete the Venn diagram to show the number of elements in each subset.
(b) Find P($A \cap C$).
(c) Find P(*B*) **given** that *C* has occurred.

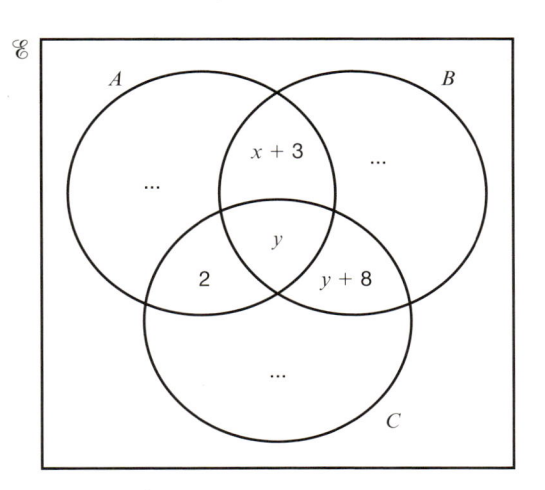

Venn diagram shows three overlapping circles *A*, *B*, *C* within universal set $\mathscr{E}$. Regions labelled: *A* only: ..., *B* only: ..., $A \cap B$ only: $x + 3$, $A \cap B \cap C$: y, $A \cap C$ only: 2, $B \cap C$ only: $y + 8$, *C* only: ...

E 4 There are 100 delegates at an international conference.

64 delegates speak English (*E*).
42 delegates speak Spanish (*S*).
60 delegates speak Mandarin (*M*).
All delegates speak at least one of these languages.
P($M \cap E$) **given** the delegate speaks Spanish = $\frac{4}{21}$,

P($E \cap S$) **given** the delegate speaks English = $\frac{3}{8}$

$n(E \cap M) = 40$ and $n(M \cap S) = 10$
(a) Complete the Venn diagram to show the number of delegates in each subset.
A delegate is chosen at random.
(b) Find the probability that
   (i) the delegate speaks Mandarin only
   (ii) the delegate speaks at least two languages
(c) A delegate who speaks English is chosen at random. Find the probability that this delegate speaks exactly two of the three languages.

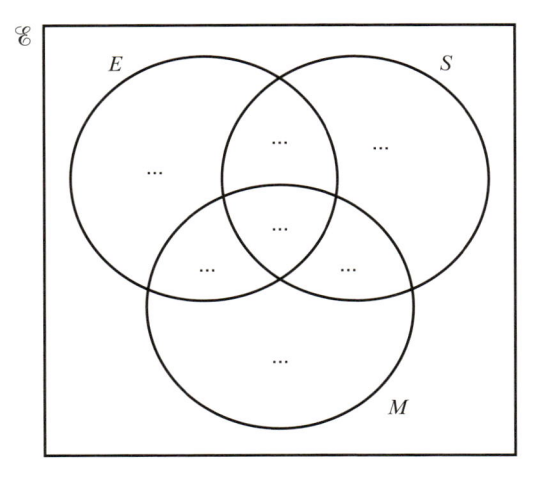

E 5 A new test is developed for an infectious disease.

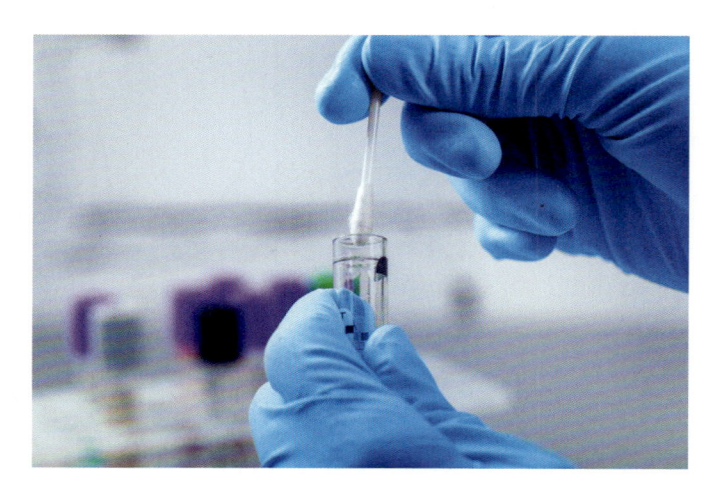

The test indicates either positive or negative.
The probability that someone with the disease will test positive is 90%.
The probability that someone without the disease will test negative is 95%.
The test is administered to a group of 200 people.
10% of this group have the disease.
D = {people with the disease}
ND = {people without the disease}
P = {people who tested positive}

(a) Complete the Venn diagram to show the number of people in each subset.
(b) One of the people who tested positive is selected at random. Find the probability that this person doesn't have the disease
(c) One of the people who tested negative is selected at random. Find the probability that this person has the disease.

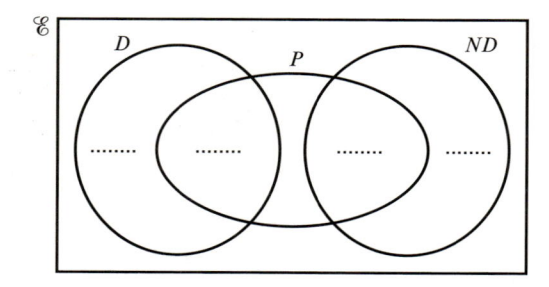

UNIT 8 NUMBER 8

- **CONVERTING MEASUREMENTS**
- **COMPOUND MEASURE**

NUMBER 8 – BASIC SKILLS EXERCISE

Give all answers correct to 3 s.f. unless otherwise stated.

Converting measurements – lengths

1. Convert
   - (a) 5 km to cm
   - (b) 8 cm to km
   - (c) 2×10^8 mm to km
   - (d) 6×10^{-4} m to mm

2. The dwarf pygmy goby is a very small fish with an average length of 0.9 cm.

   Find this length in km.

3. The length of a banana is 20 cm. Find this length in micrometres, given 1 micrometre = 10^{-6} metres.

4. The thickness of a piece of paper is 0.004 inches. The piece of paper is folded in half, then in half again and so on until it has been folded in half 50 times. (Assume it is possible to do this.)
   Find the height of the pile of paper in km, given 1 inch = 25.4 mm.

Converting measurements – areas

5. Convert
   - (a) 5×10^6 cm² to m²
   - (b) 4×10^{-3} km² to cm²
   - (c) 4 m² to mm²
   - (d) 2×10^{12} mm² to km²

6   A singles tennis court measures 78 feet by 27 feet.

Find the area in km², given 1 foot = 0.305 m

7   The black hole at the centre of our galaxy has a diameter of 23.6 million km. Assuming it is a sphere, find its surface area in cm².

8   Assuming a grain of salt is a cube of side 0.3 mm, find the surface area in km².

Converting measurements – volumes

9   Convert
(a) 2 m³ to ml
(b) 4 km³ to m³
(c) 8×10^{10} mm³ to m³
(d) 7×10^{-9} km³ to mm³

10   A drinks carton is a cuboid measuring 20 cm by 7 cm by 7 cm.
Find the volume in
(a) ml
(b) litres
(c) km³

11   Taking a rain drop to be a sphere with diameter 1.5 mm, how many rain drops are needed to fill Rutland Water, a large reservoir in England, which has a volume of 1.24×10^8 m³?

12   1 ml of a chemical contains 3×10^{22} molecules. The volume of the world's oceans is 1.5×10^9 km³. One litre of the chemical is poured into the ocean and left to mix thoroughly, then one litre of the mixture is taken out.
How many molecules of the chemical are in the one litre of mixture?

Compound measure – speed

13 The speed of sound is 343 m/s.
What is this in km/h?

14 The average speed of a garden snail is 0.048 km/h.

How far, in mm, will a snail travel in 10 seconds?

15 A train leaves London at 08:12 to travel to Cambridge, which is 49 miles away.
The average speed of the train is 25 m/s.
What time does the train arrive, given 1 mile is 1.6 km?

16 An airbag in a particular car 'explodes' at 150 miles per hour.
Taking 1 mile to be 1.6 km, how long in seconds will it take the airbag to come out to 30 cm?

17 Human hair grows at a rate of 6 inches per year.

Taking 1 inch to be 2.54 cm and a year to be 365 days, find how many millimetres human hair grows in a week.

18 The distance from Heathrow to Sydney, Australia, is 17 000 km. An aeroplane takes off from Heathrow at 17:34 on Thursday, flies non-stop, and then lands in Sydney at 23:53 local time on Friday. The time in Sydney is 11 hours ahead of the time in Heathrow.
Find the average speed of the aeroplane in m/s.

Compound measure – density

19 The mass of water in a garden pond is 5×10^4 kg. The water has a density of 1 g/cm³. Find the volume of water in the pond in m³.

20 Gold has a density of 19.3 g/cm³ and a price of £45 128 per kg.
Find the value of a gold ring that is in the shape of a hollow cylinder with internal radius 10 mm, external radius 12 mm and length 3 mm.

21 A snooker ball is a sphere with a diameter of 52.5 mm and a mass of 141 g, both figures being correct to 3 s.f.

Calculate the upper bound for the density of a snooker ball in g/cm³.

22 Material A has a density of 4.3 g/cm³, Material B has a density of 5200 kg/m³.
2 kg of Material A and 500 g of Material B are mixed to form Material C.
Calculate the density of Material C in g/cm³.

23 Three cuboids of wood, A, B and C, are thrown into water.

Cuboid	Dimensions	Mass
A	10 cm by 120 mm by 32 mm	350 g
B	0.5 m by 3 m by 10 cm	0.165 tonnes
C	40 cm by 80 cm by 60 mm	15.4 kg

The table gives information about the cuboids.
Wood will float in water if its density is less than 1 g/cm³.
Which cuboids float and which cuboids sink?

24 Liquid A has a density of a g/cm³. Liquid B has a density of b kg/m³.
Equal volumes of A and B are mixed together to form liquid C.
Find an expression for the density of liquid C.

SKILLS
ADAPTIVE LEARNING

Compound measure – pressure

25 What force is exerted by a pressure of 12 N/m² acting on a square of side 5 mm?

26 Find the pressure in N/m² exerted by a force of 640 N on a circular area of radius 10 cm.

27 What area in cm² is needed by a pressure of 4×10^4 N/m² to support a force of 400 N?

28 A cylinder of height 12 cm and weight 240 N exerts a pressure of 6400 N/m² on the surface it is resting on.
What is the volume of the cylinder in cm³?

29 Stu is pumping up his bicycle tyre with a hand pump. The pressure in the pump is 34 N/cm², and the piston area is 300 mm².

Find the force Stu needs to exert in N.

30 The pressure in a car's tyre is given as 25 pounds force per square inch.
Calculate the pressure in N/m² given that 1 inch = 2.54 centimetres and 1 pound force = 4.54 N.

31 A solid metal cylinder rests with its flat end on a table.
The cylinder has height 100 mm, radius 60 mm and density 12 tonnes/m³.

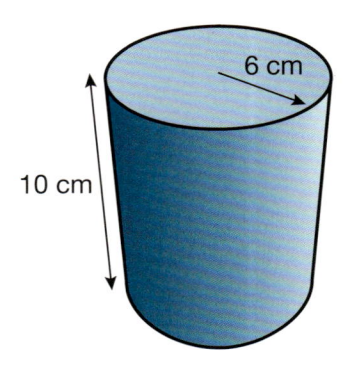

1 kg of the metal exerts a force of 10 N on the table.
Find the pressure in N/cm² exerted by the cylinder on the table.

NUMBER 8 – EXAM PRACTICE EXERCISE

1 Gold has a density of 19.3 g/cm³, silver has a density of 10.5 g/cm³.

Yulia is making a gold ring from an alloy (mixture) of gold and silver.

She makes an alloy from gold and silver in the ratio of 3 : 1 by volume.

(a) Find the density of the alloy in g/cm³.

Yulia makes a second alloy from gold and silver in the ratio of x : 1 by volume.

The density of the resulting alloy is 18.1 g/cm³.

(b) Find the value of x.

2 Candle wax has a density of 900 kg/m³.

When burning, a candle uses $\frac{1}{15}$ g of wax every minute.

A cylindrical candle has a diameter of 20 mm.
It has marks on it to show the time in hours since it was lit.

(a) How far apart, in mm, should the marks be?

Another candle is made from the same wax.
It is in the shape of a cone with base radius 40 mm and height 20 cm.

(b) Show this candle takes 3π hours to burn down to half its height.

E 3 A lorry of length l metres is travelling along a motorway at a speed of v km/h. It passes under a bridge which is w metres wide.

The time that it takes from the instant the front of the lorry passes under the bridge to the instant that the back of the lorry leaves the bridge is t seconds.

(a) Show that $t = \dfrac{18(l+d)}{5v}$

For a certain lorry, $l = 16.5$ m, $w = 60$ m and $t = 2.7$ seconds.
The speed limit is 60 mph.

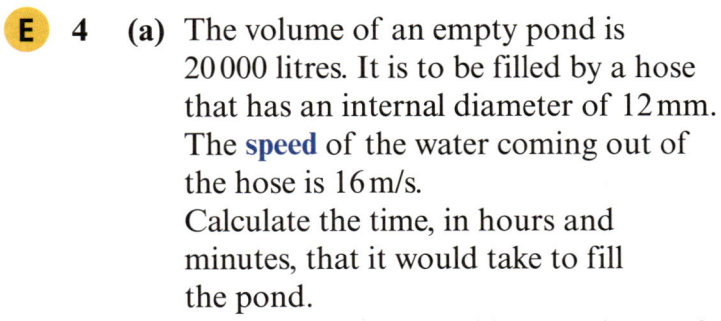

(b) Taking 1 mile as 1.6 km, calculate if the lorry is breaking the speed limit.

E 4 (a) The volume of an empty pond is 20 000 litres. It is to be filled by a hose that has an internal diameter of 12 mm. The **speed** of the water coming out of the hose is 16 m/s.
Calculate the time, in hours and minutes, that it would take to fill the pond.

(b) A second empty pond has a volume of 15 000 litres. It is to be filled by a hose that has an internal diameter of d mm.
The speed of the water coming out of the hose is 16 m/s.
The time to fill the pond needs to be 2 hours.
Calculate the value of d.
Give your answer to 3 s.f.

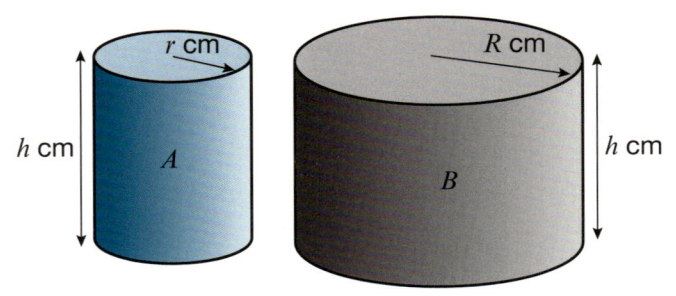

E 5 Two solid metal cylinders, A and B, rest with their flat ends on a table.

Both cylinders have the same height h cm and the same density d kg/cm³.
1 kg of the metal exerts a force of 10 N on the table.
Cylinder A has radius r cm and cylinder B has radius R cm.
Show that the pressure exerted on the table by each cylinder is $10hd$ N/cm².

UNIT 8 ALGEBRA 8

- **FUNCTION NOTATION**
- **DOMAIN AND RANGE**
- **COMPOSITE FUNCTIONS**
- **INVERSE FUNCTIONS**
- **MIXED QUESTIONS**

ALGEBRA 8 – BASIC SKILLS EXERCISE

SKILLS
INTERPRETATION

Function notation

1. Decide, giving a reason, if the graph shows a **function** or not.

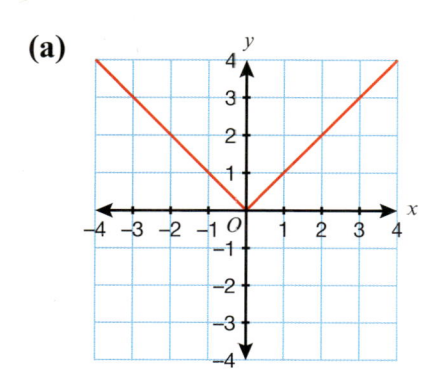

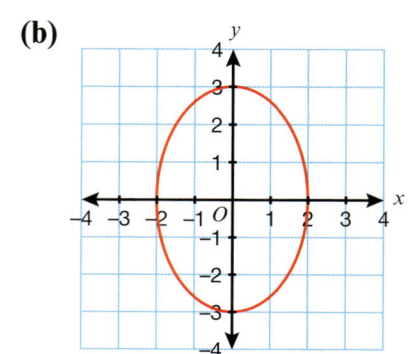

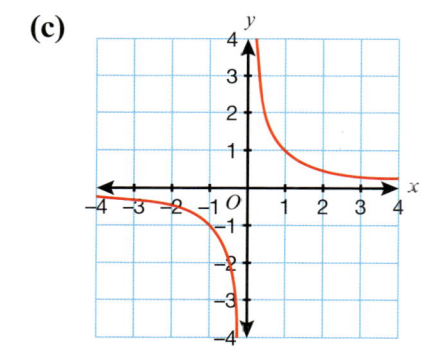

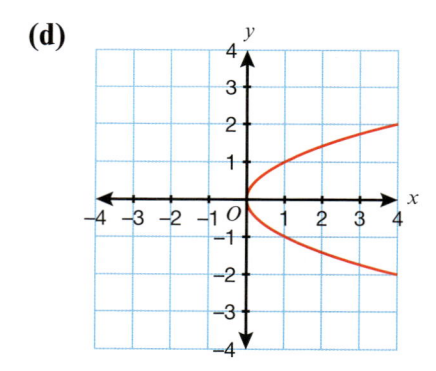

   (a)

   (b)

   (c)

   (d)

2. (a) Complete the **mapping diagram**.

0°	0
30°	1/2
60°	$\frac{\sqrt{3}}{2}$
90°	1
120°	
150°	
180°	

   $x \longrightarrow \sin(x)$

   (b) Is $\sin(x)$ a function? Justify your answer.

3. Find the function shown in this flow chart in the form $f: x \to ax^2 + bx + c$, where a, b and c are constants.

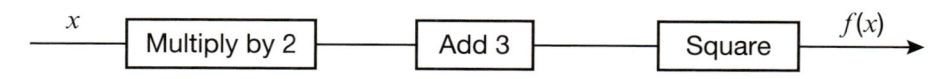

   $x \longrightarrow$ [Multiply by 2] $\longrightarrow$ [Add 3] $\longrightarrow$ [Square] $\xrightarrow{f(x)}$

4 $f(x) = 7 - 2x$
Calculate
(a) $f(3)$ (b) $f(-2)$ (c) $f(0)$ (d) $f(y^2)$

5 (a) $f(x) = x - \dfrac{1}{x}$
Calculate
(i) $f(2)$ (ii) $f(-2)$
(b) What value of x must be excluded from the domain of $f(x)$?

6 $g: x \rightarrow 5x - 4$
Calculate a if
(a) $g(a) = 6$ (b) $g(a) = -4$

7 $g: x \rightarrow 5x - x^2$
Calculate b if
(a) $g(b) = 6$ (b) $g(b) = -6$

8 $f(x) = 2x + 3$
Calculate
(a) $f(x) - 1$ (b) $f(x - 1)$

9 $f(x) = 4 + 3x$
Calculate
(a) $2f(x)$ (b) $f(2x)$

10 $f(x) = x^2 - 9$
Calculate $f(x + 3)$

11 $f(x) = x^2 - 2x + 1$
Calculate $f(2x + 1)$

12 $f: x \rightarrow 3(x - 1)$ and $g: x \rightarrow 4x + 2$
Calculate the value of a such that $f(a) = g(a)$

13 $f(x) = x^2 + 5x + 3$ and $g(x) = (2x + 1)^2$
Find the values of a such that $f(a) = g(a)$

14 $f(x) = ax^2 + bx$
If $f(1) = 2$ and $f(-2) = -16$, find a and b

15 $f(x) = ax + b$
If $f(a) = f(b)$, show that either $a = b$ or $a = 0$

Domain and range

16 State which values of x (if any) cannot be included in the domain of
(a) $f(x) = \dfrac{1}{1 - 2x}$ (b) $f(x) = 1 - \dfrac{1}{2x}$
(c) $f(x) = \sqrt{x + 3}$ (d) $f(x) = \dfrac{2}{\sqrt{3 - x}}$

17 State which values of x (if any) cannot be included in the domain of
(a) $f(x) = \sqrt{x^2 - 9}$ (b) $f(x) = \dfrac{3}{4 + x^2}$
(c) $f(x) = \dfrac{1}{\sin x}$ (d) $f(x) = \tan x$

18 Find the range of the following functions when the domain is all **real numbers**.
   (a) $f(x) = x - 1$
   (b) $g(x) = x^2 - 1$
   (c) $h(x) = (x - 1)^2$

19 Find the range of the following functions using the given domains.
   (a) $f(x) = x^2 - 1$, domain $\{-1, 0, 1, 2\}$
   (b) $g(x) = (x - 4)^2$, domain all real numbers
   (c) $h(x) = x^2 - 4$, domain all real numbers

Composite functions

20 $f(x) = 2x + 4$ and $g(x) = 5 - x$
   Calculate
   (a) $fg(1)$
   (b) $gf(-1)$
   (c) $ff(1)$
   (d) $gg(-1)$

21 $f(x) = 5x - 3$
   Solve $ff(x) = x$

22 $f(x) = kx + 2$, $g(x) = kx - 2$ and $fg(3) = 3$
   Find the values of k.

23 $f(x) = x + 2$ and $g(x) = x^2 - 4$
   Find a such that $fg(a) = gf(a)$

24 $f(x) = kx$ and $g(x) = x - 2$
   If $gf(k) = k$, find the values of k.

25 $f(x) = 1 - x$, $g(x) = 3x - 1$ and $h(x) = x^2$
   Find $fgh(x)$.

Inverse functions

26 Find the **inverse** of the following functions.
   (a) $f(x) = 7(2 - x)$
   (b) $g(x) = \sqrt{x + 5}$
   (c) $f(x) = \frac{4}{x} - 2$

27 Find the inverse of $f: x \to \frac{x - 2}{x + 1}$

28 If f is a function of x and $f^{-1}(7) = 4$, find $f(4)$.

29 $f(x) = 7x + 5$
   Find $ff^{-1}(x)$.

30 $f(x) = \frac{x}{(x - 1)}$
   (a) Find the inverse of $f^{-1}(x)$.
   (b) Describe the relationship between $f(x)$ and $f^{-1}(x)$.

31 If $f^{-1}(x) = 4x - 3$, find $f(x)$.

32 If $f^{-1}(x) = \frac{x - 1}{x}$, find $f(x)$.

ALGEBRA 8

SKILLS
INTERPRETATION, DECISION MAKING

Mixed questions

33 $f(x) = 4 - 5x$ and $g(x) = \frac{4-x}{5}$
   (a) Find the functions
      (i) $fg(x)$
      (ii) $gf(x)$
   (b) Describe the relationship between functions f and g.
   (c) Write down the exact value of $fg(\pi)$.

34 $f(x) = \sqrt{x+1}$ and $g(x) = 3x + 2$
   (a) Find
      (i) $fg(x)$
      (ii) $gf(x)$
   (b) What values should be excluded from the domain of
      (i) $fg(x)$
      (ii) $gf(x)$?

35 $f(x) = \dfrac{3x-4}{5}$ and $gf(x) = x$
    Find $g(x)$.

36 $f(x) = 2 + x$ and $g(x) = 3x - 1$
   (a) Find
      (i) $fg(x)$
      (ii) $gf(x)$
   (b) Show that $(fg)^{-1}(x) = g^{-1}f^{-1}(x)$

37 $f(x) = ax + b$, $f^{-1}(2) = 1$ and $f^{-1}(0) = 2$
    Find a and b.

38 $f(x) = 3x + 1$
    Find a such that $f(a) + f^{-1}(a) = 1$

39 $f(x) = 2x - 7$ and $fg(x) = 6x - 5$
    Find $g(x)$.

40 $f(x) = x^2$
   (a) Sketch the graph of $y = f(x)$ and state its range.
   (b) Find the inverse function, stating any restrictions on the domain.

41 $f(x) = x^2 - 2$
   (a) Sketch the graph of $y = f(x)$ and state its range.
   (b) Find the inverse function, stating any restrictions on the domain.

42 $f(x) = x^2 + 2x$
   (a) Write $f(x)$ in the form $(x + a)^2 + b$
   (b) Sketch the graph of $y = f(x)$ and state its range.
   (c) Find the inverse function, stating any restrictions on the domain.

43 $f(x) = x^2 - 2x + 4$
   (a) Write $f(x)$ in the form $(x + a)^2 + b$
   (b) Sketch the graph of $y = f(x)$ and state its range.
   (c) Find the inverse function, stating any restrictions on the domain.

44 $f(x) = 2x^2 + 4x + 6$
   (a) Write $f(x)$ in the form $a(x + b)^2 + c$
   (b) Sketch the graph of $y = f(x)$ and state its range.
   (c) Find the inverse function, stating any restrictions on the domain.

ALGEBRA 8 – EXAM PRACTICE EXERCISE

SKILLS
PROBLEM SOLVING, INTERPRETATION, DECISION MAKING

E 1 $f(x) = (x-1)^2$
$g(x) = 7 - x$
  (a) (i) Find $g^{-1}(x)$.
  (ii) What is the relationship between $g(x)$ and $g^{-1}(x)$?
  (b) Work out the range of values of x for which $f(x) < g(x)$
  Show clear algebraic working.

E 2 $f(x) = (x-1)^2$
$g(x) = 2x + 1$
  (a) If $2fg(x) = gf(x)$, show that $6x^2 + 4x - 3 = 0$
  (b) Solve $2fg(k) = gf(k)$, showing clear algebraic working.
  Give your answers in the form $\frac{p \pm \sqrt{q}}{r}$ where p, q and r are integers.

E 3 $f(x) = ax + b$
$g^{-1}(x) = 3x - 5$
$f(3) = 5$
$g(4) = f(2)$
Find $f^{-1}(7)$, showing clear algebraic working.

E 4 The graph shows two functions, f and g.
  (a) Find to 1 d.p.
   (i) $fg(2)$
   (ii) $gf(4)$
   (iii) $gf^{-1}(3)$
  (b) $g(x) - k = 0$ has two solutions.
  Find the range of possible values of k.
  Give your answer to 1 d.p.
  (c) $f^{-1}(a) = g^{-1}(a)$
  Find the values of a to 1 d.p.

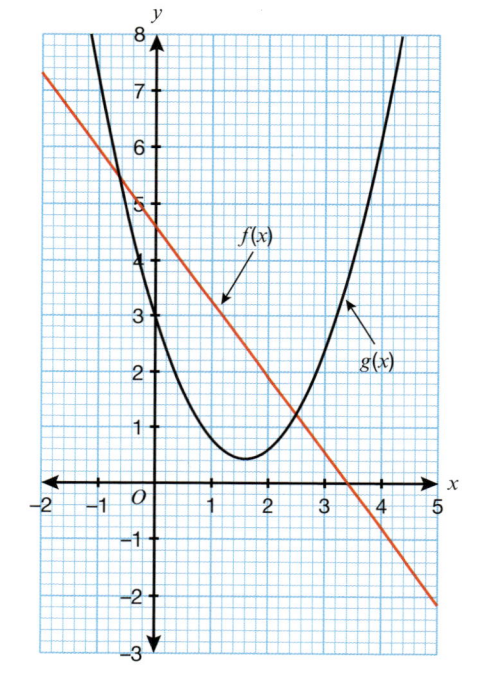

E 5 $f(x)$ is the function that gives the radius of a circle when the area is the input.
  (a) Show that $f(x) = \sqrt{\frac{x}{\pi}}$

$g(x)$ is the function that gives the circumference of a circle when the radius is the input.
  (b) Find $g(x)$.
  (c) Show that $gf(x) = 2\sqrt{\pi x}$. What does this composite function represent?
  (d) Solve $a = gf(a)$. What does your answer mean?

UNIT 8 GRAPHS 7

- **USING GRAPHS TO SOLVE QUADRATIC EQUATIONS**
- **USING GRAPHS TO SOLVE OTHER EQUATIONS**
- **USING GRAPHS TO SOLVE SIMULTANEOUS LINEAR AND NON-LINEAR EQUATIONS**

GRAPHS 7 – BASIC SKILLS EXERCISE

SKILLS

PROBLEM SOLVING

Using graphs to solve quadratic equations

1. **(a)** Draw an accurate graph of $y = x^2 - 3x + 1$ for $-2 \leq x \leq 5$
   (b) Use this graph to estimate the solutions to the following equations. Give the equation of the lines you use to do this.
   - **(i)** $x^2 - 3x - 3 = 0$
   - **(ii)** $x^2 - 4x - 1 = 0$
   - **(iii)** $x^2 - x - 3 = 0$

2. The graph of $y = x^2 - 3x + 2$ has been drawn.
   Find the equation of the lines that should be drawn on this graph to solve the following equations.
   - **(a)** $x^2 - 3x = 0$
   - **(b)** $x^2 - 3x + 1 = 0$
   - **(c)** $x^2 - 4x + 2 = 0$
   - **(d)** $x^2 - 2x - 2 = 0$

3. Find the equation in x solved by the intersection of the following pairs of graphs. Express your answer in the form $ax^2 + bx + c = 0$ where a, b and c are integers.
   - **(a)** $y = 5x^2 + 13$ and $y = 3x - 4$
   - **(b)** $y = 4x^2 + 3x - 5$ and $y = 7x + 2$
   - **(c)** $y = 2x^2 - 7x + 5$ and $y = x^2 + 2$
   - **(d)** $y = 2x - 1 - 3x^2$ and $y = 4 - x$

4. Here is the graph of $y = x^2 - 4x + 3$
   The equation $x^2 - 4x = k$ has no solutions.
   (a) Estimate the range of values of k.
   The equation $x^2 - 3x = p$ has one solution.
   (b) Estimate the value of p.

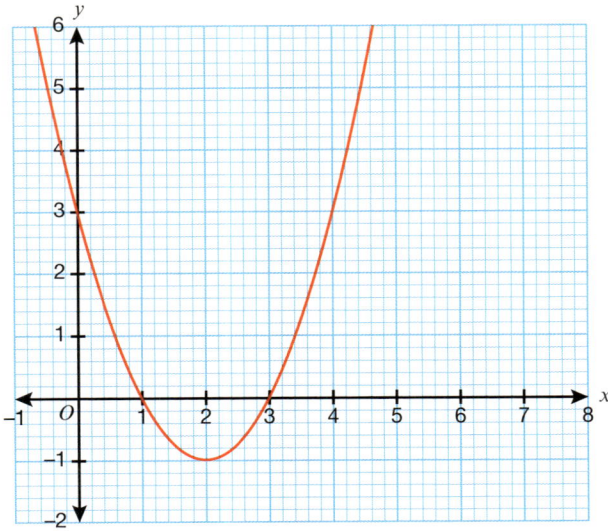

Using graphs to solve other equations

5 Here is the graph of $y = 2x - x^3$

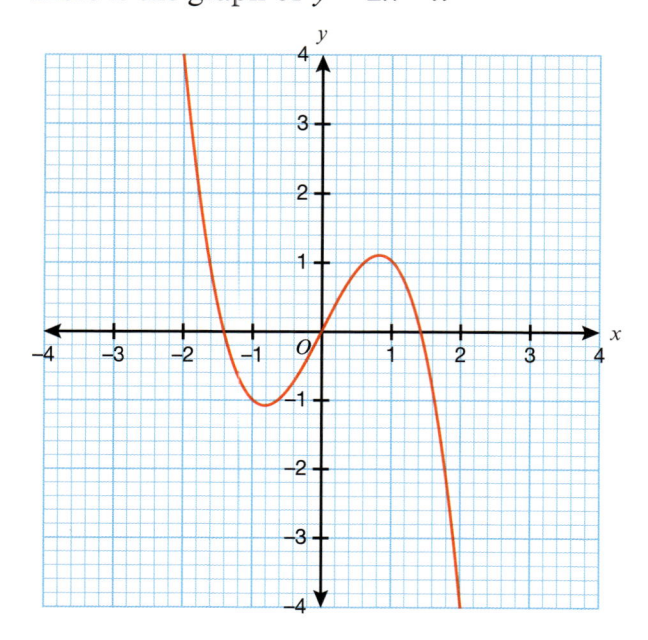

(a) Use this graph to estimate the solutions to the following equations.
Give the equations of the lines you use to do this.
   (i) $3x - x^3 = 0$
   (ii) $x - x^3 = 1$
   (iii) $x^3 + x^2 = 2x + 1$

The equation $2x - x^3 = k$ has only one solution.
(b) Estimate the range of values for k.

6 Here is the graph of $y = x + \frac{1}{x}$

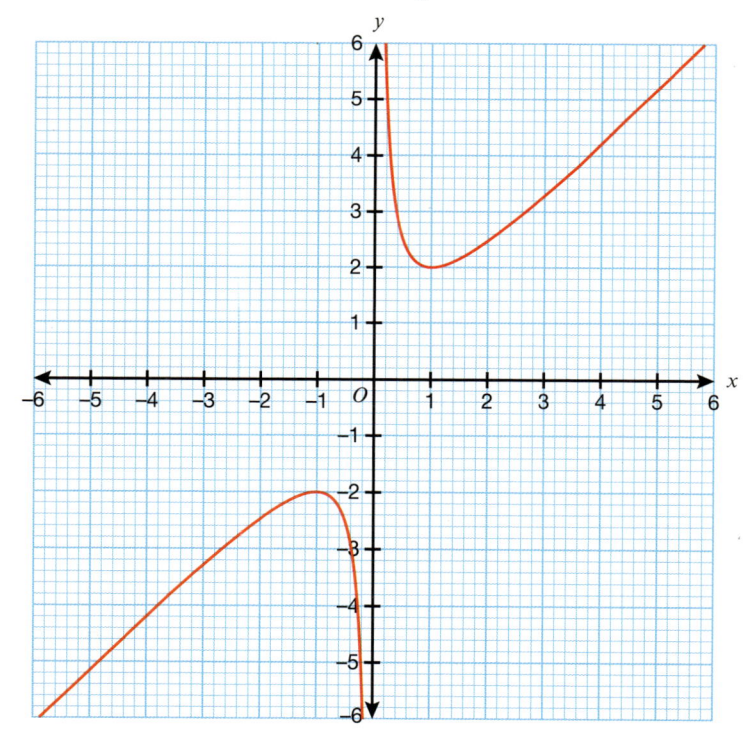

(a) Use this graph to estimate the solutions to the following equations.
Give the equation of the lines you use to do this.
   (i) $\frac{1}{x} - x = 0$
   (ii) $\frac{x}{2} + \frac{1}{x} + 2 = 0$
   (iii) $x^2 + x + \frac{1}{x} = 4$

The equation $x + \frac{1}{x} = k$ has no solutions.
(b) Estimate the range of values of k.

7 Here is the graph of $y = x^3 - 5x^2 + 6x$

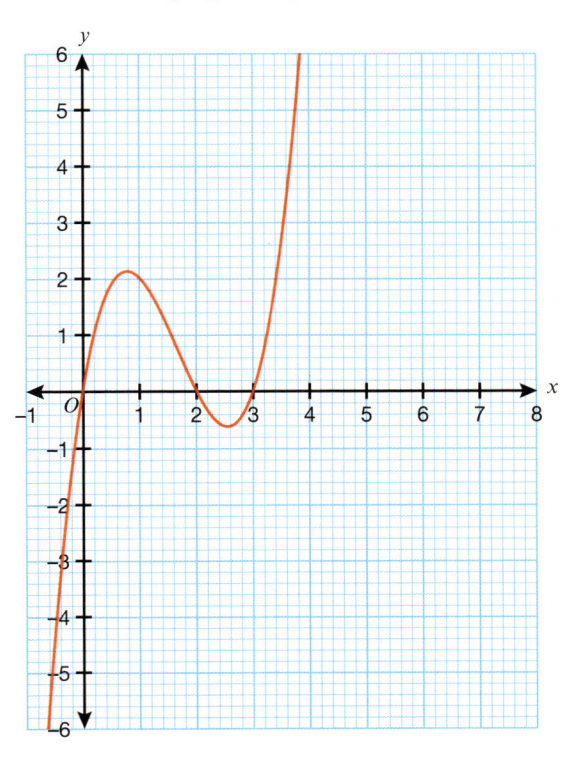

The equation $x^3 - 5x^2 + 6x + k = 0$ has three solutions.
(a) Estimate the range of values of k.
(b) Use the graph to estimate the solutions to the equation
$3x^3 - 15x^2 + 19x - 3 = 0$

Using graphs to solve simultaneous linear and non-linear equations

8 Use a graphical method to solve $y = 5 - x^2$ and $y = 2 - x$ simultaneously.

The domain for x is $-2 \leq x \leq 3$
Give your answers to 1 d.p.

9 Use a graphical method to solve $y = \frac{1}{x} - x$ and $y = x^2 - x - 3$ simultaneously.

The domain for x is $-2 \leq x \leq 3$
Give your answers to 1 d.p.

10 Use a graphical method to solve $y = x^3 - 2x$ and $y = 0.5x^2 + x - 1$ simultaneously.

The domain for x is $-2 \leq x \leq 2$
Give your answers to 1 d.p.

GRAPHS 7 – EXAM PRACTICE EXERCISE

SKILLS
CRITICAL THINKING, PROBLEM SOLVING, ANALYSIS

E 1 (a) Complete the table of values for $y = x^2 - 2x - 2$

x	-2	-1	0	1	2	3	4
y	6				-2	1	

(b) On graph paper, draw the graph of $y = x^2 - 2x - 2$
Use $-2 \leq x \leq 4$, $-5 \leq y \leq 6$ and **equal scales** for both axes.

(c) Draw a straight line on your graph to estimate the solutions (to 1 d.p.) to $x^2 - x = 3$
Give the equation of the line you draw.

The equation $x^2 - 3x + k = 0$ has only one solution.

(d) By drawing a suitable straight line on your graph, estimate the value of k to 2 s.f.

E 2 The graph of $y = -x^3 + 7x - 6$ is drawn.

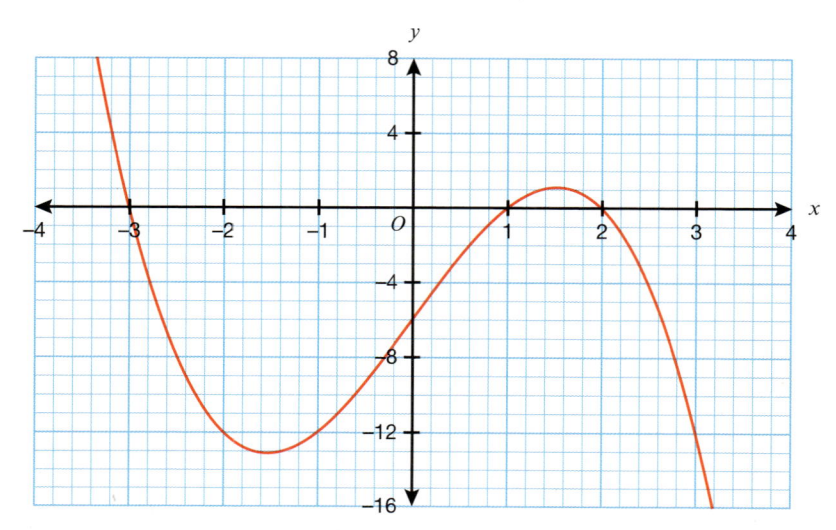

The equation $x^3 - 7x = h$ has three solutions.
(a) Estimate the range of possible values for h.
(b) Use the graph to solve, to 1 d.p., the equation $x^3 - 8x + 2 = 0$
Give the equation of any line you draw on the graph.

E 3 The graph of $y = x^3 - 3x + \frac{1}{x}$, $x \neq 0$ is drawn.

(a) The line $y = \frac{x}{2} - 1$ is added to the graph.

Show that the x values of the intersection of the two graphs are the solutions of
$2x^4 - 7x^2 + 2x + 2 = 0$

(b) Use the graph to solve the equation $2x^4 - 7x^2 + 2x + 2 = 0$, giving answers to 1 d.p.

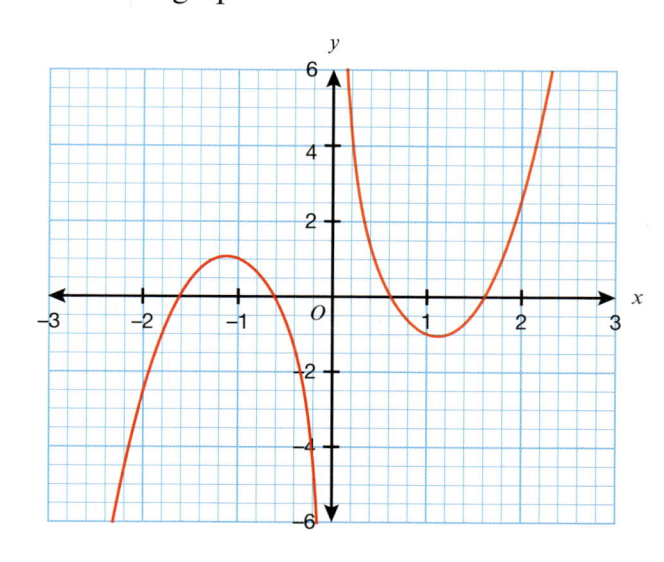

4 The graph of the circle with equation $x^2 + y^2 = 16$ is shown below.

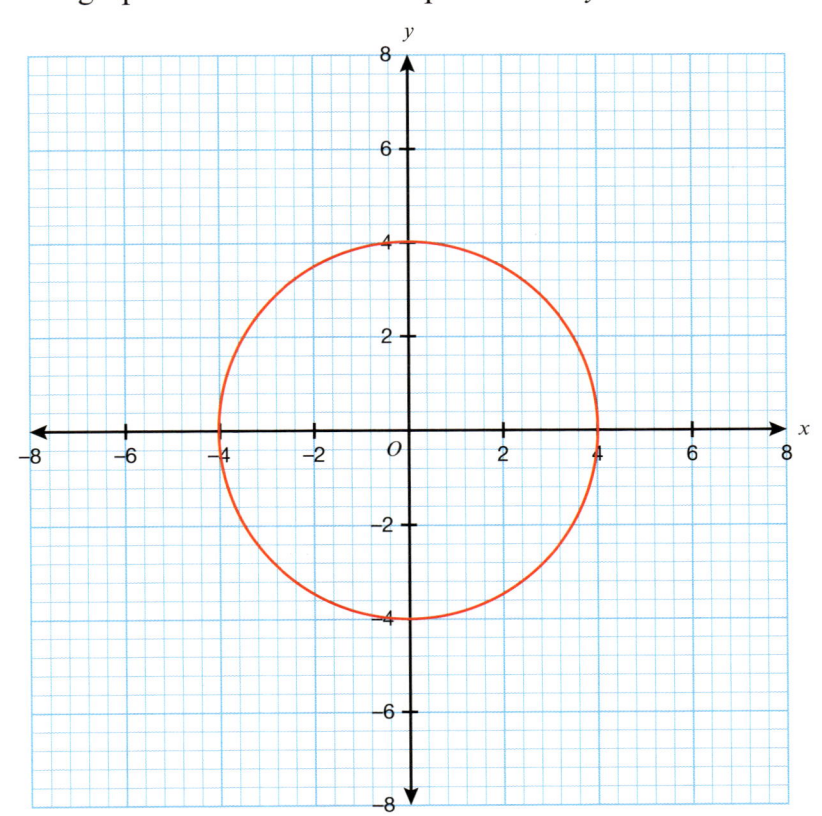

The line $x + y = 2$ is added to the graph.

(a) Show that the x values of the points of intersection of the two graphs are the solutions to the equation $x^2 - 2x - 6 = 0$

(b) Use the graph to solve the equation $x^2 - 2x - 6 = 0$, giving your answers to 1 d.p.

The simultaneous equations $x^2 + y^2 = 16$ and $x + y = a$ have only one solution.

(c) By drawing suitable straight lines on the graph, estimate the values of a, giving your answers to 1 d.p.

5 The graph of $y = 2\cos x$ for $-360° \leq x \leq 360°$ is drawn below:

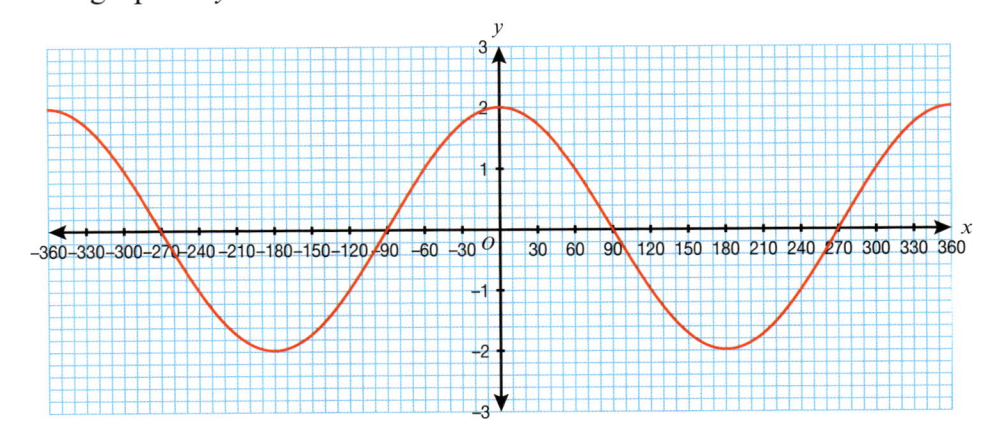

The equation $\cos x + \frac{x}{180} = \frac{1}{2}$ can be solved by finding the points of intersection of the graph of $y = 2\cos x$ with the line L.

(a) Find the equation of the line L, showing clear algebraic working.

(b) Estimate the solutions to the equation $\cos x + \frac{x}{180} = \frac{1}{2}$, giving your answers to the nearest 5°.

UNIT 8 – SHAPE AND SPACE 8

- **VECTOR OPERATIONS**
- **SIMPLE GEOMETRIC PROOFS**
- **VECTOR MODELLING**

SHAPE AND SPACE 8 – BASIC SKILLS EXERCISE

SKILLS
ANALYSIS

Vector operations

1. Given that $\mathbf{u} = \begin{pmatrix} 1 \\ 2 \end{pmatrix}$ and $\mathbf{v} = \begin{pmatrix} -2 \\ 3 \end{pmatrix}$, express **p**, **q**, **r** and **s** as **column vectors** and find their magnitudes where
   (a) $\mathbf{p} = \mathbf{u} + \mathbf{v}$
   (b) $\mathbf{q} = \mathbf{u} - \mathbf{v}$
   (c) $\mathbf{r} = 2\mathbf{u} + 3\mathbf{v}$
   (d) $\mathbf{s} = 3\mathbf{u} - 2\mathbf{v}$

2. Given that $\mathbf{u} = \begin{pmatrix} 3 \\ 1 \end{pmatrix}$, $\mathbf{v} = \begin{pmatrix} 2 \\ 5 \end{pmatrix}$ and $\mathbf{w} = \begin{pmatrix} 0 \\ -4 \end{pmatrix}$, express **p**, **q**, **r** and **s** as column vectors and find their magnitudes where
   (a) $\mathbf{p} = \mathbf{u} + \mathbf{v} + \mathbf{w}$
   (b) $\mathbf{q} = \mathbf{u} - \mathbf{v} - \mathbf{w}$
   (c) $\mathbf{r} = 2\mathbf{u} + 3\mathbf{v} + 4\mathbf{w}$
   (d) $\mathbf{s} = 2(\mathbf{u} - 2\mathbf{v} + 3\mathbf{w})$

3. $\mathbf{p} = \begin{pmatrix} 3 \\ 2 \end{pmatrix}$ and $\mathbf{q} = \begin{pmatrix} 3 \\ -5 \end{pmatrix}$. Find
   (a) (i) $\mathbf{p} + \mathbf{q}$ (ii) $2\mathbf{p} - \mathbf{q}$
   (b) the values of constants m and n such that $m\mathbf{p} + n\mathbf{q} = \begin{pmatrix} 12 \\ -13 \end{pmatrix}$
   (c) the values of constants r and s such that $\mathbf{p} + r\mathbf{q} = \begin{pmatrix} s \\ -8 \end{pmatrix}$
   (d) the values of constants u and v such that $u(\mathbf{p} + \mathbf{q}) + v(2\mathbf{p} - \mathbf{q}) = \begin{pmatrix} 0 \\ 21 \end{pmatrix}$

4. Given that $\mathbf{a} = \begin{pmatrix} 1 \\ 2 \end{pmatrix}$, $\mathbf{b} = \begin{pmatrix} 4 \\ 3 \end{pmatrix}$ and $m\mathbf{a} + n\mathbf{b} = \begin{pmatrix} -2 \\ 1 \end{pmatrix}$, where m and n are constants, find the values of m and n.

SKILLS
PROBLEM SOLVING

Simple geometric proofs

5. OAB is a triangle such that $\vec{OA} = \mathbf{a}$ and $\vec{OB} = \mathbf{b}$ and M is the midpoint of AB.
   Express the following in terms of **a** and **b**.
   (a) $\vec{AB}$
   (b) $\vec{AM}$
   (c) $\vec{OM}$

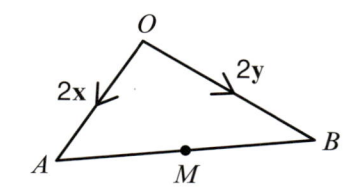

6. OAB is a triangle such that $\vec{OA} = 2\mathbf{x}$ and $\vec{OB} = 2\mathbf{y}$ and $AM : MB = 1 : 1$.
   Express the following in terms of **x** and **y**.
   (a) $\vec{AB}$
   (b) $\vec{AM}$
   (c) $\vec{OM}$

7   $ABCDEF$ is a regular hexagon with centre O. $\overrightarrow{AB} = \mathbf{p}$
    and $\overrightarrow{BC} = \mathbf{q}$. Express the following in terms of $\mathbf{p}$ and $\mathbf{q}$. 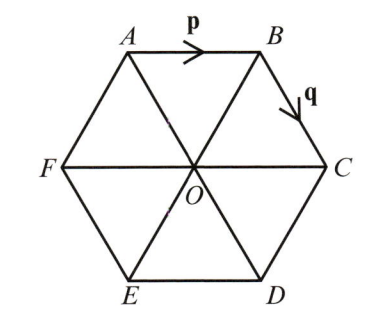
    (a) $\overrightarrow{ED}$
    (b) $\overrightarrow{DE}$
    (c) $\overrightarrow{AC}$
    (d) $\overrightarrow{AE}$

8   OPQ is a triangle. $OR : RP = 2 : 1$ and S is the midpoint
    of OQ. M is the midpoint of PQ. If $\overrightarrow{OR} = \mathbf{r}$ and
    $\overrightarrow{OS} = \mathbf{s}$, express the following in terms of $\mathbf{r}$ and $\mathbf{s}$. 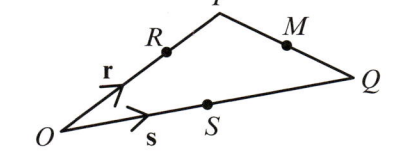
    (a) $\overrightarrow{RS}$
    (b) $\overrightarrow{OP}$
    (c) $\overrightarrow{PQ}$
    (d) $\overrightarrow{OM}$

9   OPQ is a triangle such that $\overrightarrow{OP} = \mathbf{p}$ and $\overrightarrow{OQ} = \mathbf{q}$
    $PR : RQ = 1 : 2$ 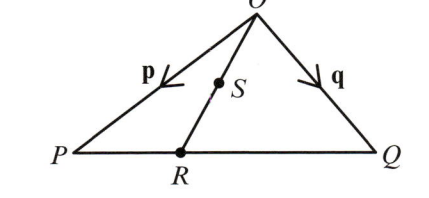
    (a) Express the following in terms of vectors $\mathbf{p}$ and $\mathbf{q}$.
        (i) $\overrightarrow{PQ}$
        (ii) $\overrightarrow{PR}$
        (iii) $\overrightarrow{QR}$
    (b) If $\overrightarrow{OS} = k\,\overrightarrow{OR}$, where k is a constant, and $OS : SR = 3 : 2$, find
        (i) k
        (ii) $\overrightarrow{OS}$ in terms of $\mathbf{p}$ and $\mathbf{q}$

10 OPQ is a triangle such that $\overrightarrow{OP} = \mathbf{p}$ and $\overrightarrow{OQ} = \mathbf{q}$
    $OM : MP = 3 : 2$ and $PN = \frac{2}{5}PQ$ 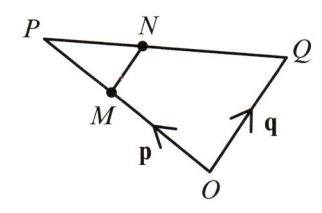
    (a) Express the following in terms of vectors $\mathbf{p}$ and $\mathbf{q}$.
        (i) $\overrightarrow{MP}$
        (ii) $\overrightarrow{PQ}$
        (iii) $\overrightarrow{PN}$
        (iv) $\overrightarrow{MN}$
    (b) How are OQ and MN related?

11 $ABCD$ is a trapezium in which $\overrightarrow{AB} = \mathbf{b}$, $\overrightarrow{BC} = \mathbf{a}$ and $\overrightarrow{AD} = 2\mathbf{a}$. The points P, Q, R and S are the midpoints of the sides AB, BC, CD and AD as shown.

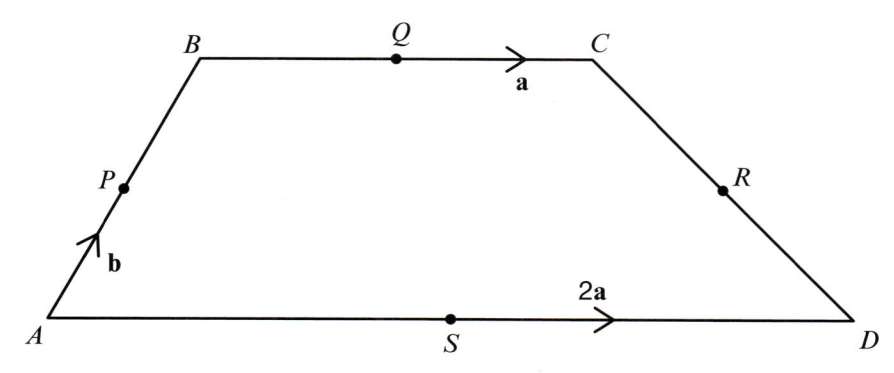

(a) Find and simplify the vectors
   (i) $\overrightarrow{AS}$ (ii) $\overrightarrow{PQ}$ (iii) $\overrightarrow{CD}$ (iv) $\overrightarrow{SR}$

(b) What can be deduced about PQ and SR?

(c) What can be deduced about the quadrilateral $PQRS$?

SKILLS

PROBLEM SOLVING, ANALYSIS

Vector modelling

12 Chen-Jui walks a route described using column vectors **p** and **q**, where the units are in km. $\mathbf{p} = \binom{1}{2}$ and $\mathbf{q} = \binom{-3}{5}$. His journey from O is given by vector **w**, where $\mathbf{w} = 2\mathbf{p} + 3\mathbf{q}$. Find

(a) the vector **w**

(b) the **magnitude** and bearing of **w**

(c) the speed of Chen-Jui's journey from O if he takes 4 hours to complete it

13 $\mathbf{p} = \binom{3}{4}$, $\mathbf{q} = \binom{-2}{1}$

(a) Express the following as column vectors as simply as possible.
   (i) $\mathbf{p} + \mathbf{q}$
   (ii) $3\mathbf{p} - 2\mathbf{q}$

(b) Calculate the magnitude of $\mathbf{p} + \mathbf{q}$.

(c) Calculate the direction of $3\mathbf{p} - 2\mathbf{q}$ as a bearing.

14 The position vector **r** of a comet with respect to an origin O, t seconds after being detected, is given by $\mathbf{r} = \binom{1}{5} + t\binom{1}{-1}$, where the units are in km.

(a) Copy and complete the table for position vector **r**.

t	0	1	2	3	4	5
r	$\binom{1}{5}$	$\binom{3}{4}$				

(b) Plot the path of the comet for $0 \leq t \leq 5$.

(c) Calculate the speed of the comet in km/h and its bearing.

SHAPE AND SPACE 8 – EXAM PRACTICE EXERCISE

SKILLS
CRITICAL THINKING,
PROBLEM SOLVING,
ANALYSIS,
DECISION MAKING

E 1 $\mathbf{a} = \begin{pmatrix} 2 \\ -1 \end{pmatrix}$ and $\mathbf{b} = \begin{pmatrix} -1 \\ 4 \end{pmatrix}$

(a) Find constants m and n such that $m\mathbf{a} - n\mathbf{b} = \begin{pmatrix} 8 \\ -11 \end{pmatrix}$.

(b) $\overrightarrow{OC} = \mathbf{a} - \mathbf{b}$
The y-axis points North.
Point D is 10 units from C on a bearing of 045°.
Show that $\overrightarrow{OD} = \begin{pmatrix} 3 + 5\sqrt{2} \\ 5\sqrt{2} - 5 \end{pmatrix}$

E 2 $\overrightarrow{OA} = \mathbf{a}$ and $\overrightarrow{OB} = \mathbf{b}$ and $AP : PB = m : n$

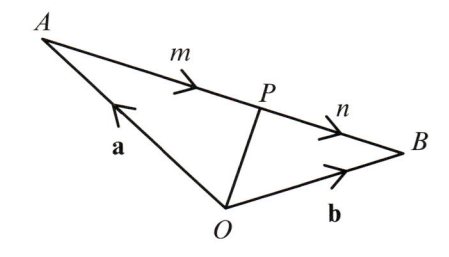

(a) Show that $\overrightarrow{OP} = \dfrac{n\mathbf{a} + m\mathbf{b}}{m + n}$

$\mathbf{a} = \begin{pmatrix} -4 \\ 3 \end{pmatrix}$, $\mathbf{b} = \begin{pmatrix} 2 \\ 1 \end{pmatrix}$ and $AP : PB = 3 : 2$

(b) Show that $|\overrightarrow{OP}| = \sqrt{\dfrac{17}{5}}$

E 3 The position vector $\mathbf{r}$ of a boat with respect to an origin O, t hours after 12:00, is given by $\mathbf{r} = \begin{pmatrix} 1 \\ 2 \end{pmatrix} + t \begin{pmatrix} -1 \\ 2 \end{pmatrix}$, where units are in km.

(a) Find the position vector $\mathbf{r}$ at
 (i) 12:00
 (ii) 16:00
(b) Show that the speed of the boat $= \sqrt{5}$ km/h
Lighthouse L is at $(4, 11)$.
(c) Find the bearing of the boat from L at 15:00 to 3 s.f.

E 4 $\overrightarrow{OA} = \mathbf{a}$ and $\overrightarrow{OB} = \mathbf{b}$
OPQ, AQB and APM are straight lines
$AP : PM = 3 : 1$
M is the midpoint of OB.

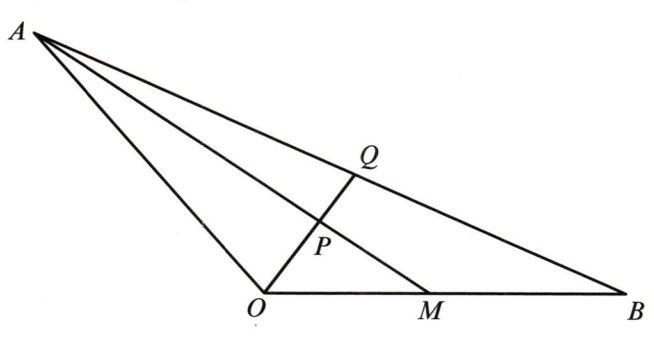

Find the ratio of $AQ : QB$.

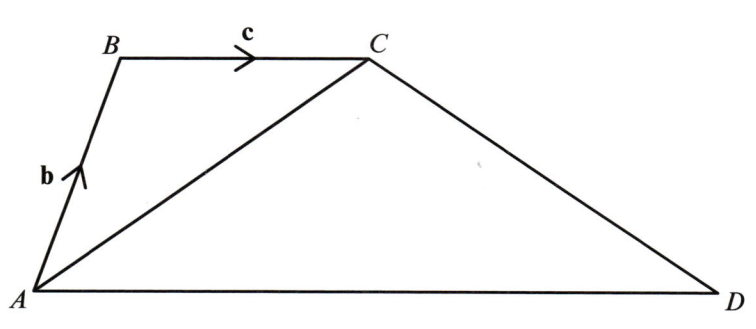

E 5

BC is parallel to AD.
$AD = 3BC$
$\overrightarrow{AB} = \mathbf{b}$, $\overrightarrow{BC} = \mathbf{c}$

(a) Find, in terms of **b** and **c**, the vector $\overrightarrow{CD}$.
Give your answer in its simplest form.

(b) A point P lies on AC such that BPD are **collinear** points.
Find the ratio of $AP : PC$.

(c) If $\mathbf{b} = \binom{4}{1}$ and $\mathbf{c} = \binom{3}{0}$, find $|\overrightarrow{CD}|$.
Give your answer as a surd in its simplest form.

UNIT 8 HANDLING DATA 5

- **MULTIPLICATION (INDEPENDENT EVENTS) AND ADDITION RULES (MUTUALLY EXCLUSIVE EVENTS)**
- **TREE DIAGRAMS (TWO BRANCHES)**

HANDLING DATA 5 – BASIC SKILLS EXERCISE

SKILLS

PROBLEM SOLVING, REASONING

Multiplication (independent events) and addition rules (mutually exclusive events)

1. Ines rolls two dice, adding their scores together.
   She then flips a fair coin to reveal a head or a tail.
   Find the probability that Ines produces
   (a) a score of 7 and a head
   (b) a prime number and a tail
   (c) a head and a square number

2. Seven discs numbered from 1 to 7 are randomly arranged face down, so that the numbers cannot be seen.

   ① ② ③ ④ ⑤ ⑥ ⑦

   Two discs, chosen at random, are turned over.
   What is the probability that the sum of the numbers on these two discs is an odd number?

3. Nine discs numbered from 1 to 9 are randomly arranged face down, so that the numbers cannot be seen.

   ① ② ③ ④ ⑤ ⑥ ⑦ ⑧ ⑨

   Three discs, chosen at random, are turned over.
   What is the probability that the sum of the revealed three numbers is even?

4. Nine cards are marked with a single letter, which is an X, a Y or a Z as shown. The cards are shuffled and then placed on a table face down. Three cards, chosen at random, are then turned over one after the other.

   X X X Y Y Y Z Z Z

   What is the probability that the three cards reveal at least one Z?

5. Scarlett is the captain of her hockey team.
   She wins the pre-match coin toss with a fair coin on at least two occasions out of three matches. Scarlett tells her team that the probability of this happening is 50%.
   Is Scarlett correct?

Tree diagrams (two branches)

6 A fair spinner is spun twice.

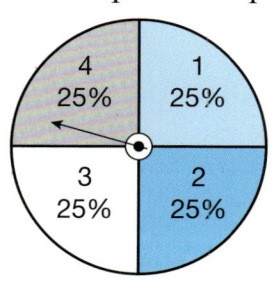

(Spinner divided into 4 equal sectors: 4 (25%), 1 (25%), 3 (25%), 2 (25%))

Use a **tree diagram** to calculate the probability of obtaining
(a) two prime numbers
(b) a prime and a non-prime number
(c) an odd and an even number in that order

7 The probability of Maria serving an ace in a game of tennis is given as $\frac{1}{15}$. She serves twice in succession.
(a) Draw a tree diagram showing all the possibilities.
(b) Find the probability of Maria serving
  (i) two aces
  (ii) no aces
  (iii) one ace

8 Box A contains apples, $\frac{1}{4}$ of which are rotten. Box B contains lemons, $\frac{4}{5}$ of which are good. A box is randomly selected and a piece of fruit is randomly taken.
(a) Draw a tree diagram showing all the possibilities.
(b) Find the probability of obtaining a good apple.
(c) Find the probability of obtaining a bad lemon.

9 Ivor has a $\frac{1}{7}$ probability of catching a cold.
If he catches a cold the probability that he catches a cough is $\frac{1}{3}$
If he does not catch a cold the probability of him not catching a cough is $\frac{3}{4}$
(a) Draw a tree diagram showing all possible outcomes for Ivor.
(b) Find the probability that Ivor
  (i) has a cold and a cough
  (ii) only has a cough
  (iii) has one of the two

HANDLING DATA 5 – EXAM PRACTICE EXERCISE

E 1 The probability of a baby Giant Panda being female is $\frac{4}{7}$
A family of Giant Pandas contains two offspring.
(a) Draw a tree diagram showing all the possibilities.
(b) Find the probability of both babies being male.
(c) Find the probability of the family containing one male and one female baby.

E 2 Ceri is a skilled and very reliable archer.
The probability of her hitting the bullseye (the centre of a target) with one of the arrows that she shoots can be found from the table.
(a) Copy and complete the table and use it to draw a tree diagram to show all possible outcomes.
Ceri shoots two arrows at the target.
(b) Find the probability of Ceri scoring
　(i) two bullseyes
　(ii) one bullseye
　(iii) at least one bullseye

	1st shot	2nd shot
Hits	$\frac{2}{3}$	
Misses		$\frac{1}{5}$

E 3 A toybox contains three teddy bears and two toy kangaroos. Jasper randomly selects one and this is *not* replaced before another is randomly taken out.
(a) Draw a tree diagram to show all possible outcomes for the two selections.
(b) Find the probability that Jasper's two toys are
　(i) two teddy bears
　(ii) a teddy bear and a kangaroo
　(iii) at least one kangaroo

E 4 Dmitri is taking his driving test.
The probability that he will pass the theory test is $\frac{3}{5}$
If he passes the theory test, he then takes the practical test.
The probability that he will pass the practical test is $\frac{1}{3}$
He must pass both tests to pass the driving test.
(a) Draw a probability tree diagram to represent this information.
(b) Hence calculate the probability that Dmitri fails his driving test.
If Dmitri passes his driving test, he can take a further advanced test to reduce the cost of his insurance. The probability that he passes this advanced test is $\frac{1}{4}$
(c) Calculate the probability that Dmitri gets reduced insurance.

E 5 A box contains 20 jewels.
The jewels are either diamonds or rubies.
Amrita randomly selects two jewels from the box without replacement and finds that they are both diamonds.
The probability of this event happening is $\frac{21}{38}$
Calculate
(a) the number of diamonds in the box
(b) the probability that she picks out a diamond and a ruby from the original box of 20 jewels

UNIT 9 NUMBER 9

- **FINANCIAL ARITHMETIC**
- **COMPARATIVE COSTS**

NUMBER 9 – BASIC SKILLS EXERCISE

SKILLS

PROBLEM SOLVING, ADAPTIVE LEARNING

Financial arithmetic

1. Lena buys a laptop computer for $550. Sales tax is then added at 20%. How much does Lena pay for the computer?

2. Zac pays $750, including 20% sales tax, for a new set of golf clubs. How much do the golf clubs cost before sales tax is added?

3. Saskia has her car serviced.
   Her bill, not including sales tax at 20%, is £580.
   Her final bill is £700. Saskia claims she has been overcharged (made to pay too much).
   Is Saskia correct? Justify your answer.

4. Asha employs some skilled workers at the rates shown in the table.

Bricklayer	£25/h
Plumber	£30/h
Electrician	£35/h

   Sales tax is added to each rate at 15%.
   Asha uses each of them for 40 hours.
   Calculate Asha's total bill.

5. Rowena is a landscape gardener who charges €45/h + sales tax at 20%.

   She charges a client €810.
   How many hours did Rowena work?

6 Michelle buys the following items for her photographic business, inclusive of sales tax at 20%.

Digital camera	$1850
Tripod	$240
2 Fluorescent lights	$380 each
Laser printer	$1350

Calculate how much Michelle paid in sales tax.

7 Krisha is paid €24/h for a 35 hour week as an IT technician, with an overtime rate of €30/h.
She works a 42 hour week and has to add sales tax of 17.5% to her bill.
Calculate how much Krisha gets paid for this week's work.

8 Liam is an online tutor who charges
€30/hour from 09:00 to 17:00
€40/hour from 19:00 to 21:00

He has to add a sales tax of 20% to his bill for each client.
One week, Liam tutors Mrs Musk from Monday to Friday from 15:00 for 2 hours per day, plus h hours after 7 pm.
He charges her a total weekly bill of €480.
Find h.

Questions 9–16 are based on the following currency conversion table:

Country	Currency	Rate per UK £1
Australia	Dollar (Aus)	1.77
Brazil	Real	7.02
China	Yuan	8.82
India	Rupee	99.50
Malaysia	Ringitt	5.48
Spain	Euro (€)	1.12
USA	Dollar (US)	1.35

9   Convert £500 into Australian dollars.

10   Convert €1000 into UK pounds.

11   Convert 500 rupees into yuan.

12   Convert $1000 (US) into reais (plural of real).

13   Convert 500 ringitts into yuan.

14   How many UK pounds is a millionaire living in India worth?

15   A Kritsal ultra-high definition TV costs the following in different countries.

Australia	$3765
Brazil	14 040 reais
Spain	€2464

In which country would a British tourist be able to buy this model of TV at the cheapest price?

16   Brad is an American tourist and he has $1000.
He travels through Malaysia, India and China.
He wishes to convert all of his money to the country he is travelling through in the ratio 1 : 1 : 3 respectively.
How much of each currency will Brad have?

Comparative costs

17 Which curry powder is the better value:
Jar A: 125 g at £3.75, or Jar B: 75 g at £2.25?

18 Which wall tiles are the better value:
Square: 10 m² for €250, or
Octagonal: 25 m² for €600?

19 Which 12 volt battery is the better value:
Everamp, for £3.60, which lasts 72 hours, or
Dynamo, for £5.25, which lasts 126 hours?

20 Which bag of rice is the better value?

White rice: 5 kg costing $9.50
Brown rice: 12 kg costing $21

NUMBER 9 – EXAM PRACTICE EXERCISE

E 1 Aria, Blake and Chloe shared €1750 between them.
Blake received 25% of Aria's amount.
Chloe got 25% more than Aria.
Calculate how much each of them received.

E 2 Kofi bought 24 boxes of lemonade.
He paid €36 for each box.
Each box contained 3024 bottles of lemonade.
He sold $\frac{2}{3}$ of the bottles for €1.80 each.
The remainder were sold at a discounted price.
Kofi made a profit of 25% overall.
Calculate how much each reduced bottle of lemonade was sold for.

E 3 Frances travels from the UK to three countries: Malaysia, India and China.
She has £7200 to convert and wishes to do so in the ratio of 1 : 2 : 3 for each country she is travelling through respectively.
The conversion rates at the airport are given as

Country	Currency	Rate per UK £1
Malaysia	Ringitt	5.48
India	Rupee	99.50
China	Yuan	8.82

(a) Calculate how much of each currency she will have for each country in her journey.

On her return journey from China, she has 25% of her yuan left.
She wishes to stop off in France.

(b) If 1€ = 8 yuan, how many euros can Frances buy?

E 4 Two mobile phone companies advertise the following rates.
Tangerine: 1 phone costing $25 and a call rate of $0.35/min.
Aardvark: 1 phone costing $90 and a call rate of $0.30/min.
Charges must have sales tax added at 17.5%.
Show that for a 24 hour period of calls Aardvark is cheaper by $p and write down the value of p.

E 5 The prices of 1 kg of two precious metals are shown in the table.

	Gold	Silver
1 January 2021	£44 940	£s
1 July 2021	£g	£600

(a) The price of gold rose by $2\frac{1}{2}$% in the first six months of 2021.
Calculate g.
(b) The price of silver fell by 4% in the first six months of 2021.
Calculate s.

Overall, in 2021 the price of gold fell by $2\frac{1}{2}$%, while the price of silver rose by 4%.
(c) Calculate the total cost of purchasing 500 g of each metal on 1 January 2022.

UNIT 9 ALGEBRA 9

- **SIMULTANEOUS EQUATIONS WITH ONE LINEAR AND ONE NON-LINEAR**
- **PROOF BY COUNTER EXAMPLE**
- **NUMBER PROOFS**
- **PROOFS USING COMPLETING THE SQUARE**
- **OTHER PROOFS**

ALGEBRA 9 – BASIC SKILLS EXERCISE

SKILLS
ANALYSIS

Simultaneous equations with one linear and one non-linear

For **questions 1–8**, solve the simultaneous equations algebraically, giving answers to 3 s.f. if appropriate.

1. $y = 8 - x$
   $y = x^2 - 4$

2. $2x = 3y$
   $x^2 + y^2 = 13$

3. $2y = x - 1$
   $x = y^2 - 3y + 5$

4. $x + y = 5$
   $xy = 6$

5. $x + 2y = 3$
   $x^2 + 2y^2 = 3$

6. $x - y = 2$
   $x^2 + xy - y^2 = 5$

7. $x + y = 5$
   $\frac{6}{y} - \frac{6}{x} = 4$

8. $x - y = 2$
   $\frac{x}{y} + \frac{y}{x} = 3$

9. A food parcel is dropped from a low flying airplane flying over sloping ground.

The path of the food parcel is given by $y = 42 + 0.2x - 0.005x^2$
The gradient of the ground is given by $y = 0.2x$
All units are in metres.
Find algebraically the coordinates of where the food parcel lands.

10 An egg is in an egg cup, resting on a table.

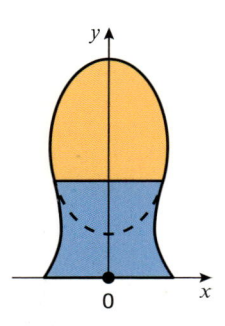

The equation of the outline of the egg is $2x^2 + y^2 - 12y + 24 = 0$
The units are in cm and the origin is as shown.
The egg cup is 4 cm high.
Find algebraically the radius of the top of the egg cup in cm.

11 Show that the line $y = 8 - 2x$ and the curve $y = 3 + 2x - x^2$ do not intersect.
Show clear algebraic working.

12 For what values of k is the line $x + y = k$ a tangent to the circle $x^2 + y^2 = 25$?

Proof by counter example

13 Nathan says that $2^p - 1$ is always a prime number when p is a positive integer greater than 1.
Find a counter example to prove Nathan wrong.

14 Find a counter example to disprove that $x^2 = x$ implies that $x = 1$

15 Find a counter example to disprove $n^3 - n^2 - 1$ is prime when n is a positive integer greater than 1.

16 Find a counter example to show that $a^2 = b^2$ implies that $a = b$ is false.

Number proofs

17 Prove that the difference between any two odd integers is always even.

18 Prove that when the sum of three consecutive odd integers is divided by 6 it leaves a remainder of 3.

19 An arithmetic series starts 1, 3, 5, 7, ….
Prove that the sum to n terms is always a square number.

20 Prove that the sum of n consecutive integers is divisible by n if n is odd.

21 Prove that the product of three consecutive odd integers is odd.

22 The product of two consecutive integers is added to the larger of the two integers.
Prove that the result is always a square number.

23 Prove that when the square of any odd integer is divided by 4 the remainder is 1.

24 Prove that the difference between the squares of any two odd integers is a multiple of 8.

25 Prove that the difference between the squares of two consecutive integers is equal to the sum of the consecutive integers.

SKILLS
ANALYSIS

Proofs using completing the square

26 Prove that $x^2 - 8x + 17 > 0$ for all real values of x.

27 Prove that $6x - 9 - x^2 \leq 0$ for all real values of x.

28 Prove that $2x^2 + 73 > 24x$ for all real values of x.

29 Prove $(x - 1)^2 + 3x(x + 2) \geq 0$ for all real values of x.

30 $x^2 + 14x + c \geq 0$ for all values of x.
    Find the range of values of c.

31 $x^2 + bx + 4 \geq 0$ for all values of x.
    Find the range of values of b.

SKILLS
ANALYSIS

Other proofs

32 Given a is a positive integer, show that $\sqrt{2a}(\sqrt{18a} + \sqrt{2a})$ is always a multiple of 8.

33 $2^{127} - 1$ is a prime number.
    Show that $2^{127} - 2$ is a multiple of 6.

34 Prove that the quadratic equation $x^2 + 2\sqrt{c}x + c = 0$ only has one solution.

35 The 3-digit number abc equals $100a + 10b + c$
    For example, $358 = (3 \times 100) + (5 \times 10) + 8$
    Prove that if $c = 5$ then abc is divisible by 5.

36 abc is a 3-digit number.
    Prove that if $a + c = b$ then abc is divisible by 11.

37 The nth term of a series is given by $n^2 - 6n + 10$
    Prove that the difference between successive terms is an odd number.

ALGEBRA 9 – EXAM PRACTICE EXERCISE

E 1 The graph shows the curve $y = x^2 - 2x + 2$ and the line $y = 4 - x$

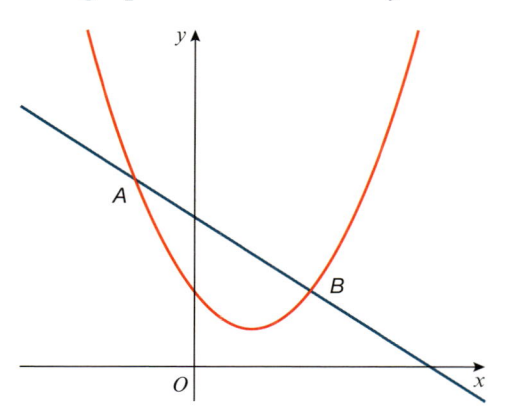

The curve and the line intersect at $A(-1, 5)$ and $B(2, 2)$.
The perpendicular bisector of AB meets the curve at C and D.
Find the coordinates of C and D, showing clear algebraic working.

Express your answers in the form $\dfrac{p \pm \sqrt{q}}{r}$ where p, q and r are integers.

E 2 The diagram shows a circle intersected by straight lines AB and AC.

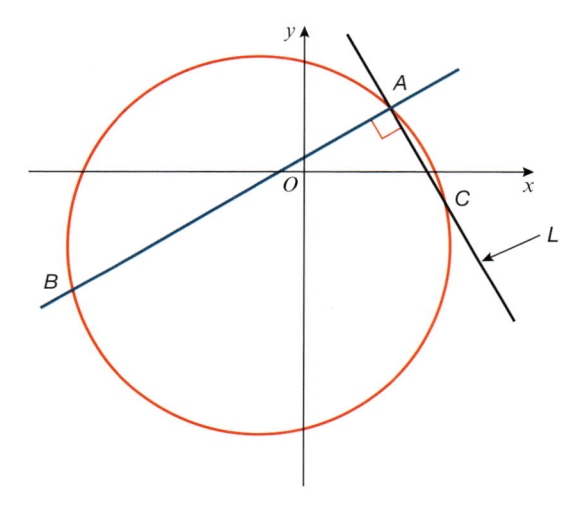

The equation of the circle is
$x^2 + y^2 + 2x + 4y = 20$
A is $(3, 1)$ and B is $(-5.8, -3.4)$.
The straight line L that passes through A and C is perpendicular to AB.
(a) Show that the equation of L is $2x + y = 7$
(b) Show that the coordinates of C are $(3.8, -0.6)$.
(c) Hence find the coordinates of the centre of the circle.

E 3 Zara is designing a pendant.

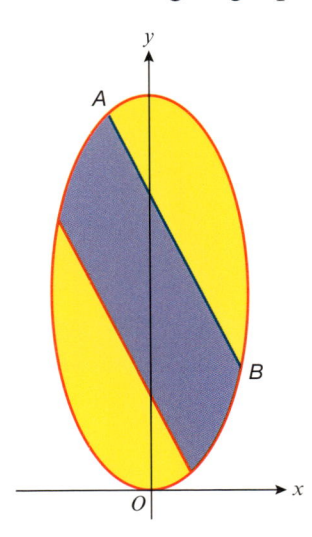

The equation of the curved outline is $4x^2 + y^2 - 4y = 0$
The equation of the line AB is $2x + y = 3$
The units are centimetres.

(a) Show that $AB = \frac{\sqrt{35}}{2}$ cm.

A cylindrical gold wire with diameter 1 mm and length $\frac{\sqrt{35}}{2}$ cm is to be placed along AB.
Gold costs £60 per gram.
The density of gold is 19.3 g/cm³.
(b) Calculate the cost of the gold wire.
Give your answer correct to 3 s.f.

E 4 (a) Prove that when any odd integer is squared, the result is one more than a multiple of 8.
(b) a and b are both integers greater than zero.
$a^2 - b^2$ is a prime number.
Prove that
(i) a and b are consecutive integers
(ii) $a + b$ is a prime number

E 5 An arithmetic series S has a first term of 2 and a common difference of 4.
(a) Prove algebraically that the sum of S to n terms is double a square number.
A new series is formed by squaring each term of S and adding 12.
(b) Prove that each term of the new series is divisible by 16.

UNIT 9 GRAPHS 8

- TANGENTS TO CURVES
- INTERPRETING TANGENTS
- TRANSFORMING GRAPHS

GRAPHS 8 – BASIC SKILLS EXERCISE

Tangents to curves

Questions 1–4 refer to the graph shown. Find estimates of the gradients by drawing tangents to the graph.

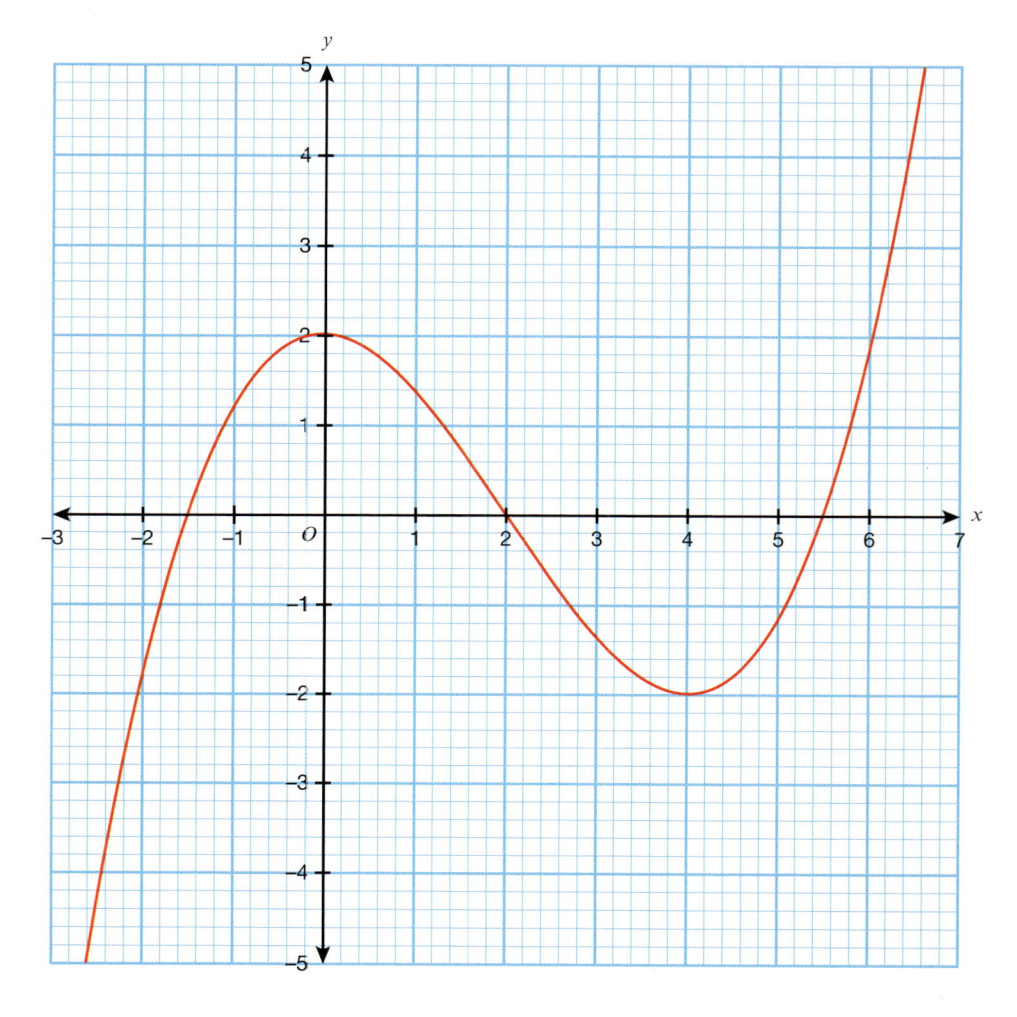

1. **(a)** Estimate the gradient when
    - (i) $x = 1$
    - (ii) $x = -1$
   (b) Estimate the points where the gradient is equal to
    - (i) -1
    - (ii) 2
    - (iii) 0

2   The curve passes through the point (3, −1.4).
   (a) Estimate the gradient at this point.
   (b) Find the equation of the tangent at this point.

3   The line $y = mx + 3$ is a tangent to the curve.
   Estimate the two possible values of m.

4   The line $y = k - x$ is a tangent to the curve.
   Estimate the two possible values of k.

SKILLS

ANALYSIS, INTERPRETATION

Interpreting tangents

5   Galileo is rolling a ball down a gentle slope.
   He finds the distance, d m, after t seconds is given by $d = 0.25t^2$
   (a) Plot an accurate graph of d against t for $0 \leq t \leq 4$
   (b) By drawing tangents, copy and complete the table giving the velocity, v m/s, after t s.

t (s)	0	1	2	3	4
v (m/s)		0.5			

   (c) Plot a graph of v against t for $0 \leq t \leq 4$
   (d) Estimate the acceleration in m/s².

6   Pedro is exercising his horse. The horse's distance, d m, from the starting point after t seconds is given by $d = \frac{t^3}{5} - 2t^2 + 5t$ for $0 \leq t \leq 8$
   (a) (i) Copy and complete the table, giving values to 2 s.f.
       (ii) Plot an accurate graph of d against t for $0 \leq t \leq 8$

t	0	1	2	3	4	5	6	7	8
d			3.6	2.4			1.2	5.6	

   (b) Describe the horse's run for $0 \leq t \leq 8$
   (c) Estimate the horse's velocity in m/s after
       (i) 1 s   (ii) 3 s
   (d) Estimate when the horse's velocity was 6 m/s.

7   The velocity, v m/s, of a skydiver after t seconds is given by $v = 10t - t^2$ for $0 \leq t \leq 5$

   (a) Draw an accurate graph of v against t for $0 \leq t \leq 5$
   (b) Estimate the acceleration in m/s² of the skydiver after
       (i) 1 s   (ii) 3 s
   (c) Estimate when the skydiver's acceleration was 5 m/s².

8 Aarav fills a flower vase with water to a depth of 20 cm.
   The level of water drops every day by 15% due to evaporation.
   (a) (i) Copy and complete the table, giving values correct to 3 s.f.
       (ii) Plot an accurate graph of d against t for $0 \leq t \leq 8$

t (days)	0	1	2	3	4	5	6	7	8
d (cm)	20		14.5					6.41	

   (b) How long does it take for the water level to drop by half?
   (c) Estimate the rate
       (i) in cm per day that the water level is dropping when $t = 2$
       (ii) in **cm per hour** that the water level is dropping when $t = 6$

Transforming graphs

9 The graph shows the function $y = f(x)$ with a maximum point at (1, 2).

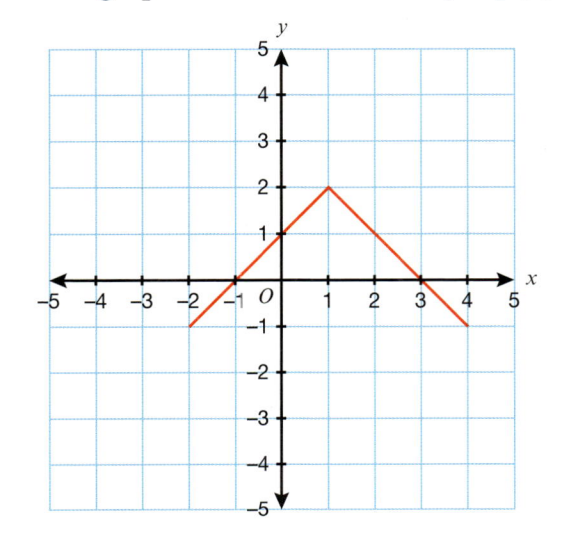

   Find the maximum point and sketch the graph of
   (a) $y = f(x) + 2$ (b) $y = f(x + 2)$ (c) $y = 2f(x)$ (d) $y = f(2x)$

10 The graph shows the function $y = f(x)$ with a **minimum point** at (−2, −2).

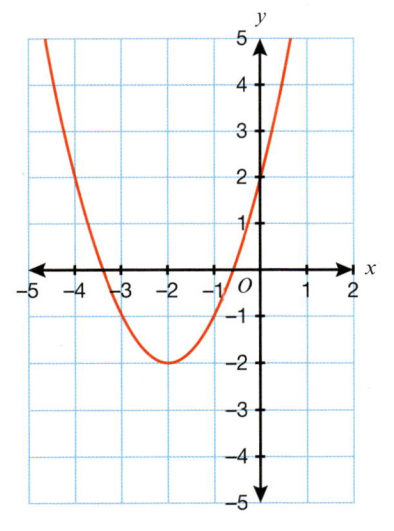

   Find the **turning points** of the following.
   (a) $y = -f(x)$ (b) $y = f(-x)$ (c) $y = \frac{1}{2}f(x)$ (d) $y = f\left(\frac{x}{2}\right)$

11 The graph shows $y = f(x)$ and a transformation of $y = f(x)$

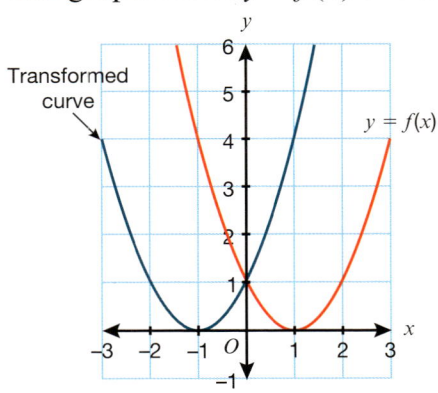

Give **two** possible equations in terms of $f(x)$ for the transformed curve.

12 The graph shows $y = 4 - x^2$ and a translation of the graph by $\begin{pmatrix} 1 \\ 0 \end{pmatrix}$.

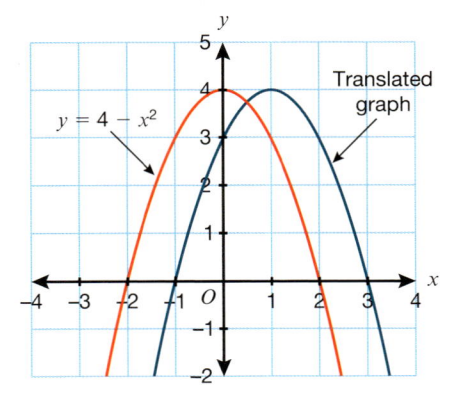

Find the equation of the translated graph in the form $y = -x^2 + bx + c$

13 Owen is designing a vase.

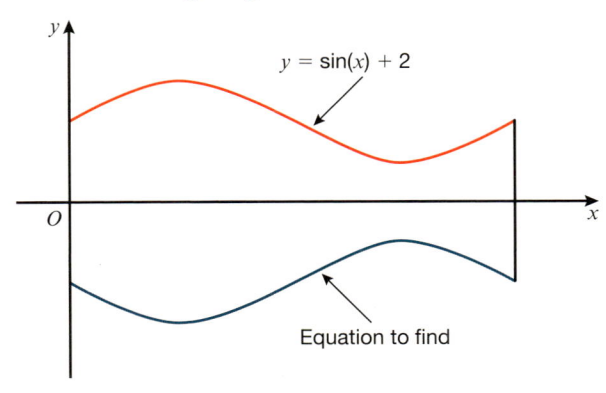

He chose $y = \sin(x) + 2$ with domain $0 \leq x \leq 360°$ as the equation to put into his computer drawing program.
The other shape is a reflection of $y = \sin(x) + 2$ in the x-axis.
Find the equation of the other shape.

14 The graph $y = x^2$ is translated by $\begin{pmatrix} -2 \\ 0 \end{pmatrix}$.

(a) Find the equation of the translated curve in the form $y = x^2 + bx + c$
The translated curve is then reflected in the y-axis.
(b) Find the equation of the reflected curve in the form $y = x^2 + dx + e$
(c) Sketch the reflected curve, stating the coordinates of the turning point.

15 Here is a sketch of $y = f(x)$ which intersects the y-axis at $(0, k)$.

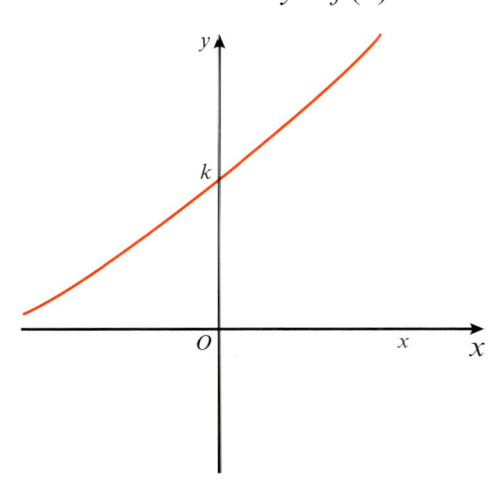

Give the coordinates of the points, in terms of k, where the following curves intersect the y-axis.

(a) $y = f\left(\dfrac{x}{2}\right)$ (b) $y = -2f(x)$ (c) $y = f(x) - 2$

16 $f(x) = kx$

Find the gradients, in terms of k, of the following graphs.

(a) $y = f(x) + 2$ (b) $y = f(2x)$ (c) $y = 2f(x)$ (d) $y = f(x + 2)$

17 $f(x) = mx + 1$

Find the gradients, in terms of m, of the following graphs.

(a) $y = f(-x)$ (b) $y = -f(x)$ (c) $y = f\left(\dfrac{x}{2}\right)$ (d) $y = 2f\left(\dfrac{x}{2}\right)$

18 $f(x) = x + p$

Find the y-intercept, in terms of p, of the following graphs.

(a) $y = f(x) - 3$ (b) $y = f(-3x)$ (c) $y = 3f(x)$ (d) $y = f(3x)$

19 The graph $y = f(x)$ has a turning point at $(6, 3)$.
 (a) The turning point of $y = f(x + a)$ is $(3, 3)$.
   What is the value of a?
 (b) The turning point of $y = f(bx)$ is $(3, 3)$.
   What is the value of b?
 (c) The turning point of $y = cf(x)$ is $(6, -3)$.
   What is the value of c?

20 (a) The point P is the only turning point on $y = f(x)$
   The point $Q\,(-2, 4)$ is the only turning point on $y = f(3x)$
   Find the coordinates of P.
 (b) The point R is the only turning point on $y = g(x)$
   The point $S(1, -3)$ is the only turning point on $y = g(-x)$
   Find the coordinates of R.

GRAPHS 8 – EXAM PRACTICE EXERCISE

SKILLS
PROBLEM SOLVING, ANALYSIS, INTERPRETATION

E 1 The graph of $y = \cos x$ for $0 \leq x \leq 360°$ is drawn.

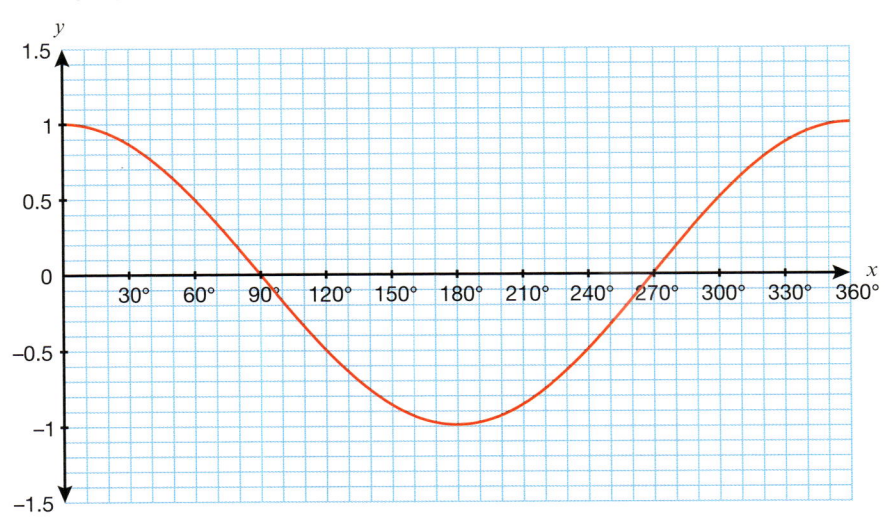

(a) By drawing a tangent, estimate the gradient m at the point where $x = 60°$.
(b) Use the symmetries of the curve to estimate the point where the gradient is $-m$.
(c) By drawing tangents, estimate the x values where the gradient is equal to $\frac{1}{100}$.
(d) State the x values where the gradient of $y = \cos x$ is equal to $\frac{1}{100}$ when $360° \leq x \leq 720°$.

E 2 The graph shows an ellipse.

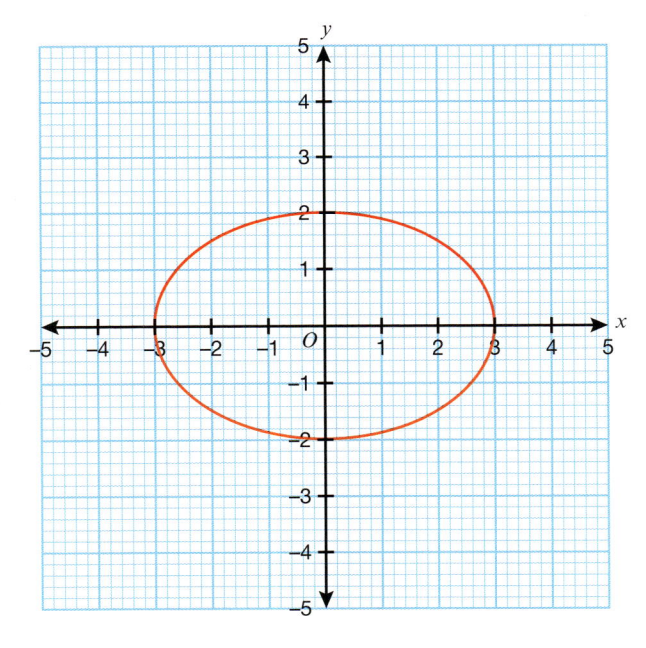

(a) $y = \frac{x}{2} + C$ is a tangent to the ellipse.
By drawing tangents, estimate the possible values of C.

(b) $y = mx - 4$ is a tangent to the ellipse.
By drawing tangents, estimate the possible values of m.

E 3 The graph of $y = f(x)$ is drawn.
The graph passes through the point $P(3, 2)$.

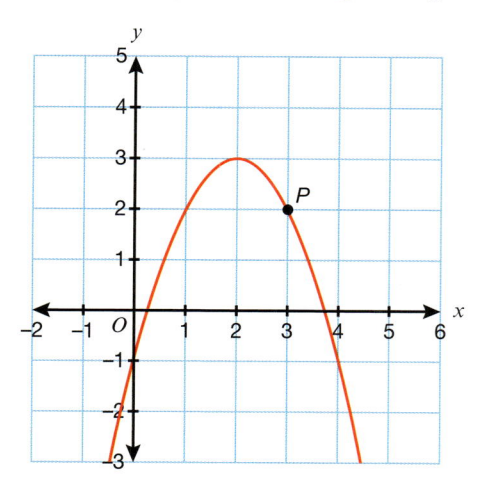

(a) By drawing a tangent, estimate the gradient at point P.
(b) Find the coordinates of the new position of P and the new gradient at P when the graph of $y = f(x)$ is transformed to the graph of
  (i) $y = f(ax)$ **(ii)** $y = f(x + a)$ **(iii)** $y = af(x)$ **(iv)** $y = f(-x)$
Give your answers in terms of a if necessary.

E 4 A particle is being accelerated in a physics experiment.
The graph shows the distance, d m, that the particle has moved after t seconds.

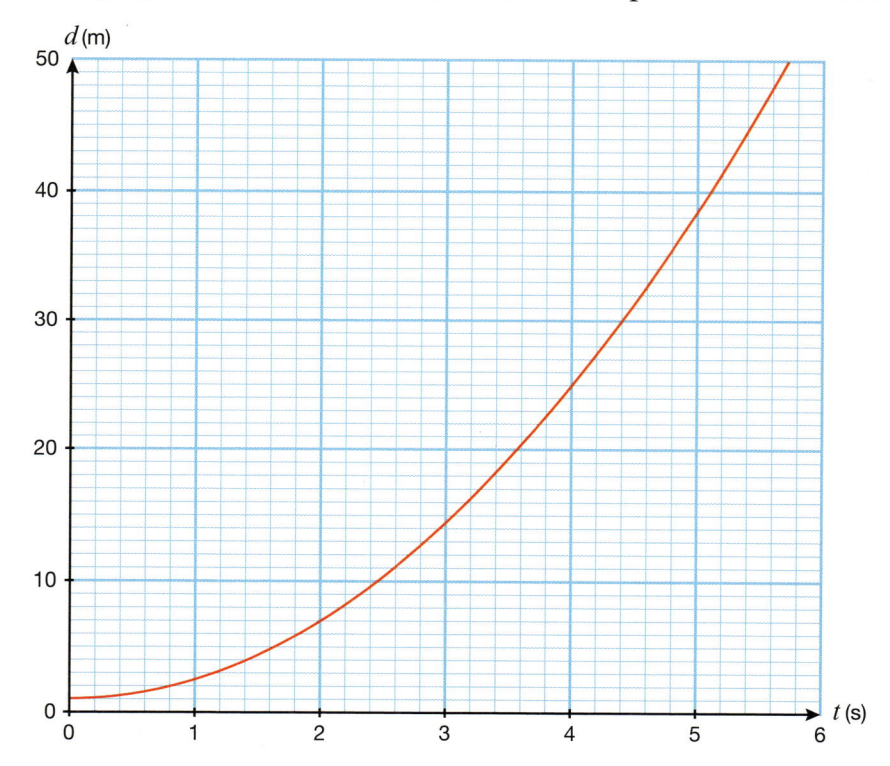

(a) Use the graph to complete the table, giving the velocity of the particle after t s.
Give values to 2 s.f.

t (s)	1	2	3	4	5
v (m/s)					

(b) Plot a graph showing v (m/s) against t (s) for $1 \leq t \leq 5$
(c) Estimate the acceleration of the particle in m/s².

E 5 (a) The graph shows $y = f(x)$

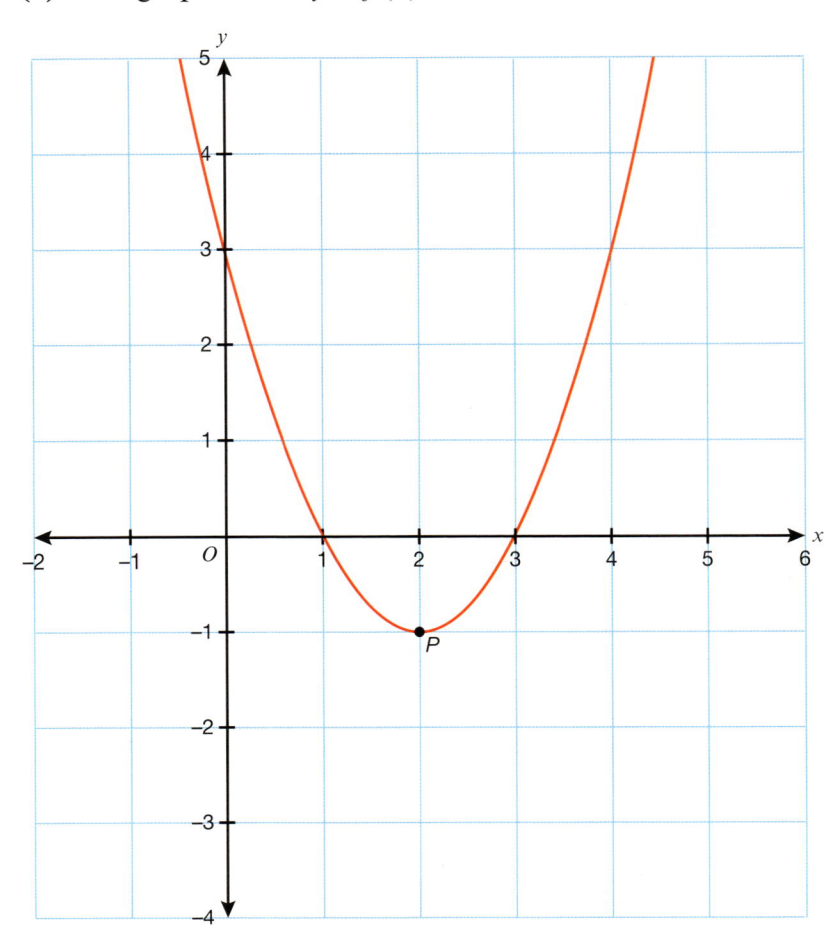

The only turning point of $y = f(x)$ is at $P(2, -1)$.
On copies of the grid, **sketch** the following curves, stating the coordinates of the turning points.

(i) $y = f(x - 2)$ (ii) $y = f\left(\frac{x}{2}\right)$ (iii) $y = -f(x)$

(b) The graph $y = 2 + g(-x)$ has one turning point at $(5, 3)$.
Find the turning point of $y = g(x)$

UNIT 9 SHAPE AND SPACE 9

- **TRIGONOMETRIC GRAPHS**
- **SINE RULE AND COSINE RULE**
- **AREA OF A TRIANGLE**

SHAPE AND SPACE 9 – BASIC SKILLS EXERCISE

SKILLS
ANALYSIS, INTERPRETATION

Trigonometric graphs

1. $f(x) = \sin(x)$ with domain $0 \leq x \leq 360°$.
   Point A is the maximum point on the curve $f(x)$.
   Write down the image of A on the curve $10f(x)$.

2. $g(x) = \cos(x)$ with domain $0 \leq x \leq 360°$.
   Point A is the minimum point on the curve $g(x)$.
   Write down the image of A on the curve $g(x) + 10$.

3. $h(x) = \tan(x)$ with domain $0 \leq x \leq 360°$, $(x \neq 90°$ or $270°)$.
   Point $A(45°, 1)$ lies on the curve $h(x)$.
   Write down the image of A on the curve $10h(x - 135°)$.

4. Solve $\sin(x) = \frac{\sqrt{3}}{2}$ for $0 \leq x \leq 360°$.

5. Solve $\cos(x) = \frac{1}{2}$ for $0 \leq x \leq 360°$.

6. Solve $\tan(x) = 1$ for $0 \leq x \leq 360°$.

SKILLS
DECISION MAKING

Sine rule and cosine rule

For **questions 7–12**, find the side marked with the letter a.
Write your answers correct to 3 s.f.

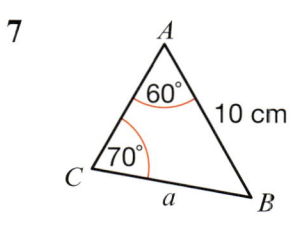

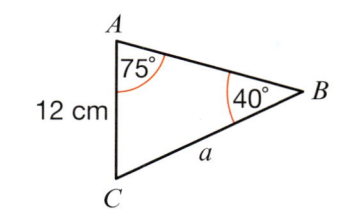

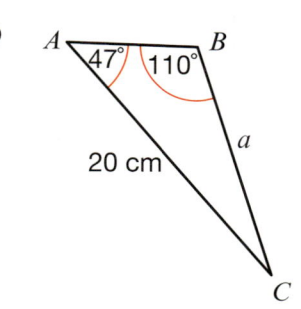

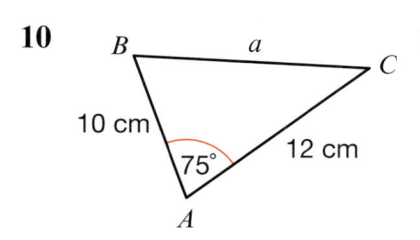

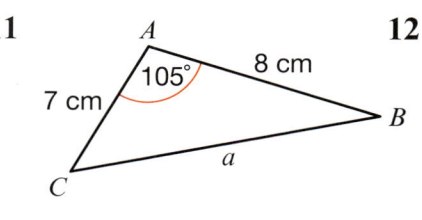

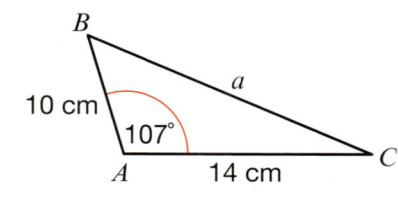

7. Triangle with angle $A = 60°$, angle $C = 70°$, side $AB = 10$ cm, side $CB = a$.

8. Triangle with angle $A = 75°$, angle $B = 40°$, side $AC = 12$ cm, side $CB = a$.

9. Triangle with angle $A = 47°$, angle $B = 110°$, side $AC = 20$ cm, side $BC = a$.

10. Triangle with angle $A = 75°$, side $AB = 10$ cm, side $AC = 12$ cm, side $BC = a$.

11. Triangle with angle $A = 105°$, side $AC = 7$ cm, side $AB = 8$ cm, side $CB = a$.

12. Triangle with angle $A = 107°$, side $AB = 10$ cm, side $AC = 14$ cm, side $BC = a$.

SHAPE AND SPACE 9   195

For **questions 13–18**, find angle *A*. Write your answers correct to 3 s.f.

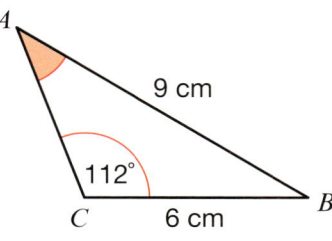

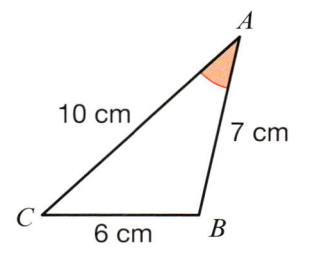

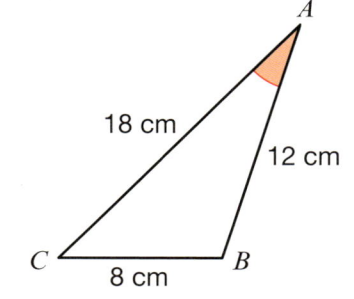

13 Triangle with B = 65°, BC = 12 cm, AC = 15 cm, find angle A.

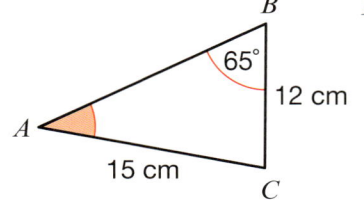

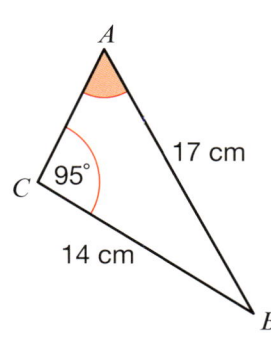

14 Triangle with C = 112°, AC (to B) = 9 cm, CB = 6 cm, find angle A.

15 Triangle with C = 95°, CA = 17 cm, CB = 14 cm, find angle A.

16 Triangle with CA = 10 cm, AB = 7 cm, CB = 6 cm, find angle A.

17 Triangle with CA = 18 cm, AB = 12 cm, CB = 8 cm, find angle A.

18 Triangle with AB = 22 cm, BC = 20 cm, AC = 18 cm, find angle A.

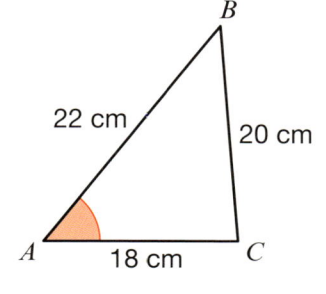

19 Find side *a* and angle *C* for

(a) Triangle with AB = 10 m, AC = 14 m, angle B = 110°, side *a* opposite A.

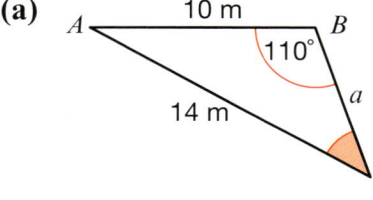

(b) Triangle with AB = 5 m, BC = 7 m, angle B = 80°, side *a* = BC.

SKILLS
ANALYSIS

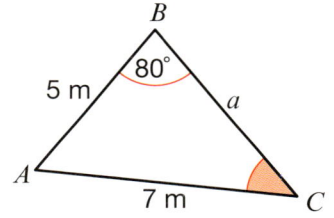

Area of a triangle

20 Find the area of each triangle *ABC* to 3 s.f.

(a) Triangle with AC = 14 m, CB = 10 m, angle C = 80°.

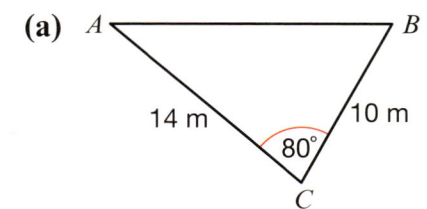

(b) Triangle with AC = 12 m, CB = 20 m, angle C = 85°.

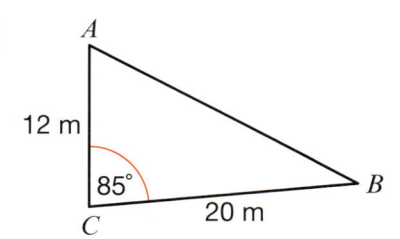

21 The area of triangle *ABC* is 250 m².
Angle *A* is greater than 90°.
Find the perimeter in m to 3 s.f.

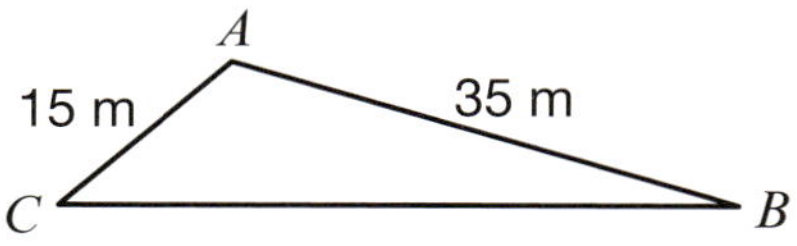

Triangle with CA = 15 m, AB = 35 m.

22 The area of an equilateral triangle is equal to the area of a circle with circumference 6π cm.
The perimeter of the triangle is *p* cm.
Show that $p = 2 \times 3^m \times n$, where *m* and *n* are constants to be found.

SHAPE AND SPACE 9 – EXAM PRACTICE EXERCISE

1 $f(x) = \sin(x)$ with domain $0 \leq x \leq 360°$.
The points P and Q on $f(x)$ are given as $(90°, 1)$ and $(180°, 0)$ respectively.

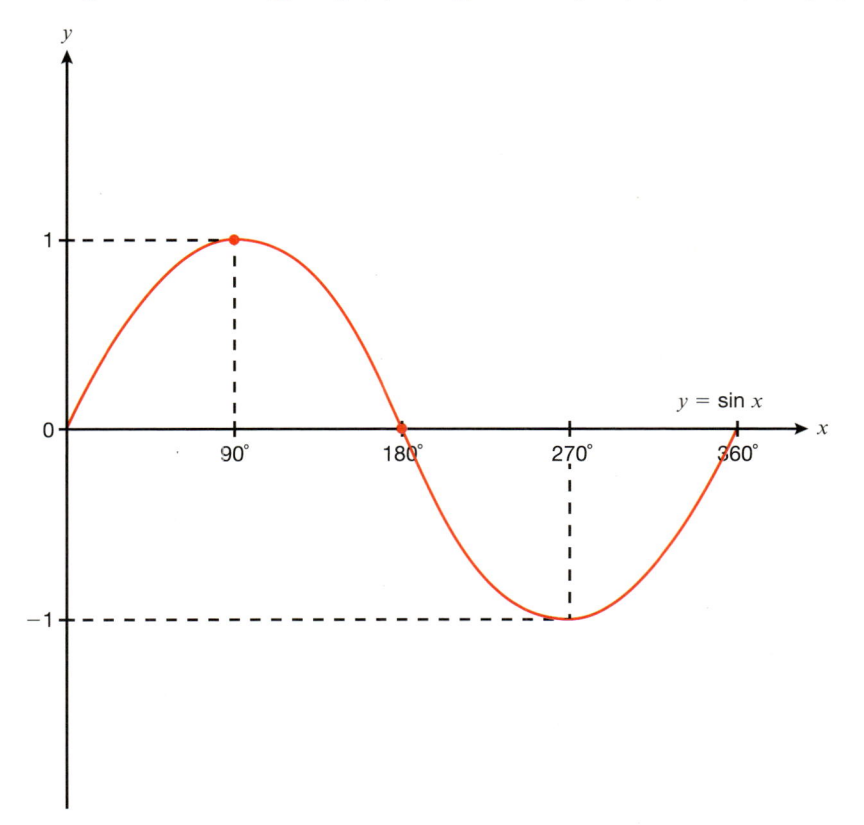

(a) Write down the equation for each function and the coordinates of P and Q after the following transformations.
 (i) $2f(x)$
 (ii) $-f(x)$
 (iii) $-2f(2x) + 2$

(b) Point R on $f(x)$ is transformed by $2f(-x)$ to $(-30°, 1)$.
Find the coordinates of R.

2 A circular clock face, centre O, has a minute hand OA and an hour hand OB.
$OA = 10$ cm
$OB = 7$ cm

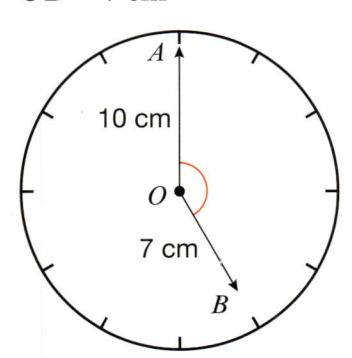

Calculate the length of AB correct to 3 s.f. at
(a) 05:00
(b) 17:50

E 3 *LMNP* is a quadrilateral.

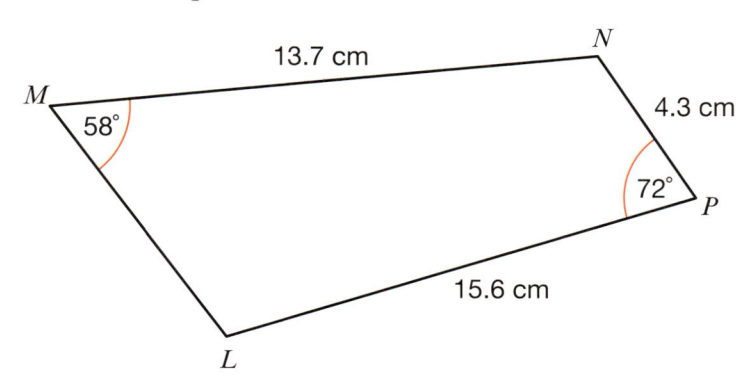

MN = 13.7 cm *NP* = 4.3 cm *LP* = 15.6 cm
angle *LMN* = 58° angle *NPL* = 72°
Calculate the area of quadrilateral *LMNP* in cm² to 3 s.f.

E 4 Here is a shape *ABCDE*.

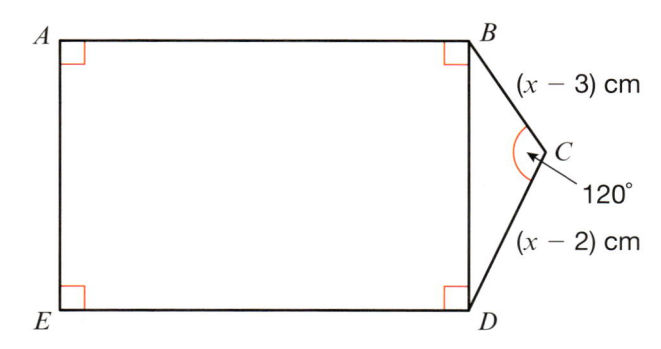

ABDE is a rectangle in which *AB* = 2*BD*
BCD is a triangle in which angle *BCD* = 120°
BC = (*x* – 3) cm and *CD* = (*x* – 2) cm
The area of rectangle *ABDE* = 14 cm²
Show that the perimeter of the shape *ABCDE* = 5 √7 + 3 cm

E 5 The sides of a triangle *PQR* are tangents to a circle.
The tangents touch the circle at the points *S*, *T* and *U*.
QS = 6 cm and *PS* = 7 cm

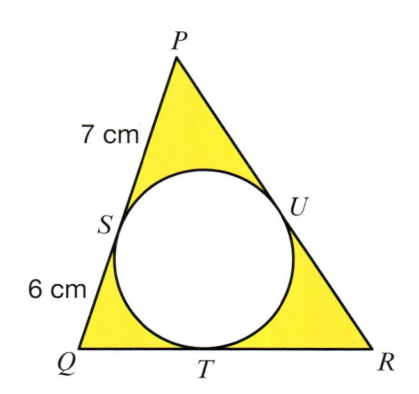

The perimeter of triangle *PQR* is 42 cm.
Calculate the shaded area in cm² to 3.s.f.

UNIT 9 HANDLING DATA 6

- **CONSTRUCTING AND INTERPRETING HISTOGRAMS (UNEQUAL CLASSES)**

HANDLING DATA 6 – BASIC SKILLS EXERCISE

SKILLS
ANALYSIS, INTERPRETATION

Constructing and interpreting histograms (unequal classes)

1 Copy and complete the following table showing the time in minutes that a group of 90 school children spent reading on a particular day.

Time, t (min)	$10 < t \leq 20$	$20 < t \leq 25$	$25 < t \leq 30$	$30 < t \leq 40$	$40 < t \leq 50$	$50 < t \leq 70$	$70 < t \leq 95$
Frequency	7	15	25		12		
Frequency density			5	1.8		0.4	

2 In an experiment the lengths of 80 daisy stalks were measured. The results are shown in the table.
   (a) Construct a histogram for these results.
   (b) Calculate an estimate of the number of daisies in this group that have a stalk length between 4 and 8 mm.
   (c) Calculate an estimate of the mean length of the daisy stalks.

Length, l (mm)	Frequency, f
$0 < l \leq 5$	5
$5 < l \leq 10$	10
$10 < l \leq 20$	22
$20 < l \leq 30$	25
$30 < l \leq 50$	18

3 40 people were asked how long it takes them to travel to work. The results are shown in the table.
   (a) Construct a histogram for these results.
   (b) Calculate an estimate of the number of people in this group who took more than 60 minutes to travel to work.
   (c) Calculate an estimate of the number of people who took less than 24 minutes to travel to work.

Time, t (min)	Frequency, f
$15 < t \leq 20$	12
$20 < t \leq 30$	12
$30 < t \leq 40$	
$40 < t \leq 70$	6

4 In an experiment the lengths of 100 cats' whiskers were measured. The results are shown in the table.
   (a) Construct a histogram for these results.
   (b) Calculate an estimate of the number of whiskers in this group that have a length between 5.5 and 8.5 mm.
   (c) Calculate an estimate of the mean length of the whiskers.

Length, l (mm)	Frequency, f
$5 < l \leq 6$	18
$6 < l \leq 6.5$	
$6.5 < l \leq 7$	21
$7 < l \leq 8$	26
$8 < l \leq 10$	20

5 The table gives the times of 50 cyclists in a race.
   (a) Construct a histogram of these results.
   (b) Calculate an estimate of the percentage of cyclists in this group that had a time of less than 48 minutes.
   (c) Calculate an estimate for the median time.

Time, t (min)	Frequency, f
$20 < t \leq 30$	5
$30 < t \leq 35$	4
$35 < t \leq 40$	9
$40 < t \leq 50$	22
$50 < t \leq 70$	7
$70 < t \leq 100$	3

UNIT 9   HANDLING DATA 6

HANDLING DATA 6 – EXAM PRACTICE EXERCISE

SKILLS
PROBLEM SOLVING, ANALYSIS, INTERPRETATION

E 1 A farmer checks the masses of a sample of apples for quality control. The unfinished table and histogram show the results.

Mass, m (g)	Frequency, f
$60 < m \leq 70$	
$70 < m \leq 80$	22
$80 < m \leq 100$	40
$100 < m \leq 120$	20
$120 < m \leq 160$	

(a) Use the histogram to complete the table.
(b) Use the table to complete the histogram.
(c) Calculate an estimate of the number of apples with a mass between 75 and 95 grams.

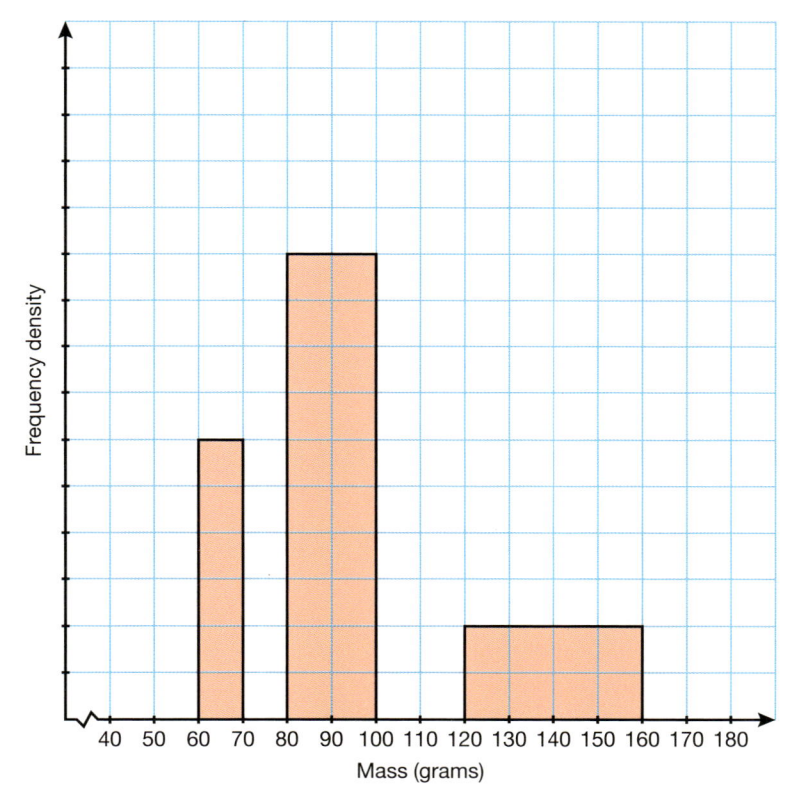

E 2 The unfinished table and histogram give the waiting times of 100 patients at a doctor's surgery. The number of patients waiting 10–12 minutes is 8 more than the number waiting 0–6 minutes.

Time, t (min)	Frequency
$0 < t \leq 6$	
$6 < t \leq 10$	26
$10 < t \leq 12$	
$12 < t \leq 14$	18
$14 < t \leq 22$	24

(a) Use the histogram to complete the table.
(b) Use the table to complete the histogram.
(c) Calculate an estimate of the percentage of patients who wait between 8 and 16 minutes.
(d) Calculate an estimate of the median waiting time.

E 3 A retailer checks the lifetimes of a sample of 200 tree lights for quality control. The unfinished table and histogram show the results.

(a) Use the histogram to complete the table.
(b) Calculate the value of x given that the **frequency density** of the last class interval is 1 light per hour.
(c) Use the table to complete the histogram.

Life, t (h)	Frequency, f
$60 < t \leq 80$	
$80 < t \leq 90$	26
$90 < t \leq 95$	20
$95 < t \leq 100$	25
$100 < t \leq 115$	
$115 < t \leq x$	51

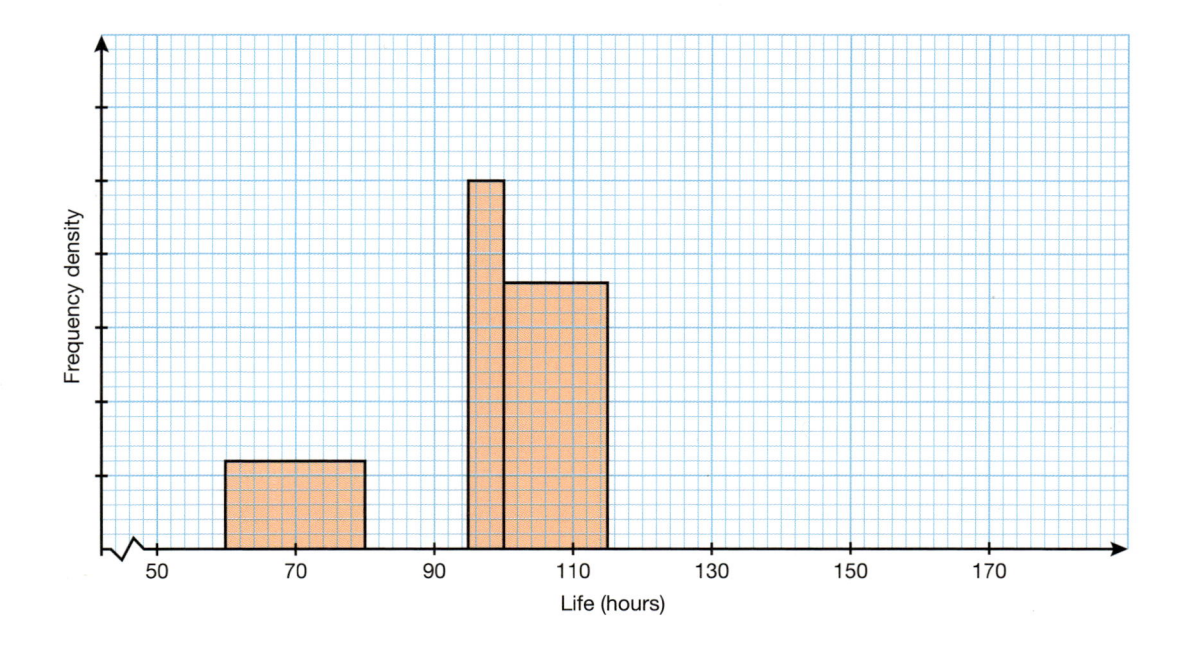

UNIT 9 **HANDLING DATA 6** 201

E 4 The unfinished table and histogram give the birth masses of 200 babies. The difference between the number of babies in the 2–3 kg class and the 3.00–3.25 kg class is 18.

Mass, *m* (kg)	Frequency
2.00 < *m* ≤ 3.00	
3.00 < *m* ≤ 3.25	
3.25 < *m* ≤ 3.50	30
3.50 < *m* ≤ 4.00	
4.00 < *m* ≤ 4.75	

(a) Use the histogram to complete the table.
(b) Use the table to complete the histogram.
(c) Calculate the probability that the birth mass is between 2.50 and 4.50 kg.
(d) Calculate an estimate of the median mass.

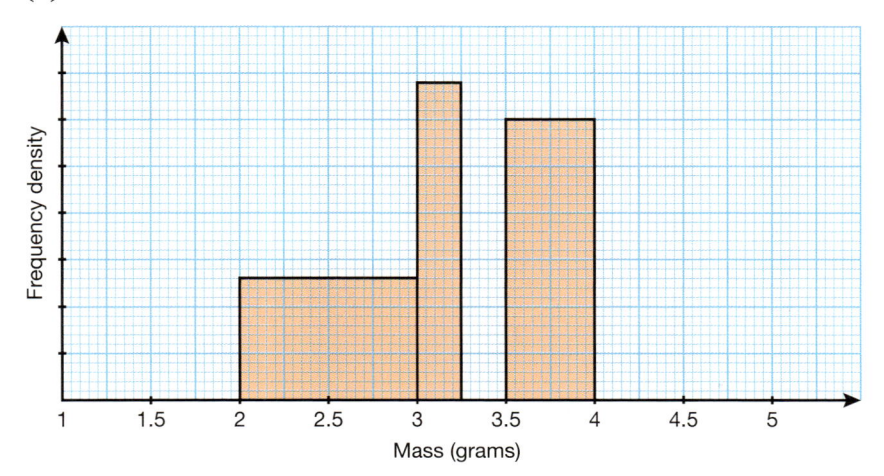

E 5 A health farm recorded the milk consumption, *m* ml, of its 180 clients one day. The table and histogram show the results.

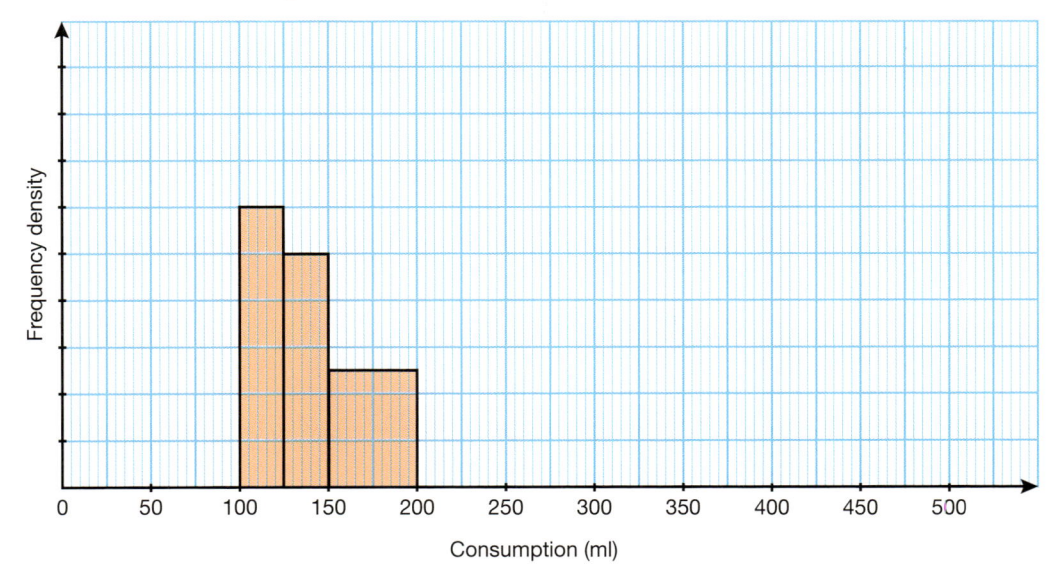

(a) Use the histogram to complete the table.
(b) Use the table to complete the histogram.
(c) Calculate an estimate of the median amount of milk consumed that day.
(d) Calculate an estimate of the percentage of clients who consumed between 70 and 170 ml of milk that day.

Consumption, *m* (ml)	Frequency, *f*
0 < *m* ≤ 50	9
50 < *m* ≤ 100	42
100 < *m* ≤ 125	30
125 < *m* ≤ 150	
150 < *m* ≤ 200	
200 < *m* ≤ 300	22
300 < *m* ≤ 500	

UNIT 10 NUMBER 10

- **RATIONAL AND IRRATIONAL NUMBERS**
- **SIMPLIFYING SURDS**
- **RATIONALISING THE DENOMINATOR**
- **MIXED QUESTIONS**

NUMBER 10 – BASIC SKILLS EXERCISE

For every question, show each step of your working.

Rational and irrational numbers

1. Which of the following are rational when k is a prime number?

    (a) $0.\dot{5}\dot{3}$ (b) $\sqrt{k} + \sqrt{k}$ (c) $\sqrt{k} + \sqrt{k}$

    (d) $\sqrt{729k^2}$ (e) π^2

2. Find a **rational number**

    (a) between $\sqrt{17}$ and $\sqrt{19}$ (b) between $\sqrt{29}$ and $\sqrt{31}$

3. Find an **irrational number**

    (a) between 11.5 and 11.75   (b) between π and $\sqrt{10}$

4. (a) Find a value of k such that $kx^2 = 3$ has rational solutions for x.
   (b) Find a value of k such that $kx^2 = 3$ has irrational solutions for x.

5. $n = \dfrac{7\sqrt{48k}}{\sqrt{27k^3}}$ where k is a prime number.

   Is n rational or irrational? Give a reason.

Simplifying surds

6. Write $3\sqrt{7k}$ as a single square root.

7. Express $\sqrt{192k^2}$ in the form $a\sqrt{b}$ where a is an integer and b is a prime number.

8. Square the following and simplify.

    (a) $a\sqrt{b}$ (b) $\dfrac{1}{2\sqrt{a}}$ (c) $\dfrac{4\sqrt{a}}{\sqrt{2b}}$

9. $\dfrac{27^{x+1}}{81^{x-1}} = 9\sqrt{3}$

   Find the value of x.

10. $\dfrac{\sqrt{k^3}}{\sqrt[3]{k^2}} = k^n$

    Find the value of n as a fraction in its simplest form.

11 Simplify as far as possible

(a) $2\sqrt{48} + 3\sqrt{27}$ (b) $\sqrt{63} - \sqrt{28}$ (c) $\sqrt{1000} - \sqrt{40} - \sqrt{90}$

12 $\dfrac{\sqrt{27} - \sqrt{12}}{2} = \dfrac{1}{\sqrt{a}}$

Find the value of a.

13 Simplify as far as possible

(a) $(\sqrt{2} + 3)(\sqrt{2} - 1)$

(b) $(3 - \sqrt{2})^2$

(c) $(\sqrt{8} + 2\sqrt{2})(2\sqrt{8} - \sqrt{2})$

14 Simplify as far as possible

(a) $\sqrt{(a^2 b)}$ (b) $(\sqrt{a} + \sqrt{b})^2$

(c) $(1 + \sqrt{a})(1 - \sqrt{a})$ (d) $(\sqrt{a} + \sqrt{a})^2$

15 Simplify $(\sqrt{a} + \sqrt{b})^2 - (\sqrt{a} - \sqrt{b})^2$

16 $(a + 5\sqrt{3})(a - 2\sqrt{3}) = b\sqrt{3} - 14$

Find the values of a and b.

Rationalising the denominator

17 Rationalise the denominator then simplify.

(a) $\dfrac{\sqrt{18}}{\sqrt{6}}$ (b) $\dfrac{4\sqrt{2}}{\sqrt{8}}$ (c) $\dfrac{10\sqrt{6}}{\sqrt{150}}$ (d) $\dfrac{81}{\sqrt{27}}$

18 Rationalise the denominator and simplify.

(a) $\dfrac{132}{7 + \sqrt{5}}$ (b) $\dfrac{\sqrt{48} + \sqrt{12}}{3 - \sqrt{3}}$ (c) $\dfrac{(3 + \sqrt{7})(3 - \sqrt{7})}{\sqrt{7} - \sqrt{5}}$

19 Rationalise the denominator and simplify.

(a) $\dfrac{2a + \sqrt{2}}{2 - \sqrt{2}}$ (b) $\dfrac{a\sqrt{a} + a}{a + \sqrt{a}}$ (c) $\dfrac{8a + 6\sqrt{a}}{2\sqrt{a}}$

20 Express $\dfrac{1}{\sqrt{2}} - \dfrac{1}{\sqrt{8}} + \dfrac{1}{\sqrt{32}}$ as a single fraction with a rational denominator.

21 Express $\dfrac{1}{\sqrt{a}} + \dfrac{1}{\sqrt{a^3}} + \dfrac{1}{\sqrt{a^5}}$ as a single fraction with a rational denominator.

22 Show that $\dfrac{3\sqrt{5}}{2\sqrt{7}}$, $\dfrac{15}{2\sqrt{35}}$ and $\dfrac{3\sqrt{35}}{14}$ all represent the same number.

Mixed questions

23 The area of a semicircle is 6π cm².

Show that the perimeter is $\sqrt{3}(4 + 2\pi)$ cm.

24 Show that the solution of the equation $x\sqrt{12} + x\sqrt{75} = 21$ is $x = \sqrt{3}$

25 Show that the solution of the equation $\frac{3x}{\sqrt{2}} + 5 = x\sqrt{8}$ is $x = 5\sqrt{2}$

26 Express $\left(\frac{4}{\sqrt{8}}\right)^5$ in the form $c\sqrt{d}$ where c and d are integers and d is prime.

27 Show that $7\sqrt{1 - \frac{1}{49}} = n\sqrt{3}$, where n is an integer, whose value is to be found.

28 Solve the equation $\sqrt{3}x^2 - \sqrt{6}x - \sqrt{12} = 0$

29 Solve the equation $\sqrt{3}x^2 - 7x + 2\sqrt{3} = 0$

30 Prove that $\sqrt{14a}\left(\sqrt{56a} + a\sqrt{28a}\right)$ is a multiple of 7.

31 Simplify fully $\dfrac{1 + a}{\frac{1}{\sqrt{a}} + \sqrt{a}}$

32 The diagram shows a right-angled triangle.

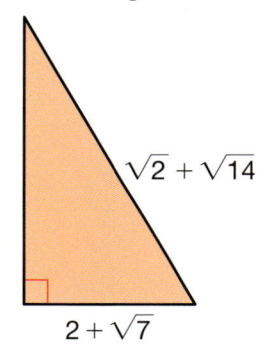

The hypotenuse measures $\sqrt{2} + \sqrt{14}$ cm.

One other side measures $2 + \sqrt{7}$ cm.

The area of the triangle is $\left(\dfrac{2 + \sqrt{7}}{2}\right)p$ cm².

Find the exact value of p.

NUMBER 10 – EXAM PRACTICE EXERCISE

SKILLS
PROBLEM SOLVING, ANALYSIS

E 1 (a) Express the following as single fractions with a rational denominator. Show each step of your working.

(i) $\dfrac{a - \sqrt{a}}{a + \sqrt{a}}$

(ii) $\dfrac{1}{\sqrt{a}} + \dfrac{1}{a} + \dfrac{1}{\sqrt{a^3}}$

(b) $p = \sqrt{125} + \sqrt{r}$ and $q = \sqrt{5} + \sqrt{s}$
The ratio $r : s = 25 : 1$
Find the ratio $p : q$ in its simplest form.
Show each step of your working.

E 2 The diagram shows a solid cylinder.

The radius is $3\sqrt{2}$ cm.

The height is $a\sqrt{2} + b\sqrt{3}$ cm.

The TOTAL surface area is $48\sqrt{6}\pi$ cm².
Find the values of a and b.
Show each step of your working.

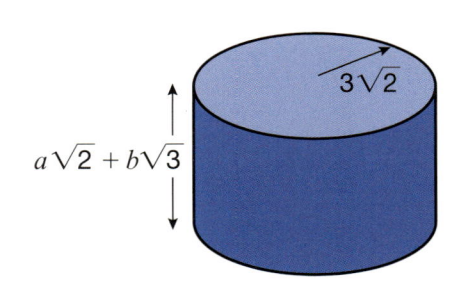

E 3 (a) Solve the equation $x^2 - \left(1 + 2\sqrt{p}\right)x + p + \sqrt{p} = 0$

Give your answers in terms of $\sqrt{p}$.
Show each step of your working.

(b) Work out $\left(a + \sqrt{b}\right)^2$, showing each step of your working.

Hence find the positive value of $\sqrt{\left(7 + \sqrt{48}\right)}$

E 4 A rectangle has a length of $a + \sqrt{2}$ cm.

The area of the rectangle is $(1 + a)\sqrt{2} + (a + 2)$ cm².
Find the width of the rectangle, showing each step of your working.

Give your answer in the form $p + q\sqrt{r}$ where p, q and r are integers and r is a prime number.

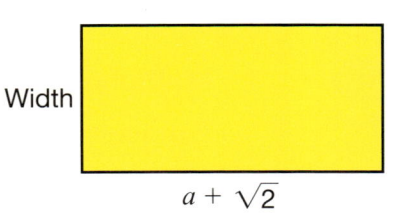

E 5 The diagram shows a right-angled triangle.

The base length is $3 - \sqrt{2}$ cm.

The area of the triangle is $\sqrt{6} + \dfrac{\sqrt{3}}{2}$ cm².

Show that the perimeter of the triangle is
$\sqrt{2}\left(\sqrt{3} - 1\right) + \sqrt{3}\left(\sqrt{3} + 1\right) + 2\sqrt{5}$ cm.
Show each step of your working.

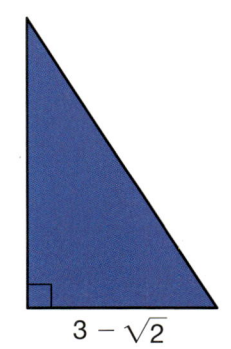

UNIT 10 ALGEBRA 10

- SIMPLIFYING ALGEBRAIC FRACTIONS
- ADDING AND SUBTRACTING ALGEBRAIC FRACTIONS
- MULTIPLYING AND DIVIDING ALGEBRAIC FRACTIONS
- EQUATIONS WITH FRACTIONS
- MIXED QUESTIONS

ALGEBRA 10 – BASIC SKILLS EXERCISE

SKILLS — ANALYSIS

Simplifying algebraic fractions

For **questions 1–8**, simplify the algebraic fractions.

1. $\dfrac{10x + 15x^2}{5x}$
2. $\dfrac{6x^2 + 9x}{2x + 3}$
3. $\dfrac{5x^2 - 15x}{3 - x}$
4. $\dfrac{(x + 6)^3}{(2x + 12)^2}$
5. $\dfrac{x^2 + 7x - 18}{3x + 27}$
6. $\dfrac{4x^2 - 4x - 80}{2x^2 - 32}$
7. $\dfrac{x^2 - 6x - 7}{x^2 - 9x + 14}$
8. $\dfrac{2x^2 + 3x - 9}{3x^2 + 11x + 6}$

SKILLS — ANALYSIS

Adding and subtracting algebraic fractions

For **questions 9–16**, write the expression as a single fraction in its simplest form.

9. $\dfrac{2(x + 3)}{7} - \dfrac{3(x - 3)}{5}$
10. $x + \dfrac{1}{1 + x}$
11. $\dfrac{2}{3} + \dfrac{3}{x - 2}$
12. $\dfrac{1}{1 - x} - \dfrac{2}{2 + x}$
13. $\dfrac{3}{2x - 1} - \dfrac{4}{3x + 1}$
14. $\dfrac{x + 3}{x + 4} - \dfrac{x + 5}{x + 6}$
15. $\dfrac{4}{3x - 18} - \dfrac{x + 5}{x^2 - x - 30}$
16. $\dfrac{x + 7}{x^2 - 2x - 15} - \dfrac{3}{2x - 10}$

SKILLS — ANALYSIS

Multiplying and dividing algebraic fractions

For **questions 17–24**, write the expression as a single simplified factorised fraction.

17. $\dfrac{x^2 - 49}{x + 3} \div \dfrac{x + 7}{x^2 - 9}$
18. $\dfrac{3x + 6}{x^2 - 3x - 10} \div \dfrac{x + 5}{x^3 - 25x}$
19. $\dfrac{x^3 - x}{x + 2} \div \dfrac{x^2 - x}{x^3 - 5x^2 - 14x}$
20. $\dfrac{x^2 + x - 2}{x^2 - 2x - 8} \times \dfrac{x^2 + x - 20}{x^2 + 6x + 5}$
21. $\dfrac{x^2 + x - 6}{x^2 - x - 2} \times \dfrac{x^2 - 3x - 4}{x^2 - x - 12}$
22. $\dfrac{4x^2 - 2x - 2}{6x + 3} \times \dfrac{9x + 6}{3x^2 - x - 2}$
23. $\dfrac{8x^2 + 2x - 1}{2x^2 + 11x + 5} \div \dfrac{4x^2 + 7x - 2}{3x + 15}$
24. $\dfrac{x^2 - 4x - 12}{x + 7} \div \dfrac{x + 2}{x^2 - 49} \times \dfrac{x + 3}{x^2 - 13x + 42}$

UNIT 10 — ALGEBRA 10

SKILLS
ANALYSIS

Equations with fractions

For **questions 25–32**, solve the equations.

25 $\dfrac{x+2}{3} = \dfrac{2x-1}{5} - 1$

26 $\dfrac{x+2}{2} - \dfrac{x+3}{3} + \dfrac{x+4}{4} = 0$

27 $\dfrac{3}{x+3} = \dfrac{9}{19-2x}$

28 $\dfrac{x-1}{x+2} + \dfrac{x+3}{x-2} = 2$

29 $\dfrac{3x+2}{x} = \dfrac{x-1}{x+2}$

30 $1 + \dfrac{2}{x} = \dfrac{24}{x^2}$

31 $\dfrac{1}{x} - \dfrac{1}{x+1} = \dfrac{1}{x+4}$

32 $\dfrac{x}{2x-4} - \dfrac{x}{3x-6} = 1$

SKILLS
ANALYSIS, DECISION MAKING

Mixed questions

33 $(x+11) : (10-x) = (x+5) : (2-x)$
   Find the value of x.

34 $(2x+1) : (x+3) = (5x-1) : (3x+3)$
   Find the possible value of x.

35 Simplify $4 - (x+1) \div \dfrac{x^2-1}{4x-5}$ fully in its simplest form.

36 Simplify $\dfrac{x^2-x-6}{3x+12} \div \dfrac{x-3}{x+4} - \dfrac{x}{3}$ fully in its simplest form.

37 $\dfrac{7-(x+5)}{2x+3} : \dfrac{x-2}{4x^2-9} = n : 1$

   Find a fully simplified expression for n.

38 Prove that $\dfrac{x^2-3x-4}{x+3} \div \dfrac{x+1}{x^2-x-12} \geq 0$

ALGEBRA 10 – EXAM PRACTICE EXERCISE

E 1 $\dfrac{3y}{x} - \dfrac{y}{x+3} = 2x + 9$

(a) Make y the subject of the expression, writing it in the form $y = (x + a)^2 + b$
(b) (i) Find the coordinates of the turning point of y.
 (ii) State if the turning point is a maximum or a minimum.

E 2 $y = t^2 - 4t$ and $x = \dfrac{t+3}{t-1}$

(a) Find y in terms of x, giving your answer in factorised form.
(b) Show that $\left(\dfrac{x+3}{x-1}\right) : y = (x-1) : (7 - 3x)$

E 3 (a) Simplify $\dfrac{2x^2 + 5x - 12}{4x^2 - 9} \div \dfrac{x^2 + 2x - 8}{2x^2 + 5x + 3}$

Give your answer as a fraction in its simplest form.

(b) Hence solve $\dfrac{2x^2 + 5x - 12}{4x^2 - 9} \div \dfrac{x^2 + 2x - 8}{2x^2 + 5x + 3} = 1 + \dfrac{x}{(x+2)}$

Show clear algebraic working.

E 4 Yara sets out on a 70 km journey in her car.

She drives the first x km of her journey at $x + 10$ km/h.
She drives the remainder at $x - 20$ km/h.
Her journey takes 1 hour.
Find the value of x correct to 3 s.f.

E 5 The area of a rectangle is $\dfrac{8x^2 + 16x - 10}{3x^2 - 3}$ cm².

One side of the rectangle is $\dfrac{2x+5}{3x-3}$ cm.
The adjacent side is y cm.

(a) Find and simplify an expression for y in terms of x.

The perimeter of the rectangle is 10 cm.
(b) Find the area of the rectangle in cm².

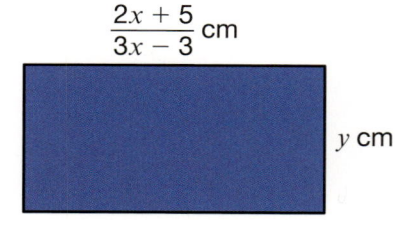

UNIT 10 GRAPHS 9

- DIFFERENTIATING INTEGER POWERS OF x
- GRADIENT OF A CURVE
- FINDING TURNING POINTS
- LINEAR KINEMATICS
- PRACTICAL PROBLEMS

GRAPHS 9 – BASIC SKILLS EXERCISE

SKILLS
ANALYSIS

Differentiating integer powers of x

1. **Differentiate** using the correct notation
   (a) $y = 3x$
   (b) $y = 10$
   (c) $y = x^3$
   (d) $y = x^4$
   (e) $y = x^5$
   (f) $y = 2x^6$
   (g) $y = 3x^5$
   (h) $y = 20x^8$

2. Differentiate using the correct notation
   (a) $y = 2x^3 + 5x^2$
   (b) $y = 7x^2 - 3x$
   (c) $y = 1 + 5x^3$
   (d) $y = 3x^4 - 5x^2$
   (e) $y = x^2(x + 5)$
   (f) $y = (x - 3)(x + 5)$
   (g) $y = (2x - 1)(x - 4)$
   (h) $y = (x + 2)^2$

3. Differentiate using the correct notation
   (a) $y = \dfrac{1}{x}$
   (b) $y = \dfrac{1}{x^2}$
   (c) $y = \sqrt{x}$
   (d) $y = x^{-3}$
   (e) $y = 4x^{-4}$
   (f) $y = \dfrac{1}{2x^2}$
   (g) $y = \dfrac{2x^3 + 3x^2 + 4}{x}$
   (h) $y = \dfrac{(x^3 + 3)(2x - 1)}{x}$

SKILLS
ANALYSIS

Gradient of a curve

4. Differentiate and then find the gradient of the tangent at the given point.
   (a) $y = 2x^2$ (1, 2)
   (b) $y = 3x - 2x^2$ (2, −2)
   (c) $y = 2x^3 + 10x^2$ (1, 12)
   (d) $y = (x + 5)(2x + 1)$ (2, 35)

5. Differentiate and then find the gradient of the tangent at the given point.
   (a) $y = \dfrac{2}{x}$ (1, 2)
   (b) $y = 2\sqrt{x} + x$ (1, 3)
   (c) $y = \left(x + \dfrac{1}{x}\right)^2$ (1, 4)
   (d) $y = \dfrac{(1 - 2x)(1 + 2x)}{2x}$ $(2, -3\tfrac{3}{4})$

6 Find the equation of the tangent to the curve $y = x + \dfrac{1}{x}$ at the point where $x = 2$

7 Find the equations of the tangents to the curve $y = x^2 - 3x$ at the points where they cut the x-axis.

8 If the curve $y = 3x^3 + \dfrac{p}{x} + 3$ has a gradient of 8 where $x = 1$, find the value of p.

9 $y = px^2 + qx + 7$ has gradient 4 when $x = 1$ and gradient -8 when $x = -1$.

Find the value of $p^3 + q^3$

SKILLS
ANALYSIS

Finding turning points

10 For the curve $y = x^3 - 3x + 2$
   (a) find $\dfrac{dy}{dx}$
   (b) find the coordinates of the curve where $\dfrac{dy}{dx} = 0$
   (c) determine whether each point is a maximum or minimum

11 For the curve $y = x^3 + 3x^2 - 9x + 1$
   (a) find $\dfrac{dy}{dx}$
   (b) find the coordinates of the curve where $\dfrac{dy}{dx} = 0$
   (c) determine whether each point is a maximum or minimum

12 (a) Find the coordinates of the **stationary points** on $y = x^3 - 2x^2 + 1$
   (b) Determine the nature of these stationary points.

SKILLS
ANALYSIS

Linear kinematics

13 The **displacement**, s metres, of a ball after t seconds is given by $s = 50 + 12t^2$
   (a) Find an expression for the ball's velocity, $v = \dfrac{ds}{dt}$
   (b) Find its velocity at $t = 2$
   (c) Find an expression for the ball's acceleration, $a = \dfrac{dy}{dt}$
   (d) Find its acceleration at $t = 2$

14 The displacement, s metres, of a particle after t seconds is given by $s = t^3 + 4t^2 - 3t + 1$
   (a) Find an expression for the particle's velocity, $v = \dfrac{ds}{dt}$
   (b) Find its velocity at $t = 10$
   (c) Find an expression for the particle's acceleration, $a = \dfrac{dv}{dt}$
   (d) Find its acceleration at $t = 10$

15 A catapult projects a small stone vertically upwards such that its height, s m, after t seconds is given by $s = 50t - 5t^2$
   (a) Find the greatest height reached by the stone.
   (b) Find the time this occurs.

16 The displacement of a comet, s km, after t seconds is given by $s = t(t^2 - 300)$ km
   (a) Find an expression for the velocity, $v = \frac{ds}{dt}$
   (b) Find the velocity of the comet after 5 seconds.
   (c) Find an expression for the acceleration, $a = \frac{dv}{dt}$
   (d) Find the acceleration of the comet after 5 seconds.
   (e) Find when the comet is momentarily at rest.

17 The displacement, s metres, of a train after t seconds is given by $s = 50 + 12t^2 + \sqrt{2}$
   (a) Find an expression for the train's velocity, $v = \frac{ds}{dt}$
   (b) Find its velocity at $t = 3$
   (c) Find an expression for the train's acceleration, $a = \frac{dv}{dt}$
   (d) Find its acceleration at $t = 3$

18 The displacement of a shooting star, s km, after t seconds is given by $s = t(t^2 - 500) + \pi$ km
   (a) Find an expression for the velocity, $v = \frac{ds}{dt}$
   (b) Find the velocity of the shooting star after 10 seconds.
   (c) Find an expression for the acceleration, $a = \frac{dv}{dt}$
   (d) Find the acceleration of the shooting star after 10 seconds.
   (e) Find when the shooting star is momentarily at rest.

Practical problems

19 The flow, Q m³/s, of a river t hours after midnight is given by the equation $Q = t^3 - 8t^2 + 14t + 10$
   (a) Differentiate to find $\frac{dQ}{dt}$
   (b) Find the rate of change of flow of the river at
      (i) midnight
      (ii) 02:00
      (iii) 05:00

20 The temperature, $C°$ Centigrade, of the sea off Brighton t months after New Year's Day is given by $C = 4t + \frac{16}{t} - 15$ and is only valid for $1 \leq t \leq 6$
   (a) Find $\frac{dC}{dt}$
   (b) Find the coolest sea temperature in this period and when it occurs.
   (c) Find the rate at which the sea temperature is cooling on 1 February.

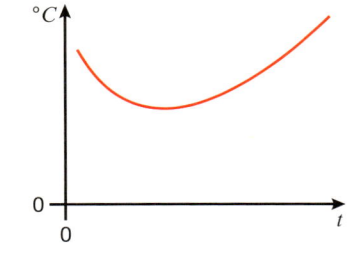

SKILLS

CRITICAL THINKING, PROBLEM SOLVING, ANALYSIS, INTERPRETATION

GRAPHS 9 – EXAM PRACTICE EXERCISE

E 1 The population, P, of a rare orchid in the Amazon rainforest over t years is modelled by $P = 5t^2 + \dfrac{10000}{t} + 10$, where $1 \leq t \leq 15$

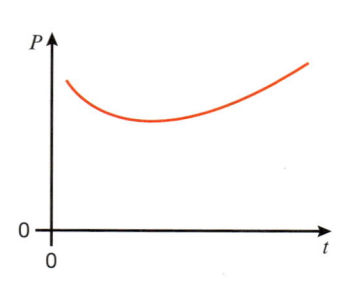

(a) Find the rate of change of P with respect to t, $\dfrac{dP}{dt}$ orchids per year for this model.

(b) Calculate when the population of orchids is at its lowest and find this value of P. Justify your answer.

E 2 (a) L is the line perpendicular to the tangent of the curve $y = x^2 - 3x$ at $x = 4$
Find the equation of line L in the form $ax + by = c$ where a, b and c are constants to be found.

(b) Line L cuts the x-axis at point A and the y-axis at point B.
O is the origin of the axes.
The area of triangle OAB = the area of a square with perimeter p.
Show that $p = \dfrac{48\sqrt{2}}{\sqrt{5}}$

E 3 The curve $y = x^3 - 6x^2 + px + q$, where p and q are constants, has a turning point at $A(1, 5)$.
(a) Find the value of constants p and q.
The curve has another turning point at B.
(b) (i) Find the coordinates of B.
(ii) State which of the points A and B are maximum or minimum. Fully justify your answers.

4 A drone takes off vertically from a point O on the ground.

At time t the velocity v m/s is given by $v = t(k - 5t)$, where k is a constant.
The acceleration at launch is 3 m/s².
(a) Find the value of k.
(b) Find the acceleration of the drone in m/s² when it is instantaneously at rest.

5 The diagram shows a right cylinder inside a cone on a horizontal base.
The cone and the cylinder have the same vertical axis.
The base of the cylinder lies on the base of the cone.
The circumference of the top face of the cylinder touches the curved surface of the cone.
The height of the cone = 12 cm
The radius of the base of the cone = 4 cm
The cylinder has radius r cm and volume V cm³.

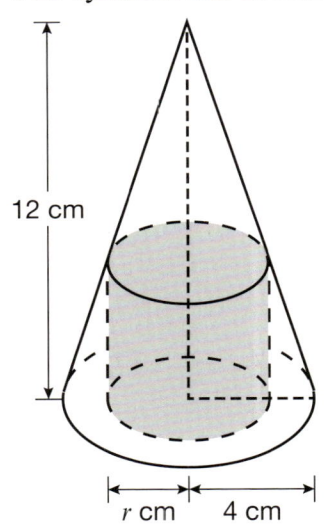

(a) Show that
   (i) $V = 3\pi r^2(4 - r)$
   (ii) $\dfrac{dV}{dr} = 3\pi r(8 - 3r)$
(b) Find
   (i) the value of r which produces a maximum value of V, fully justifying your answer
   (ii) the value of p if the maximum value of V is given by $\dfrac{256\pi}{p}$ cm³

UNIT 10 SHAPE AND SPACE 10

- **GEOMETRIC PROBLEMS**
- **NAVIGATION AND BEARINGS**

SHAPE AND SPACE 10 – BASIC SKILLS EXERCISE

SKILLS
ANALYSIS

Geometric problems

1. A bird watcher spots an eagle perched at the top of a tree of height h metres. The angle of elevation from the bird watcher's feet to the eagle is 20° and she stands 100 m from the base of the tree.
   Find h.

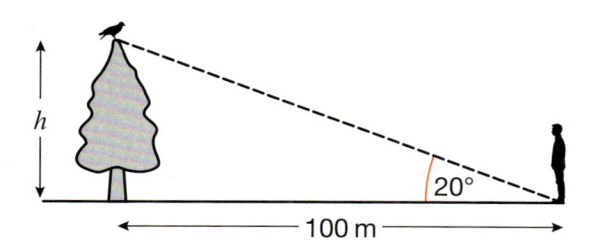

2. A telephone engineer is up a telegraph pole. Her eye is 15 m above the ground. She spots her toolbox which is x metres from the base of the pole at an angle of depression of 35°.
   Find x.

3. Rob skis down a straight slope from point A to point B. The difference in height between these two points is 125 m, and the actual distance AB as viewed on a map is 375 m.
   Calculate the angle of this ski slope.

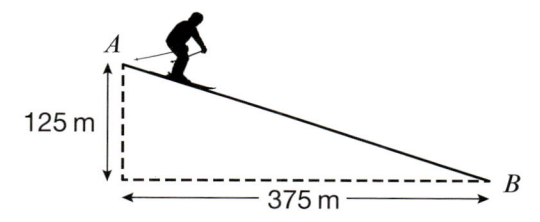

4. A 3.2 m ladder makes an angle of 15° with a vertical wall.
   Calculate the distance of the foot of the ladder from the base of the wall.

5. A straight wheelchair ramp is 12 m long and rises 225 cm.
   Find the angle the ramp makes with the horizontal.

6. The centre of a clock face is 30 m above the ground. The hour hand is 1.5 m long.
   Find the height of the hour hand above the ground at 21:30.

7. A large fun-fair swing consists of a 5 m chain at the end of which is the seat.
   Find how far above the lowest point the seat is when the chain makes an angle of 50° with the vertical.

8 The vertices of a regular hexagon lie on the circumference of a circle of radius 10 m. What percentage of the circle area is taken up by the hexagon?

9 A triangle ABC has sides of lengths which are the 4th, 5th and 6th prime numbers. Calculate for triangle ABC
(a) the smallest angle
(b) the area
Give all answers to 3 s.f.

Navigation and bearings

10 Lighthouse A is 30 km due South of lighthouse B. Port C is 60 km due West of A. Calculate the bearing of
(a) C from B
(b) B from C

11 On a map of Derbyshire, Belper is 10 cm East of Ashbourne and Derby is 7 cm South of Belper. Draw a suitable diagram and **calculate** the bearing of Derby from Ashbourne.

12 Jamila runs from point A on a constant bearing of 300° at 5 m/s for 15 minutes. She then stops at point B. Calculate how far Jamila has run
(a) North from A
(b) West from A
(c) from A

13 Raphael hikes from village A for 7 km on a bearing of 040° to village B. He then hikes 12 km on a bearing of 130° to village C. He needs to return back to A by 18:00. If he departs from C at 16:00 at 2 m/s, find
(a) the distance and bearing of Raphael's journey from C to A
(b) if Raphael arrives back at village A by 18:00

14 A ship 5 km North of an oil-rig travels on a bearing of 150°. Calculate the closest distance that the ship passes by the oil-rig.

15 A yacht, Y, is 10 km from a port, P, on a bearing of 156°, whilst a fishing boat, F, is 20 km from the port on a bearing of 044°. Find
(a) the distance of the yacht from the fishing boat
(b) the bearing of F from Y
(c) the bearing of Y from F

SHAPE AND SPACE 10 – EXAM PRACTICE EXERCISE

E 1 From the top of a cliff of height y m the angle of depression of a Channel swimmer at X is 30°. She swims directly towards the base of the cliff such that, 1 minute later, at Y, the angle of depression from the top of the cliff to the swimmer is 50°. Her speed between X and Y is 0.75 m/s. Find the height of the cliff in m to 3 s.f.

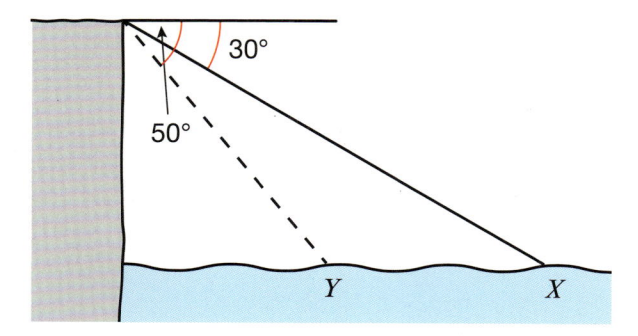

E 2 A firework travels vertically for 100 m, then for 75 m at 20° to the vertical, then 50 m at 20° to the horizontal. It then drops vertically to the ground in 1 minute. Find the average speed of its descent in m/s.

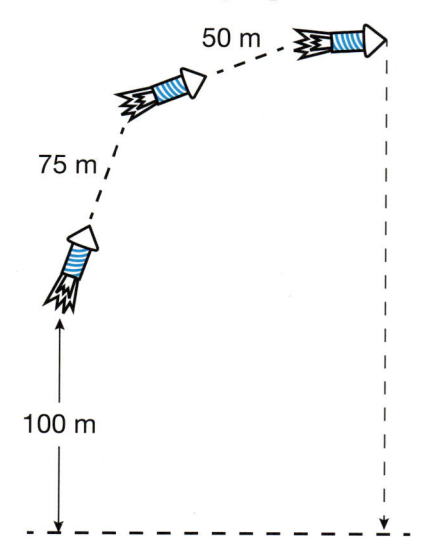

E 3 A hot-air balloon drifts 28 km from its starting point O, on a bearing of 080°, then 62 km on a bearing of 225° to reach point A.
Find
(a) the distance OA
(b) the bearing of O from A
A truck departs from O at the same time as the balloon. It travels along OA and arrives at A at the same time as the balloon. The balloon's speed is 30 km/h.
(c) Find the speed of the truck in km/h to 3 s.f.

E 4 Ship A leaves a port at 14:00 hours and sails at a speed of 15 km/h on a bearing of 130°. Ship B leaves the same port at 14:00 hours and sails at a speed of 10 km/h on a bearing of 240°.
(a) Draw a diagram to show the positions of the port and the two ships at 16:00 hours.
(b) Calculate the distance between the ships at 16:00 hours.
(c) Calculate the bearing of ship A from ship B.

E 5 Igor is at the top of a 25 m tree when he sees Jesper due East of him at an angle of depression of 25°. Simultaneously he observes Karen due North at an angle of depression of 15°. How far apart are Jesper and Karen at this moment in m to 3 s.f.?

UNIT 10 HANDLING DATA 7

- **CONDITIONAL PROBABILITY**
- **TREE DIAGRAMS (MORE THAN TWO BRANCHES)**
- **PROBABILITY TABLES**

HANDLING DATA 7 – BASIC SKILLS EXERCISE

SKILLS
ANALYSIS

Conditional probability

1. A squad of basketball players consists of six girls and four boys.
   The starting team consists of five randomly chosen players.
   Calculate the probability that there are three girls, given that the first two players chosen are boys.

2. Twelve cards are each numbered from 1 to 12.
   The cards are then turned face down and then shuffled.
   The cards are then randomly selected one by one and not replaced.
   (a) What is the probability that the second card is a prime number given that the first card was a prime number?
   (b) What is the probability that the third and fourth cards are prime given that the first two cards were not primes?

3. Eight ordinary playing cards are shown. They are turned downwards and then shuffled. Three cards are then randomly removed one at a time with without being replaced.

   (a) What is the probability that the second and third cards are a Queen given that the first card is a Queen?
   (b) What is the probability that the three cards are two Kings given that the first card is a red card?

4 Gunter is a party organiser who has prepared some shakes ready for a large children's party. However, he has forgotten to label the bottles. He knows the number of types of shake are as given in the table. He selects a bottle at random.

	Crush	Smooth
Citrus	32	15
Berry	18	45

  (a) Calculate the probability that the shake is
    (i) Crush
    (ii) Smooth
  (b) Given he takes a bottle of Crush shake, calculate the probability that the shake is
    (i) citrus
    (ii) berry
  (c) In a hurry Gunter randomly takes three bottles without replacement. Calculate to 3 s.f., the probability that he has at least one bottle of Berry Smooth shake.

5 Kylie and Masaba are taking a scuba dive leader test. If they fail the first test, only one re-test is permitted. Their probabilities of passing are given in the table.

	Boris	Gunter
P(pass on 1st test)	0.65	0.75
P(pass on 2nd test)	0.85	0.80

These probabilities are independent of each other. Find the probabilities that
  (a) Masaba becomes a dive leader on passing the second test
  (b) Kylie passes her first test whilst Masaba fails her first test
  (c) only one of the two women becomes a scuba dive leader, assuming that a re-test is taken if the first test has been failed

6 The table shows the number of students, from Years 10 and 11, taking part in different activities.

	Kayaking	Rock climbing	Mountain biking
Year 10	11	10	9
Year 11	8	15	7

  (a) A student is picked at random from the group.
    What is the probability that this student
    (i) is rock climbing
    (ii) is a Year 10 student who kayaks?
  (b) Two Year 11 students are picked at random one after the other, without replacement.
    What is the probability that both students
    (i) do mountain biking
    (ii) do not do rock climbing?

Tree diagrams (more than two branches)

SKILLS ANALYSIS

7 Linford and Alan race against each other in a competition.
If one of them wins a race, he wins the competition.
If the race is a draw, they run another race.
They run a maximum of three races.
Each time they race, the probability that Linford wins is 0.45.
Each time they race, the probability that there is a draw is 0.05.

(a) Complete the probability tree diagram.

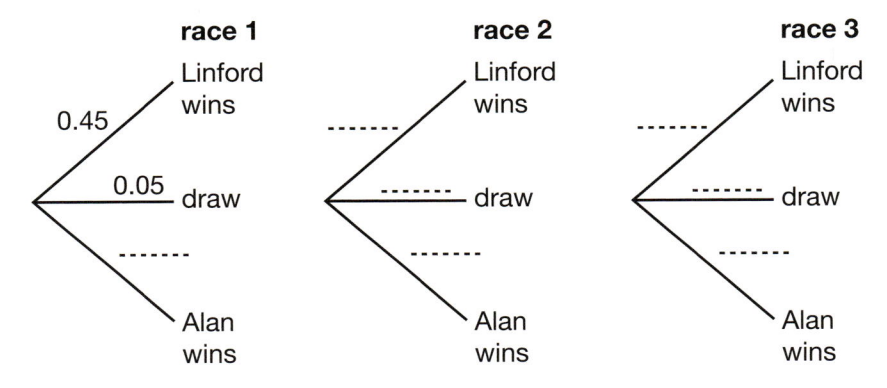

	race 1	race 2	race 3
	Linford wins (0.45)	Linford wins	Linford wins
	draw (0.05)	draw	draw
	Alan wins	Alan wins	Alan wins

(b) Calculate the probability that Alan wins the competition.

8 There are 20 coins in a bag.
10 coins are 20 cent coins
6 coins are 10 cent coins
4 coins are 5 cent coins

Emma takes at random two of the coins from the bag without replacement.

(a) Complete the probability tree diagram.

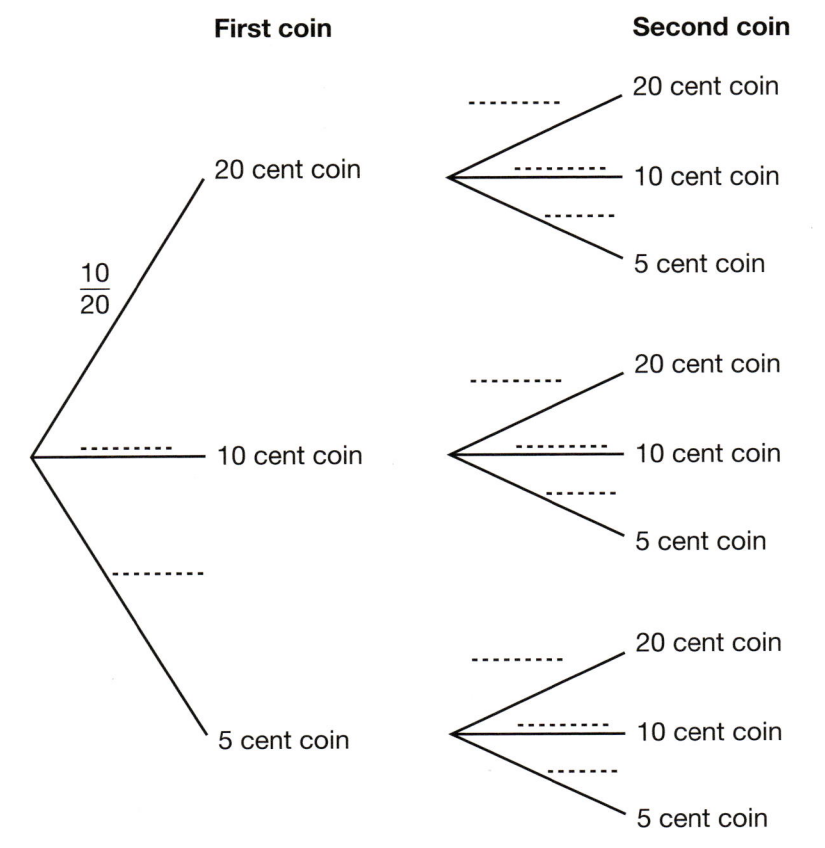

First coin → Second coin branches:
- 20 cent coin ($\frac{10}{20}$) → 20 cent coin / 10 cent coin / 5 cent coin
- 10 cent coin → 20 cent coin / 10 cent coin / 5 cent coin
- 5 cent coin → 20 cent coin / 10 cent coin / 5 cent coin

(b) Calculate the probability that Emma picks out coins worth at least 25 cents.

Probability tables

9 A biased spinner is marked with the scores 1, 2, 3, 4 and 5. The table shows the probabilities of obtaining these scores.

Score	1	2	3	4	5
Probability	0.05	x	0.15	$2x$	0.2

(a) The spinner is spun once. Work out the probability that
   (i) the score is 2 or 4
   (ii) the score is 2
(b) The spinner is now spun twice. Work out the probability that
   (i) the scores add up to 10
   (ii) the scores add up to 4

10 The probability of a red kite laying a certain number of eggs is given in the table.

Number of eggs	Probability
0	0.1
1	k
2	0.3
3	0.4
4	0.06
≥ 5	0.04

Find
(a) the value of k
(b) the probability that a red kite
   (i) lays at least two eggs
   (ii) lays at most two eggs
(c) the probability that two red kites lay a total of at least three eggs

11 A veterinary surgeon has two independent tests, X and Y, for the presence of a virus in a turkey. Tests are performed in the order X then Y.

Probabilities of a positive test	Test X	Test Y
Virus present	$\dfrac{3}{5}$	$\dfrac{5}{6}$
Virus not present	$\dfrac{4}{5}$	$\dfrac{6}{7}$

(a) Find the probability that one test will be positive and one negative on
   (i) an infected turkey
   (ii) an uninfected turkey
(b) If at least one positive test is the criterion for indicating an infected turkey, find the probability that after two tests
   (i) on an infected turkey, the criterion is not met
   (ii) on an uninfected turkey, the criterion is met

HANDLING DATA 7 – EXAM PRACTICE EXERCISE

E 1 Two pharmaceutical companies wish to test their new vaccine on a particular strain (version) of virus. The results of their **trials** are shown in the table.

Age (y years)	Success (✓) or No Change (✗)	Proton-Zenith	Neutron-Vector
y = 60	✓	12 750	14 400
	✗	7250	5600
y = 30	✓	14 800	12 400
	✗	5200	7600

(a) A person is picked randomly from these trials.
What is the probability of this person
  (i) showing a success
  (ii) being a 60-year-old showing no change
  (iii) being a 30-year-old showing a success?
(b) A second person is randomly picked from the Proton-Zenith trial.
What is the probability that this person shows a success, given that they are a 60-year-old?

E 2 Hamish has a very large herd of cows. $\frac{4}{5}$ of the cows are Jersey whilst the rest are Friesian.
He randomly picks two cows from the herd without replacement.

(a) Calculate an estimate of the probability that he has selected
  (i) two Friesian cows
  (ii) a Friesian and a Jersey cow
A third cow is randomly selected from the herd.
(b) Calculate an estimate of the probability that Hamish now has at least two Friesian cows from his sample of three.

E 3 Bag A contains a large number of garden lights which are red, green and gold in the ratio 1 : 2 : 3 respectively. Bag B also contains a large number of garden lights which are red, green and gold in the ratio 1 : 1 : 2 respectively. Helga takes one light randomly from Bag A and another one randomly from Bag B.
(a) Draw a tree diagram to show all possible outcomes for the two selections.
(b) Find the probability that Helga's two lights are
  (i) both gold
  (ii) green and gold
  (iii) at least one red

E 4 Box X contains two white and three black marbles. Box Y contains three white and two black marbles.

Box X
Box Y

A marble is randomly taken from Box X and placed into Box Y before two marbles are randomly taken from Box Y without replacement.

(a) Draw a tree diagram showing all possible outcomes for the two selections from Box Y.
(b) Find the probability that the two marbles taken from Box Y consist of
 (i) two whites
 (ii) a black and a white
 (iii) at least one black

E 5 A new test is 90% successful in detecting a weak heart in race horses.
If a weak heart is detected, the correcting operation has an 80% success rate the first time it is attempted.
If this operation is unsuccessful, it can be repeated only twice more, with success rates of 60% and 40% respectively.

(a) Draw a tree diagram illustrating all possible outcomes.
(b) Use this diagram to find the probability of a horse with a weak heart being
 (i) cured after one operation
 (ii) cured at the third operation
 (iii) cured

Examination Practice Papers 1A

Time: 2 hours

1 In the year 2010, the population of Brazil was 196 million.
Between 2010 and 2020, the population of Brazil increased by 17 million.
  (a) Find the percentage increase of the population of Brazil between 2010 and 2020 to 3 s.f. **(1)**
In 2000, the population of Brazil was 175 million.
Between 2000 and 2005, the population of Brazil increased by 6.3%.
  (b) What was the population of Brazil at the start of 2005 to the nearest million? **(2)**
Between 1990 and 2000, the population of Brazil increased by 17.4%.
  (c) What was the population of Brazil at the start of 1990 to the nearest million? **(2)**

2 (a) Simplify
    (i) $u \times u \times u \times u \times u$ **(1)**
    (ii) $3u + 2v - 7u + 4v + 11$ **(1)**
    (iii) $\dfrac{u^7 \times u^8}{u^{11}}$ **(1)**

  (b) Expand and simplify
    (i) $u(5u - 1) - u(3u - 2)$ **(1)**
    (ii) $(5u - 1)(3u - 2)$ **(2)**

3 (a) The area of the semicircle is $k\pi$ cm².

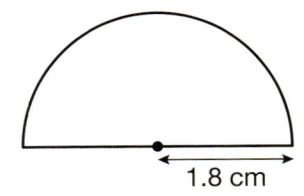

    1.8 cm

  Find the value of the constant k. **(1)**

  (b) Calculate the area of the compound shape in cm².

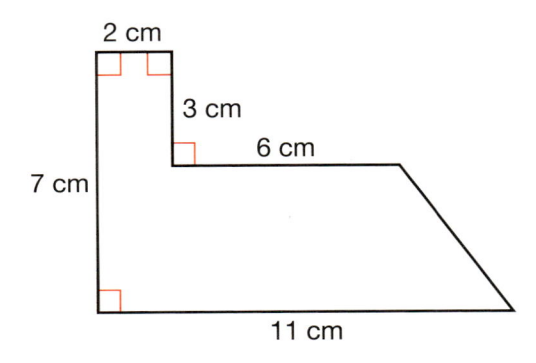

    2 cm
    3 cm
    6 cm
    7 cm
    11 cm **(2)**

4 The diagram shows a spinner.

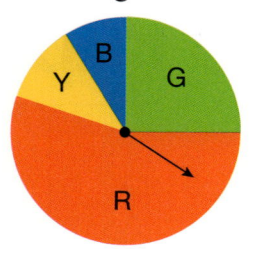

The arrow stops on red (R), green (G), blue (B) or yellow (Y) with probabilities as shown in the table.

Colour	R	G	B	Y
Probability	0.55	0.25	x	0.12

(a) Find the value of x. (1)
(b) The spinner is spun once.
Calculate the probability that the arrow will land on a red or a blue sector. (2)
(c) The spinner is spun twice.
Calculate the probability that a green and a yellow are obtained. (2)
(d) The spinner is spun 200 times.
Calculate how many times you would expect the arrow to land on yellow or red. (1)

5 a, b, c and d are different integers where $a < b < c < d$.
The sum of a, b and c is 33.
The mean of all four numbers is 15.
(a) Calculate the value of d. (1)
The range of these four numbers is 23.
(b) Calculate the median of this group of integers. (1)

6 Two points are $A(0, 4)$ and $B(-5, -2)$.
M is the midpoint of AB.
(a) Find the coordinates of M. (1)
(b) Find the equation of line AB in the form $y = mx + c$ (2)
(c) Find the equation of the perpendicular bisector of line AB in the form $ax + by + c = 0$, where a, b and c are integers. (2)

7 $\mathscr{E} = \{2, 3, 5, 7, 11, 13, 17, 19, 23, 29\}$
$P = \{2, 5, 11, 17, 23\}$
$Q = \{3, 7, 13, 19\}$
(a) Is $P \cap Q = \varnothing$? Explain your answer. (1)
(b) If $x \in \mathscr{E}$ and $x \notin P \cup Q$, what is the value of x? (1)
(c) $P \cap R = \{2, 19\}$, $Q \cap R = \{13\}$ and $P \cup Q \cup R = \mathscr{E}$
List all the elements of set R. (2)

8. The table gives the time a group of students spent on their smart phones on a Saturday.

Time t (min)	Frequency
$0 < t \leq 40$	20
$40 < t \leq 80$	35
$80 < t \leq 120$	60
$120 < t \leq 160$	33
$160 < t \leq 200$	7
$200 < t \leq 240$	5

(a) Complete the cumulative frequency table. **(1)**
(b) Draw the cumulative frequency graph on the grid below. **(2)**

Time t (min)	Frequency	Cumulative frequency
$0 < t \leq 40$	20	
$40 < t \leq 80$	35	
$80 < t \leq 120$	60	
$120 < t \leq 160$	33	
$160 < t \leq 200$	7	
$200 < t \leq 240$	5	

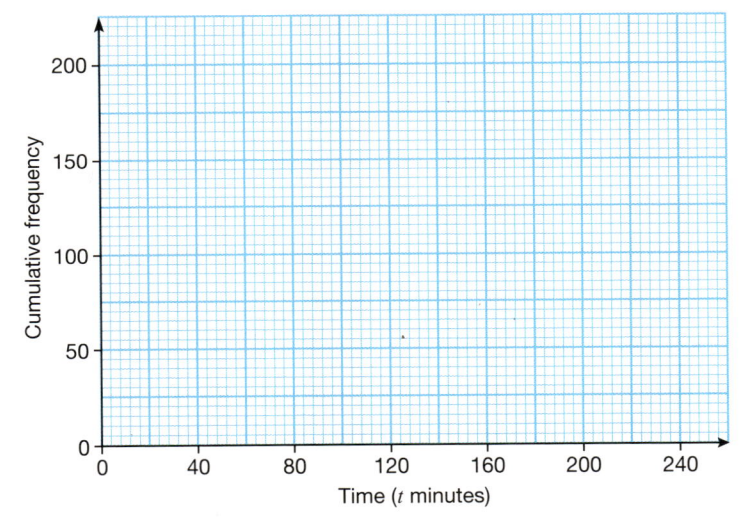

(c) Use your graph to estimate
 (i) the interquartile range of times spent on smart phones **(1)**
 (ii) the range of times of students in the top 10% **(1)**

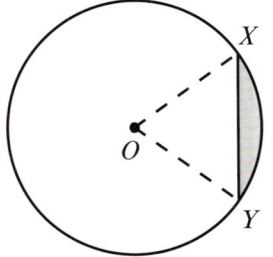

9. XY is a chord of a circle, centre O.

$OX = 7.5$ cm and angle $XOY = 70°$

Calculate to 3 s.f.
(a) the area of the shaded segment in cm² **(1)**
(b) the perimeter of the shaded segment in cm **(2)**

10 (a) Simplify

    (i) $p^7 \times p^{11}$ (1)

    (ii) $\dfrac{p^{11}}{p^7}$ (1)

    (iii) $(2p + 1)^2 - (p - 1)^2$ (2)

(b) Solve the equations, showing clear algebraic working.

    (i) $11p - 1 = 7p + 1$ (1)

    (ii) $\dfrac{11p - 1}{4} = \dfrac{4p + 1}{11}$ (2)

11 Solve the simultaneous equations, showing clear algebraic working.

$$3m - 10n = 20$$
$$5m + 2n = 6$$

(2)

12 Use algebraic methods to show that $0.4\dot{9}\dot{2} = \dfrac{164}{333}$ (2)

13

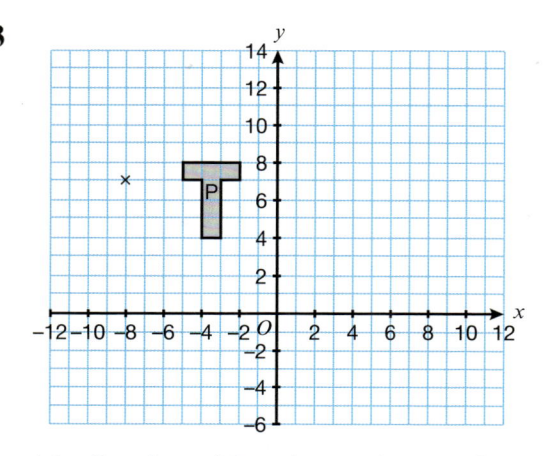

(a) On the grid, enlarge shape P by scale factor 3 and centre (–8, 7). Label the image of this transformation Q. (1)

(b) On the grid, rotate shape P through 90° clockwise about centre (–8, 7). Label the image of this transformation R. (2)

(c) Shape Q is enlarged by scale factor $\frac{1}{2}$ about 0, producing image Q_1.

Shape R is enlarged by scale factor 5 about 0, producing image R_1.
Calculate the areas of

    (i) Q_1 (1)

    (ii) R_1 (1)

14 A small crane is moving concrete blocks on a building site.

A pallet of concrete blocks has a mass of 150 kg to the nearest 10 kg.
The crane can safely lift a load of 1800 kg to 2 s.f.
Calculate the greatest number of pallets of concrete blocks that the crane can safely lift in one load. (2)

15 Show by clear algebraic working that

$$1 - \frac{2x^2 - 7x + 3}{x^2 + 2x - 15} = \frac{6 - x}{x + 5}$$ (2)

16 (a) Solve these inequalities.
  (i) $5p - 7 \geq p + 3$ (1)
  (ii) $3(2p - 7) < 2(p + 3)$ (2)
(b) Write down the full integer solution set for these simultaneous inequalities.
  $5p - 7 \geq p + 3$ and $3(2p - 7) < 2(p + 3)$ (2)

17 Light intensity I (measured in candelas, cd) is inversely proportional to the square of the distance d m from its source.
A lighthouse beam measures 1 million cd at a distance of 1 m.
(a) Find a formula for I in terms of d. (2)
(b) A boat p km from the lighthouse observes its beam has a light intensity of 4 cd.
Calculate the value of p. (1)

18 The diagram shows parts of the graphs of $y = f(x)$ and $y = g(x)$

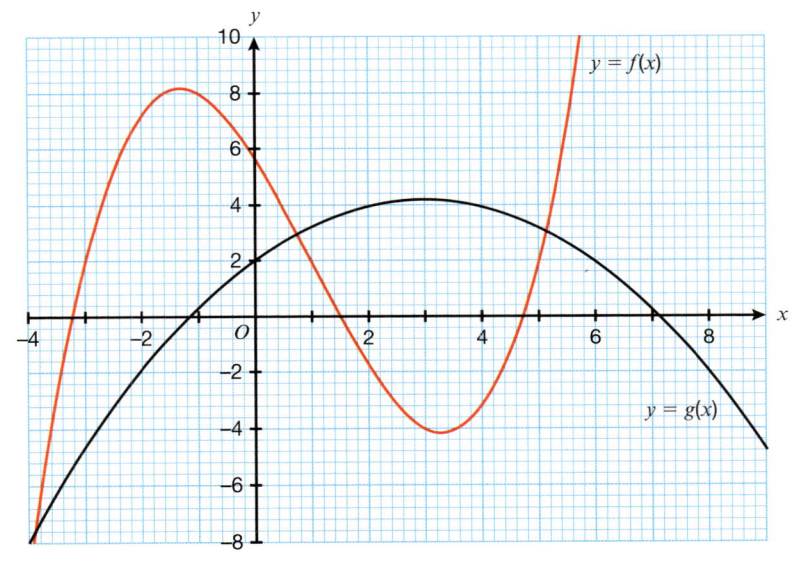

(a) Estimate the values of
  (i) $f(0)$ (1)
  (ii) $fg(0)$ (2)
(b) Use the graph to solve $f(x) = 2$ (1)
(c) Calculate an estimate for the gradient of the curve $y = g(x)$ at the point on the curve where $x = 7$ (1)

19 JKLM is a cyclic quadrilateral.
GJH is a tangent to the circle at J.
GML is a straight line.
JL and MK intersect at P.
Angle MGJ = 81°
Angle JKM = 30°
Angle HJK = 73°

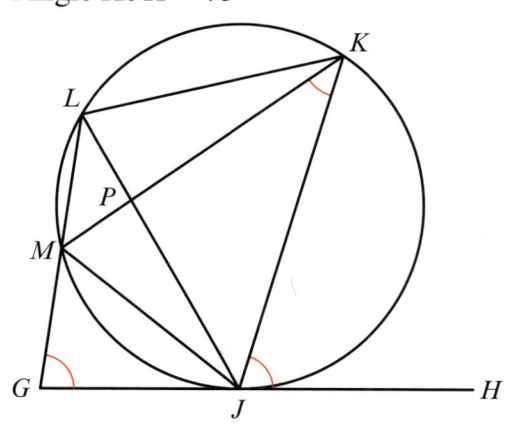

Calculate the following angles. Justify each step of your working.
(a) Angle MLJ (1)
(b) Angle JLK (2)
(c) Angle KPL (2)
(d) Angle JKL (2)

20 $f(x) = 5x^2 - 20x + 12$
(a) Show that $f(x) = a(x + b)^2 + c$ where a, b and c are constants to be found. (2)
(b) Write down the minimum point of $f(x)$. (1)

21 There are 50 children at a party.
The children have three toys to choose from: a colouring set (C), a steam train (S) and a velociraptor mask (V).
The Venn diagram shows their choices.

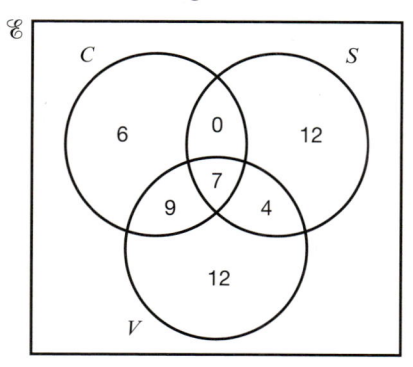

A child is picked at random from the group.
Calculate
(a) $P(C \cap S \cap V)$ (1)
(b) $P(C \cap S')$ (1)
(c) $P(S \cup V')$ (2)
(d) $P(C \mid V)$ (1)

22 $f(x) = \sin x$ for $0 \leq x \leq 360°$
$g(x) = 2f(x) + 1$
(a) Sketch $g(x)$ for $0 \leq x \leq 360°$ (1)
A is the maximum point and B is the minimum point of $g(x)$.
(b) Show A and B on your sketch. (2)
(c) Write down the exact coordinates of A and B. (2)

23 An equilateral triangle with perimeter $3a$ has an area of A.
A circle of circumference 10π has the same area as the equilateral triangle.
Show by clear algebraic working that $a^2 = \dfrac{100\pi}{\sqrt{3}}$ (2)

24 The diagram shows a closed cylindrical container.
The height is y cm.
The radius is r cm.
The volume is 240 cm³.

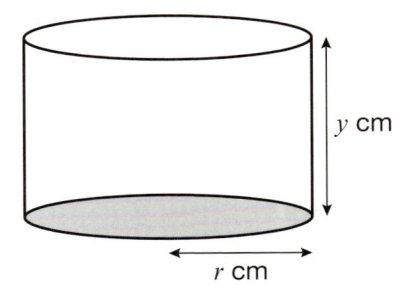

(a) Show that $y = \dfrac{240}{\pi r^2}$ (1)

The cylinder has a total surface area of A cm².

(b) Show that $A = 2\pi r^2 + \dfrac{480}{r}$ (2)

(c) By using $\dfrac{dA}{dr}$ show that the stationary point occurs when $r = \sqrt[3]{\dfrac{120}{\pi}}$ (2)

(d) Explain why this stationary point produces the minimum value of A and find its value in cm² to 3 s.f. (1)

TOTAL: 100 MARKS

Examination Practice Papers 1B

Time: 2 hours

1. Calculate the value of $\sqrt{\frac{3.1^2 + 1.3^2}{3.1^2 - 1.3^2}}$ to 3 s.f. (2)

2. Romesh has a glass of mango juice for breakfast which contains 24 mg of vitamin C. This is 60% of the total recommended daily amount of vitamin C.
Calculate the weekly amount of vitamin C in mg that Romesh should consume if he is to meet the recommended figure. (2)

3. Part of the train service timetable from Barcelona to Paris is shown.

Barcelona	16:20
Perpignon	17:45
Nimes	19:48
Paris	22:45

   The mean speed of the train from Nimes to Paris is 168 km/h.
   (a) Calculate the distance travelled by the train from Nimes to Paris to the nearest km.
   The distance by rail from Barcelona to Paris is 831 km. The mean speed of the train for the whole journey remains unchanged. (2)
   (b) Calculate the total time of stoppages for this journey to the nearest minute. (2)

4. Show that $1\frac{1}{2} \times \left(7\frac{1}{3} \div 3\frac{1}{7}\right)^2 = 8\frac{1}{6}$ (2)

5. $x = 2464$ and $y = 1372$
   (a) Write x and y as products of prime factors. (2)
   (b) (i) The highest common factor (HCF) of x and y is $2^m \times 7^n$.
   Find the values of m and n. (2)
   (ii) The lowest common multiple (LCM) of x and y is $2^p \times 7^q \times 11^r$.
   Find the value of $(p + q + r)^{(m+n)}$. (2)

6 The table gives the ingredients to make 5 loaves of brown bread.

Ingredients for 5 loaves of brown bread
2000 g of brown bread flour
500 g of white bread flour
35 g of dried yeast
$7\frac{1}{2}$ teaspoons of salt
5 tablespoons of butter

(a) Nicki wants to make 20 loaves of brown bread.
    How many grams of dried yeast is required? (2)
(b) 90 teaspoons of salt are used to make L loaves of bread.
    Find L. (2)
(c) Express the ratio of the weights of brown bread flour to white bread flour to yeast in the form of $p : q : r$ where p, q and r are integers in their lowest form. (2)

7 Lucia took part in an 800 m race at the school sports day.
The times of the other five runners were:
2 min 13.6 s, 2 min 15.9 s, 2 min 15.8 s, 2 min 18.3 s, 2 min 14.1 s
The mean time of all six runners was 2 min 15.5 s.
Gold, silver and bronze medals were awarded for the first three athletes to cross the finish line.
Calculate if Lucia was awarded a medal and, if so, which one. (3)

8 The perimeter of a semicircle is 100 cm to the nearest 10 cm.
Calculate to 3 s.f. the
(a) upper bound for the area in cm² of the semicircle (2)
(b) lower bound for the area in cm² of the semicircle (2)

9 Ship A is 40 km west and 50 km south of ship B.
(a) The distance between the ships is given by $k\sqrt{10}$
    Find the value of k. (2)
(b) Calculate the bearing of ship A from ship B.
    Give your answer to the nearest degree. (2)

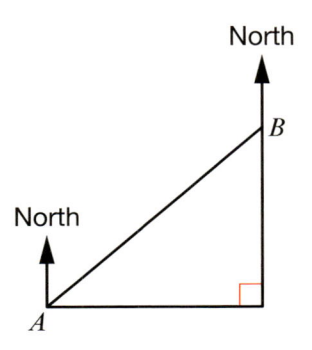

10 Solve the equation $(2x + 1)(x - 1)^2 = 1$ (3)

11 Prove that the difference between the squares of two consecutive odd numbers will always be a multiple of 8.
Show clear algebraic working. (3)

12 A thin metal pole AB fits perfectly inside a cylindrical tin.
The diameter of the tin is 8 cm.
The volume of the tin is $192\,\pi$ cm³.
AC is a diameter of the base of the tin.
B is on the top edge of the tin directly above C.
Calculate the angle between the pole and the base of the tin.
Give your answer to 3 s.f. (3)

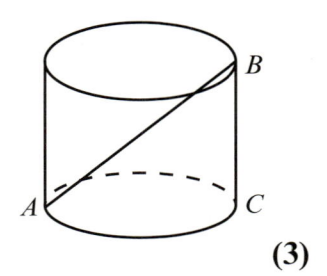

13 An n-sided regular polygon has side length L cm.
The interior angle of the polygon is 144°.
The area of the polygon is A cm².
 (a) Find the value of n and state the name of the polygon. (2)
 (b) Find the perimeter of the polygon if L is 12 cm. (2)
The polygon is enlarged such that the new perimeter is 9.6 m.
 (c) Express the area of the enlarged polygon in terms of A. (2)

14 A box contains 15 toys.
The box contains 5 teddy bears, 5 robots and 5 dolls.
Kieran randomly takes 3 toys one at a time without replacement.
Calculate the probability that Kieran takes exactly 2 of the same kind of toy. (3)

15 $g(x) = \dfrac{10}{x - 3}$ and $h(x) = \dfrac{x - 5}{x}$
 (a) Express g^{-1} in the form $g^{-1}(x) = ...$ (3)
 (b) If $gh(p) = -1$, find p, showing clear algebraic working. (3)

16 Esther invests €12 000 in a savings account for 10 years.
The savings account pays compound interest at a rate of
2.5% for the 1st year
3.5% per year for all subsequent years
 (a) How much will Esther have in her account at the end of 10 years? (3)
Ivan invests money in a savings bond which pays interest at a compound rate of 1.5% per year.
At the end of two years Ivan's savings bond is worth €1236.27.
 (b) How much money did Ivan invest in his savings bond? (3)

17 The ratio of $(x + 1) : (x + 2) = (y + 1) : (y + 3)$
Find an expression for y in terms of x, showing clear algebraic working. (3)

18 An artist makes a cylindrical platform from marble.
The diameter is 100 cm and the height is 120 cm.
The density of marble is 2710 kg/m³.
   (a) Show that the mass of the platform = $k\pi$ kg where k is a constant to be found. (3)
   (b) The force exerted on the floor by this mass = 2.5×10^4 N
Calculate the pressure on the floor in N/m² in standard form to 3 s.f. (3)

19 The equation of a circle C is given by $x^2 + y^2 = 26$
The line L has equation $2x + y - 3 = 0$
Line L intercepts circle C at two points, P and Q.
Find the exact coordinates of P and Q, showing clear algebraic working. (3)

20 Two Mars Rovers set off from their base camp at the same time to explore a level plain.
Rover A travels at x cm/s on a bearing of 040°.
Rover B travels at 4 cm/s on a bearing of 070°.
After 3 hours the Rovers are 250 m apart.
Calculate the smallest possible value of x in cm/s to 3 s.f. (4)

21 The diagram shows a parallelogram, $PQRS$.

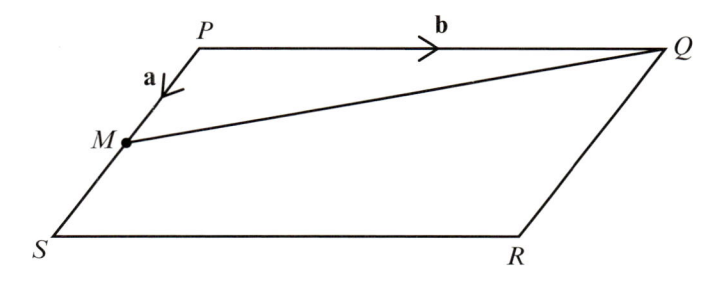

M is the midpoint of PS.
$\overrightarrow{PM} = \mathbf{a}$ and $\overrightarrow{PQ} = \mathbf{b}$
N is the point on MQ such that $MN : NQ = 1 : 2$
Prove that PNR are collinear points. (4)

22 An arithmetic progression is generated by the formula $t_n = 3n + 1$, where n is the position of each term in the sequence.
Find the sum of the first twenty terms of the arithmetic progression. (4)

23 A body is moving in a straight line passing through a fixed point O.
The displacement, s metres, of the body from O at time t seconds is given by
$s = (t-1)^3 + 3t$ metres

(a) Find, as a function of t, the
   (i)   velocity, v m/s   **(2)**
   (ii)   acceleration, a m/s^2 **(2)**

(b) Calculate the velocity of the body when its acceleration is zero. **(2)**

24 Two solid spheres, each of radius r cm, fit exactly inside a hollow cylinder.
The radius of the cylinder is r cm.
The height of the cylinder is equal to $4r$ cm.

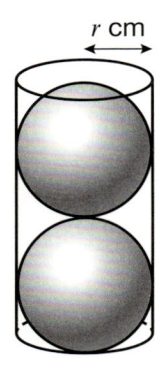

(a) Show by clear algebraic working that the volume of the space inside the cylinder, not occupied by the spheres, V, is $\frac{4\pi r^3}{3}$ cm^3. **(3)**

(b) If $V = \frac{9\pi}{2}$ cm^3, calculate the value of r in cm. **(2)**

(c) What fraction of the volume of the cylinder is not occupied by the two spheres? **(2)**

TOTAL: 100 MARKS

Examination Practice Papers 2A

Time: 2 hours

1. The bearing of the village of Moritz to the town of Kielder is 070°.
   Calculate the bearing of Moritz from Kielder. (2)

2. (a) Calculate the nth term of the sequence 10, 9.5, 9, 8.5… (2)
   (b) Find the number of terms of the sequence required such that the sum to n terms is zero. (2)

3. Find the highest common factor and the lowest common multiple of $12x^3y^2z^5$ and $21x^5y^3z^2$. (2)

4. Rearrange the formula to make v the subject.
   $$\frac{2v - w}{3} = \frac{2v + w}{5} + u$$ (2)

5. A pair of running shoes costs $92 inclusive of sales tax at 15%.
   Calculate the price of the shoes before sales tax is added. (2)

6. The straight line L passes through the points $A(1, 4)$ and $B(-3, 8)$.
   (a) Calculate the equation of L. (2)
   Line M is the perpendicular bisector of AB.
   (b) Calculate the equation of M. (2)
   Express both equations in the form $ax + by + c = 0$, where a, b and c are integers.

7. Solve the inequality $2x^2 - x - 6 \geq 0$ (2)

8 *A*, *B* and *C* are three points on the circumference of a circle with centre *O*.
DAE is a tangent to the circle at *A*.
BC = AC
Angle *ODA = x*, angle *EAB = 2x* and angle *CFD = 3x*

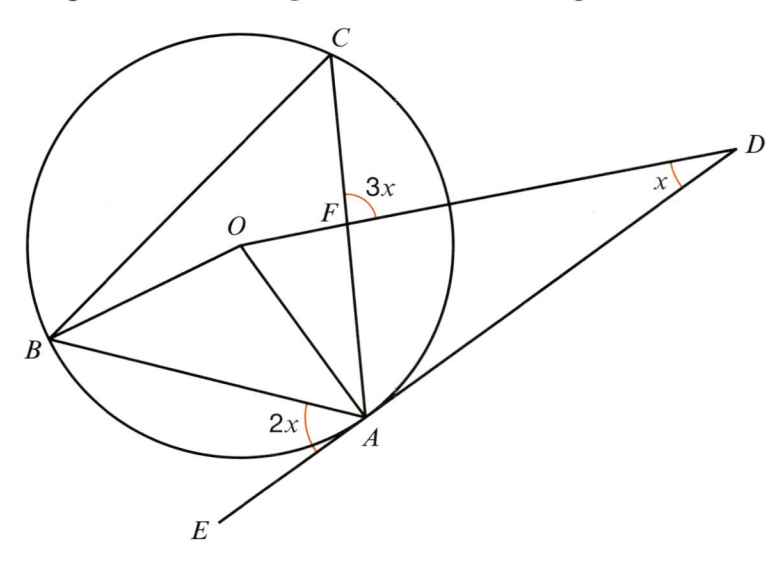

Calculate the value of *x*. State clear reasons for each stage of your working. **(2)**

9 The table shows information about the time, in minutes, spent on revising Chemistry by each of 24 students the night before their examination.

Time t (min)	Number of students
$0 < t \leq 30$	4
$30 < t \leq 60$	10
$60 < t \leq 90$	7
$90 < t \leq 120$	3

(a) Calculate the percentage of the students who spent more than 90 minutes on their Chemistry revision. **(1)**
(b) State the modal class. **(1)**
(c) Calculate an estimate of the mean revision time in minutes and seconds. **(2)**
Siri joins this class and her revision time was identical to the class mean revision time.
(d) Show, with further calculations, if the new mean revision time will increase, decrease or remain unchanged. **(2)**

10 Jana ran the school 800-m race in 2 min 20 s.
The length of the track was measured to the nearest 10 m and her time was given to the nearest 5 seconds.
Calculate correct to 3 s.f.
(a) the upper bound for her mean speed in m/s **(2)**
(b) the lower bound for her mean speed in m/s **(2)**

11 At an airport, the probability of a passenger having overweight luggage is p.
The possibilities for the first two passengers' luggage weight at the queue for the check-in desk are shown below.

(a) Copy and complete the tree diagram.

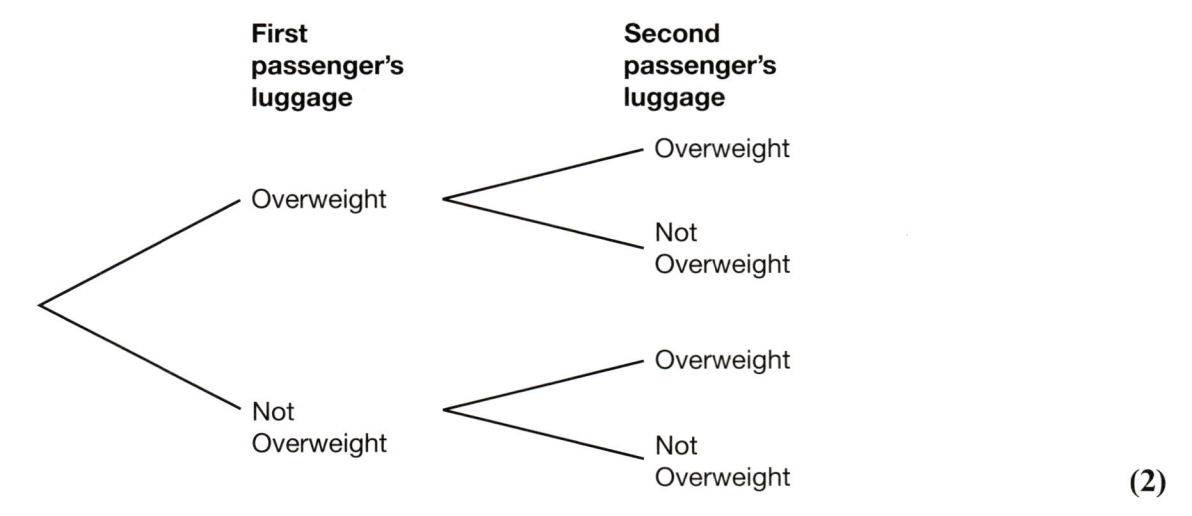

First passenger's luggage — Overweight / Not Overweight
Second passenger's luggage — Overweight / Not Overweight (from each branch)

(2)

(b) (i) Find an expression, in terms of p, for the probability that exactly one of these two passengers has overweight luggage. (2)

The probability that exactly one of these two passengers has overweight luggage is 0.05.

(ii) Find the possible values of p correct to 3 s.f. (2)

12 The numbers a, b, c and d are four consecutive odd integers, where $a < b < c < d$
Prove that $d^2 - a^2$ is divisible by 24. (3)

13 ABC is an isosceles triangle.
$AC = AB = 3$ cm
$BC = 2$ cm
M is the midpoint of CB.
$AX : XM = 3 : 1$
Show that $AX = \frac{3\sqrt{2}}{2}$ cm.

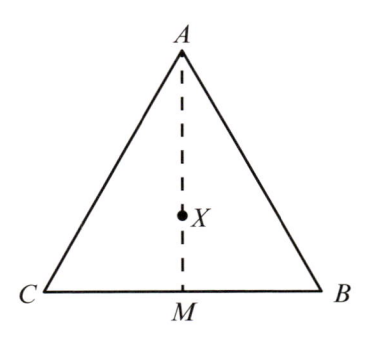

(3)

14 (a) Show by clear algebraic working that

$$1 - \frac{1}{x+a} - \frac{x-1}{x} = \frac{a}{x(x+a)}$$ (2)

(b) Solve $1 - \frac{1}{x+2} - \frac{x-1}{x} = \frac{2}{3}$ (3)

15 Priti has done a tree survey.
The diagram shows her results.

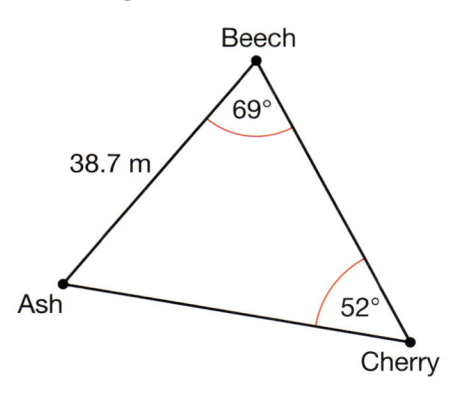

The distance between the ash and beech trees is 38.7 m correct to 3 s.f.
All angles are correct to 2 s.f.
Calculate the lower bound (minimum) distance in metres between the ash and cherry trees correct to 3 s.f. **(3)**

16 The composite shape shown consists of a semicircle of radius r cm together with a rectangle of width r cm and length $4r$ cm.

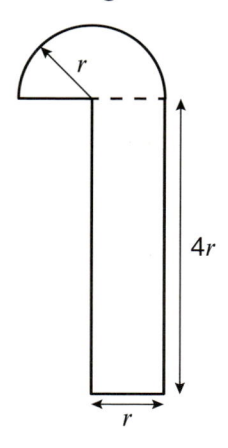

The perimeter of the shape is 50 cm.
(a) Find the area of the shape in cm². Give your answer correct to 4 s.f. **(2)**
The shape is used to make a prism of length 25 cm.
(b) (i) Find the volume of the prism in cm³ correct to 4 s.f. **(2)**
   (ii) Find the total surface area of the prism in cm² correct to 4 s.f. **(2)**
A mathematically similar prism is made using the same design of shape, but with a perimeter of 30 cm.

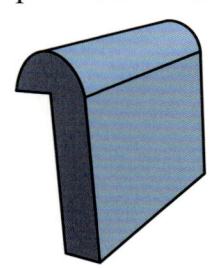

(c) (i) Find the volume of the new prism in cm³ correct to 3 s.f. **(1)**
   (ii) Find the surface area of the new prism in cm² correct to 3 s.f. **(1)**

17 $x = 3^{\frac{p}{q}}$ $\qquad$ $y = 3^{-\frac{q}{p}}$

(a) Express the following in terms of x
   (i) 3^{p-1} (2)
   (ii) 3^q (2)
(b) Express 3^p in terms of y.
$x^q : y^p = 3 : 1$ and $x^q \times y^p = 243$ (2)
(c) Show that $x = \frac{\sqrt{3}}{9}$ and $y = \sqrt[3]{9}$ (2)

18

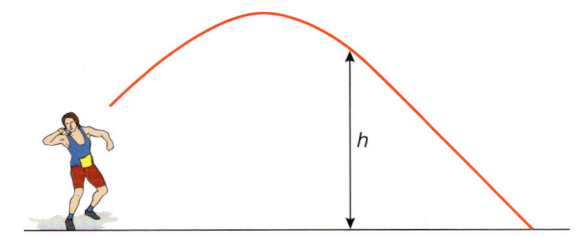

Felix is a shot putter. The formula for the height of the shot, h metres above the ground, t s after he has released the shot is $h = 2 + 6t - 5t^2$

(a) Find the value of t when the shot hits the ground correct to 3 s.f. (2)
(b) Express h in the form $h = a(t + b)^2 + c$, where a, b and c are constants to be found. (2)
(c) Hence find the greatest value of h and the time at which this occurs. (2)

19 The diagram shows two cylinders, A and B.

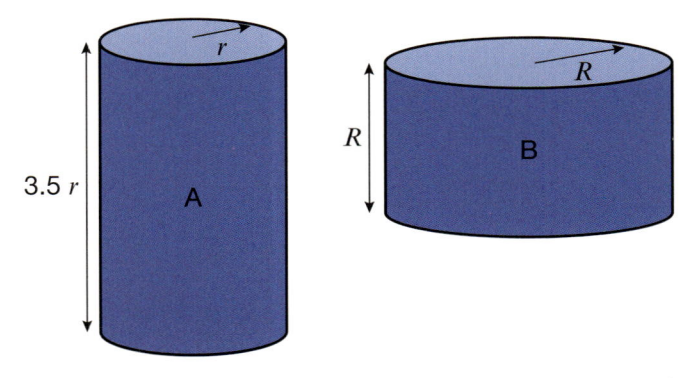

The radius of cylinder A is r cm and the height is $3.5r$ cm.
The radius of cylinder B is R cm and the height is R cm.
The total surface areas of the two cylinders are equal.
The ratio of the volume of cylinder A : volume of cylinder B $= m : n$
in its simplest form.
Find the values of m and n. (3)

20 OAB is a triangle.
OBR is a straight line.
P is a point on OA such that $OP : PA = 2 : 1$
Q is a point on AB such that $AQ : QB = 2 : 1$
R is a point on OB extended such that $OB : OR = 3 : 4$
$\overrightarrow{OA} = \mathbf{a}, \overrightarrow{OB} = \mathbf{b}$

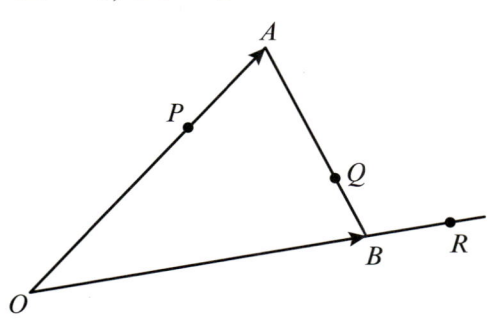

(a) Find $\overrightarrow{PQ}$ in terms of $\mathbf{a}$ and $\mathbf{b}$. (2)
(b) Prove that P, Q and R are collinear points. (2)

21 The image of point $P(x, y)$ is $Q(3, 7)$ after it has been reflected in the x-axis then translated by $\begin{pmatrix} -1 \\ 2 \end{pmatrix}$.

(a) Calculate the coordinates of P. (2)

The distance $OP = \sqrt{k}$, where O is the origin.

(b) Find the value of k. (2)

22 The diagram shows the graph of $y = f(x) = \cos(x)$, for $0 \leq x \leq 360°$

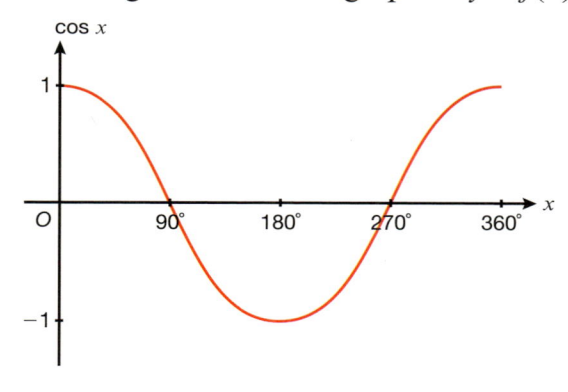

(a) Sketch the following graphs.
   (i) $y = f(x) + 1$ (2)
   (ii) $y = -f(x)$ (2)
   (iii) $y = 2f(x)$ (2)
(b) If $g(x) = x^2$, find the function $gf(\pi x) + \pi$, giving your answer in terms of $\cos(x)$. (2)

23 u, v and w are three variables.
u is directly proportional to v^2.
u is also directly proportional to $\sqrt{w}$.
Given that $v = 50$ when $w = 144$, find the value of v when $w = 625$
Give your answer in standard form correct to 3 s.f. (3)

24 A box is in the shape of a cuboid.
The height is $2x$ cm, the width is x cm and the depth is d cm.
The total surface area is 1400 cm².
Narrow tape is fastened parallel to the edges around the box as shown.

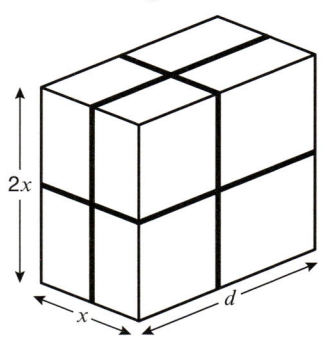

(a) Show that the length of tape, L cm, used is

$$L = \frac{28x}{3} + \frac{2800}{3x}$$

(Ignore any overlap of the tape.)
The length of tape used is the minimum possible. **(3)**

(b) Show that the volume of the box is $\frac{10\,000}{3}$ cm³ when L is a minimum. **(3)**

TOTAL: 100 MARKS

Examination Practice Papers 2B

Time: 2 hours

1. Rice is sold in two bags.
   Bag A: 2.5 kg at $2
   Bag B: 4 kg at $3.20
   Show, by calculation, which bag is the better value. **(2)**

2. Calculate the perimeter of a semicircle of area 120 cm² correct to 3 s.f. **(3)**

3. Calculate the value of $\sqrt[3]{\dfrac{\pi^3 + \pi^2 + \pi}{\left(\dfrac{\pi}{3 \times 10^{-3}}\right)}}$ in standard form correct to 3 s.f. **(2)**

4. At a school prom 45% of the students are in Year 10, the rest are in Year 11.
   60% of the Year 10 students and 30% of the Year 11 chose the fish option to eat.
   What percentage of those at the prom did not choose the fish option to eat? **(2)**

5. A sequence of fractions is defined as
   $T_n = \dfrac{t_n}{u_n}$, where $t_n = 2n - 1$, $u_n = 2n + 1$

   Calculate the product of the first four terms of the sequence T_n. **(3)**

6. A bag contains n similar beads.
   Three are white, four are black and the rest are red.
   Karen randomly selects a bead and replaces it.
   If this is repeated n times, estimate how many non-white beads she would expect to see in terms of n. **(3)**

7. Mika invests £p at a compound interest rate of 5% per year.
   After 3 years his investment is worth £1389.15.
   Calculate
   (a) the value of p **(2)**
   (b) the percentage profit gained by Mika correct to 3 s.f. **(2)**

8. A cylindrical bottle of water has a flat circular base of circumference 30 cm.
   The bottle is on a flat table and exerts a force of 15 N on the table.
   Calculate the pressure of the bottle on the table in N/m² correct to 3 s.f. **(3)**

9 Make t the subject of the formula.

$$m = \sqrt{\frac{t+1}{t-1}}$$ (3)

10 The Venn diagram shows the universal set $\mathcal{E}$ and sets A, B and C.
The numbers refer to the number of elements in the set.

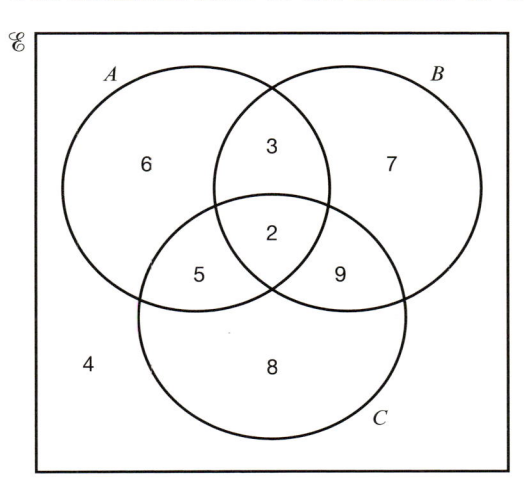

A single random selection is made from the universal set.
Calculate the following probabilities, showing your working clearly.
(a) $P(A')$ (1)
(b) $P(B \cap C')$ (1)
(c) $P(A \cup B \cup C)$ (1)
An element is selected at random from the set $A \cup B$.
(d) Calculate the probability that this element is in the set $A \cap B \cap C$ (1)

11 The diagram shows part of a tessellation of tiles.
It consists of two congruent regular pentagons and part of a regular polygon A.
Two sides of each of the regular pentagons and two sides of A meet at point P.

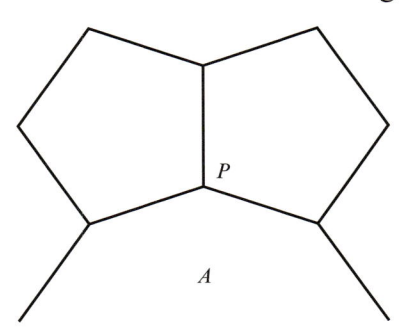

(a) How many pentagons surround polygon A? (2)
(b) Name the regular polygon A. (1)

12 Ibo ran the 100 m sprint in 12.5 s as shown by the speed–time graph.

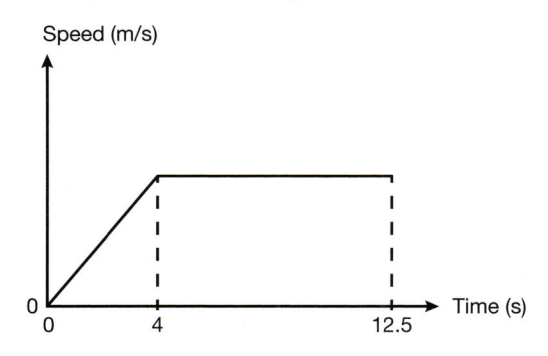

Calculate correct to 3 s.f. Ibo's
(a) maximum velocity in m/s (2)
(b) acceleration in m/s² for $0 < t < 4$ (2)

13 A, B, C and D are points on a circle.
PAB and PDC are straight lines.
$PA = 10$ cm
$PD = 8$ cm
$DC = 7$ cm

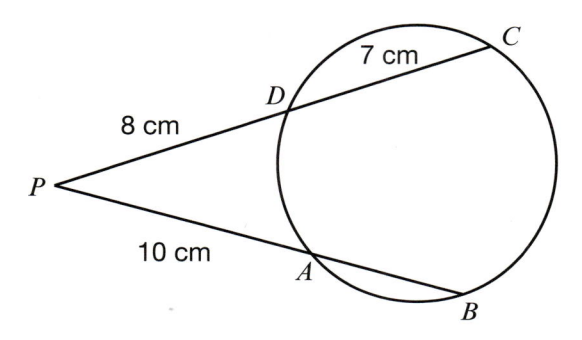

Given that angle $APD = 30°$, calculate length BC to 3 s.f. (4)

14 a and b are positive integers.
$(11\sqrt{3} - a)(3\sqrt{3} + a) = 95 + 32b\sqrt{3}$

Show that $a^2 + b^2 = \frac{17}{4}$ (3)

15 An ornamental garden lawn *ABCD*, shown shaded below, is part of a minor-sector of a circle.

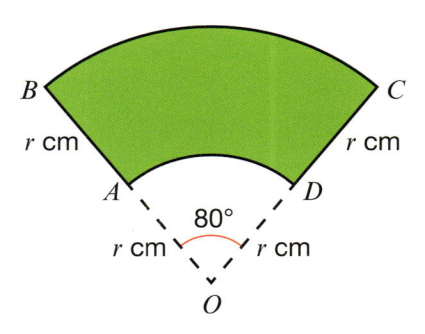

The total perimeter of the lawn is *p* m.

(a) Show that $p = \dfrac{2r(3 + 2\pi)}{3}$ (2)

The lawn is to be laid with grass turf at a cost of $18 per m^2.
The perimeter of the lawn is 18 m.

(b) Calculate the cost of the grass turf to the nearest $. (3)

16 (a) Calculate the coordinates of the point of intersection of the two lines.
$$6x - 5y = 7$$
$$4x + 3y = 11$$ (3)

(b) Solve the simultaneous equations.
$$6p^{-2} - 5q^{-1} = 7$$
$$4p^{-2} + 3q^{-1} = 11$$ (3)

17 The mast of a yacht is shown below as the vertical length *AB*.

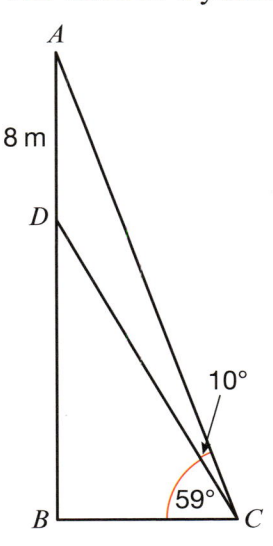

Points *A* and *B* are at the top and bottom of the mast respectively.
The angle of elevation of *A* from *C* is 69°.
The angle of elevation of *D* from *C* is 59°.
Length *AD* = 8 m
Calculate the total length of the mast in metres correct to 3 s.f. (4)

18 Three functions are defined as
$f(x) = \sin(x)$
$g(x) = \frac{x + 60}{2}$
$h(x) = 2x$

(a) Express the inverse function g^{-1} in the form $g^{-1}(x) = ...$ (2)

(b) If the domain of $f(x)$ is $0 \leq x \leq 90°$, solve $fgh(x) = 1$
Show clear algebraic working. (3)

19 A school carries out a spot-check on the number of students arriving late to the headteacher's assembly.
The results are illustrated in the incomplete frequency table and histogram.

(a) Complete the table. (2)

Minutes late, t (min)	$0 < t \leq 1$	$1 < t \leq 3$	$3 < t \leq 5$	$5 < t \leq 6$	$6 < t \leq 7$	$7 < t \leq 8$
Number of students	6	14	8			12
Frequency density	6		4			4

(b) Complete the histogram. (2)

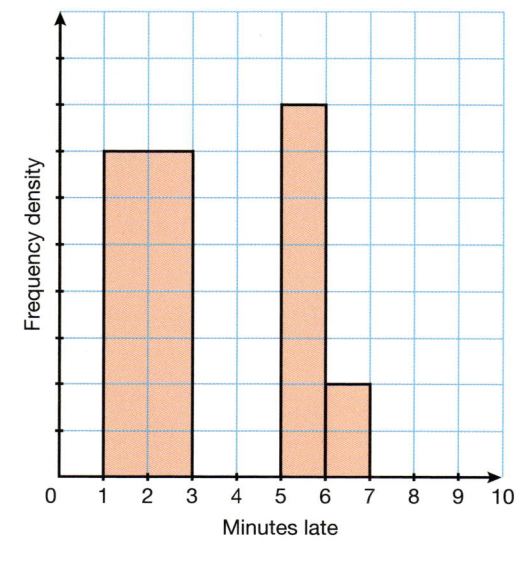

(c) Find the modal class.
A student is picked at random from this group of late students. (1)

(d) Calculate the probability that this student arrived at least $2\frac{1}{2}$ minutes late. (2)

20 Jack has a herd of llamas on his farm.
The ratio of male llamas to female llamas is 3 : 10.
One day a female llama gives birth to a litter of 3 male and 2 female crias (baby llamas).
The ratio of male to female llamas is now 1 : 3.
Calculate how many llamas are now in Jack's herd. (3)

21 (a) Complete the table of values for $y = \frac{1}{4}\left(2x + \frac{12}{x} - 5\right)$ (2)

x	0.5	1	2	3	4	5	6
y	5		1.25			1.85	

(b) Draw the graph of $y = \frac{1}{4}\left(2x + \frac{12}{x} - 5\right)$ for $0.5 \leq x \leq 6$ (2)

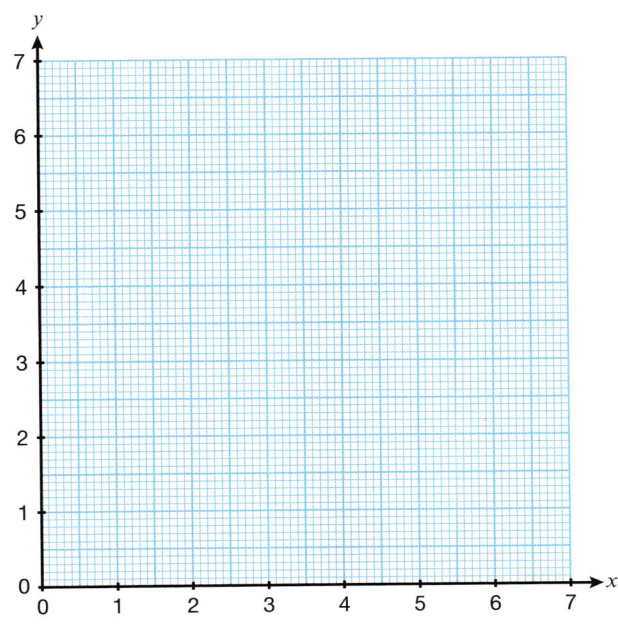

(c) Use the graph to find estimates for the solutions of the equation
$2x + \frac{12}{x} = 13$ (3)

22 A crystal is in the shape of a tetrahedron.

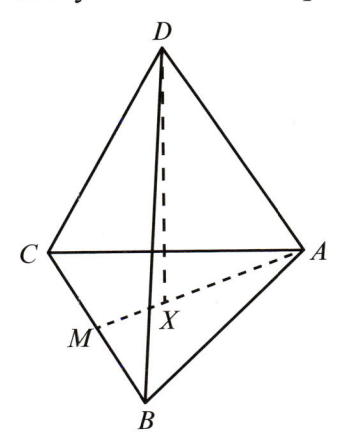

Each face of the tetrahedron is an equilateral triangle of side 2 mm.
M is the midpoint of CB and $AX : XM = 2 : 1$
The point D is vertically above the point X.

(a) Show that the volume of the crystal is $\frac{2\sqrt{2}}{3}$ mm³.

(volume of a tetrahedron = $\frac{1}{3} \times$ base area $\times$ height) (3)

(b) Find the angle DMA correct to 3 s.f. (3)

23 **(a)** Express $\dfrac{4x^2 - 9}{x + 2} \div \dfrac{2x^2 - 5x - 12}{x - 4}$ as a single fraction. (3)

(b) Hence solve $\dfrac{4x^2 - 9}{x + 2} \div \dfrac{2x^2 - 5x - 12}{x - 4} = \dfrac{x + 1}{2(x - 2)}$ (3)

24 A small stone is thrown vertically upwards from the top of a 24 m vertical cliff beside the sea.

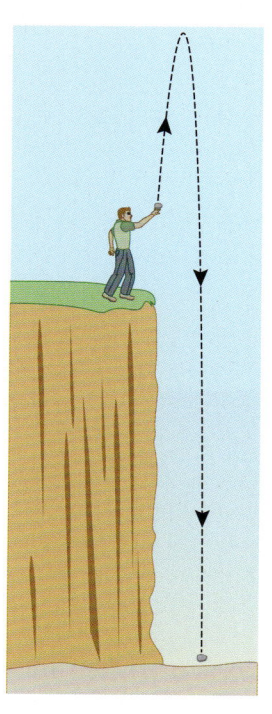

The height of the stone s metres from the point of projection, t seconds later, is given by $s = 20t - 4t^2$

(a) When does the stone hit the sea? (2)
(b) Find the velocity of the stone in m/s as it enters the water. (2)
(c) Calculate the mean speed of the stone in m/s over its entire time of flight correct to 3 s.f. (2)

TOTAL: 100 MARKS

GLOSSARY

acceleration (*noun*) the rate at which **velocity** changes with time

acute angle (*noun*) an angle that is less than 90°

adjacent (*adjective*) next to

angle of depression (*noun*) the angle measured downwards from the horizontal

angle of elevation (*noun*) the angle measured upwards from the horizontal

appreciate (*verb*) to gain value over time

arc (*noun*) part of a curve or circle

arithmetic sequence (*noun*) a sequence of numbers in which the terms increase (or decrease) by a fixed number (= **common difference**); for example, 2, 5, 8, 11, 14 (common difference = + 3)

arithmetic series (*noun*) an arithmetic sequence with the signs + or − placed between each number; for example, 2 + 5 + 8 + 11 + 14

axis of symmetry (*noun*) (or line of symmetry) a line through a shape such that each side is a mirror image of the other

bar chart (*noun*) a diagram using rectangles of equal width (bars) whose heights represent an amount or quantity

bearing (*noun*) an angle measured clockwise from north, used to describe a direction

bisect (*verb*) to divide something into two equal parts

bisector (*noun*) a straight line that divides an angle or another line into two equal parts

chord (*noun*) a straight line joining two points on a curve

circumference (*noun*) the total distance around a circle

class (*noun*) a group of data in a collection of grouped data

clear (*verb*) to remove fractions in an equation by multiplying both sides of the equation by the lowest **common denominator**

collinear (of points) (*adjective*) three or more points that all lie on the same straight line

column vector (*noun*) a vector such as $\binom{5}{8}$ used to describe a translation; the top number gives the movement parallel to the horizontal axis (to the right or left); the bottom number gives the movement parallel to the vertical axis (up or down)

common denominator (*noun*) a number that can be divided exactly by all the **denominators** (= bottom numbers) in a set of fractions

common difference (*noun*) the difference between each term in an **arithmetic sequence**

common factor (*noun*) a number (a **factor**) that two or more other numbers can be exactly divided by; for example, 2 is a common factor of 4, 6 and 8

compasses (*noun*) a V-shaped instrument with one sharp point and a pencil at the other end, used for drawing circles

complement (*noun*) the complement of a **set** is all those members (objects) which are not in that set but which are in the universal set (all members being considered)

compound interest (*noun*) interest is the extra money that you must pay back when you borrow money or money paid to you by a bank or financial institution when you keep money in an account there; compound interest is calculated on both the sum of money lent or borrowed or saved and on the unpaid interest already earned or charged

compound measure (*noun*) a measure made up of two or more different measurements; for example, speed, density and pressure

conditional probability (*noun*) the probability of a **dependent event**; that is, the probability of event A given that event B has already occurred

consecutive (*adjective*) numbers follow each other in order, with no gaps, from smallest to largest

correct to (*adjective*) accurate to; a number given correct to '…' has been rounded; for example, 3.592 is 3.6 correct to 1 decimal place and 3.59 correct to 2 decimal places

cube (*noun*) a solid object that has 6 identical square **faces** (= flat surfaces)

cubic graph (*noun*) the graph of a cubic function of the form $y = ax^3 + bx^2 + cx + d$ where a, b, c and d are numbers and the highest power of x is 3

cuboid (*noun*) a solid object that has 6 rectangular **faces** (= flat surfaces)

cumulative frequency (*noun*) the total of all the frequencies of a set of data up to any particular group of data; a 'running total' of the frequencies

cyclic quadrilateral (*noun*) a flat shape with 4 sides (= a **quadrilateral**) with all 4 vertices on the **circumference** of a circle

cylinder (*noun*) a solid with straight parallel sides and a circular cross-section; an example of a **prism**

decimal place (or **d.p.**) (*noun*) the position of a digit to the right of a decimal point

dependent event (*noun*) an event that depends on the outcome of another event

denominator (*noun*) the number below the line in a fraction

depreciate (*verb*) to lose value over time

diameter (*noun*) a straight line passing through the centre of a circle and joining two points that lie on the circle; a chord that passes through the centre of a circle

differentiate (*verb*) to find the gradient of a **function**

direct proportion (*noun*) a relationship between two quantities such that as one quantity increases the other increases at the same rate

dispersion (*noun*) a measure of the way in which a set of data is spread out

displacement (*noun*) the distance and direction of an object from a fixed point

domain (*noun*) the set of all input values of a **function**

edge (*noun*) a line segment where two faces in a 3D shape meet

equidistant (*adjective*) at an equal distance from two places or points

equilateral triangle (*noun*) a triangle whose 3 sides are all the same length and all the angles are 60°

expand (an expression) (*verb*) to **multiply out** brackets (= remove brackets)

exterior angle (*noun*) the angle formed outside a **polygon** between any one edge and the extended adjacent edge

face (*noun*) the flat surface of a solid object

factor (*noun*) a number that divides exactly into another number

factorise (*verb*) to put an expression into brackets; the reverse of expand

frequency (of a piece of data) (*noun*) the number of times each piece of data is found

frequency density (*noun*) a measure of the frequency divided by the class width:

$$\text{frequency density} = \frac{\text{frequency}}{\text{class width}}$$

the height of each bar in a **histogram**

function (*noun*) a set of rules for turning one number into another

gradient (*noun*) the measure of the slope of a straight line relative to the horizontal; for a straight line

$$\text{gradient} = \frac{\text{change in the } y \text{ coordinates}}{\text{change in the } x \text{ coordinates}} = \frac{\text{'rise'}}{\text{'run'}}$$

hemisphere (*noun*) a half of a sphere

histogram (*noun*) a diagram similar to a bar chart where the width of each bar is equal to the class width, the area of the bar represents the frequency, and the height of each bar is the **frequency density**

hypotenuse (*noun*) the longest side of a **right-angled triangle**; it is the side opposite the right angle

improper fraction (*noun*) a fraction such as $\frac{107}{8}$ in which the **numerator** (= top number) is larger than the **denominator** (= bottom number)

independent event (*noun*) an event that does not affect the probability of another event

indices (*noun*) (*plural*) (*singular* **index**) (= **powers**) a number which tells you how many times to multiply the given number or term by itself; for example, the ^{2} in 4^2 is the index

integer (*noun*) a whole number

intercept (*noun*) the point on a graph where the graph crosses an axis

interior angle (*noun*) an angle formed inside a **polygon** between two adjacent edges

interquartile range (*noun*) the difference between the upper and lower **quartiles** of a set of data

intersect (*verb*) if two lines intersect, they meet or cross over each other

inverse (*noun*) opposite in effect or the reverse of; for example, addition (+) is the inverse of subtraction (−)

inverse proportion (*noun*) a relationship between two quantities such that one quantity increases at the same rate as the other quantity decreases

irrational number (*noun*) a number that cannot be written as a fraction; for example, $\sqrt{2}$ and π

lower bound (*noun*) the value half a unit less than the rounded measurement

magnitude (of a vector) (*noun*) the length of a **vector**

map (*noun*) the connection from one set to another

map (*verb*) to translate, reflect or rotate a shape so that it fits (maps) onto another shape exactly

mapping diagram (*noun*) a diagram that lists two **sets**; arrows are used to show how the members are to be matched

mass (*noun*) a measure of how much matter is in an object

maximum point (*noun*) the highest **turning point** on a graph

mean (*noun*) the numerical value found by adding together all the separate values of a data set and dividing by how many pieces of data there are

median (*noun*) the middle value of a set of values that have been arranged in size order

midpoint (*noun*) a point that is halfway along the line segment joining two points

minimum point (*noun*) the lowest **turning point** on a graph

mixed number (*noun*) a number that consists of a whole number and a fraction; for example $7\frac{1}{4}$

modal class (*noun*) the **class** of grouped data which has the highest frequency

mode (*noun*) the piece of data that occurs most often in a set of data

multiple (of a number) (*noun*) is the product of that number and an integer (whole number)

multiply out (*verb*) (= **expand**) to remove brackets; to multiply out a bracket, multiply each term inside the bracket by the term outside the bracket; to multiply out double brackets, multiply each term in one bracket by each term in the other bracket

mutually exclusive events (*noun*) events that cannot happen at the same time

numerator (*noun*) the number above the line in a fraction; for example, 5 is the numerator in $\frac{5}{6}$

parabola (*noun*) a special curve, shaped like an arch (or upside-down arch); the path of an object that is thrown into the air follows a curve of this shape

parallelogram (*noun*) a flat shape with 4 sides (= a **quadrilateral**) in which opposite sides are parallel and the same length

perimeter (*noun*) the total distance around the edge of a shape

perpendicular (*adjective*) if one line is perpendicular to another line, they form an angle of 90° (= a **right angle**)

pie chart (*noun*) a diagram in which a circle is divided from its centre into sectors (parts) to show how the total is split up between the different categories

plane (*noun*) a flat surface

polygon (*noun*) a flat shape with 3 or more straight sides

power (*noun*) (= **index**) the small number written to the right and above another number

prime factor (*noun*) a factor that is a **prime number**

prime number (*noun*) a number that can only be divided by 1 and itself; for example, 3 and 7 are prime numbers

prism (*noun*) any solid with parallel sides that has a constant cross-section

product (*noun*) the number you get by multiplying two or more numbers

protractor (*noun*) an instrument for measuring and drawing angles

quadratic equation (or **quadratic**) (*noun*) an equation where the highest power of x is 2; for example, $3x^2 + 5x - 4 = 0$

quadratic graph (*noun*) the graph of a quadratic equation of the form $y = ax^2 + bx + c$ where a, b and c are numbers and the highest power of x is 2; its shape is that of a **parabola**

quadrilateral (*noun*) a flat shape with 4 straight sides

quartile (*noun*) each of 4 equal groups into which a data set can be divided

radius (*noun*) (*plural* **radii**) the distance from the centre to the curve which makes a circle; any straight line from the centre to the curve

random (*adjective*) happening or chosen by chance; a result is random if each possible result has the same chance of happening, and a selection is random if each object (or number) has the same chance of being chosen

range (*noun*) the difference between the lowest and highest values of a set of data

rate (*noun*) a fixed price paid or charged for something

rate (of change) (*noun*) how fast something changes over a period of time

rate (of inflation) (*noun*) percentage increase in the price of goods and services

ratio (*noun*) a ratio shows the relative sizes of two or more quantities

rationalise (the denominator) (*verb*) to remove the surd from the **denominator** (= bottom number) of a fraction

rational number (*noun*) a number that can be written as a fraction in the form $\frac{a}{b}$ where a and b are **integers** (= whole numbers) and $b \neq 0$; for example, $4 \left(\frac{4}{1}\right)$ and $0.\dot{4}\left(\frac{4}{9}\right)$

real numbers (*noun*) the set of all **rational** and **irrational numbers**

reciprocal graph (*noun*) the graph of a reciprocal function of the form $y = \frac{a}{x}$ where a is a number

recurring decimal (noun) a decimal in which one or more digits repeats; for example, 0.111 111...

relative frequency (noun) (or experimental probability) an estimate of probability based on experimental data; it is how often something happens divided by the total number of **trials** (= experiments)

retardation (noun) (= deceleration) the process of slowing down

rhombus (noun) a flat shape with 4 equal sides (= a **quadrilateral**) in which opposite sides are parallel and opposite angles are equal

right angle (noun) an angle that is 90° exactly

right-angled triangle (noun) a triangle that has a **right angle** (= 90°)

rotational symmetry (noun) the symmetry of a shape which can be turned and fitted onto itself within one full turn

round (verb) to alter an exact figure to one that is less exact

sample (noun) a small set of objects chosen from a larger set of objects which is examined to find out something about the larger set

scale (noun) a set of marks with regular spaces between them on the axes of a graph

scale (noun) a **ratio** such as 1 : 100 which shows the relationship between a length on a drawing or map and the actual length in real life

scale factor (noun) the scale factor of an enlargement is the number of times by which each original length has been multiplied

sector (noun) the part of a circle whose perimeter is an arc and two radii

segment (noun) the part of a circle that is separated from the rest of the circle when you draw a straight line across it

set (noun) a collection of objects (numbers, letters, symbols, etc.)

set builder notation (noun) mathematical notation used to describe what is in a **set**; for example, $\{x : x > 0\}$ is the set of all x such that x is greater than 0

significant figure (or **s.f.**) (noun) each of the digits of a number that are used to express it to the required accuracy, starting from the first non-zero digit from the left-hand end of the number

similar (adjective) shapes are similar when one shape is an enlargement of the other

similar triangles (noun) two triangles are similar if they are the same in shape but different in size

simplify (an expression) (verb) to collect all **like terms** so the expression is a collection of terms connected by + and − signs

simplify (a fraction) (verb) to divide the **numerator** (= top number) and **denominator** (= bottom number) by the same number (a **common factor**)

simultaneous equations (noun) two equations that are solved together to find two unknowns

sketch (verb) to make a rough drawing of a diagram, graph or shape

sketch (noun) a rough drawing of a diagram or graph which gives a general idea of the shape or relationship, or a rough drawing of a shape showing angles and lengths

standard form (noun) a number is written in standard form when it is expressed as $A \times 10^n$ where A is always between 1 and 10 and n is a positive or negative integer

stationary point (= **turning point**) (noun) a maximum or minimum point on a graph where the graph turns; the point where a curve has zero gradient

subject (noun) the **variable** (= letter) on its own, on one side of the equals sign in a formula

subset (noun) a collection of objects (= **set**) which contains part of another set

sum (noun) the total resulting from the addition of two or more numbers, amounts or items

sum (verb) to add two or more numbers or amounts together

surd (noun) a number written exactly using roots; for example, $\sqrt{3}$

tangent (noun) a straight line that touches a curve at one point only

tetrahedron (noun) a solid object that has 4 **faces** (= flat surfaces) which each have 3 edges

translation (noun) a 'sliding' movement in which all the points on the shape move the same distance in the same direction

trapezium (noun) (British English) a flat shape with 4 sides (= a **quadrilateral**) where one pair of opposite sides are parallel

tree diagram (noun) a diagram that shows two or more events with possible outcomes and their probabilities listed on branches

trial (noun) an experiment (carried out a number of times to estimate the probability of an event)

turning point (= **stationary point**) (noun) a maximum or minimum point on a graph where the graph turns; the point where a curve has zero gradient

universal set (noun) the set that contains all objects being considered

upper bound (noun) the value half a unit greater than the rounded measurement

variable (*noun*) a letter such as x or y in a term, expression, formula or equation whose value can vary; a letter used to represent an unknown quantity to solve a problem using an equation(s)

vector (*noun*) a quantity that has **magnitude** (= size) and direction

velocity (*noun*) the rate at which **displacement** changes with time

Venn diagram (*noun*) a drawing in which ovals are drawn inside a rectangle to show the relationships between **sets** (= a collection of objects)

vertices (*noun*) (*plural*) (*singular* **vertex**) points where two or more edges meet (a corner)

working (*noun*) a record of the calculations made when solving a problem

ANSWERS

NUMBER 1 – BASIC SKILLS EXERCISE

1 (a) 27
(b) 56
(c) 26
(d) 12

2 $4\frac{1}{3} = \frac{13}{3}$, $\frac{52}{12} = \frac{4 \times 13}{4 \times 3} = \frac{13}{3}$,

$\frac{6.5}{1.5} = \frac{65}{15} = \frac{5 \times 13}{5 \times 3} = \frac{13}{3}$

3 (a) $\frac{1}{3}$
(b) $\frac{10}{21}$
(c) $3\frac{5}{12}$
(d) $3\frac{5}{7}$
(e) $\frac{1}{35}$
(f) $\frac{5}{9}$

4 $3\frac{1}{2} \div 2\frac{1}{3} = \frac{7}{2} \div \frac{7}{3}$

$= \frac{7}{2} \times \frac{3}{7}$

$= \frac{3}{2}$

$= 1\frac{1}{2}$

5 $4\frac{2}{3} - 2\frac{1}{2} + 1\frac{3}{4} = \frac{14}{3} - \frac{5}{2} + \frac{7}{4}$

$= \frac{56}{12} - \frac{30}{12} + \frac{21}{12}$

$= \frac{47}{12}$

$= 3\frac{11}{12}$

6 $\frac{0.12}{32} \div \frac{0.024}{7.2} = \frac{12}{3200} \div \frac{24}{7200}$

$= \frac{12}{3200} \times \frac{7200}{24}$

$= \frac{9}{8}$

$= 1\frac{1}{8}$

7 $\frac{1}{4} - \left(\frac{1}{4} \times \frac{1}{4}\right) + \left(\frac{1}{4} \div \frac{1}{4}\right) = \frac{1}{4} - \left(\frac{1}{4} \times \frac{1}{4}\right)$

$+ \left(\frac{1}{4} \div \frac{1}{4}\right)$

$= \frac{1}{4} - \left(\frac{1}{4} \times \frac{1}{4}\right)$

$+ \left(\frac{1}{4} \times \frac{4}{1}\right)$

$= \frac{1}{4} - \frac{1}{16} + 1$

$= \frac{4}{16} - \frac{1}{16} + \frac{16}{16}$

$= \frac{19}{16}$

$= 1\frac{3}{16}$

8 $\dfrac{4}{2 + \dfrac{2}{3+4}} = \dfrac{4}{2 + \dfrac{2}{3+4}}$

$= \dfrac{4}{2 + \dfrac{2}{7}}$

$= \dfrac{4}{\dfrac{14}{7} + \dfrac{2}{7}}$

$= \dfrac{4}{\dfrac{16}{7}}$

$= \dfrac{28}{16}$

$= 1\frac{3}{4}$

ANSWERS 255

9 (a) 8
   (b) −16
   (c) − 48
   (d) $-\frac{1}{3}$
   (e) 48

10 (a) 3
   (b) 16
   (c) 8
   (d) 38
   (e) 4
   (f) 2

11 (a) 12 300
   (b) 12 400
   (c) 12 300
   (d) 439 000
   (e) 550 000
   (f) 0.0130
   (g) 1.01
   (h) 0.01000

12 (a) 1.294
   (b) 1.295
   (c) 1.295
   (d) 1.200
   (e) 0.100
   (f) 340.005
   (g) 1.000
   (h) 0.000499

NUMBER 1 – EXAM PRACTICE EXERCISE

1 (a) $4\frac{2}{3} \div 3\frac{5}{9} - 1\frac{3}{8} = \frac{14}{3} \div \frac{32}{9} - \frac{11}{8}$

   $= \frac{14}{3} \times \frac{9}{32} - \frac{11}{8} = \frac{21}{16} - \frac{22}{16} = -\frac{1}{16}$

   (b) $\frac{1}{4} = \frac{7}{28}; \frac{2}{7} = \frac{8}{28}; \frac{3}{14} = \frac{6}{28}$; so Karim eats the most.

   (c) $\frac{1}{4} + \frac{2}{7} + \frac{3}{14} = \frac{7}{28} + \frac{8}{28} + \frac{6}{28}$

   $= \frac{7+8+6}{28} = \frac{21}{28} = \frac{3}{4}$ so $\frac{3}{4}$ is eaten,

   leaving $1 - \frac{3}{4} = \frac{1}{4}$ uneaten.

2 (a) (i) 0.001⋮8548 = 0.002 to 3 d.p.
           the 8 rounds the 1 up to 2
       (ii) 0.00185⋮48 = 0.00185 to 3 s.f.
           the 4 does not round anything up
       (iii) 0.00⋮18548 = 0.00 to 2 d.p.
           the 1 does not round anything up
       (iv) 0.0018⋮548 = 0.0019 to 2 s.f.
           the 5 rounds the 8 up to 9
   (b) (i) One of the following:
       Lowest common multiple of 2 and 10 is 10, not 2 − 10
       The numerator (top) of the first fraction has not been multiplied by anything to keep the value of the fraction correct.
       (ii) $\frac{9}{2} - \frac{25}{10} = \frac{45}{10} - \frac{25}{10} = \frac{45-25}{10} = \frac{20}{10} = 2$

3 (a) $(5^2 \div 4 - 6 \times 3^2 \div 2^3) = \frac{25}{4} - \frac{6 \times 9}{8}$

   $= \frac{25}{4} - \frac{27}{4} = \frac{-2}{4} = -\frac{1}{2}$

   so $1 \div 2 \times (5^2 \div 4 - 6 \times 3^2 \div 2^3)$
   $= 1 \div 2 \times \frac{-1}{2} = \frac{1}{2} \times \frac{-1}{2} = -\frac{1}{4}$

   (b) $u = \frac{8}{3} \Rightarrow \frac{1}{u} = \frac{3}{8}; v = \frac{6}{5} \Rightarrow \frac{1}{v} = \frac{5}{6}$

   so $\frac{1}{u} + \frac{1}{v} = \frac{3}{8} + \frac{5}{6} = \frac{3 \times 3 + 5 \times 4}{24} = \frac{29}{24}$

   $\Rightarrow f = \frac{24}{29}$

4 (a) $187\frac{1}{2} = \frac{375}{2}; 3\frac{1}{8} = \frac{25}{2}$

   number of presses $= \frac{375}{2} \div \frac{25}{8}$

   $= \frac{375}{2} \times \frac{8}{25} = \frac{15}{1} \times \frac{4}{1} = 60$

   (b) Time from Granada to Antequera is 72 minutes
   Time from Granada to Sevilla is 168 minutes

   So fraction is $\frac{72}{168} = \frac{6}{14} = \frac{3}{7}$

5 **(a)** The fraction of the lower school that play football is

$\frac{5}{11} \times \frac{3}{10} = \frac{3}{22}$

$\frac{6}{11}$ of the school are in the upper school so the fraction of the upper school that play football is $\frac{6}{11} \times \frac{7}{12} = \frac{7}{22}$

⇒ fraction of school that play football is $\frac{3}{22} + \frac{7}{22} = \frac{10}{22} = \frac{5}{11}$

(b) The smallest number of students must be the smallest whole number divisible by both 45 and 12, i.e. the Lowest Common Multiple of 45 and 12.
$45 = 3^2 \times 5$, $12 = 2^2 \times 3$ therefore the LCM is $2^2 \times 3^2 \times 5 = 180$ students

ALGEBRA 1 – BASIC SKILLS EXERCISE

1. $2xy + 2xz$
2. $2xy$
3. $10a + 5$
4. $7b$
5. $9ab$
6. $7a^5$
7. $5a^6$
8. $72a^5$
9. $12a - 6b$
10. $12a + 16b$
11. $-a - b$
12. $6b - 2a$
13. 5
14. -2
15. -3
16. -9
17. 49
18. 1
19. -2
20. -1
21. $\frac{3}{2}$
22. 1.8
23. -1
24. 2
25. 3
26. -1
27. 2
28. -1
29. 3
30. 2

ALGEBRA 1 – EXAM PRACTICE EXERCISE

1. The numbers are x, $x + 2$ and $x + 4$, so $x + (x + 2) + (x + 4) = 648$
$3x + 6 = 648$, $3x = 642$
$x = 214$ so the numbers are 214, 216 and 218

2. Interior angle at B is
$180 - (145 - 6x) = 35 + 6x$
Angle $C = 35 + 6x$ as it is an isosceles triangle
Angle sum of a triangle is 180°, so
$35 + 6x + 35 + 6x + 70 - 4x = 180$
$8x + 140 = 180$, $8x = 40$
$x = 5$
so angles are 65°, 65° and 50°

3. The width of the screen is $x - 0.5$
The length of the phone is $2x$ so the length of the screen is $2x - 3$
The perimeter of the screen is 32
so $2(x - 0.5) + 2(2x - 3) = 32$
$2x - 1 + 4x - 6 = 32$
$6x = 39$
$x = 6.5$
So the screen measures 6 cm by 10 cm and the area is $6 \times 10 = 60$ cm²

4. Let x be the diameter of the circle.
The side of the square is x so the perimeter of the square is $4x$
The circumference of the circle is πx
So $4x + \pi x = 30$, $x(4 + \pi) = 30$
$x = \frac{30}{4 + \pi}$
$x = 4.20$ (3 s.f.)
So lengths are $4 \times 4.20 = 16.8$ cm and $\pi \times 4.20 = 13.2$ cm (3 s.f.)

5. **(a)** Let x be the number of minutes after 12:00
In 60 minutes the minute hand moves 360° or 6° per minute
In x minutes the minute hand moves $6x°$ from the vertical.
The hour hand moves at $\frac{1}{12}$ of the speed of the minute hand
In x minutes the hour hand moves $\frac{6x}{12} = \frac{x}{2}$ degrees from the vertical.
Angle between hands must equal
$90° \Rightarrow 6x - \frac{x}{2} = 90 \Rightarrow \frac{11x}{2} = 90 \Rightarrow x = 16.36$

$x = 16$ minutes 22 secs so time is 12:16:22 to the nearest second.

(b) Let x be the number of minutes after 12:00
In x minutes the minute hand moves $6x°$ from the vertical.
The time will be after 01:00. At 01:00 the minute hand has moved 360°, so the angle of the minute hand will be $6x - 360$ degrees from the vertical.
The hour hand will have moved $\frac{x}{2}$ degrees from the vertical.
$\Rightarrow 6x - 360 = \frac{x}{2} \Rightarrow \frac{11x}{2} = 360 \Rightarrow x = 65.45..$
$x = 1$ hour 5 minutes and 27 seconds so time is 01:05:27 to the nearest second.
OR
The time will be after 01:00
Let y be the number of minutes after 01:00.
In y minutes the minute hand moves $6y°$ from the vertical.
At 01:00 the hour hand has moved 30° from the vertical so y minutes later it has moved $30 + \frac{y}{2}$ degrees
$\Rightarrow 6y = 30 + \frac{y}{2} \Rightarrow \frac{11y}{2} = 30 \Rightarrow y = 5.45..$ or 5 mins 27 secs to nearest second
So time is 01:05:27 to the nearest second.

GRAPHS 1 – BASIC SKILLS EXERCISE

1 (a) 2   (b) $-\frac{1}{2}$
2 45 m
3 $\frac{2}{3}$ m
4 28.6
5 $p = -4$
6 No. Gradient of AB is 2, gradient of $BC \ne 2$, it is 2.02 to 3 s.f.
7 -63
8 3
9 A and D
10 The second point in the table should be (0, 3).

11

x	-3	$a = -2$	0	1	3	$c = 4$
y	11	8	2	-1	$b = -7$	-10

12 (a)

x	-2	0	2	4
$y = 3 - 2x$	7	3	-1	-5
$2y - x + 2 = 0$	-2	-1	0	1

(b)

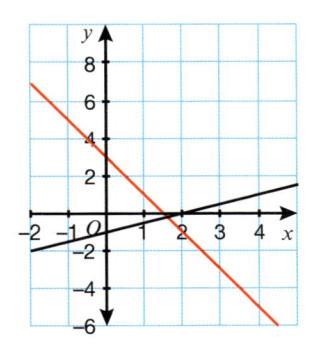

(c) $y = 3 - 2x$: gradient $= -2$, intercept $= (0, 3)$
$2y - x + 2 = 0$: gradient $= \frac{1}{2}$, intercept $= (0, -1)$
(d) $(1.6, -0.2)$

13 (a) 5 kg = 11 lbs
Draw straight line from (0, 0) to (5, 11)
(b) (i) 7.7 lbs   (ii) 1.82 kg

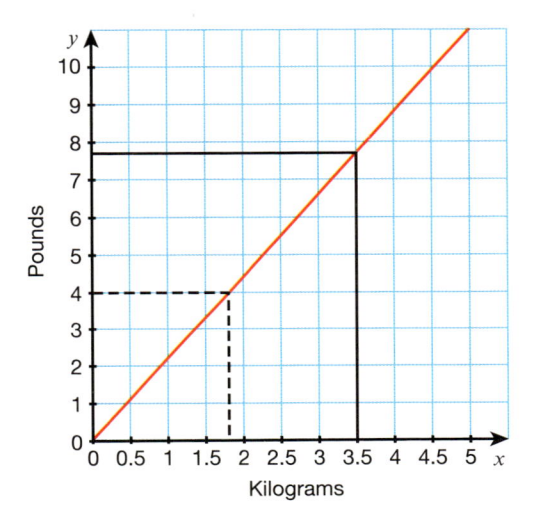

14 (a) approximately $61
(b) approximately 7.1 km
(c) approximately 1.7 km

GRAPHS 1 – EXAM PRACTICE EXERCISE

1 (a) $\frac{1}{x} = \frac{1}{3} \Rightarrow x = 3$ so width is 6 m

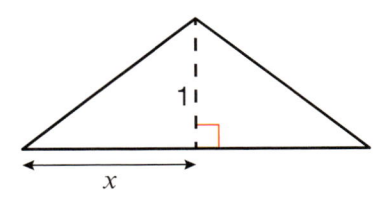

(b) Gradient $= \frac{(5p-9)-(p-9)}{(p+7)-(p-1)} = \frac{5p-p}{7+1}$
$= \frac{4p}{8} = \frac{p}{2} \Rightarrow p = 1$

258 ANSWERS

2 Sketching the position of the points shows that if it is a parallelogram $AB \parallel DC$ and $AD \parallel BC$

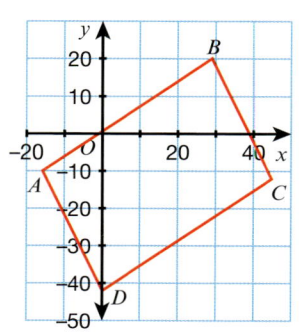

(a) Gradient of $AB = \frac{20--10}{29--16} = \frac{30}{45} = \frac{2}{3}$

gradient of $DC = \frac{-12--42}{45-0} = \frac{30}{45} = \frac{2}{3}$

$\Rightarrow AB$ is parallel to DC as the gradients are the same.

gradient of $AD = \frac{-42--10}{0--16} = \frac{-32}{16} = -2$

gradient of $BC = \frac{-12-20}{45-29} = \frac{-32}{16} = -2$

$\Rightarrow AD$ is parallel to BC as the gradients are the same.
$\Rightarrow ABCD$ is a parallelogram as it has two pairs of opposite parallel sides.

(b) Gradient of $AO = \frac{0--10}{0--16} = \frac{10}{16} = \frac{5}{8}$

As the gradient of $AO \neq$ gradient of AB, O does not lie on AB.

3 (a)

t (min)	0	300	1000	1800
C (£)	20	20	34	50

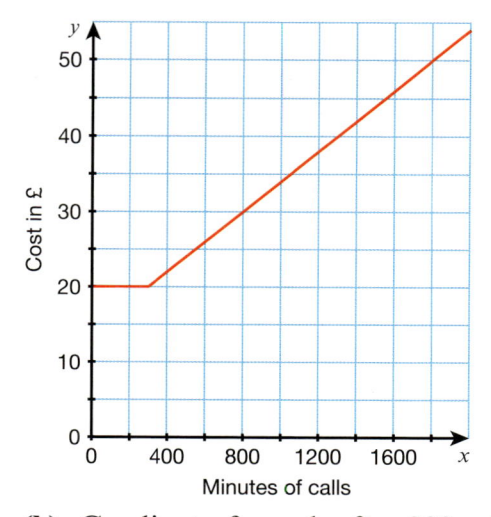

(b) Gradient of graph after 300 minutes is

$\frac{50-20}{1800-300} = \frac{30}{1500} = 0.02$

This is 0.02 £/min or 2p per minute

(c) 16 h 40 mins = 1000 mins. From graph bill should be £34, so she should complain.

4 (a) The area is decreasing by 86 000 km² per year, so the formula must be of the form $A = -86000y + c$
When $y = 0$, $A = 7.7 \times 10^6$, so the formula is $A = 7.7 \times 10^6 - 86000y$

(b)

x (year after 1980)	0	20	40
y (area in km²)	7.7×10^6	5.98×10^6	4.26×10^6

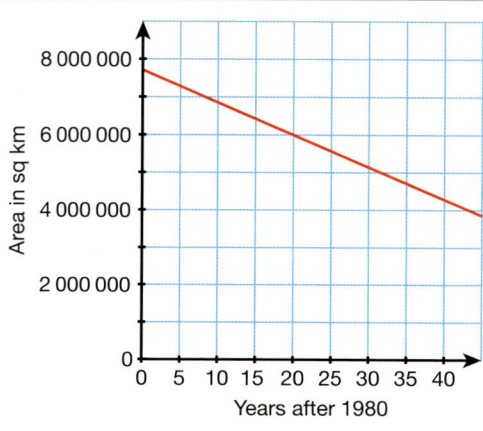

(c) (i) 600 000 km²
(ii) 2011

5 (a)

Weight, W (g)	200	1200
Length, L (m)	0	325

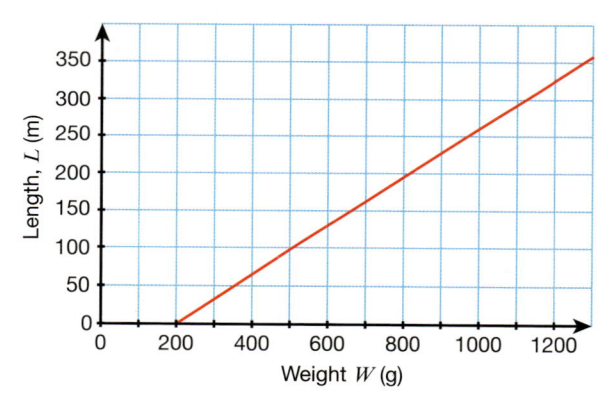

(b) Reading from graph gives
(i) 231 m
(ii) 503 g
(Note as you are reading from a graph, your answers might not be the same, but they should be within ±5 units.)

(c) Gradient is $\frac{330}{1000} = 0.33$ so equation is of the form $L = 0.33W + c$

Substituting in one of the known points, say (200, 0), gives $c = -66$
$\Rightarrow$ equation is $L = 0.33W - 66$

SHAPE AND SPACE 1 – BASIC SKILLS EXERCISE

1. $x = 36°, y = 106°, z = 38°$
2. $x = 60°, y = 30°$
3. $x = 33°, y = 33°, z = 83°$
4. $x = 75°$

5. (a) Exterior angles sum to 360
    $22x - 80 = 360, x = 20$
   (b) Angle $A = 70$, angle $B = 70$, angle $C = 40$ so isosceles with $AC = BC$

6. (a) Interior angles sum to 360°
    $x + \frac{7}{8}x + \frac{29}{24}x + \frac{2}{3}x = 360$
    $\frac{15}{4}x = 360, x = 96$
   (b) Substituting $x = 96$ gives interior angle $A = 64°, B = 96°, C = 84°$ and $D = 116°$
    $A + D = 180°$ so AB is parallel to DC (corresponding angles)
    or
    $B + C = 180°$ so AB is parallel to DC (corresponding angles)

7. Acute angle between 12 and 8 is 120°
    $\frac{1}{3} \times 360°$
    Angle between minute hand and 12 is
    $x = \frac{6}{60} \times 360 = 36°$
    Whole turn is 60 mins so 6 mins is $\frac{6}{60}$ of 360°
    Hour hand travels at $\frac{1}{12}$ speed of minute hand.
    $\Rightarrow y = \frac{1}{12} \times 36° = 3°$
    $\Rightarrow$ acute angle between hands is $120 + x - y = 153°$

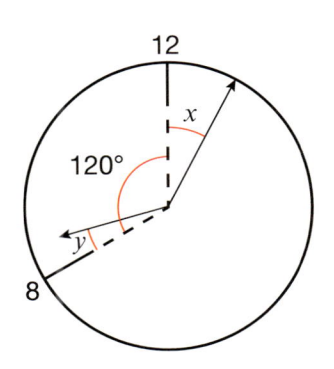

8. $x = 100°, y = 75°, z = 135°$

9. Mark all the equal sides.

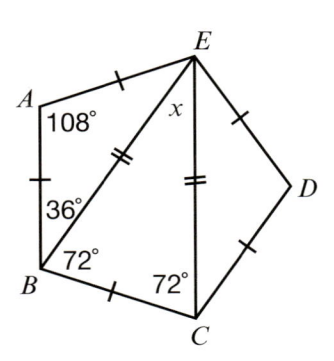

   (a) Exterior angle of a regular pentagon is $360 \div 5 = 72$
    angle $A = 180 - 72 = 108°$
    $\triangle ABE$ is isosceles,
    so $A\hat{B}C = (180 - 108) \div 2 = 36°$
    Angle $B = 108$ so $E\hat{B}C = 108 - 36 = 72°$
    $\triangle BCE$ is isosceles so $B\hat{C}E = 72°$
    By angle sum of $\triangle BCE$, $x = 36°$
   (b) $A\hat{B}E = B\hat{E}C$ so AB is parallel to CE (alternate angles)
    or
    $A\hat{B}C + B\hat{C}E = 180$ so AB is parallel to CE (corresponding angles)
    or
    $B\hat{A}E + A\hat{E}C = 180$ so AB is parallel to CE (corresponding angles)

10. Exterior angle is $360 \div 20 = 18$ so interior angle is $180 - 18 = 162°$

11. Sum of interior angles is $180(n - 2) = 3060$ so $n = 19$

12. (a) Triangle shown is isosceles so interior angle is 156°, exterior angle is 24° and number of sides is $360 \div 24 = 15$
    (b) $15 \times 156 = 2340°$

13. $a = 4.5$
14. $a = 6, b = 4.5$
15. $a = 4.5, b = 2.5$

260 ANSWERS

16 (a) and (b)

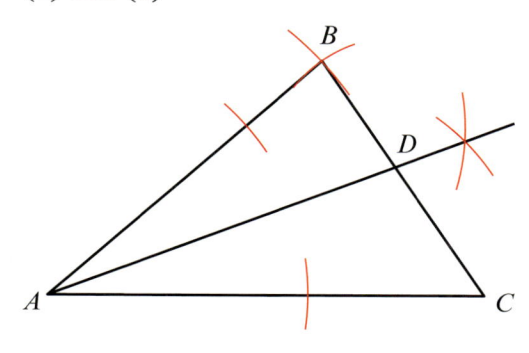

(c) 4.36 cm

17 (a) and (b)

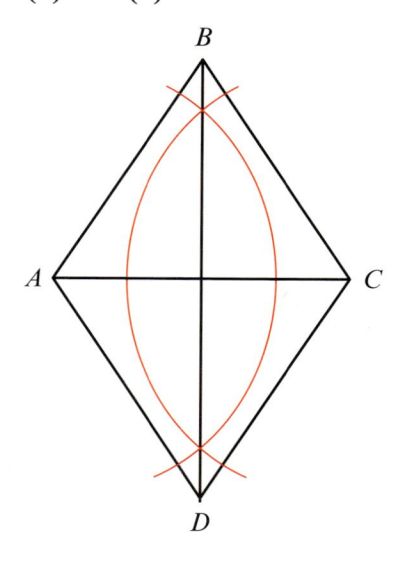

(c) 7.21 cm

18 (a) and (b) CP = 4.9 so CP = 9.8 m

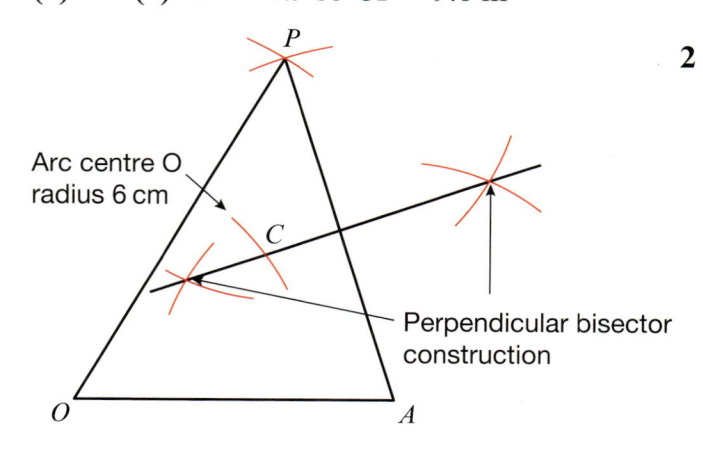

SHAPE AND SPACE 1 – EXAM PRACTICE EXERCISE

1 (a) Using isosceles triangle properties and angle sum on a straight line gives the angles shown in the diagram.

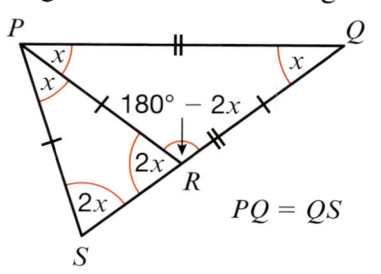

$PQ = QS$

$5x = 180$ (angle sum of PRS)
$x = 36°$

(b) Draw out the similar triangles as shown.

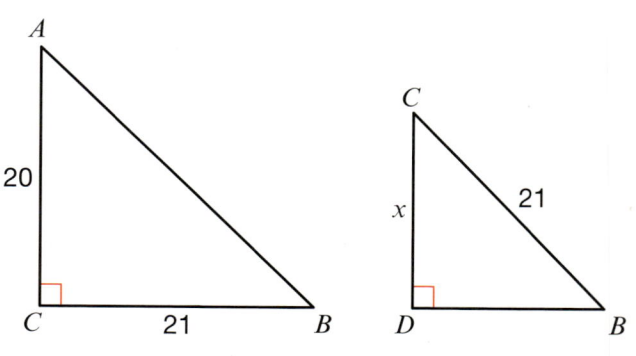

$AB^2 = 20^2 + 21^2 \Rightarrow AB = 29$ Pythagoras

$\frac{x}{21} = \frac{20}{29}$

$x = \frac{420}{29}$

2 (a) 35 km ≡ 7 cm, 28 km ≡ 5.6 cm. Draw HN, then construct a 60° angle at H. Bisect this to give 30° and measure 7 cm to find B. From B construct the perpendicular to HN and measure 5.6 cm to find F.

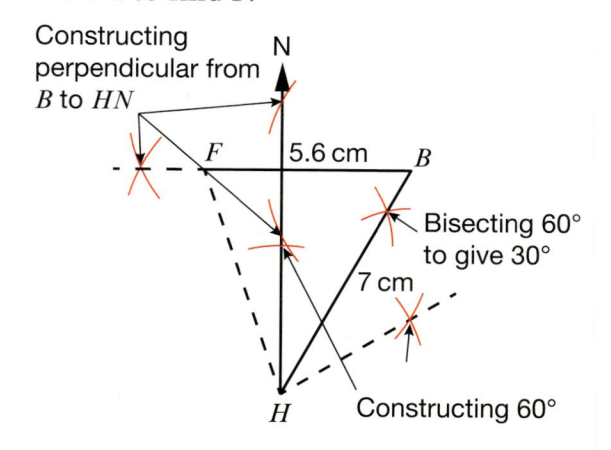

(b) *FH* measures 6.4 cm and angle *FHN* measures 14°
So bearing is 180 − 14 = 166°
FH represents 6.4 × 5 = 32 km
So It took 32 ÷ 4 = 8 h

3 (a) The interior angle at *D* is 360 − 4*x*
Due to the rotational symmetry, all the interior angles are the same.
The sum of the interior angles of a 10-sided polygon is (10 − 2) × 180 = 1440°
5*x* + 5(360 − 4*x*) = 1440
5*x* + 1800 − 20*x* = 1440
15*x* = 360
x = 24°

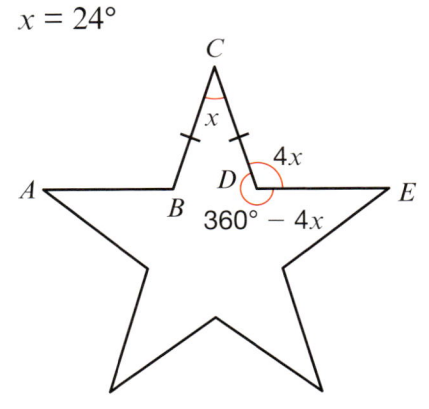

(b) Calculate the angles as shown.
Triangle *BCD* is isosceles.

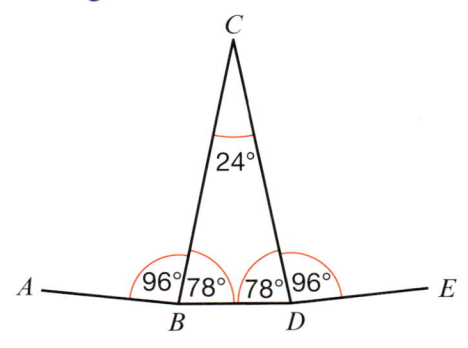

Angle sum at *B* is 174° so *ABD* is not a straight line.
Angle sum on a straight line is 180°.
OR Extend *AB* and *DE* to intersect at *F*. Show the angle at *F* is not 180°.

4 The interior angles of a pentagon sum to 3 × 180 = 540
By symmetry the angle in the yellow pentagon at *G* is 130

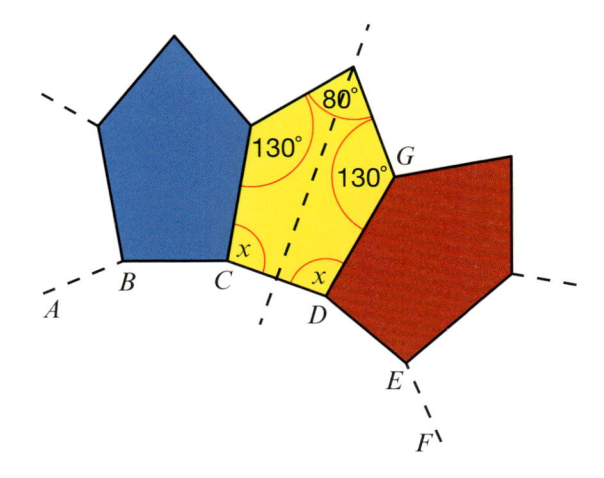

Let the angle in the yellow pentagon at *C* be *x*
The angle in the yellow pentagon at *D* is *x* by symmetry
2*x* + 130 + 130 + 80 = 540
x = 100°
The angle in the blue pentagon at *C* is also 100°
The interior angle of the polygon is 360 − 100 − 100 = 160°
exterior angle of polygon = 20°
number of sides = 360 ÷ 20 = 18°

5 Add marks showing equal sides
Mark in 60° angles in equilateral triangle
ABE is isosceles, so angle at *A* is *x* and angle at *B* is 180 − 2*x* (angle sum of triangle)
Angles at *B* and *C* sum to 180° (*AB* parallel to *CD*, complementary angles)
180 − 2*x* + 60 + 60 + *y* = 180
y = 2*x* − 120
Triangle *CDE* is isosceles
2*z* + 2*x* − 120 = 180
z = 150 − *x*
Angles at *E* sum to 360 so
AED + *x* + 60 + 150 − *x* = 360
AED = 150°

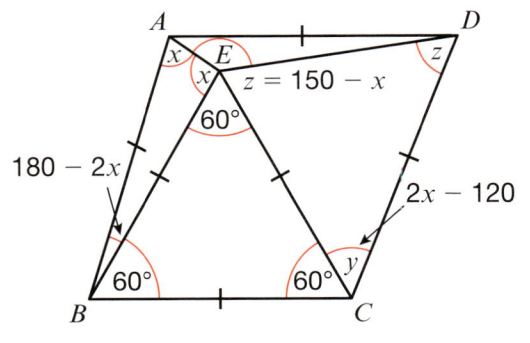

SETS 1 – BASIC SKILLS EXERCISE

1. (a) Any multiples of 3
   (b) Any negative integers
   (c) Any sport
   (d) Any make of car

2. (a) {multiples of 3}
   (b) {negative integers}
   (c) {sports}
   (d) {makes of car}

3. (a) {2, 4, 6, 8}
   (b) {4, 9, 16}
   (c) {January, June, July}
   (d) {Red, Amber (or Orange), Green}

4. (a) True
   (b) False
   (c) False
   (d) True

5. a, b and d

6. (a) [Venn diagram: A contains B; B contains 4, 8; A contains 2, 6, 10; outside 1 3 5 7 9 11]
   (b) {1, 3, 5, 7, 9, 11},
       odd numbers between 1 and 11 inclusive
       OR odd numbers between 0 and 12
   (c) 8
   (d) Yes. All multiples of 4 are also multiples of 2

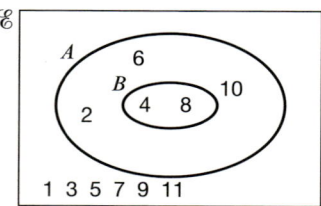

7. (a) Because 10 is not a member of ξ
   (b) {5, 15}
   (c) 2   Factors are 1 and 5
   (d) {5}

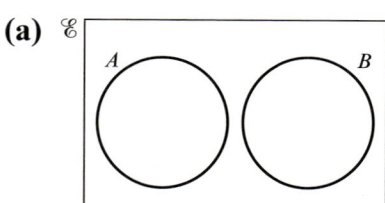

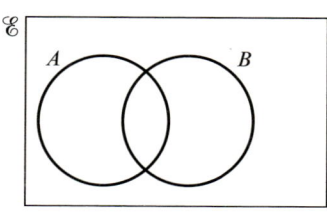

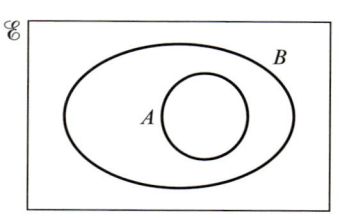

8. (a) [Venn diagram: A and B disjoint]
   (b) [Venn diagram: A and B intersecting]
   (c) [Venn diagram: A inside B]
   (d) [Venn diagram: B inside A]

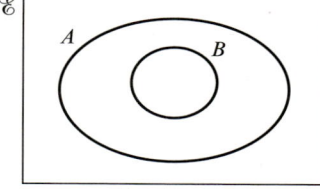

9. (a) $W = \{A, E, I, U\}$, $W' = \{O\}$,
       $S = \{O, U\}$, $S' = \{A, E, I\}$
   (b) [Venn diagram: W contains A E I; intersection U; S contains O]
   (c) (i) {A, E, I, O, U} or ξ
       (ii) {U}

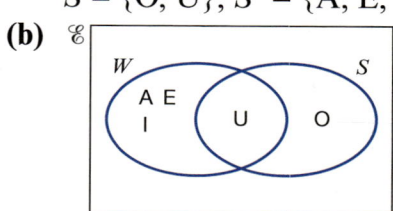

10. (a) [Venn diagram: T contains 3; intersection 6; B contains 4; outside 2]
    (b) 15

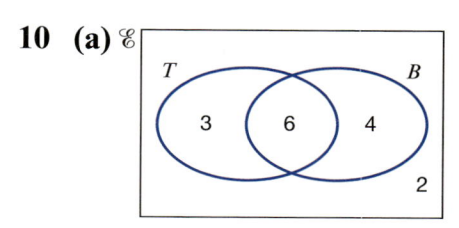

SETS 1 – EXAM PRACTICE EXERCISE

1. (a) (i)   False
       (ii) True
       (iii) False
       (iv) False
   (b) (i) $A \cap C = \emptyset$
       (ii) $C \cup D = C$
       (iii) $A \cap B \neq \emptyset$

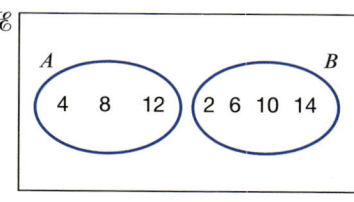

2. (a) [Venn diagram: A contains 4 8 12; B contains 2 6 10 14]

   $A \cup B = \xi$

ANSWERS 263

(b) (i) 8
(ii) 2
(iii) In the Venn diagram, x can be any number between 0 and 9

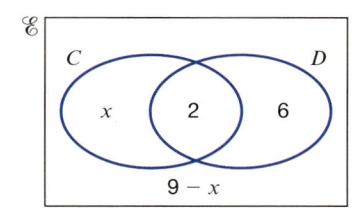

[Venn diagram with sets C and D: x in C only, 2 in intersection, 6 in D only, $9-x$ outside]

3 (a) [Venn diagram with sets A and B: 2 in A only, 20 in intersection, 5 in B only, 3 outside]

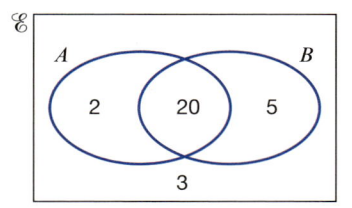

(b) 20

4 (a) [Venn diagram with sets I and R, empty]

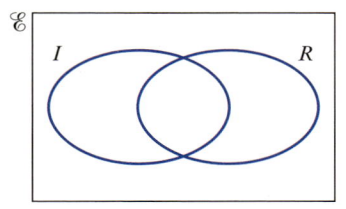

(b) $I \cap R$ is the set of isosceles right-angled triangles, so angles are 90°, 45° and 45°

(c) [Venn diagram with I, R and E as subset of I]

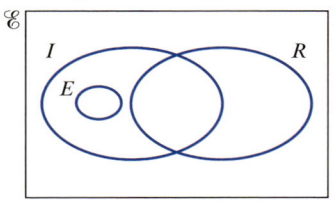

All equilateral triangles are isosceles, so E is a subset of I

5 (a) [Venn diagram: $n(\mathscr{E}) = 33$, $n(A) = x$, $n(B) = 2x+7$, $\frac{x}{2}$ in A only, $\frac{x}{2}$ in intersection, $17-x$ outside]

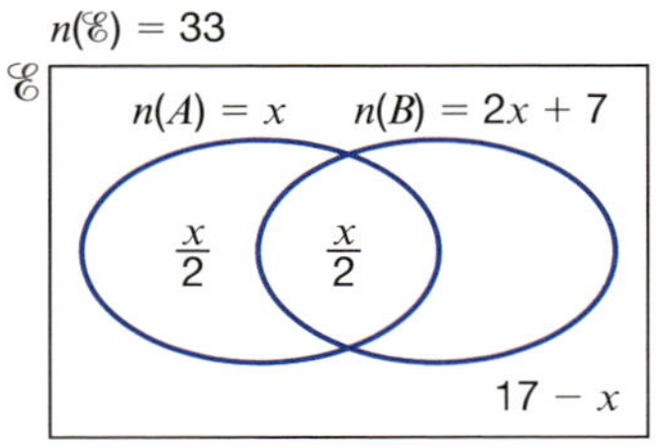

As $n(A) = x$ and $n(A \cap B) = \frac{x}{2}$ then
$n(A \cap B') = \frac{x}{2}$

$\frac{x}{2} + 2x + 7 + 17 - x = 33$

$\frac{3x}{2} = 9$

$x = 6$
$n(B) = 19$, $n(A \cap B) = 3$
$n(A' \cap B) = 19 - 3 = 16$

(b) (i) [Venn diagram: $B = \frac{3}{4}$, intersection $\frac{5}{24}$, outside 2, universal set I]

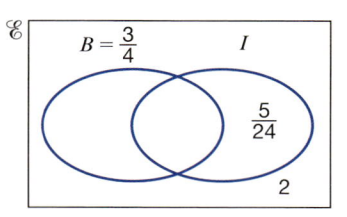

Fraction using B and I is
$\frac{3}{4} + \frac{5}{24} = \frac{23}{24}$

2 students are $\frac{1}{24}$ of the group
number of students is $24 \times 2 = 48$

(ii) Turn the fractions into numbers and fill in the Venn diagram

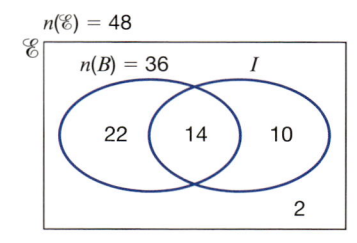

[Venn diagram: $n(\mathscr{E}) = 48$, $n(B) = 36$, 22 in B only, 14 in intersection, 10 in I only, 2 outside]

From the Venn diagram $n(B \cap I) = 14$

NUMBER 2 – BASIC SKILLS EXERCISE

1 (a) 1.45×10^5
(b) 1.23×10^8
(c) 1×10^6
(d) 1×10^9

2 (a) 1.38×10^5
(b) 9.74×10^8
(c) 3.13×10^3
(d) 3.16×10^4

3 (a) 350
(b) 5750
(c) 1 250 000
(d) 93 210

4 6×10^{199}
5 4×10^1
6 2.8×10^{100}
7 3.2×10^{100}
8 2×10^{50}
9 4×10^{200}
10 2.89×10^{50}

11 (a) 1×10^{-1}
(b) 5×10^{-3}
(c) 2.5×10^{-1}
(d) 7×10^{-6}

264 ANSWERS

12. (a) 1.23×10^{-2}
    (b) 1.24×10^{-2}
    (c) 1.60×10^{-4}
    (d) 8.89×10^{-3}
13. (a) 0.035
    (b) 0.005 75
    (c) 0.000 001 25
    (d) 0.000 932 1
14. 6×10^{-199}
15. 4×10^{-1}
16. -1.7×10^{-99}
17. 2.3×10^{-99}
18. 2×10^{-50}
19. 4×10^{-200}
20. 1.85×10^{-6}
21. 2.66×10^{-22}
22. 2.41×10^{-6}
23. 1.62×10^{-3}
24. 1.38×10^{-2}
25. (a) 4.08×10^{-7}
    (b) 1.76×10^{-9}
    (c) 3.87×10^{-11}
    (d) 4.83×10^{-4}
26. 2.90×10^{-5} km
27. (a) 3.02×10^{30} mm²
    (b) 1.69×10^{-8} %
28. 6.32×10^{-13} km/s
29. 9.46×10^{12} km/year
30. (a) $\frac{1}{4}$
    (b) $\frac{1}{10}$
    (c) $\frac{3}{4}$
    (d) $\frac{3}{5}$
    (e) $\frac{7}{20}$
31. 150 m
32. $360
33. 42 g
34. 8%
35. 0.01 %
36. loss of 37.5% or −37.5% increase
37. 12%
38. 1650 m
39. 528 kg
40. $912
41. 21 250 cm²
42. $90
43. €897
44. £56.25
45. (a) 56.7 s
    (b) 19% improvement
46. (a) 1.39 m
    (b) 14%
47. (a) €11 880
    (b) €120 000 $\times \left(1 + \frac{x}{100}\right) \left(1 - \frac{x}{100}\right)$
48. $x \times \left(1 + \frac{y}{100}\right)$
49. $x \times \left(1 - \frac{y}{100}\right)$
50. +44%

NUMBER 2 – EXAM PRACTICE EXERCISE

1. (a) (i) Let V be volume of all five planets:
   $V = 1.43 \times 10^{24} + 8.27 \times 10^{23} + 1.08 \times 10^{21} + 1.63 \times 10^{20} + 7.15 \times 10^{18}$
   $= 2.2582... \times 10^{24}$ m³
   $= 2.26 \times 10^{24}$ m³ (3 s.f.)
   (ii) Volume of Jupiter − Volume of Pluto $= 1.43 \times 10^{24} - 7.15 \times 10^{18}$
   $= 1.4299... \times 10^{24}$ m³
   $= 1.43 \times 10^{24}$ m³
   (b) Volume Mars $\times k =$ Volume Earth
   $1.63 \times 10^{20} \times k = 1.08 \times 10^{21}$
   $k = \frac{1.08 \times 10^{21}}{1.63 \times 10^{20}} = 7$
   (nearest integer)

2. (a) (i) DNA molecule width − Water molecule width $= 2.15 \times 10^{-9} - 2.70 \times 10^{-10}$
   $= 0.000 000 001 88$ m
   $= 1.88 \times 10^{-9}$ m
   (ii) Grain of sand width − Human hair width $= 5.25 \times 10^{-4} - 7.50 \times 10^{-5}$
   $= 0.000 45$
   $= 4.50 \times 10^{-4}$ m
   (b) Width Covid-19 virus : Human hair
   $= 1.60 \times 10^{-7} : 7.50 \times 10^{-5} = 1 : \frac{7.50 \times 10^{-5}}{1.60 \times 10^{-7}}$
   $= 468.75$
   $= 1 : n$ where $n = 469$ to the nearest integer

3. 1 January 2022:
   Maira account $= \$15 000 \times 1.08 - (0.08 \times \$15 000 \times 0.40) = \$15 720$

(Multiply by 1.08 to increase by 8%.
Multiply by 0.08 to find 8% of $15 000.
Multiply by 0.40 to find 40% of the profit.)
Jurgen account = $18 000 × 0.88 = $15 840
Jurgen has $15 840 − $ 15 720 = $ 120 more in his account than Maira on 1 Jan 2022.
(Multiply by 0.88 to decrease by 12%)

4 (a) London's population in 1900 as a percentage of its population in 2000
    $= \frac{5}{7.27} \times 100 = 68.8\%$
    (x as a % of $y = \frac{x}{y} \times 100$)
   (b) (i) Percentage change in London's population from 1950 to 2000 $= \frac{7.27 - 8.2}{8.2}$
       $\times 100 = -11.3\%$
       (ii) Percentage change in London's population from 1900 to 2020
       $= \frac{9.3 - 5}{5} \times 100 = +86.0\%$
       (% change $= \frac{\text{change}}{\text{original}} \times 100$)

5 (a) Percentage of female doctors by country:
    England: $\frac{98\,974}{98\,974 + 107\,221} \times 100 = 48\%$
    Scotland: $\frac{11\,012}{11\,012 + 9766} \times 100 = 53\%$
    Wales: $\frac{4711}{4711 + 5531} \times 100 = 46\%$
    Northern Ireland: $\frac{3337}{3337 + 3207} \times 100 = 51\%$
    Scotland has the highest percentage of female doctors in 2019.
   (b) Number of male doctors = 125 725
       New number of male doctors = 130 754
       125 725 × p = 130 754,
       so $p = \frac{130\,754}{125\,725} = 1.04$, so $k = 4$

ALGEBRA 2 – BASIC SKILLS EXERCISE

1 $\frac{4}{x}$
2 $2a$
3 $\frac{2x}{y}$
4 $4x^2$
5 $\frac{5ad}{7b}$
6 4
7 z
8 1
9 $4bc$
10 b
11 $\frac{17x}{12}$
12 $\frac{7}{6x}$
13 $\frac{14z}{15}$
14 $\frac{3}{5x}$
15 $\frac{(4x - x^2)}{6}$
16 $\frac{x^2}{6}$
17 $a^2 + b^2$
18 $\frac{a + b^3}{b}$
19 ±4
20 ±4
21 ±3
22 3
23 ±2
24 4
25 9
26 4
27 9
28 4
29 3^{10}
30 a^6
31 5^7
32 x^2
33 4^6
34 y^{18}
35 7^4
36 z^3
37 (a) 2 > −2
   (b) −2 > −5
   (c) 20% < $\frac{1}{4}$
   (d) −0.3 > −$\frac{1}{3}$
38 (a) 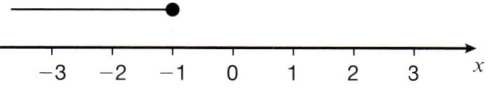
   (b) 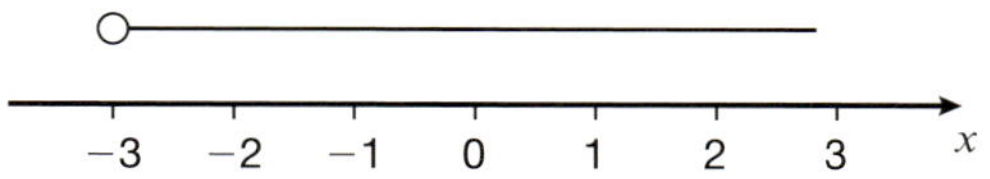
   (c) 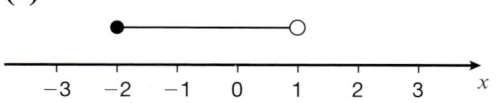
39 (a) −2 ≤ x < 2
   (b) x ≤ −1 or x > 2

266 ANSWERS

40   $x \leq 2$
41   $x > 4$
42   $x < -2$
43   $-4 < x \leq 0$

ALGEBRA 2 – EXAM PRACTICE EXERCISE

1   **(a)** $\dfrac{12x^3y^2z}{5x^2y^4} \div \dfrac{8xz}{15y^3} \times \dfrac{yz}{9x^2}$

$= \dfrac{12x^3y^2z}{5x^2y^4} \times \dfrac{15y^3}{8xz} \times \dfrac{yz}{9x^2}$ To divide, 'turn upside down and multiply'

$= \dfrac{12y^2z}{5y^4} \times \dfrac{15y^3}{8z} \times \dfrac{yz}{9x^2}$ 'Cancelling' x

$= \dfrac{12y^2z}{5} \times \dfrac{15}{8z} \times \dfrac{z}{9x^2}$ 'Cancelling' y

$= \dfrac{12y^2}{5} \times \dfrac{15}{8} \times \dfrac{z}{9x^2}$ 'Cancelling' z

$= \dfrac{y^2z}{2x^2}$ 'Cancelling' the numbers

  (b) $\left(\dfrac{1}{x} - \dfrac{3x}{x^2}\right) = \dfrac{1}{x} - \dfrac{3}{x} = \dfrac{-2}{x}$

Deal with $\left(\dfrac{1}{x} - \dfrac{3x}{x^2}\right)$ first (BIDMAS)

$\Rightarrow \dfrac{1}{x^2} \div \left(\dfrac{1}{x} - \dfrac{3x}{x^2}\right) = \dfrac{1}{x^2} \times \dfrac{x}{-2} = \dfrac{-1}{2x}$

To divide, turn fraction upside down and multiply

$\Rightarrow 1 - \left[\dfrac{1}{x^2} \div \left(\dfrac{1}{x} - \dfrac{3x}{x^2}\right)\right] = 1 - \dfrac{-1}{2x}$

$= \dfrac{2x}{2x} + \dfrac{1}{2x} = \dfrac{2x+1}{2x} \Rightarrow a = 2.$

2   **(a)** Ava's age $= y$, Ben's age $= y - 4$,
Charlie's age $= 2(y - 4)$
Sum of ages $= y + y - 4 + 2(y - 4) = 4y - 12$
$4y - 12 > 27$ and $4y - 12 < 41$
(or $27 < 4y - 12 < 41$)

  (b) $4y - 12 < 41$
$4y < 53 \Rightarrow y < 13.25$ y is an integer
Ava is 13, Ben is 9 and Charlie is 18.

  (c) $4y - 12 > 27$
$4y > 39$
$y > 9.75$ y is an integer
Ava is 10, Ben is 6 and Charlie is 12

3   **(a)** Method 1: $a^4 \div a^3 = a^1$ Subtracting indices rule

$\sqrt{x+1} = 4$
$x + 1 = 16$
$x = 15$

Method 2: $\dfrac{a^{\sqrt{x+1}}}{a^3} = a$ Multiplying both sides by a^3

$a^{\sqrt{x+1}} = a^4$
$\sqrt{x+1} = 4$
$x + 1 = 16$
$x = 15$

  (b) (i) $1 + \dfrac{1}{a} = \dfrac{a}{a} + \dfrac{1}{a} = \dfrac{a+1}{a}$

Simplify denominator first

$\dfrac{1}{1 + \dfrac{1}{a}} = 1 \div \dfrac{a+1}{a}$

$= 1 \times \dfrac{a}{a+1} = \dfrac{a}{a+1}$

    (ii) $\dfrac{1}{1 + \dfrac{1}{1 + \dfrac{1}{a}}} = \dfrac{1}{1 + \dfrac{a}{a+1}}$ Using result from part i

$1 + \dfrac{a}{a+1} = \dfrac{a+1+a}{a+1} = \dfrac{2a+1}{a+1}$

Simplify denominator first

$\dfrac{1}{1 + \dfrac{a}{a+1}} = 1 \div \dfrac{2a+1}{a+1}$

$= 1 \times \dfrac{a+1}{2a+1} = \dfrac{a+1}{2a+1}$

4   First third of journey is x km at a speed of 60 km/h

Time taken for the first third of the journey is $\dfrac{x}{60}$ hours.   Time $= \dfrac{\text{distance}}{\text{speed}}$

Remaining two-thirds of journey is $2x$ km at 40 km/h

Time taken for remaining two-thirds is $\dfrac{2x}{40}$ hours.   Time $= \dfrac{\text{distance}}{\text{speed}}$

$\dfrac{x}{60} + \dfrac{2x}{40} = \dfrac{3}{2}$ total journey time is 1.5 hours or $\dfrac{3}{2}$ hours

$\dfrac{x}{60} + \dfrac{2x}{40} = \dfrac{3}{2}$

$\frac{2x}{120} + \frac{6x}{120} = \frac{180}{120}$ multiplying both sides by 120

$2x + 6x = 180$

$x = \frac{180}{8}$

$3x = \frac{3 \times 180}{8}$ $3x$ is total length of journey

$= 67.5$ km

5 (a) $\frac{1}{R} = \frac{b}{ab} + \frac{a}{ab} = \frac{b+a}{ab} \Rightarrow R = \frac{ab}{a+b}$

(b) a becomes $a + 1$, b becomes $b - 1$

Substitute these values into $R = \frac{ab}{a+b}$

$R_{new} = \frac{(a+1)(b-1)}{a+1+b-1} = \frac{(a+1)(b-1)}{a+b}$

Change in R is $R_{new} - R = \frac{(a+1)(b-1)}{a+b}$

$-\frac{ab}{a+b} = \frac{ab+b-a-1-ab}{a+b} = \frac{b-a-1}{a+b}$

% change $= \frac{b-a-1}{a+b} \div \frac{ab}{a+b} \times 100$

% change is $\frac{\text{Change in } R}{\text{Original } R} \times 100$

$= \frac{b-a-1}{a+b} \times \frac{a+b}{ab} \times 100$

$= \frac{b-a-1}{ab} \times 100$

GRAPHS 2 – BASIC SKILLS EXERCISE

1 $y = 3x - 1$

2 $y = -\frac{1}{4}x + 2$

3 $y = x$

4 $y = 2x + 1$

5 $y = -\frac{1}{3}x + 4$

6 $y = 4x - 2$

7 $y = -0.4x + 1$

8 $y = 0.2x$

9 $y = -2x + 12$

10 $y = \frac{x}{3} + \frac{5}{3}$

11 $y = -\frac{x}{2} - 1$

12 $y = 3x - 5$

13 3, 2

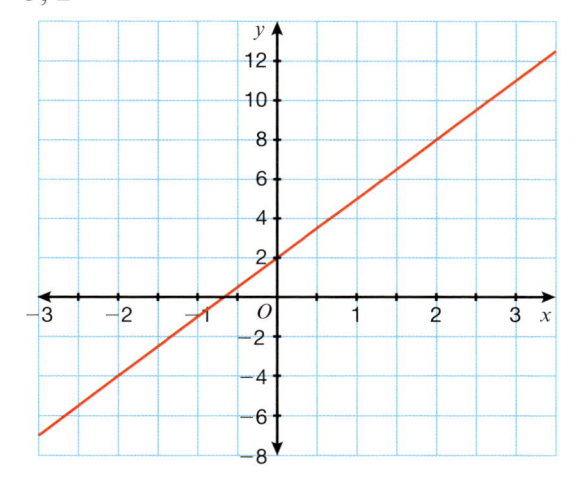

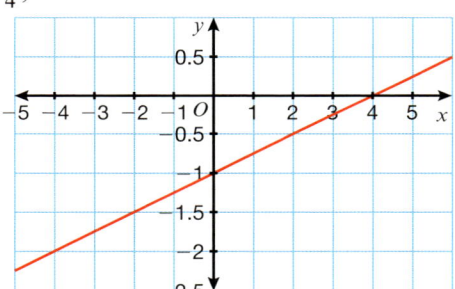

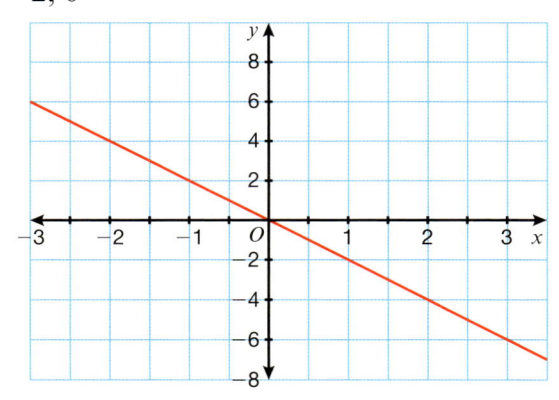

14 $\frac{1}{4}, -1$

15 $-2, 0$

16 −1, 2

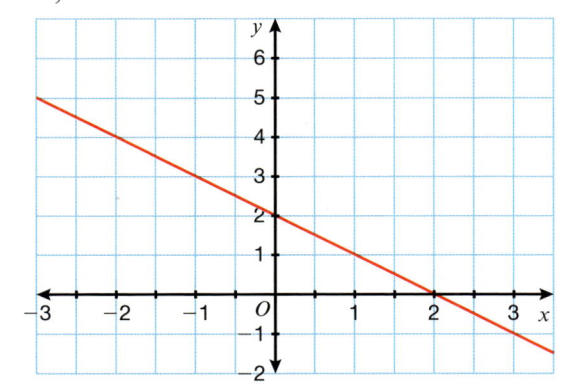

17 (3, 0), (0, 12)

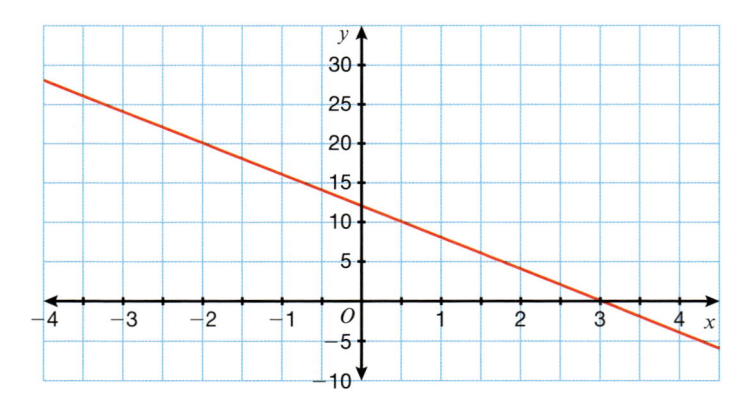

18 (15, 0), (0, 5)

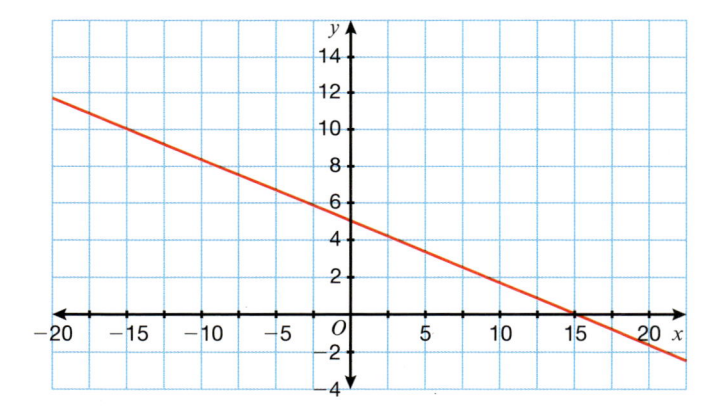

19 (10, 0), 0, −2)

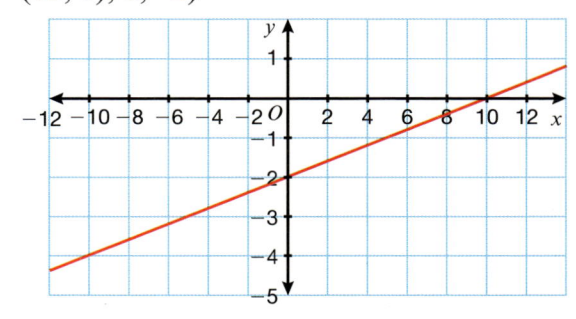

20 $\left(\frac{1}{2}, 0\right), \left(0, -\frac{1}{7}\right)$

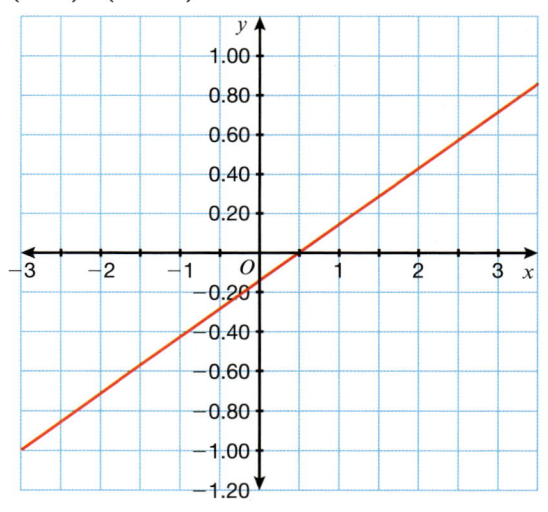

21 (1.5, 4.5)

x	0	3	6
y = x + 3	3	6	9

x	0	3	6
y = 6 − x	6	3	0

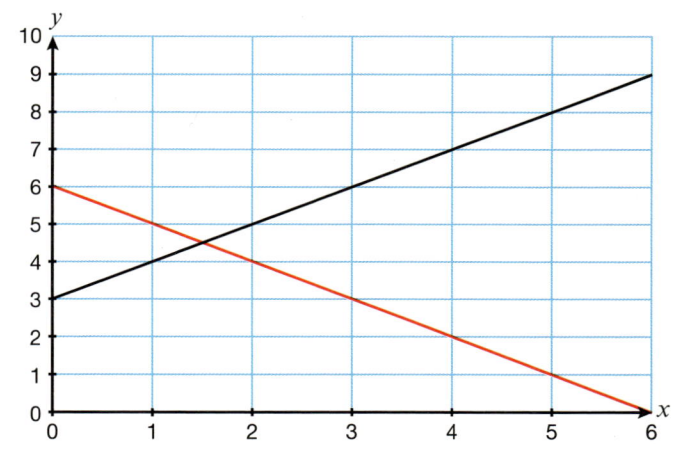

ANSWERS 269

22 $\left(\frac{7}{3}, \frac{2}{3}\right)$

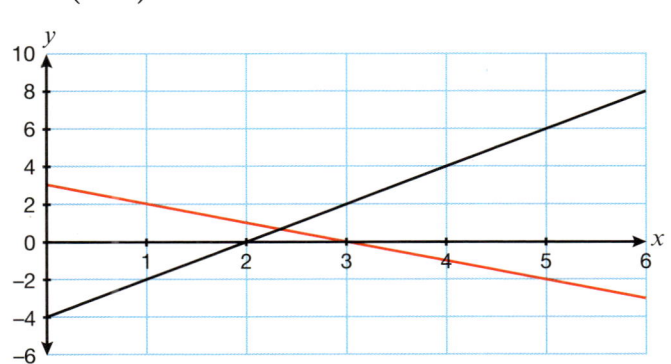

23 (2, 1)

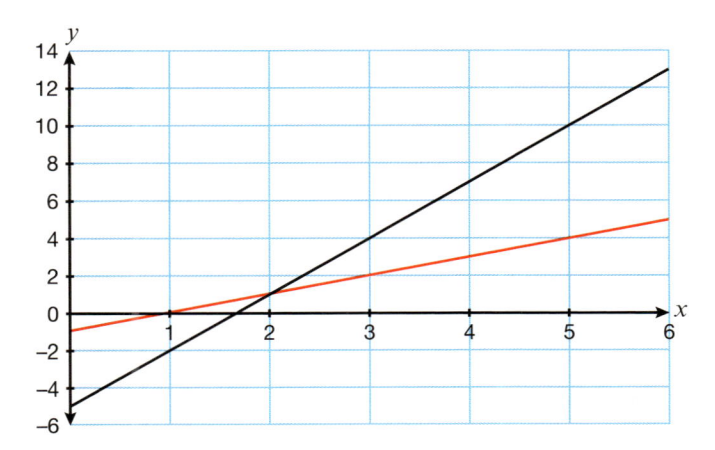

24 (4, 2)

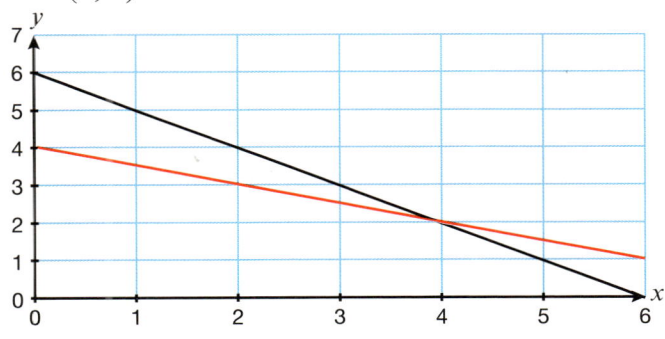

25 (5.3, 3.3)

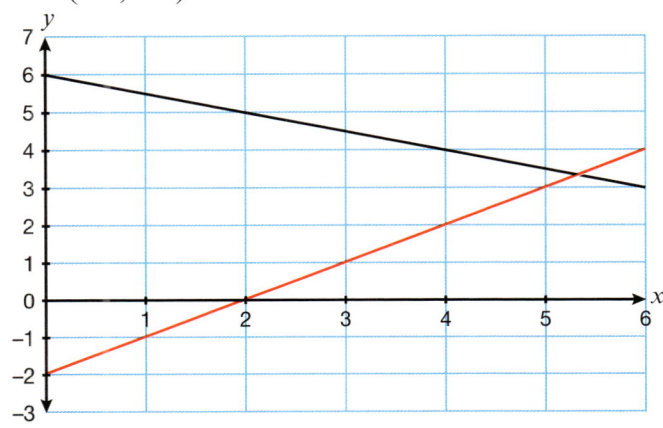

26 (3.2, −0.4)

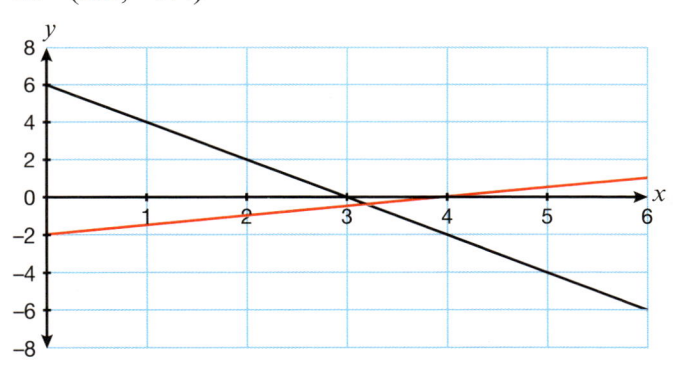

GRAPHS 2 – EXAM PRACTICE EXERCISE

1

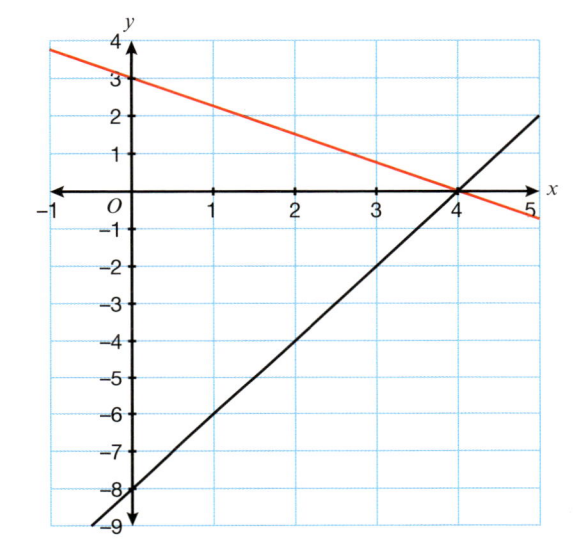

(a) $y = 2x - 4$ has gradient 2 so L_2 must be $y = 2x + c$
L intersects the x-axis at (4, 0)
Substituting $x = 4$, $y = 0$ into $y = 2x + c$ gives
$c = -8$ so M is $y = 2x - 8$

(b) L intersects the y-axis at (0, 3), M intersects the y-axis at (0, −8) and they both intersect the x-axis at (4, 0)
Area = $\frac{1}{2} \times 11 \times 4 = 22$ square units

2 (a) Rearrange the equations as
$A: y = \frac{1}{2}x + 2$, $B: y = -2x + 2$
$C: y = \frac{1}{2}x - \frac{1}{2}$, $D: y = -2x + 7$

270 ANSWERS

A sketch helps you to understand and answer the question.

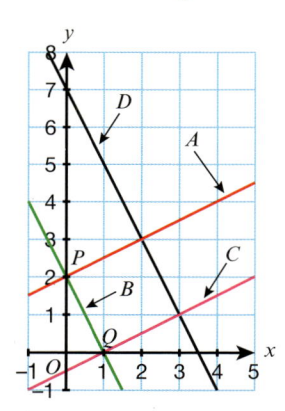

A and *C* have the same gradient of $\frac{1}{2}$ so they are parallel and one pair of opposite sides.

B and *D* have the same gradient of -2 so they are parallel and the other pair of opposite sides.

(b) *A* and *B* have a common point, *P*, (0, 2) so this is a vertex

B and *C* have a common point, *Q*, (1, 0) so this is a vertex.

$PQ^2 = 1^2 + 2^2 = 5$ Pythagoras' Theorem
$PQ = \sqrt{5}$ so perimeter $= 4\sqrt{5}$

3 (a)

Age (years)	Mia	Priya
Now	x	y
10 years ago	$x - 10$	$y - 10$
10 years' time	$x + 10$	$y + 10$

Ages 10 years ago were $x - 10$, $y - 10$
$x - 10 = 6(y - 10)$
$x - 10 = 6y - 60$
$x + 50 = 6y$
Ages in 10 years' time will be $x + 10$, $y + 10$
$x + 10 = 2(y + 10)$
$x + 10 = 2y + 20$
$x - 10 = 2y$

(b) Some points for $x + 50 = 6y$ are (10, 10), (22, 12) and (46, 16)
Some points for $x - 10 = 2y$ are (10, 0), (30, 10) and (50, 20)
or rearrange equations as $y = \frac{x}{6} + \frac{50}{6}$ and $y = \frac{x}{2} - 5$ and make a table of values using 3 widely spaced values of x

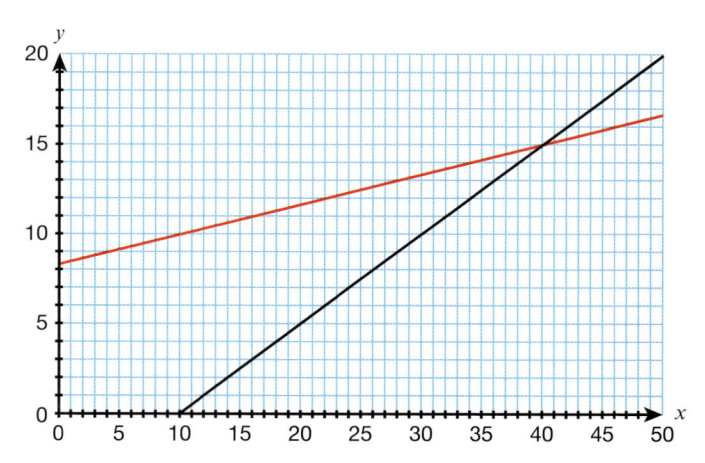

The graphs intersect at (40, 15) so Mia is 40 years old and Priya is 15 years old.

4 (a) 200 minutes on the phone costs 200*p* cents and 200 texts cost 200*t* cents.
$200p + 200t = 2800$
Cost of $28 must be expressed in cents
$p + t = 14$
100 minutes on the phone costs 100*p* cents and 300 texts cost 300*t* cents.
$100p + 300t = 2200$
Cost of $22 must be expressed in cents
$p + 3t = 22$

(b) Table of values for $p + t = 14$

p	0	7	14
t	14	7	0

Table of values for $p + 3t = 22$

p	1	7	22
t	7	5	0

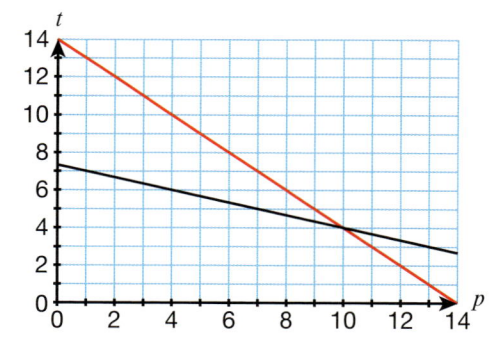

(c) The graphs intersect at $p = 10$, $t = 4$, so 150 minutes on the phone will cost 150×10 cents, 250 texts will cost 250×4 cents.
Total cost is 2500 cents or $25.

5 (a) Let equation of *L* be $y = mx + c$, then equation of *K* is $y = 2mx + c$
Gradient of *K* is twice gradient of *L* and they both have the same *y* intercept.

L: Substituting (−2, 4) gives $4 = -2m + c$
K: Substituting (4, −1) gives
$-1 = 2m \times 4 + c$ so $-1 = 8m + c$

(b) Subtract the two equations:
$4 - (-1) = -2m - 8m$
$5 = -10m$
$m = -\frac{1}{2}$
and $c = 3$

(c) Equation of *L* is $y = -\frac{x}{2} + 3$

L intersects the *x*-axis at (6, 0) and the *y*-axis at (0, 3)
Equation of *K* is $y = -x + 3$
K intersects the *x*-axis at (3, 0) and the *y*-axis at (0, 3)

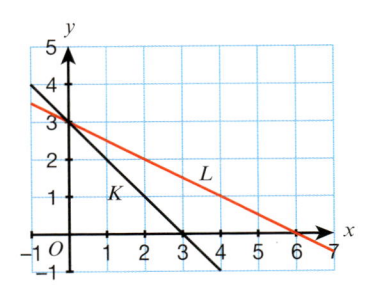

$A = \frac{1}{2} \times 3 \times 3 = 4.5$ square units

SHAPE AND SPACE 2 – BASIC SKILLS EXERCISE

1. $a = 6.40$
2. $b = 4.47$
3. $c = 15.0$
4. $AC = 36.6$
5. $a = 5.39$
6. $a = 5.20$
7. **(a)** $r = 11.7$
   (b) $a = 18.7$
8. **(a)** $XC = 2$ cm
   (b) $AC = 4.47$ cm
9. $k = 3$ Using Pythagoras', horizontal distance is 3 and vertical distance is 15 gives hypotenuse of $3\sqrt{26}$
10. Using Pythagoras', (length of square)^2 = $(a-c)^2 + (b-d)^2$. But area is (length of square)^2
    So $A = (a-c)^2 + (b-d)^2$
11. $a = 5, b = 17$ or vice-versa. Use Pythagoras' with horizontal distance 20 and vertical distance 90
    $20^2 + 90^2 = 8500$ so $OP = 10\sqrt{85}$. 5 and 17 are prime numbers which multiply to give 85.
12. $k = 3$ Use Pythagoras' (length of base diagonal)$^2 = (10x)^2 + (10x)^2 = 200x^2$
    (internal diagonal)$^2 = 200x^2 + 100x^2 = 300x^2$
    so internal diagonal = $10\sqrt{3}\ x$ so $k = 3$
13. $a = 90°, b = 30°$
14. $a = 70°, b = 20°$
15. $a = 55°, b = 70°$
16. $a = 90°, b = 45°$
17. $2a = 36°, 3a = 54°$
18. $x = 70°, y = 55°, z = 35°$
19. $a = 60°$
20. $a = 140°$
21. $a = 50°$
22. $a = 140°$
23. $a = 100°$
24. $a = 80°$
25. $a = 290°$
26. $a = 102°$
27. $x = 130°, y = 25°, z = 65°$
28. $a = 40°, b = 20°$
29. $a = 120°, b = 30°$
30. $a = 40°, b = 60°$
31. $a = 35°, b = 25°$
32. $a = 65°, b = 115°$
33. $a = 50°, y = 130°$
34. $a = 110°, b = 70°$
35. $a = 60°, b = 60°$
36. $x = 130°, y = 65°, z = 115°$

SHAPE AND SPACE 2 – EXAM PRACTICE EXERCISE

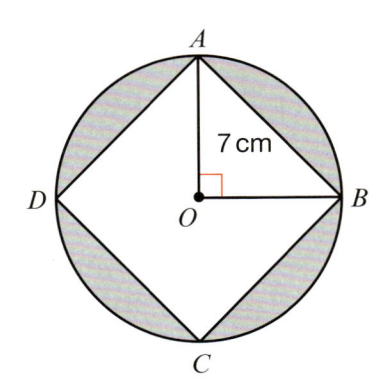

1. **(a)** Let *O* be the centre of the circle, so triangle *AOB* is a right-angled triangle.
   If $AO = BO = r$, then from Pythagoras' Theorem: $7^2 = r^2 + r^2 = 2r^2$, so $r^2 = \frac{49}{2}$
   area of the shaded segments = circle area − square area = $\pi \frac{49}{2} - 7^2 = 49(\frac{\pi}{2} - 1)$
   $= 49(\frac{\pi - 2}{2})$

percentage of shaded area of area of

circle = $\dfrac{49\left(\frac{\pi-2}{2}\right)}{\pi \frac{49}{2}} \times 100 = \dfrac{100}{\pi}(\pi - 2)$

$= m(\pi - 2), m = \dfrac{100}{\pi}$

(b) Area of one of the original circle

shaded segments = $\dfrac{49\left(\frac{\pi-2}{2}\right)}{4}$

$= 49\left(\dfrac{\pi-2}{8}\right) = \dfrac{49}{8}(\pi - 2) = a$

Let segment of the enlarged circle be A, so if the scale factor of enlargement = 4

$A = 4^2 \times a = 16 \times \dfrac{49}{8}(\pi - 2) = 98(\pi - 2)$

$= n(\pi - 2), n = 98$

2

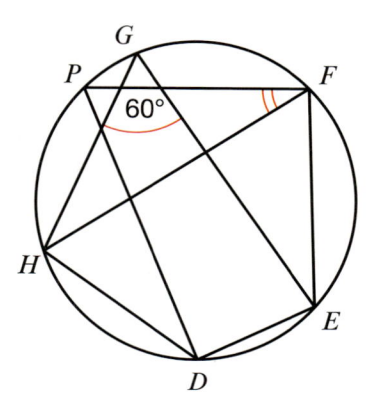

Angle $HDE = 180° - 0° = 120°$
(GHDE is a cyclic quadrilateral: Opposite angles in a cyclic quadrilateral sum to 180°)
Angle $HDP = \dfrac{1}{3} \times 120° = 40°$

(Angle HDE: Angle $EDP = 1 : 2$)
Angle HDP = Angle $HFP = 40°$
(Both angle HDP and angle HFP are formed in the same segment off chord HP: Angles in the same segment are equal).

3

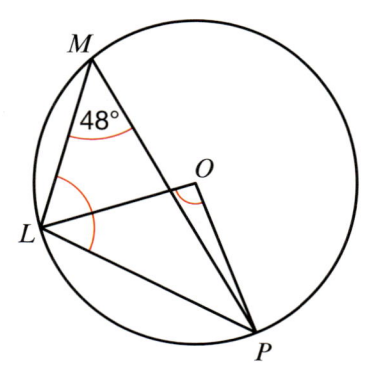

Angle $LOP = 2 \times 48° = 96°$
(Angle at centre = 2 × angle at circumference off the same chord in the same segment)
Angle OLP = Angle $OPL = \dfrac{180° - 96°}{2} = 42°$
(Triangle OLP is isosceles, so the base angles are equal)
Angle $MPL = \dfrac{2}{3} \times 42° = 28°$
Angle $MLP = 180° - 48° - 28° = 104°$
(Angle sum of a triangle = 180°)

4

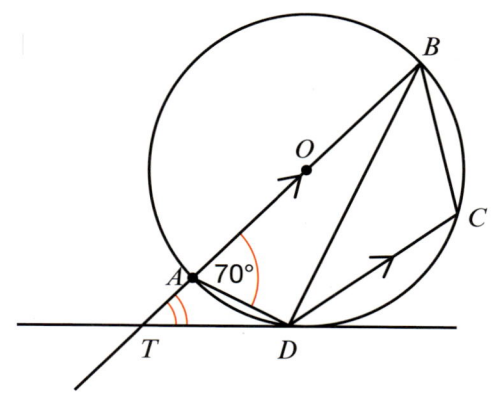

(a) Angle $ADB = 90°$
(Angle in a semicircle is 90°. AB is the diameter of the circle)
Angle $ABD = 20°$
(Angle sum of a triangle = 180°)
Angle $BDC = 20°$
(Angle ABD and Angle BDC are alternate angles)
Angle $ADC = 110°$
(Angle BAD and Angle ADC are also co-interior angles that sum to 180°)

(b) Angle ADT = Angle $ABD = 20°$
(Alternate segment theorem)
Angle $ATD = 180° - 110° - 20° = 50°$
(Angle sum of a triangle = 180°)

5

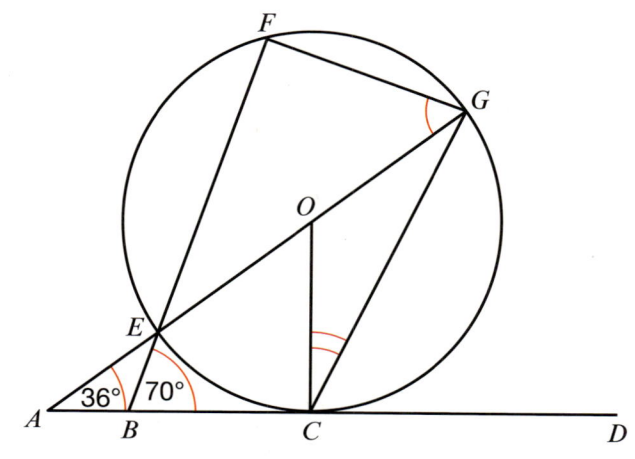

(a) Angle $OCA = 90°$ (Radius OC is perpendicular to tangent AD.)
Angle $AOC = 180° - 90° - 36° = 54°$
(Angle sum of a triangle = 180°)
Angle $COG = 180° - 54° = 126°$
(Sum of angles in a straight line = 180°)
Angle $OCG = \frac{180° - 126°}{2} = 27°$
(Triangle OCG is isosceles, so the base angles are equal.)

(b) Angle $BEO = 360° - 70° - 90° - 54° = 146°$
(Angle sum of a quadrilateral = 360°)
Angle $FEO = 180° - 146° = 34°$
(Sum of angles in a straight line = 180°)
Angle $FGO = 180° - 90° - 34° = 56°$
(Angle sum of a triangle = 180°. Angle in a semi-circle is 90°. AB is the diameter of the circle.)

(c) Triangle ECG is a right-angled triangle as EG is a diameter of the circle.
Using Pythagoras': $EG^2 = EC^2 + CG^2$,
$(2r)^2 = EC^2 + (4s)^2$
$EC^2 = 4r^2 - 16s^2 = 4(r^2 - 4s^2) = 4(r + 2s)(r - 2s)$ – using a difference of squares
$EC = \sqrt{4(r + 2s)(r - 2s)}$
$= 2\sqrt{(r + 2s)(r - 2s)}$ as required.

HANDLING DATA 1 – BASIC SKILLS EXERCISE

1   (a) Phone make – categorical
    (b) Number of goals scored – discrete
    (c) Height of a horse – continuous
    (d) Number of coins – discrete
    (e) Time to eat a pizza – continuous
    (f) Hair colour – categorical

2   (a)

Number	Tally	Frequency
1	ⵏⵏⵏⵏ I	6
2	ⵏⵏⵏⵏ ⵏⵏⵏⵏ I	11
3	II	2
4	IIII	4
5	ⵏⵏⵏⵏ II	7

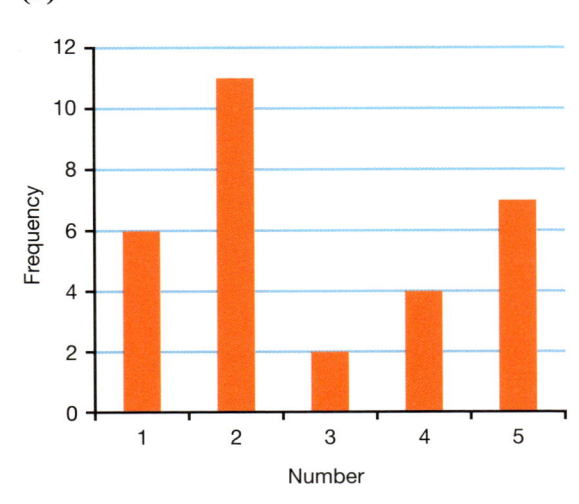

(b) [bar chart: Frequency vs Number 1–5, values 6, 11, 2, 4, 7]

(c) Does not appear very random, but the sample is too small to draw any definite conclusions.

3   (a)

Number of guides	Tally	Frequency
1–5	ⵏⵏⵏⵏ I	6
6–10	III	3
11–15	II	2
16–20	ⵏⵏⵏⵏ II	7
21–25	ⵏⵏⵏⵏ IIII	9
26–30	III	3

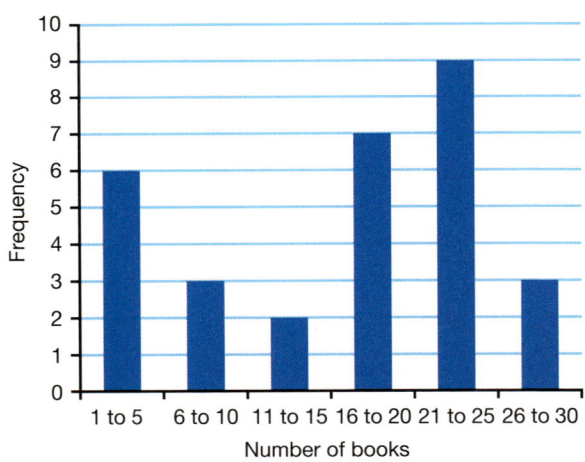

(b) [bar chart: Frequency vs Number of books, categories 1 to 5, 6 to 10, 11 to 15, 16 to 20, 21 to 25, 26 to 30, values 6, 3, 2, 7, 9, 3]

(c) There are many students with a lot of revision guides, quite a few with not many guides, but not many students with a middling number of guides.

4 (a)

	January–April	May–August	September–December	Total
Year 1	64	42	72	178
Year 2	55	24	37	116
Total	119	66	109	294

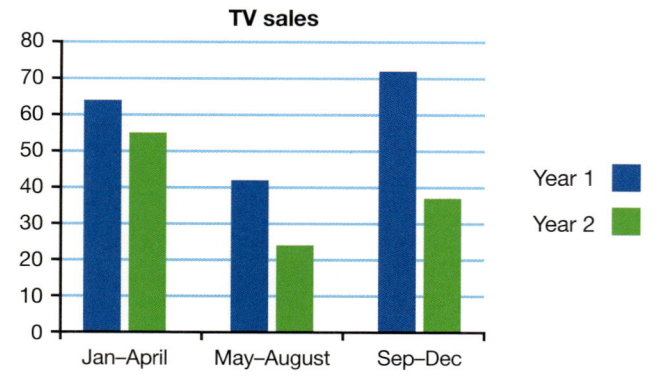

(b) TV sales bar chart (Year 1 and Year 2 for Jan–April, May–August, Sep–Dec)

(c) Year 2 sales were worse overall, especially from April–December

5 (a) 7.5% had a rabbit
Percentages must sum to 100'
or '% must sum to 100

(b) Angle for cat = $\frac{55}{100} \times 360° = 198°$

Angle for bird = $\frac{30}{100} \times 360° = 108°$

Angle for rabbit = $\frac{7.5}{100} \times 360° = 27°$

Angle for fish = $\frac{5}{100} \times 360° = 18°$

Angle for other = $\frac{2.5}{100} \times 360° = 9°$

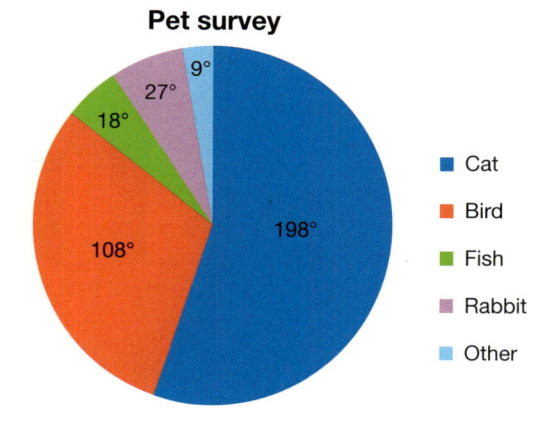

Pet survey pie chart: Cat 198°, Bird 108°, Fish 18°, Rabbit 27°, Other 9°

6 Orange juice is 56°

$\frac{56}{14} = 4$ so 4° corresponds to 1 person

Coffee $\frac{88}{4} = 22$ people

Tea $\frac{104}{4} = 26$ people

Milk $\frac{72}{4} = 18$ people

Other $\frac{40}{4} = 10$ people

7 Data in order is 0, 1, 2, 3, 4, 5, 6, 7, 7, 7, 7, 9
mean = 4.83, median = 4.5 and mode = 7

8 Data in order:
0 0 0 0 0 0 0
1 1 1 1 1 2 2
2 2 3 3 3 3 4
4 4 4 4 5 5 6
6 6

(a) Sum of data = 73
mean is 73 ÷ 30 = 2.43 (3 s.f.)
median is 2 and mode is 0

(b) She would probably use the mode as this is the lowest average.

9 Total sent over the week = 7 × 32 = 224
Total sent over the first 6 days = 176
Number sent on seventh day = 224 – 176 = 48

10 Data in order: 0, 0, 0, 0, 0, 1, 1, 1, 2, 3
(a) Mean = 0.8, median is 0.5 and mode is 0
(b) Goals scored this season = 12 × 1.25 = 15,
goals last season = 8
Total goals = 23, total matches = 22,
mean = 23 ÷ 22 = 1.05 (3 s.f.)

11 Total points needed: 857 × 7 = 5999
Total so far: 6 × 840 = 5040
Points needed: 5999 – 5040 = 959

12

State	A	B	C	Total
Population in millions	21	26	18	65
Mean	0.1	0.09	0.15	
Number infected in millions	2.1	2.34	2.7	7.14

Mean for whole country = $\frac{7.14}{65} = 0.11$ (2 d.p.)

13 $x = 56, y = 73$

14 $x = 7, y = 42$

15 Sum of the first 19 prime numbers squared
= 19 × 1314 = 24 966

mean is $\frac{24\,966 + 71^2}{20} = 1500.35$

ANSWERS

HANDLING DATA 1 – EXAM PRACTICE EXERCISE

1 (a) Data in order are 29, 32, 32, 35, 83, 86, 95
Mean = $\frac{392}{7}$ = 56, median is 35 and mode = 32

(b) Mode cannot be calculated as frequencies are not known.
Median cannot be calculated as the distribution of sales is not known.
Mean can be calculated. Total sales for the first week are 392.
Total sales for the next three weeks (21 days) are 60 × 21 = 1260.
Total sales for the four-week period of 28 days are 392 + 1260 = 1652
mean is $\frac{1652}{28}$ = 59

2 (a) Two of the following:
The vertical axis does not start at zero.
The vertical axis has no zig-zag line to show it does not start at zero.
The bars are not of equal widths.
The size of the type is not the same.

(b)

Tablet sales

(Bar chart: Sales in millions vs Burn, Apricot, Song; values approximately 5, 4.9, 4.8)

Note: Bars must not touch each other and the vertical scale must be linear.

3 $t = 50°$ (Angles must sum to 360)
50° corresponds to 40 pupils so 10° corresponds to 40 ÷ 5 = 8 pupils
100° corresponds to 8 × 10 = 80 pupils = p
60° corresponds to 8 × 6 = 48 pupils = q
70° corresponds to 8 × 7 = 56 pupils = r
80° corresponds to 8 × 8 = 64 pupils = s

4 (a) New mean is $\frac{12a + 16a + 21a + 27a}{4}$

$= \frac{a(12 + 16 + 21 + 27)}{4} = a × 19$

The mean has been multiplied by a.

(b) Let s be the total of the numbers in set A, then $x = \frac{s}{n}$ and $s = xn$

Let t be the total of the numbers in set B, then $y = \frac{t}{m}$ and $t = my$

The total of all $n + m$ numbers in set C is $s + t = nx + my$ so the mean is $\frac{nx + my}{n + m}$

5 (a) Range is $d - 6 = 15$ so $d = 25$
Median is the mean of b and 14 so $b = 12$
Mode is 8 so $a = 8$
Mean = 14 so the sum of the numbers is 8 × 14 = 112
Sum of the numbers is 94 + c so $c = 18$
$a = 8$, $b = 12$, $c = 18$ and $d = 25$

(b) Mean = 17 so
$\frac{w + x + y + z}{4} = 17$
$w + x + y + z = 17 × 4 = 68$ (equation 1)
Range = 8 so $z - w = 8$ (equation 2)
Median = 16 so $\frac{x+y}{2} = 16$ so
$x + y = 16 × 2 = 32$ (equation 3)
Substitute equation 3 into equation 1
$w + 32 + z = 68$ so
$w + z = 68 - 32 = 36$ (equation 4)
Add equations 2 and 4 to get
$2z = 44$
$z = 22$ and $w = 14$
$x + y = 32$ so $x = 15$ and $y = 17$ since the median is 16
Integers are 14, 15, 17 and 22.

NUMBER 3 – BASIC SKILLS EXERCISE

1 (a) 7, 14, 21, 28
(b) 11, 22, 33, 44
(c) 17, 34, 51, 68

2 (a) 1, 3, 5, 15
(b) 1, 2, 4, 5, 10, 20
(c) 1, 2, 7, 14, 49, 98

3 (a) $3^3 × 5 × 7$
(b) $2^3 × 3^4 × 5 × 7$
(c) $3^9 × 5^3 × 7^3$
(d) $2^2 × 3^3 × 5^3 × 7$

4 (a) $2^7 × 3^4 × 5^2 × 7^4$
(b) $2^8 × 3^4 × 5^2 × 7^4$

5 $N = 2^9 × 3^2 × 5^6$ therefore the largest odd factor is $3^2 × 5^6 = 140\,625$

276 ANSWERS

6 (a) $60 = 2^2 \times 3 \times 5$, $70 = 2 \times 5 \times 7$ therefore
      HCF = $2 \times 5 = 10$
      LCM = $2^2 \times 3 \times 5 \times 7 = 420$
   (b) $140 = 2^2 \times 5 \times 7$, $84 = 2^2 \times 3 \times 7$
      therefore HCF = $2^2 \times 7 = 28$
      LCM = $2^2 \times 3 \times 5 \times 7 = 420$
   (c) $525 = 3 \times 5^2 \times 7$, $40 = 2^3 \times 5$ $441 = 3^2 \times 7^2$
      therefore HCF = 1
      LCM = $2^3 \times 3^2 \times 5^2 \times 7^2 = 88\,200$

7 HCF = 3, LCM = $2^4 \times 3^2 \times 5^2 \times 7^2 \times 11^2$

8 15, 21

9 (a) HCF = $5pq$, LCM = $140\,pq$
   (b) HCF = $2xyz$, LCM = $12x^2y^2z^2$
   (c) HCF = $6a^2b^3c^2$, LCM = $36a^4b^3c^4$

10 (a) 1, 2, 3, 4, 6, 12
   (b) Factors of 12

11 $48 = 2^4 \times 3$, $45 = 3^2 \times 5$ therefore
   LCM = $2^4 \times 3^2 \times 5 = 720$ s or 12 minutes

12 $88 = 2^3 \times 11$, $110 = 2 \times 5 \times 11$ therefore
   LCM = $2^3 \times 5 \times 11 = 440$ so 4.4 seconds

13 (a) 5 : 11
   (b) 1 : 5 : 17
   (c) 3 : 4 : 70
   (d) $x : 4y : 20$

14 (a) 1 : 24
   (b) 3 : 1440 = 1 : 480
   (c) 4 : 1000 = 1 : 250
   (d) $10 : \frac{900\,000}{60 \times 60} = 1 : 25$

15 $\frac{3}{x} = \frac{x}{27}$ so $x^2 = 81$ so $x = 9$ or $x = -9$

16 (a) $\frac{360}{9} = 40$ so 160 : 200
   (b) $\frac{133}{7} = 19$ so 19 : 38 : 76
   (c) $\frac{1000}{10} = 100$ so 100 : 200 : 300 : 400
   (d) $\frac{352}{11} = 32$ so 64 : 96 : 192

17 $\frac{3450}{15} = 230$ so shares are £460, £1380 and £1610 so difference is £1150

18 $\frac{9}{4} \times 12 = 27$ therefore Petra is 27 years old

19 $x : y = 175 : 100 = 7 : 4$

20 $\frac{9}{7} \times 3.5 = 4.5$ therefore longest charging time is 4 h 30 mins

21 $\frac{3}{103} \times 51.5 = 1.5$ therefore the distance swum is 1.5 km

22 $\frac{5}{8} - \frac{3}{8} = \frac{1}{4}$ therefore $\frac{1}{4}$ of the weight of both sloths is 6 kg and the total weight is 24 kg hence 9 kg and 15 kg

23 $\frac{5}{10} - \frac{2}{10} = \frac{3}{10}$ so $\frac{3}{10}$ of total length is 120 cm and the total length is 400 cm.

24 Total no of parts is 16.
   Sugar : milk : flour is 4 : 5 : 7
   $\frac{5}{16} - \frac{4}{16} = \frac{1}{16} = 60$ g so the total weight
   $= 60 \times 16 = 960$ g
   therefore the weight of flour $= \frac{7}{16} \times 960 = 420$ g

25 LCM of 2 and 9 is 18, 1 : 2 = 9 : 18 and
   9 : 5 = 18 : 10 so $a : b : c = 9 : 18 : 10$

26 $a : b = 2 : 3 = 8 : 12$, $b : c = 12 : 15$
   so $a : c = 8 : 15$

27 Angles A and C are $\frac{2}{3}$ of the angle sum of the triangle
   $\frac{8}{8+x} = \frac{2}{3}$
   $24 = 16 + 2x$
   $x = 4$

28 LCM of 3 and 7 is 21, 2 : 3 = 14 : 21 and
   7 : 5 = 21 : 15 so $P : W : R = 14 : 21 : 15$.
   $14 + 21 + 15 = 50 =$ therefore the fraction of roses that are red is $\frac{15}{50} = \frac{3}{10}$ and hence the number is $\frac{3}{10}r$

29 Area of the circle is πr^2
   Area of square is $4 \times \frac{1}{2} r^2 = 2r^2$

   The square is made up of 4 right-angled triangles with base and height of r.
   Alternatively calculate the length of the side of the square using Pythagoras' Theorem, length $\sqrt{r^2 + r^2} = \sqrt{2r^2}$
   Area = length × length = $2r^2$.

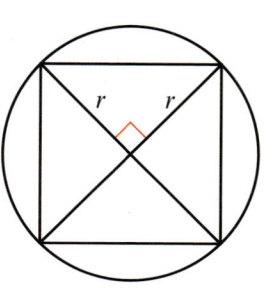

   Ratio is $\pi r^2 : 2r^2 = \pi : 2$

30 Let F be father's age and S be son's age
$F = 3S$ and $F + 12 = 2(S + 12)$
$3S + 12 = 2S + 24$
$S = 12, F = 36$
In 36 years, $F = 72, S = 48$
So $3 : 2$

NUMBER 3 – EXAM PRACTICE EXERCISE

1 (a) $10^6 = 2^6 \times 5^6$ therefore the greatest is 5^6
 $= 15\,625$ An odd factor cannot contain any power of 2
 (b) $525 = 3 \times 5^2 \times 7$, $21 = 3 \times 7$,
 $3150 = 2 \times 3^2 \times 5^2 \times 7$
 $x = 2 \times 3^2 \times 7 = 126$

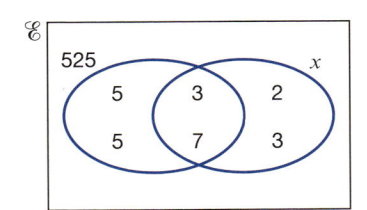

2 (a) $60 = 2^2 \times 3 \times 5$ $x = 2^2 \times 3 = 12$,
 $y = 3 \times 5 = 15$
 x and y must share the factor 3, but not the factors 2 or 5
 (b) $45\,360 = 2^4 \times 3^4 \times 5 \times 7$, $36 = 2^2 \times 3^2$
 There are two possible cases, shown in the Venn diagrams.

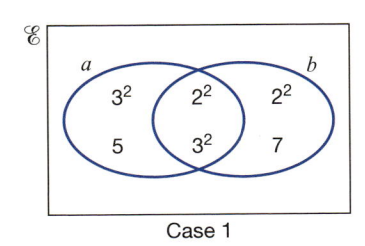

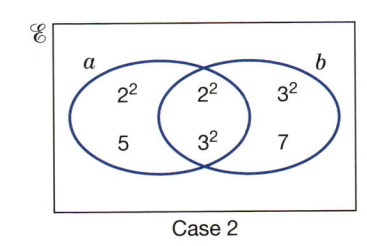

 Case 1 $a = 2^2 \times 3^4 \times 5 = 1620$,
 $b = 2^4 \times 3^2 \times 7 = 1008$

 Case 2 $a = 2^4 \times 3^2 \times 5 = 720$,
 $b = 2^2 \times 3^4 \times 7 = 2268$

 As $a < b$, Case 2 applies so $x = 4$ and $y = 2$

(3) (a) $1 + 3 = 4$ and $11 + 13 = 24$, so multiply the first ratio by 6 so they can be directly compared, i.e. $6 : 18$ and $11 : 13$.

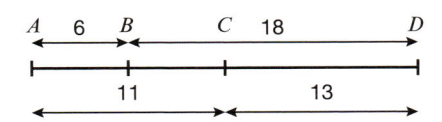

The diagram shows that $BC = 5$, so $AB : BC : CD = 6 : 5 : 13$

(b) (i) $11 : 3 = 22 : 6$ and $5 : 2 = 15 : 6$ so men : women : children $= 22 : 15 : 6$
 (ii) $22 + 15 + 6 = 43$ so the fractional difference of men and women is
 $\frac{22}{43} - \frac{15}{43} = \frac{7}{43}$

Total population is $42 \times \frac{43}{7} = 258$ therefore the number of children is $\frac{6}{43} \times 258 = 36$

4 Number of V, C and M is $0.6 \times 140 = 84$
60% are not Mushroom
Ratio of $2 : 5 : 7$ is a total of 14 parts
number of Meat is $\frac{7}{14} \times 84 = 42$
number of Veggie is $\frac{2}{14} \times 84 = 12$
difference is $42 - 12 = 30$ pizzas

5 $720 = 2^4 \times 3^2 \times 5$, $1260 = 2^2 \times 3^2 \times 5 \times 7$,
$1800 = 2^3 \times 3^2 \times 5^2$

HCF of 720, 1260 and 1800 is $2^2 \times 3^2 \times 5 = 180$ so 180 parcels

Number of pints of milk is $\frac{720}{180} = 4$

Number of loaves of bread is $\frac{1260}{180} = 7$

Number of cans of beans is $\frac{1800}{180} = 10$

180 parcels each with 4 pints of milk, 7 loaves of bread and 10 cans of beans

ALGEBRA 3 – BASIC SKILLS EXERCISE

1 $a(7 - a)$
2 $3x(1 - 4x)$
3 $ab(a + b)$
4 $4xy(1 - 2xy)$
5 $\frac{1}{3} pqr (qr^2 + 2p^2q)$
6 $(x + 1)(2x - 5)$

7    $x + 4$
8    $1 + a$
9    $2x$
10   $\frac{5}{xy}$
11   $\frac{2(x+2)}{7}$
12   x^2y
13   6
14   $\frac{3}{5}$
15   11
16   4
17   14
18   15
19   $\frac{1}{5}$
20   $\frac{2}{3}$
21   -49
22   $\frac{3}{4}$
23   ± 4
24   ± 8
25   $1\frac{1}{5}$
26   6
27   Let £x be Zazoo's winnings $\Rightarrow$ Yi's winnings are £$3x$ and Xavier's are £$\frac{3x}{2}$

$\Rightarrow x + 3x + \frac{3x}{2} = 11000 \Rightarrow \frac{11x}{2} = 11000$

$\Rightarrow \frac{x}{2} = 1000 \Rightarrow x = 2000$

$\Rightarrow$ Zazoo gets £2000, Yi gets £6000 and Xavier gets £3000.

28   (4, 1)
29   (3, 2)
30   (1, 2)
31   (1, 1)
32   (1, 4)
33   (1, 8)
34   (3, 1)
35   (6, 2)
36   (2, 1)
37   (2, 1)
38   (−1, 5)
39   (−0.4, −9.2)
40   $x = 24$, $y = 15$
41   6 stools

ALGEBRA 3 – EXAM PRACTICE EXERCISE

1   (a)   (i) $\frac{2}{5}p^2r^2(r - 2p)$

         (ii) $(x - 1)(3 - x)$

    (b)   (i) $\frac{10x^2 + 5x}{5x} - 1 = \frac{5x(2x+1)}{5x} - 1$

              $= (2x + 1) - 1 = 2x$

         (ii) $\frac{3x^3y + 9x^2y^2}{x^2 + 3xy} = \frac{3x^2y(x+3y)}{x(x+3y)}$

              $= 3xy$

    (c) $\frac{x^2 - xy}{xy^2 + y^3} \div \frac{xy - y^2}{x^3 + x^2y}$

       $= \frac{x^2 - xy}{xy^2 + y^3} \times \frac{x^3 + x^2y}{xy - y^2}$

       $= \frac{x(x-y)}{y^2(x+y)} \times \frac{x^2(x+y)}{y(x-y)} = \frac{x^3}{y^3}$

       $= \left(\frac{x}{y}\right)^3$ so $n = 3$

2   (a)   (i) $\frac{2(x+1)}{5} - \frac{3(x+1)}{10} = x$

           $\frac{4x + 4 - 3x - 3}{10} = x$

           $x + 1 = 10x$

           $x = \frac{1}{9}$

         (ii) $\frac{36}{x} - 4x = 0$

            $36 - 4x^2 = 0$

            $36 = 4x^2$

            $x^2 = 9$

            $x = \pm 3$

    (b)   Let C be the amount Carla gets.
Then Bobbie gets $1.4C$
To increase by 40%, multiply by 1.4
And Anna gets $0.7C + 500$
$0.7C + 500 + 1.4C + C = 16\,000$
$3.1C = 15500$
$C = 5000$
Anna gets $4000, Bobbie gets $7000 and Carla gets $5000.

3   $4y - 2x - 15 = 2x + y$ simplifies to $3y - 4x = 15$
$x : y = 3 : 5$ so $5x = 3y$
Substituting gives
$5x - 4x = 15$
$x = 15$
$y = 25$
angle B = angle C = 55° so angle A = 70°
Ratio angle A : angle B = 70 : 55 = 14 : 11

4 (a) $12 = 2^2 + 2a + b$
$-6 = (-1)^2 - a + b$
$2a + b = 8$
$b - a = -7$
$3a = 15$
$a = 5$
$b = -2$
equation of curve is $y = x^2 + 5x - 2$

(b) Let a be number of ash trees and b be the number of beech trees.
$20a + 30b = 3100$
$30a + 20b = 2900$
$2a + 3b = 310$
$3a + 2b = 290$
$6a + 9b = 930$
$6a + 4b = 580$
$5b = 350$
$b = 70$
$a = 50$
Ash costs $50, beech costs $70

5 $(x + 100) : (y + 100) = 4 : 3$
$\frac{x + 100}{y + 100} = \frac{4}{3}$
$3(x + 100) = 4(y + 100)$
$3x - 4y = 100$ equation 1
$(x - 100) : (y - 100) = 11 : 7$
$\frac{x - 100}{y - 100} = \frac{11}{7}$
$7(x - 100) = 11(y - 100)$
$7x - 11y = -400$ equation 2
$21x - 28y = 700$ equation 1 × 7
$21x - 33y = -1200$ equation 2 × 3
$5y = 1900 \Rightarrow y = 380$
$x = 540$
Bike costs $540, laptop costs $380

GRAPHS 3 – BASIC SKILLS EXERCISE

1 8 m/s
2 –4 m/s
3 (a) 15 m/s
 (b) 4 s
 (c) –9 m/s
4 (a)

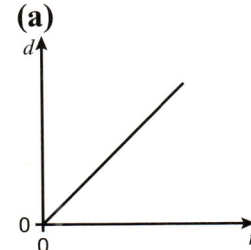

(b)

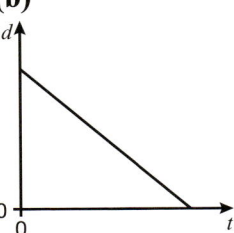

5 (a)

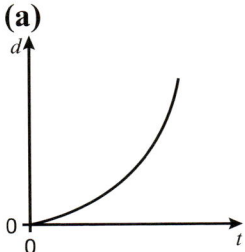

(b)

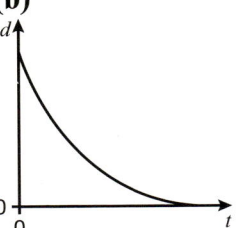

6

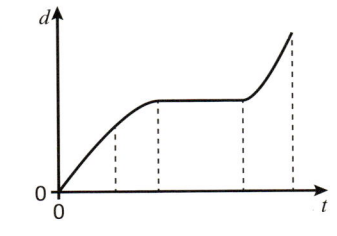

7 5 m/s²
8 –0.5 m/s²
9 (a) 3 m/s²
 (b) 0 m/s²
 (c) 2 m/s²
 (d) 43.3 m/s
10 (a)

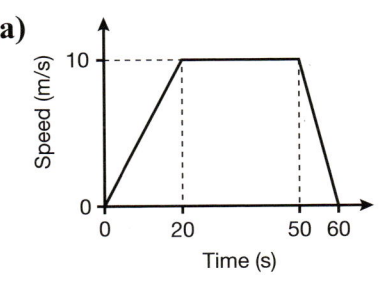

(b) (i) 0.5 m/s²
 (ii) –1 m/s²
 (iii) 7.5 m/s

11 (a) [graph: V vs t, linear increasing from origin]

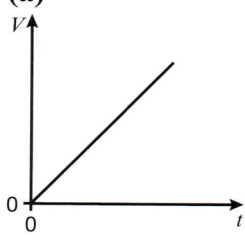

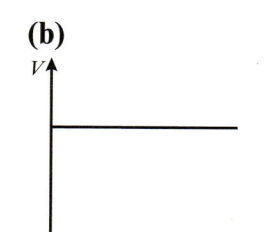

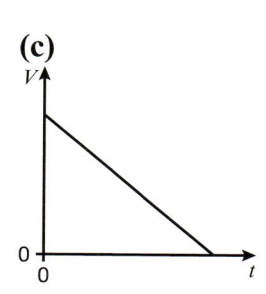

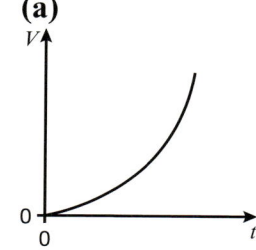

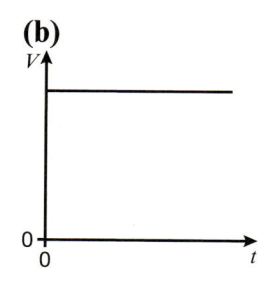

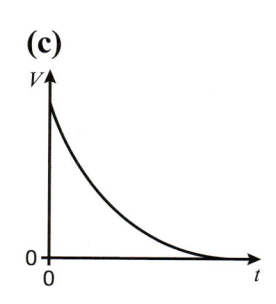

(b) [graph: V vs t, horizontal line]

(c) [graph: V vs t, linear decreasing to t-axis]

12 (a) [graph: V vs t, curve increasing (concave up)]

(b) [graph: V vs t, horizontal line]

(c) [graph: V vs t, exponential decay curve]

GRAPHS 3 – EXAM PRACTICE EXERCISE

1 Gradient of a distance–time graph = velocity

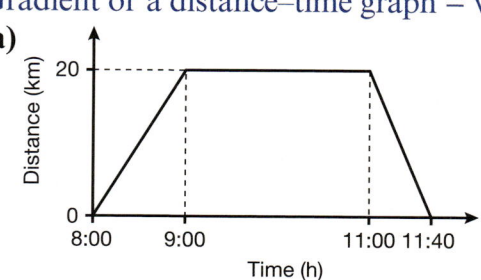

(a) [graph: Distance (km) vs Time (h); rises from 0 at 8:00 to 20 at 9:00, flat to 11:00, falls to 0 at 11:40]

(b) 11: 40 (Return speed = 30 km/h, $30 = \frac{20}{t}$, $t = \frac{2}{3}$ hr = 40 min)

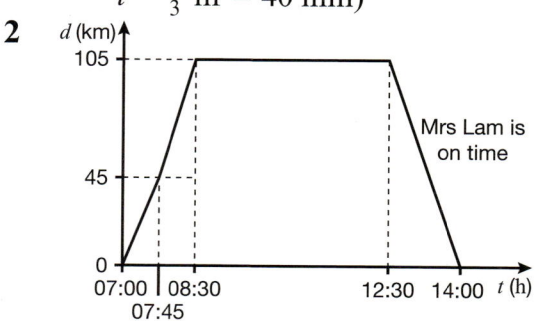

2 [graph: d (km) vs t (h); rises from 0 at 07:00 through 45 at 07:45 to 105 at 08:30, flat to 12:30, falls to 0 at 14:00; labelled "Mrs Lam is on time"]

3 (a) Area under a speed–time graph = distance travelled
Gradient of a speed–time graph = acceleration

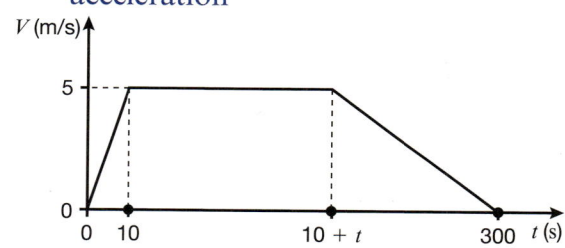

[graph: V (m/s) vs t (s); rises from 0 to 5 at t=10, flat to 10+t, falls to 0 at 300]

(b) (i) 1 km = 1000 m
Area under graph = Distance travelled
$1000 = \frac{1}{2}(t + 300)5$
$400 = t + 300$
$t = 100$ s

(ii) Acceleration, $a = -\frac{5}{300 - 110}$

$a = -0.0263$ m/s² (3 s.f.)

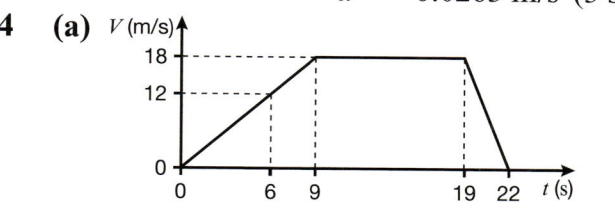

4 (a) [graph: V (m/s) vs t (s); rises from 0 to 18 at t=9 (passing 12 at t=6), flat to 19, falls to 0 at 22]

(b) Initial acceleration = 2 m/s², so final retardation = 6 m/s²

(c) Mean speed of the hawk =
$\frac{\text{area under the speed – time graph}}{\text{time of travel}}$

Area under graph = 0.5 × 6 × 12 + 0.5 × (12 + 18) × 3 + 0.5 × (10 + 13) × 18
= 288 m

Mean speed of the hawk = 288 ÷ 22 = 13.1 m/s

5   (a) Be careful to work in consistent units.
1 km = 1000 m
1 hour = 3600 s
    (i) 400 ÷ 62.5 = 6.4 m/s
    (ii) $\frac{0.4 \times 60 \times 60}{62.5}$ = 23.04 ≈ 23.0 km/h
  (b) Area under speed-time graph = 400 m
400 = 0.5 × (50.5 + 62.5) × S_{max},
so S_{max} = 7.08 m/s
  (c) Initial acceleration = gradient of first phase = (7.0796…) ÷ 12 = 0.58997…
= 0.590 m/s²

SHAPE AND SPACE 3 – BASIC SKILLS EXERCISE

1   x = 8.39 m, y = 3.53 m
2   x = 12.1 cm, y = 5.12 cm
3   x = 6.53 cm, y = 1.55 cm
4   x = 34.6 cm, y = 29.1 cm
5   θ = 43.6°
6   θ = 5.20°
7   θ = 59.6°
8   θ = 16.1°
9   71.6°
10 144 cm
11 x = 7.71, y = 7.96
12 x = 14.3, y = 24.9
13 x = 17.3, y = 34.6
14 x = 17.3, y = 6
15 θ = 16.8°
16 θ = 59.5°
17 θ = 50.2°
18 θ = 11.0°
19 3.95 m
20 (a) 4.5 km
    (b) 2.25 km
    (c) 3.90 km

SHAPE AND SPACE 3 – EXAM PRACTICE EXERCISE

1   (a)

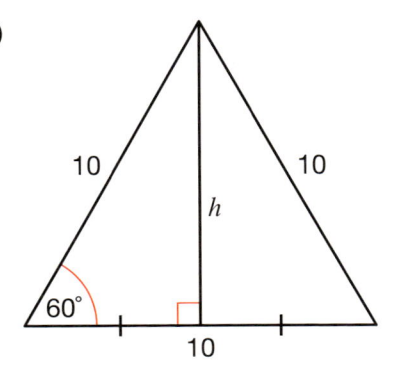

Area of triangle = $\frac{1}{2} \times 10 \times h$
= $\frac{1}{2} \times 10 \times (10 \times \sin 60°)$ = $25\sqrt{3}$
Area of circle = $\pi r^2 = 25\sqrt{3}$, $r^2 = \frac{25\sqrt{3}}{\pi}$
so $r = \frac{5\sqrt[4]{3}}{\sqrt{\pi}}$
Circumference of circle = $2\pi r = 2\pi \times \frac{5\sqrt[4]{3}}{\sqrt{\pi}}$ =
$10\sqrt{\pi} \times \sqrt[4]{3} = 10 \times \pi^{\frac{1}{2}} \times 3^{\frac{1}{4}} = 10 \times \pi^a \times 3^b$
$a = \frac{1}{2}, b = \frac{1}{4}$

2   (a)

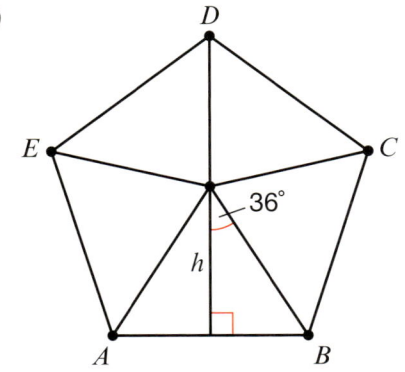

Angle at centre of pentagon = 360°, so angle of each triangle at centre of pentagon
= $\frac{360}{5}$ = 72°
$AB = 2 \times 6.8 \times \sin(36°)$ = 7.9939…cm
Perimeter = 5 × 7.9939 = 39.969…cm = 40.0 cm (3 s.f.)
(b) Let shaded area be A
$A = \frac{\text{area of circle} - \text{area of pentagon}}{5}$
$= \frac{\pi \times 6.8^2 - 5 \times 6.8 \times \sin(36°) \times 6.8 \times \cos(36°)}{5}$
= 7.0650…cm²
$p = \frac{7.0650}{\pi \times 6.8^2} \times 100$ = 4.8635…% = 4.86%
The value of p is 4.86.

3

Triangle OAB:
$\sin(35°) = \frac{OB}{7}$, so $OB = 7 \times \sin(35°)$
= 4.0150…cm
$\sin \theta = \frac{\text{opposite side}}{\text{hypotenuse}}$
Area of circle = $\pi \times 4.0150^2$ = 50.6440…cm²
area of circle = πr^2

Area of triangle $BCD = \frac{1}{2} \times BC \times DC$

(Angle $BCD = 90°$ as angles in a semi-circle are right-angles)

Triangle BCD:

$\sin(70°) = \frac{CD}{2 \times 4.01503}$,

so $CD = 2 \times 4.01503 \times \sin(70°) = 7.5458...$cm

$\sin\theta = \frac{\text{opposite side}}{\text{hypotenuse}}$

$\cos(70°) = \frac{BC}{2 \times 4.01503}$,

so $BC = 2 \times 4.01503 \times \cos(70°) = 2.7464...$cm

$\cos\theta = \frac{\text{adjacent side}}{\text{hypotenuse}}$

Area of triangle BCD

$= \frac{1}{2} \times 2.7464 \times 7.5458 = 10.362...$cm² or

Area $= \frac{1}{2} \times BD \times BC \times \sin 70°$

Area in circle and outside of triangle BCD

$= 50.644 - 10.362 = 40.282$ cm²

% of whole circle not occupied by triangle

$BCD = \frac{40.282}{50.644} \times 100 = 79.540...$%

So value of $p = 79.5$ (3 s.f.)

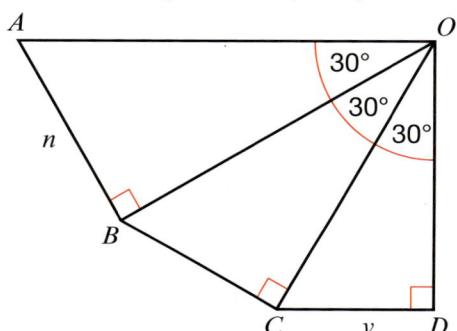

4

(a) Triangle OAB

$\tan 30° = \frac{n}{OB}$, so $OB = \frac{n}{\tan 30°} = \sqrt{3}n$

$\tan\theta = \frac{\text{opposite side}}{\text{adjacent side}}$

$\tan 30° = \frac{1}{\sqrt{3}}$

Triangle OBC

$\cos(30°) = \frac{OC}{\sqrt{3}n}$,

so $OC = \cos 30° \times \sqrt{3}n = \frac{3}{2}n$

$\cos\theta = \frac{\text{adjacent side}}{\text{hypotenuse}}$

$\cos 30° = \frac{\sqrt{3}}{2}$

Triangle OCD

$\sin 30° = \frac{y}{\frac{3}{2}n}$, so $y = \frac{3}{2}n \times \sin 30° = \frac{3}{4}n$

as required.

$\sin\theta = \frac{\text{opposite side}}{\text{hypotenuse}}$

$\sin 30° = \frac{1}{2}$

(b) Let area of the pentagon be A.

A = area of triangle OAB + area of triangle OBC + area of triangle OCD

Area of triangle OAB

$= \frac{1}{2} \times n \times \sqrt{3}n$

$= \frac{\sqrt{3}}{2} n^2$

Area of triangle $OBC = \frac{1}{2} \times BC \times OC$

$= \frac{1}{2} \times (\sqrt{3}n \times \sin(30°)) \times \frac{3}{2}n = \frac{3\sqrt{3}}{8}n^2$

Area of triangle $OCD = \frac{1}{2} \times CD \times OD$

$= \frac{1}{2} \times \frac{3}{4}n \times \left(\frac{3}{2}n \times \cos(30°)\right) = \frac{9\sqrt{3}}{32}n^2$

So $A = \frac{\sqrt{3}}{2}n^2 + \frac{3\sqrt{3}}{8}n^2 + \frac{9\sqrt{3}}{32}n^2$

$= \frac{16\sqrt{3}}{32}n^2 + \frac{12\sqrt{3}}{32}n^2 + \frac{9\sqrt{3}}{32}n^2$

$= \frac{37\sqrt{3}}{32}n^2$

If $A = \frac{37\sqrt{3}}{2} = \frac{37\sqrt{3}}{32}n^2$, $n^2 = 16$, $n = 4$

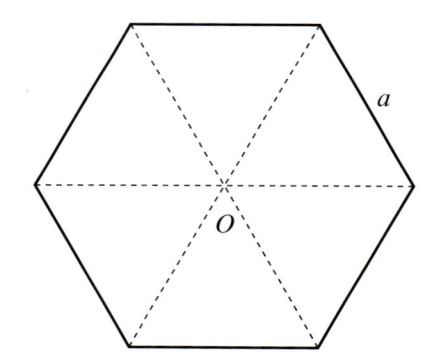

5

Pentagon $PQRSTU$ is regular so each triangle is equilateral.

Area of triangle $OST = \frac{1}{2} \times a \times (a \times \sin 60°)$

$= \frac{\sqrt{3}}{4}a^2$

Area of pentagon $= 6 \times \frac{\sqrt{3}}{4}a^2 = \frac{3\sqrt{3}}{2}a^2$ as required.

6

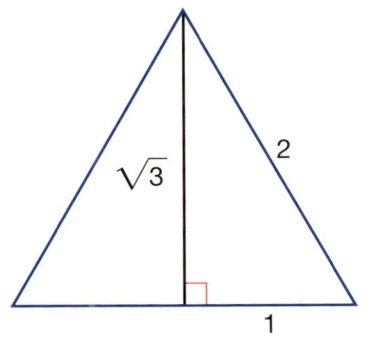

Pythagoras' theorem: Let height of equilateral triangle = h

$2^2 = h^2 + 1^2$, $h = \sqrt{3}$

If area of equilateral triangle = area of regular pentagon

$\frac{1}{2} \times 2 \times \sqrt{3} = \frac{3\sqrt{3}}{2} a^2$, $1 = \frac{3}{2} a^2$, $a^2 = \frac{2}{3}$,

$a = \sqrt{\frac{2}{3}}$

$P = 6a = 6 \times \sqrt{\frac{2}{3}} = 3 \times 2 \times \frac{\sqrt{2}}{\sqrt{3}} = \sqrt{3} \times 2 \times 2^{\frac{1}{2}}$

$= \sqrt{3} \times 2^{\frac{3}{2}} = \sqrt{3} \times 2^k$, so $k = \frac{3}{2}$

HANDLING DATA 2 – BASIC SKILLS EXERCISE

1 (a)

Time	Frequency
$40 \le t < 45$	12
$45 \le t < 50$	5
$50 \le t < 55$	8
$55 \le t < 60$	4
$60 \le t < 65$	2
$65 \le t < 70$	10
$70 \le t < 75$	4
$75 \le t < 80$	5

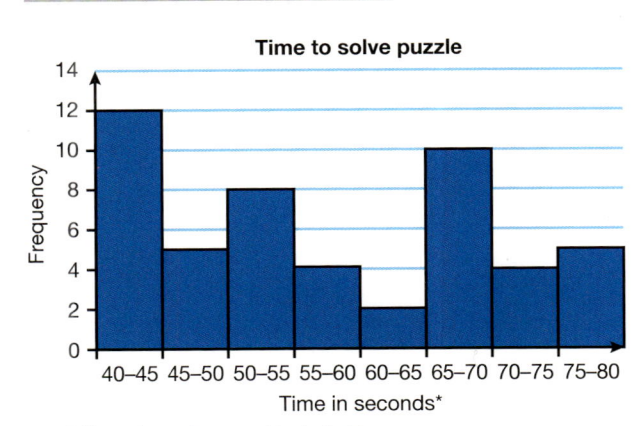

(b) 58%

2 (a) 85

(b)

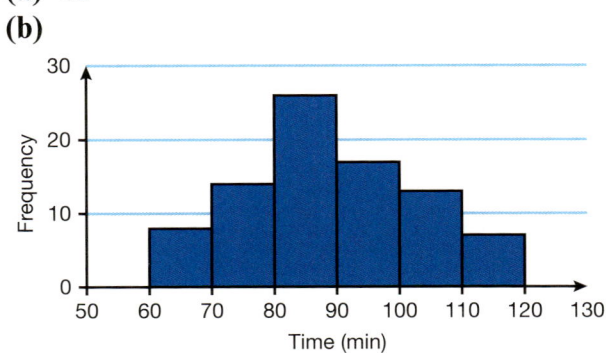

* Upper bounds are not included in groups

(c) 23.5%

3 (a)

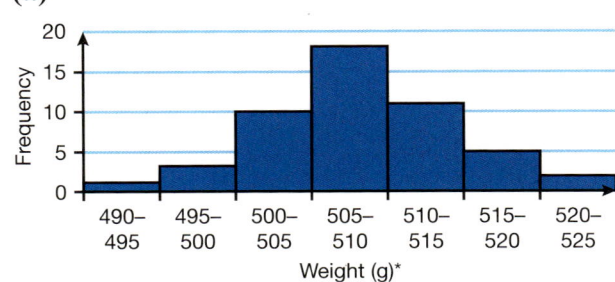

* Upper bounds are not included in groups

(b) Evidence suggests the mean is between 505 and 510 so 500 is probably minimum weight.

4 (a) 126

(b)

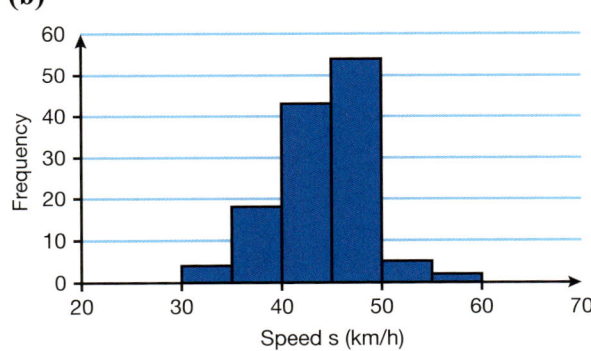

* Upper bounds are not included in groups

(c) Speed limit is probably 50 km/h as there is a sharp cut off at that speed.

5 (a) 15

(b)

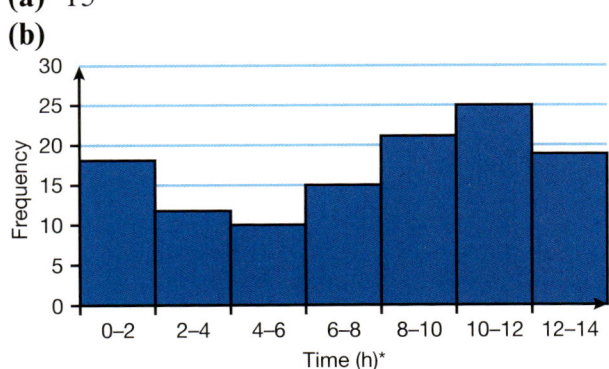

* Upper bounds are not included in groups

(c) 38.3 – assuming that the 4 is included and not the 10

284 ANSWERS

6. (a) 50 lessons
   (b) 16–20
   (c) 15.3
7. (a) 24
   (b) $4 < m \leq 6$
   (c) 4.75 kg
8. (a) 25
   (b) $17.5 < w \leq 20.5$
   (c) 17.9 minutes
   (d) $17.5 < w \leq 20.5$
9. (a) 32
   (b) $14 \leq w < 15$
   (c) 14.3
   (d) Decrease as 13 is below the mean
10. (a) mean = 1.69, median = 1.72
    (b) new mean = 1.76
11. (a) 14.2 m
    (b) 1.40 m
12. (a) mean = 7.45, median = 7.45
    (b) new mean = 8.2
13. 1.74 m
14. (a) 83 cm
    (b) 9.37 cm
15. 21 m 56 s
16. (a) 126 s
    (b) 129 s

HANDLING DATA 2 – EXAM PRACTICE EXERCISE

1. Treat the number of calls as continuous data as we only have the data in class intervals.
   (a) February is the only month with 28 days.
   (b) 16–20 calls
   (Modal class in the one with the highest frequency)
   (c)

Number of Calls	Frequency (f)	Midpoint (x)	f × x
1–5	2	3	2 × 3 = 6
6–10	4	8	4 × 8 = 32
11–15	7	13	7 × 13 = 91
16–20	9	18	9 × 18 = 162
21–25	6	23	6 × 23 = 138
	Σf = 28		Σfx = 429

Estimated mean = $\frac{429}{28}$ = 15.3 calls

(Estimated mean = , where x is the mid-point of each class interval.)

2. Treat the length of words as continuous data as we only have the data in class-intervals.
   (a) 1000 students
   (b) 601–800 words
   (Modal class in the one with the highest frequency)
   (c)

Number of Words	Frequency (f)	Midpoint (x)	f × x
401–600	150	500.5	150 × 500.5 = 75 075
601–800	425	700.5	425 × 700.5 = 297 712.5
801–1000	350	900.5	350 × 900.5 = 315 175
1001–1200	75	1100.5	75 × 1100.5 = 82 537.7
	Σf = 1000		Σfx = 770 500.5

Estimated mean = $\frac{770\,500.5}{1000}$ = 770.5 words

(Estimated mean = $\frac{\Sigma fx}{\Sigma f}$, where x is the mid-point of each class interval.)

3. (a) 540 Munros
   (b) 3000–3300 ft
   (Modal class in the one with the highest frequency)
   (c)

Height (h feet)	Frequency (f)	Midpoint (x)	f × x
$3000 < h \leq 3300$	300	3150	300 × 3150 = 945 000
$3300 < h \leq 3600$	135	3450	135 × 3450 = 465 750
$3600 < h \leq 3900$	80	3750	80 × 3750 = 300 000
$3900 < h \leq 4200$	20	4050	20 × 4050 = 81 000
$4200 < h \leq 4500$	5	4350	5 × 4350 = 21 750
	Σf = 540		Σfx = 1 813 500

Estimated mean = $\frac{1\,813\,500}{540}$ = 3358.3...

= 3360 ft (nearest 10 ft)

(Estimated mean = $\frac{\Sigma fx}{\Sigma f}$, where x is the mid-point of each class interval.)

4 (a) $\Sigma f = 50 = x + 23 + p + 5 = 28 + x + p$,
       so $p = 22 - x$

(b)

Speed (s mph)	Frequency (f)	Midpoint (x)	$f \times x$
$90 < s \leq 100$	x	95	$x \times 95 = 95x$
$100 < s \leq 110$	23	105	$23 \times 105 = 2415$
$110 < s \leq 120$	$22 - x$	115	$(22 - x) \times 115$
$120 < s \leq 130$	5	125	$5 \times 125 = 625$
	$\Sigma f = 50$		$\Sigma fx = 5570 - 20x$

Estimated mean $= 107.8 = \frac{5570 - 20x}{50}$

$107.8 \times 50 = 5570 - 20x$, so $x = 9$

(Estimated mean $= \frac{\Sigma fx}{\Sigma f}$, where x is the mid-point of each class interval.)

5 (a)
(b)

Delay (d mins)	Midpoint (x)	Frequency (f)	$f \times x$
$0 \leq d < 30$	15	10	$10 \times 15 = 150$
$30 \leq h < 60$	45	14	$14 \times 45 = 630$
$60 \leq h < 90$	75	16	$16 \times 75 = 1200$
$90 \leq h < 120$	105	11	$11 \times 105 = 1155$
$120 \leq h < 150$	135	8	$8 \times 135 = 1080$
$150 \leq h < 180$	165	1	$1 \times 165 = 165$
		$\Sigma f = 60$	$\Sigma fx = 4380$

Estimated mean $= \frac{4380}{60} = 73$ mins

(Estimated mean $= \frac{\Sigma fx}{\Sigma f}$, where x is the mid-point of each class interval.)

(c) Estimate because midpoints used as there are no exact values.
(d) Median class interval is $60 \leq d < 90$ as this is where the 30th value must be placed.

NUMBER 4 – BASIC SKILLS EXERCISE

1 (a) $535
   (b) $572.45
   (c) $612.52
   (d) $655.40

2 (a) £104
   (b) £108.16
   (c) £121.67
   (d) £148.02

3 (a) ฿26 250
   (b) ฿27 562.50
   (c) ฿31 907.04
   (d) ฿66 332.44

4 (a) ¥41 000
   (b) ¥38 088
   (c) ¥29 658.67
   (d) ¥19 547.48

5 (a) €3345.56
   (b) 12 years

6 (a) €1343.92
   (b) 14 years

7 20.2 years

8 ₹10 675

9 (a) $60 \times 0.94^{10} = 32.3$ km
   (b) $60 \times 0.94^{30} = 9.38$ km

10 (a) $100 \times 0.98 = 98$ g
   (b) $100 \times .98^5 = 90.39 \approx 90.4$ g
   (c) $100 \times .98^{10} = 81.7$ g

11 $2 \times 0.9975^{60} = 1.72$ litres

12 0.5% monthly increase hence
   $1.005^{120} = 1.819$ so 81.9% increase which is not enough.
   0.52% monthly increase gives
   $1.0052^{120} = 1.86$ so 86% increase which is enough.

13 €7366.96

14 (a) $4255.70
   (b) $5978.95

15 €652.70

16 (a) £16 769.97
   (b) £13 887.21

17 $\frac{150}{125} \times 100 = \$120$

18 $\frac{24}{120} \times 100 = \$20$

19 $\frac{2125}{85} \times 100 = €2500$

20 80 s

21 $600

22 12

23 $4329

24 €1811.59

25 £409.36

26 €2573.53

27 $1283.76

28 $888 889

29 €6863.56

30 £2326.24

31 Let Q be the factor of depreciation in the first year, then $Q - 0.1$ is the factor for the second year.
$60\,000(Q)(Q + 0.1) = 30\,000$
$60\,000Q(Q - 0.1) = 30\,000$
$Q^2 + 0.1Q - 0.5 = 0$
$Q^2 - 0.1Q - 0.5 = 0$
$Q = 0.75987...$
$Q \approx 0.76$
$R = (1 - 0.759...) \times 100 = 24.1\%$ (3 s.f.)

32 Final radius is $\sqrt{\frac{730}{\pi}} = 15.24356...$

Original area was $\frac{730}{1.15} = 634.7826...$

therefore original radius is $\sqrt{\frac{634.78...}{\pi}} = 14.2146959...$

Fractional increase in radius is $\frac{15.24356...}{14.21469...} = 1.07238...$ therefore

percentage increase is 7.24%

33 (a) $\frac{120\,000}{0.9875^{48}} = 219\,482$ so the lost area is $219\,482 - 120\,000 = 99\,500$ hectares

(b) $120\,000 \times 0.9875^{48} = 65\,608$ so the lost area is $120\,000 - 65\,608 = 54\,400$ hectares

34 (a) $\frac{412}{1.005^{20}} = 373$ ppm

(b) $412 \times 1.005^{20} = 455$ ppm

NUMBER 4 – EXAM PRACTICE EXERCISE

1 Total amount in account after 5 years $= \$50\,000 \times 1.035^5 = \$59\,384.32$
Interest after 35% deduction of interest $= (\$59\,384.32 - \$50\,000) \times 0.65 = \$6099.81$
Percentage gained from original investment $= \frac{6099.81}{50\,000} \times 100 = 12.2\%$ (3 s.f.)

2 Total amount in account after first 3 years $= €12\,000 \times 1.0325^3 = €13\,208.44$
Total amount in account after final 7 years $= €13\,208.44 \times 1.0225^7 = €15\,434.57$
Total interest gained after 10 years $= €15\,434.57 - €12\,000 = €3434.57$
Percentage gained from original investment $= \frac{3434.57}{12\,000} \times 100 = 28.6\%$ (3 s.f.)

3 Let Q be the factor of depreciation each year. After three years' depreciation
£50\,000 $\times Q^3 =$ £25\,000
So, $Q^3 = 0.5$, $Q = \sqrt[3]{0.5} = 0.7937...$
Therefore, % depreciation each year $= (1 - 0.793\,7) \times 100 = 20.6\%$ (3 s.f.)

4 (a) Let H be the height of the tree.
$H \times (1.075)^3 = 12$, so $H = \frac{12}{1.075^3}$
$= 9.66$ m (3 s.f.)
(b) $x \times 1.075 \times 1.05 \times 1.025 = 1.8$
$x = 1.56$ metres (3 s.f.)

5 (a) Let required price be £P
$P =$ £46\,800 $\times (1 - 0.152) =$ £39\,686.40
$P =$ £39\,686 (nearest £)
(b) Let required price be €Q
18% = €3848, so 1% = €213.78,
so 100% = €21\,377.78
$Q = €21\,378$ (nearest €)

ALGEBRA 4 – BASIC SKILLS EXERCISE

Note that answers can be correct but look different to the answer given. For example, the two answers given for Q1 and Q6 are just different rearrangements of the same expression.

1 $b - \frac{c^2}{a}$ or $\frac{ab - c^2}{a}$

2 $\frac{cd - b}{a}$

3 $\frac{a + c}{bd}$

4 $\sqrt{a(b+c)}$

5 $\sqrt{\dfrac{a}{c-b}}$

6 $\left(\dfrac{c}{a}+b\right)^2$ or $\left(\dfrac{ab+c}{a}\right)^2$

7 $\left(\dfrac{c}{a}\right)^2+b$

8 $\dfrac{c-f}{d+e}$

9 $\dfrac{a-bc}{c-1}$ or $\dfrac{bc-a}{1-c}$

10 $\dfrac{ab+cd}{a+c}$

11 $t(p^2-s)$

12 $\dfrac{rs}{r+s}$

13 $h=\dfrac{3V}{\pi r^2}$

14 $r=\sqrt[3]{\dfrac{3V}{4\pi}}$

15 $s=\dfrac{v^2-u^2}{2a}$

16 $h=\dfrac{A}{2\pi r}-r$

17 $a=\dfrac{s}{n}-\dfrac{d(n-1)}{2}$

18 $a=\dfrac{2(s-ut)}{t^2}$

19 $a=\dfrac{S(1-r)}{1-r^n}$

20 $x=a\sqrt{1-\dfrac{y^2}{b^2}}$ or $\dfrac{a}{b}\sqrt{b^2-y^2}$

21 $t=g\left(\dfrac{T}{2\pi}\right)^2$

22 $r=\sqrt{\dfrac{GmM}{F}}$

23 $d=\left(\dfrac{F}{k}\right)^3$

24 $r=\dfrac{6a}{5m^2-1}$

25 $b=\dfrac{2A}{a\sin C}$, $b=4$

26 $a=\dfrac{2A-bh}{h}$, $a=8$

27 $\sin A=\dfrac{a\sin B}{b}$, $A=48.6°$ (3 s.f.)

28 $\cos A=\dfrac{b^2+c^2-a^2}{2bc}$ or $\dfrac{a^2-b^2-c^2}{-2bc}$, $\cos A=0.7$

29 $v=\dfrac{fu}{u-f}$, $v=6\dfrac{2}{3}$

30 $c=\dfrac{b^2-(2ax+b)^2}{4a}$, $c=-3$

ALGEBRA 4 – EXAM PRACTICE EXERCISE

1 (a) Perimeter of room is 18 m so the wall area is $18\times 2.6=46.8$ m²
   $N=2+0.4\times 46.8=20.72$ so she needs to buy 21 rolls.

   (b) Making A the subject of the formula:
   $A=\dfrac{N-2}{0.4}$
   Substituting $N=15$ gives $A=32.5$ m²
   If A is just less than 32.5 m², say 32 m², Juan will still need 15 rolls as $A\leq 32.5$ m²
   Substituting $N=14$ gives $A=30$ m² and if A is greater than 30 then 15 rolls are needed.
   30 m² $< A \leq 32.5$ m²

2 (a) The diagram shows n cubes joined together.

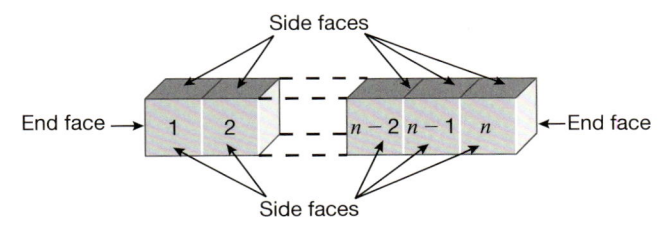

   There are two end faces each with an area of 1 cm² so the end face area = 2 cm²
   Each cube has 4 side faces exposed, each of area 1 cm² so each cube's side face area = 4 cm²
   n cubes have a total side face area of $4n$ cm²
   $A=4n+2$

   (b) Making n the subject of the formula gives $n=\dfrac{A-2}{4}$
   Substituting $A=214$ gives $n=53$

   (c) n is an integer. In the formula $n=\dfrac{A-2}{4}$, if A is odd then $A-2$ is also odd and an odd number divided by 4 (an even number) can never be an integer.

3 (a) Substitute $C = \frac{100N}{33}$ into $F = \frac{9C + 160}{5}$ gives

$$9C = 9 \times \frac{100N}{33} = \frac{300N}{11}$$

$$F = \frac{\frac{300N}{11} + 160}{5}$$

$$= \frac{60N}{11} + 32$$

$$= \frac{60N + 11 \times 32}{11}$$

$$= \frac{60N + 352}{11}$$

(b) Let the temperature where they read the same be T

then $T = \frac{60T + 352}{11}$

Substituting T for F and N

in $F = \frac{60N + 352}{11}$ gives

$11T = 60T + 352$
$49T = -352$
$T = -7.2$ (1 d.p.)

4 (a) $t = 2\pi\sqrt{\frac{l}{9.8}}$

$\frac{t}{2\pi} = \sqrt{\frac{l}{9.8}}$

$\left(\frac{t}{2\pi}\right)^2 = \frac{l}{9.8}$

$l = 9.8\left(\frac{t}{2\pi}\right)^2$

($l = \frac{9.8t^2}{4\pi^2}$ is also correct)

(b) Method 1:
Actual length $= 1.05 \times 9.8\left(\frac{1}{2\pi}\right)^2$
$= 0.26065$ m (to 5 s.f.)

$t = 2\pi\sqrt{\frac{0.26065}{9.8}} = 1.0247$ s (5 s.f.)

Increase is 0.0247 s $\Rightarrow$ % increase

$= \frac{0.0247}{1} \times 100 = 2.47 \approx 2.5\%$ (2.s.f.)

Method 2: Let l be the length of the second pendulum; then the length of the manufactured pendulum is $1.05l$. Let t_1 and t_2 be the times of swings respectively (note $t_1 = 1$)

$\frac{t_2}{t_1} = \left(2\pi\sqrt{\frac{1.05l}{9.8}}\right) \div \left(2\pi\sqrt{\frac{l}{9.8}}\right)$

$= \sqrt{1.05}$
$= 1.0247$
So the % increase is 2.5% (2 s.f.)
1.025 is multiplier for 2.5% increase

5 (a) The heights of each trapezium are calculated by substituting $x = 0, 1$ and 2 respectively into $y = ax^2 + bx + c$

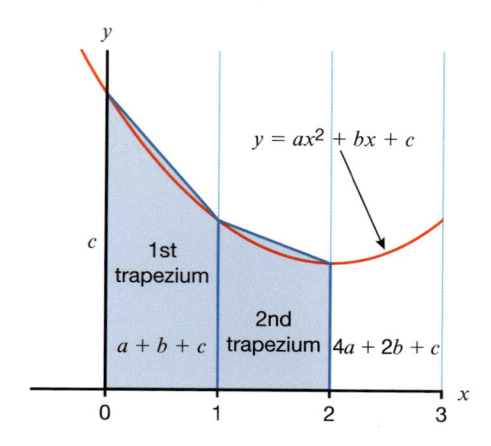

When $x = 0$, $y = c$
When $x = 1$, $y = a + b + c$
When $x = 2$, $y = 4a + 2b + c$

The area of a trapezium $= \frac{1}{2}(a + b)h$

In this case $h = 1$
Area of first trapezium
$= \frac{1}{2}(c + a + b + c)$

$= \frac{1}{2}(a + b + 2c)$

Area of second trapezium
$= \frac{1}{2}(a + b + c + 4a + 2b + c)$

$= \frac{1}{2}(5a + 3b + 2c)$

Total area
$= \frac{1}{2}(a + b + 2c + 5a + 3b + 2c)$

$= \frac{1}{2}(6a + 4b + 4c) = 3a + 2b + 2c$

(b) Difference in areas

$= (3a + 2b + 2c) - \left(\frac{8a}{3} + 2b + 2c\right) = \frac{a}{3}$

Percentage error $= \dfrac{\frac{a}{3}}{\frac{8a}{3} + 2b + 2c} \times 100$

$= \dfrac{a}{8a + 6b + 6c} \times 100 = \dfrac{100a}{8a + 6b + 6c}\%$

GRAPHS 4 – BASIC SKILLS EXERCISE

1.
x	-2	-1	0	1	2	3
y	5	3	3	5	9	15

2.
x	-2	-1	0	1	2	3
y	-3	-5	-5	-3	1	7

3.
x	-3	-2	-1	0	1	2	3	4
y	10	7	6	7	10	15	22	31

4.
x	-3	-2	-1	0	1	2	3	4
y	-4	-6	-6	-4	0	6	14	24

5.
x	-3	-2	-1	0	1	2	3
y	10	4	0	-2	-2	0	4

$x = -1$ or 2

6.
x	-4	-3	-2	-1	0	1	2	3	4
y	6	0	-4	-6	-6	-4	0	6	14

$x = -3$ or 2

7.
x	-3	-2	-1	0	1	2	3	4	5
y	7	0	-5	-8	-9	-8	-5	0	7

$x = -2$ or 4

8. **a, b** $x \approx -0.3$ or 1.8 for both equations.

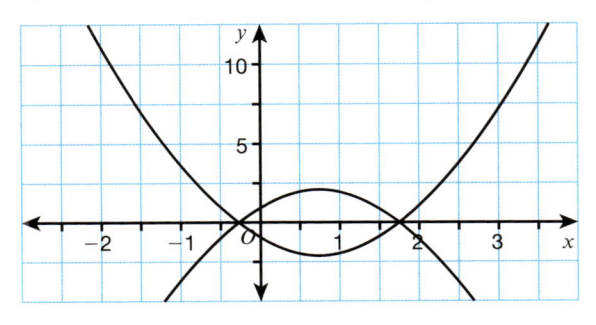

GRAPHS 4 – EXAM PRACTICE EXERCISE

1. (a)
t	0	1	2	3	4	5
y	0	5	20	45	80	125

(b) (i) 61 m
    (ii) 2.2 s

2. Substitute $x = 0$ into formula for y to produce $y = 5$ and hence solve for $p = 5$.
(a) $p = 5$
(b)
x	0	1	2	3	4	5
y	5	0	-1	2	9	20

(c) $x = 1$ or 2.5

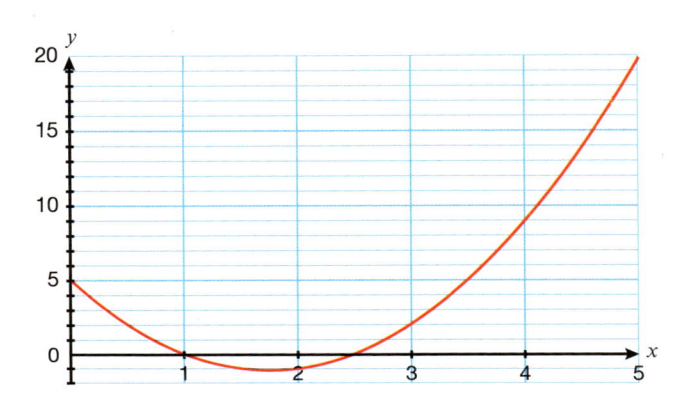

3. Substitute $x = 0$ and $y = -3$, $x = 4$ and $y = 13$ to produce simultaneous equations:
$-3 = q$

$13 = 32 + 4p + q$

Solve them to find p and q.

(a) $p = -4$, $q = -3$
(b)
x	-2	-1	0	1	2	3	4
y	13	3	-3	-5	-3	3	13

(c) $x \approx -0.6$ or 2.6

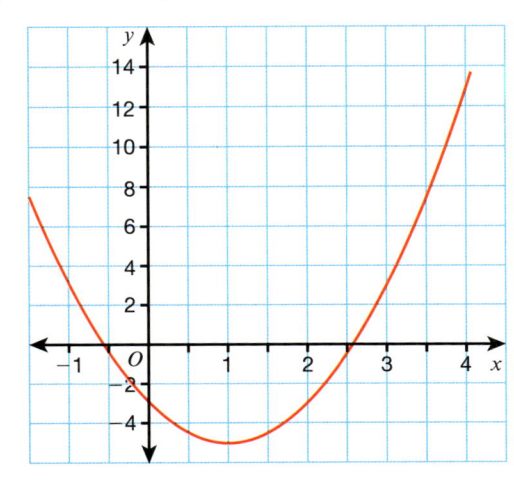

4   Substitute $t = 1$ into formula for p to produce $p = 7$ to solve for $k = 3$.
   (a) $k = 3$
   (b)

t	0	1	2	3	4
p	0	7	8	3	−8

   (c) (i) £8333 @ $t = 1.7$ months
       (ii) $t > 3.3$ months

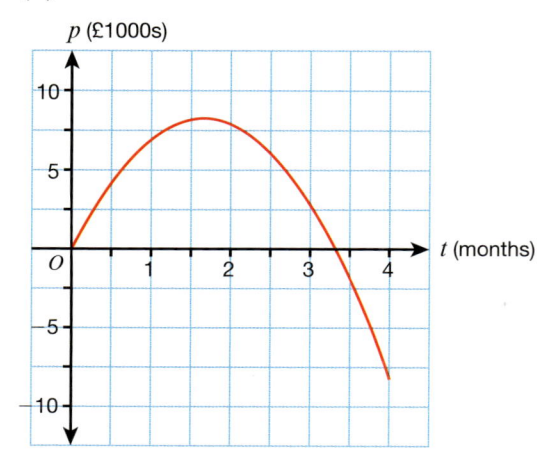

5 (a) 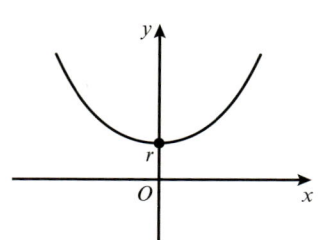
   (b) 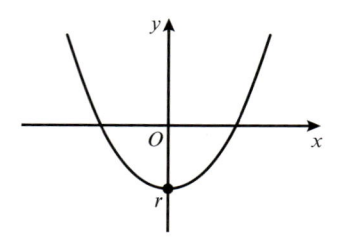
   (c) 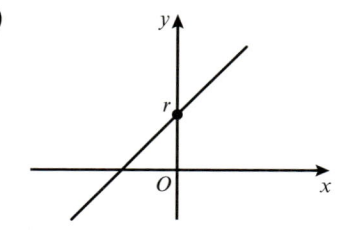
   (d)

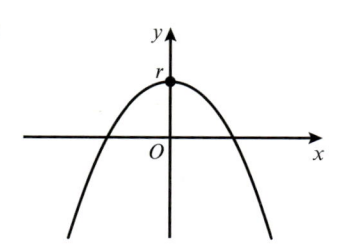

SHAPE AND SPACE 4 – BASIC SKILLS EXERCISE

1 (a) 22.4 cm
   (b) 26.4 cm
   (c) 32.1°

2 (a) 70.7 m
   (b) 60.4 m
   (c) 41.8°
   (d) 9038 m²

3 (a) 16.7°
   (b) $DF = 94.3$ m
   (c) 9.03°
   (d) 2.19 m/s

4 79.2 m

5 Show by clear working that area = 600 cm², by Pythagoras' theorem.

6 The diagram shows a tetrahedron.
   AD is perpendicular to both AB and AC.
   $AB = 10$ cm. $AC = 8$ cm. $AD = 5$ cm.
   Angle $BAC = 90°$
   Let angle $BDC = \theta$
   Area of triangle $BDC = \frac{1}{2} \times BD \times CD \times \sin(\theta)$

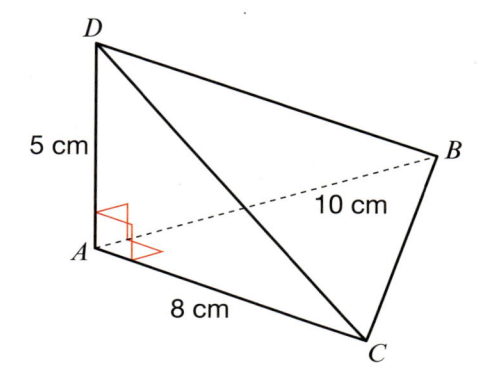

   (Area of a triangle = $\frac{1}{2} ab \sin C$)

   Triangle ACD:
   $CD^2 = 5^2 + 8^2 = 89$, $CD = 9.4340…$ cm
   Triangle ABD:
   $BD^2 = 5^2 + 10^2 = 125$, $BD = 11.180…$ cm
   Triangle ABC:
   $BC^2 = 8^2 + 10^2 = 164$, $BD = 12.806…$ cm
   Triangle BCD:
   (Cosine Rule : $a^2 = b^2 + c^2 - 2bc \cos A$)
   $164 = 125 + 89 - 2 \times 11.180 \times 9.4340 \times \cos \theta$
   (Rearrange to make $\cos \theta$ the subject and find θ)
   $\cos \theta = 0.23703…$, so $\theta = 76.289…°$

Area of triangle BDC
$= \frac{1}{2} \times 11.180 \times 9.4340 \times \sin(76.289°)$
$= 51.2$ cm² (3 s.f.)

SHAPE AND SPACE 4 – EXAM PRACTICE EXERCISE

1 (a)

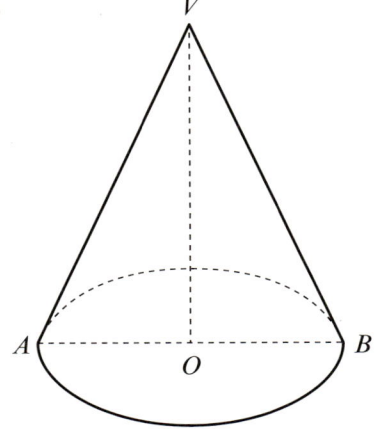

(Total surface area of solid cone
= Area of circular base + curved
surface area) $= \pi r^2 + \pi r l$
$75\pi = \pi \times 5^2 + \pi \times 5 \times l$
$50\pi = 5\pi l, l = 10$ cm

(b) Let angle $AVB = 2\theta$
Triangle OVB:
$\sin(\theta) = \frac{OB}{VB} = \frac{5}{10}$ $\left(\cos\theta = \frac{\text{opposite side}}{\text{hypotenuse}}\right)$
$\theta = 30°$, so angle $AVB = 60°$

2

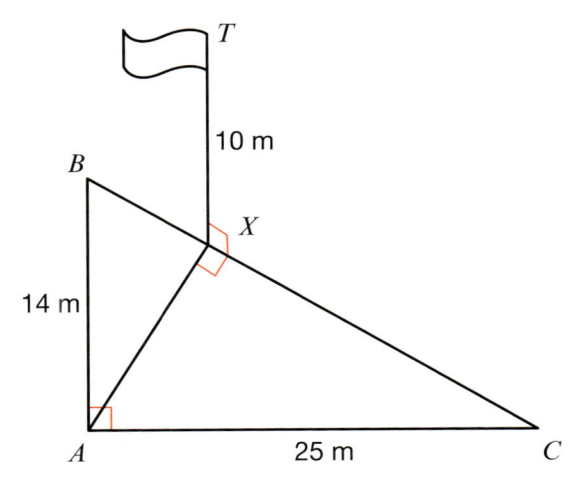

Triangle ABC:
Let angle $ACX = \theta$
$\tan(\theta) = \frac{AB}{AC} = \frac{14}{25}$ $\left(\tan\theta = \frac{\text{opposite side}}{\text{adjacent side}}\right)$
$\theta = 29.249...°$

Triangle AXC:
$\cos(\theta) = \frac{XC}{AC} = \frac{XC}{25}$ $\left(\cos\theta = \frac{\text{adjacent side}}{\text{hypotenuse}}\right)$
$XC = 21.813...$m
$XM : MC = 3 : 1 = 16.360 : 5.453$
Triangle TXM:

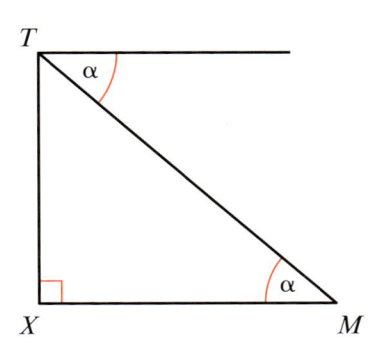

Calculate angle $XMT = \alpha$
(Alternate angles)

$\tan(\alpha) = \frac{TX}{XM} = \frac{10}{16.360}$
$\left(\tan\theta = \frac{\text{opposite side}}{\text{adjacent side}}\right)$
$\alpha = 31.435...° = 31.4°$ (3 s.f.)
But angle of depression is angle
$XTM = 45° - 31.4° = 13.6°$
This could have been calculated immediately
using $\tan(\ ) = \frac{XM}{TX}$

3 (a)

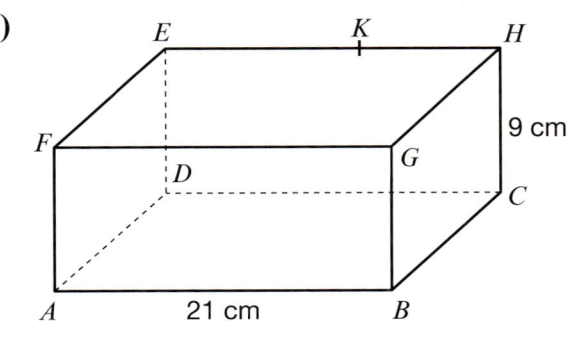

$EK : KH = 2 : 1 = 14 : 7$, so $EK = 14$ cm,
$KH = 7$ cm
$BC : CH = 4 : 3 = 12 : 9$, so $BC = 12$ cm
Drop a perpendicular line from K to DC
to point L.
Triangle BCL:
$LB^2 = 7^2 + 12^2$, $LB = 13.892...$cm
Triangle KLB:
$KB^2 = LB^2 + KB^2$, $KB^2 = 13.892^2 + 9^2$,
$KB = 16.553...$cm
Triangle ADL:

$LA^2 = 14^2 + 12^2$, $LA = 18.439...$cm
Triangle KLA:
$KA^2 = LA^2 + KL^2$, $KA^2 = 18.439^2 + 9^2$,
$KA = 20.518...$cm
Now consider triangle AKB:
Let angle $AKB = \theta$
(Cosine rule : $a^2 = b^2 + c^2 - 2bc \cos A$)
$21^2 = 20.518^2 + 16.553^2 - 2 \times 20.518 \times 16.553 \times \cos\theta$
(Re-arrange to make $\cos\theta$ the subject and find θ)
$\cos\theta = 0.37392...$, so $\theta = 68.043°$, so angle $AKB = 68.0°$ (3 s.f.)

(b) Let required angle $KAL = \alpha$
Triangle KAL:
$\tan(\alpha) = \frac{KL}{AL} = \frac{9}{18.439}$

$\left(\tan\theta = \frac{\text{opposite side}}{\text{adjacent side}}\right)$

$\alpha = 26.017...°$, so angle $KAL = 26.0°$ (3 s.f.)

4

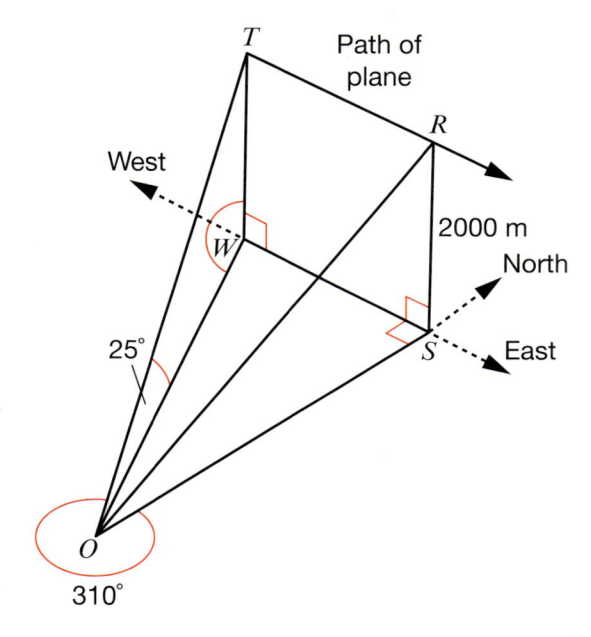

(a) Triangle OWT:

$\tan(25°) = \frac{TW}{OW} = \frac{2000}{OW}$

$\left(\tan\theta = \frac{\text{opposite side}}{\text{adjacent side}}\right)$

$OW = \frac{2000}{\tan(25°)} = 4289.0...$m

$= 4290$ m (3 s.f.)
Triangle OWS:
Angle $WOS = 360 - 310 = 50°$
(Plan view on base triangle OWS)
$\cos(50°) = \frac{OS}{OW} = \frac{OS}{4289.0...}$

$\left(\cos\theta = \frac{\text{adjacent side}}{\text{hypotenuse}}\right)$

$OS = 4289.0 \times \cos(50°) = 2757.0...$ m
$= 2760$ m (3 s.f.)

(b) Triangle ROS:

Let required angle $ROS = \theta$

$\tan(\theta) = \frac{RS}{OS} = \frac{2000}{2757.0}$

$\left(\tan\theta = \frac{\text{opposite side}}{\text{adjacent side}}\right)$

$\theta = 35.958... = 36.0°$ (3 s.f.)

(c) Speed $= \frac{\text{distance}}{\text{time}} = \frac{WS}{1} = ...$m/min

(Units required to be in km and hours to give an answer of speed in km/h)
Triangle SOW:
$OW^2 = OS^2 + SW^2$
(Pythagoras' theorem)
$4289.0^2 = 2757.0^2 + SW^2$

$SW = \sqrt{4289.0^2 - 2757.0^2} = 3285.5...$m

Speed $= \frac{3.2855}{\frac{1}{60}} = 197.13...\frac{\text{km}}{\text{hr}}$

$= 197$ km/h (3 s.f.)

5 (a)

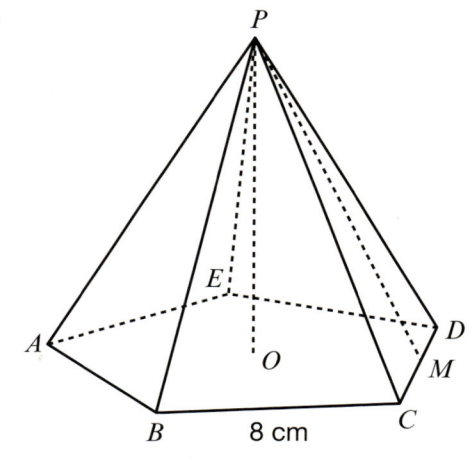

The base of the pyramid is a regular pentagon, so angle $DOC = \frac{360°}{5} = 72°$

Triangle OCM:

$\tan(36°) = \frac{CM}{OM} = \frac{4}{OM}$

$\left(\tan\theta = \frac{\text{opposite side}}{\text{adjacent side}}\right)$

$OM = \frac{4}{\tan(36°)} = 5.5055...\text{cm}$

Triangle POM:

Required angle is $PMO = \alpha$

$\tan(\alpha) = \frac{PO}{OM} = \frac{10}{5.5055} = 1.8164...$,

so angle $PMO = 61.2°$ (3 s.f.)

(b) Weight of pyramid + weight of water = 1000 g

Area of pyramid base
= 5 × area of triangle ODC
= $5 \times \frac{1}{2} \times 8 \times 5.5055$
= 110.11...cm²

(Volume of pyramid
= $\frac{1}{3} \times$ base area × perpendicular height)

Volume of pyramid = $\frac{1}{3} \times 110.11 \times 10$
= 367.03...cm³

$\left(\text{Density} = \frac{\text{Mass}}{\text{Volume}}\right)$

1000 kg/m³ = 1 g/cm³

Weight of water = density × volume
= 1 × 367.03 g.
So $w + 367.03 = 1000$
(working in units of g)
$w = 633$ g (3 s.f.)

HANDLING DATA 3 – BASIC SKILLS EXERCISE

1

Median	Q_1	Q_3	Range	IQR
6	1	7	8	6

2

Median	Q_1	Q_3	Range	IQR
5	1	6	9	5

3

Median	Q_1	Q_3	Range	IQR
4	1.5	7	11	5.5

4

Median	Q_1	Q_3	Range	IQR
62	48	83	69	35

5

Median	Q_1	Q_3	Range	IQR
6	5	8	9	3

6

Median	Q_1	Q_3	Range	IQR
3.9	2.1	9.0	9	6.0

7

Median	Q_1	Q_3	Range	IQR
67	42	77	84	35

8

Median	Q_1	Q_3	Range	IQR
0.56	0.46	0.68	0.7	0.22

9

Median	Q_1	Q_3	Range	IQR
2	1	3	5	2

10

Median	Q_1	Q_3	Range	IQR
2	1	2.5	5	1.5

11 (a)

Time (t mins)	C.F.
$0 < t \leq 10$	3
$10 < t \leq 20$	10
$20 < t \leq 30$	25
$30 < t \leq 40$	52
$40 < t \leq 50$	71
$50 < t \leq 60$	80

(b)

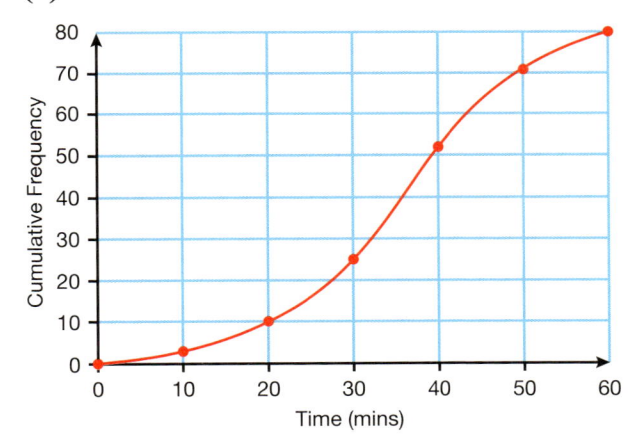

(c) $Q_2 = 36$, $Q_1 = 27$, $Q_3 = 43$, IQR = 16

(d) 50 students

12 (a)

Speed s (m.p.h)	C.F.
$s \leq 55$	0
$55 < s \leq 60$	6
$60 < s \leq 65$	25
$65 < s \leq 70$	71
$70 < s \leq 75$	85
$75 < s \leq 80$	90

(c) $Q_2 = 67$, $Q_1 = 64.5$, $Q_3 = 69.5$, IQR = 5

(d) 18%

294 ANSWERS

13 (a)

Weight w (kilograms)	Country A Cum. freq.	Country B Cum. freq.
w ≤ 2.0	0	0
2.0 < w ≤ 2.5	14	0
2.5 < w ≤ 3.0	43	3
3.0 < w ≤ 3.5	66	23
3.5 < w ≤ 4.0	80	74
4.0 < w ≤ 4.5	80	80

(c) Country A: $Q_2 = 2.95$, $Q_1 = 2.62$, $Q_3 = 3.37$, IQR = 0.75
Country B: $Q_2 = 3.65$, $Q_1 = 3.45$, $Q_3 = 3.78$, IQR = 0.33

(d) Babies heavier in country B, more variation in weight in country A

HANDLING DATA 3 – EXAM PRACTICE EXERCISE

1 Median = 23.5, $Q_1 = 17.5$, $Q_3 = 31$, range = 28, IQR = 13.5

2 (a)

Weight w (g)	Cum. freq.
66 < w ≤ 68	5
68 < w ≤ 70	18
70 < w ≤ 72	36
72 < w ≤ 74	46
74 < w ≤ 76	54
76 < w ≤ 78	60

(c) $Q_2 = 71.4$, IQR = 4.1
(d) 15%

3 (a)

Time t (min)	Cum. freq.
0 < t ≤ 20	3
20 < t ≤ 40	10
40 < t ≤ 60	21
60 < t ≤ 80	31
80 < t ≤ 100	52
100 < t ≤ 120	77
120 < t ≤ 140	100

(c) $Q_2 = 98$, $Q_1 = 68$, $Q_3 = 119$, IQR = 51
(d) 35%

4 (a)

Time t (milliseconds)	Cum. freq. before drink	Cum. freq. after drink
t ≤ 160	0	0
160 < t ≤ 180	10	0
180 < t ≤ 200	45	0
200 < t ≤ 220	76	8
220 < t ≤ 240	80	49
240 < t ≤ 260	80	74
260 < t ≤ 280	80	80

(c) Before drink $Q_2 = 197$, $Q_1 = 189$, $Q_3 = 206$, IQR = 17

After drink $Q_2 = 237$, $Q_1 = 229$, $Q_3 = 245$, IQR = 16

(d) Drink lengthens reaction times by approximately 40 milliseconds, but doesn't after the spread. This possibly means that everybody is equally affected.

5 (a)

Diameter d (cm)	Frequency Short Wood	Frequency Waley Wood
0 < d ≤ 10	6	2
10 < d ≤ 20	15	5
20 < d ≤ 30	27	12
30 < d ≤ 40	50	50
40 < d ≤ 50	71	92
50 < d ≤ 60	85	98
60 < d ≤ 70	95	100
70 < d ≤ 80	100	100

(c) Short Wood $Q_2 = 40$, $Q_1 = 29$, $Q_3 = 53$, IQR = 24

Waley Wood $Q_2 = 40$, $Q_1 = 36$, $Q_3 = 46$, IQR = 10

(d) Waley Wood is much more uniform in size. This possibly means it is a plantation with all the trees having been planted at the same time. Short Wood is more diverse in size, possibly a wild wood.

ANSWERS

NUMBER 5 – BASIC SKILLS EXERCISE

1. 1×10^8
2. 4×10^{13}
3. 5×10^{15}
4. 1×10^{11}
5. 2×10^2
6. 2×10^3
7. 5×10^7
8. 5×10^8
9. 3×10^{14}
10. 3×10^{15}
11. 1×10^3
12. 2×10^{10}
13. 2×10^6
14. 4×10^{-3}
15. 2×10^{-12}
16. 5×10^7
17. 2×10
18. 8×10^{-3}
19. upper bound = 3.52, lower bound = 2.93
20. upper bound = 4.08, lower bound = 3.15
21. upper bound = 2.33, lower bound = 1.73
22. upper bound = 1.71, lower bound = 1.50
23. upper bound = 2.29, lower bound = 2.15
24. upper bound = 0.159, lower bound = 0.09832
25. upper bound = 3.38, lower bound = 2.59
26. (a) upper bound = 15.9 m², lower bound = 9.62 m²
    (b) upper bound = 14.1 m, lower bound = 11.0 m
27. upper bound = 12.1, lower bound = 11.7
28. upper bound = 104, lower bound = 78
29. upper bound = 17 N/cm², lower bound = 15 N/cm²
30. upper bound = 75 000 mm², lower bound = 64 000 mm²

NUMBER 5 – EXAM PRACTICE EXERCISE

1. $a_{max} = 2.5$ m, $b_{max} = 100.5$ m, $\alpha_{max} = 40.5°$
   $a_{min} = 1.5$ m, $b_{min} = 99.5$ m, $\alpha_{min} = 39.5°$
   (a) upper bound of h
   $$= a_{max} + (b_{max} \times \tan(\alpha_{max}))$$
   $$\left(\tan \theta = \frac{\text{opposite side}}{\text{adjacent side}}\right)$$
   $= 2.5 + 100.5 \times \tan(40.5°) = 88.335...$ m
   $= 88.3$ m (3 s.f.)
   (b) lower bound of h
   $$= a_{min} + (b_{min} \times \tan(\alpha_{max}))$$
   $$\left(\tan \theta = \frac{\text{opposite side}}{\text{adjacent side}}\right)$$
   $= 1.5 + 99.5 \times \tan(39.5°) = 83.521...$ m
   $= 83.5$ m (3 s.f.)

2. Let area of the base be A cm² and force be F N.
   $A_{max} = 12.5 \times 12.5 = 156.25$ cm², $F_{max} = 55$ N
   $A_{min} = 11.5 \times 11.5 = 132.25$ cm², $F_{min} = 45$ N
   (a) upper bound of $P = \dfrac{F_{max}}{A_{min}} = \dfrac{55}{132.25}$
   $= 0.41587...$ N/cm²
   $= 0.416$ N/cm²
   (b) lower bound of $P = \dfrac{F_{min}}{A_{max}} = \dfrac{45}{156.25}$
   $= 0.288$ N/cm²

3. $d_{max} = 2.55$ m, $t_{max} = 2.75$ s
   $d_{min} = 2.45$ m, $t_{min} = 2.25$ s
   (speed $= \dfrac{\text{distance}}{\text{time}}$, Circumference of a circle $= 2\pi r$)
   (a) upper bound of $V = \dfrac{d_{max}}{t_{min}} = \dfrac{2 \times \pi \times 0.5 \times 2.55}{2.25}$
   $= 3.5604...$ m/s $= 3.6$ m/s (2 s.f.)
   (b) lower bound of $V = \dfrac{d_{min}}{t_{max}} = \dfrac{2 \times \pi \times 0.5 \times 2.45}{2.75}$
   $= 2.7988...$ m/s $= 2.8$ m/s (2 s.f.)

4. $R_{max} = 12.85$ cm, $r_{max} = 10.35$ cm
   $R_{min} = 12.75$ cm, $r_{min} = 10.25$ cm
   (Area of a circle $= \pi r^2$)
   $A_{max} = \pi R_{max}^2 - \pi r_{min}^2 = \pi(R_{max}^2 - r_{min}^2)$
   $= \pi(12.85^2 - 10.25^2) = 60.06\pi$ cm²
   $A_{min} = \pi R_{min}^2 - \pi r_{max}^2 = \pi(R_{min}^2 - r_{max}^2)$
   $= \pi(12.75^2 - 10.35^2) = 55.44\pi$ cm²

So, if $p\pi \le A < q\pi$
$55.44\pi \le A < 60.06\pi$
$p = 55, q = 60$ (2 s.f.)

5 $a_{max} = 12.55$, $b_{max} = 3.255$, $c_{max} = 1.755$ and $d_{max} = 3.855$
$a_{min} = 12.45$, $b_{min} = 3.245$, $c_{min} = 1.745$ and $d_{min} = 3.845$

(a) $Z_{max} = \dfrac{a_{max} - b_{min}}{c_{min} + d_{min}} = \dfrac{12.55 - 3.245}{1.745 + 3.845}$
$= 1.6645$, upper bound of $T = 10^{Z_{max}}$
$= 46$ (2 s.f.)

(b) $Z_{min} = \dfrac{a_{min} - b_{max}}{c_{max} + d_{max}} = \dfrac{12.45 - 3.255}{1.755 + 3.855}$
$= 1.6390\ldots$, lower bound of $T = 10^{Z_{min}}$
$= 44$ (2 s.f.)

ALGEBRA 5 – BASIC SKILLS EXERCISE

1 $x^2 - 3x - 10$
2 $x^2 + 16x + 64$
3 $x^4 - 10x^2 + 25$
4 $8x^2 + 2x - 6$
5 $10x^3 + x^2 - 2x$
6 $x^3 - 4x^2 - 3x + 18$
7 $9x^3 - 18x^2 - 25x + 50$
8 $8x^3 - 36x^2 + 54x - 27$
9 $x^2 - 5$
10 -9

For questions 11–14, there is no need to multiply out the brackets.

11 $(x^2 + 3)$ is a common factor.
$(x^2 + 3)(2x + 1) + (x^2 + 3)(1 - 2x)$
$= (x^2 + 3)[2x + 1 + 1 - 2x] = 2(x^2 + 3)$

12 $(4x + 1)$ is a common factor.
$(4x + 1)^2 - (4x + 1)(x + 1)$
$= (4x + 1)[(4x + 1) - (x + 1)]$
$= (4x + 1)[4x + 1 - x - 1] = 3x(4x + 1)$

13 $(4x + 3)$ is a common factor.
$\pi(4x + 3) - 3(4x + 3) = (4x + 3)(\pi - 3)$

14 $(1 - \cos x)$ is a common factor.
$2x(1 - \cos x) - 3(1 - \cos x)$
$= (1 - \cos x)(2x - 3)$

15 $(x - 3)(x - 4) = 0$, $x = 3$ or 4
16 $(x - 1)(x + 9) = 0$, $x = 1$ or -9
17 $x(x - 11) = 0$, $x = 0$ or 11
18 $(x - 4)(x + 5) = 0$, $x = 4$ or -5
19 $(3x - 5)(x + 2) = 0$, $x = \frac{5}{3}$ or -2
20 $(4x + 3)(x - 2) = 0$, $x = -\frac{3}{4}$ or 2
21 $(2x - 3)(3x - 2) = 0$, $x = \frac{3}{2}$ or $-\frac{2}{3}$
22 $(5x - 8)(2x + 5) = 0$, $x = \frac{8}{5}$ or $-\frac{5}{2}$
23 $(x - 4)(x + 6) = 0$, $x = 4$ or -6
24 $2(x - 1)(x + 3) = 0$, $x = 1$ or -3
25 $2(2x + 1)(x - 5) = 0$, $x = \frac{1}{2}$ or 5
26 $2x(2x + 3)(x + 2) = 0$, $x = 0, -\frac{3}{2}$ or -2
27 $(x^2 - 9)(x^2 - 4) = 0$, $x = \pm 3$ or ± 2
28 $7(x + 2) = 0$ so $x = -2$
29 $(x - 4)(x - 1)$ so $x = 4$ or $x = 1$
30 $(3x + 1)(2x - 1) = 0$ so $x = \frac{1}{2}$ or $-\frac{1}{3}$

31 $\frac{1}{2} \times 2x \times x = 3x(x - 3)$

The areas are the same.
$x^2 = 3x^2 - 9x$
$2x^2 - 9x = 0$
$x(2x - 9) = 0$
$x = 0$ or 4.5
$x = 0$ is not a real-life solution so $x = 4.5$

32 $x(x + 2) = 15$
$x^2 + 2x - 15 = 0$
$(x + 5)(x - 3)$
$x = 3$
$x = -5$ is not a real-life solution

33 The coconut hits the ground when $x = 14$ so
$5t^2 + 3t = 14$
$5t^2 + 3t - 14 = 0$
$(5t - 7)(t + 2) = 0$ so $t = \frac{7}{5}$
$t = -2$ is not a real-life solution

34 Let one integer be x, then the other integer is $x + 4$ ($x − 4$ is also correct − see later)
$x^2 + (x + 4)^2 = 208$
$x^2 + x^2 + 8x + 16 = 208$
$2x^2 + 8x − 192 = 0$
$x^2 + 4x − 96 = 0$
$(x + 12)(x − 8) = 0$
$x = −12$ or $8 \Rightarrow$ numbers are $−12$ and $−8$ or 8 and 12
If using $x − 4$:
$x^2 + (x − 4)^2 = 208$
$x^2 + x^2 − 8x + 16 = 208$
$2x^2 − 8x − 192 = 0$
$x^2 − 4x − 96 = 0$
$(x − 12)(x + 8) = 0$
$x = 12$ or $−8 \Rightarrow$ numbers are 12 and 8 or $−8$ and $−12$

35 $(4x − 3)^2 (x + 1)^2 + (2x + 4)^2$
Pythagoras' theorem
$16x^2 − 24x + 9 = x^2 + 2x + 1 + 4x^2 + 16x + 16$
$11x^2 − 42x − 8 = 0$
$(11x + 2)(x − 4) = 0$
$x = 4$ as $x = −\frac{2}{11}$ is not a real-life solution
triangle sides are 5, 12 and 13 so area is
$\frac{1}{2} \times 5 \times 12 = 30$ cm²

36 (a) $(a + b)(a − b)$
(b) $2^{24} − 1^2 = (2^{12} + 1)(2^{12} − 1)$
so suitable integers are $2^{12} + 1 = 4097$ and $2^{12} − 1 = 4095$

ALGEBRA 5 – EXAM PRACTICE EXERCISE

1 Internal angle sum of a quadrilateral is 360°
$8x^2 − 32 + 22x − 16 + 20x + 4 + 6x^2 + 12 = 360$
$14x^2 + 42x − 392 = 0$
$x^2 + 3x − 28 = 0$ Dividing by 14
$(x − 4)(x + 7) = 0 \Rightarrow x = 4$
$x = −7$ is not a real-life solution
angles are $A = 96°$, $B = 72°$, $C = 84°$ and $D = 108°$
it is cyclic as $A + C = 180°$ or $B + D = 180°$

2 (a) $\frac{1}{2}(3x + 5 + x + 1) \times (x + 3) = 35$
See formula sheet for area of a trapezium.
$(2x + 3)(x + 3) = 35$
$2x^2 + 9x − 26 = 0$
$(x − 2)(2x + 13) = 0$
$x = 2$ $x = −\frac{13}{2}$ is not a real-life solution.
(b) $(x − 2)^2 + (2x + 6)^2 = (3x − 2)^2$
Pythagoras' theorem.
$x^2 − 4x + 4 + 4x^2 + 24x + 36 = 9x^2 − 12x + 4$
$4x^2 − 32x − 36 = 0$
$x^2 − 8x − 9 = 0$ Dividing equation by 4
$(x − 9)(x + 1) = 0$
$x = 9$ $x = −1$ is not a real-life solution
Sides are 7, 24 and 25 so perimeter is 56 cm

3 (a) $(x + 2)(x + a) = x^2 + px + 6$
$\Rightarrow x^2 + ax + 2x + 2a = x^2 + px + 6$
$2a = 6$
$a = 3$
factors are $(x + 2)$ and $(x + 3)$
$(x + 2)(x + 3) = x^2 + 5x + 6$
$p = 5$
(b) (i) $(2x + 3)(x − 7)$
(ii) $2\left(x + \frac{1}{2}\right)^2 − 11\left(x + \frac{1}{2}\right) = 21$
$2\left(x + \frac{1}{2}\right)^2 − 11\left(x + \frac{1}{2}\right) − 21 = 0$
Compare this with $2x^2 − 11x − 21 = 0$
so replace x by $\left(x + \frac{1}{2}\right)$ in b.
This gives $\left(2\left(x + \frac{1}{2}\right) + 3\right)\left(\left(x + \frac{1}{2}\right) − 7\right) = 0$
$(2x + 4)\left(x − 6\frac{1}{2}\right) = 0$
$x = −2$ or $x = 6\frac{1}{2}$

4 (a) $(x − 5)\left(x + \frac{2}{3}\right) = 0$
$(x − 5)(3x + 2) = 0$ Multiplying by 3
$3x^2 − 13x − 10 = 0$ Any multiple of this equation is correct

(b) To have one solution, when factorised the equation must be $(x - a)(x - a) = 0$
$(x - a)^2 = 0$
$x^2 - 2ax + a^2 = 0$
$2a = 6$
$a = 3$
$p = 9$
equation is $(x - 3)^2 = 0$ so the solution is $x = 3$

5 (a) Let x be the number of jars she bought so each jar costs $\frac{2000}{x}$ cents.

In the other shop, each jar costs $\frac{2000}{x} - 20$ and she could have bought $x + 5$ jars.

$(x + 5)\left(\frac{2000}{x} - 20\right) = 2000$

$2000 - 20x + \frac{10000}{x} - 100 = 2000$

$\frac{10000}{x} - 20x - 100 = 0$

$10000 - 20x^2 - 100x = 0$ Multiplying equation by x

$20x^2 + 100x - 10000 = 0$ Multiplying by -1 and re-arranging

$x^2 + 5x - 500 = 0$ Dividing by 20

(b) $x^2 + 5x - 500 = 0$
$(x + 25)(x - 20) = 0$
$x = 20$ $x = -25$ is not a real-life solution

Priti bought 20 jars.

(c) Each jar costs $\frac{2000}{x} = 100$ cents or \$1

GRAPHS 5 – BASIC SKILLS EXERCISE

1 $y > -3$

2 $x < 2$ or $x \geq 4$

3 $x + y \geq 5$

4 $y < 2x + 2$

5 $x \geq 0$, $y \geq 0$ and $x + 2y < 6$

6 $x + y \geq -4$, $y - 3x > -4$ and $3y - x \leq 4$

7

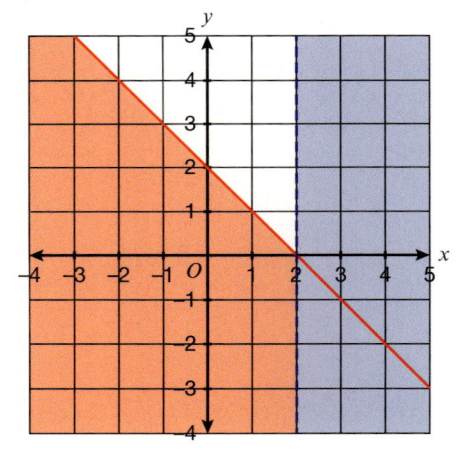

8

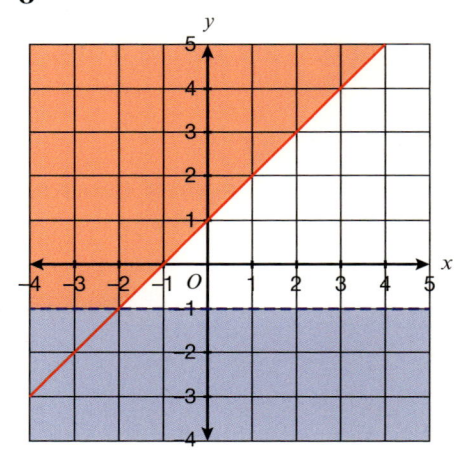

9

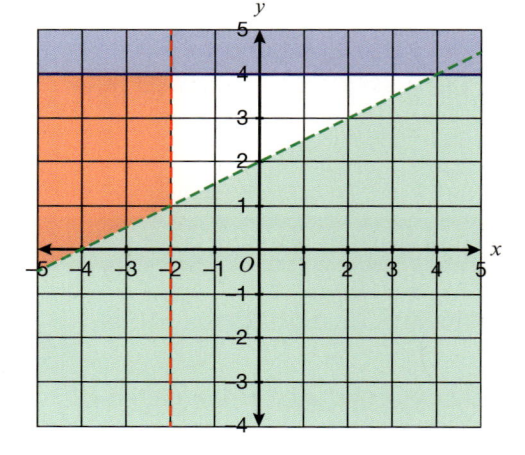

ANSWERS

10

11 (a) $-\frac{3}{4}, \frac{4}{3}$

(b) $\frac{6}{7}, \frac{-7}{6}$

12 a and d, b and c

13 Sketch shows right angle is at A.

Gradient of $AB = \frac{1}{3}$, gradient of $AC = -3$,

$\frac{1}{3} \times -3 = -1$ hence AB is perpendicular to AC

14 Gradient of L is $-\frac{3}{7}$, gradient of M is

$\frac{12 - -9}{5 - -4} = \frac{21}{9} = \frac{7}{3}$

$-\frac{3}{7} \times \frac{7}{3} = -1$ so L is perpendicular to M

15 $9y + 5x = 18$

16 -5

17 (a) $\left(-2, -1\frac{1}{2}\right)$

(b) $\left(11\frac{1}{2}, -13\right)$

18 $(-2, 3)$

19 Sketch shows diagonals are AC and BD.

Midpoint of AC is $\left(\frac{7-4}{2}, \frac{1+1}{2}\right) = \left(1\frac{1}{2}, 1\right)$,

Midpoint of BD is $\left(\frac{4-1}{2}, \frac{3-1}{2}\right) = \left(1\frac{1}{2}, 1\right)$

As midpoint is the same, diagonals bisect each other.

20 Gradient of AB is $\frac{1}{3}$ so a perpendicular gradient is -3
The midpoint of AB is $(1,0)$
Equation is $y = -3x + 3$

21 A lies on $2y = x + 2$ so the median passes through A and midpoint of BC.

The midpoint of BC is $\left(\frac{5-1}{2}, \frac{1+3}{2}\right) = (2, 2)$

which lies on $2y = x + 2$ hence it is a median.

22 (a) 13
(b) 15

23 Centre of circle is $C(3, 0)$. $AC = 5$ so the radius is 5. $CP = \sqrt{2^2 + 21} = 5$ and P lies on circle.

24 $AB^2 = (2\sqrt{3})^2 + 2^2 = 12 + 4 = 16$
$AB = 4$. $BC = 1 - {}^-3 = 4$
$AC^2 = (2\sqrt{3})^2 + (-2)^2 = 12 + 4 = 16$
$AC = 4$
As all sides are equal, triangle is equilateral.

25 $CT^2 = 3^2 + 2^2$ so the radius is $\sqrt{13}$

The gradient of CT is $-\frac{2}{3}$ and the gradient of the tangent is $\frac{3}{2}$

The equation of tangent is $y = \frac{3x}{2} + c$

Substitute $(2, -1)$ hence $c = -4$ and the tangent is $2y = 3x - 8$

26 Let the coordinates of B be $(2k, k)$

B lies on $2y = x$

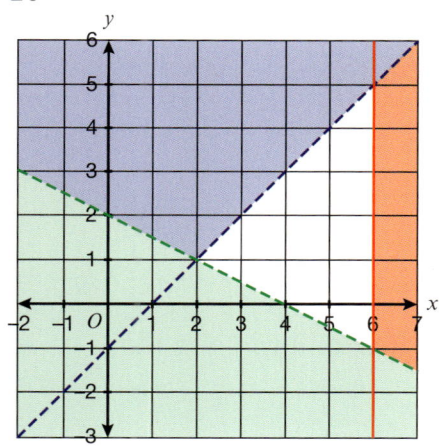

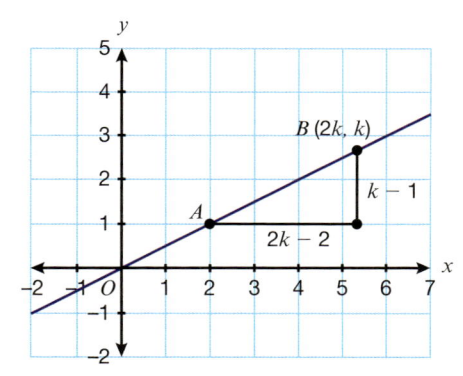

A sketch will help you to answer Q11–Q25

$AB^2 = (k-1)^2 + (2k-2)^2$
$20 = k^2 - 2k + 1 + 4k^2 - 8k + 4$
$5k^2 - 10k - 15 = 0$
$k^2 - 2k - 3 = 0$
$(k+1)(k-3) = 0$
$k = -1$ or 3

Coordinates of B are $(-2, -1)$ or $(6, 3)$

GRAPHS 5 – EXAM PRACTICE EXERCISE

1 The gradient of the line passing through $(-2, 0)$ and $(0, 4)$ is 2
The equation of the line is $y = 2x + 4$
One required inequality is $y \leq 2x + 4$
$\leq$ as the line is solid
The gradient of the line passing through $(0, -1)$ and $(2, 0)$ is $\frac{1}{2}$
The equation of the line is $y = \frac{x}{2} - 1$ or $2y + 2 = x$
One required inequality is $2y + 2 \geq x$
$\geq$ as the line is solid
The gradient of the line passing through $(0, 6)$ and $(8, 0)$ is $-\frac{3}{4}$
The equation of the line is $y = -\frac{3x}{4} + 6$ or $4y + 3x = 24$
One required inequality is $4y + 3x < 24$
$<$ as the line is dotted
The three inequalities are:
$y \leq 2x + 4$, $2y + 2 \geq x$, $4y + 3x < 24$

2 A sketch with a guess for k will help you understand the problem. Axes need to be equal aspect so that the two lines look as though they are at right angles

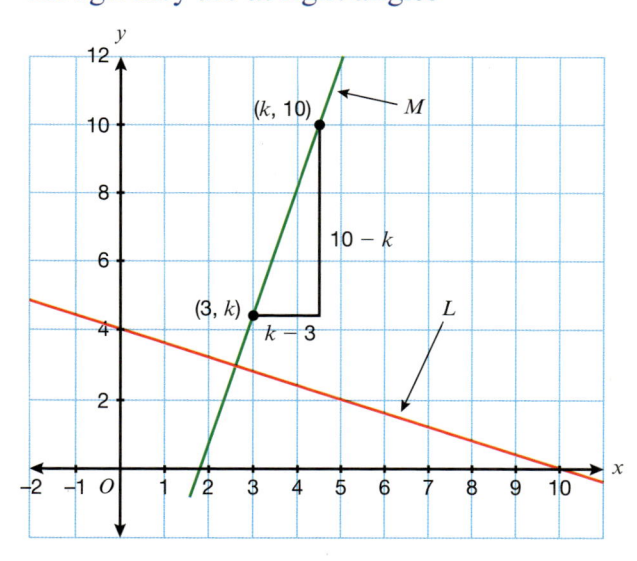

The gradient of L is $-\frac{2}{5}$

Rearranging L gives $y = -\frac{2}{5}x + \frac{23}{5}$

The gradient of M is $\frac{5}{2}$ $-\frac{2}{5} \times \frac{5}{2} = -1$

The gradient of line joining the two points is $\frac{10-k}{k-3}$

$\frac{k-10}{3-k}$ is also correct and will give the same answer.

$\frac{10-k}{k-3} = \frac{5}{2}$

$2(10 - k) = 5(k - 3)$
$20 - 2k = 5k - 15$
$7k = 35$
$k = 5$

3 A sketch shows that AB and AC will be the equal sides.

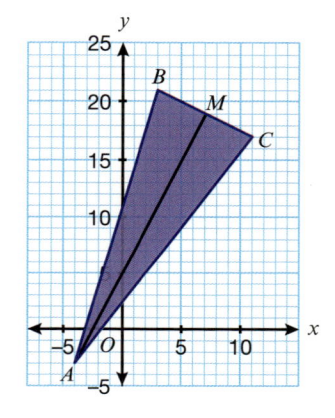

(a) $AB^2 = (21 + 3)^2 + (3 + 4)^2 = 625$
$AB = 25$
$AC^2 = (17 + 3)^2 + (11 + 4)^2 = 625$
$AC = 25$
So ABC is an isosceles triangle.

(b) M is $\left(\frac{3+11}{2}, \frac{21+17}{2}\right) = (7, 19)$

Gradient of AM is $\frac{19+3}{7+4} = 2$

Gradient of BC is $\frac{17-21}{11-3} = -\frac{1}{2}$

Product of gradients is $2 \times \frac{-1}{2} = -1$

So AM is perpendicular to BC

4   Let the point R be (k, k)
    R lies on $y = x$ so coordinates are equal.
    A rough sketch helps.

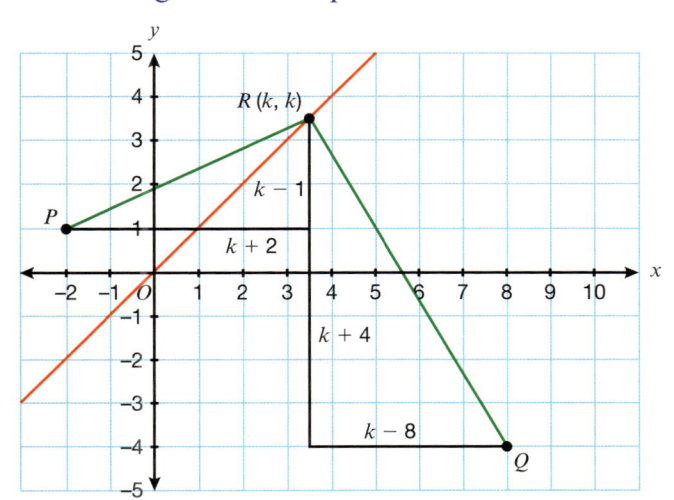

Gradient of PR is $\frac{k-1}{k--2} = \frac{k-1}{k+2}$

$\frac{1-k}{-2-k}$ is also correct

Gradient of QR is $\frac{k--4}{k-8} = \frac{k+4}{k-8}$

$\frac{-4-k}{8-k}$ is also correct

As PR is perpendicular to QR

$\frac{k-1}{k+2} \times \frac{k+4}{k-8} = -1$

$(k-1)(k+4) = -(k+2)(k-8)$
$k^2 - 3k - 4 = -k^2 + 6k + 16$
$2k^2 - 3k - 20 = 0$
$(2k+5)(k-4) = 0$
$k = 4$ or $k = -\frac{5}{2}$

R is (4, 4) or (−2.5, −2.5)

5   Shortest distance is along the perpendicular to the road passing through (7, −2).

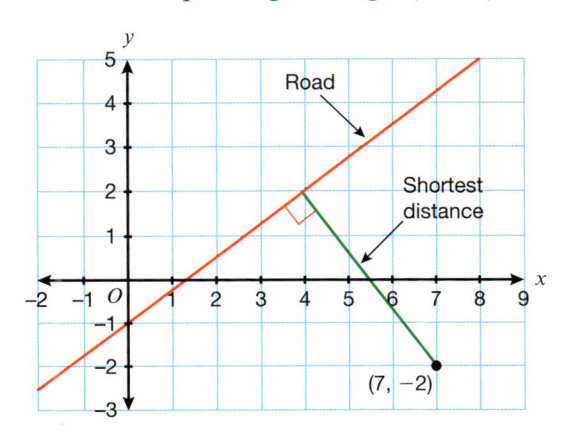

Gradient of the line (road) is $\frac{3}{4}$

Rearranging $4y + 4 = 3x$ gives $y = \frac{3}{4}x - 1$

The gradient of perpendicular is

$-\frac{4}{3} - \frac{4}{3} \times \frac{3}{4} = -1$

The equation of perpendicular is

$y = -\frac{4}{3}x + c$ or $3y + 4x = d$

Substituting $x = 7$, $y = -2$ gives $d = 22$ so equation of perpendicular is $3y + 4x = 22$
Intersection is given by solving $3y + 4x = 22$ and $4y + 4 = 3x$ simultaneously.
$3y + 4x = 22$ (1)
$4y + 4 = 3x$ (2)
$9y + 12x = 66$ (3)
(3) is (1) multiplied by 3

$16y - 12x = -16$ (4)

(4) is (2) rearranged and multiplied by 4

$25y = 50$ Add (3) and (4)

$y = 2$, $x = 4$ so the lines intersect at (4, 2)

Distance from (7, −2) to (4, 2) is

$\sqrt{(7-4)^2 + (-2-2)^2} = \sqrt{25} = 5$

Kyle must walk 500 m.

SHAPE AND SPACE 5 – BASIC SKILLS EXERCISE

1   (6, 10)
2   (2, 11)
3   $\begin{pmatrix} 2 \\ 2 \end{pmatrix}$
4   13 units
5   (1, −2)
6   (−3, 4)
7   (6, 5)
8   (1, 8)
9   (2, −1)
10 (−4, 3)
11 Rotation of 180° about 0

302 ANSWERS

12 Rotation 90° clockwise about centre (6, 8)

13 (2, 4)

14 (9, 12)

15 100

16 40

17 (a) (3, −4)
    (b) (−3, 4)
    (c) (4, −3)
    (d) (10, −2)

18 (a) (−3, −5)
    (b) (3, 5)
    (c) (−5, −3)
    (d) (−8, 8)

19

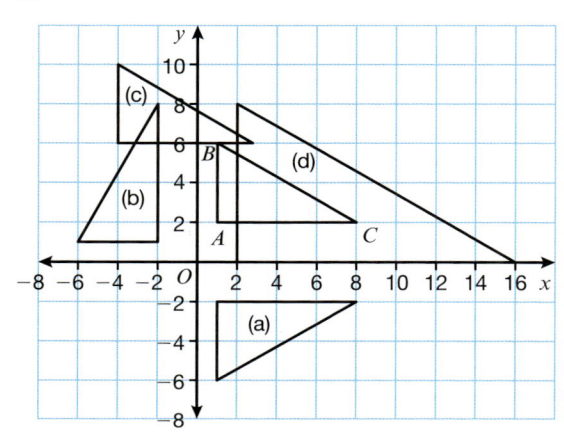

(a) $A'(1, −2), B'(1, −6), C'(8, −2)$
(b) $A'(−2, 1), B'(−6, 1), C'(−2, 8)$
(c) $A'(−4, 6), B'(−4, 10), C'(3, 6)$
(d) $A'(2, 0), B'(2, 8), C'(16, 0)$

20

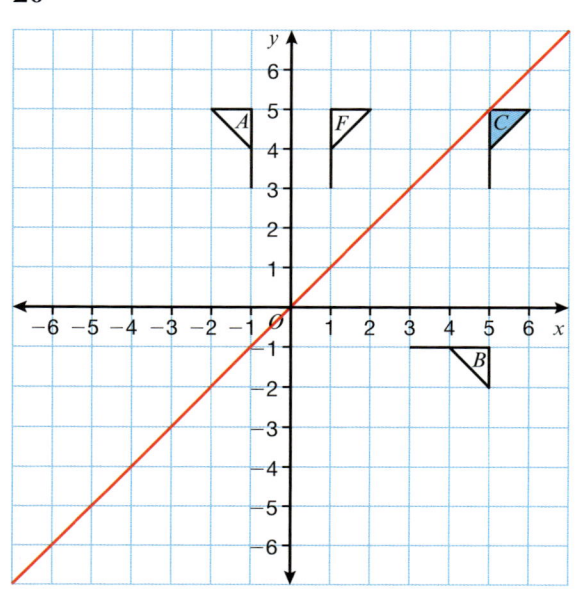

(c) Rotation of 90° clockwise around 0

(e) Translation along $\begin{pmatrix} 4 \\ 0 \end{pmatrix}$

SHAPE AND SPACE 5 – EXAM PRACTICE EXERCISE

1 $x = −11, y = −1$
   Perform the inverse operation of each translation in reverse order on point (4, 8).
   1. Translate along vector $\begin{pmatrix} -3 \\ 3 \end{pmatrix}$
   2. Rotation of 90° in an anticlockwise direction about 0
   3. Reflection in x-axis

2 $A(1, −5), B(−1, −5), C(1, −9)$
   Perform the inverse operation of each translation in reverse order on triangle JKL.
   1. Translate along vector $\begin{pmatrix} 3 \\ -4 \end{pmatrix}$
   2. Rotation of 90° in a clockwise direction about 0
   3. Reflection in y-axis

3

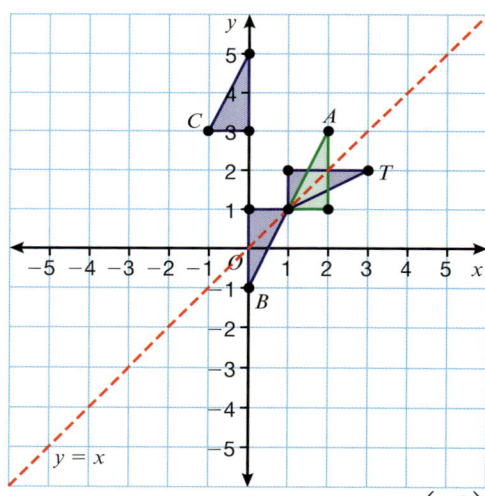

A translates to C along vector $\begin{pmatrix} -2 \\ 2 \end{pmatrix}$

ANSWERS

4

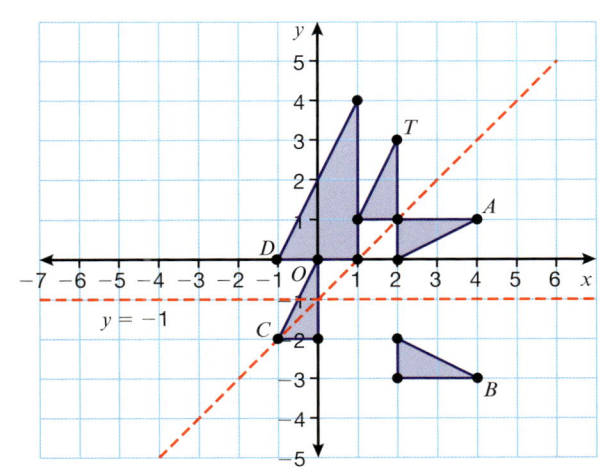

(e) Rotation of 90° clockwise about centre (0, −1)

(f) Enlargement of scale factor +2 about centre (−1, −4)

5 (a) The image of A after the translation along vector $\binom{6}{6}$ is at $(7, 6 + \sqrt{3})$

(b) The image hexagon would have a new perimeter of $6 \times 12 = 72$.
Each triangle within the original hexagon is an equilateral triangle of side 2.
Area of whole hexagon image
$= 6 \times$ area of an equilateral triangle side $12 = 6 \times A_1$

$A_1 = \frac{1}{2} \times 12 \times 12 \times \sin(60°)$

(Area of triangle $= \frac{1}{2}ab\sin C$)

$= \frac{1}{2} \times 12 \times 12 \frac{\sqrt{3}}{2}$
$= 36\sqrt{3}$

$= 2^2 \times 3^2 \times 3^{\frac{1}{2}} = 2^2 \times 3^{\frac{5}{2}}$

So the total hexagon area $= 6 \times A_1$
$= (3 \times 2) \times 2^2 \times 3^{\frac{5}{2}} = 2^3 \times 3^{\frac{7}{2}}$

$a = 3, b = \frac{7}{2}$

HANDLING DATA 4 – BASIC SKILLS EXERCISE

1 0.8

2 (a) $\frac{1}{2}$

(b) $\frac{5}{6}$

(c) 1

(d) 0

3 (a) $\frac{3}{29}$

(b) $\frac{9}{58}$

(c) $\frac{17}{29}$

(d) 0

4 (a) 0

(b) $\frac{9}{25}$

(c) $\frac{16}{25}$

(d) $\frac{9}{25}$

5 (a) $\frac{1}{13}$

(b) $\frac{2}{13}$

(c) $\frac{3}{4}$

(d) $\frac{3}{26}$

6 (a) $\frac{1}{8}$

(b) $\frac{1}{2}$

(c) $\frac{3}{4}$

(d) $\frac{5}{8}$

7 (a) RG GR GG

(b) $\frac{2}{3}$

ANSWERS

8 (a)

×	1	2	3	4	5	6
1	1	2	3	4	5	6
2	2	4	6	8	10	12
3	3	6	9	12	15	18
4	4	8	12	16	20	24
5	5	10	15	20	25	30
6	6	12	18	24	30	36

(b) (i) $\frac{1}{36}$

(ii) 0

(iii) $\frac{11}{36}$

(iv) $\frac{2}{9}$

9 (a)

	10	30	50
9	10	30	50
16	16	30	50
25	25	30	50
36	36	36	50

(b) (i) $\frac{1}{12}$

(ii) 0

(iii) $\frac{11}{12}$

(iv) $\frac{1}{3}$

10 (a) $\frac{25}{28}$

(b) $\frac{1}{6}$

(c) Number not cured =

$\frac{1}{9} \times 90 + \frac{3}{14} \times 84 + \frac{1}{10} \times 99 = 10 + 18 + 9.9$

≈ 38 horses

11 (a)

		Pink Box		
		△	○	☆
Blue Box	□	□△	□○	□☆
	□	□△	□○	□☆
	☆	☆△	☆○	☆☆

(b) (i) $\frac{5}{9}$

(ii) $\frac{4}{9}$

12 10

13 $\frac{3}{5}$

14 40

15 5

16 $\frac{1}{245}$

17 (a)

	2	3	5	7	11
13	15	16	18	20	24
17	19	20	22	24	28
19	21	22	24	26	30
23	25	26	28	30	34
29	31	32	34	36	40

(b) P(number with a zero) = $\frac{5}{25}$, expected

numbers with a zero = $50 \times \frac{5}{25} = 10$

18 72 letters with a line of symmetry

HANDLING DATA 4 – EXAM PRACTICE EXERCISE

1 (a) $8x = 1$

$x = \frac{1}{8}$, so P(black) = $\frac{3}{8}$

(Sum of all probabilities = 1)

(b) P(not red or green) = $6x = \frac{6}{8}$

P(not red or green) = $\frac{3}{4}$

(c) If the spinner lands 25 times on one colour its probability must be $\frac{1}{4}$ which leads to the conclusion that it is most likely to have been blue as P(blue) = $\frac{1}{4}$.

2 (a) P(4) = 0.35

P(prime) = p (2 or 3 or 5)
= 0.1 + 0.05 + 0.2

P(prime) = 0.35

(b) Li throws two numbers a total number of 40 times from 100. The probability of this event must = 0.4

The only two numbers which have a probability sum of 0.4 is 3 and 4.
(P(3) = 0.05, P(4) = 0.35)

Most likely numbers are 3 and 4.

3 (a)

	Milkshake	Orange juice	Tea	Coffee	Total
Year 10	2	10	7	5	24
Year 11	3	12	4	7	26
Total	5	22	11	12	50

(b) (i) P(year 10, milkshake) = $\frac{2}{50} = \frac{1}{25}$

(ii) P(year 11, not tea or coffee) = $\frac{3+12}{50} = \frac{15}{50} = \frac{3}{10}$

(c) P(not milkshake/year 10) = $\frac{22}{24} = \frac{11}{12}$

4 (a)

	35	42	120
20	5	2	20
63	7	21	3
96	1	6	24

(b) (i) P(even) = $\frac{4}{9}$

(ii) P(prime or triangular) = $\frac{2}{3}$

(Triangle numbers are 1, 3, 6, 10, 15, 21...)

(c) P(odd) = $\frac{5}{9}$, therefore the expected number of odds from 90 choices
= $\frac{5}{9} \times 90 = 50$

5 Let the number of purple jellyfish be x

P(purple) = $\frac{x}{60}$

P(white) = $\frac{60-x}{60}$

If 40 white jellyfish are added:
P(purple) = $\frac{x}{100}$, P(white) = $\frac{100-x}{100}$

$\frac{100-x}{100} = 3 \times \frac{60-x}{60}$

$20(100 - x) = 100(60 - x)$
$100 - x = 300 - 5x$
$4x = 200, x = 50$

P(purple) = $\frac{50}{100} = \frac{1}{2}$

NUMBER 6 – BASIC SKILLS EXERCISE

1 (a) $\frac{126}{3} = \frac{294}{7}$ so yes

(b) $\frac{275}{50} \neq \frac{500}{80}$ so yes

(c) $\frac{254}{12} = \frac{317.5}{15}$ so yes

2 $\frac{1227 \times 1.9}{1.2}$ = 1942.75 seconds or 32 minutes 22.75 seconds

3 Brand A $\frac{60}{25}$ = €2.4/ml, Brand B $\frac{70}{30}$
= €2.3̇/ml so Brand B is cheaper

4 (a) $\frac{104.5 \times 60}{9.5}$ = 660 tonnes in one minute

(b) $\frac{297 \times 9.5}{104.5}$ = 27 seconds

5 (a) $\frac{12\,000}{11 \times 24 \times 60}$ = 758 m (3 s.f.)

(b) $\frac{11 \times 534}{12\,000}$ = 0.4895 days or 11 hours 45 mins

6 (a)

Number of people	50	80	160	200
Cost in £	125	200	400	500

(b) $\frac{50}{125} \times 875$ = 350 people

7 Between 0−5 mins temperature drop is 1° C/min, between 5−15 mins it is 0.9° C/min and between 15−30 mins it is 0.867° C. Temperature drop is not constant so Kit is wrong.

8 1 square contains $\frac{30}{100} \times \frac{1}{20} \times 85$ = 1.275 g of solids.
15 g of solids needs $\frac{15}{1.275}$ = 11.76 squares so at least 12 squares are needed.

9 $x \times y$ = constant if x and y are in inverse proportion

x	2	3	4	6
y	18	12	10	6
xy	36	36	40	36

(4, 10) is not in inverse proportion.

10 Number of scarves × temperature = constant as they are in inverse proportion. Constant = 32 × 15 = 480

Number of scarves	120	60	40	32	24
Temperature (°C)	4	8	12	15	20

11 (a) $\frac{24}{64}$ = 0.375 seconds

   (b) $\frac{15}{0.25}$ = 60 Mbs

12 Number of cleaners × days = constant as they are in inverse proportion
Constant = 3 × 8 = 24
(a) 2 × 12 = 24 so 12 days
(b) 4 × 6 = 24 so 4 window cleaners

13 Number of desks × time = constant as they are in inverse proportion. $\frac{3}{4}$ h = 45 min, constant = 3 × 45 = 135. Easier to work in minutes.
(a) 5 × 27 = 135 so 27 minutes
(b) n × 15 = 135 so n = 9 desks

14 Time × temperature = constant as they are in inverse proportion
Constant = 20 × 9 = 180
(a) t × 15 = 180 so t = 12 minutes
(b) 24 × T = 180 so T = 7.5°C

15 Number of waiters × time = constant as they are in inverse proportion
Constant = 12 × 3 = 36 (for 60 people)
(a) 18 × 2 = 36 therefore 18 waiters
(b) 24 × 1.5 = 36 therefore 24 waiters are needed to serve 60 people in 1.5 minutes
90 secs = 1.5 mins
24 × $\frac{100}{60}$ = 40 waiters needed to serve 100 people in 90 seconds

16 (a) 150 km of flight produces 1 g so
150 × 1000 = 150 000 km produces 1 kg
1000 g = 1 kg mean distance per bee is
150 000 ÷ 10 000 = 15 km
(b) 12 × 150 000 km will produce 12 kg
number of bees = 12 × 150 000 ÷ 45
= 40 000

17 $\frac{1}{25}$

18 $\frac{1}{27}$

19 $\frac{1}{16}$

20 $\frac{1}{49}$

21 $\frac{1}{5}$

22 $\frac{1}{108}$

23 $\frac{9}{8}$ or $1\frac{1}{8}$

24 1

25 9

26 $\frac{2}{3}$

27 $\frac{1}{7}$

28 $\frac{1}{16}$

29 $\frac{8}{125}$

30 $\frac{8}{27}$

31 $\frac{9}{4}$

32 $\frac{5}{3}$

33 1

34 $\frac{1}{3}$

35 16

36 9

37 4

38 0

39 $\frac{1}{2}$

40 $-\frac{2}{3}$

41 0

42 $\frac{3}{4}$

43 $\frac{1}{2}$

44 1 or −2

NUMBER 6 – EXAM PRACTICE EXERCISE

1 One machine produces $\frac{3000}{5} = 6000$ shoes in 20 days

One machine produces $\frac{6000}{20} = 300$ shoes every day

Five machines working for 6 days produce $5 \times 6 \times 300 = 9000$ shoes

To complete the order, 27 000 shoes must be produced in 10 days. $36\,000 - 9\,000 = 27\,000$

1 machine will produce $300 \times 10 = 3000$ shoes in 10 days

To produce 27 000 shoes in 10 days will take $\frac{27000}{3000} = 9$ machines

Kiko must order an extra $9 - 5 = 4$ machines

2 Temperature decreases by 10°C in 500 m hence 2°C in 100 m and 14°C in 700 m
so the temperature at 700 m is $20 - 14 = 6°C$
Below 700 m, let T be temperature in °C and d be depth in metres
$T \times d =$ constant as T and d are in inverse proportion
$T \times d = k$
$k = 6 \times 700 = 4200$
$T \times d = 4200$
If $T = 4$, then $d = \frac{4200}{4} = 1050$ m

3 (a) $(5^4)^{\frac{3}{8}} \times (5^{10})^{-\frac{1}{4}} \div 100^{\frac{1}{2}} = 5^{\frac{3}{2}} \, 5^{-\frac{5}{2}} \div 10^{-1}$
$= 5^{-1} \times 10$
$= \frac{1}{5} \times 10$
$= 2$

(b) $27\sqrt{27} = 3^3 \times (3^3)^{\frac{1}{2}}$
$= 3^3 \times 3^1 \times 3^{\frac{1}{2}}$
$= 3^4 \times 3^{\frac{1}{2}}$
$= 81\sqrt{3}$

(c) $27\sqrt{27} = (3^3)^k$
$3^3 \times 3^{\frac{3}{2}} = 3^{2k}$
$3^{\frac{9}{2}} = 3^{2k}$
$k = \frac{9}{4}$

4 (a) $2^3 = (2^2)^k$ so $2k = 3$ and $k = \frac{3}{2}$

(b) $2\sqrt{32} = 4^k$
$2^1 \times (2^5)^{\frac{1}{2}} = (2^2)^k$
$2^{\frac{7}{2}} = 2^{2k}$
$k = \frac{7}{4}$

(c) $\frac{1}{32} = 8^k$
$32^{-1} = (2^3)^k$
$(2^5)^{-1} = 2^{3k}$
$2^{-5} = 2^{3k}$
$k = \frac{-5}{3}$

5 (a) (i) $6 = 2 \times 3$
$= (2^3)^{\frac{1}{3}} \times (3^2)^{\frac{1}{2}}$
$= x^{\frac{1}{3}} \times y^{\frac{1}{2}}$

(ii) $4\sqrt{3} = 2^2 \times 3^{\frac{1}{2}}$
$= (2^3)^{\frac{2}{3}} \times (3^2)^{\frac{1}{4}}$
$= x^{\frac{2}{3}} \times y^{\frac{1}{4}}$

(iii) $\frac{1}{3\sqrt{4}} = 3^{-1} \times 4^{-\frac{1}{2}}$
$= 3^{-1} \times (2^2)^{-\frac{1}{2}}$
$= 3^{-1} \times 2^{-1}$
$= (3^2)^{-\frac{1}{2}} \times (2^3)^{-\frac{1}{3}}$
$= x^{-\frac{1}{3}} \times y^{-\frac{1}{2}}$

(b) $\frac{3\sqrt{6}}{8} = 3 \times \sqrt{2} \times \sqrt{3} \times 2^{-3}$
$= 3 \times 2^{\frac{1}{2}} \times 3^{\frac{1}{2}} \times 2^{-3}$
$= 2^{-\frac{5}{2}} \times 3^{\frac{3}{2}}$
$2^a \times 3^b = 2^{-\frac{5}{2}} \times 3^{\frac{3}{2}}$
$a = \frac{-5}{2}, b = \frac{3}{2}$

ALGEBRA 6 – BASIC SKILLS EXERCISE

1. (a) $y = 9x$
   (b) $y = 90$
   (c) $x = 5$

2. $a = 20b$

b	10	5	30
a	200	300	600

3. (a) $y = 8x$
   (b) $y = 80$
   (c) $x = 5$

4. (a) $y = \left(\frac{x}{4}\right)^3$
   (b) $y = 512$

5. (a) $y = 0.4x^2$
   (b) $y = 90$
   (c) $x \approx 6.12$

6. (a) $p = 20\sqrt{q}$
   (b) $p = 160$
   (c) $q = 6.25$

7. (a) $d = 5t^2$
   (b) $d = 20$ m
   (c) $t \approx 4.24$ s

8. (a) $p = 1.5n^2$
   (b) $p = €216$
   (c) $n = 20$

9. (a) $y = 4x^3$
   (b) $y = 256$
   (c) $x = 6$

10. (a) $e = 0.5v^2$
    (b) $e = 1250$ kJ
    (c) $v = 1414$ m/s

11. (a) $A = 15h^2$
    (b) $A = 135$ m²
    (c) $h = 6$ m

12. (a) $y = \frac{48}{x}$
    (b) $y = 6$
    (c) $x = 4$

13. (a) $p = \frac{50}{q}$
    (b) $p = 2.5$
    (c) $q = 2.5$

14. (a) $y = \frac{80}{x^2}$
    (b) $y = 5$
    (c) $x = 12.6$

15. (a) $p = \frac{2500}{\sqrt{q}}$
    (b) $p = 250$
    (c) $q = 2500$

16. (a) $p^2 = \frac{800}{q^3}$
    (b) $p = 3.54$
    (c) $q = 3.17$

17.
b	125	8	1
a	2	5	10

18. (a) $N = \frac{9000}{d^2}$
    (b) $N = 2250$
    (c) $d = 3$

19. $\frac{1}{2}$

20. -1

21. -2

22. -3

23. $\frac{1}{3}$

24. $-\frac{1}{2}$

25. $-\frac{1}{3}$

26. $-\frac{1}{4}$

27. $\frac{1}{2}$

28. 2

29. 3

30. 3

31. -5

32. -4

33. -4

34. -3

35. 1

36 $\frac{1}{2}$

37 1

38 $\frac{1}{4}$

39 2

40 2

41 −1

42 10^4

43 $a^{-2} = \frac{1}{a^2}$

44 $b^{-1} = \frac{1}{b}$

45 c^2

46 d^2

47 $e^{-1} = \frac{1}{e}$

48 $f^{-2} = \frac{1}{f^2}$

49 $g^{-\frac{1}{3}} = \frac{1}{\sqrt[3]{g}}$

50 h^2

51 $x = \frac{3}{10}, y = -\frac{9}{10}$

52 $x = \frac{3}{4}, y = 0$

53 $x = 2, y = -\frac{3}{5}$

54 $x = \frac{3}{5}, y = \frac{7}{3}$

55 $x = \frac{1}{2}$

56 $x = 3$ or 4

ALGEBRA 6 – EXAM PRACTICE EXERCISE

1 (a) $C \propto d, C = kd$
   If $d = 49$ cm, $C = \$60$
   $60 = k \times 49, k = 1.2$
   $C = 1.2d$
   (b) If $d = 65$ cm
   $C = 1.2 \times 65 = \$78$
   (c) If $C = \$80$
   $80 = 1.2 \times d, d = 66.\dot{6}$ cm

2 (a) $n \propto \frac{1}{t^2}, n = \frac{k}{t^2}$
   If $n = 10^3, t = 0.5$
   $10^3 = \frac{k}{0.5^2}$
   $k = 2.5 \times 10^2$
   $n = \frac{2.5 \times 10^2}{t^2}$
   (b) If $t = 2$
   $n = \frac{2.5 \times 10^2}{2^2} = 62.5$
   (c) If $n = 1$
   $1 = \frac{2.5 \times 10^2}{t^2}, t = \sqrt{2.5 \times 10^2} = 15.8$ yrs

3 (a) $v \propto \sqrt{d}, v = k\sqrt{d}$
   If $d = 10$ m, $v = 9.8$ m/s
   $9.8 = k \times \sqrt{10}, k = \frac{9.8}{\sqrt{10}}$
   $v = \frac{9.8\sqrt{d}}{\sqrt{10}} = 9.8\sqrt{\frac{d}{10}}$
   (b) (i) If $d = 50$ m, $v = 9.8\sqrt{\frac{50}{10}}$
   $= 21.9$ m/s (3 s.f.)
   (ii) If $d = 1000$ m, $v = 9.8\sqrt{\frac{1000}{10}}$
   $= 98$ m/s
   (c) If $v = 1$ m/s
   $1 = 9.8\sqrt{\frac{d}{10}}, \frac{1}{9.8} = \sqrt{\frac{d}{10}}, \left(\frac{1}{9.8}\right)^2 = \frac{d}{10}$
   $d = 10 \times \left(\frac{1}{9.8}\right)^2 = 0.104$ m (3 s.f.)
   (d) 790 km/h $= \frac{790 \times 1000}{60 \times 60} = 219.4$ m/s
   (Convert 790 km/h into m/s)
   $219.4 = 9.8\sqrt{\frac{d}{10}}, \frac{219.4}{9.8} = \sqrt{\frac{d}{10}},$
   $\left(\frac{219.4}{9.8}\right)^2 = \frac{d}{10}$
   $d = 10 \times \left(\frac{219.4}{9.8}\right)^2 = 5010$ m (3 s.f.)

4 $x = k_1 z^3$ and $x = k_2 y^2$, where k_1 and k_2 are constants
   So $x = k_1 z^3 = k_2 y^2$ therefore $k_1 z^3 = k_2 y^2$,
   $z^3 = \frac{k_2}{k_1} \times y^2, 50^3 = \frac{k_2}{k_1} \times 25^2, \frac{k_2}{k_1} = 200$
   $z^3 = 200 \times 10^2$, so $z^3 = 20\,000, z = 27.1$ (3 s.f.)

ANSWERS

5 $ab = 125$ implies that $5^m \times 5^n = 5^3$
so $m + n = 3$ (1)
$a^4b^{-2} = 5^{-9}$ implies that $5^{4m} \times 5^{-2n} = 5^{-9}$
so $4m - 2n = -9$ (2)
Solving equations (1) and (2):
(1): $m = 3 - n$
substituting into (2) gives
$4(3 - n) - 2n = -9$
$12 - 4n - 2n = -9$
$21 = 6n$
$n = 3.5$
substituting into (1) gives
(1): $m + 3.5 = 3$
$m = -0.5$

SEQUENCES 1 – BASIC SKILLS EXERCISE

1 16, 19.5, 23 (add 3.5)

2 0.2, 0, −0.2 (subtract 0.2)

3 $\frac{1}{16}, \frac{1}{32}, \frac{1}{64}$ $\left(\frac{1}{2^{n-1}}\right)$

4 0.32, 0.064, 0.0128 (divide by 5)

5 −9, 27, −81 (multiply by −3)

6 35, 48, 63 $n^2 - 1$

7 −2, 4, 10, 16, …

8 80, 76, 72, 68

9 $-\frac{1}{3}, 0, \frac{1}{3}, \frac{2}{3}$

10 $2, \frac{5}{2}, \frac{10}{3}, \frac{17}{4}$

11 3, 10, 21, 36

12 $\frac{1}{3}, -\frac{1}{4}, -\frac{3}{5}, -\frac{5}{6}$

13 56, 76, 99

14 2, −8, −21

15 4, 10, 18

16 74, 100, 130

17 8, 5, 1

18 −6, −4, −1

19 $2n + 3$

20 $29 - 3n$

21 $\frac{n-1}{n+1}$

22 $3n - 2$

23 $13 - 4n$

24 2^{n-1}

25 No, $78 - 3n = -218 \Rightarrow n = 98.67 \ldots$

26 $-23 + 5n > 1000 \Rightarrow n > 204.6$ 205th term is 1002

27 First sequence is $4n - 7$, second sequence is $3n + 9$. $4n - 7 = 3n + 9$ so $n = 16$

28 2nd sequence is $11n + 8$ so $n^2 - 4 = 11n + 8$
and $n^2 - 11n - 12 = 0$
$(n + 1)(n - 12) = 0$
$n = 12$
The term is 140

29 17th term $= \frac{1}{52}$ or $0.0192\ldots$

30 $n = 1$ gives $1 + a + b = 3$
$n = 2$ gives $4 + 2a + b = 3$ so $a = -3, b = 5$

31 $a = 6, d = 5, n = 20$ so $S_{20} = 1070$

32 $a = -2, d = -4, a + (n-1)d = -46$
$n = 12$
$S_{12} = -288$

33 $S_{38} \frac{38}{2}(1 + 297) = 5662$

34 $a = 4, d = 4, n = 100$
$S_{100} = 20\,200$

35 First term $= 461 - 7 \times 67 = -8$ $S_{68} = \frac{68}{2}(-16 + 67 \times 7) = 15\,402$

36 (a) $120 = \frac{10}{2}[6 + (10 - 1)d]$ so $d = 2$

(b) $120 = \frac{10}{2}[2a + (10 - 1)3]$ so $a = -\frac{3}{2}$

37 $a + 6d = 37, a + 17d = 92$ so $a = 7, d = 5$
$S_{20} - S_9 = \frac{20}{2}(14 + 19 \times 5) - \frac{9}{2}(14 + 8 \times 5) = 847$

38 $270 = \frac{n}{2}[12 + (n - 1)3]$
$n^2 + 3n - 180 = 0$
$(n + 15)(n - 12) = 0$
$n = 12$

39 Sum of first 80 even numbers = $\frac{80}{2}$
$(4 + 79 \times 2) = 6480$

Even multiples of 3 are multiples of 6. Need to subtract $6 + 12 + 18 + \ldots + 156$
Number of terms given by $6 + (n - 1)$
$6 = 156$ so $n = 26$
Sum of $6 + 12 + 18 + \ldots + 156 = \frac{26}{2}$
$(12 + 25 \times 6) = 2106$

answer is $6480 - 2106 = 4374$

40 $935 = \frac{17}{2}(a + 103)$ so $a = 7$ and

$d = \frac{103 - 7}{17 - 1} = 6$

41 $a = -11$, $d = 2$ gives
$540 = \frac{n}{2}[-22 + (n - 1)2]$
$n^2 - 12n - 540 = 0$
$(n - 30)(n + 18) = 0$
$n = 30$
last term is $-11 + 29 \times 2 = 47$

42 $145 = \frac{10}{2}(2a + 9d)$ (1)

Sum of first 20 terms is $145 + 645 = 790$
$790 = \frac{20}{2}(2a + 19d)$ (2)

Solving (1) and (2) simultaneously gives
$a = -8$, $d = 5$

43 $64 = a + 11d$ and $504 = \frac{12}{2}(2a + 11d)$
so $a = 20$, $d = 4$
$S_{24} = \frac{24}{2}(40 + 23 \times 4) = 1584$

44 First term ($k = 1$) is 3, common difference is 4
$S_n = \frac{n}{2}[6 + (n - 1)4] = n(2n + 1)$

45 (a) $0 = 48 + (k - 1)(-3)$ so $k = 17$
(b) After the 17th term, terms are negative and thus reducing the sum of the series.
largest sum is $S_{17} = \frac{17}{2}[96 + 16 \times (-3)]$
$= 408$
Note S_{16} is also correct as the 17th term is zero.

SEQUENCES 1 – EXAM PRACTICE EXERCISE

1 (a) The common difference is 4 so the sequence continues as 21, 25, 29, nth term is $4n - 3$
(b) 25 is a square number and is 7th in the sequence.
Next square number is 36. $4n - 3$ is always odd so 36 is not a member of the sequence.
or $4n - 3 = 36$ so $n = 9.75$ and hence 36 is not a member of the sequence.
Next square number is 49 so $4n - 3 = 49$ and $n = 13$
(c) T is the sequence 1, 3, 7, 13, …
Table of differences shows 2nd difference is constant and equal to 2

1   3   7   13
  2   4   6
    2   2

Extending the table gives (shown in red)

1   3   7   13   21   31
  2   4   6   8   10
    2   2   2   2

T is 1, 3, 7, 13, 21, 31, …
the sixth square number in S is in the 31st position.
Substituting $n = 31$ into $4n - 3$ gives the value as 121 (or 11^2)

2 (a) $\frac{n + 1}{2n + 1}$

(b) $n + 1 = 99$ so $n = 98$
$2n + 1 = 195$
$n = 97$
$\frac{99}{195}$ is not a member of the sequence
$\frac{n + 1}{2n + 1}$

(c) $\frac{n + 1}{2n + 1} = 0.52 \Rightarrow n + 1 = (2n + 1)(0.52)$
$= 1.04n + 0.52$
$0.04n = 0.48$
$n = 12$
so 13th term is the first with a value less than 0.52.
12th term equals 0.52 so is not less than 0.52

312 ANSWERS

3 Subtracting two consecutive terms gives d
$(10x - 9) - (4x + 10) = d$
$6x - 19 = d$
$(12x - 10) - (10x - 9) = d$
$2x - 1 = d$
$6x - 19 = 2x - 1$
$4x = 18$
$x = 4.5$
$d = 8$ and $a = 28$
Sum from the 20th to the 30th terms
$= S_{30} - S_{19}$ Sum includes the 20th term
$S_{30} = \frac{30}{2}(56 + 29 \times 8) = 4320$
$S_{19} = \frac{19}{2}(56 + 18 \times 8) = 1900$
$S_{30} - S_{19} = 4320 - 1900 = 2420$

4 $a + 4d = 56$ (1)   5th term is $a + 4d$
$\frac{5}{2}(2a + 4d) = 300$ $S_5 = \frac{5}{2}[2a + (5-1)d]$
$a + 2d = 60$ (2)

Solving (1) and (2) simultaneously gives
$a = 64, d = -2$
$S_5 : S_n = 6 : 11$
$S_n = \frac{11}{6} \times 300 = 550$
$\frac{n}{2}[128 - 2(n-1)] = 550$
$64n - n^2 + n = 550$
$n^2 - 65n + 550 = 0$
$(n - 55)(n - 10) = 0$
$n = 55$ or $n = 10$

5 (a) $1 + 2 + 3 + \ldots + 99 + 100 = 5050$
smallest share is $\frac{1}{5050} \times 10100 = £2$
largest share is $\frac{100}{5050} \times 10100 = £200$

(b) $1 + 2 + 3 + 4 + \ldots + n =$
$\frac{n}{2}[2 + (n-1) \times 1] = \frac{n}{2}(n+1) = \frac{n(n+1)}{2}$

Smallest share is $1 \div \left[\frac{n(n+1)}{2}\right]$ of the
amount $= A \times \frac{2}{n(n+1)} = \frac{2A}{n(n+1)}$

Largest share is $n \div \left(\frac{n(n+1)}{2}\right)$ of the
amount $= A \times n \times \frac{2}{n(n+1)} = \frac{2A}{n+1}$

SHAPE AND SPACE 6 – BASIC SKILLS EXERCISE

1   12
2   3
3   8
4   8
5   4
6   3
7   5
8   4
9   6
10 3
11 8
12 5
13 4
14 4
15 (a) $x = 16$
    (b) $x = 10$
16 62°
17 55°
18 124°
19 132°
20 54°
21 66°
22 30°
23 222°
24 57°
25 112°
26 68°
27 42°
28 44°

29 42°

30 228°

31 44°

32 (a) $x = 60°, y = 60°, z = 55°$
(b) $x = 40°, y = 70°, z = 40°$

SHAPE AND SPACE 6 – EXAM PRACTICE EXERCISE

1

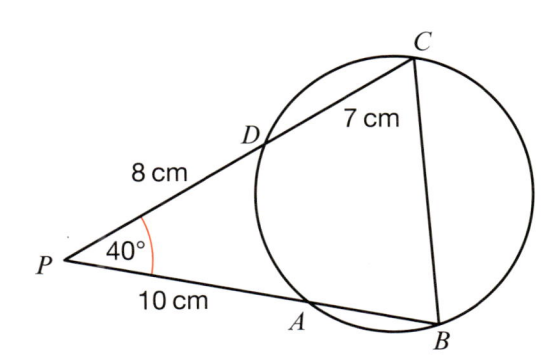

(a) $PB \times PA = PC \times PD$ (intersecting chords theorem)
$PB \times 10 = 15 \times 8$
$PB = \frac{15 \times 8}{10} = 12$ cm, so AB
$= 12 - 10 = 2$ cm

(b) If angle $DPA = 40°$, BC can be found from the cosine rule.
(cosine rule: $a^2 = b^2 + c^2 - 2bc\cos(A)$)
$BC^2 = PC^2 + PB^2 - 2 \times PC \times PB \times \cos(40°)$
$= 15^2 + 12^2 - 2 \times 15 \times 12 \times \cos(40°)$
$BC = 9.6553...$cm $= 9.66$ cm (3 s.f.)

(c) Angle BCD can be found from the sine rule.
(sine rule: $\frac{a}{\sin A} = \frac{b}{\sin B} = \frac{c}{\sin C}$)

$\frac{BC}{\sin(DPA)} = \frac{PB}{\sin(BCD)}$,

$\frac{9.6553}{\sin(40°)} = \frac{12}{\sin(BCD)}$

$\sin(BCD) = \frac{12 \times \sin(40°)}{9.6553} = 0.79888....,$

$BCD = 53.0°$ (2 s.f.)

2

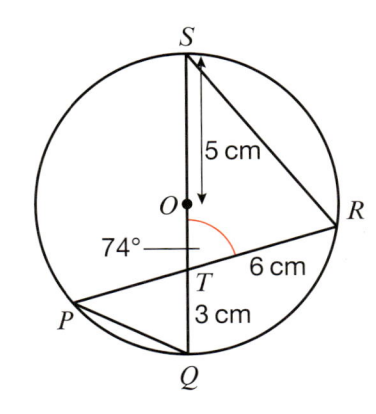

(a) $PT \times RT = ST \times QT$ (intersecting chords theorem)
$PT \times 6 = 7 \times 3$
$PT = \frac{7 \times 3}{6} = 3.5$ cm, so $PR = 3.5 + 6$
$= 9.5$ cm

(b) If the angle $OTR = 74°$, consider triangle RST and use the cosine rule
(cosine rule: $a^2 = b^2 + c^2 - 2bc\cos(A)$)
$RS^2 = RT^2 + ST^2 - 2 \times RT \times ST \times \cos(74°)$
$= 6^2 + 7^2 - 2 \times 6 \times 7 \times \cos(74°)$
$RS = 7.8643...$cm $= 7.86$ cm (3 s.f.)

(c) angle QPT = angle TSR
(Angles in the same segment are equal.)
So consider triangle RST to find angle TSR hence finding angle QPT.
(cosine rule: $a^2 = b^2 + c^2 - 2bc\cos(A)$)
$RT^2 = RS^2 + ST^2 - 2 \times RS \times ST \times \cos(RST)$
$6^2 = 61.846 + 7^2 - 2 \times 61.846 \times 7 \times \cos(RST)$
$\cos(RST) = \frac{61.846 + 7^2 - 6^2}{2 \times 61.846 \times 7}$, so angle
$RST = 85.041°...,$
So angle RST = angle $QPT = 85.0°$ (3 s.f.)

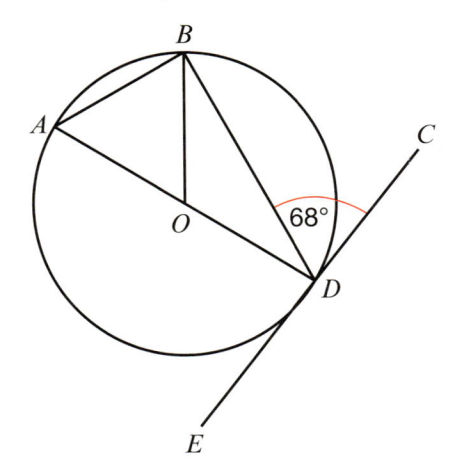

3

(a) angle $BAO = 68°$ (alternate segment theorem)
angle BAO = angle $ABO = 68°$ (triangle ABO is isosceles)
angle $AOB = 180° - 2 \times 68° = 44°$ (angle sum of triangle = 180°)
angle $BOD = 180° - 44° = 136°$ (angle sum of a straight line = 180°)

(b) angle $ABD = 90°$ (angles in a semi-circle = 90° at the circumference)
So triangle ABD is a right-angled triangle.
$AD^2 = AB^2 + BD^2$, $(2r)^2 = (2s)^2 + BD^2$
$BD^2 = 4r^2 - 4s^2 = 4(r^2 - s^2) = 4(r+s)(r-s)$
$BD = \sqrt{4(r+s)(r-s)} = 2\sqrt{(r+s)(r-s)}$
as required

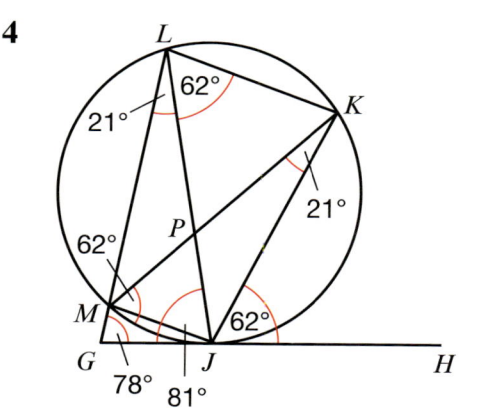

4

(a) angle $PLK = 62°$ (alternate segment theorem)
angle PLK = angle $PMJ = 62°$ (angles in the same segment are equal)
angle MLP = angle $PKJ = 21°$ (angles in the same segment are equal)
Triangle GLJ:
angle $LJG = 180° - (21° + 78°) = 81°$ (angle sum of a triangle = 180°)
angle $LJK = 180° - (81° + 62°) = 37°$ (angle sum of a straight line = 180°)

(b) angle LMK = angle $KJL = 37°$ (angles in the same segment are equal)
angle $GMJ = 180° - (37° + 62°) = 81°$ (angle sum of a straight line = 180°)
angle GMK = angle GMJ + angle PMJ $= 81° + 62° = 143°$

5

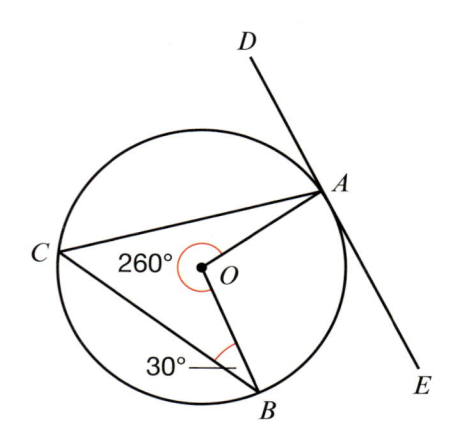

(a) (i) Draw line AB on diagram as shown.
angle $BOA = 100°$ (angle sum in a circle = 360°)
angle $ACB = 50°$ (angle at centre of circle = 2 × angle at circumference off the same chord)
angle $CAO = 360° - (50° + 260° + 30°) = 20°$ (angle sum of a quadrilateral = 360°)

(ii) angle $ABO = \dfrac{180° - 100°}{2} = 40°$ (triangle ABO is isosceles so base angles are equal.)

angle ABC = angle ABO + angle OBC
$= 40° + 30° = 70°$

(b) angle EAB = angle $ACB = 50°$ (alternate segment theorem)
angle $FAB = 25°$ (line FA bisects angle BAE)
angle $AFB = 180° - 50° = 130°$ (opposite angles in a cyclic quadrilateral = 180°)
angle $FBA = 180° - 130° - 25° = 25°$ (angle sum of a triangle = 180°)

SETS 2 – BASIC SKILLS EXERCISE

1 (a)

(b)

ANSWERS 315

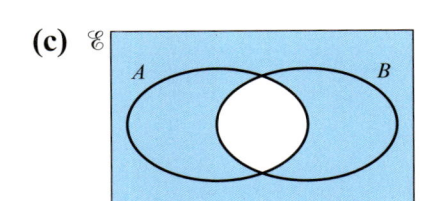

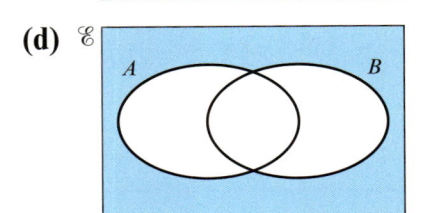

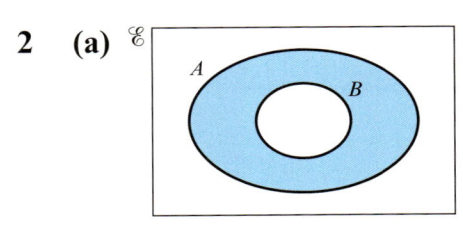

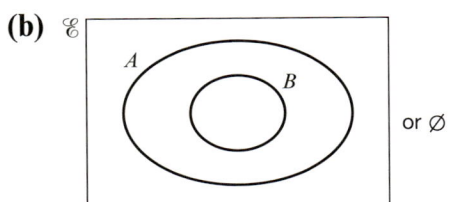

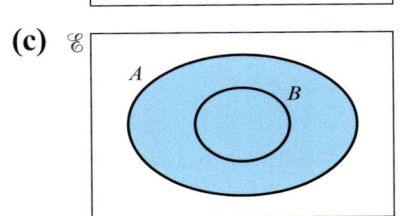

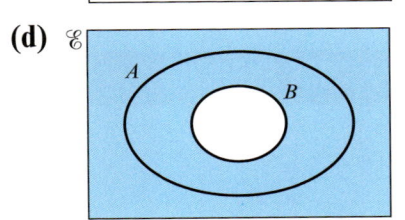

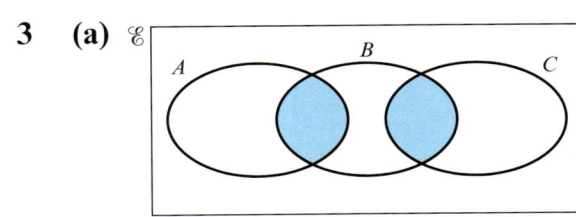

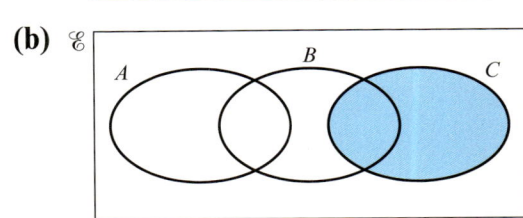

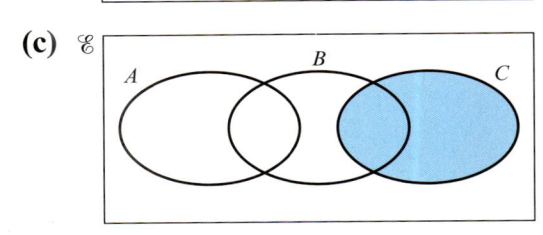

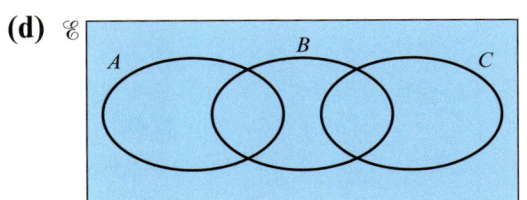

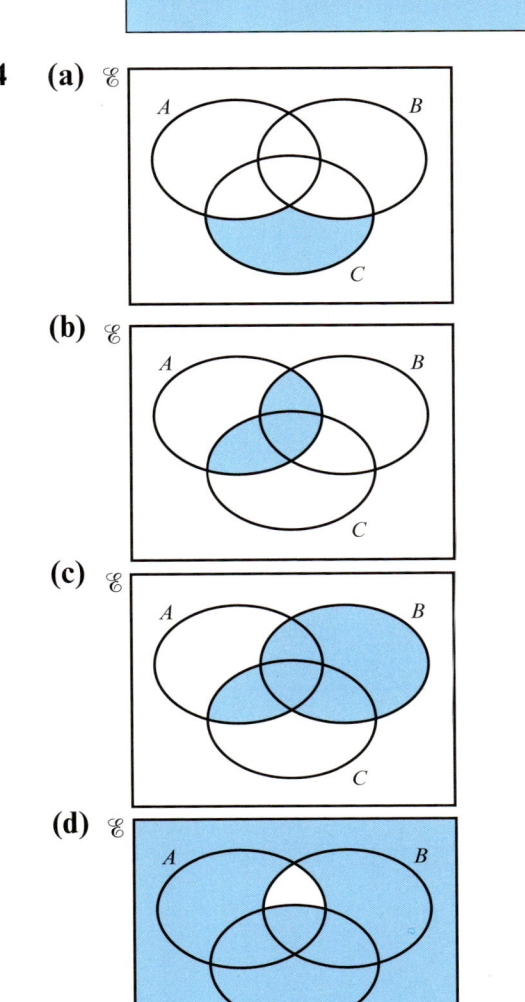

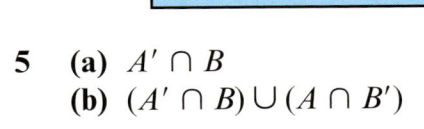

(c) [Venn diagram: A ∪ B complement region shaded, i.e., everything except A ∩ B]

(d) [Venn diagram: everything shaded]

2 (a) [A only shaded (A with B inside, ring shaded)]

(b) [nothing shaded] or ∅

(c) [A shaded including B]

(d) [everything except B shaded]

3 (a) [(A ∩ B) ∪ (B ∩ C) shaded]

(b) [C only and B∩C region shaded]

(c) [C only shaded]

(d) [three overlapping circles with everything shaded]

4 (a) [C only region shaded]

(b) [A∩B and A∩C regions shaded]

(c) [B ∪ (A∩C) type region shaded]

(d) [everything shaded except A∩B∩C-ish middle top]

5 (a) $A' \cap B$
   (b) $(A' \cap B) \cup (A \cap B')$

6 (a) $A' \cup B$
   (b) $(A \cap B') \cup C$

7 (a) There are no tabby cats over 10 years old.
   (b) There are some non-tabby cats under 10 years old.

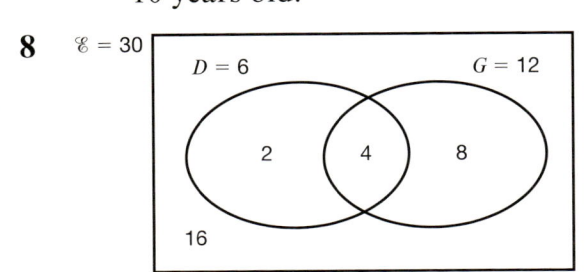

8 $\mathscr{E} = 30$

[Venn diagram with $D = 6$, $G = 12$; regions: 2, 4, 8; outside: 16]

16 play neither.

316 ANSWERS

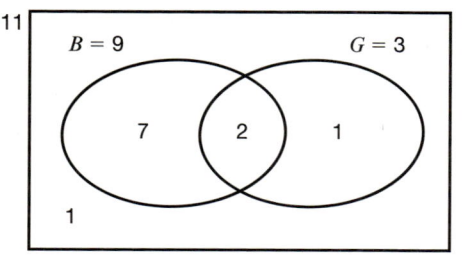

9 $\mathscr{E} = 11$

$B = 9$, $G = 3$: 7 | 2 | 1; outside: 1

2 have both.

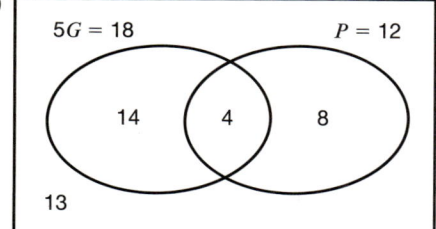

10 $\mathscr{E} = 39$

$5G = 18$, $P = 12$: 14 | 4 | 8; outside: 13

8 cannot.

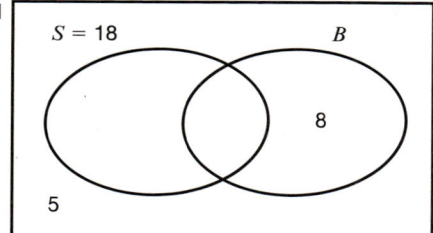

11 $\mathscr{E} = 31$

$S = 18$, B: 8; outside: 5

31 animals are in the field.

12 (a) 21
(b) 13

Venn diagram with sets A, B, C: 5, 4, 2, 7, 3, 6

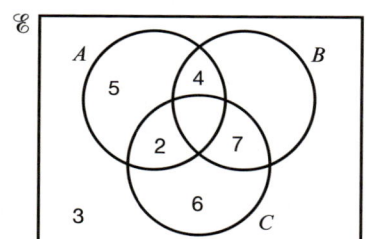

13 I = Isosceles triangles
E = Equilateral triangles
R = Right-angled triangles

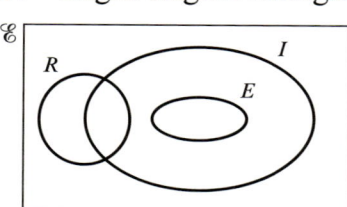

(Venn diagram with E inside I, and R overlapping I)

14 $\mathscr{E}$

$B = 40$, $G = 55$, $T = 30$: 23, 7, 30, 5, 5, 13, 7, 8

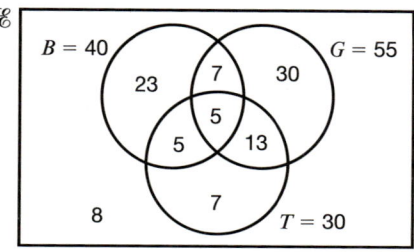

Number of pensioners =
$23 + 7 + 30 + 5 + 5 + 13 + 7 = 90$

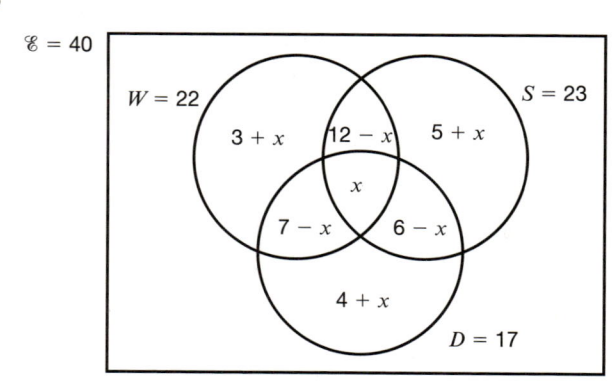

15 $\mathscr{E} = 40$

$W = 22$, $S = 23$, $D = 17$
Regions: $3 + x$, $12 - x$, $5 + x$, x, $7 - x$, $6 - x$, $4 + x$

$(3 + x) + (12 - x) + (5 + x) + (7 - x) + (6 - x) + (4 + x) + x = 40$
$x = 3$ so 3 teenagers enjoy all three sports.

16 (a) $A = \{-1, 0, 1\}$
(b) $B = \{3, 4, 5\}$
(c) $C = \{-1, 0, 1\}$
(d) $D = \{1, 2, 3, 4\}$
(e) $E = \{-2, 2\}$
(f) $F = \{0, 1, 2, 3, 4, 5, 6\}$

17 (a) $A = \{x: x < 5\}$
(b) $B = \{x: x \geq -8\}$
(c) $C = \{x: -2 < x < 4\}$
(d) $D = \{x: 3 \leq x \geq 8\}$
(e) $E = \{x: -2 \leq x \leq 2\}$ or $C = \{x: -3 < x < 3\}$
(f) $F = \{x: x = 2y \text{ and } 2 \leq y \leq 4\}$ or $D = \{x: x = 2y \text{ and } 1 < y < 5\}$

SETS 2 – EXAM PRACTICE EXERCISE

1 (a) (i) $(A \cup B') =$

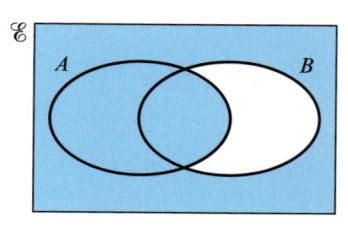

(Venn diagram with everything except B-only shaded)

so $(A \cup B')' =$

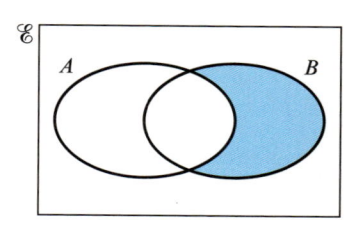

(Venn diagram with only B-only region shaded)

(ii) $A' \cap B' =$

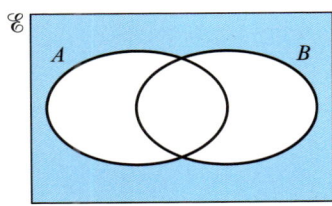

(b) (i) Largest intersection is 39% when swimming is a subset of jogging.

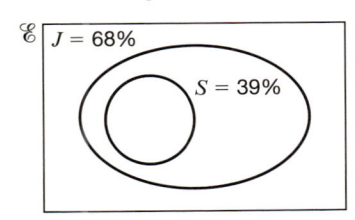

(b) (ii) Smallest intersection is when the percentage not in J or S is 0%.
Let the % in $J \cap S$ be x, then $(68 - x) + x + (39 - x) = 100$
$\Rightarrow x = 7\% \Rightarrow$ smallest percentage is 7%.

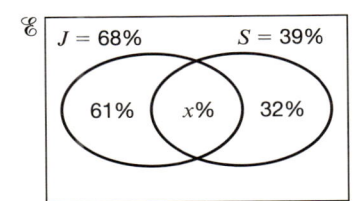

2 (a) Suzie has some green T shirts.
(b) All Suzie's dresses are green.
(c)

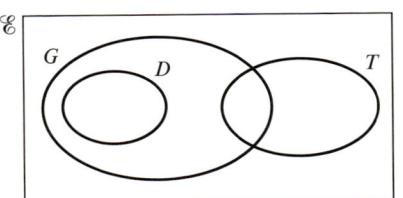

3 The Venn diagram shows H representing horses, D representing donkeys and NM representing non-microchipped
H and D do not intersect.

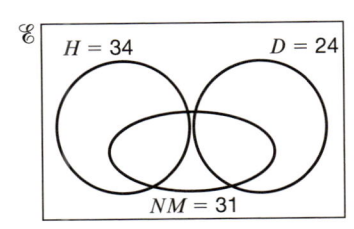

Let x be the number of horses with microchips so $2x$ is the number donkeys with microchips
$\Rightarrow 34 - x$ is the number of horses without microchips, $24 - 2x$ is the number of donkeys without microchips

Putting these into the Venn diagram gives:

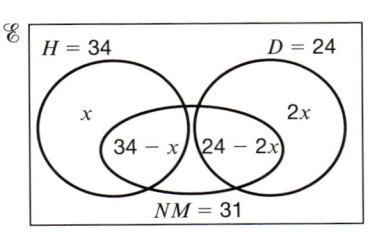

$\Rightarrow 34 - x + 24 - 2x = 31 \Rightarrow 3x = 27 \Rightarrow x = 9$
$\Rightarrow$ horses without microchips = $34 - x = 25$

4 Let B represent blue cars, G green cars and S soft tops.
The numbers represent the numbers of cars.
B and G do not intersect.

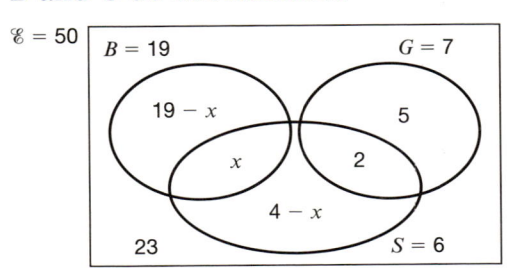

The total number of cars is 50
$19 - x + x + 4 - x + 2 + 5 + 23 = 50$
$x = 3$

5 (a) Of the 6 that like peppermint and chocolate, some might like toffee.
Of the 9 that like chocolate and toffee, some might like peppermint.
Let P represent peppermint lovers, C chocolate lovers and T toffee lovers.
The numbers represent the numbers of teenagers.

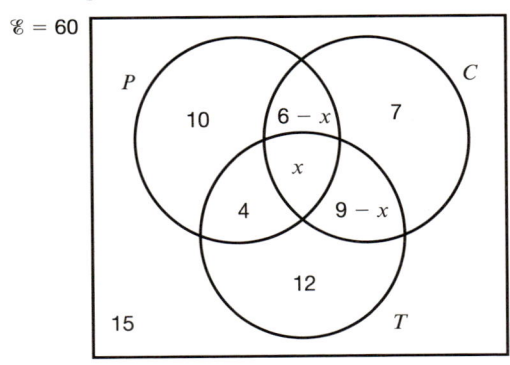

(b) $6 - x$ from the Venn diagram
(c) All the numbers must sum to 60.
$10 + (6 - x) + x + 4 + 7 + (9 - x) + 12 + 15 = 60$
$x = 3$ so 3 teenagers like all three.

NUMBER 7 – BASIC SKILLS EXERCISE

1. 2.64
2. 4.37
3. 0.245
4. 6.75
5. 5.94
6. 0.314
7. 27.3
8. 2 400 000
9. 26 200
10. 15.6
11. 755 000
12. 25.5
13. 862 000
14. 2.79
15. 2.31
16. 5.68
17. 14.7
18. 0.104
19. $\frac{1}{9}$
20. $\frac{2}{9}$
21. $\frac{1}{3}$
22. $\frac{4}{11}$
23. $\frac{7}{11}$
24. $\frac{17}{99}$
25. $\frac{71}{99}$
26. 1
27. $\frac{4}{33}$
28. $\frac{34}{99}$
29. $\frac{1}{45}$
30. $\frac{7}{90}$
31. $\frac{25}{333}$
32. $\frac{41}{333}$
33. $\frac{1234}{9999}$
34. $\frac{2468}{9999}$
35. $\frac{11}{15}$
36. $\frac{17}{45}$
37. $\frac{2}{1125}$
38. $\frac{211}{9000}$

NUMBER – 7 EXAM PRACTICE EXERCISE

1. (a) 6.99×10^4
   (b) 7.85×10^7
   (c) 2.90×10^3

2. (a) 3.16×10^0
   (b) 1.11×10^1
   (c) 2.87×10^7

3. (a) 0.773
   (b) 0.992
   (c) 0.129

4. Let $x = 0.0\dot{2}\dot{3}$
   $10x = 0.2323…$
   $1000x = 23.2323…$
   $990x = 23$, so $x = \frac{23}{990}$

   Let $y = 0.1\dot{7}$
   $10y = 1.777…$
   $100y = 17.777…$
   $90y = 16$, so $y = \frac{16}{90}$

   $x + y = \frac{23}{990} + \frac{16}{90} = \frac{199}{990}$, so
   $p = 199, q = 990$

5 (a) Let $p = 0.xyxy...$
   $100p = xy.xyxy...$
   $99p = xy = 10x + y$, so $p = \frac{10x + y}{99}$,
   as required.
   (The number xy means there are 10 x's and 1y)

   (b) Let $p = 5.xyzxyz...$
   $1000p = 5xyz.xyzxyz...$
   (The number xyz means there are 100 x's, 10 y's and 1z)
   $999p = 5xyz - 5 = 5000 + 100x + 10y + z - 5 = 4995 + 100x + 10y + z$
   so $p = \frac{4995 + 100x + 10y + z}{999}$, as required.

ALGEBRA 7 – BASIC SKILLS EXERCISE

1   5, 6
2   −1, 5
3   −1, 4
4   −4, −3
5   2
6   2, 0
7   −3, 5
8   −4, 8
9   $-3 \pm \sqrt{3}$
10 $\frac{-3 \pm \sqrt{3}}{2}$
11 $3 \pm \sqrt{\frac{23}{2}}$
12 $2 \pm \sqrt{5}$
13 $-1 \pm \sqrt{\frac{8}{3}}$
14 $3 \pm \sqrt{\frac{53}{5}}$
15 1.59, 4.41
16 −0.257, 2.59
17 3.11, −1.61
18 −57.9, −4.29
19 −3.30, 0.379
20 −2.45, −0.147
21 $x < -5$ or $x > 3$
22 $-2 \leq x \leq 7$
23 $-\frac{1}{3} < x < \frac{1}{2}$
24 $x < -3.45$ or $x > 1.45$
25 $2 - \sqrt{2} < x < 2 + \sqrt{2}$
26 $-4 \leq x \leq -2$ or $3 \leq x \leq 6$ $x \geq 6$ or $x \leq 4$ or $-1.65 \leq x \leq 3.64$
27 $b = 6, c = -7$
28 $(x + 3\pi)(x - \pi) = 0$, $x = -3\pi$ or $x = \pi$
29 $(x + p)(x + q) = 0$, $x = -p$ or $x = -q$
30 $9 - (x - 3)^2$
31 $b = -2, c = -4$
32 $x^2 + (x + 2)^2 = 202$, 9 and 11 or −11 and −9
33 $x(x + 3) = 9 \times 5$, $x = 5.37$
34 (a) $(x - 2)^2 + 5$
    (b) $x = 2$
    (c) 5
35 $b = -5, c = 6$
36 8 m by 5 m
37 $x^2 + (5 - x)^2 = 4^2$ so the sides are 1.18 cm and 3.82 cm (3 s.f.)
38 $\pi(w + 2)^2 - \pi 2^2 = \pi 2^2$
    The width of the path is 0.828 m (3 s.f.)
39 $A + B + C + D = 360°$
    $3x^2 + 24x - 315 = 0$
    $x^2 + 8x - 105 = 0$
    $(x - 7)(x + 15) = 0$
    $x = 7$
    The angles are $A = 60°$, $B = 120°$, $C = 135°$ and $D = 45°$
    $A + B = 180°$ therefore a trapezium (or $C + D = 180°$)

320 ANSWERS

40 $600 < 3x(x + 5) < 700$, $11.9 < x < 13.0$

$(x - 3)(2x + 3) > \frac{1}{2}(x + 2)(2x - 6)$

$x^2 - 2x - 3 > 0$

$x > 3$

41 Area of Rectangle = $(2x + 3)(x - 3)$
$= 2x^2 - 6x + 3x - 9 = 2x^2 - 3x - 9$
Area of Triangle = half × base × height
$= 0.5(2x - 6)(x + 2)$
$= 0.5(2x^2 + 4x - 6x - 12)$
$= 0.5(2x^2 - 2x - 12) = x^2 - x - 6$
For Area of Rectangle > Area of Triangle, then:
$2x^2 - 3x - 9 > x^2 - x - 6$
$2x^2 - x^2 - 3x + x - 9 + 6 > 0$
$x^2 - 2x - 3 > 0$
$(x + 1)(x - 3) > 0$
Solving, $x < -1$ or $x > 3$. As x must be greater than zero then $x > 3$ for the area of the rectangle to be greater than the area of the triangle.

ALGEBRA 7 – EXAM PRACTICE EXERCISE

1 (a) $f(x) = -3[x^2 + 4x - 1] = -3[(x + 2)^2 - 5]$
$= -3(x + 2)^2 + 15$

(b) $-3(x + 2)^2 + 15 = 0$
$3(x + 2)^2 = 15$
$(x + 2)^2 = 5$
$x = -2 \pm \sqrt{5}$

(c)

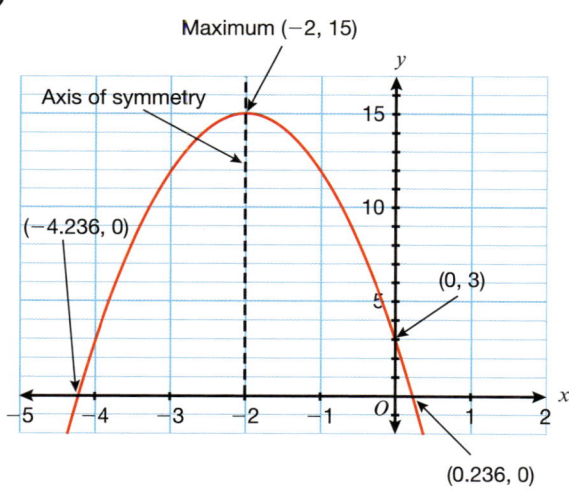

Maximum (−2, 15)
Axis of symmetry
(−4.236, 0)
(0, 3)
(0.236, 0)

2 (a) Formula sheet: Curved surface area of cylinder = $2\pi rh$, surface area of sphere = $4\pi r^2$

Surface area of cylinder = $2\pi r \times 20 = 40\pi r$
The two hemispherical ends have a surface area equal to the surface area of a sphere.
Surface area of ends = $4\pi r^2$
$4\pi r^2 + 40\pi r \leq 800\pi$
$r^2 + 10r - 200 \leq 0$
Dividing both sides by 4π and rearranging.
$(r + 20)(r - 10) \leq 0$
$0 < r \leq 10$ as $r > 0$

(b) Maximum volume is when $r = 10$
Volume of cylinder = $\pi \times 10^2 \times 20$
$= 2000\pi$
Volume of two hemispheres
$= \frac{4}{3} \times \pi \times 10^3 = \frac{4000}{3}\pi$

Volume of a sphere = $\frac{4}{3}\pi r^3$

Total volume $\frac{10\,000}{3}\pi = 10\,500$ cm³ to 3 s.f.

3 (a) The sum of the internal angles = 360°
$2x^2 + 50 + 3x^2 - 18 + 3x + 40 + 12x + 18 = 360$
$5x^2 + 15x - 270 = 0$
$x^2 + 3x - 54 = 0$
$(x + 9)(x - 6) = 0$
$x = 6$ or $x = -9$
When $x = -9$ the angle $D = -90$ so $x \neq -9$
Substituting $x = 6$ gives $A = 122°$, $B = 90°$, $C = 58°$ and $D = 90°$
Since $B + D = 180°$, $ABCD$ is cyclic (or $A + C = 180°$)

(b) Since $B = 90°$, AC is a diameter.

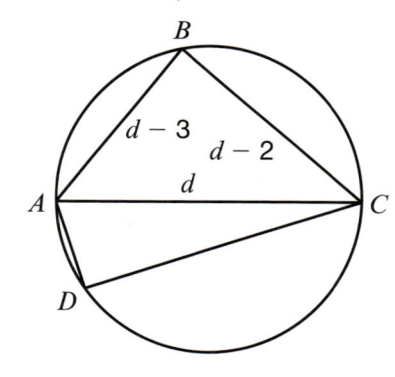

By Pythagoras' theorem in triangle ABC
$(d - 3)^2 + (d - 2)^2 = d^2$
$d^2 - 6d + 9 + d^2 - 4d + 4 = d^2$
$d^2 - 10d + 13 = 0$

Using the quadratic formula gives

$d = \frac{10 \pm \sqrt{100 - 4 \times 13}}{2}$

$d = \frac{10 \pm \sqrt{48}}{2}$

$d = \frac{10 \pm \sqrt{16 \times 3}}{2}$

$d = \frac{10 \pm 4\sqrt{3}}{2}$

$d = 5 \pm 2\sqrt{3}$

$d = 5 - 2\sqrt{3} \approx 1.5$ means AB and BC are negative so $d = 5 + 2\sqrt{3}$ cm

4 (a) Area of garden $= 6 \times 8 = 48$ m²
Total area of the flower beds
$= (6 - x)(8 - x) = 48 - 14x + x^2$
$\Rightarrow$ area of path $= 48 - (48 - 14x - x^2)$
$= 14x - x^2$
Or: area of one path is $6x$, area of the other path is $8x$. When added together the overlap of area x^2 is counted twice, so area is $6x + 8x - x^2 = 14x - x^2$.

(b) $(14x - x^2) : 48 = 1 : 4 \Rightarrow \frac{14x - x^2}{48} = \frac{1}{4}$
$\Rightarrow \frac{14x - x^2}{12} = \frac{1}{1} \Rightarrow 14x - x^2 = 12$ or
$x^2 - 14x + 12 = 0$

Using the formula to solve $x^2 - 14x + 12 = 0$, $a = 1, b = -14, c = 12$
$\Rightarrow x = \frac{14 \pm \sqrt{196 - 48}}{2} \Rightarrow x = 7 \pm \sqrt{37}$
$\Rightarrow x = 13.1$ or 0.917 (3 s.f.)
$x < 6 \Rightarrow x = 0.917$ m
If $x > 6$ m path takes up more than the width of the garden.

5 (a) Volume of sweet is $[\pi(r + 5)^2 - \pi r^2] \times 3$
Volume of hole is $\pi r^2 \times 3$
Ratio of volumes is $4 : 1$
so $[\pi(r + 5)^2 - \pi r^2] \times 3 = 4\pi r^2 \times 3$
$r^2 + 10r + 25 - r^2 = 4r^2$
Dividing both sides by π and 3 and simplifying
$4r^2 - 10r - 25 = 0$

(b) $r = \frac{10 \pm \sqrt{100 + 4 \times 4 \times 25}}{2 \times 4}$

$= \frac{10 \pm \sqrt{500}}{8}$

$= \frac{5 \pm 5\sqrt{5}}{4}$

The positive value of $r = 4.0451\ldots$
Volume of sweet is $= 4 \times \pi \times 4.0451^2 \times 3$
Volume of sweet is 4 times the volume of the hole
Volume of sugar is $0.6 \times 4 \times \pi \times 4.0451^2 \times 3$
$= 370$ mm³ (3 s.f.)
370 mm³ $= 0.370$ cm³ (3.s.f.)

GRAPHS 6 – BASIC SKILLS EXERCISE

1 (a)

x	−2	−1	0	1	2	3	4
y	−17	−1	3	1	−1	3	19

(b)

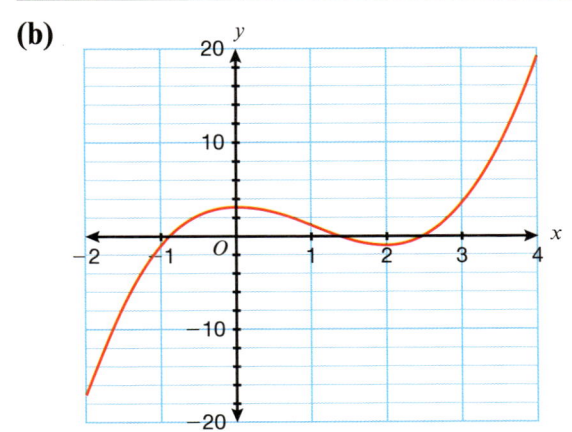

2 (a)

x	−2	−1	0	1	2	3	4
y	−19	0	1	−4	−3	16	65

(b)

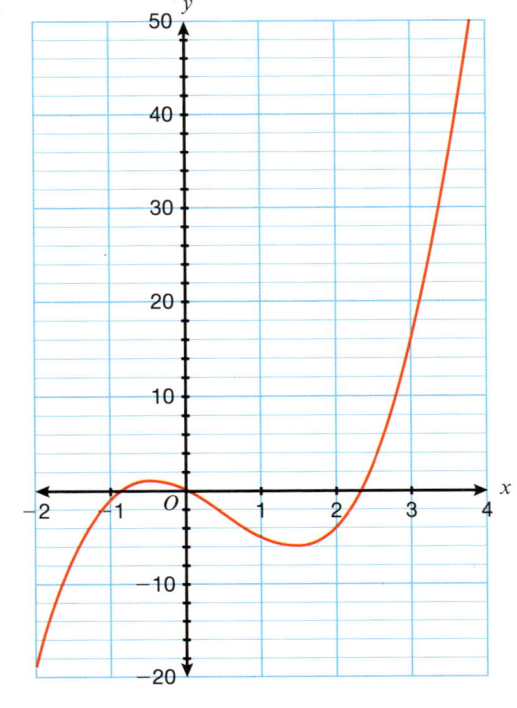

3 (a) $a = -5$

x	−2	−1	0	1	2	3	4	5
y	−23	1	9	7	1	−3	1	18

(b)

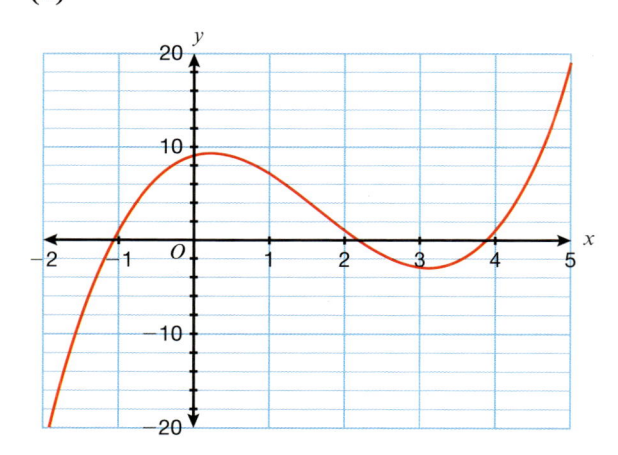

(c) $x \approx -1.1$, 2.2 or 3.8

4 (a) $a = -7$, $b = 8$

x	-1	0	1	2	3	4	5	6
y	-9	8	11	6	-1	-4	3	26

(b)

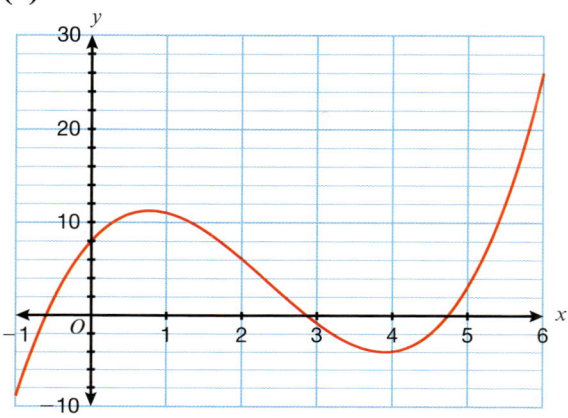

(c) $x \approx -0.6$, 2.8 or 4.7

5 (a)

t	1	2	4	6	8	10	12
p	20	10	5	3.3	2.5	2	1.7

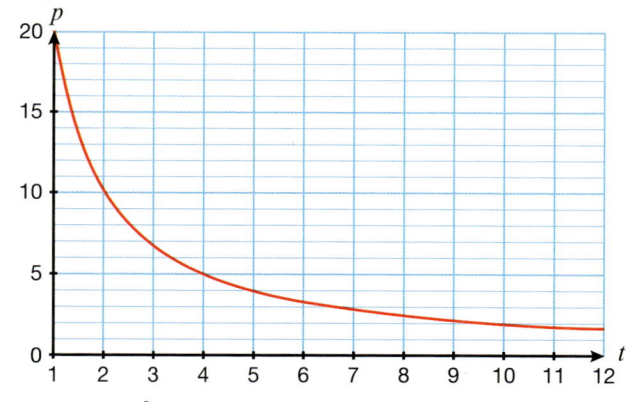

(b) (i) $1\frac{2}{3}$ months
 (ii) $2222

(c) $x = 80$

6 Substitute $x = 6$ into formula for y to find value of $k = 12$

(a) $k = 12$

x	1	2	3	4	5	6
y	12	6	4	3	2.4	2

(b)

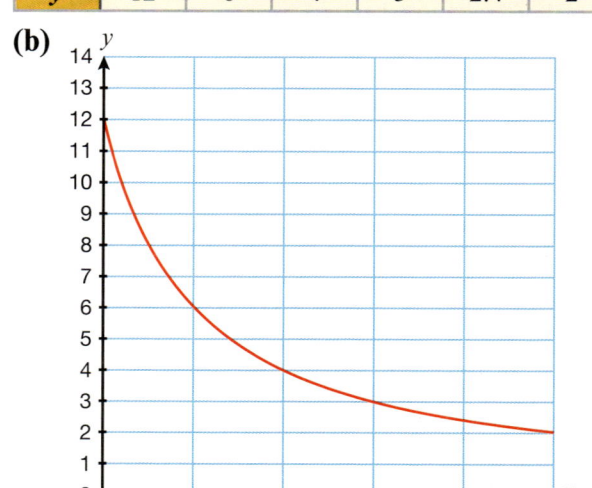

7 Substitute $x = 1$ into formula for y to find value of $a = 4$

(a) $a = 4$

x	1	2	3	4	5	6
y	8	10	13.3	17	20.8	24.7

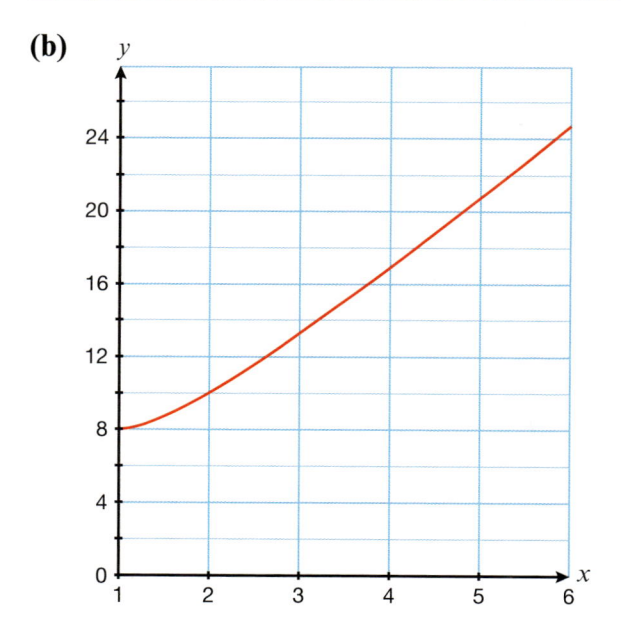

(b)

(c) $x = 1$, $y = 8$

8 (a)

x	1	2	3	4	5	6	7
y	9	252	294	284	237	155	34.3

(b)

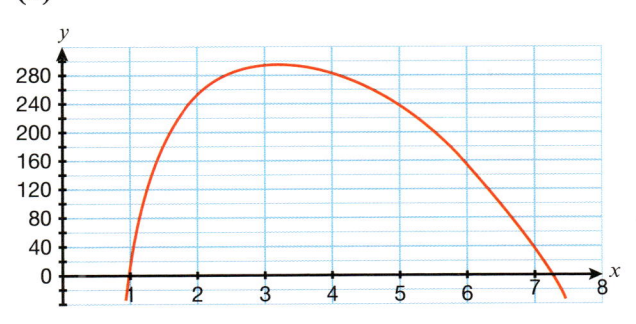

[Graph showing curve peaking around x=3 at y≈290, crossing x-axis near x=1 and x=7]

(c) (i) By inspection $y_{max} \approx 295$

(ii) $x^2 + \frac{200}{x} + \frac{200}{x^2} = 210$,

$-x^3 - \frac{200}{x} - \frac{200}{x^2} + 410 = 200$

Draw $y = 200$ and x values in the domain are $x \approx 1.6$ or 5.5

GRAPHS 6 – EXAM PRACTICE EXERCISE

1 (a)

t	0	1	2	3	4	5	6
d	18	23	18	9	2	3	18

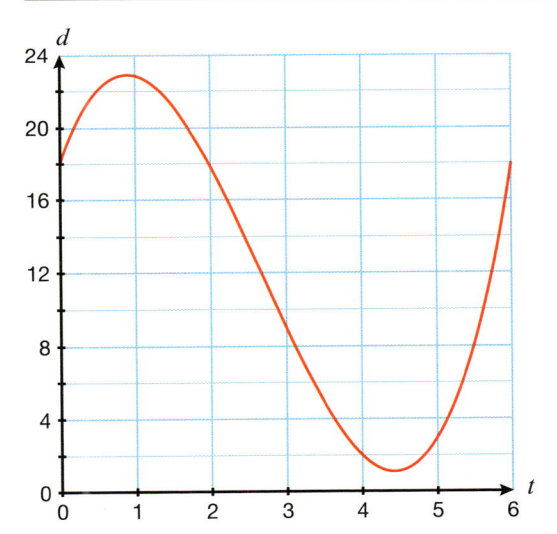

[Graph of d vs t, curve starting at 18, peaking near 23 at t=1, minimum near t=4.5, back up to 18]

(b) 23.1 m depth at 00:54

(c) $02:54 \leq t \leq 05:36$

2 (a) Substitute $t = 0$ into formula for T to find value of b, then substitute $t = 5$ into formula for T to find value of a.

(a) $a = -6, b = 10$

t	0	1	2	3	4	5
T	10	13	10	7	10	25

(b)

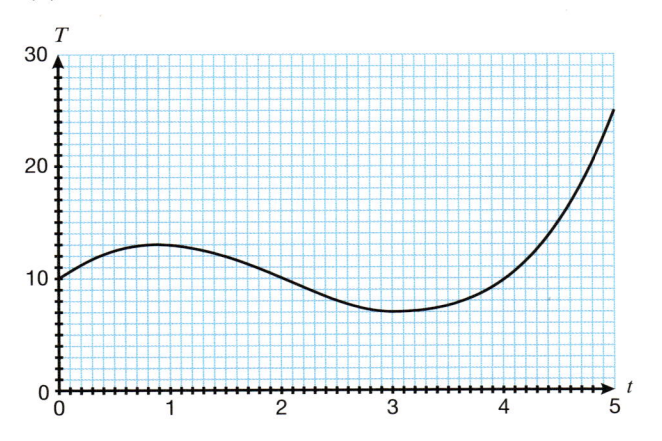

[Graph of T vs t]

(c) $T = 6.9°C$, $t = 10:12$

3 (a)

t	0	1	2	3	4	5	6
w	25	24	17	10	9	20	49

(b)

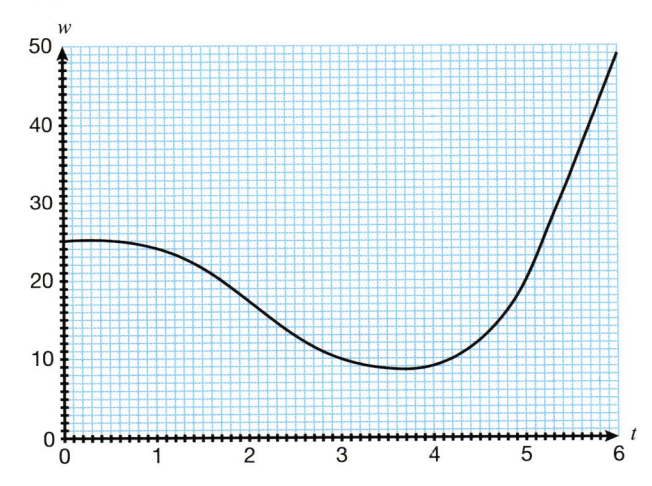

[Graph of w vs t]

(i) 12.6 mph
(ii) 01:40, 05:00

4 (a)

t	1	2	3	4	5	6
w	2000	1000	667	500	400	333

(b)

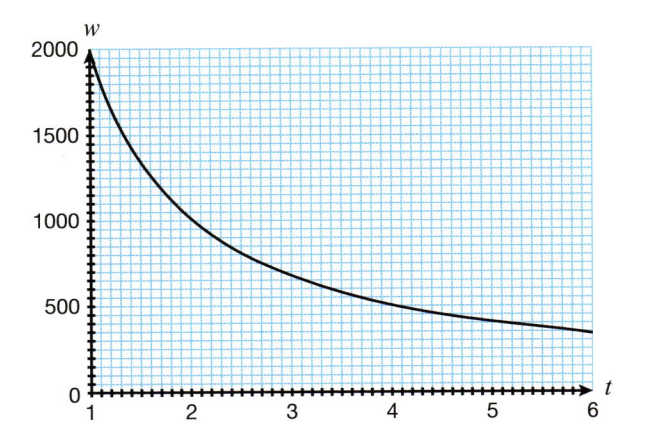

[Graph of w vs t, decreasing curve]

(i) 571 approx
(ii) 15 March approx

5   Substitute $t = 1$ and $t = 10$ into formula for V to form two simultaneous equations:
$25 = a + b$ [1]
$52 = 10a + \frac{b}{10}$ [2]
Solve these equations to find values of a and b.
(a) $a = 5, b = 20$

t	1	2	4	6	8	10
v	25	20	25	33.3	42.5	52

(b)

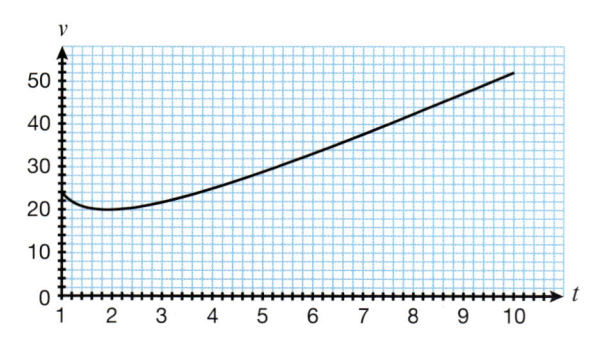

(c) (i) $v = 20$ m/s, $t = 2$. Time = 12:02
(ii) $t \geq 4$. Time for speed to be at least 25 m/s is: $12:04 \leq$ time $\leq 12:10$

SHAPE AND SPACE 7 – BASIC SKILLS EXERCISE

1 (a) $A = 9.72$ cm², $P = 14.3$ cm
   (b) $A = 49.1$ cm², $P = 28.6$ cm
   (c) $A = 13.1$ cm², $P = 28.2$ cm

2 $r = 4.67$ cm, $A = 34.2$ cm²

3 $x = 100°$, $P = 18$ cm

4 $A = 92.47$ cm²

5 18.5 cm²

6 $P = 153$ mm $A = 625$ mm²

7 $r = 6$ cm, $V = 144\pi$ or 452 cm³

8 4 : 5

9 (a) $A = 2369$ mm²
   (b) $V = 8247$ mm³

10 (a) $V = 320$ cm³
   (b) $A = 341$ cm²

11 (a) $x = 25.5°$
   (b) $V = 126$ cm³
   (c) $A = 190$ cm²

12 $V = 24$ cm³

13 (a) $P = 20$ cm
   (b) $A = 31.4$ cm²

14 $x = 4.5$ cm

15 $\frac{4a}{21}$ cm²

16 (a) $V = 2048$ cm³, (b) $A = 1875$ cm²

17 $n = 3$

18 (a) Diameter of Moon = 3480 km
   (b) surface area of Earth = 5.09×10^8 km²

SHAPE AND SPACE 7 – EXAM PRACTICE EXERCISE

1 Let r be the radius of the circle so $\pi r^2 = k\pi$ hence $r = \sqrt{k}$

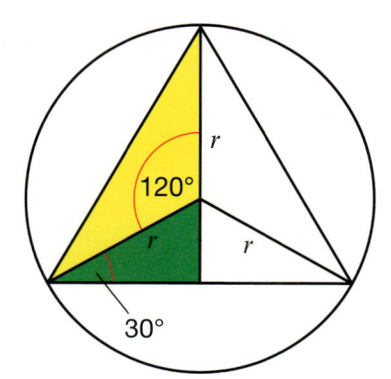

Area of red triangle is $\frac{1}{2} \times r \times r \times \sin 120°$
$= \frac{r^2}{2} \sin 60° = \frac{\sqrt{3}}{4} r^2$
Area of a triangle = $\frac{1}{2} ab\sin C$, $\sin 60° = \frac{\sqrt{3}}{2}$
The area of the equilateral triangle is $\frac{3\sqrt{3}}{4} r^2 = \frac{3\sqrt{3}}{4} k$

OR

The base of the green triangle is $r\cos 30° = \frac{r\sqrt{3}}{2}$
Height of the the green triangle is $r\sin 30° = \frac{r}{2}$
The area of the green triangle is
$\frac{1}{2} \times \frac{r\sqrt{3}}{2} \times \frac{r}{2} = \frac{\sqrt{3}}{8} r^2$

The area of the equilateral triangle is
$6 \times \frac{\sqrt{3}}{8} r^2 = \frac{3\sqrt{3}}{4} r^2 = \frac{3\sqrt{3}}{4} k$

Six green triangles make up the equilateral triangle.

There are other equally valid ways of calculating the area of the triangle.

The blue area is $k\pi - \frac{3\sqrt{3}}{4}k$

$= k\left(\pi - \frac{3\sqrt{3}}{4}\right)$ cm²

2 (a) Curved surface area of a cylinder
$= 2\pi rh$
Inside height is $d = 2r \Rightarrow$
Curved surface area $= 2\pi r \times 2r = 4\pi r^2$
Total inside surface area
$= \pi r^2 + 4\pi r^2 = 250$ Base is πr^2
$5\pi r^2 = 250$
$r = \sqrt{\frac{50}{\pi}} = 3.989...$ cm

Volume of a cylinder $= \pi r^2 h$
Volume $= \pi r^2 \times 2r = 2\pi r^3 = 400$ cm³ (2 s.f.)

(b) Area scale factor $= \frac{360}{250} = \frac{36}{25}$
Length scale factor $= \sqrt{\frac{36}{25}} = \frac{6}{5}$
Volume scale factor $= \left(\frac{6}{5}\right)^3 = \frac{216}{125}$
or 216 : 215

3 The maximum number of pieces is when the cube has maximum volume, the cylinder has minimum outside diameter and maximum inside diameter and the pieces have minimum length.
Therefore, the cube side length is 3.05 cm, the cylinder has outside diameter 4.95 mm and inside diameter 3.05 mm and piece length of 5.95 mm.
Working in mm
$30.5^3 = \frac{\pi}{4}(4.95^2 - 3.05^2) \times l$
$l = 2376.65...$
number of pieces = 2376.65.... ÷ 5.95 = 399.4...
Number of pieces must be an integer so number is 399.

4 (a) Flat end area is
$\pi(kr)^2 - \pi r^2 = \pi r^2 (k^2 - 1)$
$A = 2\pi r^2 (k^2 - 1)$
Remember there are two flat end faces.
Curved outer area is
$2\pi kr \times r = 2\pi krz^2$
Curved area = circumference × height

Curved inner area is
$2\pi r \times r = 2\pi r^2$
$B = 2\pi kr^2 + 2\pi r^2$
$= 2\pi r^2 (k + 1)$
$A : B = \frac{2\pi r^2(k^2 - 1)}{2\pi r^2(k + 1)}$
$= \frac{(k + 1)(k - 1)}{(k + 1)}$
$= k - 1$
$k^2 - 1 = (k + 1)(k - 1)$
'difference of two squares'

(b) Length scale factor = 2 so the area scale factor = 4.
Both areas will be 4 times larger so the ratio will not change.

5 (a) The cone that is removed is similar to the original cone.
The area scale factor is $= \frac{a}{4} \div a = \frac{1}{4}$
The length scale factor $= \sqrt{\frac{1}{4}} = \frac{1}{2}$
i.e. removed cone is half the height of the original cone.
Volume scale factor $= \left(\frac{1}{2}\right)^3 = \frac{1}{8}$
So the removed cone has a volume $= \frac{1}{8}V$
Therefore, the volume of truncated cone $= \frac{7}{8}V$ cm³

(b) The total surface area of the removed cone $= \frac{A}{4}$ Area scale factor is $\frac{1}{4}$
Curved surface area of removed cone
$= \frac{A}{4} - \frac{a}{4}$
Base area of removed cone $= \frac{a}{4}$
Surface area of truncated cone is surface area of original cone less curved surface of removed cone plus surface area of top of truncated cone.
Surface area of truncated cone
$A - \left(\frac{A}{4} - \frac{a}{4}\right) + \frac{a}{4} = A - \frac{A}{4} + \frac{a}{4} + \frac{a}{4}$
$= \frac{3A}{4} + \frac{a}{2}$

SETS 3 – BASIC SKILLS EXERCISE

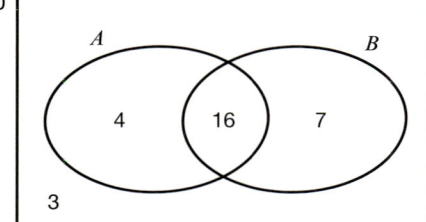

1 (a) $n(\mathcal{E}) = 30$

Venn diagram: A and B overlapping. A only: 4, intersection: 16, B only: 7, outside: 3.

(b) (i) $\frac{16}{30} = \frac{8}{15}$

(ii) $\frac{11}{30}$

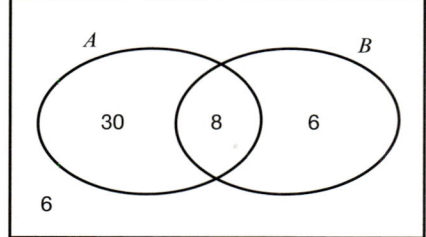

2 (a) $n(\mathcal{E}) = 50$

Venn diagram: A only: 30, intersection: 8, B only: 6, outside: 6.

(b) (i) $P(B) = \frac{14}{50} = 0.28$

(ii) $P(A \cup B) = \frac{44}{50} = 0.88$

(iii) $P(A \cap B) = \frac{8}{50} = 0.16$

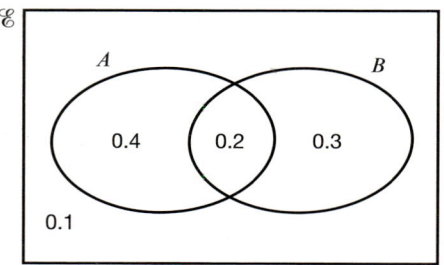

3 Venn diagram: A only: 0.4, intersection: 0.2, B only: 0.3, outside: 0.1.

(a) $P(A \cap B) = 0.2$
(b) $P(A \cup B') = 0.7$

4 (a) 45
(b) (i) 29
(ii) 11
(c) (i) $\frac{20}{45} = \frac{4}{9}$

(ii) $\frac{7}{45}$

(iii) $\frac{16}{45}$

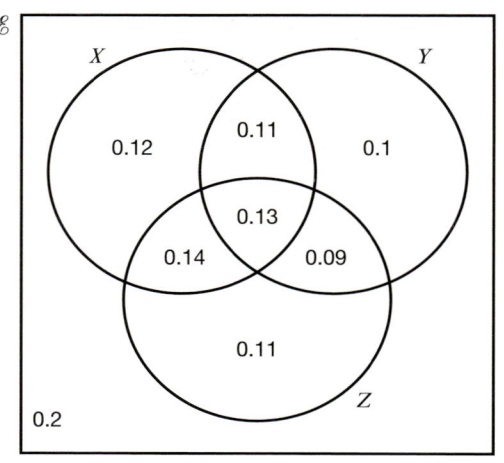

5 Venn diagram with three sets X, Y, Z: X only: 0.12, X∩Y only: 0.11, Y only: 0.1, X∩Z only: 0.14, X∩Y∩Z: 0.13, Y∩Z only: 0.09, Z only: 0.11, outside: 0.2.

(a) $P(X \cup Y) = 0.69$
(b) $P(Y \cap Z') = 0.21$
(c) $P(X \cap (Y \cup Z')) = 0.36$

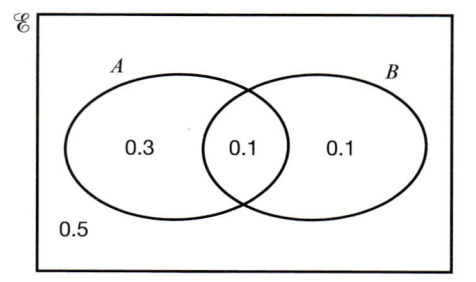

6 Venn diagram: A only: 0.3, intersection: 0.1, B only: 0.1, outside: 0.5.

(a) $P(B) = 0.2$
(b) $P(B|A) = \frac{0.1}{0.4} = \frac{1}{4} = 0.25$

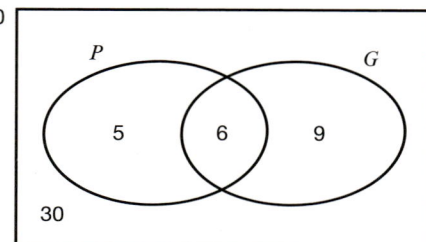

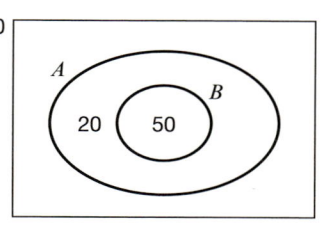

7 $n(\mathcal{E}) = 50$

Venn diagram: P only: 5, intersection: 6, G only: 9, outside: 30.

$\frac{6}{11}$

8 $n(\mathcal{E}) = 100$

Venn diagram: B inside A. A only: 20, B: 50, outside: 30.

(a) $P(A|B) = \frac{50}{50} = 1$

(b) $P(B|A) = \frac{50}{70} = \frac{5}{7}$

9 (a) $n(\mathcal{E}) = 100$

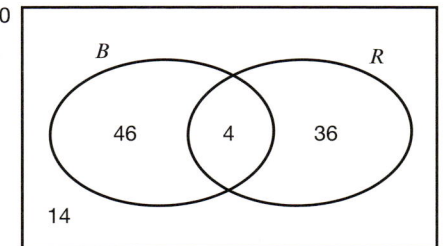

[Venn diagram with sets B and R: B only = 46, B∩R = 4, R only = 36, outside = 14]

(b) $P((B \cup R)') = \frac{14}{100} = 0.14$

(c) $P(R|B) = \frac{4}{50} = 0.08$

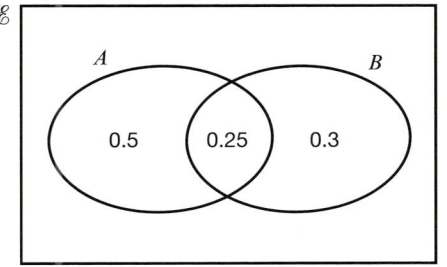

10 [Venn diagram with sets A and B: A only = 0.5, A∩B = 0.25, B only = 0.3]

(a) $P(B) = 0.55$

(b) $P(A'|B) = \frac{0.3}{0.55} = \frac{6}{11}$

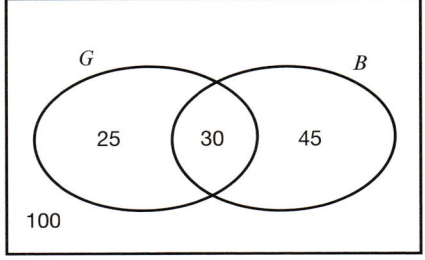

11 $n(\mathcal{E}) = 200$

[Venn diagram with sets G and B: G only = 25, G∩B = 30, B only = 45, outside = 100]

(a) $(2x + 1) + (3x - 6) + (4x - 3) + 100 = 200$
    $x = 12$

(b) $P(B) = \frac{75}{200} = \frac{3}{8} = 0.375$

(c) $P(B|G) = \frac{30}{55} = \frac{6}{11}$

(d) $P(G|B) = \frac{30}{75} = \frac{2}{5} = 0.4$

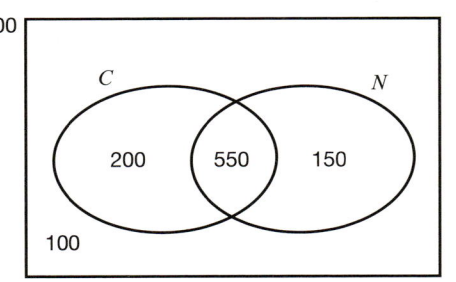

12 $n(\mathcal{E}) = 1000$

[Venn diagram with sets C and N: C only = 200, C∩N = 550, N only = 150, outside = 100]

(a) $\frac{370}{1000} = \frac{37}{100}$

(b) $\frac{370}{570} = \frac{37}{57}$

(c) $\frac{200}{530} = \frac{20}{53}$

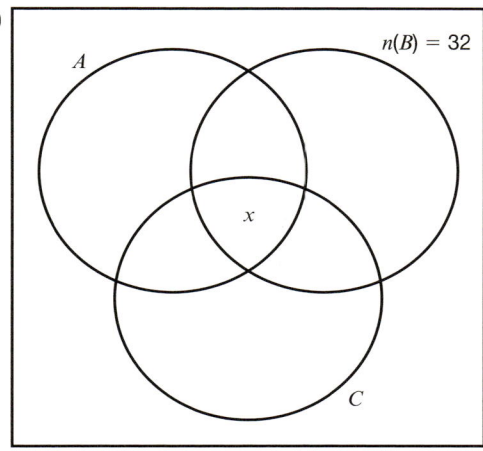

13 $n(\mathcal{E}) = 100$, $n(B) = 32$

[Three-set Venn diagram with sets A, B, C and x in A∩B∩C]

$P((A \cap C)|B) = \frac{1}{8} = \frac{x}{32}$ so $x = 4$

$P(A \cap B \cap C) = \frac{4}{100} = \frac{1}{25} = 0.04$

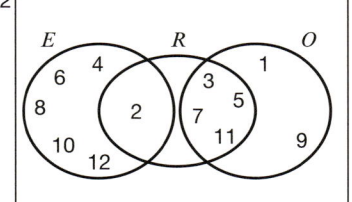

14 (a) $n(\mathcal{E}) = 12$

[Venn diagram with sets E, R, O: E only contains 6, 8, 10; E∩R contains 4, 2; R only contains 3, 7; R∩O contains 5, 11; O only contains 1, 9; outside contains 12]

(b) (i) $P(R \cap E) = \frac{1}{12}$

(ii) $P(R \cap E \cap O) = 0$

(iii) $P((R \cup E)') = \frac{2}{12} = \frac{1}{6}$

(c) $P(R|O) = \frac{4}{6} = \frac{2}{3}$

15 (a) Let $x = n(B \cap S \cap F)$

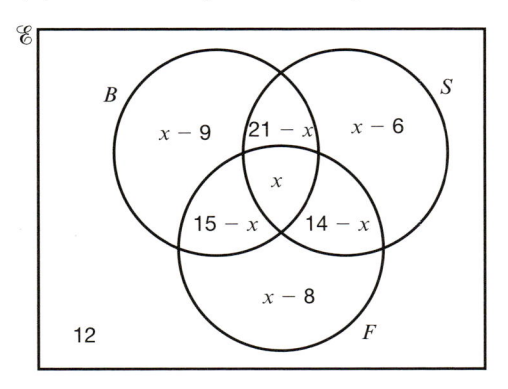

[Three-set Venn diagram with sets B, S, F: regions labelled x−9, 21−x, x−6, 15−x, x, 14−x, x−8, outside = 12]

Summing, putting expression = 48 and solving gives $x = 9$

(b)

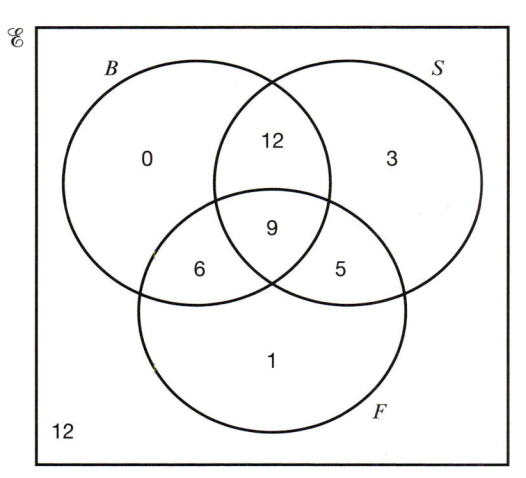

[Venn diagram with universal set ℰ, sets B, S, F. Values: B only 0, B∩S only 12, S only 3, B∩F only 6, B∩S∩F 9, S∩F only 5, F only 1, outside 12]

(i) $\frac{9}{48} = \frac{3}{16}$

(ii) $\frac{23}{48}$

(c) $\frac{27}{36} = \frac{3}{4}$

SETS 3 – EXAM PRACTICE EXERCISE

1 (a) $2x(x + 1) + 10x + x^2 + 6x + 160 = 1000$
    Number of spectators sums to 1000
    $3x^2 + 18x - 840 = 0$
    $x^2 + 6x - 240 = 0$
    $(x + 20)(x - 14) = 0$
    $x = 14$ or use quadratic formula
    $x = -20$ is not possible

Venn diagram becomes (numbers represent number of spectators)

[Venn diagram: n(ℰ) = 1000, H and S overlap, H only 420, H∩S 140, S only 280, outside 160]

(b) (i) $\frac{420 + 140 + 280}{1000} = \frac{840}{1000} = 0.84$

or $\frac{1000 - 160}{1000} = \frac{840}{1000} = 0.84$

(ii) $\frac{420 + 280}{1000} = \frac{700}{1000} = 0.7$

(c) $\frac{140}{140 + 280} = \frac{140}{420} = \frac{1}{3}$

2 (a)

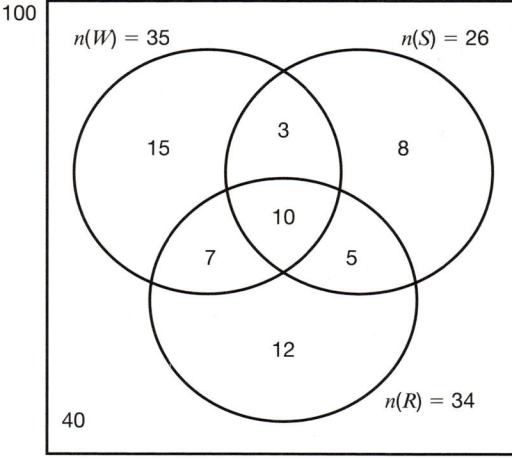

[Venn diagram: n(ℰ) = 100, n(W) = 35, n(S) = 26, n(R) = 34. W only 15, W∩S only 3, S only 8, W∩R only 7, W∩S∩R 10, S∩R only 5, R only 12, outside 40]

(b) (i) $\frac{34}{100} = \frac{17}{50} = 0.34$

(ii) $\frac{12}{100} = \frac{3}{25} = 0.12$

(iii) $\frac{7}{100} = 0.07$

(c) $P(S|R) = \frac{15}{34}$

3 (a) $P(A|B) = 0.2$
    $\frac{x + 3 + y}{70} = 0.2$
    $P(C|A) = 0.32$
    $\frac{2x + y}{50} = 0.32$

Simplifying gives:
$x + y = 11$
$2x + y = 16$
Solving simultaneously gives
$x = 5$ and $y = 6$
The Venn diagram can now be filled in.

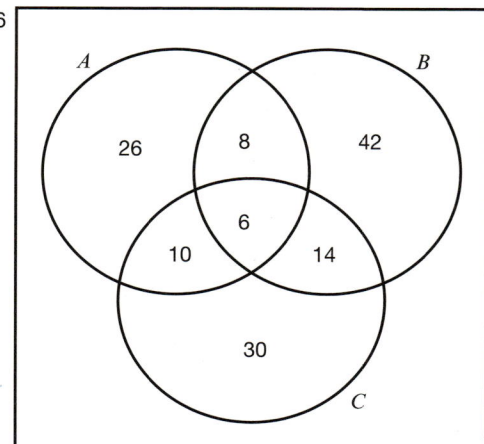

[Venn diagram: n(ℰ) = 136, sets A, B, C. A only 26, A∩B only 8, B only 42, A∩C only 10, A∩B∩C 6, B∩C only 14, C only 30]

Total number of elements = 136

(b) $P(A \cap C) = \frac{16}{136} = \frac{2}{17}$

(c) $P(B|C) = \frac{20}{60} = \frac{1}{3}$

4 (a) $P((M \cap E)|S) = \frac{4}{21}$
$\frac{x}{42} = \frac{4}{21}$
$x = 8$
$P((E \cap S)|E) = \frac{3}{8}$
$\frac{y+8}{64} = \frac{3}{8}$
$y = 16$
$n(E \cap M) = 40$
$z + 8 = 40$
$z = 32$
$n(M \cap S) = 10$
$w + 8 = 10$
$w = 2$
$n(E) = 64$
$p = 8$
$n(S) = 42$
$q = 16$
$n(M) = 60$
$r = 18$

(b) (i) $\frac{18}{60} = \frac{3}{10} = 0.3$

(ii) $\frac{w+x+y+z}{100} = \frac{16+8+32+2}{100}$
$= \frac{58}{100} = \frac{29}{50} = 0.58$

(c) $\frac{y+z}{64} = \frac{48}{64} = \frac{3}{4} = 0.75$

5 (a) $n(D) = 0.1 \times 200 = 20$
$n(ND) = 200 - 20 = 180$ or 0.9×200
$\frac{x}{20} = 0.9 \Rightarrow x = 18$ $\frac{y}{180} = 0.95 =$
$h \Rightarrow y = 171$

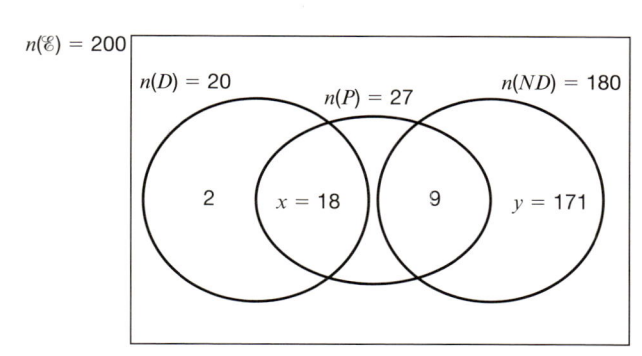

(b) $\frac{9}{9+18} = \frac{1}{3}$

(c) $\frac{2}{2+171} = \frac{2}{173}$

NUMBER 8 – BASIC SKILLS EXERCISE

1 (a) 5×10^5 cm
 (b) 8×10^{-5} km
 (c) 200 km
 (d) 0.6 mm

2 9×10^{-6} km

3 2×10^5 micrometres

4 Number of thicknesses of paper = 2^{50}
height = $2^{50} \times 0.004 \times 25.4 \times 10^{-6}$
= 1.14×10^8 km

5 (a) 5×10^2 m²
 (b) 4×10^7 cm²
 (c) 4×10^6
 (d) 2 km²

6 1.96×10^{-4} km²

7 1.75×10^{25} cm²

8 5.40×10^{-13} km²

9 (a) 2×10^9 ml
 (b) 4×10^9 m³
 (c) 80 m³
 (d) 7×10^9 mm³

10 (a) 980 ml
 (b) 0.98 litres
 (c) 9.8×10^{-13} km³

11 Volume of rain drop = $\frac{4}{3} \times \pi \times 0.75^3$ mm³,
volume of reservoir = $1.24 \times 10^8 \times 10^9$ mm³.
The number of raindrops
= $(1.24 \times 10^8 \times 10^9)$
$\div \left(\frac{4}{3} \times \pi \times 0.75^3\right) = 7.02 \times 10^{16}$

12 1 litre of a chemical contains $3 \times 10^{22} \times 10^3 = 3 \times 10^{25}$ molecules.
Volume of ocean is $1.15 \times 10^{10} \times 10^9$ m³ = $1.5 \times 10^9 \times 10^9 \times 10^3$ litres = 1.5×10^{21} litres
Number of molecules per litre is
$(3 \times 10^{25}) \div (1.5 \times 10^{21}) = 2 \times 10^4$ or 20 000

13 1230 km/h

14 133 mm

15 0904

16 4.5×10^{-3} seconds

17 2.92 mm

18 Time taken is 19 h 19 mins,
average speed = 880 km/h = 244 m/s

19 50 m³

20 £361.18

21 1.87 g/cm³

22 4.45 g/cm³

23 Density of A is 0.911 (floats), of B is 1.1 (sinks), of C is 0.802 (floats)

24 $\frac{a + 0.001b}{2}$

25 3×10^{-4} N

26 20 400 N/m²

27 1 000 000 cm²

28 4500 cm³

29 102 N

30 1.76×10^5 N/m²

31 Cylinder volume = $\pi \times 6^2 \times 10$
= 360π cm³
Dimensions changed to cm.
12 tonnes/m³ = $\frac{12 \times 1000}{10^6}$
= 1.2×10^{-2} kg/cm³
Mass of cylinder = $360\pi \times 1.2 \times 10^{-2}$
= $\frac{108}{25} \pi$ kg.
This exerts a force of $10 \times \frac{108}{25} \pi = \frac{216}{5} \pi$
N on the table.

Area in contact with the table = $\pi \times 6^2$
= 36π cm²
The pressure is $\frac{216}{5} \pi \div 36\pi = \frac{6}{5}$ N/cm²
or 1.2 N/cm²

NUMBER 8 – EXAM PRACTICE EXERCISE

1 (a) mass = density × volume
3 cm³ of gold has a mass of 3×19.3
= 57.9 g
1 cm³ of silver has a mass of 10.5 g.
4 cm³ of the alloy has a mass of
57.9 + 10.5 = 68.4 g
density of alloy is $\frac{68.4}{4}$ = 17.1 g/cm³

(b) x cm³ of gold has a mass of $x \times 19.3$ g
1 cm³ of silver has a mass of 10.5 g
$1 + x$ cm³ of the alloy has a mass of
$19.3x + 10.5$ g
density of alloy is $\frac{19.3x + 10.5}{1 + x}$
= 18.1 g/cm³
solving for x gives
$19.3x + 10.5 = 18.1(1 + x)$
$19.3x + 10.5 = 18.1 + 18.1x$
$1.2x = 7.6$
$x = \frac{19}{3}$

2 (a) The candle uses $\frac{1}{15} \times 60 = 4$ g of wax every hour
The wax has a density of $900 \times \frac{1000}{10^9}$
= 9×10^{-4} g/mm³
4 g of wax has a volume of $\frac{4}{9 \times 10^{-4}}$
= 4444.4... mm³
Let the distance between marks be x mm
Volume of cylinder is $\pi r^2 h$ and $r = 10$ mm
$\Rightarrow x \times \pi \times 10^2 = 4444.4.. \Rightarrow x = 14.147...$
or 14.1 mm to 3 s.f.

(b) Volume of cone = $\frac{1}{3} \pi r^2 h$, top half has
$r = 20$ mm and $h = 100$ mm
OR work out volume of whole cone,
top half has $\left(\frac{1}{2}\right)^3 = \frac{1}{8}$ of volume by similarity
Volume of top half of cone
= $\frac{1}{3} \times \pi \times 20^2 \times 100 = \frac{40\,000\pi}{3}$ mm³

Weight of top half of cone
$= \frac{40\,000\pi}{3} \times 9 \times 10^{-4} = 12\pi$ g

Time taken $12\pi \div 4 = 3\pi$ hours
Uses 4 g of wax every hour (see part a)

3 (a) The diagram shows the lorry just as the front passes under the bridge and just when the back leaves the bridge.

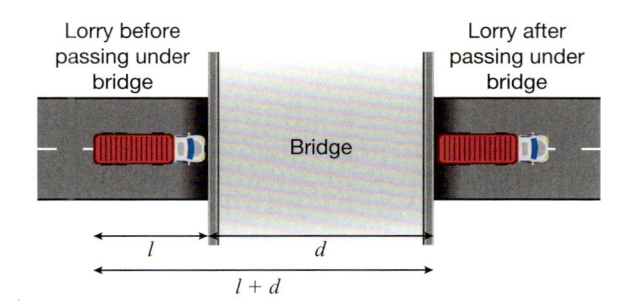

Lorry before passing under bridge

Bridge

Lorry after passing under bridge

l d
$l + d$

The back of the lorry travels a distance $l + d$ metres in a time of t seconds
OR the front of the lorry travels a distance $l + d$ metres in a time of t seconds
$\Rightarrow t = \frac{l+d}{\text{speed}}$

Speed must be in consistent units, i.e. m/s
v km/h $= 1000v$ m/h $= \frac{1000v}{3600} = \frac{5v}{18}$ m/s
$t = \frac{18(l+d)}{5v}$

(b) $t = \frac{18(l+d)}{5v}$
$vt = \frac{18(l+d)}{5}$
$v = \frac{18(l+d)}{5t}$

Substituting values gives
$v = \frac{18(16.5 + 60)}{5 \times 2.7}$
$v = 102$ km/h
Units in the expression are lengths in metres, time in seconds and speed in km/h
102 km/h $= \frac{102}{1.6} = 63.75$ mph,
so it is breaking the speed limit

4 (a) Area of hose $= \pi \times 6^2$ mm²
16 m/s = 16 000 mm
volume of water that comes out of hose in one second
$= \pi \times 6^2 \times 16\,000$ mm³
$= (\pi \times 6^2 \times 16\,000) \div 1000$ cm³
$= 576\pi$ cm³
1000 cm³ = 1 litre so 576π cm³
$= 0.576\pi$ litres/s
Time taken to fill pond $= \frac{20\,000}{0.576\pi}$ seconds
$= \frac{20\,000}{0.576 \times \pi \times 60}$ minutes
$= 184.207\ldots$ minutes $= 3$ hours 4 minutes (and 12.4 seconds)

(b) Area of the hose $= \pi \times \frac{d^2}{4}$ mm²
16 m/s = 16 000 mm/s
Volume of water that comes out of the hose every second is $= \pi \times \frac{d^2}{4} \times 16\,000$
$= 4000\pi d^2$ mm³ $= 4000\pi d^2 \div 1000$ cm³
$= 4\pi d^2$ cm³ $= 4\pi d^2 \div 1000$ litres
$= 0.004\pi d^2$ litres
2 hours is $2 \times 60 \times 60$ seconds
$= 7200$ seconds
$7200 = 15\,000 \div 0.004\pi d^2 \Rightarrow d^2$
$= \frac{15\,000}{7200 \times 0.004\pi} = 165.78\ldots$
$d = 12.9$ (3 s.f.)

5 Volume of A $= \pi \times r^2 \times h$ cm³ so the mass of A $= \pi r^2 hd$ kg
Force A exerts on table $= 10\pi r^2 hd$ N
Each kg exerts a force of 10N
Area of A in contact with table $= \pi r^2$ cm²
pressure exerted by A on table =
$\frac{10\pi r^2 hd}{\pi r^2} = 10hd$ N/cm²

Volume of B $= \pi \times R^2 \times h$ cm³ so the mass of A $= \pi R^2 hd$ kg
Force B exerts on table $= 10\pi R^2 hd$ N
Each kg exerts a force of 10N
Area of B in contact with table $= \pi R^2$ cm²
The pressure exerted by B on table =
$\frac{10\pi R^2 hd}{\pi R^2} = 10hd$ N/cm²

The pressure exerted by each cylinder is the same and equal to $10hd$ N/cm²

ALGEBRA 8 – BASIC SKILLS EXERCISE

1. **(a)** Function as any vertical line only cuts the graph once
   (b) Not a function as a vertical line can cut the graph more than once
   (c) Not a function as there is no value when $x = 0$
   (d) Not a function as a vertical line can cut the graph more than once

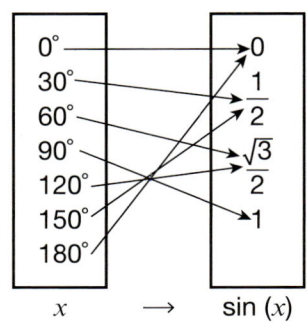

2. **(a)**

x	$\rightarrow$	$\sin(x)$
0°	→	0
30°	→	$\frac{1}{2}$
60°	→	$\frac{\sqrt{3}}{2}$
90°	→	1
120°		
150°		
180°		

   (b) It is a function as it is a many-to-one mapping.

3. $f : x \rightarrow 4x^2 + 12x + 9$

4. **(a)** 1
   (b) 11
   (c) 7
   (d) $7 - 2y^2$

5. **(a)** **(i)** 1.5
       (ii) 2.5
   (b) 0 as $1 \div 0$ is undefined

6. **(a)** 2
   (b) 0

7. **(a)** 2, 3
   (b) $-1, 6$

8. **(a)** $2x + 2$
   (b) $2x + 1$

9. **(a)** $8 + 6x$
   (b) $4 + 6x$

10. $f(x) = x^2 + 6x$

11. $f(x) = 4x^2$

12. -5

13. 1 or $-\frac{2}{3}$

14. $a = -2, b = 4$

15. $f(a) = a^2 + b, f(b) = ab + b$
    $f(a) = f(b)$
    $a^2 + b = ab + b$
    $a^2 - ab = 0$
    $a(a - b) = 0$
    $a = 0$ or $a = b$

16. **(a)** $x = \frac{1}{2}$
    (b) $x = 0$
    (c) $x < -3$
    (d) $x \geq 3$

17. **(a)** $-3 < x < 3$
    (b) None
    (c) $x = 180n$, n is an integer
    (d) $x = 90 + 180n$, n is an integer

18. **(a)** All real numbers
    (b) $g(x) \geq -1$
    (c) $h(x) \geq 0$

19. **(a)** range $= \{-1, 0, 3\}$
    (b) Range is all real numbers ≥ 0
    (c) Range is all real numbers ≥ -4

20. **(a)** 12
    (b) 3
    (c) 16
    (d) -1

21. $x = \frac{3}{4}$

22. $k = 1$ or $k = -\frac{1}{3}$

23. $-\frac{1}{2}$

24. $k = 2$ or $k = -1$

25. $2 - 3x^2$

26. **(a)** $2 - \frac{x}{7}$
    (b) $x^2 - 5$
    (c) $\frac{4}{x + 2}$

27. $f : x \rightarrow \frac{x + 2}{1 - x}$

28. 7

29. $f(x) = x$

30. **(a)** $f^{-1}(x) = \frac{x}{x - 1}$
    (b) Self inverse

31 $f(x) = \frac{x+3}{4}$

32 $f(x) = \frac{1}{1-x}$

33 (a) (i) x
(ii) x
(b) Inverse of each other
(c) π

34 (a) (i) $\sqrt{(3x+3)}$
(ii) $3\sqrt{(x+1)} + 2$ or $3\sqrt{x+5}$
(b) (i) $x < -1$
(ii) $x < 0$

35 $g(x) = \frac{5x+4}{3}$ $g(x)$ is the inverse of $f(x)$

36 (a) (i) $1 + 3x$
(ii) $5 + 3x$
(b) $(fg)^{-1}(x) = g^{-1}f^{-1}(x) = \frac{x-1}{3}$ because
$g^{-1}(x) = \frac{x+1}{3}$ and $f^{-1}(x) = x - 2$

37 $a = -2, b = 4$

38 $a = \frac{1}{10}$

39 $g(x) = 3x + 1$ $g(x) = [(6x - 5) + 7] \div 2$

40 (a) Range is $\{y : y \geq 0\}$

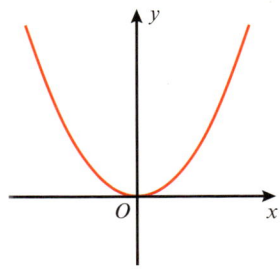

(b) $y = \sqrt{x}$, Restriction on domain $x \geq 0$

41 (a) Range is $\{y : y \geq -2\}$

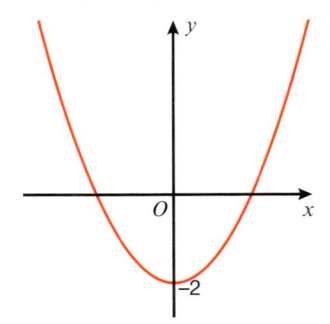

(b) $y = \sqrt{x+2}$, Restriction on domain $x \geq -2$

42 (a) $f(x) = (x+1)^2 - 1$
(b) $\{y : y \geq -1\}$

(c) $y = (x+1)^2 - 1 \Rightarrow (x+1)^2$
$= y + 1 \Rightarrow x = \sqrt{y+1} - 1 \Rightarrow f^{-1}(x)$
$= \sqrt{x+1} - 1$

Restriction on domain $x \geq -1$

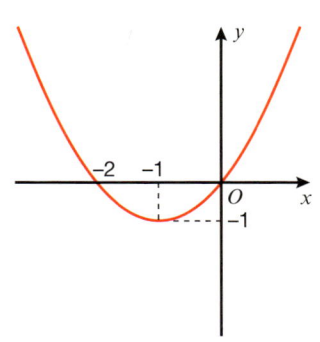

43 (a) $f(x) = (x-1)^2 - 1 + 4 = (x-1)^2 + 3$
(b) Function is a positive quadratic, minimum value at $(1, 3)$
Cuts the y axis at $(0, 4)$
Range is $\{y : y \geq 3\}$
(c) $y = (x-1)^2 + 3 \Rightarrow y - 3 = (x-1)^2$
$\Rightarrow x - 1 = \sqrt{y-3} \Rightarrow x = \sqrt{y-3} + 1$
$\Rightarrow f^{-1}(x) = \sqrt{x-3} + 1$
Restriction on domain $x \geq 3$

44 (a) $f(x) = 2[x^2 - 2x + 3]$
$= 2[(x-1)^2 + 2] = 2(x-1)^2 + 4$
(b) $\{y : y \geq 4\}$

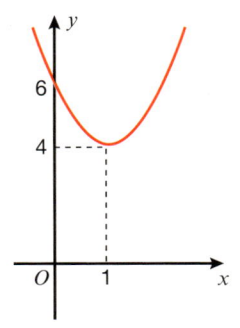

(c) $y = 2(x-1)^2 + 4 \Rightarrow \frac{y-4}{2} = (x-1)^2$
$\Rightarrow x = \sqrt{\frac{y-4}{2}} + 1$
$\Rightarrow f^{-1}(x) = \sqrt{\frac{x-4}{2}} + 1$
Restriction on domain $x \geq -4$

ALGEBRA 8 – EXAM PRACTICE EXERCISE

1. (a) (i) $y = 7 - x$
     $x = 7 - y$
     $f^{-1}(x) = 7 - x$
   (ii) $g(x)$ and $g^{-1}(x)$ are self inverse
   (b) $(x - 1)^2 < 7 - x$
     $x^2 - x - 6 < 0$
     $(x - 3)(x + 2) < 0$
     $-2 < x < 3$
     A sketch of $y = (x + 2)(x - 3)$ is a positive quadratic passing through $(-2, 0)$ and $(3, 0)$ showing $x < 0$ for $-2 < x < 3$

2. (a) $fg(x) = f(2x + 1)$
     $= (2x + 1 - 1)^2$
     $= 4x^2$
     $gf(x) = g[(x - 1)^2]$
     $= 2(x - 1)^2 + 1$
     $= 2(x^2 - 2x + 1) + 1$
     $= 2x^2 - 4x + 3$
     $2fg(x) = gf(x)$
     $8x^2 = 2x^2 - 4x + 3$
     $6x^2 + 4x - 3 = 0$
   (b) $2fg(k) = gf(k)$
     $6k^2 + 4k - 3 = 0$
     Solving for k using the quadratic formula
     $k = \dfrac{-4 \pm \sqrt{4^2 - 4 \times 6 \times -3}}{2 \times 6}$
     $= \dfrac{-4 \pm \sqrt{88}}{12}$
     $= \dfrac{-4 \pm \sqrt{4 \times 22}}{12}$
     $= \dfrac{-4 \pm 2\sqrt{22}}{12}$
     $= \dfrac{-2 \pm \sqrt{22}}{6}$
     So $p = -2$, $q = 22$ and $r = 6$

3. $f(3) = 5$
   $5 = 3a + b$ Equation 1
   $g(4) = f(2)$ so $g(4) = 2a + b$
   $g^{-1}(x) = 3x - 5$
   $y = 3x - 5$
   $3x = y + 5$
   $x = \dfrac{y + 5}{3}$
   $g(x) = \dfrac{x + 5}{3}$
   $g(4) = 3$
   $3 = 2a + b$ Equation 2

   Solving Equation 1 and Equation 2 simultaneously
   $5 = 3a + b$ (1)
   $3 = 2a + b$ (2)
   $2 = a$ Subtracting (2) from (1)
   $b = -1$ Subtracting $a = 2$ into either (1) or (2)
   $f(x) = 2x - 1$
   $7 = 2x - 1$
   $x = 4$
   $f^{-1}(7) = 4$
   Or
   $f^{-1}(x) = \dfrac{x + 1}{2}$
   $f^{-1}(7) = 4$

4. Answers will differ as read from a graph.
   (a) (i) $fg(2) = 3.8$
     (ii) $gf(4) = 6.2$
     (iii) $gf^{-1}(3) = 0.57$
   (b) $k > 0.4$
   (c) -0.6 or 2.5

5. (a) Let $f(x)$ be the radius and x the area.
     $f(x)$ is the output of a function, x the input
     $\pi[f(x)]^2 = x$ $\pi r^2 = A$
     $[f(x)]^2 = \dfrac{x}{\pi}$
     $f(x) = \sqrt{\dfrac{x}{\pi}}$
   (b) Let $g(x)$ be the circumference and x the radius
     $f(x)$ is the output of a function, x the input
     $g(x) = 2\pi x$ $C = 2\pi r$
   (c) $gf(x) = g[f(x)] = g\left[\sqrt{\dfrac{x}{\pi}}\right] = 2\pi\sqrt{\dfrac{x}{\pi}}$
     $= 2\sqrt{\dfrac{\pi^2 x}{\pi}} = 2\sqrt{\pi x}$
     $gf(x)$ gives the circumference of a circle when the area is the input
   (d) $a = 2\sqrt{\pi a}$
     $a^2 = 4\pi a$
     $a^2 - 4\pi a = 0$
     $a(a - 4\pi) = 0$
     $a = 0$ or $a = 4\pi$
     $a = 0$ is not a real-world solution, so
     $a = 4\pi$
     4π is the only value where the area and circumference are numerically the same

GRAPHS 7 – BASIC SKILLS EXERCISE

1 **(a)**

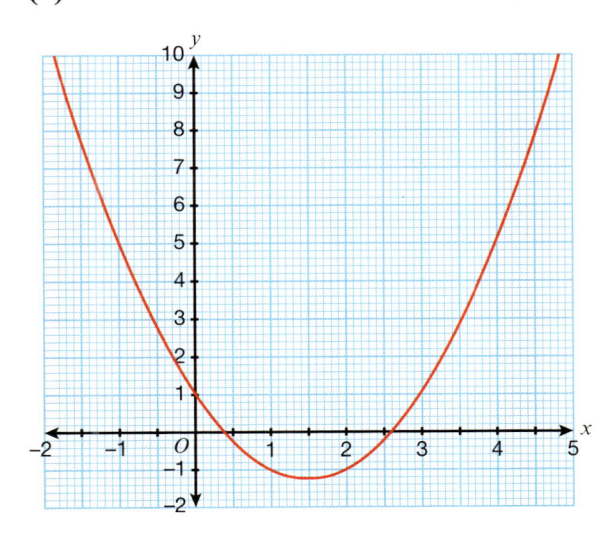

(b) (i) −0.79, 3.8, $y = 4$
(ii) −0.24, 4.2, $y = x + 2$
(iii) −1.3, 2.3, $y = 4 - 2x$

2 (a) $y = 2$
(b) $y = 1$
(c) $y = x$
(d) $y = 4 - x$

3 (a) $5x^2 - 3x + 17 = 0$
(b) $4x^2 - 4x - 7 = 0$
(c) $x^2 - 7x + 3 = 0$
(d) $3x^2 - 3x + 5 = 0$

4 (a) No solutions if $x^2 - 4x + 3 < -1$
$\Rightarrow x^2 - 4x < -4 \Rightarrow k < -4$
(b) $x^2 - 3x = p$
$x^2 - 4x + 3 = 3 + p - x$
There is one solution if $y = -x + 3 + p$ is a tangent to the curve.
$y = -x + 3 + p$ is a straight line with gradient −1 and intercept $3 + p$.
Using a ruler, the intercept is approximately 0.75 so $p = -2.25$

5 (a) (i) −1.7, 0, 1.7, $y = -x$
(ii) −1.325, $y = x + 1$
(iii) −1.8, −0.45, 1.2, $y = x^2 - 1$
(b) $k < -1.1$ or $k > 1.1$

6 (a) (i) −1, 1, $y = 2x$
(ii) −3.4, −0.59, $y = \frac{x}{2} - 2$
(iii) −2.7, 0.27, 1.4, $y = 4 - x^2$
(b) $-2 < k < 2$

7 (a) $-0.6 < k < 2.1$
(b) $3x^3 - 15x^2 + 19x - 3 = 0$
$3x^3 - 15x^2 + 18x = 3 - x$
$x^3 - 5x^2 + 6x = 1 - \frac{x}{3}$, find intersections
with $y = 1 - \frac{x}{3}$, $x = 0.2, 1.8, 3$

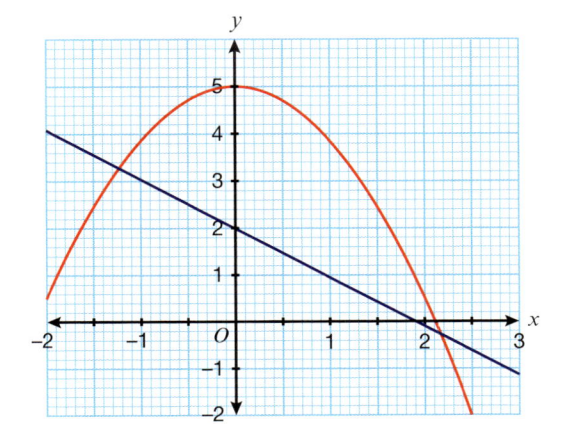

8 (−1.3, 3.3), (2.3, −0.3)

9 (−1.5, 0.9), (−0.3, −2.5), (1.9, −1.3)

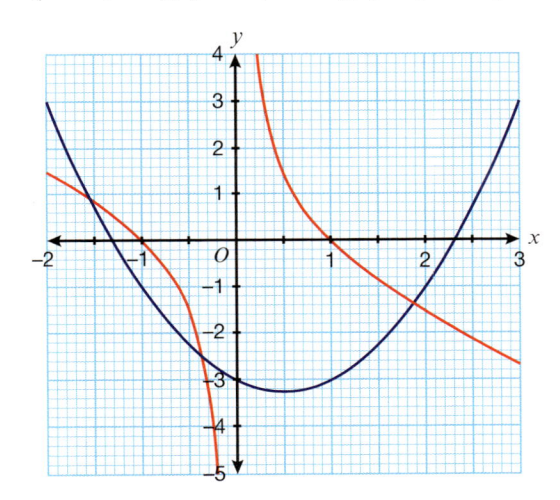

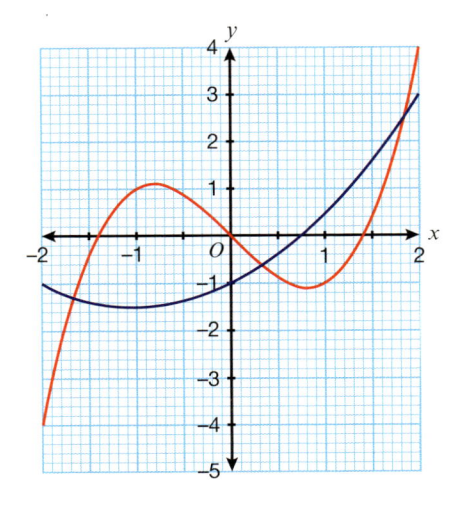

10 (−1.7, −1.3), (0.3, −0.6), (1.8, 2.5)

GRAPHS 7 – EXAM PRACTICE EXERCISE

1 (a)

x	−2	−1	0	1	2	3	4
y	6	1	−2	−3	−2	1	6

(b)

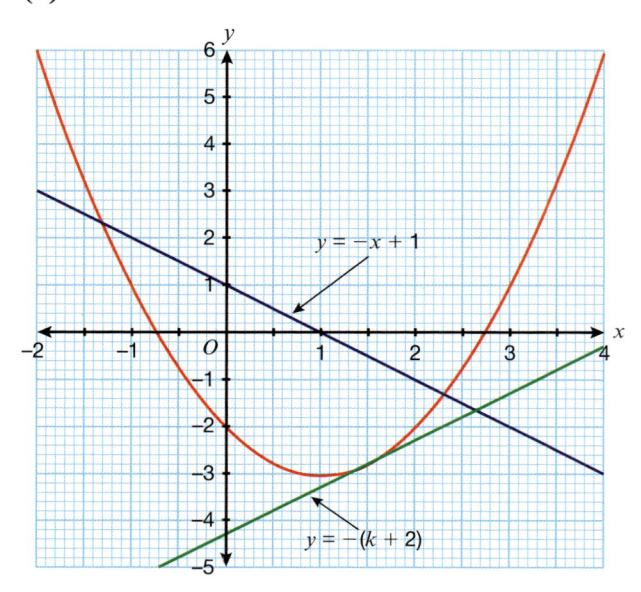

(c) $x^2 - x = 3$
$x^2 - 2x + x - 2 + 2 = 3$
$x^2 - 2x - 2 = -x + 1$
The line to plot is $y = -x + 1$
Solutions are $x = -1.3$ or 2.3
x values of the intersection points are the solutions

(d) $x^2 - 3x + k = 0$
$x^2 - 2x - x + k - 2 + 2 = 0$
$x^2 - 2x - 2 = x - k - 2$
$x^2 - 2x - 2 = x - (k + 2)$
The line to plot is $y = x - (k + 2)$
This is a straight line with gradient 1 and y intercept of $-(k + 2)$
This line must be a tangent to the graph of $y = x^2 - 2x - 2$
Place a ruler on the graph at a gradient of 1, move it until it is a tangent to the curve
The intercept is $-4.25 = -(k + 2)$
so $k = 2.25$
$2 \leq k \leq 2.5$ is acceptable providing a tangent is drawn on the graph

2 (a) Draw two horizontal lines on the graph as shown, one touching the maximum point, the other the minimum point. Any horizontal line drawn between these two lines will intersect the graph at 3 points giving three solutions.

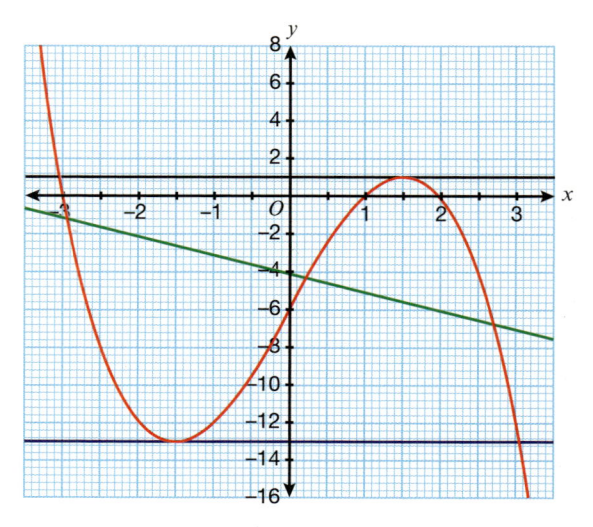

$x^3 - 7x = h$
$-x^3 + 7x = -h$
$-x^3 + 7x - 6 = -h - 6$
$-x^3 + 7x - 6 = -h - 6$ has three solutions if $-13.13 < -h - 6 < 1.13$
$-13.13 < -h - 6 < 1.13$
$\Rightarrow -1.13 < h + 6 < 13.13$
$\Rightarrow -7.13 < h < 6.13$
Values within 0.3 are acceptable

(b) $x^3 - 8x + 2 = 0$
$-x^3 + 8x - 2 = 0$
$-x^3 + 7x + x - 6 + 4 = 0$
$-x^3 + 7x - 6 = -x - 4$
Solutions are the x values of the intersections of $y = -x^3 + 7x - 6$ and $y = -x - 4$
$x = -2.9$ or $x = 0.3$ or $x = 2.7$

3 (a) The x values of the intersection of the two graphs are given by

$x^3 - 3x + \frac{1}{x} = \frac{x}{2} - 1$

$x^4 - 3x^2 + 1 = \frac{x^2}{2} - x$

Multiplying both sides by x
$2x^4 - 6x^2 + 2 = x^2 - 2x$
Multiplying both sides by 2
$2x^4 - 7x^2 + 2x + 2 = 0$

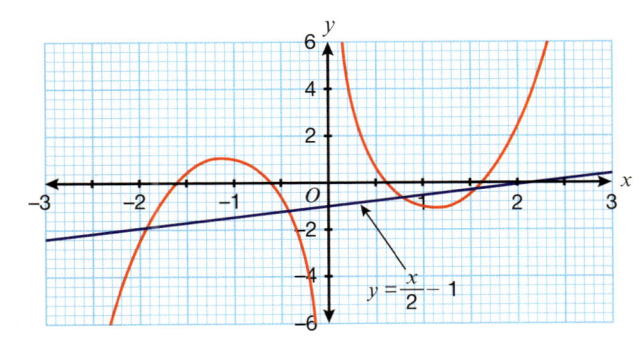

(b) Adding the line $y = \frac{x}{2} - 1$ to the graph shows there are 4 solutions.
Reading from the graph,
$x = -1.9, -0.4, 0.8, 1.6$ to 1 d.p.

4 (a) The y values of the points of intersection of the graphs $x^2 + y^2 = 16$ and $y = x^2 - 5$ are given by eliminating x between the two equations.
$x^2 = y + 5$
$y^2 + y + 5 = 16$
$y^2 + y = 11$

(b) Reading the y values from the points of intersection gives $y = -3.8\ (3.9)$ or $y = 2.8\ (2.9)$

(c) $y = x^2 + k$ is a parabola with vertex on the y-axis at $(0, k)$. If the vertex is on the y-axis and within the circle, then there will be exactly two intersections with the circle.
$-4 < k < 4$

5 (a) $\sin x - 2\cos x = 1$ so $\sin x - 1 = 2\cos x$ and the x values of the points of intersection of the two graphs are the solutions.
$x = -270°, -145°, 90°, 215°$
Solutions within 5° are acceptable

(b) $\cos x + \frac{x}{180} = \frac{1}{2}$

$2\cos x + \frac{x}{90} = 1$

$2\cos x = -\frac{x}{90} + 1$

L is $y = -\frac{x}{90} + 1$

SHAPE AND SPACE 8 – BASIC SKILLS EXERCISE

1 (a) $\mathbf{p} = \begin{pmatrix} -1 \\ 5 \end{pmatrix}$, $\sqrt{26}$

(b) $\mathbf{q} = \begin{pmatrix} 3 \\ -1 \end{pmatrix}$, $\sqrt{10}$

(c) $\mathbf{r} = \begin{pmatrix} -4 \\ 13 \end{pmatrix}$, $\sqrt{185}$

(d) $\mathbf{s} = \begin{pmatrix} 7 \\ 0 \end{pmatrix}$, 7

2 (a) $\mathbf{p} = \begin{pmatrix} 5 \\ 0 \end{pmatrix}$, $\sqrt{29}$

(b) $\mathbf{q} = \begin{pmatrix} 1 \\ 0 \end{pmatrix}$, 1

(c) $\mathbf{r} = \begin{pmatrix} 12 \\ 1 \end{pmatrix}$, $\sqrt{145}$

(d) $\mathbf{s} = \begin{pmatrix} -2 \\ -42 \end{pmatrix}$, $\sqrt{1768}$

3 (a) (i) $\mathbf{p} + \mathbf{q} = \begin{pmatrix} 6 \\ -3 \end{pmatrix}$

(ii) $2\mathbf{p} - \mathbf{q} = \begin{pmatrix} 6 \\ 4 \end{pmatrix} - \begin{pmatrix} 3 \\ -5 \end{pmatrix} = \begin{pmatrix} 3 \\ 9 \end{pmatrix}$

(b) $m\mathbf{p} + n\mathbf{q} = \begin{pmatrix} 12 \\ -13 \end{pmatrix} = m\begin{pmatrix} 3 \\ 2 \end{pmatrix} + n\begin{pmatrix} 3 \\ -5 \end{pmatrix}$

$= \begin{pmatrix} 12 \\ -13 \end{pmatrix}$

$3m + 3n = 12$
$m + n = 4$ \quad (1)
$2m - 5n = -13$ \quad (2)
(1): $m = 4 - n \rightarrow$ (2)
(2): $2(4 - n) - 5n = -13$
$8 - 2n - 5n = -13$
$-7n = -21$
$n = 3, m = 1$

(c) $\mathbf{p} + r\mathbf{q} = \begin{pmatrix} s \\ -8 \end{pmatrix} = s\begin{pmatrix} 3 \\ 2 \end{pmatrix} + r\begin{pmatrix} 3 \\ -5 \end{pmatrix}$

$= \begin{pmatrix} 5 \\ -8 \end{pmatrix}$

$3 + 3r = 5$ \qquad (1) × 5 → (3)
$2 - 5r = -8$ \qquad (2) × 3 → (4)
$15 + 15r = 5s$ \qquad (3)
$6 - 15r = -24$ \qquad (4)
(3) + (4): $21 = 5s - 24$
$4s = 5s$, $s = 9, r = 2$

(d) $u(\mathbf{p} + \mathbf{q}) + r(2\mathbf{p} - \mathbf{q}) = r\begin{pmatrix} 0 \\ 21 \end{pmatrix}$

$u\begin{pmatrix} 6 \\ -3 \end{pmatrix} + v\begin{pmatrix} 3 \\ 9 \end{pmatrix} = \begin{pmatrix} 0 \\ 21 \end{pmatrix}$

$= 6u + 3v = 0$ \qquad (1)
$-3u + 9v = 21$ \qquad (2) × 2 → (3)
$-6u + 18v = 42$ \qquad (3)
(1) + (3): $21v = 42$,
$v = 2, u = -1$

4   $m = 2, n = -1$

5   (a) $\overrightarrow{AB} = -\mathbf{a} + \mathbf{b}$
    (b) $\overrightarrow{AM} = -\frac{1}{2}(\mathbf{b} - \mathbf{a})$
    (c) $\overrightarrow{OM} = -\frac{1}{2}(\mathbf{a} + \mathbf{b})$

6   (a) $\overrightarrow{AB} = -2\mathbf{x} + 2\mathbf{y}$
    (b) $\overrightarrow{AM} = \mathbf{y} - \mathbf{x}$
    (c) $\overrightarrow{OM} = \mathbf{x} + \mathbf{y}$

7   (a) $\overrightarrow{ED} = \mathbf{p}$
    (b) $\overrightarrow{DE} = -\mathbf{p}$
    (c) $\overrightarrow{AC} = \mathbf{p} + \mathbf{q}$
    (d) $\overrightarrow{AE} = 2\mathbf{q} - \mathbf{p}$

8   (a) $\overrightarrow{RS} = -\mathbf{r} + \mathbf{s}$
    (b) $\overrightarrow{OP} = \frac{3}{2}\mathbf{r}$
    (c) $\overrightarrow{PQ} = -\frac{3}{2}\mathbf{r} + 2\mathbf{s}$
    (d) $\overrightarrow{OM} = \mathbf{s} + \frac{3}{4}\mathbf{r}$

9   (a) (i) $\overrightarrow{PQ} = \mathbf{q} - \mathbf{p}$
        (ii) $\overrightarrow{PR} = \frac{1}{3}(\mathbf{q} - \mathbf{p})$
        (iii) $\overrightarrow{OR} = \mathbf{p} + \frac{1}{3}(\mathbf{q} - \mathbf{p})$
                $= \mathbf{p} + \frac{1}{3}\mathbf{q} - \frac{1}{3}\mathbf{p}$
                $= \frac{2}{3}\mathbf{p} + \frac{1}{3}\mathbf{q} = \frac{1}{3}(2\mathbf{p} + \mathbf{q})$
    (b) (i) $\overrightarrow{OS} = k\overrightarrow{OR}$
                $= \frac{3}{5}\overrightarrow{OR} = -k = \frac{3}{5}$
        (ii) $\overrightarrow{OS} = \frac{3}{5} \times \frac{1}{3}(2\mathbf{p} + \mathbf{q}) = \frac{1}{5}(2\mathbf{p} + \mathbf{q})$

10 (a) (i) $\overrightarrow{MP} = \frac{2}{5}\mathbf{p}$
        (ii) $\overrightarrow{PQ} = \mathbf{q} - \mathbf{p}$
        (iii) $\overrightarrow{PN} = \frac{2}{5}(\mathbf{q} - \mathbf{p})$
        (iv) $\overrightarrow{MN} = \overrightarrow{MP} + \overrightarrow{PN}$
                $= \frac{2}{5}\mathbf{p} + \frac{2}{5}(\mathbf{q} - \mathbf{p})$
                $= \frac{2}{5}\mathbf{q}$
    (b) $\overrightarrow{OQ} = \mathbf{q}$ } OQ is parallel to MN
        $\overrightarrow{MN} = \frac{2}{5}\mathbf{q}$ } MN = $\frac{2}{5}$ OQ or
        OQ = $\frac{5}{2}$ MN

11 (a) (i) $\mathbf{a}$
        (ii) $\frac{1}{2}(\mathbf{a} + \mathbf{b})$
        (iii) $\mathbf{a} - \mathbf{b}$
        (iv) $\frac{1}{2}(\mathbf{a} + \mathbf{b})$

    (b) Parallel and equal lengths
    (c) PQRS is a trapezium

12 (a) $\mathbf{w} = \begin{pmatrix} -7 \\ 19 \end{pmatrix}$
    (b) $\sqrt{410}$, 339.8°
    (c) 5.06 km/h

13 (a) $\begin{pmatrix} 1 \\ 5 \end{pmatrix}$
    (b) $\begin{pmatrix} 13 \\ 10 \end{pmatrix}$
    (c) 5.10
    (d) 052.4°

14 (a)

t	0	1	2	3	4	5
r	$\begin{pmatrix}1\\5\end{pmatrix}$	$\begin{pmatrix}3\\4\end{pmatrix}$	$\begin{pmatrix}5\\3\end{pmatrix}$	$\begin{pmatrix}7\\2\end{pmatrix}$	$\begin{pmatrix}9\\1\end{pmatrix}$	$\begin{pmatrix}11\\0\end{pmatrix}$

    (b)

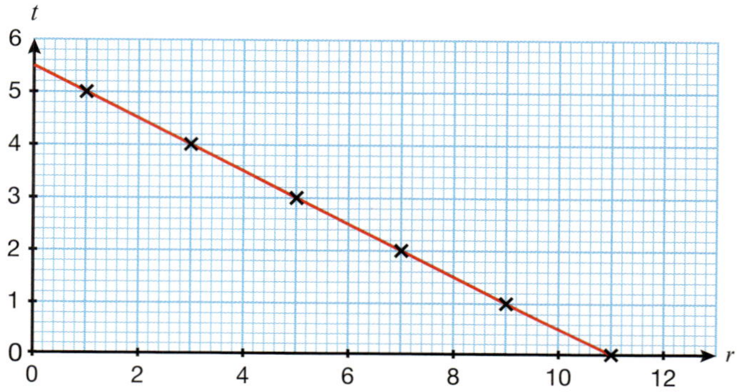

    (c) 8050 km/h, 117°

SHAPE AND SPACE 8 – EXAM PRACTICE EXERCISE

1   (a) $m\mathbf{a} - n\mathbf{b} = \begin{pmatrix} 8 \\ -11 \end{pmatrix} = \mathbf{c}$, so
        $2m + n = 8$ (1)
        $-m - 4n = -11$ (2)
        (2) × 2: $-2m - 8n = -22$ (3)
        (1) + (3): $-7n = -14$, so $n = 2$ and $m = 3$
    (b) If $m = 1$, $n = 1$ and $c = \begin{pmatrix} 3 \\ -5 \end{pmatrix}$.
    (c)

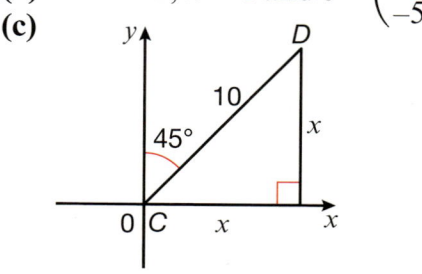

$10^2 = 2x^2$
$x^2 = 50$
$x = \sqrt{50}$
$= 5\sqrt{2}$

So vector $\mathbf{d} = \begin{pmatrix} 3 \\ -5 \end{pmatrix} + \begin{pmatrix} 5\sqrt{2} \\ 5\sqrt{2} \end{pmatrix}$

$= \begin{pmatrix} 3 + 5\sqrt{2} \\ 5\sqrt{2} - 5 \end{pmatrix}$

2 (a) $\overrightarrow{OP} = \overrightarrow{OA} + \overrightarrow{AP}$
$= \overrightarrow{OA} + \frac{m}{m+n}\overrightarrow{AB}$

$= \mathbf{a} + \frac{m}{m+n}(\mathbf{b} - \mathbf{a}) = \frac{(m+n)\mathbf{a} + m(\mathbf{b} - \mathbf{a})}{m+n}$

$= \frac{n\mathbf{a} + m\mathbf{b}}{m+n}$

(b) $\overrightarrow{OP} = \dfrac{2\begin{pmatrix}-4\\3\end{pmatrix} + 3\begin{pmatrix}2\\1\end{pmatrix}}{3+2}$

$= \dfrac{\begin{pmatrix}-2\\9\end{pmatrix}}{5}$

$\overrightarrow{OP} = \frac{1}{5}\sqrt{(-2)^2 + 9^2}$

$= \frac{1}{5}\sqrt{85}$

$= \frac{1}{5}\sqrt{5 \times 17}$

$= \sqrt{\frac{17}{5}}$

as required

3 (a) (i) $t = 0$, $\mathbf{r} = \begin{pmatrix} 1 \\ 2 \end{pmatrix}$

(ii) $t = 4$, $\mathbf{r} = \begin{pmatrix} -3 \\ 10 \end{pmatrix}$

(b) (Each hour that passes, the boat travels along vector $\begin{pmatrix} -1 \\ 2 \end{pmatrix}$ km, so the length of this vector is the distance travelled in 1 h)

Speed $= \sqrt{(-1)^2 + 2^2} = \sqrt{5}$ km/h

(c) At 15:00, $t = 3$, $\mathbf{r} = \begin{pmatrix} -2 \\ 8 \end{pmatrix}$ km

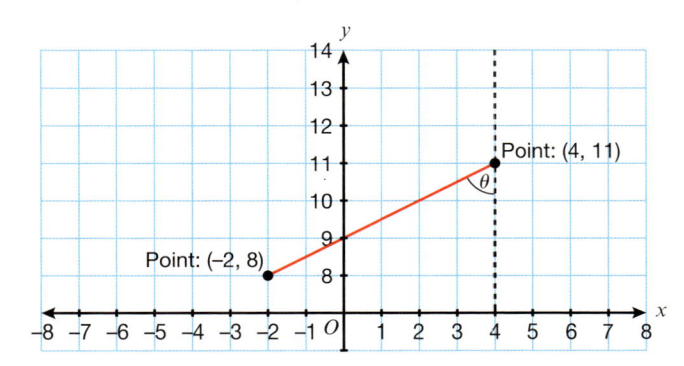

Bearing of boat from $L = 180° + \theta°$

$\tan(\theta) = \frac{6}{3} = 2$, so $\theta = 63.43°\ldots$

Bearing of boat from
$L = 180° + 63.43°\ldots = 243°$ (3 s.f.)

4 $\overrightarrow{AQ} = k\overrightarrow{AB} = k(\mathbf{b} - \mathbf{a})$

$\overrightarrow{OP} = \overrightarrow{OA} + \frac{3}{4}\overrightarrow{AM} = \mathbf{a} + \frac{3}{4}\left(\frac{1}{2}\mathbf{b} - \mathbf{a}\right)$

$= \frac{1}{4}\mathbf{a} + \frac{3}{8}\mathbf{b}$

$\overrightarrow{OQ} = \mathbf{a} + \lambda(\mathbf{b} - \mathbf{a}) = \mathbf{a} + \lambda\mathbf{b} - \lambda\mathbf{a}$
$= (1 - \lambda)\mathbf{a} + \lambda\mathbf{b}$

(If vector $m\mathbf{p}$ is collinear with vector $n\mathbf{q}$, then $\frac{m}{n}$ = a constant)

Now OPQ are collinear so:

$\dfrac{\lambda}{1-\lambda} = \dfrac{\frac{3}{8}}{\frac{1}{4}} = \dfrac{3}{2}$

$2\lambda = 3 - 3\lambda$
$5\lambda = 3$
$\lambda = \frac{3}{5}$

$\overrightarrow{AQ} = \overrightarrow{AO} + \overrightarrow{OQ} = -\mathbf{a} + \left(1 - \frac{3}{5}\right)\mathbf{a} + \frac{3}{5}\mathbf{b}$

$= -\frac{3}{5}\mathbf{a} + \frac{3}{5}\mathbf{b}$

$= \frac{3}{5}(\mathbf{b} - \mathbf{a})$

$= \frac{3}{5}\overrightarrow{AB}$

$AQ : QB = 3 : 2$

5 (a) $\overrightarrow{CD} = \overrightarrow{CB} + \overrightarrow{BA} + \overrightarrow{AD}$
      $= -\mathbf{c} - \mathbf{b} + 3\mathbf{c} = 2\mathbf{c} - \mathbf{b}$
   (b) If BPD are collinear $\overrightarrow{BP} = k\overrightarrow{BD}$
      $\overrightarrow{BD} = \overrightarrow{BC} + \overrightarrow{CD} = \mathbf{c} + 2\mathbf{c} - \mathbf{b} = 3\mathbf{c} - \mathbf{b}$
      Now $\overrightarrow{BP} = \overrightarrow{BA} + \lambda\overrightarrow{AC} = -\mathbf{b} + \lambda(\mathbf{b} + \mathbf{c})$
      $= (\lambda - 1)\mathbf{b} + \lambda\mathbf{c}$ (1)

      (If vector $m\mathbf{p}$ is collinear with vector $n\mathbf{q}$, then $\frac{m}{n}$ = a constant)

      $\frac{\lambda}{\lambda - 1} = \frac{3}{-1}$, $\lambda = \frac{3}{4}$, so from (1)
      $\overrightarrow{BP} = \frac{1}{4}(3\mathbf{c} - \mathbf{b})$ so $\overrightarrow{BP} = \frac{1}{4}\overrightarrow{BD}$
      $\overrightarrow{AP} = \overrightarrow{AB} + \overrightarrow{BP} = \mathbf{b} + \frac{1}{4}(3\mathbf{c} - \mathbf{b})$
      $= \frac{3}{4}(\mathbf{b} + \mathbf{c}) = \frac{3}{4}\overrightarrow{AC}$

      $AP : PC = 3 : 1$

   (c) $\overrightarrow{CD} = 2\mathbf{c} - \mathbf{b} = 2\begin{pmatrix}3\\0\end{pmatrix} - \begin{pmatrix}4\\1\end{pmatrix} = \begin{pmatrix}2\\-1\end{pmatrix}$
      $|\overrightarrow{CD}| = \sqrt{(2)^2 + (-1)^2} = \sqrt{5}$

HANDLING DATA 5 – BASIC SKILLS EXERCISE

1 (a) $\frac{1}{12}$
   (b) $\frac{5}{24}$
   (c) $\frac{7}{24}$

2 $P(O_1E_2 \text{ or } E_1O_2) = P(O_1E_2) + P(E_1O_2)$
   $= \frac{4}{7} \times \frac{3}{6} + \frac{3}{7} \times \frac{4}{6} = \frac{24}{42} = \frac{4}{7}$

   $P(A \text{ or } B) = P(A) + P(B)$ if A and B are mutually exclusive

3 Either all 3 discs are even or 1 is even and two are odd to sum an even number.
   $P(E_1E_2E_3 \text{ or } E_1O_2O_3 \times 3)$
   $= P(E_1E_2E_3) + P(E_1O_2O_3) \times 3$
   $= \frac{4}{9} \times \frac{3}{8} \times \frac{2}{7} + \frac{4}{9} \times \frac{5}{8} \times \frac{4}{7} \times 3$
   $= \frac{264}{504}$
   $= \frac{11}{21}$

   $P(A \text{ or } B) = P(A) + P(B)$ if A and B are mutually exclusive

4 Let Z be the number of Z's that are revealed
   $P(Z \geq 1) + P(Z = 0) = 1$
   $P(Z \geq 1) = 1 - P(Z = 0)$
   $= 1 - P(Z'_1 Z'_2 Z'_3)$
   $= 1 - \frac{6}{9} \times \frac{5}{8} \times \frac{4}{7}$
   $= 1 - \frac{5}{21}$
   $= \frac{16}{21}$

5 $P(W < 2) + P(W \geq 2) = 1$
   $P(W \geq 2) = 1 - P(W < 2)$
   $= 1 - [P(W = 0) + P(W = 1)]$
   $= 1 - \left[\left(\frac{1}{2} \times \frac{1}{2} \times \frac{1}{2}\right) + 3 \times \left(\frac{1}{2} \times \frac{1}{2} \times \frac{1}{2}\right)\right]$
   $= \frac{1}{2}$

   Scarlett is correct.

6 (a) $\frac{1}{4}$
   (b) $\frac{1}{2}$
   (c) $\frac{1}{4}$

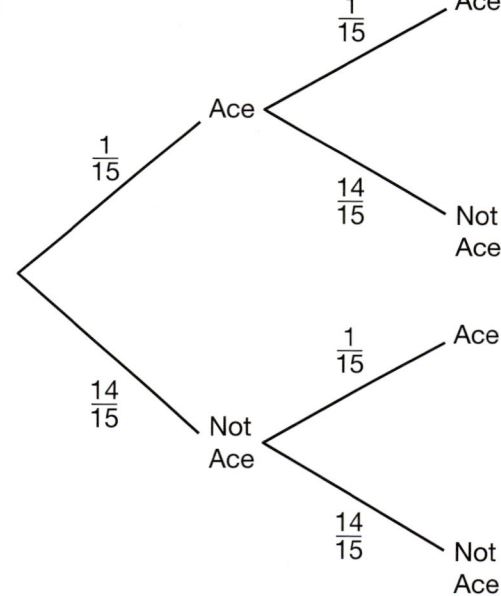

7 (a) [tree diagram: first branch Ace $\frac{1}{15}$ → Ace $\frac{1}{15}$, Not Ace $\frac{14}{15}$; Not Ace $\frac{14}{15}$ → Ace $\frac{1}{15}$, Not Ace $\frac{14}{15}$]

   (b) (i) $\frac{1}{225}$
       (ii) $\frac{196}{225}$
       (iii) $\frac{28}{225}$

ANSWERS 341

8 (a)

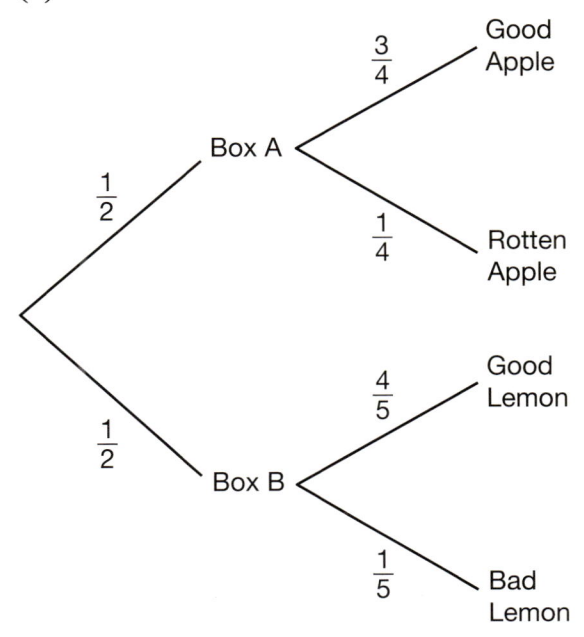

Tree diagram:
- $\frac{1}{2}$ Box A
  - $\frac{3}{4}$ Good Apple
  - $\frac{1}{4}$ Rotten Apple
- $\frac{1}{2}$ Box B
  - $\frac{4}{5}$ Good Lemon
  - $\frac{1}{5}$ Bad Lemon

(b) $\frac{3}{8}$

(c) $\frac{1}{10}$

9 (a)

Tree diagram:
- $\frac{1}{7}$ Cold
  - $\frac{1}{3}$ Cough
  - $\frac{2}{3}$ No Cough
- $\frac{6}{7}$ No Cold
  - $\frac{1}{4}$ Cough
  - $\frac{3}{4}$ No Cough

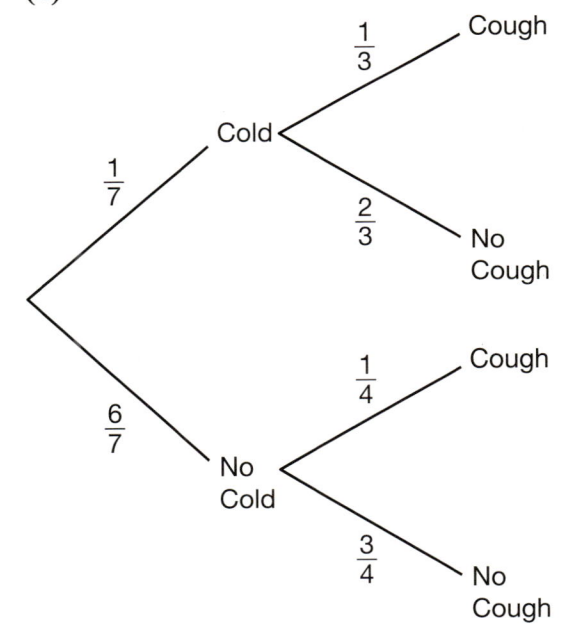

(b) (i) $\frac{1}{21}$

(ii) $\frac{3}{14}$

(iii) $\frac{13}{42}$

HANDLING DATA 5 – EXAM PRACTICE EXERCISE

1 (a) Let event F be a female baby giant panda.
Let event M be a male baby giant panda.

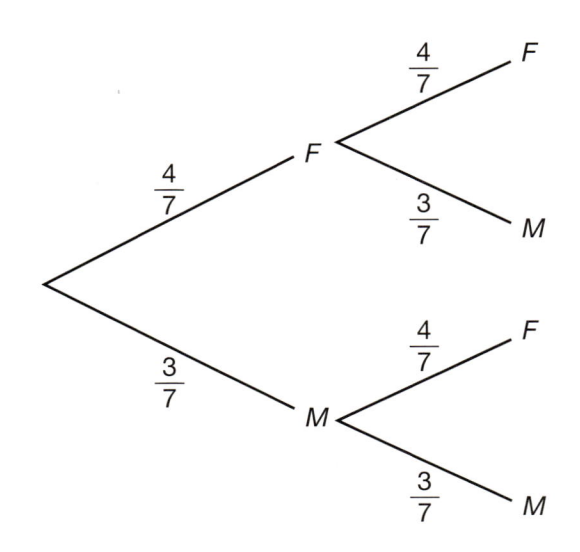

Tree diagram:
- $\frac{4}{7}$ F
  - $\frac{4}{7}$ F
  - $\frac{3}{7}$ M
- $\frac{3}{7}$ M
  - $\frac{4}{7}$ F
  - $\frac{3}{7}$ M

(b) $P(M_1 M_2) = P(M_1) \times P(M_2)$
$= \frac{3}{7} \times \frac{3}{7} = \frac{9}{49}$

$P(A \text{ and } B) = P(A) \times P(B)$

(c) $P(M_1 F_2 \text{ or } F_1 M_2)$
$= P(M_1 F_2) + P(F_1 M_2)$
$= \frac{3}{7} \times \frac{4}{7} + \frac{4}{7} \times \frac{3}{7} = \frac{24}{49}$

$P(A \text{ or } B) = P(A) + P(B)$ if A and B are mutually exclusive

2 (a)

	1st Shot	2nd Shot
Hits	$\frac{2}{3}$	$\frac{4}{5}$
Misses	$\frac{1}{3}$	$\frac{1}{5}$

Table completed as $P(E) + P(E') = 1$
Let event H be a hit of the bullseye.
Let event M be a miss of the bullseye.

342 ANSWERS

1st Shot   **2nd Shot**

- $\frac{2}{3}$ H
  - $\frac{4}{5}$ H
  - $\frac{1}{5}$ M
- $\frac{1}{3}$ M
  - $\frac{4}{5}$ H
  - $\frac{1}{5}$ M

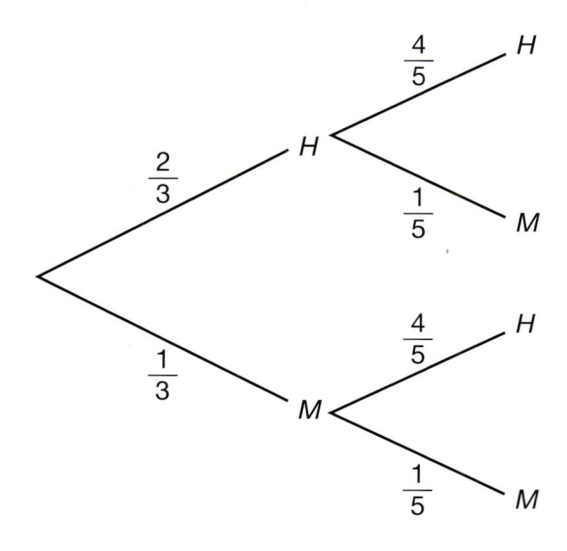

(b) (i) $P(H_1 H_2) = P(H_1) \times P(H_2)$
$$= \frac{2}{3} \times \frac{4}{5} = \frac{8}{15}$$
$P(A \text{ and } B) = P(A) \times P(B)$

(ii) $P(H = 1) = P(H_1 M_2 \text{ or } M_1 H_2)$
$= P(H_1 M_2) + P(M_1 H_2)$
$= \frac{2}{3} \times \frac{1}{5} + \frac{1}{3} \times \frac{4}{5} = \frac{6}{15} = \frac{2}{5}$
$P(A \text{ or } B) = P(A) + P(B)$ if A and B are mutually exclusive

iii) $P(H \geq 1) + P(H = 0) = 1$
$P(H \geq 1) = 1 - P(H = 0)$
$= 1 - P(M_1 M_2)$
$P(E) + P(E') = 1$
$= 1 - \frac{1}{3} \times \frac{1}{5}$
$= 1 - \frac{1}{15}$
$= \frac{14}{15}$

3 (a) Let event T be a teddy bear is selected.
Let event K be a kangaroo is selected.

1st Pick   **2nd Pick**

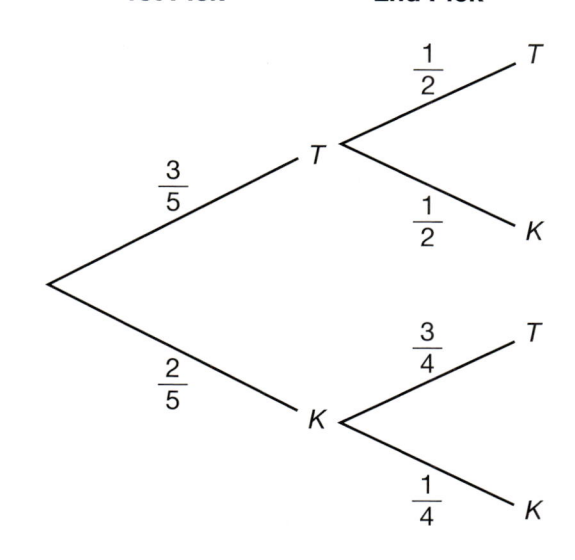

- $\frac{3}{5}$ T
  - $\frac{1}{2}$ T
  - $\frac{1}{2}$ K
- $\frac{2}{5}$ K
  - $\frac{3}{4}$ T
  - $\frac{1}{4}$ K

(b) (i) $P(T_1 T_2) = P(T_1) \times P(T_2)$
$$= \frac{3}{5} \times \frac{1}{2} = \frac{3}{10}$$
$P(A \text{ and } B) = P(A) \times P(B)$

(ii) $P(T_1 K_2 \text{ or } K_1 T_2)$
$= P(T_1 K_2) + P(K_1 T_2)$
$= \frac{3}{5} \times \frac{1}{2} + \frac{2}{5} \times \frac{3}{4}$
$= \frac{12}{20} = \frac{3}{5}$
$P(A \text{ or } B) = P(A) + P(B)$ if A and B are mutually exclusive

(iii) $P(K \geq 1) + P(K = 0) = 1$
$P(K \geq 1) = 1 - P(K = 0)$
$= 1 - P(T_1 T_2)$
$P(E) + P(E') = 1$
$= 1 - \frac{3}{10} = \frac{7}{10}$

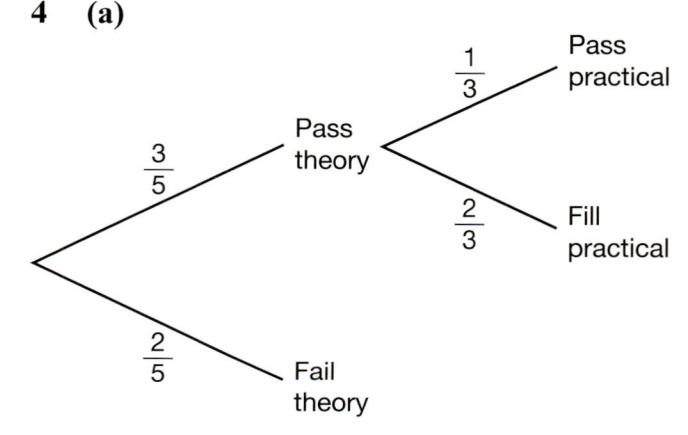

4 (a)

- $\frac{3}{5}$ Pass theory
  - $\frac{1}{3}$ Pass practical
  - $\frac{2}{3}$ Fill practical
- $\frac{2}{5}$ Fail theory

(b) $P(FT \text{ or } PT,FP) = P(FT) + P(PT,FP)$
$= \frac{2}{5} + \frac{3}{5} \times \frac{2}{3} = \frac{4}{5}$
$P(A \text{ or } B) = P(A) + P(B)$ if A and B are mutually exclusive

(c) $P(PT,PP,PA) = \frac{3}{5} \times \frac{1}{3} \times \frac{1}{4} = \frac{1}{20}$
$P(A \text{ and } B) = P(A) \times P(B)$

5 (a) Let d be the number of diamonds in the box
Let r be the number of rubies in the box
$P(D_1 D_2) = P(D_1) \times P(D_2)$
$= \frac{d}{20} \times \frac{d-1}{19} = \frac{21}{38}$
$P(A \text{ and } B) = P(A) \times P(B)$
$d(d-1) = 210$
$d^2 - d - 210 = 0$
$(d-15)(d+14) = 0$
$d = 15$ and $r = 5$

(b) P(D₁R₂ or R₁D₂) = P(D₁R₂) + P(R₁D₂)

$= \frac{15}{20} \times \frac{5}{19} + \frac{5}{20} \times \frac{15}{19} = \frac{30}{76} = \frac{15}{38}$

P(A or B) = P(A) + P(B) if A and B are mutually exclusive

NUMBER 9 – BASIC SKILLS EXERCISE

1. $660
2. $625
3. Yes. Saskia has been over charged by £4.
4. €4140
5. 15 hours
6. $700
7. €1233.75
8. 2 h 30 mins
9. $885 (Aus)
10. £892.86
11. 44.32 yuan
12. 5200 reais
13. 804.74 yuan
14. £10 050.25
15. Australia: £2127.12
    Brazil: £2000
    Spain: £2200
    Cheapest purchase is in Brazil.
16. Malaysia : India : China = $200 : $200 : $600
    811.85 ringitts, 14 740.74 rupees, 3920 yuan
17. A: 33.3 g/£, B: 33.3 g/£ so same value!
18. Square: €25/m², Octagonal: €24/m², Octagonal are better value.
19. Everamp: 20 h/£, Dynamo: 24 h/£, Dynamo is better value.
20. kg bag $1.90 per kg, 21 kg bag $1.75 per kg so 12 kg bag better value per kg.

NUMBER 9 – EXAM PRACTICE EXERCISE

1. Let €x be the amount that Aria receives.
   Aria   Blake   Chloe
   x   0.25x   1.25x
   So, 1750 = x + 0.25x + 1.25x = 2.5x
   x = 700
   So Aria: €700   Blake: €175   Chloe: €875

2. Total amount paid by Kofi
   = 24 × €36 = €864
   Money received by Kofi
   $= \frac{2}{3} \times 24 \times 30 \times €1.80 = €864$
   Kofi's overall profit = 0.25 × €864 = €216
   Number of bottles left
   $= \frac{1}{3} \times 24 \times 30 = 240$
   So price of each bottle to secure 25% profit
   $= \frac{€216}{240} = €0.90$ per bottle

3. (a) Total parts = 6, so 1 part of £7200
       = £1200
       Malaysia: £1200 = 5.48 × £1200
                  = 6576 ringitts
       India: £2400 = 99.50 × £2400
                  = 238 800 rupees
       China: £3600 = 8.82 × £3600
                  = 31 752 yuan
   (b) Return journey: 25% of 31752 yuan
       = 7938 yuan
       If 1€ = 8 yuan, 1 yuan = €$\frac{1}{8}$, so
       7938 yuan = 7938 × $\frac{1}{8}$ euros
       = €992.25

4. Tangerine cost = $25 + $0.35 × 60 × 24
   = $529 × 1.175 = $621.58
   Aardvark cost = $90 + $0.30 × 60 × 24
   = $522 × 1.175 = $613.35
   So Aardvark is cheaper by $8.23 and is therefore better value assuming the quality of service is the same.
   p = 8.23

5. (a) g = 1.025 × £44 940, so g = £46 063.50
   (b) s × 0.96 = £600, so s = £625
   (c) Price of 1 kg of gold on 1 Jan 2022
       = 0.975 × £44 940 = £43 816.50
       Price of 1 kg of silver on 1 Jan 2022
       = 1.04 × £625 = £650
       500 g of gold = 0.5 × £43 816.50
       = £21 908.25
       500 g of silver = 0.5 × £650 = £325
       Total price = £22 233.25

ALGEBRA 9 – BASIC SKILLS EXERCISE

1. $(-4, 12), (3, 5)$

2. $(3, 2), (-3, -2)$

3. $(3, 1), (9, 4)$

4. $(2, 3), (3, 2)$

5. $(1, 1)$

6. $(-4.16, -6.16), (2.16, 0.162)$

7. $(3.92, 1.08), (-1.92, 6.92)$

8. $(3.24, 1.24), (-1.24, -3.24)$

9. $(91.65, 18.33)$

10. Equation of top of egg cup is $y = 4$
    Intersection at $(-2, 4)$ and $(2, 4)$,
    radius $= 2$ cm

11. Eliminating y gives $x^2 - 4x + 5 = 0$. Using quadratic formula $b^2 - 4ac = 16 - 20 = -4$

12. Substituting $y = k - x$ into $x^2 + y^2 = 25$ gives $2x^2 - 2kx + (k^2 - 25) = 0$. This has one solution if, using quadratic formula, $b^2 - 4ac = 0$. Substituting values gives
    $4k^2 = 4 \times 2 \times (k^2 - 25)$
    $k^2 = 50$
    $k = \pm 5\sqrt{2}$

13. $p = 4, 2^4 - 1 = 15$

14. $x = 0$

15. $n = 5$ gives 99 which is not prime.

16. False if a and b are of opposite signs; for example, $(-2)^2 = (2)^2$ but $-2 \neq 2$

17. $(2m + 1) - (2n + 1) = 2(m - n)$ which is even.

18. $(2n - 1) + (2n + 1) + (2n + 3) = 6n + 3$ this leaves remainder 3 when divided by 6
    or $(2n + 1) + (2n + 3) + (2n + 5)$
    $= 6(n + 1) + 3$

19. $S = \frac{n}{2}[2 + (n - 1)2] = \frac{n}{2}[2n] = n^2$

20. Sum $= \frac{n}{2}[2a + (n - 1)]$. Let $n = 2p + 1$
    $S = (2p + 1)\left[a + \frac{2p + 1 - 1}{2}\right] = (2p + 1)$
    $(a + p)$ which is divisible by $n = (2p + 1)$

21. $(2n - 1)(2n + 1)(2n + 3)$
    $= 8n^3 + 12n^2 - 2n - 3$
    $= 2(4n^3 + 6n^2 - n - 1) - 1$

22. $n(n + 1) + (n + 1) = n^2 + 2n + 1 = (n + 1)^2$

23. $(2n + 1)^2 = 4n^2 + 4n + 1 = 4(n^2 + n) + 1$

24. $(2m + 1)^2 - (2n + 1)^2 = 4(m^2 + m - n^2 - n)$
    $= 4[m(m + 1) - n(n + 1)]$
    Either m or $m + 1$ is even with a factor of 2, likewise n and $n + 1$ hence 8 is a factor.

25. $(n + 1)^2 - n^2 = 2n + 1 = (n + 1) + n$

26. $(x - 4)^2 + 1$

27. $-(x - 3)^2$

28. $2x^2 - 24x + 73 = 2(x - 6)^2 + 1 > 0$

29. $(2x + 1)^2 \geq 0$

30. $x^2 + 14x + c = (x + 7)^2 - 49 + c$
    $c - 49 \geq 0$
    $c \geq 49$

31. $x^2 + bx + 4 = \left(x + \frac{b}{2}\right)^2 - \frac{b^2}{4} + 4$
    $4 - \frac{b^2}{4} \geq 0$
    $b^2 \leq 16$
    $-4 \leq b \leq 4$

32. $\sqrt{3a}(\sqrt{18a} + \sqrt{2a}) = \sqrt{36a^2} + 2a = 6a + 2a = 8a$

33. $2^{127} - 2 = 2(2^{126} - 1)$
    $2^{127} - 2$ has a factor of 2.
    $2^{127} - 2, 2^{127} - 1, 2^{127}$ are three conecutive integers. 2^{127} is even, $2^{127} - 1$ is prime, $2^{127} - 2$ has a factor of 3 as one of any three consecutive integers has a factor of 3.
    $2^{127} - 2$ has a factor of 6.

34. Using the quadratic formula gives $b^2 - 4ac = (2\sqrt{c})^2 - 4c = 0$ therefore there is only one solution.

35. $abc = 100a + 10b + 5 = 5(20a + 2b + 1)$

36. $100a + 10b + c = 100a + 10(a + c) + c$
    $= 110a + 11c = 11(10a + c)$

37. $[(n + 1)^2 - 6(n + 1) + 10] - [n^2 - 6n + 10]$
    $= n^2 + 2n + 1 - 6n - 6 + 10 - n^2 + 6n - 10$
    $= 2n - 5$ which is an odd number.

ALGEBRA 9 – EXAM PRACTICE EXERCISE

1

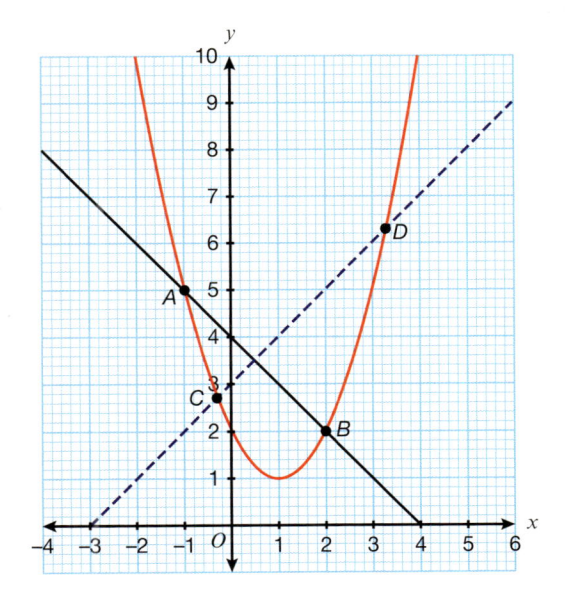

Midpoint of AB is $\left(\dfrac{-1+2}{2}, \dfrac{5+2}{2}\right) = \left(\dfrac{1}{2}, \dfrac{7}{2}\right)$

Midpoint is mean of the coordinates.
Gradient of AB is -1
gradient of perpendicular is 1
equation of CD is $y = x + C$
For perpendicular lines, product of gradients $= -1$
Substituting midpoint gives $\dfrac{7}{2} = \dfrac{1}{2} + C$
$C = 3$ so equation of CD is $y = x + 3$
Therefore, the coordinates of C and D are given by the solutions to the simultaneous equations
$y = x^2 - 2x + 2$ and $y = x + 3$
$x^2 - 2x + 2 = x + 3$
$x^2 - 3x - 1 = 0$
Using the quadratic formula with $a = 1$, $b = -3$ and $c = -1$ gives
$x = \dfrac{3 \pm \sqrt{9+4}}{2} = \dfrac{3 \pm \sqrt{13}}{2}$
Substituting into $y = x + 3$ gives
$C = \left(\dfrac{3 - \sqrt{13}}{2}, \dfrac{9 - \sqrt{13}}{2}\right)$ and
$D = \left(\dfrac{3 + \sqrt{13}}{2}, \dfrac{9 + \sqrt{13}}{2}\right)$

2

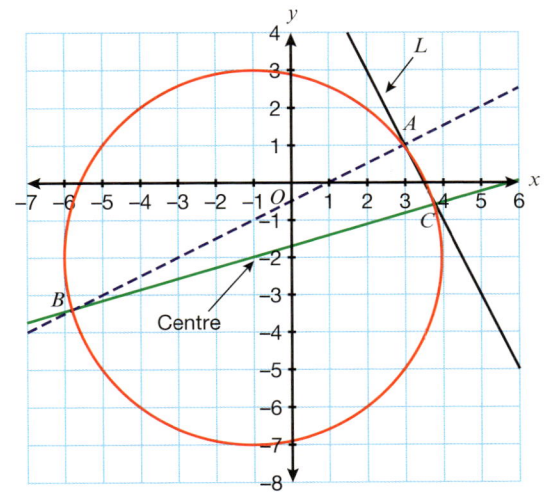

(a) Gradient of AB is $\dfrac{1 + 3.4}{3 + 5.8} = \dfrac{1}{2}$
gradient of L is -2
For perpendicular lines, product of gradients $= -1$
Equation of L is $y = -2x + C$
Substituting the coordinates of A gives
$1 = -2 \times 3 + C$
$C = 7$ hence L is $y = -2x + 7$

(b) Coordinates of where L intersects the circle are given by the solutions to the simultaneous equations
$x^2 + y^2 + 2x + 4y = 20$ and
$y = -2x + 7$
$y = -2x + 7 \Rightarrow 4y = -8x + 28$ and
$y^2 = 4x^2 - 28x + 49$
Substituting into
$x^2 + y^2 + 2x + 4y = 20$ gives
$x^2 + 4x^2 - 28x + 49 + 2x - 8x + 28 = 20$
$5x^2 - 34x + 57 = 0$
$(5x - 19)(x - 3) = 0$
$x = 3$ or $\dfrac{19}{5}$
Or use quadratic formula to solve.
Substituting into $y = -2x + 7$ gives
$C = \left(\dfrac{19}{5}, \dfrac{-3}{5}\right)$ or $(3.8, -0.6)$

(c) AB and AC are chords intersecting at right angles therefore BC is a diameter of the circle.
The midpoint of BC is the centre of the circle $= \left(\dfrac{3.8 - 5.8}{2}, \dfrac{-0.6 - 3.4}{2}\right) = (-1, -2)$
B is $(-5.8, -3.4)$ given in question.

3 (a) Coordinates of A and B are given by the solutions to the simultaneous equations
$4x^2 + y^2 - 4y = 0$ and $2x + y = 3$
$2x + y = 3$
$y = 3 - 2x$
$y^2 = 9 - 12x + 4x^2$
Substituting into $4x^2 + y^2 - 4y = 0$ gives
$4x^2 + 9 - 12x + 4x^2 - 12 + 8x = 0$
$8x^2 - 4x - 3 = 0$
Solving using the quadratic formula gives $x = \frac{1 \pm \sqrt{7}}{4}$

When $x = \frac{1 + \sqrt{7}}{4}$,
$y = 3 - 2 \times \frac{1 + \sqrt{7}}{4} = \frac{5 - \sqrt{7}}{2}$
so the coordinates of B are
$\left(\frac{1+\sqrt{7}}{4}, \frac{5-\sqrt{7}}{2}\right)$

When $x = \frac{1 - \sqrt{7}}{4}$,
$y = 3 - 2 \times \frac{1 - \sqrt{7}}{4} = \frac{5 + \sqrt{7}}{2}$
so the coordinates of A are
$\left(\frac{1-\sqrt{7}}{4}, \frac{5+\sqrt{7}}{2}\right)$

Distance in the x direction between A and B is $\frac{1+\sqrt{7}}{4} - \frac{1-\sqrt{7}}{4} = \frac{\sqrt{7}}{2}$
Distance in the y direction between A and B is $\frac{5+\sqrt{7}}{2} - \frac{5-\sqrt{7}}{2} = \sqrt{7}$
$AB^2 = \left(\frac{\sqrt{7}}{2}\right)^2 + (\sqrt{7})^2 = \frac{7}{4} + 7 = \frac{35}{4}$
$AB = \frac{\sqrt{35}}{2}$ cm

(b) Volume of wire $= \pi \times 0.05^2 \times \frac{\sqrt{35}}{2}$
$= 0.03285...$ cm³
1 mm = 0.1 cm $\Rightarrow$ radius is 0.05 cm
Weight of gold $= 0.03285... \times 19.3$
$= 0.6341...$ g
Cost of gold $= 0.6341 \times 60 = 38.04...$
$= £38.0$ (3 s.f.)

4 (a) Any odd number is given by $2n + 1 \Rightarrow$
$(2n + 1)^2 = 4n^2 + 4n + 1 = 4n(n + 1) + 1$
one of n or $n + 1$ must be even so
$n(n + 1)$ has a factor of 2 hence
$4n(n + 1)$ has a factor of 8 and
$4n(n + 1) + 1$ is 1 more than a multiple of 8

(b) $a^2 - b^2 = (a + b)(a - b)$
  (i) As $a^2 - b^2$ is a prime number then one of the factors $(a + b)$ or $(a - b)$ must equal 1.
  $a + b = 1$ so $a = 1 - b$ implies that a is negative as $b > 0$. But $a > 0$ so $a + b \neq 1$
  $a - b = 1$ so $a = 1 + b$ implies that a and b are consecutive integers.
  (ii) $a^2 - b^2 = (a + b) \times 1 \Rightarrow a + b = a^2 - b^2$ which is prime, so $a + b$ is also prime.

5 (a) From the formula sheet, the sum to n terms is given by $S = \frac{n}{2}[2a + (n - 1)d]$ where a is the first term and d the common difference.
$S = \frac{n}{2}[2 \times 2 + (n - 1)4] = \frac{n}{2}[4 + 4(n - 1)]$
$= \frac{4n}{2}[1 + n - 1] = 2n^2$ which is double a square number.

(b) The nth term of S is $a + (n - 1)d$
$= 2 + 4(n - 1) = 4n - 2$
nth term squared $= (4n - 2)^2$
$= 16n^2 - 16n + 4$
nth term squared $+ 12 = 16n^2 - 16n + 4 + 12 = 16(n^2 - n + 1)$ which is divisible by 16

GRAPHS 8 – BASIC SKILLS EXERCISE

1 (a) (i) -1.2
   (ii) 1.8
(b) (i) $(3.2, -1.6)$ and $(0.8, 1.6)$
   (ii) $(5.1, -1.0)$ and $(-1.1, 1.0)$
   (iii) $(4.0, -2.1)$ and $(0, 2.1)$

2 (a) -1.2
(b) $y = -1.2x + 2.1$

3 1.76 and -1.5

4 2.4 and 1.5

ANSWERS

5 (a)

t	0	1	2	3	4
d	0	0.25	1	2.25	4

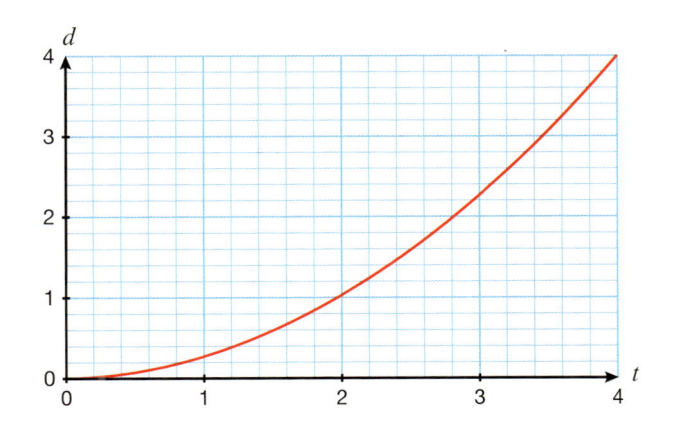

(b) Gradient gives velocity
  (i) 0 m/s
  (ii) 0.5 m/s
  (iii) 1 m/s
  (iv) 1.5 m/s
  (v) 2 m/s

(c)

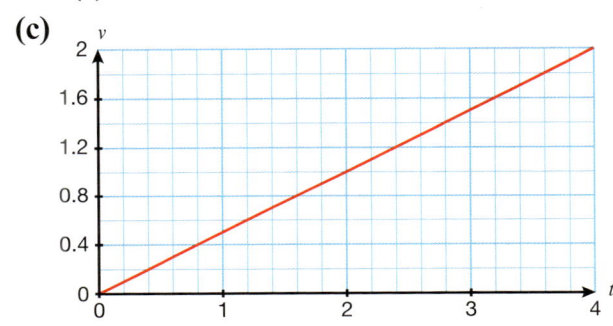

(d) Gradient gives acceleration
    Acceleration is constant and equal to 0.5 m/s²

6 (a) (i)

t	0	1	2	3	4	5	6	7	8
d	0	3.2	3.6	2.4	0.8	0	1.2	5.6	14.4

(ii)

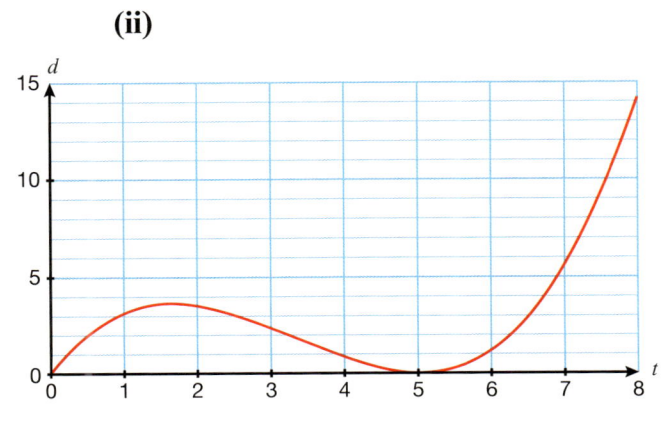

(b) Starts off, slows down and stops after approximately 1.5 s, returns to start after 5 s then sets off at increasing speed

(c) Gradient gives velocity
  (i) 1.6 m/s
  (ii) −1.6 m/s
(d) 6.9 s

7 (a)

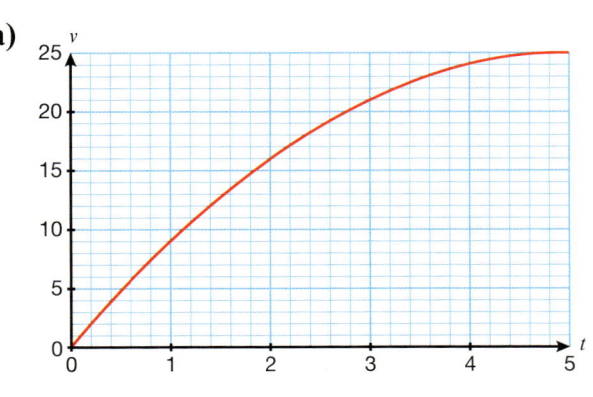

(b) Gradient gives acceleration
  (i) 8 m/s²
  (ii) 4 m/s²
(c) 2.5 s

8 (a) (i)

t (days)	0	1	2	3	4	5	6	7	8
d (cm)	20	17	14.5	12.3	10.4	8.87	7.54	6.41	5.45

(ii)

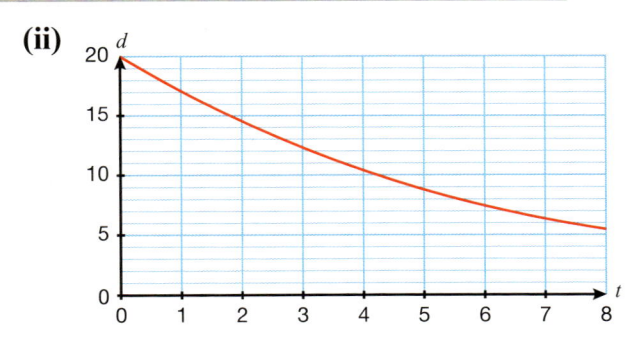

(b) Approximately 4.3 days
(c) 2.3 cm/day
(d) 61.2 cm/day = 0.05 cm/h

9 (a) (1, 4)

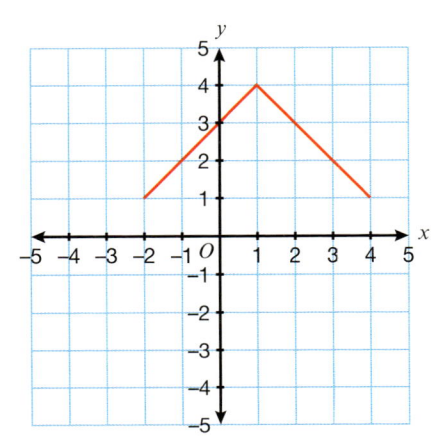

(b) (−1, 2)

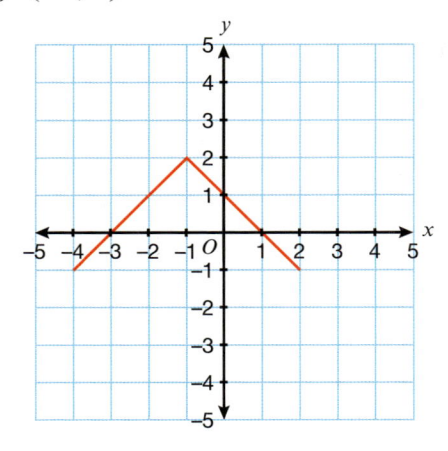

(c) (1, 4)

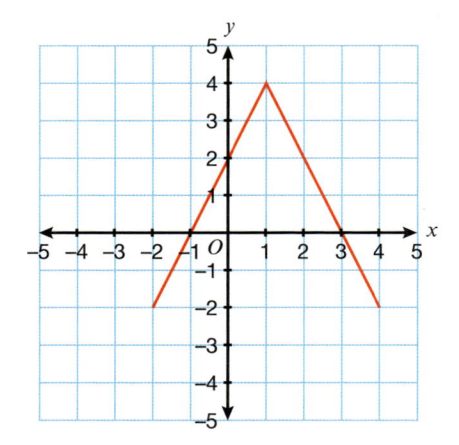

(d) (0.5, 2)

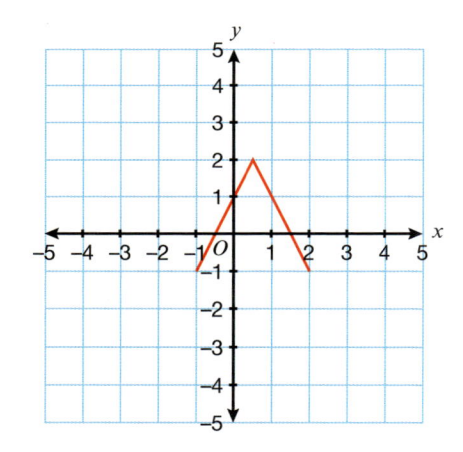

10 (a) (−2, 2)
   (b) (2, −2)
   (c) (−2, −1)
   (d) (−4, −2)

11 $y = f(x + 2)$ and $y = f(-x)$

12 $y = -x^2 + 2x + 3$

13 $y = -[\sin(x) + 2] = -\sin(x) - 2$

14 (a) $y = x^2 + 4x + 4$
   (b) $y = x^2 - 4x + 4$

(c) Minimum (2, 0)

15 (a) $(0, k)$
   (b) $(0, -2k)$
   (c) $(0, k - 2)$

16 (a) k
   (b) $2k$
   (c) $2k$
   (d) k

17 (a) $-m$
   (b) $-m$
   (c) $\frac{m}{2}$
   (d) m

18 (a) $(0, p - 3)$
   (b) $(0, p)$
   (c) $(0, 3p)$
   (d) $(0, p)$

19 (a) 3
   (b) 2
   (c) −1

20 (a) (−6, 4)
   (b) (−1, −3)

GRAPHS 8 – EXAM PRACTICE EXERCISE

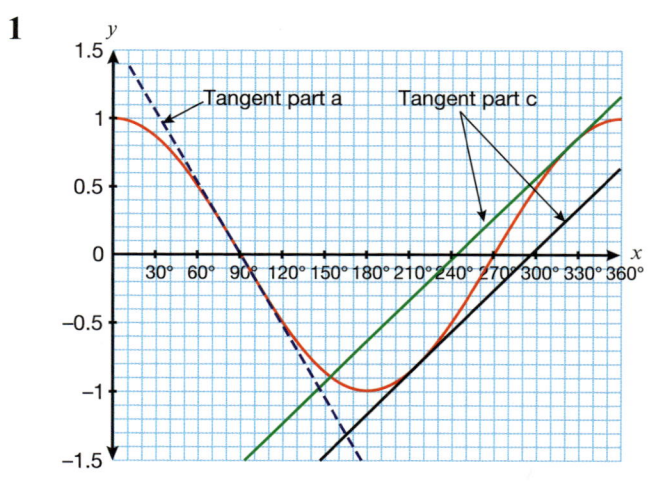

1

(a) Gradient is approximately −0.017 5
(b) Gradient −m at (330°, 0.5)
(c) See graph. $x = 215°$ or $325°$

(d) The cosine curve is periodic with period 360°
x = 215 + 360 = 575° or
x = 325 + 360 = 685°

2

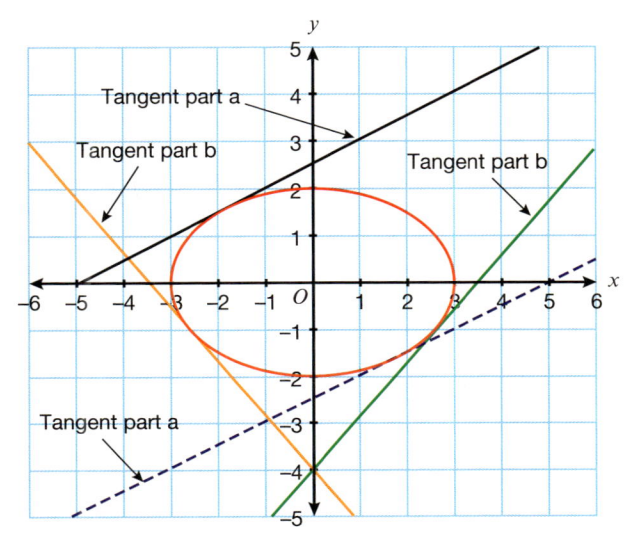

(a) C = approximately 2.5 or
C = approximately −2.5 (see graph)
(b) m = approximately 1.1 or
m = approximately −1.1 (see graph)

3

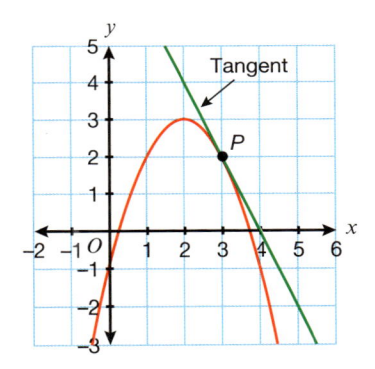

(a) See graph. Gradient is −2
(b) (i) Stretch with scale factor $\frac{1}{a}$ parallel to the x-axis
so P becomes $\left(\frac{3}{a}, 2\right)$, gradient is $a \times -2 = -2a$
(ii) Translation of $\begin{pmatrix} -a \\ 0 \end{pmatrix}$ so P becomes (3 − a, 2), gradient is unchanged = −2
(iii) Stretch scale factor a parallel to the y axis so P becomes (3, 2a), gradient is $a \times -2 = -2a$
(iv) Reflection in the y-axis so P becomes (−3, 2), gradient becomes 2.

4 (a)

t (s)	1	2	3	4	5
v (m/s)	3	6	9	12	15

(b)

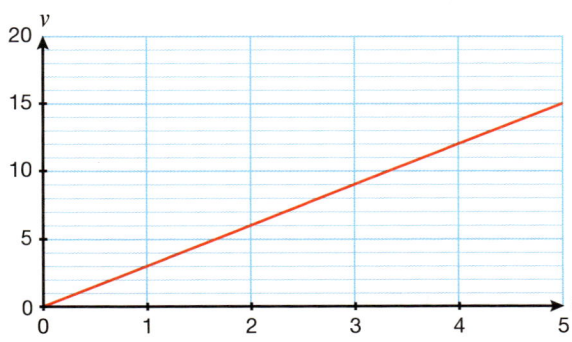

(c) Gradient is equal to 3 therefore the acceleration is 3 m/s²

5 (a) (i) Translation of $\begin{pmatrix} 2 \\ 0 \end{pmatrix}$

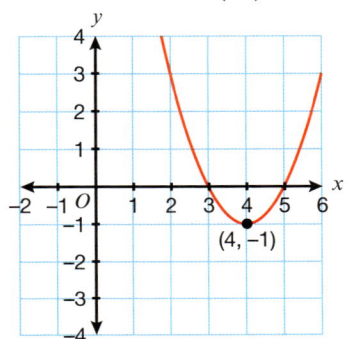

(ii) Stretch scale factor 2 parallel to x-axis

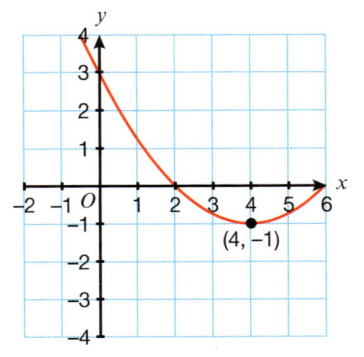

(iii) Reflection in the x-axis

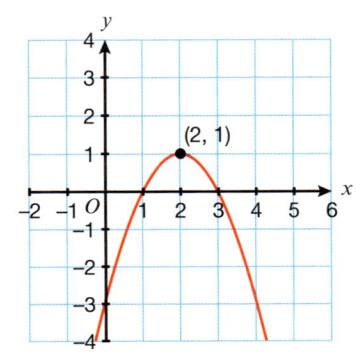

(b) $g(x)$ has been reflected in the y-axis then translated by $\begin{pmatrix} 0 \\ 2 \end{pmatrix}$.

The reverse of this is translate by $\begin{pmatrix} 0 \\ -2 \end{pmatrix}$ then reflect in the y-axis.

$(5, 3)$ translated by $\begin{pmatrix} 0 \\ -2 \end{pmatrix}$ gives $(5, 1)$.

$(5,1)$ reflected in the y-axis gives $(-5, 1)$

$\Rightarrow$ turning point is $(-5, 1)$

SHAPE AND SPACE 9 – BASIC SKILLS EXERCISE

1 $A'(90°, 10)$
2 $A'(180°, 9)$
3 $A'(180°, 10)$
4 $x = 60°, 120°$
5 $x = 60°, 300°$
6 $x = 45°, 225°$
7 9.22 cm
8 18.0 cm
9 15.6 cm
10 13.5 cm
11 11.9 cm
12 19.4 cm
13 46.5°
14 38.2°
15 55.1°
16 36.2°
17 20.7°
18 59.0°
19 (a) $C = 42.2°$, $a = 6.96$ m
   (b) $C = 44.7°$, $a = 5.84$ m
20 (a) 68.9 m²
   (b) 120 m²
21 92.1 m

22 Circle area = triangle area
Circumference of circle = $6\pi = 2\pi r$, $r = 3$
Area of circle = $\pi r^2 = \pi \times 3^2 = 9\pi$
Let equilateral triangle have side x, so perimeter $p = 3x$
(Area of triangle = $\frac{1}{2} ab\sin C$)

$9\pi = \frac{1}{2} \times x \times x \times \sin(60°) = \frac{\sqrt{3}x^2}{4}$

$x^2 = \frac{36\pi}{\sqrt{3}} = \frac{3^2 \times 4 \times \pi}{\sqrt{3}} = 3^{\frac{3}{2}} \times 4 \times \pi$

$x = \sqrt{3^{\frac{3}{2}} \times 4 \times \pi} = 3^{\frac{3}{4}} \times 2 \times \pi^{\frac{1}{2}} = 2 \times \sqrt{\pi} \times 3^{\frac{3}{4}}$

$((a^m)^n = a^{mn})$

$p = 3x = 3 \times \left(2 \times \sqrt{\pi} \times 3^{\frac{3}{4}}\right) = 2 \times 3^{\frac{7}{4}} \times \sqrt{\pi}$

$= 2 \times 3^m \times n$

So $m = \frac{7}{4}$, $n = \sqrt{\pi}$

SHAPE AND SPACE 9 – EXAM PRACTICE EXERCISE

1 **(a) (i)** $2f(x) = 2\sin(x°)$
       ($2f(x)$ stretches the function by scale factor 2 parallel to y-axis)
       P is transformed to $(90°, 2)$, Q is transformed to $(180°, 0)$
   (ii) $-f(x) = -\sin(x°)$
       ($-f(x)$ reflects the function in the x-axis)
       P is transformed to $(90°, -1)$, Q is transformed to $(180°, 0)$
   (iii) $-2f(2x) + 2 = -2\sin(2x°) + 2$
       The function $-2f(2x) + 2$
       (i) stretches the function by scale factor $\frac{1}{2}$ parallel to x-axis.
       (ii) stretches the function by scale factor 2 parallel to the y-axis.
       (iii) reflects the function in the x-axis.
       (iv) translates the function along vector $\begin{pmatrix} 0 \\ 2 \end{pmatrix}$
       P is transformed to $(45°, 0)$, Q is transformed to $(90°, 2)$
   (b) R is at $(30°, 0.5)$

2

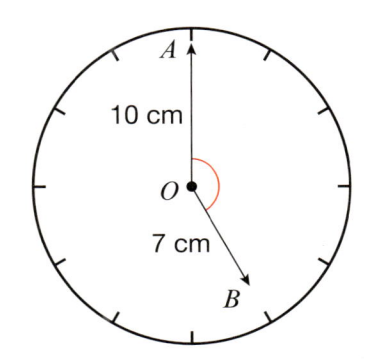

(a) Triangle OAB at 05:00 angle AOB
$= 5 \times 30° = 150°$
$AB^2 = 10^2 + 7^2 - 2 \times 10 \times 7 \times \cos(150°)$
(cosine rule: $a^2 = b^2 + c^2 - 2bc\cos A$)
$AB = 16.4$ cm (3 s.f.)

(b) Triangle OAB at 17:50 angle AOB
$= 4 \times 30° + (30° - \frac{50}{60} \times 30) = 125°$
$AB^2 = 10^2 + 7^2 - 2 \times 10 \times 7 \times \cos(125°)$
(cosine rule: $a^2 = b^2 + c^2 - 2bc\cos A$)
$AB = 15.1$ cm (3 s.f.)

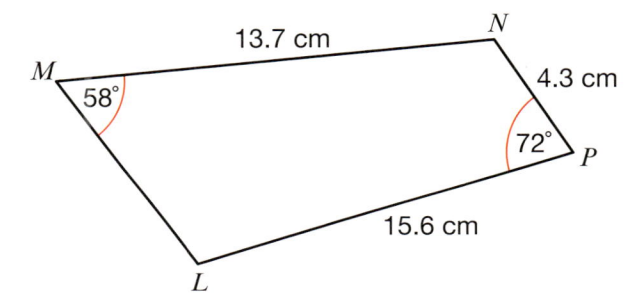

3

Let required area $LMNP =$
Area of triangle LNP + Area of triangle LMN
Area of triangle LNP
$= \frac{1}{2} \times 15.6 \times 4.3 \times \sin(72°) = 31.898...$ cm^2

(area of triangle $= \frac{1}{2} ab\sin C$)

Triangle LNP:
$LN^2 = 15.6^2 + 4.3^2 - 2 \times 15.6 \times 4.3 \times \cos(72°)$
(cosine rule: $a^2 = b^2 + c^2 - 2bc\cos A$)
$LN = 14.846...$ cm
Triangle LMN:

$\frac{\sin(MLN)}{13.7} = \frac{\sin(58°)}{14.846}$

$\left(\text{sine rule: } \frac{a}{\sin A} = \frac{b}{\sin B} = \frac{c}{\sin C}\right)$

$\sin(MLN) = 0.78259...$,
angle $MLN = 51.498°...$
angle $MNL = 180 - 58 - 51.498 = 70.502°...$
(angle sum of a triangle $= 180°$)

Area triangle LMN

$= \frac{1}{2} \times 13.7 \times 14.846 \times \sin(70.502°)$

$= 95.863$ cm^2...

Area $LMNP = 31.898 + 95.863$
$= 127.761$ cm^2... $= 128$ cm^2 (3 s.f.)

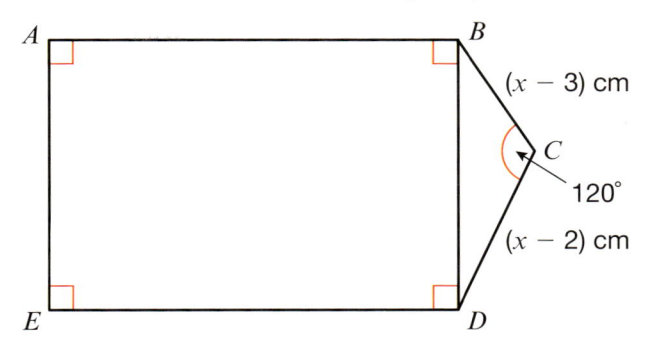

4

$ABDE$ is a rectangle in which $AB = 2BD$
Triangle BCD:
$BD^2 = (x-3)^2 + (x-2)^2 - 2(x-3)(x-2)\cos(120°)$
(cosine rule: $a^2 = b^2 + c^2 - 2bc\cos A$)
$= (x^2 - 6x + 9) + (x^2 - 4x + 4) + (x^2 - 5x + 6)$
$= 3x^2 - 15x + 19$
Alternative: $AB \times BD = 14$ so $2(BD)^2 = 14$
and $BD^2 = 7$
$3x^2 - 15x + 19 = 7$ etc
Area $ABDE = 14 = AB \times BD = 2BD \times BD =$
$2(BD)^2 = 2(3x^2 - 15x + 19) = 6x^2 - 30x + 38$
$0 = 6x^2 - 30x + 24$
$0 = x^2 - 5x + 4$
$0 = (x-4)(x-1)$
$x = 4$ or $x = 1$
Discard $x = 1$ as the sides lengths are > 0.
If $x = 4$, $BC = 1$, $DC = 2$, $BD^2 = 7$,
$BD = \sqrt{7}$, $AB = 2\sqrt{7}$
Required perimeter of pentagon
$ABCDE = 2AB + AE + BC + CD$
$= 4\sqrt{7} + \sqrt{7} + 1 + 2 = 5\sqrt{7} + 3$ cm

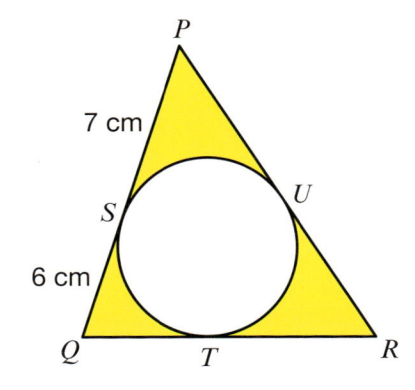

5

Perimeter of triangle $PQR = 42$ cm
$PS = PU = 7$ cm
$QS = QT = 6$ cm
$RT = RU = 8$ cm
Triangle PQR
$15^2 = 13^2 + 14^2 - 2 \times 13 \times 14 \times \cos(SQT)$
(Cosine rule: $a^2 = b^2 + c^2 - 2bc\cos A$)

352 ANSWERS

$\cos(SQT) = \frac{13^2 + 14^2 - 15^2}{2 \times 13 \times 14} = \frac{5}{13}$,

angle $SQT = 67.380°...$

Let required area be A cm².
A = Area of triangle PQR − Area of circle
Area of triangle PQR
$= \frac{1}{2} \times 13 \times 14 \times \sin(67.380°) = 84.000...$cm²

(Area of triangle = $\frac{1}{2} ab \sin C$)

Consider circle centre O and triangle QSO.
Angle $OSQ = 90°$, so triangle QSO is a right-angled triangle.
OS = radius of circle r
$\tan\left(\frac{1}{2} \times 67.380°\right) = \frac{r}{6}$

$r = 4$ cm
Area of circle = $\pi \times 4^2 = 50.265...$cm²
$A = 84.000 - 50.265 = 33.7$ cm² (3 s.f.)

HANDLING DATA 6 – BASIC SKILLS EXERCISE

frequency density = $\frac{\text{frequency}}{\text{class width}}$

Be careful with the class widths when the data is continuous (i.e. time, weight, length, volume…)

1

Time, t	$10 < t \le 20$	$20 < t \le 25$	$25 < t \le 30$	$30 < t \le 40$	$40 < t \le 50$	$50 < t \le 70$	$70 < t \le 95$
Frequency	7	15	25	18	12	8	5
Frequency density	0.7	3	5	1.8	1.2	0.4	0.2

2 (a)

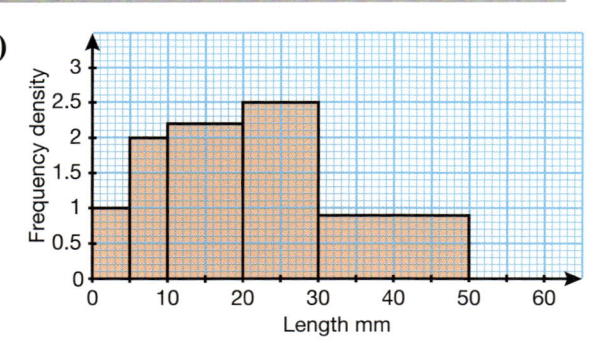

Length, l (mm)	Frequency density
$0 < l \le 5$	1
$5 < l \le 10$	2
$10 < l \le 20$	2.2
$20 < l \le 30$	2.5
$30 < l \le 50$	0.9

(b) 7
(c) 22.0 mm

3 (a)

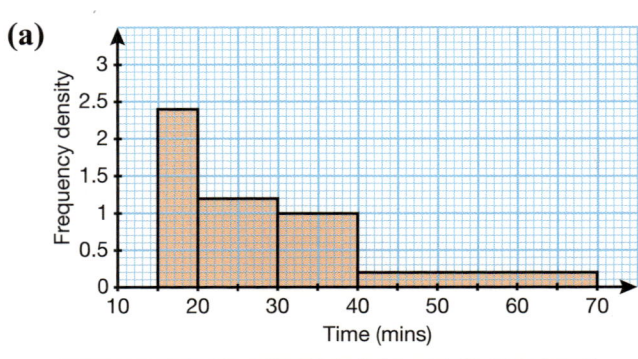

Time, t (min)	Frequency density
$15 < t \le 20$	2.4
$20 < t \le 30$	1.2
$30 < t \le 40$	1
$40 < t \le 70$	0.2

(b) 2
(c) 17 (16.8)

4 (a)

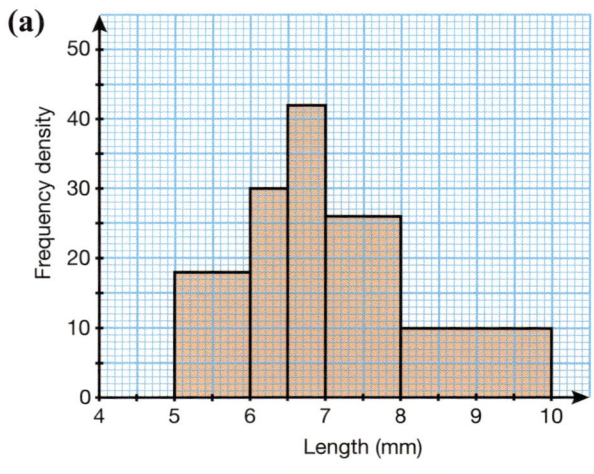

Length, l (mm)	Frequency density
$5 < l \le 6$	18
$6 < l \le 6.5$	30
$6.5 < l \le 7$	42
$7 < l \le 8$	26
$8 < l \le 10$	10

(b) 76
(c) 7.10 mm

5 (a)

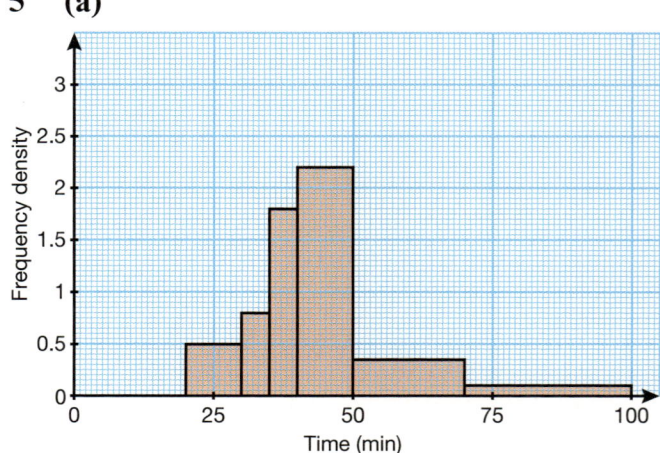

ANSWERS 353

Time, t (min)	Frequency density
$20 < t \le 30$	0.5
$30 < t \le 35$	0.8
$35 < t \le 40$	1.8
$40 < t \le 50$	2.2
$50 < t \le 70$	0.35
$70 < t \le 100$	0.1

(b) 71.2%
(c) 43.2 mins

HANDLING DATA 6 – EXAM PRACTICE EXERCISE

Frequency density = $\frac{\text{frequency}}{\text{class-width}}$

Be careful with the class widths when the data is continuous (i.e. time, weight, length, volume…)

1 (a) (b)

Mass, m (g)	Frequency	Frequency density
$60 < m \le 70$	12	1.2
$70 < m \le 80$	22	2.2
$80 < m \le 100$	40	2
$100 < m \le 120$	20	1
$120 < m \le 160$	16	0.4

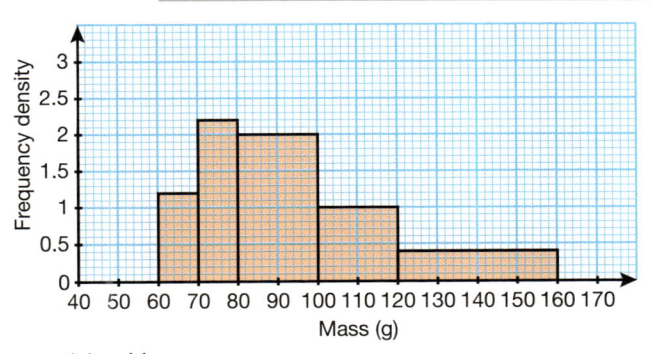

(c) 41

2 (a)

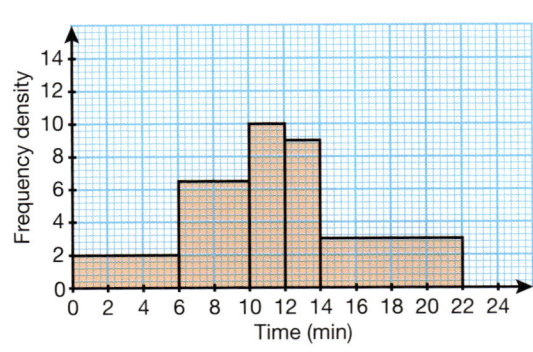

(b)

Time, t (min)	Frequency	Frequency density
$0 < t \le 6$	12	2
$6 < t \le 10$	26	6.5
$10 < t \le 12$	20	10
$12 < t \le 14$	18	9
$14 < t \le 22$	24	3

(c) 57%
(d) 11.2 min

3 (a)

Life, t (h)	Frequency	Frequency density
$60 < t \le 80$	24	1.2
$80 < t \le 90$	26	2.6
$90 < t \le 95$	20	4
$95 < t \le 100$	25	5
$100 < t \le 115$	54	3.6
$115 < t \le x$	51	1

(b) $x = 166$
(c)

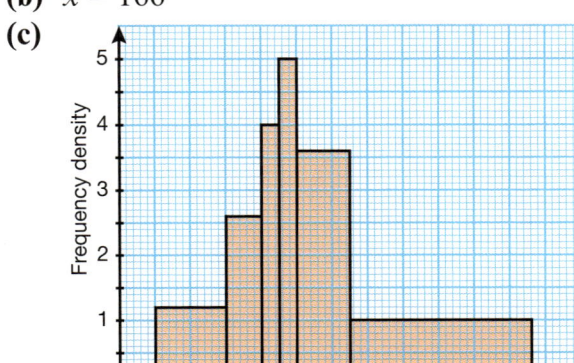

4 (a)

Mass, m kg	Frequency	Frequency density
$2 < m \le 3$	52	52
$3 < m \le 3.25$	34	136
$3.25 < m \le 3.5$	30	120
$3.5 < m \le 4$	60	120
$4 < m \le 4.75$	24	32

(b)

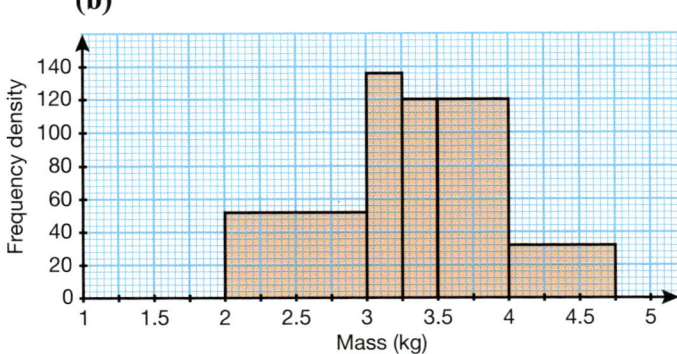

(c) 0.83
(d) 3.37 kg

5 (a)

Consumption, m (ml)	Frequency
$0 < m \le 50$	9
$50 < m \le 100$	42
$100 < m \le 125$	30
$125 < m \le 150$	25
$150 < m \le 200$	25
$200 < m \le 300$	22
$300 < m \le 500$	27

(b)

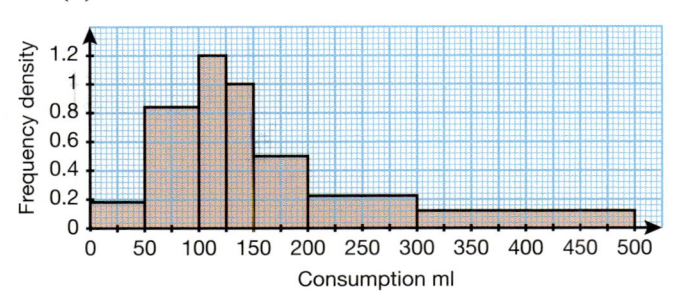

(c) 134 ml
(d) 50.1%

NUMBER 10 – BASIC SKILLS EXERCISE

1. a, b and d
2. (a) e.g. 4.2
   (b) e.g. 5.4
3. (a) e.g. $\sqrt{137}$
   (b) e.g. $\sqrt{9.9}$
4. (a) e.g. $k = 3$
   (b) e.g. $k = 1$
5. $n = \frac{28}{3k}$ therefore rational
6. $\sqrt{63k}$
7. $8k\sqrt{3}$
8. (a) $a^2 b$
   (b) $\frac{1}{4a}$
   (c) $\frac{8a}{b}$
9. 4.5
10. $\frac{1}{2}$
11. (a) $17\sqrt{3}$
    (b) $\sqrt{7}$
    (c) $5\sqrt{10}$
12. $a = 12$
13. (a) $2\sqrt{2} - 1$
    (b) $11 - 6\sqrt{2}$
    (c) 24
14. (a) $a\sqrt{b}$
    (b) $a + b + 2\sqrt{a}\sqrt{b}$
    (c) $1 - a$
    (d) $4a$
15. $4\sqrt{ab}$
16. $a = 4, b = 12$
17. (a) $\sqrt{3}$
    (b) 2
    (c) 2
    (d) $9\sqrt{3}$
18. (a) $\frac{22(7 - \sqrt{5})}{7}$
    (b) $3 + 3\sqrt{3}$
    (c) $\sqrt{7} + \sqrt{5}$
19. (a) $2a + 1 + \sqrt{2}(a + 1)$
    (b) $\sqrt{a}$
    (c) $4\sqrt{a} + 3$
20. $\frac{3\sqrt{2}}{8}$
21. $\frac{\sqrt{a}(a^2 + a + 1)}{a^3}$
22. All are equal to $\frac{3\sqrt{35}}{14}$
23. Radius = $\sqrt{12} = 2\sqrt{3} \Rightarrow$
    Perimeter = $2 \times 2\sqrt{3} + \pi 2\sqrt{3}$
24. $x\sqrt{12} + x\sqrt{75} = 21$
    $x(2\sqrt{3} + 5\sqrt{3}) = 21$
    $x = \frac{21 \times \sqrt{3}}{(7\sqrt{3}) \times \sqrt{3}} = \sqrt{3}$
25. $x2\sqrt{2} - \frac{3x}{\sqrt{2}} = 5$
    $4x - 3x = 5\sqrt{2}$
    $x = 5\sqrt{2}$
26. $4\sqrt{2}$
27. $n = 4$
28. $x = \frac{2 \pm \sqrt{10}}{2}$
29. $x = 2\sqrt{3}$ or $x = \frac{\sqrt{3}}{3}$
30. $7(4a + 2\sqrt{2}a^2)$
31. $\sqrt{a}$

32 Let h be the third side of the triangle

$(\sqrt{2} + \sqrt{14})^2 = h^2 + (2 + \sqrt{7})^2$

Pythagoras' theorem

$16 + 2\sqrt{2}\sqrt{14} = h^2 + 11 + 4\sqrt{7}$

$5 + 4\sqrt{7} = h^2 + 4\sqrt{7}$ $\qquad \sqrt{14} = \sqrt{2}\sqrt{7}$

$h^2 = 5$

$h = \sqrt{5}$

area $= \frac{1}{2}(2 + \sqrt{7}) \times \sqrt{5}$

Area of a triangle $= \frac{1}{2}$ base $\times$ height

area $= \left(\frac{2 + \sqrt{7}}{2}\right)\sqrt{5}$, so $p = \sqrt{5}$

NUMBER 10 – EXAM PRACTICE EXERCISE

1 **(a)** **(i)**

$\dfrac{a - \sqrt{a}}{a + \sqrt{a}} = \dfrac{(a - \sqrt{a})(a - \sqrt{a})}{(a + \sqrt{a})(a - \sqrt{a})}$

$= \dfrac{a^2 - 2a\sqrt{a} + a}{a^2 - a}$

$= \dfrac{a(a - 2\sqrt{a} + 1)}{a(a - 1)}$

$= \dfrac{a + 1 - 2\sqrt{a}}{a - 1}$

(ii)

$\dfrac{1}{\sqrt{a}} + \dfrac{1}{a} + \dfrac{1}{\sqrt{a^3}} = \dfrac{1}{\sqrt{a}} + \dfrac{1}{\sqrt{a}\sqrt{a}} + \dfrac{1}{\sqrt{a}\sqrt{a}\sqrt{a}}$

$= \dfrac{a + \sqrt{a} + 1}{\sqrt{a^3}}$

$= \dfrac{\sqrt{a^3}(a + \sqrt{a} + 1)}{\sqrt{a^3}\sqrt{a^3}}$

$= \dfrac{a^2\sqrt{a} + a^2 + a\sqrt{a}}{a^3}$

$= \dfrac{a\sqrt{a} + a + \sqrt{a}}{a^2}$

$= \dfrac{a + \sqrt{a}(a + 1)}{a^2}$

(b) $r = 25s$

$\dfrac{p}{q} = \dfrac{\sqrt{125} + \sqrt{25s}}{\sqrt{5} + \sqrt{s}}$

$= \dfrac{5\sqrt{5} + 5\sqrt{s}}{\sqrt{5} + \sqrt{s}}$

$= \dfrac{5(\sqrt{5} + \sqrt{s})}{\sqrt{5} + \sqrt{s}}$

$= 5$

$p : q = 5 : 1$

2 Total surface area is two ends plus curved surface area $= 2\pi r^2 + 2\pi rh$

$2\pi(3\sqrt{2})^2 + 2\pi(3\sqrt{2})(a\sqrt{2} + b\sqrt{3}) = 48\sqrt{6}\pi$

Divide both sides by π

$36 + 2(6a + 3b\sqrt{6}) = 48\sqrt{6}$

$36 + 12a + 6b\sqrt{6} = 48\sqrt{6}$

equating rational numbers and irrational numbers separately

$36 + 12a = 0$ and $6b = 48$

$a = -3$ and $b = 8$

3 **(a)** Using the quadratic formula with

$a = 1$, $b = -(1 + 2\sqrt{p})$ and $c = p + \sqrt{p}$

$b^2 - 4ac = (1 + 2\sqrt{p})^2 - 4(p + \sqrt{p})$

$= 1 + 4p + 4\sqrt{p} - 4p - 4\sqrt{p} = 1$

$x = \dfrac{(1 + 2\sqrt{p}) \pm 1}{2}$

$x = \dfrac{2 + 2\sqrt{p}}{2}$ or $x = \dfrac{2\sqrt{p}}{2}$

$x = 1 + \sqrt{p}$ or $x = \sqrt{p}$

(b) $(a + \sqrt{b})(a + \sqrt{b}) = a^2 + b + 2a\sqrt{b}$

$a^2 + b + 2a\sqrt{b} = 7 + \sqrt{48}$

$a^2 + b = 7(1)$ and $2a\sqrt{b} = \sqrt{48}(2)$

equating rational values and irrational values separately

(1) $a^2 = 7 - b$, (2) $a^2 b = 12$

Substituting (1) into (2) gives

$(7 - b)b = 12$

$b^2 - 7b + 12 = 0$

$(b - 4)(b - 3) = 0$

$b = 4$ or $b = 3$

$a^2 = 3$ or $a^2 = 4$

$a = \pm\sqrt{3}$ or $a = \pm 2$

$\sqrt{7 + \sqrt{48}} = \pm 2 \pm \sqrt{3}$

The positive possible values are $2 + \sqrt{3}$ or $2 - \sqrt{3}$

$(2 + \sqrt{3})^2 = 7 + 4\sqrt{48} = 7 + \sqrt{48}$ Correct

$(2 - \sqrt{3})^2 = 7 - 4\sqrt{3} = 7 - \sqrt{48}$ Incorrect

Positive value of $\sqrt{7 + \sqrt{48}} = 2 + \sqrt{3}$

4 Let w be the width

$w(a + \sqrt{2}) = (1 + a)\sqrt{2} + (a + 2)$

$w = \dfrac{(1 + a)\sqrt{2} + (a + 2)}{a + \sqrt{2}}$

$= \dfrac{[(1 + a)\sqrt{2} + (a + 2)](a - \sqrt{2})}{(a + \sqrt{2})(a - \sqrt{2})}$

$= \dfrac{a\sqrt{2} + a^2\sqrt{2} + a^2 + 2a - 2 - 2a - a\sqrt{2} - 2\sqrt{2}}{a^2 - 2}$

$= \dfrac{a^2(1 + \sqrt{2}) - 2(1 + \sqrt{2})}{a^2 - 2}$

$= \dfrac{(a^2 - 2)(1 + \sqrt{2})}{a^2 - 2}$

$= 1 + \sqrt{2}$ cm

5 Let h be the height of the triangle

$\frac{1}{2}(3 - \sqrt{2}) \times h = \sqrt{6} + \dfrac{\sqrt{3}}{2}$

$\sqrt{6} + \dfrac{\sqrt{3}}{2} = \dfrac{2\sqrt{6} + \sqrt{3}}{2}$

$h = \dfrac{2\sqrt{6} + \sqrt{3}}{3 - \sqrt{2}}$

$= \dfrac{(2\sqrt{6} + \sqrt{3})(3 + \sqrt{2})}{(3 - \sqrt{2})(3 + \sqrt{2})}$

$= \dfrac{6\sqrt{6} + 3\sqrt{3} + 2\sqrt{2}\sqrt{6} + \sqrt{6}}{9 - 2}$

$2\sqrt{2}\sqrt{6} = 2\sqrt{2}\sqrt{2}\sqrt{3}$

$= 4\sqrt{3}$

$h = \dfrac{7\sqrt{6} + 7\sqrt{3}}{7}$

$= \sqrt{6} + \sqrt{3}$ cm

Let H be the hypotenuse of triangle.

$H^2 = (3 - \sqrt{2})^2 + (\sqrt{6} + \sqrt{3})^2$

$\quad = 11 - 6\sqrt{2} + 9 + 2\sqrt{3}\sqrt{6}$

$2\sqrt{3}\sqrt{6} = 2\sqrt{3}\sqrt{2}\sqrt{3} = 6\sqrt{2}$

$\quad = 20$

$H = \sqrt{20}$

Perimeter $= (3 - \sqrt{2}) + (\sqrt{6} + \sqrt{3}) + \sqrt{20}$

$= \sqrt{3}\sqrt{3} - \sqrt{2} + \sqrt{2}\sqrt{3} + \sqrt{3} + \sqrt{4}\sqrt{5}$

$= \sqrt{2}(\sqrt{3} - 1) + \sqrt{3}(\sqrt{3} + 1) + 2\sqrt{5}$ cm

ALGEBRA 10 – BASIC SKILLS EXERCISE

1 $2 + 3x$

2 $3x$

3 $-5x$

4 $\dfrac{x + 6}{4}$

5 $\dfrac{x - 2}{3}$

6 $\dfrac{2(x - 5)}{x - 4}$

7 $\dfrac{x + 1}{x - 2}$

8 $\dfrac{2x - 3}{3x + 2}$

9 $\dfrac{93 - 11x}{35}$

10 $\dfrac{x^2 + x + 1}{x + 1}$

11 $\dfrac{2x + 5}{3(x - 2)}$

12 $\dfrac{3x}{(1 - x)(2 + x)}$

13 $\dfrac{x + 7}{(2x - 1)(3x + 1)}$

14 $\dfrac{-2}{(x + 4)(x + 6)}$

15 $\dfrac{1}{3(x - 6)}$

16 $\dfrac{-1}{2(x + 3)}$

17 $(x - 7)(x - 3)$

18 $3x$

19 $\dfrac{x}{(x + 1)(x - 7)}$

20 $\dfrac{x - 1}{x + 1}$

21 1

22 2

23 $\dfrac{3}{x + 2}$

24 $x + 3$

25 $x = 28$

26 $x = -2.427$, $x = 2$

28 $x = -8$

29 $x = -\frac{1}{2}$ or -4

30 $x = -6$ or $x = 4$

31 $x = \pm 2$

32 $x = 2.4$

33 $x = -2$

34 $x = 2$ or $x = 3$

35 $\frac{1}{x-1}$

36 $\frac{2}{3}$

37 $3 - 2x$

38 $\frac{x^2 - 3x - 4}{x + 3} \div \frac{x + 1}{x^2 - x - 12} = \frac{(x - 4)(x + 1)}{x + 3}$

$\times \frac{(x - 4)(x + 3)}{x + 1} = (x - 4)^2 \geq 0$

ALGEBRA 10 – EXAM PRACTICE EXERCISE

1 (a) $\frac{3y}{x} - \frac{y}{x + 3} = y\left(\frac{3}{x} - \frac{1}{x + 3}\right)$

$= y\left(\frac{3(x + 3) - x}{x(x + 3)}\right) = y\left(\frac{2x + 9}{x(x + 3)}\right)$

$\frac{3y}{x} - \frac{y}{x + 3} = 2x + 9$

$y\left(\frac{2x + 9}{x(x + 3)}\right) = 2x + 9$

$y = \frac{x(x + 3)(2x + 9)}{(2x + 9)}$

$y = x(x + 3)$

$y = x^2 + 3x$

$y = \left(x + \frac{3}{2}\right)^2 - \frac{9}{4}$

(b) (i) $\left(-\frac{3}{2}, -\frac{9}{4}\right)$, **(ii)** a minimum

y is a positive quadratic

2 (a) $x = \frac{t + 3}{t - 1}$

$x(t - 1) = t + 3$

$xt - x = t + 3$

$t(x - 1) = x + 3$

$t = \frac{x + 3}{x - 1}$

Substituting gives $y = \left(\frac{x + 3}{x - 1}\right)^2 - 4\left(\frac{x + 3}{x - 1}\right)$

$y = \frac{(x + 3)^2 - 4(x - 1)(x + 3)}{(x - 1)^2}$

$y = \frac{x^2 + 6x + 9 - 4x^2 - 8x + 12}{(x - 1)^2}$

$y = \frac{-3x^2 - 2x + 21}{(x - 1)^2}$

$y = \frac{-(3x - 7)(x + 3)}{(x - 1)^2}$ or $\frac{(7 - 3x)(x + 3)}{(x - 1)^2}$

(b) $\left(\frac{x + 3}{x - 1}\right) \div y$

$= \left(\frac{x + 3}{x - 1}\right) \times \frac{(x - 1)^2}{(7 - 3x)(x + 3)}$

$= \frac{x - 1}{7 - 3x}\left(\frac{x + 3}{x - 1}\right) : y = (x - 1) : (7 - 3x)$

3 (a) $\frac{2x^2 + 5x - 12}{4x^2 - 9} \div \frac{x^2 + 2x - 8}{2x^2 + 5x + 3}$

$= \frac{2x^2 + 5x - 12}{4x^2 - 9} \times \frac{2x^2 + 5x + 3}{x^2 + 2x - 8}$

$= \frac{(2x - 3)(x + 4)}{(2x + 3)(2x - 3)} \times \frac{(2x + 3)(x + 1)}{(x + 4)(x - 2)}$

$= \frac{x + 1}{x - 2}$

(b) $\frac{2x^2 + 5x - 12}{4x^2 - 9} \div \frac{x^2 + 2x - 8}{2x^2 + 5x + 3}$

$= 1 + \frac{x}{x + 2}$

$\frac{x + 1}{x - 2} = 1 + \frac{x}{x + 2}$

Using the result from part a.

$\frac{x + 1}{x - 2} = 1 + \frac{x}{x + 2}$

$(x + 1)(x + 2) = (x - 2) + x(x + 2) + x(x - 2)$

Multiplying both sides by $(x - 2)(x + 2)$

$x^2 + 3x + 2 = x^2 - 4 + x^2 - 2x$

$x^2 - 5x - 6 = 0$

$(x + 1)(x - 6) = 0$

$x = -1$ or $x = 6$

4 Time taken to travel x km at $x + 10$ km/h is $\frac{x}{x+10}$ h

Time taken to travel $70 - x$ km at $x - 20$ km/h is $\frac{70-x}{x-20}$ h

$\frac{x}{x+10} + \frac{70-x}{x-20} = 1$

Multiply both sides by $(x+10)(x-20)$
$x(x-20) + (x+10)(70-x) = (x+10)(x-20)$
$x^2 - 20x - x^2 + 60x + 700 = x^2 - 10x - 200$
$x^2 - 50x - 900 = 0$
Solving using the quadratic formula gives
$x = 25 + 5\sqrt{61}$ or 64.1 to 3 s.f.

5 (a) $y = \frac{8x^2 + 16x - 10}{3x^2 - 3} \div \frac{2x+5}{3x-3}$

$= \frac{2(2x-1)(2x+5)}{3(x-1)(x+1)} \times \frac{3(x-1)}{(2x+5)}$

$= \frac{2(2x-1)}{x+1}$

(b) Half perimeter is $\frac{2x+5}{3x-3} + \frac{2(2x-1)}{x+1} = 5$

Multiply both sides by $3(x-1)(x+1)$
$(2x+5)(x+1) + 2(2x-1)3(x-1) = 5 \times 3(x-1)(x+1)$
$2x^2 + 7x + 5 + 12x^2 - 18x + 6 = 15x^2 - 15$
$x^2 + 11x - 26 = 0$
$(x-2)(x+13) = 0$
$x = 2$
sides are $\frac{4+5}{6-3} = 3$ and $\frac{2(4-1)}{3} = 2$

area $= 3 \times 2 = 6$ cm²

GRAPHS 9 – BASIC SKILLS EXERCISE

1 (a) $\frac{dy}{dx} = 3$

(b) $\frac{dy}{dx} = 0$

(c) $\frac{dy}{dx} = 3x^2$

(d) $\frac{dy}{dx} = 4x^3$

(e) $\frac{dy}{dx} = 5x^4$

(f) $\frac{dy}{dx} = 12x^5$

(g) $\frac{dy}{dx} = 15x^4$

(h) $\frac{dy}{dx} = 160x^7$

2 (a) $\frac{dy}{dx} = 6x^2 + 10x$

(b) $\frac{dy}{dx} = 14x - 3$

(c) $\frac{dy}{dx} = 15x^2$

(d) $\frac{dy}{dx} = 12x^3 - 10x$

(e) $\frac{dy}{dx} = 3x^2 + 10x$

(f) $\frac{dy}{dx} = 2x + 2$

(g) $\frac{dy}{dx} = 4x - 9$

(h) $\frac{dy}{dx} = 2x + 4$

3 (a) $\frac{dy}{dx} = -x^{-2} = -\frac{1}{x^2}$

(b) $\frac{dy}{dx} = -2x^{-3} = -\frac{2}{x^3}$

(c) $\frac{dy}{dx} = \frac{1}{2}x^{-\frac{1}{2}} = \frac{1}{2\sqrt{x}}$

(d) $\frac{dy}{dx} = -3x^{-4} = -\frac{3}{x^4}$

(e) $\frac{dy}{dx} = -16x^{-5} = -\frac{16}{x^5}$

(f) $\frac{dy}{dx} = -x^{-3} = -\frac{1}{x^3}$

(g) $\frac{dy}{dx} = 4x + 3 - 4x^{-2}$

(h) $\frac{dy}{dx} = 2 + 3x^{-2}$

4 (a) $\frac{dy}{dx}$ (at $x = 1$) $= 4$

(b) $\frac{dy}{dx}$ (at $x = 1$) $= -5$

(c) $\frac{dy}{dx}$ (at $x = 1$) $= 26$

(d) $\frac{dy}{dx}$ (at $x = 2$) $= 19$

5 (a) -2

(b) 2

(c) 0

(d) $\frac{-17}{8}$

6 $4y = 3x + 4$

7 $y = -3x, y = 3x - 9$

8 $p = 1$

9    $p = 3$, $q = -2$, so $p^3 + q^3 = 27 - 8 = 19$

10   (a) $\frac{dy}{dx} = 3x^2 - 3$

     (b) $(1, 0)$, $(-1, 4)$
     (c) $(-1, 4)$ is max, $(1, 0)$ is min.

11   (a) $\frac{dy}{dx} = 3x^2 + 6x - 9$

     (b) $(-3, 28)$, $(1, -4)$

     (c) $(-3, 28)$ is max, $(1, -4)$ is min.

12   (a) $(0, 1)$, $(4/3, -0.185185...)$

     (b) $x = 0$ is a max, $x = \frac{4}{3}$ is a min.

13   (a) $v = 24t$ m/s

     (b) 48 m/s

     (c) $a = 24$ m/s^2

     (d) 24 m/s^2

14   (a) $v = 3t^2 + 8t - 3$ m/s

     (b) 377 m/s

     (c) $a = 6t + 8$ m/s^2

     (d) 68 m/s^2

15   (a) $s = 125$ m

     (b) $t = 5$

16   (a) $v = \frac{ds}{dt} = 3t^2 - 300$ km/s

     (b) at $t = 5$, $v = -225$ km/s

     (c) $a = \frac{dv}{dt} = 6t$ km/s^2

     (d) at $t = 5$, $a = 30$ km/s^2

     (e) $t = 10$ s

17   (a) $v = 24t$ m/s

     (b) 72 m/s

     (c) $a = 24$ m/s^2, (constant)

     (d) 24 m/s^2

18   (a) $v = 3t^2 - 500$ km/s

     (b) at $t = 10$ s, $v = -200$ km/s

     (c) $a = 6t$ km/s^2

     (d) at $t = 10$ s, $a = 60$ km/s^2

     (e) $t = \left(\frac{\sqrt{500}}{3}\right)^{0.5}$ s, 12.9 s

19   (a) $\frac{dQ}{dt} = 3t^2 - 16t + 14$

     (b) (i)   14 m^3/s^2
          (ii)   −6 m^3/s^2
          (iii) 9 m^3/s^2

20   (a) $\frac{dC}{dt} = 4 - 16t^{-2} = 4 - \frac{16}{t^2}$

     (b) $t = 2$, $C = 1$

     (c) −12°C/month

GRAPHS 9 – EXAM PRACTICE EXERCISE

1   (a) $P = 5t^2 + \frac{10000}{t} + 10$

          $P = 5t^2 + 10000t^{-1} + 10$

          (Rewrite P in index form so differentiation is easier.)

          $\frac{dP}{dt} = 10t - 10000t^{-2}$ flowers/year

          (Now equate this to zero and solve for t.)

     (b) $\frac{dP}{dt} = 0 = 10t - \frac{10000}{t^2}$

          (Multiply by t^2.)
          $0 = 10t^3 - 10000$
          $10000 = 10t^3$
          $1000 = t^3$
          $t = 10$ yrs
          (From the graph, the gradient of the curve is zero at $t = 10$ yrs.)
          At $t = 10$, $P = 1510$
          (Substitute $t = 10$ into equation for P.)

2   (a) $y = x^2 - 3x$ (Differentiate to find the gradient function.)

          $\frac{dy}{dx} = 2x - 3$ (Find the gradient to the curve at $x = 4$.)

          At $x = 4$, $\frac{dy}{dx} = 5$

          Gradient of normal $= -\frac{1}{5}$

          (If m_1 is gradient of tangent and m_2 is gradient of normal, $m_1 \times m_2 = -1$)

          Equation of normal at $x = 4$ is

          $y = -\frac{1}{5}x + c$

(Equation of a straight line is $y = mx + c$)

At $x = 4$, $y = 4$ (The y-value is found by substituting $x = 4$ into $y = x^2 - 3x$)

$4 = -\frac{1}{5} \times 4 + c$ (Point (4, 4) is on the normal so it must satisfy the equation.)

$c = 4\frac{4}{5}$, so equation of normal is

$y = -\frac{1}{5}x + 4\frac{4}{5}$

$x + 5y = 24$ (Multiply the equation $y = -\frac{1}{5}x + 4\frac{4}{5}$ by 5 and re-arrange.)

$a = 1$, $b = 5$, $c = 24$

(b) At A, $y = 0$, so $x = 24$

At B, $x = 0$, so $y = \frac{24}{5}$

Area of triangle $OAB = \frac{1}{2} \times$ base $\times$ height

$= \frac{1}{2} \times 24 \times \frac{24}{5} = \frac{288}{5}$ units^2

So $\frac{288}{5}$ = area of a square side x

$x = \sqrt{\frac{288}{5}} = \frac{12\sqrt{10}}{5}$, $p = 4x$

so $p = \frac{48\sqrt{10}}{5} = \frac{48\sqrt{2}}{\sqrt{5}}$ as required

$\left(\frac{48\sqrt{10}}{5} = \frac{48\sqrt{5} \times \sqrt{2}}{\sqrt{5} \times \sqrt{5}}\right)$

3 (a) At $A(1, 5)$: $5 = 1 - 6 + p + q$

so $p + q = 10$ (1)

(Substitute coordinates of A into equation)

If A is a turning point $\frac{dy}{dx} = 0$
$= 3x^2 - 12x + p$
So at $x = 1$, $0 = 3 - 12 + p$,
so $p = 9$ and $q = 1$ (Using equation (1))

(b) $y = x^3 - 6x^2 + 9x + 1$

$\frac{dy}{dx} = 3x^2 - 12x + 9$

$0 = x^2 - 4x + 3$

(Gradient = 0 at turning points)
$0 = (x - 1)(x - 3)$
$x = 1$ or $x = 3$, so $y = 5$ or 1 so $A(1, 5)$, $B(3, 1)$

Due to the shape of the cubic curve, the smallest x value is the maximum point on the function.
So $A(1, 5)$ max point and $B(3, 1)$ min point.

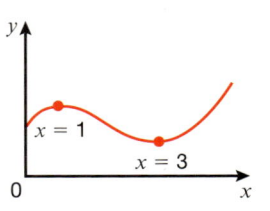

4 (a) $v = t(k - 5t) = kt - 5t^2$

$a = \frac{dv}{dt} = k - 10t$

(Differentiate velocity function to get acceleration function)
$t = 0$, $a = 3$, so $3 = k - 10 \times 0$,
$k = 3$

(b) $v = 3t - 5t^2 = 0 = t(3 - 5t)$, so $t = 0$ or 0.6 s
$a = 3 - 10t = 3 - 10(0.6)$
(Take the value of $t = 0.6$ s)
$a = -3$ m/s^2

5 (a) (i) $V = \pi r^2 h$
$12 : 4 = h : (4 - r)$
(Similar triangles…)
$h = 3(4 - r)$
$V = \pi r^2 \times 3(4 - r) = 3\pi r^2(4 - r)$ as required

(ii) $V = 12\pi r^2 - 3\pi r^3$

$\frac{dV}{dr} = 24\pi r - 9\pi r^2 = 3\pi r(8 - 3r)$

as required

(b) (i) $\frac{dV}{dr} = 0 = 3\pi r(8 - 3r)$

(Gradient of curve is flat at V_{max})
$r = 0$ or $\frac{8}{3}$, so $r = \frac{8}{3}$ cm
(Ignore $r = 0$ as it does not fit the model)

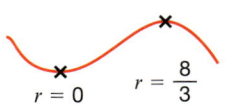

(Negative cubic curves will have this shape)

(ii) When $r = \frac{8}{3}$ cm, $V = 3\pi \left(\frac{8}{3}\right)^2 \left(4 - \frac{8}{3}\right)$

$= \frac{256\pi}{9}$ cm^3, so $p = 9$

SHAPE AND SPACE 10 – BASIC SKILLS EXERCISE

1. 36.4 m
2. 21.4 m
3. 18.4°
4. 0.828 m
5. 10.8°
6. 10.39 m
7. 1.79 m
8. 82.7%
9. (a) 32.6°
   (b) 38.5 units²
10. (a) 243°
    (b) 63.4°
11. 125°
12. (a) 2250 m
    (b) 3897 m
    (c) 4500 m
13. (a) 13.9 km   279.7°
    (b) He travels at 7.2 km/h so he does arrive by 18:00
14. 2.5 km
15. (a) 25.5 km
    (b) 022.7°
    (c) 203°

SHAPE AND SPACE 10 – EXAM PRACTICE EXERCISE

1. Let cliff height WZ be h metres

   Speed = $\frac{\text{Distance}}{\text{Time}}$

   $0.75 = \frac{ZX - ZY}{60}$ [1]

   Triangle WZX:
   $\tan(60°) = \frac{ZX}{h}$, so $ZX = h\tan(60°)$ [2]

   Triangle WZY:
   $\tan(40°) = \frac{ZY}{h}$, so $ZY = h\tan(40°)$ [3]

   Subs [2] and [3] into [1]

   [1] $0.75 = \frac{h\tan(60°) - h\tan(40°)}{60}$

   $= \frac{h[\tan(60°) - \tan(40°)]}{60}$

   So $0.75 \times 60 = h[\tan(60°) - \tan(40°)]$

   $h = \frac{45}{\tan(60°) - \tan(40°)}$

   $h = 50.4$ m (3 s.f.)

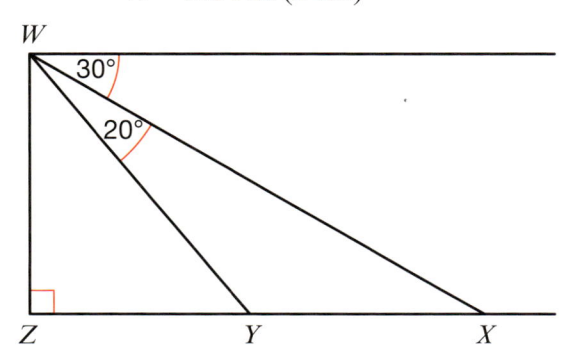

2. speed = $\frac{\text{distance}}{\text{time}}$

   speed of descent = $\frac{100 + h_1 + h_2}{60}$ m/s

   Motion from A to B:
   $\sin(70°) = \frac{h_1}{75}$, $h_1 = 75 \times \sin(70°) = 70.4769\ldots$m

   Motion from B to C:
   $\sin(20°) = \frac{h_2}{50}$, $h_2 = 50 \times \sin(20°) = 17.1010\ldots$m

   speed of descent = $\frac{100 + 70.4769 + 17.1010}{60}$

   $= 3.1263\ldots$m/s $= 3.13$ m/s (3 s.f.)

3

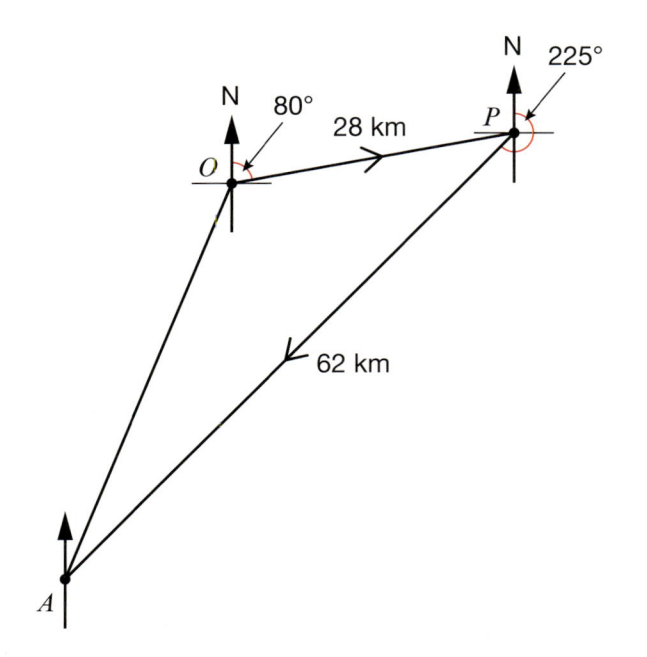

(a) Angle $OPA = 80° - 45° = 35°$
(alternate angles, North to South = 180°)
cosine rule   (SSSA condition so cosine rule)
$OA^2 = 28^2 + 62^2 - 2 \times 28 \times 62 \times \cos(35°)$
$= 1783.9041...$
$OA = 42.2363...$ km
$OA = 42.2$ km (3 s.f.)

(b) Bearing of O from A:
sine rule   (SASA condition so sine rule)
Let angle $OAP = \theta$
$\frac{\sin \theta}{28} = \frac{\sin(35°)}{42.2363}$

so $\sin \theta = \frac{\sin(35°)}{42.2363} \times 28$

$= 0.38024...$
$\theta = 22.349°...$
Angle $AOP = 180° - 35° - 22.349°$
$= 122.651°...$
Bearing of O from $A = (80° + 122.651°) - 180°$ (alternate angles)
Bearing of O from $A = 022.7°$ (3 s.f.)

(c) speed $= \frac{\text{distance}}{\text{time}}$

balloon: $30 = \frac{28 + 62}{t}$, so $t = \frac{90}{30} = 3$ h

truck: speed $= \frac{42.2363}{3} = 14.0787$ km/h...

Speed $= 14.1$ km/h (3 s.f.)

4 (a)

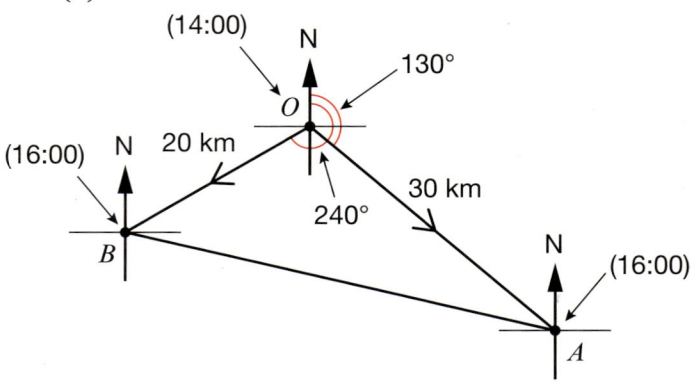

(b) Angle $BOA = 240° - 130° = 110°$
cosine rule
(SSSA condition so cosine rule)
$AB^2 = 20^2 + 30^2 - 2 \times 20 \times 30 \times \cos(110°) = 1710.4241...$ km
$AB = 41.3573...$ km
$AB = 41.4$ km (3 s.f.)

(c) Bearing of A from B:
sine rule   (SASA condition so sine rule)
Let angle $OBA = \theta$
$\frac{\sin \theta}{30} = \frac{\sin(110°)}{41.3573}$

$\sin \theta = \frac{\sin(110°)}{41.3573} \times 30$

$= 0.68163...$
$\theta = 42.9719°...$
Bearing of A from $B = 060° + 042.9719°$
(alternate angles)
Bearing of A from $B = 103°$ (3 s.f.)

5

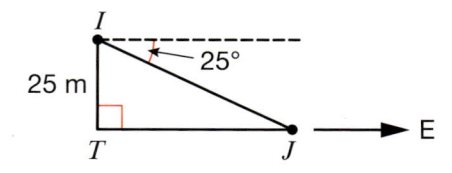

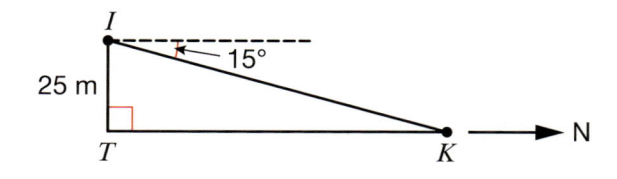

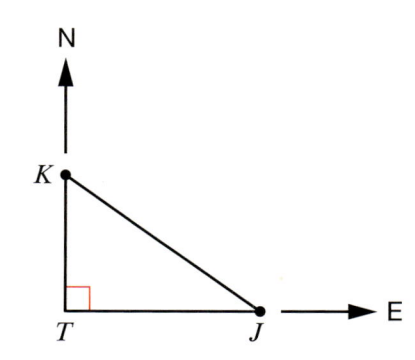

Triangle *ITJ*:

$\tan(65°) = \frac{TJ}{25}$ $\left(\tan \theta = \frac{\text{opposite side}}{\text{adjacent side}}\right)$

$TJ = 25 \times \tan(65°)$
$= 53.6127...$ m

Triangle *ITK*:

$\tan(75°) = \frac{TK}{25}$

$TK = 25 \times \tan(75°)$
$= 93.3013...$ m

Plan view on triangle *KTJ*:

$KJ^2 = KT^2 + TJ^2$
   (Pythagoras' theorem)
$= 53.6127^2 + 93.3013^2$
$= 11\,579.45...$
$KJ = 107.608...$ m
$KJ = 107.6$ m (1 d.p.)

HANDLING DATA 7 – BASIC SKILLS EXERCISE

1 $\frac{5}{14}$

2 (a) $\frac{4}{11}$

(b) $\frac{2}{9}$

3 (a) $\frac{2}{7}$

(b) $\frac{1}{3}$

4 (a) (i) $\frac{5}{11}$

(ii) $\frac{6}{11}$

(b) (i) $\frac{16}{25}$

(ii) $\frac{9}{25}$

(c) 0.798 (3 s.f.)

5 (a) 0.2

(b) 0.1625

(c) 0.097 25

6 (a) (i) $\frac{5}{12}$

(ii) $\frac{11}{60}$

(b) (i) $\frac{7}{145}$

(ii) $\frac{7}{29}$

7 (a)

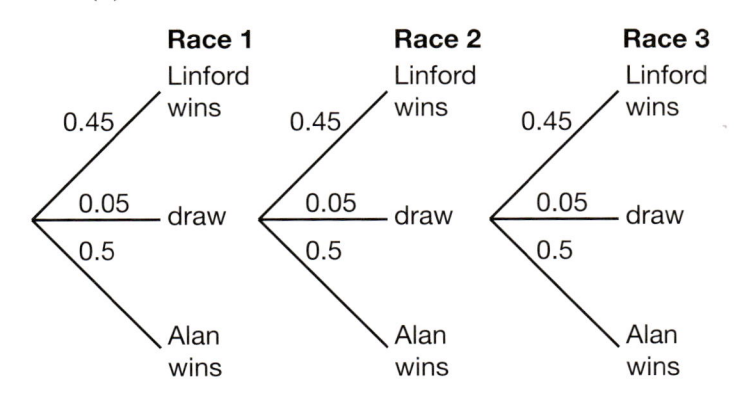

	Race 1	Race 2	Race 3
	Linford wins (0.45)	Linford wins (0.45)	Linford wins (0.45)
	draw (0.05)	draw (0.05)	draw (0.05)
	Alan wins (0.5)	Alan wins (0.5)	Alan wins (0.5)

(b) P(Alan wins) = P(Alan wins 1st race)
or P(draw then Alan wins 2nd race) or
P(draw and Alan wins 3rd race)
$= 0.5 + 0.05 \times 0.5 + 0.05 \times 0.05 \times 0.5$
$= 0.526$

8 (a)

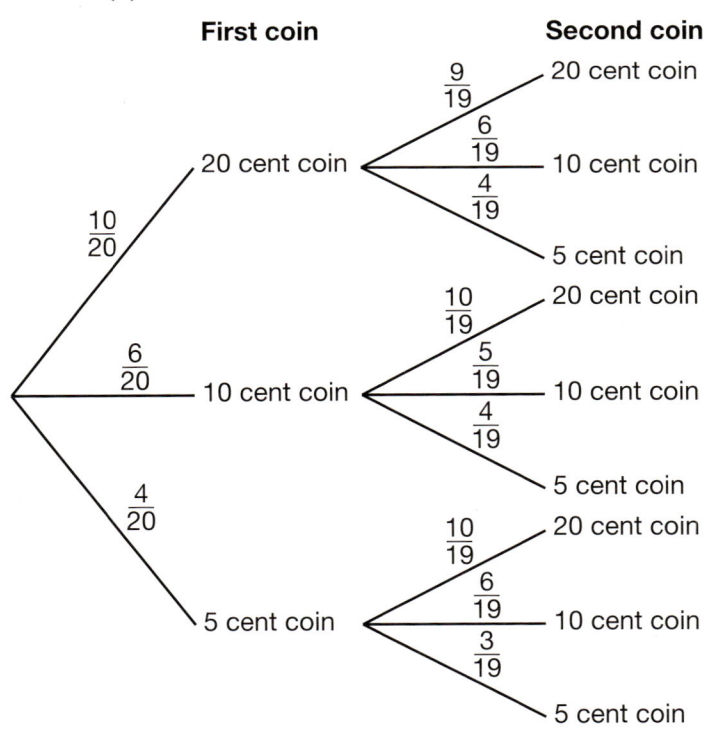

First coin branches:
- 20 cent coin ($\frac{10}{20}$) → 20 cent ($\frac{9}{19}$), 10 cent ($\frac{6}{19}$), 5 cent ($\frac{4}{19}$)
- 10 cent coin ($\frac{6}{20}$) → 20 cent ($\frac{10}{19}$), 10 cent ($\frac{5}{19}$), 5 cent ($\frac{4}{19}$)
- 5 cent coin ($\frac{4}{20}$) → 20 cent ($\frac{10}{19}$), 10 cent ($\frac{6}{19}$), 5 cent ($\frac{3}{19}$)

(b) Let *X* be Emma's score.
$P(X \geq 25) = 1 - P(X < 25)$
$= 1 - P(X \leq 20)$
$P(E) + P(E') = 1$
$= 1 - [P(X = 10) + P(X = 15) + P(X = 20)]$

$$= 1 - \left[\left(\tfrac{4}{20} \times \tfrac{3}{19}\right) + \left(\tfrac{6}{20} \times \tfrac{4}{19}\right) + \tfrac{4}{20} \times \tfrac{6}{19}\right) + \left(\tfrac{6}{20} \times \tfrac{5}{19}\right)\right] = \tfrac{29}{38}$$

(P(A and B) = P(A) × P(B))
(P(A or B) = P(A) + P(B) if A and B are mutually exclusive)

9 (a) (i) 0.6
 (ii) 0.2
 (b) (i) 0.04
 (ii) 0.055

10 (a) $k = 0.1$
 (b) (i) 0.8
  (ii) 0.5
 (c) 0.9

11 (a) (i) $\tfrac{13}{30}$
  (ii) $\tfrac{2}{7}$
 (b) (i) $\tfrac{1}{15}$
  (ii) $\tfrac{34}{35}$

HANDLING DATA 7 – EXAM PRACTICE EXERCISE

1 (a) (i) P(success)
$$= \tfrac{12\,750 + 14\,400 + 14\,800 + 12\,400}{80\,000}$$
$$= \tfrac{54\,350}{80\,000} = \tfrac{1087}{1600}$$

 (ii) P(60-year old no change)
$$= \tfrac{7250 + 5600}{80\,000} = \tfrac{257}{1600}$$

 (iii) P(30-year old success)
$$= \tfrac{14\,800 + 12\,400}{80\,000}$$
$$= \tfrac{17}{50}$$

 (b) P(Success/60 yr old) $= \tfrac{12\,750}{20\,000} = \tfrac{51}{80}$

2 (a) As the herd has a very large number of cows, the proportions will be approximately the same when one, two or three cows are removed.

 (i) $P(F_1) \times P(F_2) = \tfrac{1}{5} \times \tfrac{1}{5} = \tfrac{1}{25}$

(P(A and B) = P(A) × P(B))

 (ii) $P(F_1J_2 \text{ or } J_1F_2) = P(F_1J_2) + P(J_1F_2)$
$= \tfrac{1}{5} \times \tfrac{4}{5} + \tfrac{4}{5} \times \tfrac{1}{5} = \tfrac{8}{25}$

(P(A or B) = P(A) + P(B) if A and B are mutually exclusive)

 (b) $P(F \geq 2) = P(F = 2) + P(F = 3)$
$= 3 \times p(F_1F_2J_3) + P(F_1F_2F_3)$
$= 3 \times \tfrac{1}{5} \times \tfrac{1}{5} \times \tfrac{4}{5} + \tfrac{1}{5} \times \tfrac{1}{5} \times \tfrac{1}{5} = \tfrac{13}{125}$

3 (a) Bag A Red (R) : Green (G) : Gold (g) = 1 : 2 : 3

  Bag B Red (R) : Green (G) : Gold (g) = 1 : 1 : 2

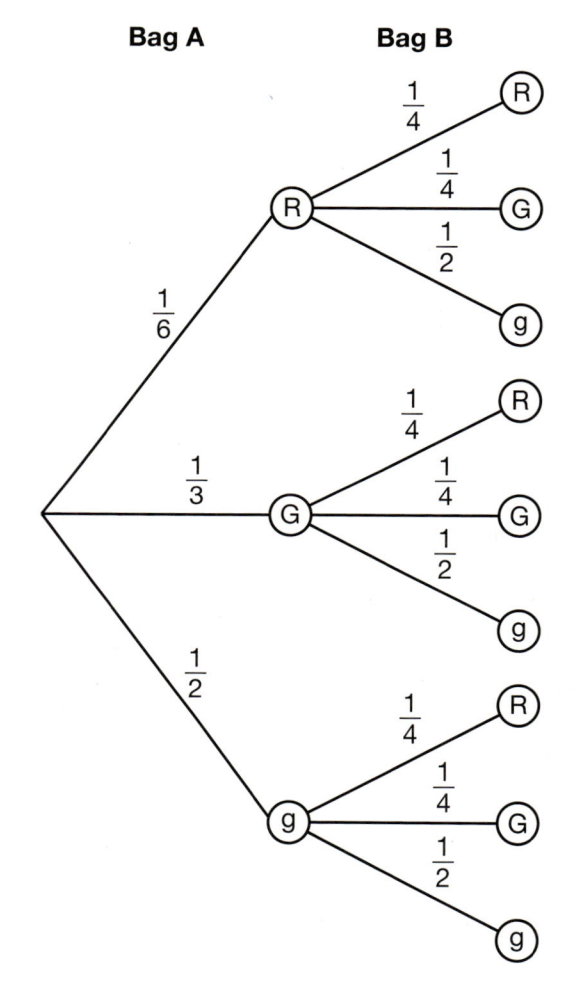

 (b) (i) $P(g_1) \times P(g_2) = \tfrac{1}{2} \times \tfrac{1}{2} = \tfrac{1}{4}$

(P(A and B) = P(A) × P(B))

  (ii) $P(Gg) = P(G_1g_2) + P(g_1G_2)$
$= \tfrac{1}{3} \times \tfrac{1}{2} + \tfrac{1}{2} \times \tfrac{1}{4} = \tfrac{7}{24}$

(P(A or B) = P(A) + P(B) if A and B are mutually exclusive)

(iii) $P(R) P(R \geq 1) + P(R = 0) = 1$
$P(R \geq 1) = 1 - P(R = 0)$
$\qquad = 1 - P(R'_1 R'_2)$
$\qquad \quad (P(E) + P(E') = 1)$
$\qquad = 1 - \frac{5}{6} \times \frac{3}{4}$
$\qquad = 1 - \frac{15}{24}$
$\qquad = \frac{9}{24}$
$\qquad = \frac{3}{8}$

4 (a)

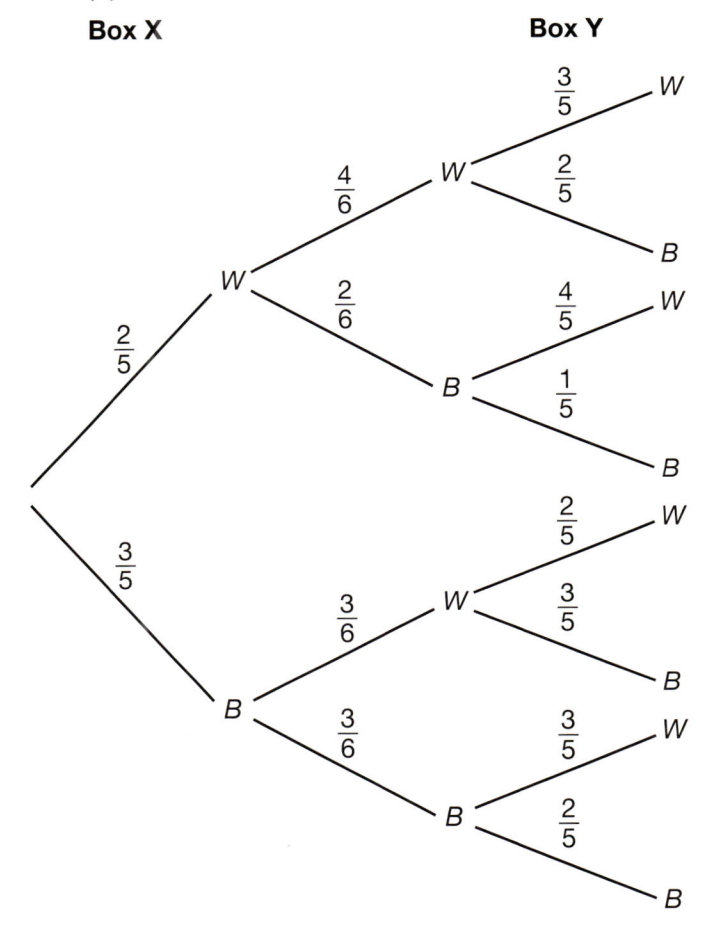

Box X   Box Y

(tree diagram with branches: from start, $\frac{2}{5}$ to W and $\frac{3}{5}$ to B in Box X; from W: $\frac{4}{6}$ to W then $\frac{3}{5}$ W, $\frac{2}{5}$ B; $\frac{2}{6}$ to B then $\frac{4}{5}$ W, $\frac{1}{5}$ B; from B: $\frac{3}{6}$ to W then $\frac{2}{5}$ W, $\frac{3}{5}$ B; $\frac{3}{6}$ to B then $\frac{3}{5}$ W, $\frac{2}{5}$ B)

(b) (i) $P(WW$ from Box Y$) = P(W) \times P(W_1)$
$\times P(W_2) + P(B) \times P(W_1) \times P(W_2)$
$= \frac{2}{5} \times \frac{4}{6} \times \frac{3}{5} + \frac{3}{5} \times \frac{3}{6} \times \frac{2}{5} = \frac{7}{25}$

$(P(A \text{ and } B) = P(A) \times P(B))$

(ii) $P(BW$ from Box Y$) = P(W) \times P(W_1)$
$\times P(B_2) + P(W) \times P(B_1) \times P(W_2)$
$+ P(B) \times P(W_1) \times P(B_2) + P(B) \times P(B_1) \times P(W_2)$
$= \frac{2}{5} \times \frac{4}{6} \times \frac{2}{5} + \frac{2}{5} \times \frac{2}{6} \times \frac{4}{5} + \frac{3}{5} \times \frac{3}{6} \times \frac{3}{5}$
$+ \frac{3}{5} \times \frac{3}{6} \times \frac{3}{5}$
$= \frac{43}{75}$

$(P(A \text{ or } B) = P(A) + P(B)$ if A and B are mutually exclusive$)$

(iii) $P(B \geq 1) + P(B = 0) = 1$
$P(B \geq 1) = 1 - P(B = 0)$
$\qquad = 1 - P(B'_1 B'_2) \quad (P(E) + P(E') = 1$
$P(B'_1 B'_2) = P(WW$ from Box Y$)$
$= \frac{7}{25} \quad P(B \geq 1) = 1 - \frac{7}{25} = \frac{18}{25}$

5 (a)   1st Operation   2nd Operation   3rd Operation

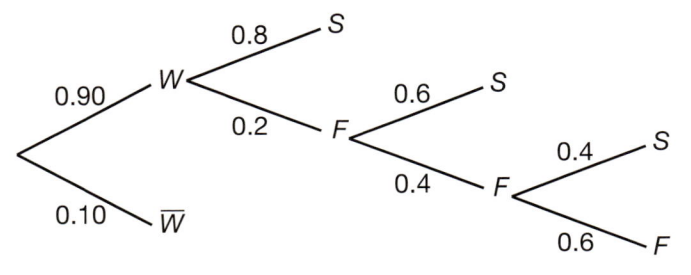

(tree diagram: 0.90 to W, 0.10 to $\overline{W}$; from W: 0.8 to S, 0.2 to F; from F: 0.6 to S, 0.4 to F; from F: 0.4 to S, 0.6 to F)

(b) (i) P(Cured 1st operation)
$= P(W) \times P(S) = 0.90 \times 0.8 = 0.72$
$(P(A \text{ and } B) = P(A) \times P(B))$

(ii) P(Cured 3rd operation)
$= P(W) \times P(F) \times P(F) \times P(S)$
$= 0.9 \times 0.2 \times 0.4 \times 0.4 = 0.0288$

(iii) P(Cured) = P(Cured 1st operation)
+ P(Cured 2nd operation) +
P(Cured 3rd operation)
$= 0.72 + P(W) \times P(F) \times P(S) + 0.0288$
$= 0.72 + 0.90 \times 0.2 \times 0.6 + 0.0288$
$= 0.8568$

$(P(A \text{ or } B) = P(A) + P(B)$ if A and B are mutually exclusive$)$

ANSWERS

EXAMINATION PRACTICE PAPERS 1A SOLUTIONS

1 (a) $\frac{17}{196} \times 100 = 8.6734... = 8.67\%$ (3 s.f.)

   (a as % of $b = \frac{a}{b} \times 100$)

   (b) $175 \times (1.063) = 186.025$ million
   $= 186$ million (nearest million)
   Increase a by $b\% = a \times \left(1 + \frac{b}{100}\right)$

   (c) Let population in 1990 be p million
   $p \times 1.174 = 175$
   $p = \frac{175}{1.174} = 149.06...$ million
   $= 149$ (nearest million)

2 (a) (i) $u \times u \times u \times u \times u = u^5$ ($a^m \times a^n = a^{m+n}$)
   (ii) $3u + 2v - 7u + 4v + 11 = 3u - 7u + 2v + 4v + 11 = -4u + 6v + 11$
   (iii) $\frac{u^7 \times u^8}{u^{11}} = \frac{u^{15}}{u^{11}} = u^4$ ($a^m \div a^n = a^{m-n}$)

   (b) $u(5u - 1) - u(3u - 2)$
   $= 5u^2 - u - 3u^2 + 2u = 2u^2 + u$

   (c) $(5u - 1)(3u - 2) = 5u(3u - 2) - 1(3u - 2)$
   $= 15u^2 - 10u - 3u + 2 = 15u^2 - 13u + 2$

3 (a)

   1.8 cm

   Area $= \frac{1}{2} \times \pi \times 1.8^2 = 1.62\pi$ cm²,
   so $k = 1.62$
   (area of circle $= \pi r^2$)

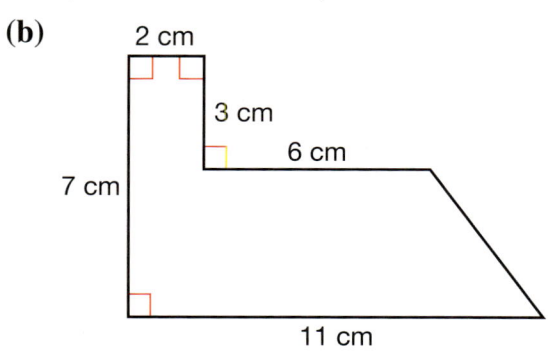

   (b)

   2 cm, 3 cm, 6 cm, 7 cm, 11 cm

   Let required area be A = area of trapezium + area of rectangle
   $A = 2 \times 3 + \frac{1}{2}(8 + 11) \times 4 = 44$ cm²
   (trapezium area $= \frac{1}{2}(a + b)h$)

4 (a) $P(B) = 1 - 0.55 - 0.25 - 0.12$
   $= 0.08$, $x = 0.08$
   (sum of all probabilities of an event = 1)

   (b) $P(R \text{ or } B) = P(R) + P(B) = 0.55 + 0.08$
   $= 0.63$
   ($P(A \text{ and } B) = P(A) + P(B)$ if A and B are mutually exclusive)

   (c) $P(GY) = P(GY \text{ or } YB)$
   $= P(GY) + P(YB)$
   $= 0.25 \times 0.12 + 0.12 \times 0.25 = 0.06$
   ($P(A \text{ and } B) = P(A) \times P(B)$ if A and B are independent)

   (d) Let $E(YR)$ be expected number of times spinner lands on a Y or R.
   $E(YR) = 200 \times 0.67 = 134$ times
   (Expected number of outcomes = probability of event × number of trials)

5 (a) Mean $= \frac{a + b + c + d}{4} = 15$

   $\left(\text{mean} = \frac{\text{sum of numbers}}{\text{number of numbers}}\right)$

   $60 = a + b + c + d = 33 + d$
   $d = 27$

   (b) Range $= 23 = d - a = 27 - a$
   $a = 4$
   (range = largest score − smallest score)
   Sum $= 60 = 4 + b + c + 27$, $b + c = 29$,
   so median $= \frac{b + c}{2} = \frac{29}{2} = 14.5$
   (Median is mean of the central pair in an even group of numbers arranged in ascending or descending order)

6 (a) Let M be midpoint of AB
   $M = \left(\frac{0 + (-5)}{2}, \frac{4 + (-2)}{2}\right)$
   $M\left(-2\frac{1}{2}, 1\right)$

   (midpoint of $A(x_1, y_1)$ and $B(x_2, y_2)$
   $= \left(\frac{x_1 + x_2}{2}, \frac{y_1 + y_2}{2}\right)$)

(b) Let m be the gradient of AB

$m = \frac{-2-4}{-5-0} = \frac{-6}{-5} = \frac{6}{5}$

$\left(\text{Gradient of } AB = \frac{\text{rise}}{\text{run}} = \frac{y_2 - y_1}{x_2 - x_1}\right)$

(c) $y = \frac{6}{5}x + 4$

(Equation of straight line: $y = mx + c$; m is gradient, c is y-axis intercept)

(d) Let perpendicular bisector of AB be line L

Gradient of line $L = -\frac{5}{6}$

(Products of the gradients of two perpendicular lines $= -1$; $m_1 \times m_2 = -1$)

Equation of line L:

$y = -\frac{5}{6}x + c$

(Line L passes through point $M\left(-2\frac{1}{2}, 1\right)$. M must satisfy the equation.)

$1 = -\frac{5}{6} \times \left(-2\frac{1}{2}\right) + c$, so $c = -1\frac{1}{12}$

$= -\frac{13}{12}$

$y = -\frac{5}{6}x - \frac{13}{12}$ or $10x + 12y + 13 = 0$

(multiply through by 12 to produce $ax + by + c = 0$)

7 (a) $P \cap Q = \emptyset$ as there are no members of set P that are also in set Q
(Sets P and Q are mutually exclusive)

(b) $x = 29$
(29 is NOT a member of $P \cup Q$ but is in $\in$)

(c) $R = \{2, 13, 19\}$

8 (a)

Time t (minutes)	Cumulative frequency
$0 < t \le 40$	20
$0 < t \le 80$	55
$0 < t \le 120$	115
$0 < t \le 160$	148
$0 < t \le 200$	155
$0 < t \le 240$	160

(b)

(Plot end points: (40, 20), (80, 55)…)

(c) (i) Interquartile range (IQR)
= upper quartile – lower quartile
= $Q_3 - Q_1$
lower quartile $Q_1 \approx 65$ mins
(LQ at $\frac{1}{4} \times n =$ 40th position)
upper quartile $Q_3 \approx 125$ mins
(UQ at $\frac{3}{4} \times n =$ 120th position)
IQR $\approx 125 - 65 \approx 60$ mins

(ii) Bottom of the top 10th percentile (T_{10}) is at 144th position which is at 155 mins. Top 10th percentile is from 155 minutes $\le t \le 240$ minutes.

9 (a) Let shaded segment area be A
$A =$ Area of sector XYZ – Area of triangle XYZ

$= \frac{70}{360} \times \pi \times 7.5^2 - \frac{1}{2} \times 7.5^2 \times \sin(70°)$

(Area sector angle $\theta = \frac{\theta}{360°}\pi r^2$, area of triangle $= \frac{1}{2}ab\sin C$)

$= 7.9323…\text{cm}^2$
$= 7.93 \text{ cm}^2$ (3 s.f.)

(b) Let shaded segment perimeter be P
$P =$ Chord XZ + Arc XZ

$= 2 \times 7.5 \times \sin(35°) + \frac{70}{360} \times 2\pi \times 7.5$

$= 17.7666…\text{cm}$
$= 17.8 \text{ cm}$ (3 s.f.)

(Arc length of sector angle θ
$= \frac{\theta}{360°} \times 2\pi r$)

368 ANSWERS

10 (a) (i) $p^7 \times p^{11} = p^{18}$ $(a^m \times a^n = a^{m+n})$
    (ii) $p^{11} \div p^7 = p^4$ $(a^m \div a^n = a^{m-n})$
    (iii) $(2p + 1)^2 - (p - 1)^2$
    $= (2p + 1)(2p + 1) - (p - 1)(p - 1)$
    $= (4p^2 + 4p + 1) - (p^2 - 2p + 1)$
    $= 3p^2 + 6p = 3p(p + 2)$

(b) (i) $11p - 1 = 7p + 1$
    $4p = 2$
    (Do same operation to both sides to isolate p)
    $p = \frac{2}{4} = \frac{1}{2}$

(ii) $\frac{11p-1}{4} = \frac{4p+1}{11}$

(multiply both sides by 44)
$11(11p - 1) = 4(4p + 1)$
$121p - 11 = 16p + 4$
$105p = 15$
$p = \frac{15}{105} = \frac{1}{7}$

11 $3m - 10n = 20$ (1)
    $5m + 2n = 6$ (2) $\times 5 =$ (3)
    $25m + 10n = 30$ (3)

(Decision made to eliminate n, so make n values 'same'. Other variable m could also be eliminated by making m values 'same')

(3) + (1): $28m = 50$, $m = \frac{50}{28} = \frac{25}{14} = 1\frac{11}{14}$

(Substitute $m = 1\frac{11}{14}$ into any equation to find n, say (2))

(2): $5 \times 1\frac{11}{14} + 2n = 6$, $2n = -\frac{41}{14}$, $n = -\frac{41}{28} = -1\frac{13}{28}$

Point of intersection of the two lines is $\left(1\frac{11}{14}, -1\frac{13}{28}\right)$

(Modern calculators allow checking of your answers, so questions of this type can be produced with more efficiency)

12 Let $x = 0.\overline{492} = 0.492\,492\,492...$ (1)
    ($\times$ by 1000 as there are 3 recurring decimals)
    $1000x = 492.492492492...$ (2)
    $999x = 492$
    ((2) – (1) to eliminate recurring decimals)
    $x = \frac{492}{999} = \frac{164}{333}$ as required
    (Divide numerator and denominator by 3)

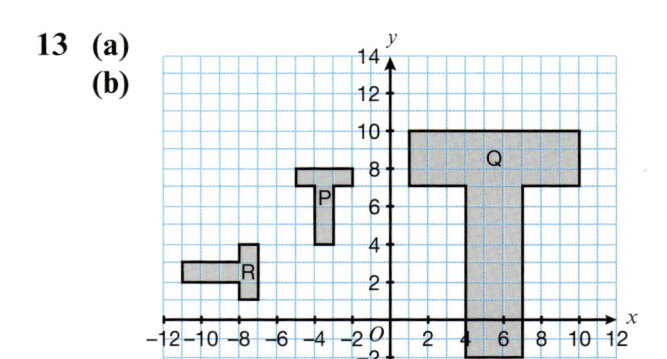

13 (a)
   (b)

(c) (Enlargements: Area of object $\times k^2$ = Area of image, if k is the scale factor of enlargement)
   (i) Area of $Q_1 = 54 \times \left(\frac{1}{2}\right)^2 = 13\frac{1}{2}$ units^2
   (ii) Area of $R_1 = 6 \times 5^2 = 150$ units^2

14 Upper bound mass = 155 kg
    Greatest number of cases lifted 'safely', n, is worst case i.e. when the safe loading is minimised and the case weight is maximised.
    $n = \frac{1750}{155} = 11.290...$ say 11

15 $1 - \frac{2x^2 - 7x + 3}{x^2 + 2x - 15}$
    $= \frac{(x + 5)(x - 3) - (2x - 1)(x - 3)}{(x + 5)(x - 3)}$
    $= \frac{(x + 5) - (2x - 1)}{(x + 5)} = \frac{6 - x}{x + 5}$

(Express as a single fraction with a common denominator of $(x + 5)(x - 3)$)

16 (a) (i) $5p - 7 \geq p + 3$, $4p \geq 10$, $p \geq 2.5$
   (ii) $3(2p - 7) < 2(p + 3)$
       $6p - 21 < 2p + 6$
       $6p - 2p < 6 + 21$
       $4p < 27$
       $p < 6.25$
   (b) The full solution set is $2.5 \leq p < 6.25$, so the integer solution set = {3, 4, 5, 6}

17 (a) $I \propto \frac{1}{d^2}$, so $I = \frac{k}{d^2}$, where k is a constant of proportionality
    $10^6 = \frac{k}{1^2}$, so $k = 10^6$, $I = \frac{10^6}{d^2}$
   (b) At $I = 4cd$, $4 = \frac{10^6}{d^2}$, $d = 500$, so $p = 0.5$

ANSWERS

18 (a) (i) $f(0) = 6$
  (ii) $fg(0) = f(2) = -2$
  (Find $g(0)$ first from the $g(x)$ graph and substitute into $f(x)$)
(b) $f(x) = 2$, $x = -3, 1, 5$ (Draw $y = 2$ on graph and find where it intercepts $y = f(x)$).
(c) On $y = g(x)$ gradient at $x = 7$, $m \approx -\frac{4}{2}$
   $= -2 \left(\text{gradient} = \frac{\text{rise}}{\text{run}}\right)$

19 (a) Angle $MLJ = 30°$
   (angles in the same segment)
(b) Angle $JLK = 73°$
   (alternate segment theorem)
(c) Angle $GJM = 30°$
   (alternate segment theorem)
   Angle $GMJ = 69°$
   (angle sum of a triangle = 180°)
   Angle $LMP = 38°$
   (angle sum in a straight line = 180°)
   Angle $MPL = 112°$
   (angle sum of a triangle = 180°)
   Angle $KPL = 68°$
   (angle sum in a straight line = 180°)
(d) Angle $JKL = 69°$ (opposite angles in a cyclic quadrilateral add up to 80°)

20 (a) $5x^2 - 20x + 12 = 5\left[x^2 - 4x + \frac{12}{5}\right]$
  $= 5\left[(x-2)^2 - 4 + \frac{12}{5}\right]$
  $= 5\left[(x-2)^2 - \frac{8}{5}\right]$
  $= 5(x-2)^2 - 8$
  so $a = 5$, $b = -2$ and $c = -8$
(b) $f(x)_{min}$ occurs at $x = 2$, $y = -8$
   min point is $(2, -8)$

21 (a) $P(C \cap S \cap V) = \frac{7}{50}$ $\left(P(E) = \frac{n(E)}{n(\mathcal{E})}\right)$
(b) $P(C \cap S') = \frac{6+9}{50} = \frac{15}{50} = \frac{3}{10}$
(c) $P(S \cup V') = \frac{12+4+7+6}{50} = \frac{29}{50}$
(d) $P(C|V) = \frac{n(C \cap V)}{n(V)} = \frac{9+7}{(9+7+4+12)}$
   $= \frac{16}{32} = \frac{1}{2}$

   (Sample space is reduced from $n(\mathcal{E})$ to $n(V)$)

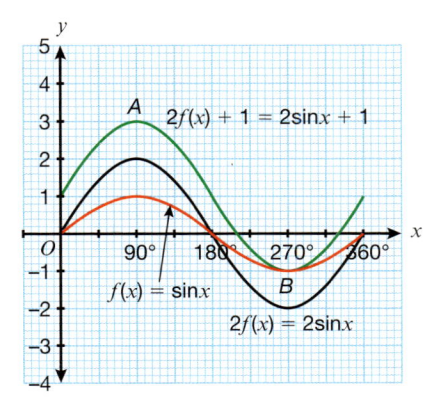

22

(If $g(x) = 2f(x)$, $g(x)$ is a stretch of $f(x)$ parallel to the y-axis of scale factor 2 and $2f(x) + 1$ is $g(x) + 1$ which is a translation of $g(x)$ along vector $\begin{pmatrix} 0 \\ 1 \end{pmatrix}$)
A is the maximum point of $g(x)$ in the domain which is (90°, 3)
B is the minimum point of $g(x)$ in the domain which is (270°, −1)

23 Area of triangle = area of circle of circumference 10π
Circumference of circle = 10π

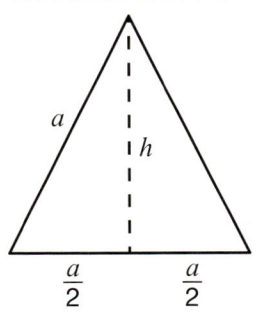

$10\pi = \pi d$ ($c = \pi d$)
$r = 5$
Area of circle, $A = \pi \times 5^2 = 25\pi$ ($A = \pi r^2$)
Area of triangle, $A = \frac{1}{2} \times a \times h$
(Area of triangle = $\frac{1}{2} \times$ base $\times$ perpendicular height)
$a^2 = h^2 + \left(\frac{a}{2}\right)^2$, $h^2 = a^2 - \left(\frac{a}{2}\right)^2 = \frac{3a^2}{4}$, $h = \frac{a\sqrt{3}}{2}$
(Pythagoras' theorem)
$A = \frac{1}{2} \times a \times \frac{a\sqrt{3}}{2} = \frac{a^2\sqrt{3}}{4}$
Both areas are equal so, $25\pi = \frac{a^2\sqrt{3}}{4}$
$a^2 = \frac{100\pi}{\sqrt{3}}$

24 (a) $240 = \pi r^2 y$, so $y = \frac{240}{\pi r^2}$
(b) $A = 2\pi r^2 + 2\pi ry = 2\pi r^2 + 2\pi r \times \frac{240}{\pi r^2}$

ANSWERS

$A = 2\pi r^2 + \frac{480}{r}$ as required
(cylinder: Volume $= \pi r^2 h$, Curved surface area $= 2\pi rh$)

(c) $A = 2\pi r^2 + 480r^{-1}$, so $\frac{dA}{dr} = 4\pi r - 480r^{-2}$
$= 0$ at stationary point
(Stationary points occur when the gradient is 0, i.e. $\frac{dy}{dx} = 0$)
$4\pi r = 480r^{-2} = \frac{480}{r^2}$, $r^3 = \frac{480}{4\pi} = \frac{120}{\pi}$, so
$r = \sqrt[3]{\frac{120}{\pi}}$ ($= 3.36...$)

(d) Take a small step to the left of
$r = \sqrt[3]{\frac{120}{\pi}}$, say $r = 3.3$
$\frac{dA}{dr}$ at $r = 3.3$ is equal to $-2.6...$
Take a small step to the right of
$r = \sqrt[3]{\frac{120}{\pi}}$, say $r = 3.4$ $\frac{dA}{dr}$
at $r = 3.4$ is equal to $+1.2...$
The curve shape around the stationary point is a U shape, so A will be a minimum value when $r = \sqrt[3]{\frac{120}{\pi}}$
$A = 2\pi r^2 + \frac{480}{r}$, $A_{min} = 213.79...\text{cm}^2$
$A_{min} = 214 \text{ cm}^2$ (3 s.f.)
(Efficient use of the 'Ans' button on the calculator is helpful for part d)

EXAMINATION PRACTICE PAPERS 1B SOLUTIONS

1 $\sqrt{\frac{3.1^2 + 1.3^2}{3.1^2 - 1.3^2}} = 1.1944... = 1.19$ (3 s.f.)

2 24 mg = 60%
(Find 1%, so that 100% can be calculated)
$\frac{24}{60} = 1\%$
Daily recommended daily dose:
$100\% = 100 \times \frac{24}{60} = 40$ g
so recommended weekly vitamin C dose
$= 7 \times 40$ g $= 280$ g

3 (a) speed $= \frac{\text{distance}}{\text{time}}$, $168 = \frac{d}{22.75 - 19.80}$,
$d = 168 \times 2.95 = 495.6$ km $= 496$ km (nearest km)
(Time from Nimes to Paris = 22 h 45 min − 19 h 48 min = 2.95 h)

(b) speed $= \frac{\text{distance}}{\text{time}}$, time $= \frac{831}{168}$
$= 4.9464...h = 4$ h 56 min 47 s
Timetable time for journey
$= 22:45 - 16:20 = 6$ h 25 min
Total stoppage time
$= 6$ h 25 min $- 4$ h 56 min 47 s
$= 1$ h 28 min 13 s
$= 1$ h 28 min

4 $1\frac{1}{2} \times \left(7\frac{1}{3} \div 3\frac{1}{7}\right)^2 = \frac{3}{2} \times \left(\frac{22}{3} \times \frac{7}{22}\right)^2$
$= \frac{3}{2} \times \frac{49}{9} = \frac{49}{6} = 8\frac{1}{6}$

5 (a) $x = 2464 = 2^5 \times 7 \times 11$, $y = 1372 = 2^2 \times 7^3$
(Long division by prime factors should be shown)

(b) (i) HCF $= 2^2 \times 7$, so $m = 2$, $n = 1$
(ii) LCM $= 2^5 \times 7^3 \times 11$, so $p = 5$, $q = 3$, $r = 1$
$(p + q + r)^{(m+n)} = 9^3 = 729$

6 (a) Yeast grams $= \frac{20}{5} \times 35 = 140$ g

(b) $L = \frac{90}{7.5} \times 5 = 60$, $L = 60$

(c) Brown flour : White flour : Yeast
$= 2000 : 500 : 35 = 400 : 100 : 7$
$p = 400$, $q = 100$, $r = 7$

7 Total time of all six runners is
$= 6 \times (2$ min 15.5 s$) = 12$ min $+ 6 \times 15.5$ s $=$
12 min $+ 93$ s $= 13$ min 33 s
Total time of the other 5 runners is
5×2 min $+ (13.6 + 15.9 + 15.8 + 18.3 + 14.1)$ s $= 10$ min $+ 77.7$ s $= 11$ min 17.7 s
(Mean $= \frac{\text{sum of all scores}}{\text{number of scores}}$)
Lucia's time = 13 min 33 s − 11 min 17.7 s
= 2 min 15.3 s
All the times in order are
1st 2 min 13.6 s
2nd 2 min 14.1 s
3rd 2 min 15.3 s
4th 2 min 15.8 s
5th 2 min 15.9 s
6th 2 min 18.3 s
So Lucia came 3rd and was awarded the bronze medal.

8 Let perimeter of a semi-circle be
p = diameter + half of circumference
$p = 2r + \pi r = r(2 + \pi)$
$p_{max} = 105$ cm, $p_{min} = 95$ cm
Let area of semi-circle be A
$A = \frac{1}{2}\pi r^2$

(a) A_{max} occurs when radius is r_{max}
$105 = r_{max}(2 + \pi)$,
$r_{max} = \frac{105}{2+\pi}$, so $A_{max} = \frac{1}{2}\pi \left(\frac{105}{2+\pi}\right)^2$
$= 655.09327...$ cm² $= 655$ cm² (3 s.f.)

(b) A_{min} occurs when radius is r_{min}
$95 = r_{min}(2 + \pi)$,
$r_{min} = \frac{95}{2+\pi}$, so $A_{min} = \frac{1}{2}\pi \left(\frac{95}{2+\pi}\right)^2$
$= 536.2554..$ cm²
$= 536$ cm² (3 s.f.)

9 (a)

Let $AB = d$
$d^2 = 40^2 + 50^2 = 4100$
(Pythagoras' theorem)
$d = \sqrt{4100} = \sqrt{41} \times \sqrt{100} = 10\sqrt{41}$,
so $k = 10$

(b) Bearing of ship A from ship B is $180° + \theta$
(Bearing is clockwise from North)
$\tan \theta = \frac{40}{50}$, ($\tan \theta = \frac{\text{opposite side}}{\text{adjacent side}}$)
so $\theta = 38.65...°$ so, bearing of ship
A from ship $B = 219°$ (nearest degree)

10 $(2x + 1)(x - 1)^2 = 1$
$(2x + 1)(x^2 - 2x + 1) = 1$
$2x(x^2 - 2x + 1) + 1(x^2 - 2x + 1) = 1$
$2x^3 - 4x^2 + 2x + x^2 - 2x + 1 = 1$
$2x^3 - 3x^2 = 0$
$x^2(2x - 3) = 0$

Either $x^2 = 0$, $x = 0$
Or $2x - 3 = 0$, $x = \frac{3}{2} = 1\frac{1}{2}$

11 If n is an integer.
A general term for an odd number $= 2n + 1$
The next odd number $= (2n + 1) + 2 = 2n + 3$
The difference between the squares of these numbers
$= (2n + 3)^2 - (2n + 1)^2$
$= (2n + 3)(2n + 3) - (2n + 1)(2n + 1)$
$= (4n^2 + 12n + 9) - (4n^2 + 4n + 1)$
$= 8n + 8 = 8(n + 1)$ which is a multiple of 8

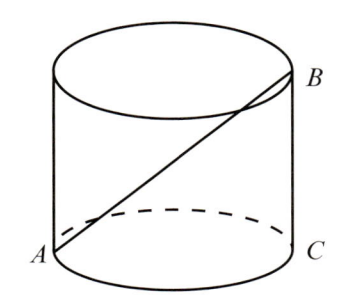

12

$192\pi = \pi \times 4^2 \times BC$
(Volume of cylinder $= \pi r^2 h$)
$BC = \frac{192\pi}{16\pi} = 12$ cm
Required angle $= BAC$, triangle BAC is right-angled
Let angle $BAC = \theta$
$\tan(\theta) = \frac{BC}{AC} = \frac{12}{8}$, so $\theta = 56.3°$ (3 s.f.)

($\tan \theta = \frac{\text{opposite side}}{\text{adjacent side}}$)

13 (a) The exterior angle of the polygon $= 180° - 144° = 36°$
(n-sided regular polygon: exterior angle $= \frac{360°}{n}$)
So $36° = \frac{360°}{n}$, $n = 10$
The shape has 10 sides so is a decagon.

(b) Perimeter $= 10 \times 12 = 120$ cm

(c) The polygons are similar figures
Scale factor of length $= \frac{960}{120} = 8$
(Similar figures: small area $\times k^2 =$ larger area, where k is length scale factor)
Enlarged area $= 8^2 \times A = 64A$

372 ANSWERS

14 The toys are not replaced.
Let X be the number of toys that are the same from 3 random picks.
T: Teddy bears, R: Robots, D: Dolls
$P(X = 2) = 3 \times P(TTT') + 3 \times P(RRR') + 3 \times P(DDD')$
($\times 3$ as the 'not' option can occur in 3 places)
($P(A$ or $B) = P(A) + P(B)$ if A and B are mutually exclusive)
($P(A$ and $B) = P(A) \times P(B)$ if A and B are independent)
$P(X = 2) = 3 \times \frac{5}{15} \times \frac{4}{14} \times \frac{10}{13} +$

$3 \times \frac{5}{15} \times \frac{4}{14} \times \frac{10}{13} +$

$3 \times \frac{5}{15} \times \frac{4}{14} \times \frac{10}{13}$

$= 9 \times \frac{5}{15} \times \frac{4}{14} \times \frac{10}{13} = \frac{60}{91}$

15 (a) If $g(x) = \frac{10}{x-3}$:

$y = \frac{10}{x-3}$

(Re-write in terms of $y = \ldots$)

$x = \frac{10}{y-3}$

(Switch x and y variables)

$y - 3 = \frac{10}{x}, y = \frac{10}{x} + 3 = \frac{10+3x}{x}$

(Re-arrange to make y the subject)

$g^{-1}(x) = \frac{10+3x}{x}$

(Replace y with $g^{-1}(x)$)

(b) If $gh(p) = -1$, $g\left(\frac{p-5}{p}\right) = -1$,

$\frac{10}{\left(\frac{p-5}{p}\right) - 3} = -1$

(Find $h(p)$ first and input this into $g(x)$)

$\frac{10}{\frac{(p-5)-3p}{p}} = -1, \frac{10p}{-2p-5} = -1,$

so $10p = 2p + 5$, $8p = 5$,

$p = \frac{5}{8}$

16 (a) Esther's investment =
€12 000 × 1.025 × 1.035⁹ = €16 763.64
(Increase a by $b\%$ for n years compound
interest = $a \times \left(1 + \frac{b}{100}\right)^n$)

(b) Let €p be the amount Ivan invests
$p \times 1.015^2 = $ €1236.27,
so $p = \frac{1236.27}{1.015^2} = 1200$
Ivan invests €1200 into his Savings Bond.

17 $(x + 1) : (x + 2) = (y + 1) : (y + 3)$

$\frac{x+1}{x+2} = \frac{y+1}{y+3}$

$(x + 1)(y + 3) = (x + 2)(y + 1)$
$xy + 3x + y + 3 = xy + x + 2y + 2$
$y = 2x + 1$

18 (a) (Density = $\frac{\text{Mass}}{\text{Volume}}$,

Volume of cylinder = $\pi r^2 h$)
Mass = Density × Volume
= 2710 × π × 0.5² × 1.20 = 813π kg
$k = 813$

(b) (Pressure = $\frac{\text{Force}}{\text{Area}}$)

Pressure = $\frac{2.5 \times 10^4}{\pi \times 0.5^2} = 31830.98\ldots$ N/m²

= 3.18 × 10⁴ N/m² (3 s.f.)

19 $x^2 + y^2 = 26$ [1]
$y = 3 - 2x$ [2]
(subs into [1])
[1] $x^2 + (3 - 2x)^2 = 26$
(expand out brackets)
$x^2 + (3 - 2x)(3 - 2x) = 26$
$x^2 + 9 - 12x + 4x^2 = 26$
$5x^2 - 12x - 17 = 0$
$(5x - 17)(x + 1) = 0$, so $5x - 17 = 0$
or $x + 1 = 0$
$x = \frac{17}{5} = 3\frac{2}{5}$, $x = -1$

(substitute into [2])
[2] $y = 3 - 2\left(\frac{17}{5}\right) = -\frac{19}{5} = -3\frac{4}{5}$, $y = 3 - 2(-1) = 5$

$P\left(3\frac{2}{5}, -3\frac{4}{5}\right)$, $Q(-1, 5)$

(Write answers as coordinate pairs)
P & Q are interchangeable!

20 After 3 hours Rover B has travelled
$\frac{3 \times 4 \times 60 \times 60}{100} = 432$ m

(Draw a sketch of the situation. There are two possible positions for Rover A, shown as A and A' on the sketch.)
(Using the sine rule in triangle ABC with the usual notation.)

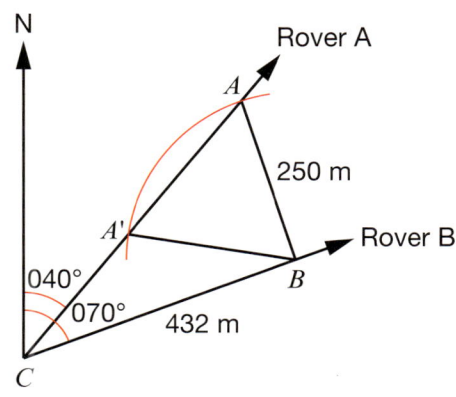

$\frac{\sin(A)}{432} = \frac{\sin(30°)}{250}$ $\sin(A) = 0.864$ $A = 59.77°$

or $120.23°$ (2 d.p.)

The smallest possible value of x is given by Rover A being at position A' on the sketch, corresponding to $A' = 120.23°$
When $A' = 120.23°$, $B = 180 - 30 - 120.23 = 29.77°$

$\frac{b}{\sin(29.77°)} = \frac{250}{\sin(30°)}$ $b = 248.26$ m (2 d.p.)

speed is $\frac{248.26}{3}$ m/h $= \frac{248.26 \times 100}{3 \times 60 \times 60}$

$= 2.30$ cm/s (3 s.f.)

21 $\overrightarrow{PS} = 2\mathbf{a}$
$\overrightarrow{PR} = 2\mathbf{a} + \mathbf{b}$
$\overrightarrow{MQ} = -\mathbf{a} + \mathbf{b} = \mathbf{b} - \mathbf{a}$
If PNR is a straight line $\overrightarrow{PR} = k\overrightarrow{PN}$
$\overrightarrow{PN} = \overrightarrow{PM} + \frac{1}{3}\overrightarrow{MQ} = \mathbf{a} + \frac{1}{3}(\mathbf{b} - \mathbf{a}) = \frac{1}{3}(2\mathbf{a} + \mathbf{b})$
$= \frac{1}{3}\overrightarrow{PR}$, so $\overrightarrow{PR} = 3\overrightarrow{PN}$

PNR in a straight line as $k = 3$

22 $t_n = 3n + 1$
$t_1 = 4, t_2 = 7, t_3 = 10$ ... so sequence is an arithmetic progression with $a = 4, d = 3$, $n = 20$
($S_n = \frac{n}{2}\{2a + (n-1)d\}$ Sum to n terms for an arithmetic progression)
$S_{20} = \frac{20}{2}\{2 \times 4 + (20-1) \times 3\} = 650$

23 (a) (i) $s = (t-1)^3 + 3t = (t-1)(t-1)^2 + 3t$
$= (t-1)(t^2 - 2t + 1) + 3t$
$= t(t^2 - 2t + 1) - 1(t^2 - 2t + 1) + 3t$
$= (t^3 - 2t^2 + t - t^2 + 2t - 1) + 3t$
$= t^3 - 3t^2 + 6t - 1$

$v = \frac{ds}{dt} = 3t^2 - 6t + 6$ m/s

(ii) $a = \frac{dv}{dt} = 6t - 6$ m/s²

(b) $a = 6t - 6, t = 1$
At $t = 1, v = 3 \times (1)^2 - 6 \times 1 + 6 = 3$ m/s

24 (a) Volume of space $V =$ Volume of cylinder $V_c -$ Volume of spheres V_s
$V_c = \pi(r)^2 \times 4r = 4\pi r^3$
(radius of cylinder $= r$, height of cylinder $= 4r$)
$V_s = 2 \times \frac{4}{3} \times \pi \times r^3 = \frac{8\pi r^3}{3}$
$V = 4\pi r^3 - \frac{8\pi r^3}{3} = \frac{12\pi r^3}{3} - \frac{8\pi r^3}{3} = \frac{4\pi r^3}{3}$
as required

(b) $\frac{4\pi r^3}{3} = \frac{9\pi}{2}$

So, $\frac{4r^3}{3} = \frac{9}{2}$, $8r^3 = 27$, $r^3 = \frac{27}{8}$,

$r = \sqrt[3]{\frac{27}{8}} = \frac{\sqrt[3]{27}}{\sqrt[3]{8}} = \frac{3}{2} = 1.5$ cm

(c) Required fraction $= \frac{\frac{4\pi r^3}{3}}{4\pi r^3} = \frac{4\pi r^3}{3} \div 4\pi r^3$
$= \frac{4\pi r^3}{12\pi r^3} = \frac{1}{3}$

EXAMINATION PRACTICE PAPERS 2A SOLUTIONS

1

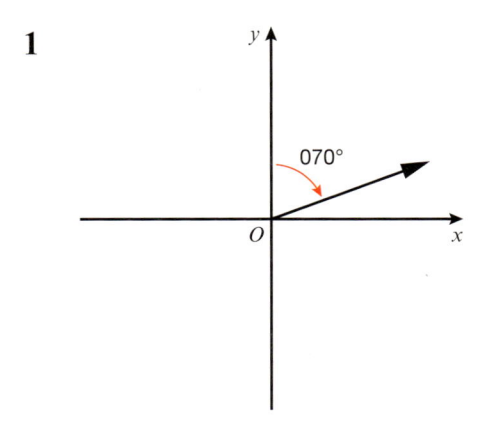

Let required bearing of Moritz to Kielder be θ.
So $\theta = 180° + 70° = 250°$
(Bearings are measured clockwise from North)

374 ANSWERS

2 (a) Sequence 10, 9.5, 9, 8.5…is an arithmetic progression with:
$a = 10, d = -0.5$
$t_n = 10 + (n - 1) \times (-0.5) = 10 - 0.5n + 0.5 = 10.5 - 0.5n = 0.5(21 - n)$
($t_n = a + (n - 1)d$ is the nth term of an arithmetic progression)

(b) If $S_n = 0$
($S_n = \frac{n}{2}[2a + (n - 1)d]$ is the sum to n terms of an arithmetic progression)
$0 = \frac{n}{2}[2 \times 10 + (n - 1) \times (-0.5)]$
(Divide both sides by $\frac{n}{2}$)
$0.5(n - 1) = 20$
$40 = n - 1$
$n = 41$

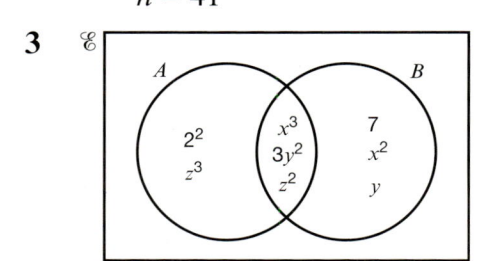

3 Let A: $12x^3y^2z^5$
   B: $21x^5y^3z^2$
HCF = $3x^3y^2z^2$ (Intersection: A ∩ B)
LCM = $84x^5y^3z^5$ (Union: A ∪ B)

Venn diagram: A contains $2^2, z^3$; intersection contains $x^3, 3y^2, z^2$; B contains $7, x^2, y$.

4 $\frac{2v - w}{3} = \frac{2v + w}{5} + u$

(multiply both sides of the equation by 15)
$5(2v - w) = 3(2v + w) + 15u$
$10v - 5w = 6v + 3w + 15u$
(Expand out brackets both sides)
$4v = 8w + 15u$
(Isolate v on the LHS of the equation)
$v = \frac{8w + 15u}{4}$
(Divide both sides of equation by 4)

5 Let price of shoes before sales tax be $\$p$.
$p \times 1.15 = 92$
(Increase a by $b\% = a \times (1 + \frac{b}{100})$)
$p = \frac{92}{1.15}$, $p = \$80$

6 (a) Equation of a straight line: $y = mx + c$
(m: gradient, c: y intercept)
$m = \frac{8 - 4}{-3 - 1} = \frac{4}{-4} = -1$

(Gradient of $AB = \frac{\text{rise}}{\text{run}} = \frac{y_2 - y_1}{x_2 - x_1}$)

so $y = -x + c$, so (1, 4) satisfies the equation as it is on the line.
$4 = -1 + c$, so $c = 5$, equation of
$L: y = -x + 5$,
$x + y - 5 = 0; a = 1, b = 1, c = -5$

(b) Midpoint of $AB = \left(\frac{1 - 3}{2}, \frac{4 + 8}{2}\right) = (-1, 6)$

(Midpoint of $A(x_1, y_1)$ and $B(x_2, y_2)$
$= \left(\frac{x_1 + x_2}{2}, \frac{y_1 + y_2}{2}\right)$)
Let gradient of L be m_1 and gradient of M be m_2
$m_1 \times m_2 = -1, -1 \times m_2 = -1, m_2 = 1$,
(Product of the gradients of two perpendicular lines $= -1$; $m \times m_2 = -1$)
Equation of $M: y = x + c$, so $(-1, 6)$ satisfies the equation as it is on the line.
Therefore $6 = -1 + c$, $c = 7$, $y = x + 7$,
$-x + y - 7 = 0, a = -1, b = 1, c = -7$

7 Let $y = 2x^2 - x - 6 = (2x + 3)(x - 2)$
(Factorising helps sketch the curve)
At the x-axis $y = 0$, so $0 = (2x + 3)(x - 2)$,
$x = 2$ or $-\frac{3}{2}$

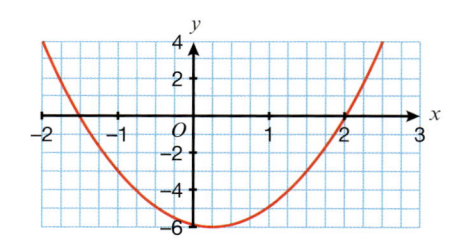

So $2x^2 - x - 6 \geq 0$ when $x \leq -\frac{3}{2}, x \geq 2$

(y-values above or on the x-axis satisfy the inequality)

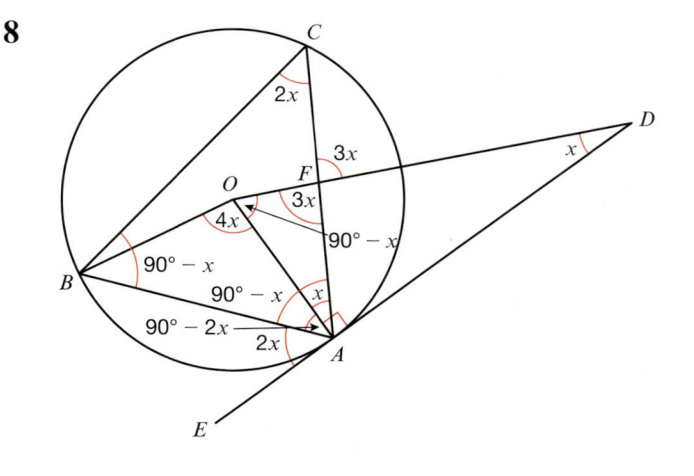

8 Circle diagram with points B, C, D, A, E, centre O, point F, with angles $2x$ at C, $3x$ and $3x$ at F, $4x$ at O, x at D, $90° - x$, $90° - x$, $90° - 2x$, $2x$ marked.

Angle $OFA = 3x$ (opposite angles)
Angle $AOF = 90 - x$
(ΔAOD is a right angled Δ as AD is a tangent and OA is a radius)
Angle $ACB = 2x$
(alternate segment theorem)
Angle $BAC = \frac{1}{2}(180 - 2x) = 90 - x$
(ΔACB is isosceles)
Angle $AOB = 4x$
($2 \times$ angle BCA, angle subtended at centre is twice angle at circumference)
Angle $OAB = \frac{1}{2}(180 - 4x) = 90 - 2x$
(ΔOAB is isosceles)
Angle $OAF = (90 - x) - (90 - 2x) = x$
$x + (90 - x) + 3x = 180$
(Angle sum of ΔOAF)
$3x = 90 \quad x = 30$

9 (a) Percentage > 90 mins $= \frac{3}{24} \times 100 = 12.5\%$

   (b) Modal class is $30 < x \leq 60$
   (Most popular group)

   (c) Mean $= \frac{\Sigma fx}{\Sigma f}$, where is the midpoint of each class

   Mean $=$
   $\frac{4 \times 15 + 10 \times 45 + 7 \times 75 + 3 \times 105}{24}$
   $= \frac{1350}{24} = 56.25$ mins $= 56$ mins 15 s

   (d) New mean $= \frac{1350 + 56.25}{25} = 56.25$ mins, so remains unchanged

10 (a) speed$_{max} = \frac{\text{distance}_{max}}{\text{time}_{min}} = \frac{805}{137.5} = 5.85454...$
   $= 5.85$ m/s (3 s.f.)

   (b) speed$_{min} = \frac{\text{distance}_{min}}{\text{time}_{max}} = \frac{795}{142.5} = 5.5789...$
   $= 5.58$ m/s (3 s.f.)

11 (a)

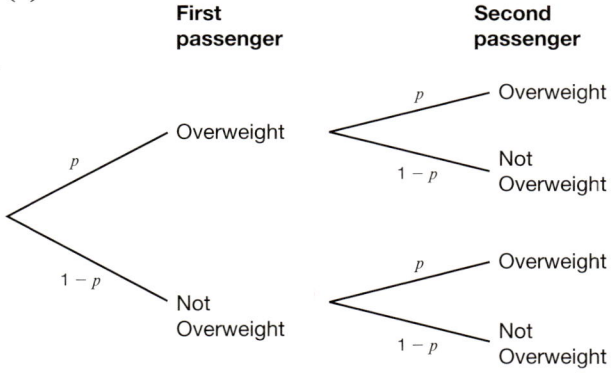

   First passenger — Second passenger

   p Overweight
   p Overweight $\langle$
   $1-p$ Not Overweight

   $1-p$ Not Overweight $\langle$
   p Overweight
   $1-p$ Not Overweight

   (b) (i) Branches required are:
       'Overweight – Not overweight' and
       'Not overweight – overweight'
       Probability $= p \times (1 - p) + (1 - p) \times p$
       $= 2p(1 - p)$ or $2p - 2p^2$

   (ii) $2p - 2p^2 = 0.05$
        $2p^2 - 2p + 0.05$
        $= p^2 - p + 0.025 = 0$
        (Solving this quadratic using the quadratic formula.)
        $p = \frac{1 \pm \sqrt{12 - 4 \times 1 \times 0.025}}{2 \times 1} = \frac{1 \pm \sqrt{0.9}}{2}$
        $p = 0.974$ or $p = 0.0257$

12 Let $a = 2n + 1$, $b = 2n + 3$, $c = 2n + 5$ and $d = 2n + 7$
   (If n is an integer, $2n$ is always even, so $2n + 1$ is odd)
   $d^2 - a^2 = (2n + 7)^2 - (2n + 1)^2$
   $= 4n^2 + 28n + 49 - (4n^2 + 4n + 1)$
   $= 4n^2 + 28n + 49 - 4n^2 - 4n - 1$
   $= 24n + 48 = 24(n + 2)$
   $24(n + 2)$ is divisible by 24
   so, $d^2 - a^2$ is divisible by 24.

13 (AM is a line of symmetry, so ΔABM is a right-angled triangle. M is midpoint of BC so $BM = 1$)
   $AM^2 + BM^2 = AB^2$ (Pythagoras' theorem)
   $AM^2 + 1 = 3^2$
   $AM^2 = 8$
   $AM = \sqrt{8}$
   $= 2\sqrt{2}$
   $AX = \frac{3}{4} AM$
   $AX = \frac{3}{4} \times 2\sqrt{2}$
   $= \frac{3\sqrt{3}}{2}$ cm

14 (a) $1 - \dfrac{1}{x+a} - \dfrac{x-1}{x}$

$= \dfrac{x(x+a) - x - (x-1)(x+a)}{x(x+a)}$

(Lowest common denominator is $x(x+a)$)

$= \dfrac{x^2 + ax - x - (x^2 - x + ax - a)}{x(x+a)}$

$= \dfrac{x^2 + ax - x - x^2 + x - ax + a}{x(x+a)}$

$= \dfrac{a}{x(x+a)}$

(b) By inspection $a = 2$, $\dfrac{2}{x(x+2)} = \dfrac{2}{3}$,

$6 = 2x(x+2) = 2x^2 + 4x$
$0 = x^2 + 2x - 3 = (x+3)(x-1)$,
$x = 1$ or $x = -3$

15 Using the sine rule gives $\dfrac{AC}{\sin(69°)} = \dfrac{38.7}{\sin(52°)}$

$AC = \dfrac{38.7 \times \sin(69°)}{\sin(52°)}$

The minimum value of AC will be given when 38.7 is a minimum, $\sin(69°)$ is a minimum and $\sin(52°)$ is a maximum.

38.7 is correct to 3 s.f. so the minimum value is 38.65

69° is correct to 2 s.f. so the minimum value is 68.5°

52° is correct to 2 s.f. so the maximum value is 52.5°

Minimum value of $AC = \dfrac{38.65 \times \sin(68.5°)}{\sin(52.5°)}$

$= 45.327... = 45.3$ m to 3 s.f.

16 (a) The perimeter $= r + 4r + r + 4r + \pi r$
$= 10r + \pi r$

(Curved length of a semicircle $= \pi r$)

$10r + \pi r = 50$, $r(10 + \pi) = 50$,

$r = \dfrac{50}{10 + \pi} = 3.8047...$

Area of shape $= \dfrac{\pi r^2}{2} + 4r \times r = r^2\left(\dfrac{\pi}{2} + 4\right)$

$= (3.8047...)^2\left(\dfrac{\pi}{2} + 4\right) = 80.64$ cm² (4 s.f.)

(b) (i) Volume $= 80.64... \times 25$
$= 2016$ cm³ (4 s.f.)

(ii) (Surface area excluding the flat ends
$=$ perimeter $\times 25$)
Surface area $= 50 \times 25 + 2 \times 80.64...$
$= 1411$ cm² (4 s.f.)

(c) (i) Length scale factor $= \dfrac{30}{50}$

$= 0.6$ volume scale factor $= 0.6^3$
Volume of new shape is 2016×0.6^3
$= 435$ cm³ (3 s.f.)

(ii) Area scale factor $= 0.6^2$
Area of new shape is 1411×0.6^2
$= 508$ cm² (3 s.f.)

17 (a) (i) $3^{\frac{p}{q}} = x \Rightarrow \left(3^{\frac{p}{q}}\right)^q$

$= x^q \Rightarrow 3^p = x^q \; 3^{p-1}$

$= 3^p \times 3^{-1} \Rightarrow 3^{p-1} = \dfrac{x^q}{3}$

(ii) $3^{\frac{p}{q}} = x \Rightarrow \left(3^{\frac{p}{q}}\right)^{\frac{q^2}{p}} = x^{\frac{q^2}{p}} \Rightarrow 3^q = x^{\frac{q^2}{p}}$

(b) $3^{\frac{-q}{p}} = y \Rightarrow \left(3^{\frac{-q}{p}}\right)^{-q} = y^{-q} \Rightarrow 3^{\frac{p^2}{q}} = y^{\frac{-p^2}{q}}$

(c) $x^q = \left(3^{\frac{p}{q}}\right)^q = 3^p$ $y^p = \left(3^{\frac{-q}{p}}\right)^p = 3^{-q}$

$x^q : y^p = 3 : 1 \Rightarrow \dfrac{3^p}{3^{-q}} = 3 \Rightarrow 3^p \div 3^{-q}$
$= 3 \Rightarrow 3^{p+q} = 3^1 \Rightarrow p + q = 1$ (1)

$x^q \times y^p = 243 \Rightarrow 3^p \times 3^{-q} = 243 \Rightarrow$
$3^{p-q} = 3^5 \Rightarrow p - q = 5$ (2)
Add (1) and (2) gives $2p = 6$ $p = 3$, $q = -2$

$x = 3^{\frac{3}{-2}} = \dfrac{1}{3^{\frac{3}{2}}} = \dfrac{1}{\sqrt{3^3}} = \dfrac{1}{3\sqrt{3}} = \dfrac{\sqrt{3}}{9}$

$y = 3^{\frac{2}{3}} = 9^{\frac{1}{3}} = \sqrt[3]{9}$

18 (a) Shot hits the ground when $h = 0$, so
$5t^2 - 6t - 2 = 0$ (Rearrange formula to make squared part positive)
$A = 5$, $B = -6$, $C = -2$

(Using quadratic formula: $x = \dfrac{-b \pm \sqrt{b^2 - 4ac}}{2a}$)

$t = \dfrac{-(-6) \pm \sqrt{(-6)^2 - 4(5)(-2)}}{2(5)} = 1.47$ s (3 s.f.)

(b) $h = -5\left[t^2 - \frac{6t}{5} - \frac{2}{5}\right] = -5\left[\left(t-\frac{3}{5}\right)^2 - \frac{9}{25} - \frac{10}{25}\right]$

$= -5\left[\left(t-\frac{3}{5}\right)^2 - \frac{19}{25}\right] = -5\left[\left(t-\frac{3}{5}\right)^2 - \frac{9}{25}\right]$

$= -5\left(t-\frac{3}{5}\right)^2 + \frac{19}{5}$

Therefore $a = -5$, $b = -\frac{3}{5}$, $c = 3\frac{4}{5}$

(c) $h_{max} = 3.8$ m at $t = \frac{3}{5}$ s

19 Total surface area is the sum of the areas both ends plus the curved surface area
Curved surface area = circumference × height
Total surface area of $A = 2 \times \pi r^2 + 2\pi r \times 3.5r$
$= 9\pi r^2$

Total surface area of $B = 2 \times \pi R^2 + 2\pi R \times R$
$= 4\pi R^2$

$9\pi r^2 = 4\pi R^2$ Surface areas are equal

$r^2 = \frac{4\pi R^2}{9\pi}$ $r = \frac{2R}{3}$ (1)

Square rooting both sides
Volume of $A = \pi r^2 \times 3.5r = 3.5\pi r^3$
Volume of $B = \pi R^2 \times R = \pi R^3$

$\frac{\text{Volume of } A}{\text{Volume of } B} = \frac{3.5\pi r^3}{\pi R^3}$

From (1) $r^3 = \left(\frac{2R}{3}\right)^3 = \frac{8R^3}{27}$

$\frac{\text{Volume of } A}{\text{Volume of } B} = \frac{3.5\pi r^3}{\pi R^3} = \frac{3.5 \times 8R^3}{R^3 \times 27} = \frac{28}{27}$

ratio 28 : 27
so $m = 28$, $n = 27$

20 (a) $\overrightarrow{PA} = \frac{1}{3}\mathbf{a}$, $\overrightarrow{AB} = \mathbf{b} - \mathbf{a}$, $\overrightarrow{AQ} = \frac{2}{3}(\mathbf{b} - \mathbf{a})$

$\overrightarrow{PQ} = \overrightarrow{PA} + \overrightarrow{AQ} = \frac{1}{3}\mathbf{a} + \frac{2}{3}(\mathbf{b} - \mathbf{a})$

$= \frac{2}{3}\mathbf{b} - \frac{1}{3}\mathbf{a}$

(b) $\overrightarrow{QB} = \frac{1}{3}\overrightarrow{AB} = \frac{1}{3}(\mathbf{b} - \mathbf{a})$ $\overrightarrow{BR} = \frac{1}{3}\mathbf{b}$

$\overrightarrow{QR} = \overrightarrow{QB} + \overrightarrow{BR} = \frac{1}{3}(\mathbf{b} - \mathbf{a}) + \frac{1}{3}\mathbf{b}$

$= \frac{2}{3}\mathbf{b} - \frac{1}{3}\mathbf{a}$

$\overrightarrow{PQ} = \overrightarrow{QR}$, PQ and QR are parallel with a common point Q, so PQR is a straight line and therefore P, Q and R are collinear points.

21 (a) Let reflection in x-axis be R and translation be T, so $TR(P) = Q$

(Undo the translation first and then the reflection by using their inverses)

$\begin{pmatrix} 3 \\ 7 \end{pmatrix} + \begin{pmatrix} 1 \\ -2 \end{pmatrix} = \begin{pmatrix} 4 \\ 5 \end{pmatrix}$ (This point is then reflected in x-axis)

$P\begin{pmatrix} 4 \\ -5 \end{pmatrix}$

(b) $OP = \sqrt{4^2 + (-5)^2} = \sqrt{16 + 25} = \sqrt{41}$
(Pythagoras' theorem)
$k = 41$

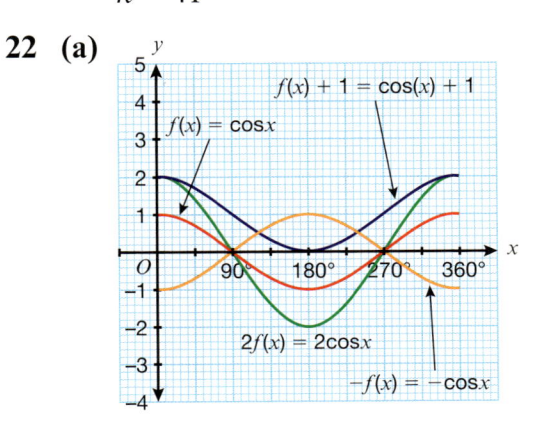

22 (a)

(i) $f(x) + 1 = \cos(x) + 1$

(Translation along vector $\begin{pmatrix} 0 \\ 1 \end{pmatrix}$)

(ii) $-f(x) = -\cos(x)$ (Reflection in x-axis)

(iii) $2f(x) = 2\cos(x)$
(Stretch parallel to y-axis scale factor 2)

(b) If $g(x) = x^2$
$= gf(\pi x) + \pi$
$= g(\cos(\pi x)) + \pi$
$= (\cos(\pi x))^2 + \pi$
$= \cos^2(\pi x) + \pi$

23 $u = k_1 v^2$, $u = k_2 \sqrt{w}$, so $k_1 50^2 = k_2 \sqrt{144}$,

$\frac{k_1}{k_2} = \frac{\sqrt{144}}{50^2} = \frac{\sqrt{w}}{v^2} = \frac{\sqrt{625}}{v^2}$

$= \frac{12}{2500} = \frac{3}{625} = \frac{25}{v^2}$

$v^2 = \frac{25 \times 625}{3}$, $v = \sqrt{\frac{25^3}{5}} = 72.168...$

$= 7.22 \times 10^1$ (3 s.f.)

24 (a) Total surface area
$= 2x^2 + 2x^2 + 2xd + 2xd + xd + xd$
$= 4x^2 + 6xd$
$4x^2 + 6xd = 1400, 2x^2 + 3xd = 700$
$$d = \frac{700 - 2x^2}{3x} \quad (1)$$
Length of tape used
$L = 2 \times 3x + 2(d + x) + 2(2x + d)$
$= 12x + 4d \quad (2)$

(Substituting d from (1) into (2))
$L = 12x + 4 \times \frac{700 - 2x^2}{3x}$
$= 12x + \frac{2800}{3x} - \frac{8x^2}{3x}$
$= 12x - \frac{2800}{3x} - \frac{8x}{3}$
$= \frac{28x}{3} + \frac{2800}{3x}$

(b) To minimise L, differentiate with respect to x
$\frac{dL}{dx} = \frac{28}{3} - \frac{2800}{3x^2}$

(Derivative of $\frac{1}{x} = x^{-1} = -x^{-2} = -\frac{1}{x^2}$)

For a maximum or minimum, $\frac{dL}{dx} = 0$
$\frac{dL}{dx} = 0$
$\frac{28}{3} - \frac{2800}{3x^2} = 0$
$\frac{28}{3} = \frac{2800}{3x^2}$
$x^2 = 100$
$x = 10$
and $L = 186\frac{2}{3}$
When $x = 9$, $L = 187.7...$, when $x = 11$, $L = 187.5...$

It is a minimum as the graph of L against x is continuous for $x > 0$ and the shape of the graph of L against x is a U shape.

When $x = 10$, $d = \frac{700 - 2 \times 10^2}{3 \times 10} = \frac{50}{3}$

Using (1)
Dimensions of box are $10 \text{ cm} \times 20 \text{ cm} \times \frac{50}{3}$ cm
Volume of box $= \frac{10000}{3}$ cm³

EXAMINATION PRACTICE PAPERS 2B SOLUTIONS

1 Bag A: kg per \$ $= \frac{2.5}{2} = 1.25$ kg/\$

Bag B: kg per \$ $= \frac{4}{3.20} = 1.25$ kg/\$

Same value for money for both bags.
Alternatively:

Bag A: \$ per kg $= \frac{2}{2.5} = 0.80$ \$/kg

Bag B: \$ per kg $= \frac{3.20}{4} = 0.80$ \$/kg

2 Area of whole circle = 240 cm²

$A = \pi r^2 = 240 = \pi r^2, \frac{240}{\pi} = r^2, r = \sqrt{\frac{240}{\pi}}$
$= 8.74039...$cm

Perimeter of semi-circle $= \frac{1}{2} \times 2\pi r + 2r$
$= \pi r + 2r = r(\pi + 2) = 44.9$ cm (3 s.f.)

3 Let expression be E,
$E = 0.347\ 695... = 3.48 \times 10^{-1}$ (3 s.f.)

4 40% of the girls and 70% of the boys did not choose the fish option

$\frac{40}{100} \times \frac{45}{100} + \frac{70}{100} \times \frac{55}{100} = \frac{56.5}{100} = 56.5\%$

(55% are boys)
OR percentage who chose fish is

$\frac{60}{100} \times \frac{45}{100} + \frac{30}{100} \times \frac{55}{100} = \frac{43.5}{100} = 43.5\%$

(55% are boys)
percentage who did not choose fish is
$100\% - 43.5\% = 56.5\%$

5 $T_n = \frac{t_n}{u_n} = \frac{2n - 1}{2n + 1}$

$T_1 = \frac{1}{3}, T_2 = \frac{3}{5}, T_3 = \frac{5}{7}, T_4 = \frac{7}{9}$

$T_1 \times T_2 \times T_3 \times T_4 = \frac{1}{9}$

6 Expected number of non-white
= p(non-white) × number of trials
$= \frac{n-3}{n} \times n = n - 3$

ANSWERS

7 (a) $p \times (1.05)^3 = £1389.15$
(Divide both sides by 1.05^3)
$p = \frac{1389.15}{1.05^3} = 1200$

(b) % profit $= \frac{1389.15 - 1200}{1200} \times 100$

$= 15.7625 = 15.8\%$ (3 s.f.)

(% profit $= \frac{\text{change}}{\text{original}} \times 100$)

8 Pressure $= \frac{\text{Force}}{\text{Area}} = \frac{15}{\pi r^2}$

(Area of circle $= \pi r^2$)
Circumference $= 2\pi r$, so $30 = 2\pi r$
(Divide both sides by 2π)
$r = \frac{30}{2\pi} = 4.7746...\text{cm} = 0.047746...\text{m}$

(100 cm = 1 m)

pressure $= \frac{15}{\pi \times 0.047746^2} = 2094.4...N/m^2$

$= 2090 \, N/m^2$ (3 s.f.)

9 $m = \sqrt{\frac{t+1}{t-1}}$

(Square both sides)
$m^2 = \frac{t+1}{t-1}$

(multiply both sides by $(t-1)$)
$m^2(t-1) = t+1$
$m^2 t - m^2 = t + 1$
(add m^2 and subtract t from both sides)
$m^2 t - t = m^2 + 1$
(factorise LHS for t)
$t(m^2 - 1) = m^2 + 1$
(divide both sides by $(m^2 - 1)$)
$t = \frac{m^2+1}{m^2-1} = \frac{m^2+1}{(m+1)(m-1)}$

10 (a) $p(A') = \frac{28}{44} = \frac{7}{11}$

(Set A' are all elements not in A)

(b) $p(B \cap C') = \frac{10}{44} = \frac{5}{22}$

(Elements in B and also not in C)

(c) $p(A \cup B \cup C)' = \frac{4}{44} = \frac{1}{11}$

(Elements not in A or B or C)

(d) $) = p((A \cap B \cap C)/(A \cup B)) = \frac{2}{32} = \frac{1}{16}$

(Sample space is reduced to $A \cup B$)

11 (a)

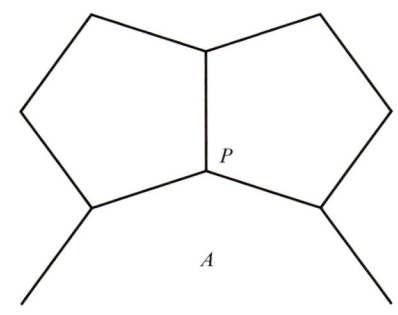

Regular pentagon exterior
angle $= \frac{360°}{5} = 72°$

(Exterior angle of a regular n-sided
pentagon $= \frac{360°}{5}$)

Regular pentagon interior angle
$= 180° - 72° = 108°$
Angle at point P:
Interior angle of $A = 360° - 2 \times 108°$
$= 144°$
Exterior angle of $A = 180° - 144° = 36°$
$36° = \frac{360°}{n}$, $n = 12$ so 12 pentagons will
surround polygon A.

(b) The 12-sided polygon is a regular dodecagon.

12 (a) $100 = \frac{1}{2}(8.5 + 12.5) \times V_{max}$

(Area under speed–time graph =
distance travelled)

$V_{max} = \frac{200}{21} = 9.5238...\text{m/s} = 9.52 \text{ m/s}$

(3 s.f.)

(b) Acceleration $= \frac{9.5238}{4} = 2.3809...\text{m/s}^2$

$= 2.38 \text{ m/s}^2$ (3 s.f.)
(Gradient of speed–time graph = acceleration)

13

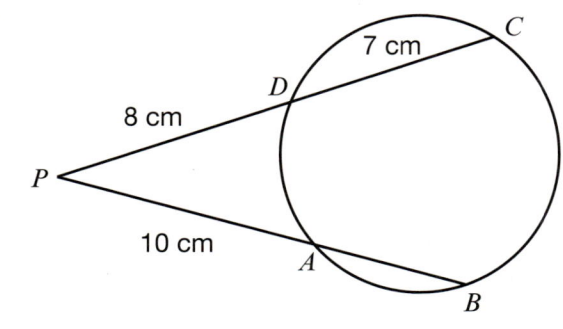

$PC \times PD = PB \times PA$
(intersecting chords theorem)
Let $AB = p$
$15 \times 8 = (10 + p)10$
$120 = 100 + 10p$
(Subtract 100 from both sides)
$20 = 10p$
(Divide both sides by 10)
$p = 2$, so $AB = 2$ cm
Now angle $APD = 30°$
Triangle BPC:
(Cosine Rule: $a^2 = b^2 + c^2 - 2bc\cos A$)
$BC^2 = 15^2 + 12^2 - 2 \times 15 \times 12 \times \cos(30°)$
$BC = 7.5651\ldots$ cm $= 7.57$ cm (3 s.f.)

14 $(11\sqrt{3} - a)(3\sqrt{3} + a) = 95 + 32b\sqrt{3}$
(Expand out the LHS and compare irrational and rational parts)
LHS $= 99 + 11\sqrt{3}\,a - 3\sqrt{3}\,a - a^2$
$= 99 - a^2 + 8a\sqrt{3}$
$= 95 + 32b\sqrt{3}$
(Rational) $99 - a^2 = 95$, $4 = a^2$, $a = 2$
(Irrational) $8 \times 2\sqrt{3} = 32b\sqrt{3}$, $b = \frac{1}{2}$
$a^2 + b^2 = 4 + \frac{1}{4} = \frac{17}{4}$ as required.

15 (a) $p = 2r + \frac{80}{360} \times 2\pi(2r) + \frac{80}{360} \times 2\pi r$

$= 2r + \frac{4\pi}{9} = (2r + r) = 2r + \frac{4\pi r}{3}$

$= \frac{2r(3 + 2\pi)}{3}$

(b) $p = 18 = \frac{2r(3 + 2\pi)}{3}$, $r = \frac{27}{3 + 2\pi}$

$= 2.9084\ldots$ m

Let area of lawn be $A = \frac{80}{360} \times \pi(4r^2 - r^2)$

$= \frac{2}{3}\pi r^2$

At $r = 2.9084\ldots$ m, $A = \frac{2}{3}\pi(2.9084)^2$

$= 17.716\ldots$ m²
Cost $= \$18 \times 17.716 = \$318.89$
$= \$319$ (nearest \$)

16 (a) $6x - 5y = 7$ $\quad$ [1] × 3 = [3]
$4x + 3y = 11$ $\quad$ [2] × 5 = [4]
$18x - 15y = 21$ $\quad$ [3]
$20x + 15y = 55$ $\quad$ [4]
[3] + [4]: $38x = 76$, so $x = 2$ substitutes into [2]
[2]: $8 + 3y = 11$, so $3y = 3$, $y = 1$
Lines intersect at point (2, 1)

(b) Let $x = p^{-2} = \frac{1}{p^2}$ and $y = q^{-1} = \frac{1}{q}$

So $2 = \frac{1}{p^2}$, $p^2 = \frac{1}{2}$, $p = \pm\frac{1}{\sqrt{2}}$

Also $\quad 1 = \frac{1}{q} =$, $q = 1$

17

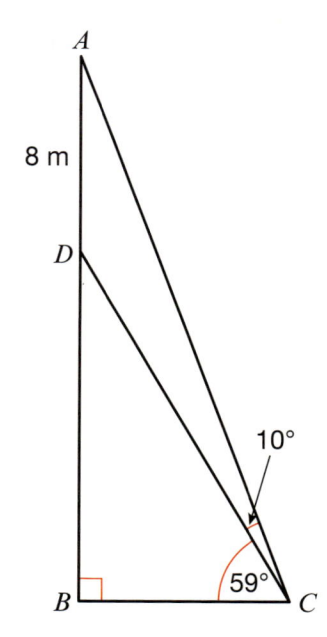

$AB = 8 + BD$
Triangle BCD: $\tan(59°) = \frac{BD}{BC}$ $\quad$ [1]

Triangle ABC: $\tan(69°) = \frac{BD + 8}{BC}$ $\quad$ [2]

Let [1] = [2] = BC:

$BC = \frac{BD}{\tan(59)} = \frac{BD + 8}{\tan(69)}$

$BD \times \tan(69) = (BD + 8) \times \tan(59)$
$BD \times \tan(69) - BD \times \tan(59) = 8 \times \tan(59)$
(Expand and factorise for BD)
$BD \times (\tan(69) - \tan(59)) = 8 \times \tan(59)$

$BD = \frac{8 \times \tan(59)}{(\tan(69) - \tan(59))} = 14.1518...\text{m}$

so $AB = 8 + 14.1518...$
$= 22.151...\text{m} = 22.2 \text{ m (3 s.f.)}$

18 (a) If $g(x) = \frac{x + 60}{2}$

$y = \frac{x + 60}{2}$

(Re-write in terms of $y = ...$)

$x = \frac{y + 60}{2}$

(Switch x and y variables)
$2x = y + 60, y = 2x - 60$
(Re-arrange to make y the subject)
$g^{-1}(x) = 2x - 60$

(b) $fgh(x) = fg(2x) = f\left(\frac{2x + 60°}{2}\right)$

$= \sin\left(\frac{2x + 60°}{2}\right) = 1$

If the domain for $f(x)$ is $0 \leq x \leq 90°$
$\sin(x) = 1$ gives one solution which is
$x = 90°$

$\frac{2x + 60}{2} = 90°, 2x + 60 = 180°,$

$2x = 120°, x = 60°$

19 Complete the table:

Minutes late t (min)	$0 < t \leq 1$	$1 < t \leq 3$	$3 < t \leq 5$	$5 < t \leq 6$	$6 < t \leq 7$	$7 < t \leq 10$
Number of pupils	6	14	8	8	2	12
Frequency density	6	7	4	8	2	4

(b) (The second class has a frequency density of 7 so it is now possible to calibrate the vertical scale.)

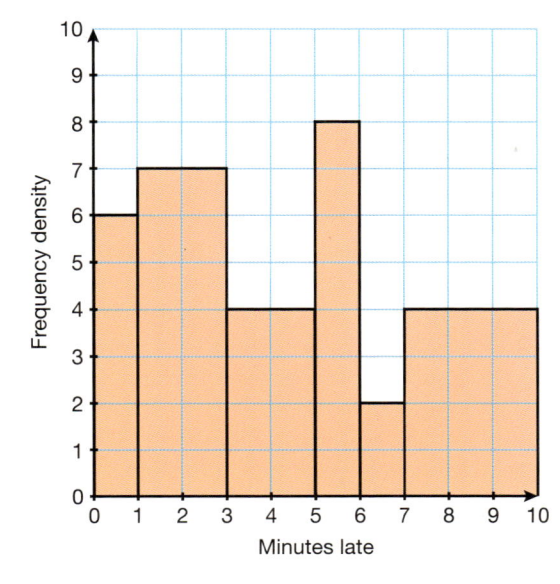

(c) Modal class is the most popular group with the highest frequency density:
$5 < t \leq 6$

(d) Area of the histogram = total frequency
Area representing $t \geq 2.5$
$= 0.5 \times 7 + 2 \times 4 + 1 \times 8 + 1 \times 2 + 3 \times 4$
$= 33.5$
$P(t \geq 2.5) = \frac{33.5}{50} = \frac{67}{100}$

20 Let m be the original number of males llamas
Let f be the original number of female llamas
$m : f = 3 : 10, \frac{m}{f} = \frac{3}{10}, m = \frac{3f}{10}, f = \frac{10m}{3}$ (1)

After the birth, number of male llamas is $m + 3$, the number of female llamas is $f + 2$

$(m + 3) : (f + 2) = 1 : 3, \frac{m + 3}{f + 2} = \frac{1}{3},$
$3(m + 3) = f + 2$ (2)
Substituting (1) into (2)
$3(m + 3) = \frac{10m}{3} + 2$

$9(m + 3) = 10m + 6$

$9m + 27 = 10m + 6$

$m = 21, f = \frac{10 \times 21}{3} = 70$ there were 91 llamas before the birth.

There are now $91 + 5 = 96$ llamas in the herd.

382 ANSWERS

21 (a)

x	0.5	1	2	3	4	5	6
y	5	2.25	1.25	1.25	1.5	1.85	2.25

(b)

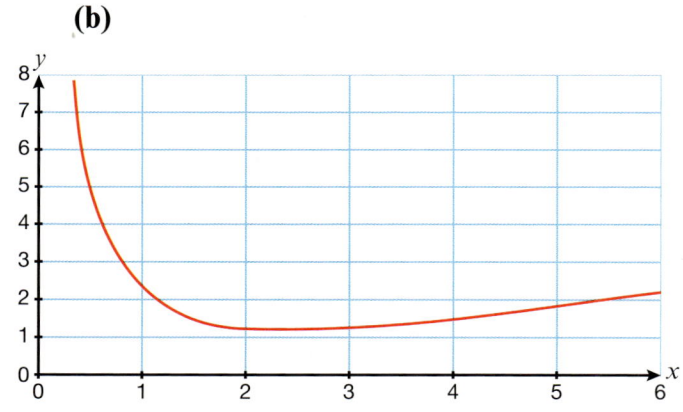

(c) $2x + \frac{12}{x} = 13$

$2x + \frac{12}{x} - 5 = 8$

$\frac{1}{4}\left(2x + \frac{12}{x} - 5\right) = 2$ so draw line $y = 2$

Solutions are where line intersects the curve at ≈ 1.1 or $x \approx 5.4$

22 (AM is a line of symmetry, so $\triangle ABM$ is a right-angled triangle. M is midpoint of BC so $BM = 1$)

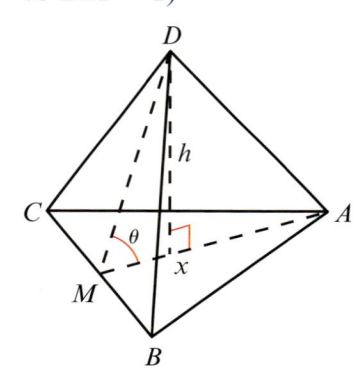

$AM^2 + BM^2 = AB^2$
(Pythagoras' theorem)
$AM^2 + 1 = 2^2$
$AM^2 = 3$
$AM = \sqrt{3}$

$AX = \frac{2}{3} AM$

$AX = \frac{2\sqrt{3}}{3}$ mm

(a) Area of base (triangle ABC) is
$\frac{1}{2} \times 2 \times \sqrt{3} = \sqrt{3}$

$h^2 + AX^2 = 2^2 \qquad AD = 2$ mm

$h^2 = 4 - \left(\frac{2\sqrt{3}}{3}\right)^2 = 4 - \frac{4 \times 3}{9} = \frac{8}{3}$

$h = \sqrt{\frac{8}{3}} = \frac{2\sqrt{2}}{\sqrt{3}}$ or $\frac{2\sqrt{2}\sqrt{3}}{3}$ or $\frac{2\sqrt{6}}{3}$

Volume $= \frac{1}{3} \times \sqrt{3} \times \frac{2\sqrt{2}}{\sqrt{3}} = \frac{2\sqrt{2}}{3}$ mm³

(b) Angle required is θ (see sketch)

$\tan(\theta) = \frac{h}{MX} = \frac{2\sqrt{2}}{\sqrt{3}} \div \frac{\sqrt{3}}{3}$

$= \frac{2\sqrt{2}}{\sqrt{3}} \times \frac{3}{\sqrt{3}} = 2\sqrt{2}, \theta = 70.5°$

$MX = \frac{1}{3} \times AM$

or $\sin(\theta) = \frac{h}{DM} = \frac{2\sqrt{2}}{\sqrt{3}} \div \frac{2\sqrt{3}}{3}$

$= \frac{2\sqrt{2}}{\sqrt{3}} \times \frac{3}{2\sqrt{3}} = \frac{2\sqrt{2}}{3} \theta$

$= 70.5°$

$DM = AM$

or $\cos(\theta) = \frac{MX}{DM} = \frac{\sqrt{3}}{3} \div \sqrt{3}$

$= \frac{\sqrt{3}}{3} \times \frac{1}{\sqrt{3}} = \frac{1}{3}$

$\theta = 70.5°$

$MX = \frac{1}{3} \times AM, DM = AM$

23 (a) $\frac{4x^2 - 9}{x + 2} \div \frac{2x^2 - 5x - 12}{x - 4}$

$= \frac{4x^2 - 9}{x + 2} \times \frac{x - 4}{2x^2 - 5x - 12}$

$= \frac{(2x - 3)(2x + 3)}{x + 2} \times \frac{x - 4}{(2x + 3)(x - 4)}$

$= \frac{2x - 3}{x + 2}$

(b) $\frac{4x^2 - 9}{x + 2} \div \frac{2x^2 - 5x - 12}{x - 4}$

$= \frac{2x - 1}{x + 4}, \frac{2x - 3}{x + 2} = \frac{x + 1}{2(x - 2)}$

(Using previous result)

$\frac{2x - 3}{x + 2} = \frac{x + 1}{2(x - 2)}$

$2(2x - 3)(x - 2) = (x + 1)(x + 2)$
(Multiplying both sides by $2(x + 2)(x - 2)$)
$4x^2 - 14x + 12 = x^2 + 3x + 2$
$3x^2 - 17x + 10 = 0$
$(x - 5)(3x - 2) = 0$
$x = 5$ or $x = \frac{2}{3}$

24 (a) Stone hits the sea when
$s = -24 = 20t - 4t^2$
(Stone is 24m <u>below</u> the cliff top)
so $4t^2 - 20t - 24 = 0$
(Divide both sides by 4)
$t^2 - 5t - 6 = 0$, $(t - 6)(t + 1) = 0$, $t = 6$
(Note $t \neq -1$)

(b) $v = \frac{ds}{dt} = 20 - 8t$, at $t = 6$,
$v = 20 - 8 \times 6 = -28$ m/s

(c) Mean speed $= \frac{\text{distance}}{\text{time}}$
distance = distance to top $\times 2 + 24$
speed at top is when $v = 0 = 20 - 8t$,
$t = \frac{5}{2}$ s
at $t = \frac{5}{2}$, $s = 20 \times \frac{5}{2} - 4 \times \left(\frac{5}{2}\right)^2 = 25$m

Mean speed $= \frac{2 \times 25 + 24}{6}$
$= 12.3$ m/s (3 s.f.)